FUNDAMENTALS OF FINANCIAL MANAGEMENT

THIRD EDITION

Vyuptakesh Sharan

Associate Editor – Acquisitions: Anshul Yadav
Senior Production Editor – Production: Vamanan Namboodiri

ISBN: 978-81-317-6142-7

First Impression, 2012
Current Impression, 2026

Published by Pearson India Education Services Pvt. Ltd, CIN: U72200TN2005PTC057128.

Head Office: 1st Floor, Berger Tower, Plot No. C-001A/2, Sector 16B, Noida - 201 301, Uttar Pradesh, India.

Registered Office: 6th Floor, Tower A, Unit A and B, International Tech Park, CapitaLand Chennai, 200 Feet Radial Road,Zamin Pallavaram, Old Pallavaram Chennai – 600117, Tamil Nadu, India

Website: in.pearson.com; Email: companysecretary.india@pearson.com

Digitally printed in India by Trinity Academy for Corporate Training Ltd, New Delhi in the year of 2026.

To,

My mother, Kalyani Devi, and father, Sri Hrishikesh Sharan

PREFACE TO THE THIRD EDITION

This edition is the outcome of the positive response and valuable feedback from readers. While retaining the essence of the previous edition, this edition presents certain new features. These are as follows:

- 'Points to Remember', consisting of questions and short answers to enable readers to grasp the fundamentals of each chapter.
- Examples depicting real-life situations as box items to help readers understand concepts better.
- Case studies in most of the chapters link the theoretical concepts with real-world scenarios.
- A large number of solved numerical problems at the end of each chapter to make it easier for students to comprehend the subject.

Finally, the text has been revised, wherever required, to make this book more topical and interesting.

VYUPTAKESH SHARAN

PREFACE

Corporate financial management, which emerged as an independent branch of study about half a century ago, has experienced phenomenal changes in respect of theoretical content as well as the tools being used for taking financial decisions and their implementation. The purpose of the book is to acquaint professionals and students of business studies with the contents and tools of corporate financial management.

There are a number of books on the subject of corporate financial management. A few of them are fairly comprehensive. Nevertheless, the present textbook is expected to serve better the interest of the readers who are not well versed in the terminology of business studies. The reason is that the explanation has been made greatly lucid, with a good number of examples in order to suit the needs of such readers. Moreover, the volume of the text has intentionally been limited to suit the time framework of the readers. If a reader would like to go deeper into a particular topic, he or she can take advantage of the select reading list given at the end of each chapter. Objective-type questions and numerical problems are provided at the end of each chapter and their answers at the end of the book. In all, the present text is extremely reader friendly.

I am thankful to my students and my colleagues for their valuable suggestions. I would particularly like to thank my wife, Roopa Sharan, who has contributed in many ways to the completion of the present textbook, as also Lokesh and Archana who spared time to solve some of the numerical problems.

I would appreciate suggestions from readers to help make the book more useful.

VYUPTAKESH SHARAN

CONTENTS

PART III WORKING CAPITAL MANAGEMENT

ABOUT THE AUTHOR

Vyuptakesh Sharan, Former Professor and Dean, Faculty of Commerce, Magadh University, is currently a Professor Emeritus at Chandragupt Institute of Management Patna (CIMP) which is an autonomous institution of Government of Bihar. Previously he was Emeritus Fellow at School of International Studies, Jawaharlal Nehru University, New Delhi, UGC Visiting Professor at the MIB Programme, Department of Commerce, Delhi School of Economics, University of Delhi and AICTE Visiting Professor at Global Business Operations Post-Graduate Programme, Sri Ram College of Commerce, University of Delhi.

Professor Sharan teaches international business and international finance. He has delivered special lectures in a number of Indian universities and abroad. He has to his credit six reference books and three text books mostly published by international publishers. He has also contributed a large number of articles to national and international journals, and has chaired more than half a dozen national seminars.

Part I

Fundamental Concepts of Financial Management

Part I familiarises the reader with the fundamental concepts of corporate financial management. It deals with:

1. Nature of financial decisions, factors influencing financial decisions and the objectives of financial decisions;
2. Time value of money, which incorporates the process of the computation of the future and present value of cash flows;
3. The concept of risk and return in the context of a single investment and also a portfolio of investments;
4. Various concepts of corporate valuation and the process of valuation of corporate securities.

1

NATURE AND GOAL OF FINANCIAL DECISIONS

OBJECTIVES

To explain the nature of corporate financial decisions

To explain factors—both microeconomic and macroeconomic—influencing financial decisions

To analyse the concept of profit maximisation as the goal of financial decisions

To explain and appraise the concept of maximisation of corporate wealth as a more appropriate goal of financial decisions

Finance lies at the root of economic activity. In the corporate form of organisation, financial decisions play a significant role in the management of operations. It is, therefore, significant to know what financial decisions really mean, what factors influence such decisions and what ultimate objective they have. These issues are explained here at some length in order to form a background for a detailed discussion of various financial decisions that will follow in the subsequent chapters.

1.1 NATURE OF FINANCIAL DECISIONS

The nature of financial decisions would be clear when we try to understand the operation of a firm. At the very outset, the promoter makes an appraisal of various investment proposals and selects one or more of them, depending upon the net benefit derived from each as well as on the availability of funds. When a particular project is selected or the area of operation is finalised, the requirements for long-term assets as well as current assets are determined, and accordingly, the quantum and the sources of finance are sorted out. The firm raises funds to finance fixed assets like land and building, plant and machinery, etc., and current assets like inventory, etc. The operation starts. An optimum trade-off between profitability and liquidity is maintained throughout the operations so as to ensure smooth operation. At the end of every accounting year, profits or losses are accounted for. A part of profit (if any) is retained with the firm for re-investment and the other part is distributed as dividend. This is the normal course of operation in a firm. Now it is evident that this process of operation involves the following financial decisions:

1. Selection of long-term investment proposals, known as the long-term investment decision;
2. Determination of working capital requirements, known as the working capital decision;
3. Raising of funds to finance the assets, known as the financing decision;
4. Allocation of profits for dividend payment, known as the dividend decision.

These four decisions form the subject matter of corporate finance, although financial tools, such as financial analysis, planning and control instruments that facilitate the above decisions are also an integral part of the theme of corporate financial management.

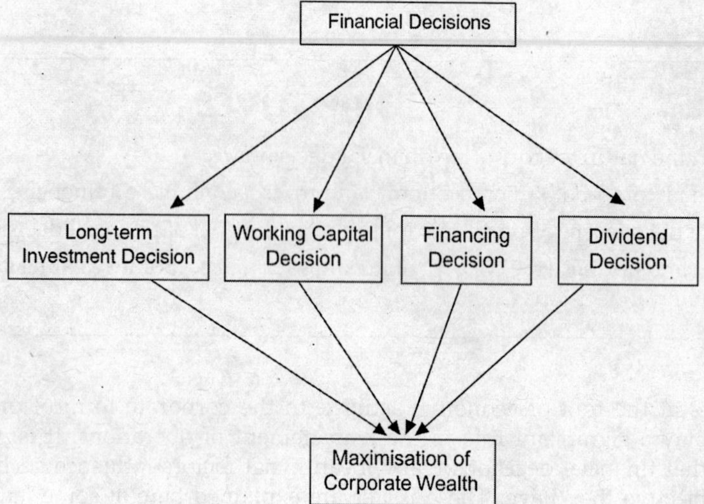

1.1.1 Long-term Investment Decision

The long-term investment decision, which is also known as capital budgeting, is concerned with the selection of a long-term investment proposal/proposals and the investment of funds in the selected proposal or proposals. Here it needs to be explained that only those proposals are selected that assure a higher return than the required rate of return. Also, since the expected return cannot be thought of in isolation of the business risk, it is the risk-adjusted return that is compared with the required rate of return. The required rate of return is also known as the cut-off rate. The computation of the risk-adjusted return and the required rate of return and, on that basis, the selection of the project form the subject matter of the investment decision.

Long-term investment decisions may be both internal and external. In the former, the finance manager has to determine which capital expenditure projects have to be undertaken, the amount of funds to be committed and the ways in which the funds are to be allocated among different investment outlets. In the latter, the finance manager is concerned with the investment of funds outside the business for merger with, or acquisition of, another firm. This is very important in the sense that mergers and acquisitions provide the firm an opportunity for fast expansion.

Unfortunately, the study of corporate finance did not pay attention to the long-term investment decision till the early 1950s. But then a number of models were developed, indicating that only those projects should be selected that assure a net positive contribution to corporate wealth. With limited funds in hand, projects are ranked on the basis of their net contribution and are selected beginning from the top till the funds are exhausted. More recent studies have also taken into account social benefits and costs, in so far as the firm has social obligations too.

The long-term investment decision, which is also known as capital budgeting, is concerned with the selection of an investment proposal/ proposals and the investment of funds in the selected proposal or proposals.

1.1.2 Working Capital Decision

The working capital decision takes into account the management of current assets and current liabilities. The management of current assets involves a couple of issues. The first being the size of current assets, or in other words, what the size of cash holdings, short-term marketable securities, account receivables and inventory should be. The firm can maintain a certain level of operation with a smaller size of current assets that may raise profitability, however, the danger of illiquidity then looms large. On the other hand, a larger investment in current assets may ensure sufficient liquidity but then profitability may tend to decline. This is why working capital decisions always seek to maintain a balance between liquidity and profitability.

The size of current assets can be pruned to raise profitability, through shortening of the operating cycle. The operating cycle denotes the period during which cash takes the form of cash again after moving through inventory and accounts receivable. Cash allows the purchase of raw material; raw material is processed into finished goods. Finished goods are sold on credit terms that create bills receivable. The bills receivable take the form of cash after credit amount is paid. Thus, if the operating cycle is shortened through better management of current assets, the size of the required current assets will be lower and profitability will get a boost.

The second issue is related to the share of current liabilities in total liabilities. This is because current assets are financed by a mix of long-term capital and short-term capital. Here, again, a similar balance needs to be maintained between liquidity and profitability. Short-term capital is often less costly but does not provide sufficient liquidity. On the contrary, long-term capital is generally costly but provides sufficient liquidity. The working capital decision takes care of an optimal balance between liquidity and profitability.

The working capital decision takes into account the management of current assets and current liabilities.

1.1.3 Financing Decision

The financing decision is concerned with the raising of funds that finance assets. Funds should be adequate to procure the assets necessary for operation; at the same time, if the funds are more than required, the excess would remain unutilised making no contribution to output but adding to the financing cost, thereby considerably eroding profitability. In other words, the financing decision should ensure optimum capitalisation.

The financing decision is concerned with the raising of funds that finance assets.

Again, it is not only the amount of capital but also the proportion mix of different forms of capital that is crucial from the viewpoint of the financing decision. The reason being that different forms of capital carry varying costs. So it is important that the proportion mix of different forms of capital owners' funds and borrowed funds, should be such that the weighted average cost of capital is minimised.

The major sources of long-term capital are shares and debentures. Funds can also be obtained in the form of term loans and leases, as the latter serves as an alternative to borrowing. If sufficient funds are not raised domestically, they are obtained from sources abroad.

1.1.4 Dividend Decision

The dividend decision helps determine how much of profit is distributed as dividend and how much is retained with the firm.

A part of profit is distributed as dividend and the rest is retained with the firm for the purpose of investment. It is the dividend decision that helps determine how much of profit is distributed as dividend and how much is retained with the firm. There are divergent views in this respect. One view is that the investors are often indifferent vis-à-vis dividend and capital gains. The other view however rejects the idea of investors' indifference. It states that profits should first be invested in profitable channels and dividend is only a passive residual. However, there is yet another view that prefers dividend inasmuch as the payment of dividend meets shareholders' expectations of receiving some return on their investment. Moreover, stability in dividend has a positive effect on the market price of the firm's shares, as stable dividends tend to resolve uncertainty in the minds of investors, particularly when earning per share shows a declining trend. Additionally, the investors interested in current periodic income find utility in a stable dividend. Thus the dividend decision is concerned with the allocation of profit between dividend payment and its retention.

1.2 FACTORS INFLUENCING FINANCIAL DECISIONS

The nature of financial decisions varies from one firm to the other. It may also be different for the same firm over a period of time. The reason is that the nature of financial decisions is influenced by the prevailing microeconomic and macroeconomic conditions. These factors need some explanation here.

1.2.1 Microeconomic Factors

Microeconomic factors are related to the internal conditions of the firm. Important among these conditions are:

1. Nature and size of the enterprise;
2. Level of risk and stability in earnings;
3. Liquidity position;
4. Asset structure and pattern of ownership;
5. Attitude of the management.

If a firm is engaged in manufacturing operations or in the provision of public utility services, its investment in fixed assets is large and hence the capital structure has a large share of long-term capital. The share of long-term capital in the capital structure is also large in firms producing capital goods. On the other hand, in trading concerns, a greater part of the investment is found in current assets. With a greater ratio of current assets, the ratio of current liabilities rises. Similarly, concerns that are larger in size need a large capital. Small firms may obtain their fixed assets on lease, but large firms would need to construct their own building and assemble their own plant. Small firms have lower goodwill in the capital market and so their financing decisions are different from that of large firms. It is because of the lack of sufficient goodwill in the capital market that small firms are largely dependent on internal finances and this is one of the reasons that their dividend decisions are different from that of large firms.

The nature of financial decisions is influenced by the prevailing microeconomic and macroeconomic conditions.

Risk is another important factor influencing financial decisions. The greater the risk, the higher the discount factor. Thus, risk influences the long-term investment decision or capital budgeting decision. Again, if risk is higher or income is not stable, the finance manager tries to impress on the shareholders for more retention of earnings rather than adopting a liberal dividend policy. But with stable income or lower risk, the financial decision will be just the reverse. In such cases, the fixed-cost capital, such as preference shares and debentures, may be preferred and also the firm may adopt a liberal dividend policy.

The third factor influencing financial decisions is the liquidity position. Since dividend is normally paid out of cash, firms with a sound liquidity position adopt a liberal dividend policy. But if, in such cases, the working capital requirements are very large or the firm has to meet significant past obligations, it will have to follow a conservative dividend policy. Any tilt towards illiquidity will alter the nature of financing and dividend decisions.

Again, in a closely-held company where the ownership lies in a few hands, the management does not find it difficult to persuade the owners to accept a conservative dividend policy in the interests of the firm. But in cases where there are many shareholders, their wishes matter considerably.

Last but not least is the management's attitude. A conservative finance manager will attach greater importance to liquidity rather than to the profitability. On the other hand an aggressive finance manager will stress on the latter, and financial decisions will be taken accordingly. For example, a conservative finance manager attempts to tread a beaten path, preferring to avoid fixed obligations for raising additional capital even if debt financing is advantageous. The preference is to maintain a large volume of current assets. However, an aggressive finance manager is ready to bear the risk involved in debt financing or that involved in maintaining lower current assets. However, a prudent finance manager would prefer a compromise between risk and return or between profitability and liquidity.

1.2.2 Macroeconomic Factors

Macroeconomic factors are the environmental factors that are beyond the control of the firm's management. They relate primarily to:

1. The state of the economy;
2. Governmental policy.

Macroeconomic factors are the environmental factors that are beyond the control of the firm's management.

The state of the economy changes from time to time and the financial decisions of a firm conform to these changes. When the economy is growing or proceeding towards recovery, the finance manager should be eager to avail of investment opportunities. But when the economy is facing a slump, the finance manager should proceed with care. For example, in such a situation it would not be advisable to go for an expansion programme. Similarly, when the economy is experiencing an uptrend, the finance manager can opt for trading on equity as larger profits are assured. But in times of a downtrend, the stress should be on internal financing. Again, during an uptrend, higher dividends can be declared, but during a downtrend conservation of cash is necessary and therefore a strict dividend policy should be followed.

The state of economy is also denoted by the structure of capital and money markets. If the capital market is well developed having a multitude of financial institutions and venturesome investors, the finance manager will find it easy to select the proportion-mix of capital structure and, accordingly, financing decisions will be broader. He can manage with a comparatively lower amount of cash as he can get funds whenever he desires. The dividend policy too is broad in such cases as the shareholders are not necessarily interested in regular and large dividends. But if the investors are not venturesome, they will wish for large dividends and the finance manager will have to adopt a liberal dividend policy, and will not be able to opt for trading on equity to any great extent. Similarly, if the financial institutions provide concessional assistance for priority projects, the investment decisions will be influenced in favour of such projects. Moreover, if the financial institutions stress on a particular debt-equity ratio, the financing decisions will be so influenced.

Apart from the state of economy, governmental policy is no less significant in influencing corporate financial decisions. State intervention or state regulation is found in almost all countries, although its degree varies. In India where economic policies have become more liberal since the 1990s, entrepreneurs are comparatively free to take up any venture that pleases them. Thus corporate investment decisions are governed by the nature and extent of state regulations.

Again, the Indian Companies Act, 1956, provides certain dividend declaration and payment rules which have to be followed by finance managers. Taxation rules framed by the government also shape corporate decisions. Since taxation absorbs a good part of a firm's income, the finance manager normally has to find out how to minimise the tax burden. Thus he shapes the firm's depreciation policy, inventory valuation and capital structure, distributes bonus shares that are exempted from tax and takes a variety of financial decisions in accordance with the rules and regulations.

However, there is always scope to manoeuvre and this can be availed of by experienced finance managers. Their experience or prudence absorbs, at least to some extent, the influences of the internal and external factors explained hitherto.

1.3 OBJECTIVE OF CORPORATE FINANCIAL DECISIONS

At the very outset, it should be made clear that the ultimate goal of corporate financial decisions is the maximisation of owners' economic welfare. Although there is unanimity on the achievement of this goal, the literature on the subject contains divergent views on its achievement. Whereas, earlier views have suggested profit maximisation, later

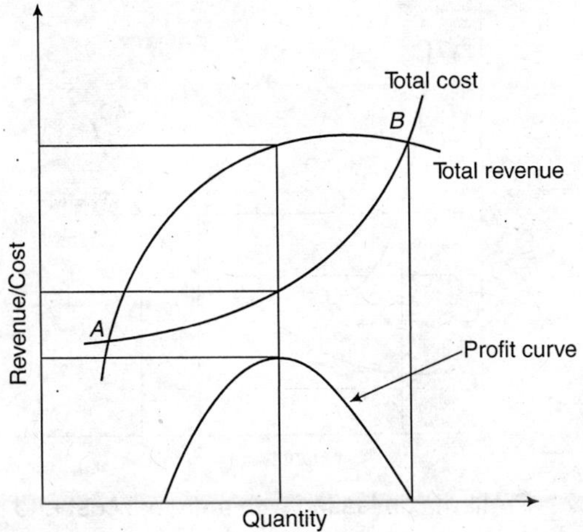

FIG. 1.1 Profit maximisation

views suggest wealth maximisation as a means to achieving the maximisation of owners' economic welfare.

1.3.1 Profit Maximisation

Total Revenue and Total Cost: Profit maximisation simply means maximising the income of the firm. Traditionally, a business firm is regarded as an economic entity whose fundamental objective is the maximisation of profits. Economists are of the view that profits can be maximised when the difference of total revenue over total cost is maximum; or in other words, total revenue is greater than total cost by the greatest amount (Baumol, 1959).

As shown in Fig. 1.1, the firm expands its sales up to Point A just to cover cost. Sales beyond this point give rise to profits. But economies of scale are reaped only upto a certain point, beyond which total revenue tends to decline and is equal to the cost again at Point B. So profit is possible only between the two points, A and B. It is the highest where the difference of the revenue over the cost is the largest. The trend of the profit is shown with the help of the profit curve.

Average Cost: Although the difference between total cost and total revenue is a reasonable way of showing profit maximisation, it is a bit clumsy for accurate measurement. Therefore, the usual and more accurate analysis of the firm's profit maximising output is carried out in terms of unit cost and revenue.

Hall and Hitch (1949) are of the view that firms aim at long-term profit maximisation and, therefore, set their price (P) or output on the average cost principle in order to cover average variable cost (AVC), average fixed cost (AFC) and a normal profit margin.

$$P = AVC + AFC + \textit{profit margin} \qquad ...(1.1)$$

The use of average cost is preferable to the use of marginal cost insofar as firms do not know with certainty the prospective demand and the marginal cost. Moreover, firms believe that full-cost price is the right price that allows a fair profit and covers the cost of production - when plant is normally utilised.

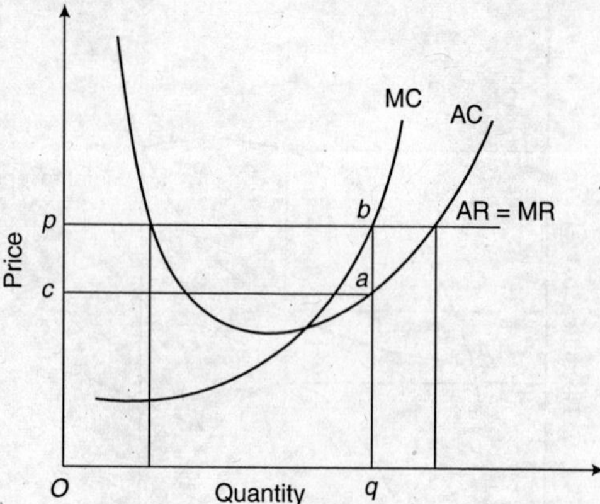

FIG. 1.2 Profit maximisation with marginal cost and revenue

Marginal Cost and Marginal Revenue: Empirical studies show that it is the equality of marginal cost and marginal revenue that determines maximum profit (Earley, 1955; 1956). Profits can be maximised where the marginal cost is equal to marginal revenue.To take the simplest case, where marginal revenue is constant or the sale of the last unit of output on account of constant prices does not lead to a lowering of the price of the product, the marginal revenue curve would be straight horizontal as shown in Fig. 1.2. Maximum profits are earned at output q where marginal revenue is equal to marginal cost. At any point of output less than that, marginal revenue is greater than marginal cost which means that increasing output will provide more revenue than the cost of production.

Output can be increased only up to point *q* because beyond that point, marginal cost would be greater than the marginal revenue and profits will decline. At point *q*, the profit per unit is equal to price, *p*, minus average cost, *c*, and the total profit would be shown by the area of the rectangle, *abpc*. However, Machlup (1967) is of the view that the marginal tools should give the same results as the average tools and lead to the same unique price-output combination that maximises profit.

Merits and Demerits: The concept of profit maximisation is deeply rooted in economic theory. Its appropriateness is justified on the following grounds:

1. This concept is analogous to rational behaviour of a firm.
2. It ensures that the ultimate survivor in the corporate world is the profit maximiser.
3. It helps in the acquiring of monopoly powers in the imperfect product market.

However, the concept of profit maximisation has been facing vehement refutations in recent decades. It is often argued that this concept held good in the nineteenth century in the case of single entrepreneur firms where the same person was the owner, manager and the financer. The only aim of the single owner was to increase his individual wealth. But, nowadays, firms are characterised by limited liability and by a divorce between management and ownership, and even the management is not concentrated in the person of one man. There exist different interest groups associated with a firm, whose interests do not coincide. For example, while the interest of the equity-holders lies in high dividend, that of the creditors lies in timely payment of interest and in secured repayment of their loans. The managers, on the contrary, are interested in professional achievements and not necessarily in higher profits. Similarly, the sales executives may be more interested in total volume of sales rather than in profits. The objective of profit maximisation fails to serve such multi-dimensional interests and so it is regarded as inappropriate.

Again, the concept of profit maximisation was appropriate in the eighteenth or nineteenth century when long-term investment was a rare phenomenon. Short-term profitability was used by firms as the only yardstick of success. Naturally, the distinction between investments for current profits and those for future pay-off was never stressed upon. But with technological advancement, it is now possible to think of projects requiring long-term investment that necessitate long-term profit planning, taking into consideration risk factors and the qualitative aspects of future activities. Unfortunately, the objective of profit maximisation proves incapable of making a distinction between returns received in different time periods as also of analysing the risk factor.

Yet again, the accounting profit that appears in the profit and loss account does not reflect opportunity cost. Sometimes it is argued that the profit and loss account shows the missed opportunities in an indirect way if failure to acquire an asset generates lower profits. But it does not provide an absolute figure against which one can compare profits with the result that it is very difficult to know whether profits are lower than they ought to be.

Last but not least, the criticism laid against the profit maximization objective is that the computation of profits is not accurate in the generality of cases. Their accuracy depends upon perfect cost estimates that are seldom correct insofar as the allocation of overheads is not properly made.

1.3.2 Objective of Wealth Maximisation

In view of the limitations to the objective of profit maximisation, it is suggested that the objective of the corporate financial decisions should be the maximisation of the value of the firm or of the corporate wealth. The value of corporate wealth may be interpreted in terms of the value of the company's total assets. The value of total assets is the sum of the firm's productive assets, (A) and the value of wealth created by the firm through the use of productive assets, (W). The value of corporate wealth, (V) can be expressed in the form of an equation as follows:

$$V = A + W \qquad \text{...(1.2)}$$

The amount of wealth created is nothing but the present value of the future net proceeds of the firm's present and future assets.

Alternatively, the value of corporate wealth (V) is represented by the market value of claim against the assets. The claims are represented by the market value of debt (D) and equity capital (E). The value of corporate wealth can thus be expressed by the following equation:

$$V = D + E \qquad \text{...(1.3)}$$

Thus the value of corporate wealth can be interpreted in two ways, and this does not imply any divergence. It is rather two sides of the same coin. Bringing together the two equations, we can write:

$$V = D + E = A + W \qquad \text{...(1.4)}$$

The value of equity depends directly on the amount of wealth creation. The larger the wealth creation, the greater the market value of the equity shares. Therefore, the value of total assets is equal to the value of debt and equity shares. The valuation of equity and debt is explained in Chapter 4 and that of assets is discussed in Chapter 5. It is suggested that the readers go through the relevant portions in these chapters.

1.3.3 Appraisal of the Objective of Maximisation of Corporate Wealth

The objective of maximisation of corporate wealth is acceptable to all the parties—shareholders, creditors, employees, management and society—directly or indirectly related to the firm. The shareholders benefit by the higher value of their shares. As far as the firm's creditors are concerned, any increase in corporate wealth provides them greater protection with respect to interest and repayment of the loan. This is particularly because the creditors have a prior claim on the firm's earnings and assets. The interest of the employees is better served with an increase in corporate wealth, because the firm can only increase or maximise its wealth in harmony with increased benefits to its employees. Moreover, employees are a part of the firm, thus with an increase in the size of the corporate cake, their share is automatically larger. The wealth of a firm is a part of society's wealth. When the former is maximised there is a positive contribution to the latter. However, the extent to which a firm contributes to society's wealth depends upon how far the gain is equally distributed among the different sections of society and how far the firm is committed to its social obligations. Last but not least, the existence of the management depends upon the prosperity of the firm. Maximisation of corporate wealth therefore serves the interests of the management.

However, there are a couple of problems related to the objective of maximising corporate wealth. First, this objective may not always be compatible with the firm's social obligations. And, second, more importantly, there exists the agency problem that needs some explanation.

1.3.4 The Agency Problem

The agency problem demonstrates the conflict of interest between the principal and the agent. In a corporate structure, the principal means the shareholders and their agents are the managers. Thus the agency problem arises when the managers do not necessarily act in the best interests of the shareholders with the sole purpose of benefiting themselves in form of greater perks, etc. However, the literature on the subject extends the concept of the agency problem to the relationship between the shareholders and the creditors (Jensen and Meckling, 1976). Therefore, the agency problem also arises when the interest of the shareholders clashes with those of the creditors.

> The agency problem arises when the managers do not necessarily act in the best interests of the shareholders with the sole purpose of benefiting themselves.

When corporate financial decisions are motivated in order to favour the managers, these decisions are not optimal. Sub-optimal decisions allow the leakage of wealth from the firm with the result that they fail to raise corporate wealth to the extent desired. To be precise, the agency problem arises when:

1. Excessive perquisites are allowed to managers.
2. There is informational asymmetry that keeps the shareholders unaware of the financial decisions in the firm.

3. The managers' tenure is short. In such cases, decisions may be taken that are gainful in the short run but not necessarily gainful in the long run.
4. The managers attach greater importance to liquidity. They prefer greater retention of earnings which may not always be in the interests of the shareholders, especially when profitable investment opportunities for the firm do not exist.
5. The creditors put restrictive covenants on debt agreements in order to protect their own interests vis-à-vis the interests of the shareholders.

These are only some examples of how an agency problem could arise. There are many ways creating an agency problem in the wake of which corporate wealth is not maximised.

However, there is a question as to who bears the brunt of this problem (i.e., the agency cost). The managers who do not act in the best interests of the company, fail to create substantial wealth in the company. Naturally, they are not able to share a substantial amount of wealth. Thus it would not be wrong to say that the agency cost is often borne by the managers or the agents.

If the agency cost is to be controlled, the shareholders must maintain a strict vigil over the functioning of the company. The managers should be rewarded for acting in the interest of the shareholders. At the same time, the managers should maintain a balance between the interest of the shareholders and that of the creditors.

To sum up, the objective of the financial decisions is to maximise the corporate wealth along with maintaining good corporate governance.

SUMMARY

Corporate financial decisions relate mainly to long-term investment of funds, management of working capital, raising of funds and allocation of profits, although the tools used for taking financial decisions, such as financial analysis, planning and forecasting, etc., do form an essential segment of corporate financial decisions. Long-term investment decisions begin from the conceiving of proposals and their evaluation and proceed through the management of fixed assets. The working capital decision is concerned with the determination of the size of current assets and their financing. Similarly, financing decisions are concerned with the size and form of resources and the sources from where they are raised. The dividend decisions are taken in the area of allocation of profits—how much of the profits should be retained with the firm and how much should be distributed as dividend. All these decisions take care of a proper balance between risk and returns and between profitability and liquidity and are influenced by a number of microeconomic and macroeconomic factors, such as size of the enterprise, level of risk, liquidity position, asset structure, attitude of the management, governmental policy and the conditions of the economy in general.

As far as the objective of corporate financial decisions is concerned, it was traditionally the maximisation of profits. It rested on the belief that it is the profit maximiser that ultimately survives. However, it is now widely believed that the maximisation of corporate wealth should be the basic objective as it not only increases shareholders' wealth but also serves the interests of different groups directly or indirectly related to the firm. However, it is often the agency problem that comes in the way of corporate wealth maximisation.

POINTS TO REMEMBER

1. What are the major financial decisions taken by a finance manager?
   - Long-term investment decision
   - Working capital decision
   - Financing decision
   - Dividend decision
2. Enumerate factors influencing a financial decision.
   - Micro-economic factors, such as nature and size of enterprise, level of risk, liquidity position, asset structure and ownership pattern, and attitude of management.
   - Macro-economic factors, such as state of the economy and the governmental policy.
3. What are the objectives of financial decisions?
   - Profit maximisation
   - Maximisation of corporate wealth
4. When is profit maximised? Is it a suitable objective of financial decisions?
   - Profit is the maximum at a point of output when revenue exceeds the cost by the widest margin or when MR = MC.
   - Although profit maximisation is in conformity with the rational behaviour of a firm and it helps firm achieve monopoly powers in an imperfect product market, it does not consider long-term period, nor does it consider the opportunity cost. Moreover, the measure of profit is often inaccurate.
5. How is corporate wealth measured?
   - CW = D + E = A + W
6. Why is corporate wealth maximisation a suitable objective?
   - It benefits all the different parties related to the firm, such as shareholders, creditors, managers, employees, consumers, etc.
7. Is there any problem in maximising corporate wealth?
   - It is the agency problem when the managers do not act in the best interest of the shareholders, and also the creditors clash with the shareholders.

8. How can agency problem be controlled?
   - Constant vigil on the functioning of the managers
   - Reward to managers working in the interest of the shareholders

DESCRIPTIVE QUESTIONS

1. Explain the different types of financial decisions that form the subject-matter of corporate financial management.
2. In what way do the microeconomic and macroeconomic factors influence corporate financial decisions?
3. "The objective of corporate financial decisions is to maximise profits". Comment on this statement.
4. "It is not profit maximisation but the maximisation of corporate wealth that is the ultimate objective of corporate financial decisions". Discuss.
5. What do you mean by the agency problem? Does it come in the way of corporate wealth maximisation? If so, how can it be controlled?

OBJECTIVE-TYPE QUESTIONS

1. Mark true or false.
   (a) The capital budgeting and long-term investment decision are synonymous.
   (b) Short-term capital provides greater liquidity than long-term capital.
   (c) Dividend policy takes into account the decision on retention of earnings for the purpose of profitable investment.
   (d) State regulation influences the nature of a firm's financial decisions.
   (e) The concept of profit maximisation takes into account the long-term returns on capital invested.
   (f) Corporate wealth is the sum of the value of total assets and the present value of the wealth created through the assets.
2. Choose the most suitable answer.
   (a) Corporate financial decisions are based on:
      (i) microeconomic factors only
      (ii) macroeconomic factors only
      (iii) both micro-and macroeconomic factors
   (b) Value of corporate wealth is equal to:
      (i) value of equity minus debt
      (ii) value of equity plus value of debt
      (iii) neither of the above

(c) The agency problem manifests in the relationship between:
  (i) shareholders and managers
  (ii) different sections of shareholders
  (iii) managers at different levels
(d) Profit is maximised where:
  (i) marginal cost = marginal revenue
  (ii) marginal cost < marginal revenue
  (iii) marginal cost > marginal revenue

STUDY TOPIC: MANAGING AGENCY PROBLEM

Any divergence between the firm's owners and the managers (agents) is known as the agency problem. So if the two interests are aligned, the agency problem will either be the minimum or be over. A number of management scientists feel that it can be done either through agents' equity ownership or through restructuring their compensation (Dalton et al., 2007; Fama and Jensen, 1983). To be precise, the agents' economic reward should go side by side with those of the shareholders. Stock ownership and other compensation mechanisms try to link the interest of the two groups. The board of directors may grant stock, stock options or bonus as a discretionary award for good performance. The stock options may be re-priced subsequently highlighting their gain. Besides the stock options and the pricing of the stock, there may be non-equity components too.

It has been found that financial alignment, managerial preferences and other such actions help reduce the agency cost. Nyberg and Gerhart (2010) analyse the data taken from Standard and Poor's Compustat and ExecuComp data base and from Thomson Financial Services and test the hypothesis whether financial alignment exists and, if exists, it impacts the future performance of the firms. Their study finds that the financial alignment exits in a sizeable measure and so the existing conception that the agency problem is a serious problem in the corporate form of organisation does not hold good.

Again, Nyberg and Gerhart (2010) find that the financial alignment has a positive impact on the corporate performance. It is statistically significant predictor of subsequent shareholders' return. On an average, companies are creating financial alignment through the long-term use of equity-based pay and policies and are reaping positive benefits from doing so.

REFERENCES

Baumol, W.J. (1959). *Business Behaviour, Value and Growth.* New York: Macmillan.

Dalton, D.R., M.A. Hitt, S.C. Certo and C.M. Dalton (2007). "The Fundamental Agency Problem and its Mitigation", in J.F. Walsh and A.P. Brief (eds.), *Academy of Management Annals, vol.* 1 (1–64).

Earley, J.S. (1955). "Recent Developments in Cost Accounting and the Marginal Analysis", *Journal of Political Economy*, 63 (2): 220–32.

__________(1956). "Marginal Policies of Excellently Managed Companies", *American Economic Review*, 46 (3): 526–36.

Fama, E.F. and M.C. Jensen (1983). "Separation of Ownership and Control", *Journal of Law and Economics*, 26 (2): 301–26.

Hall, and Hitch (1949). "Price Theory and Business Behaviour", *Oxford Economic Papers*, 2 (1): 26–43.

Jensen, M.C. and W.H. Meckling (1976). "Theory of the Firm, Managerial Behaviour, Agency Costs and Ownership Structure", *Journal of Financial Economics*, 3 (4): 305–60.

Machlup, F. (1967). "Theories of Firm: Marginalist, Managerialist, Behavioural", *American Economic Review*, 57 (3): 419–27.

Nyberg, A.J. and B. Gerhart (2010). "Agency Theory Revisited: CEO Return and Shareholder Interest Alignment", *Academy of Management Journal*, 53 (5): 1029–49.

SELECT FURTHER READINGS

Altman, E.I. and M.G. Subrahmanyam (1985). *Recent Advances in Corporate Finance*. Homewood, Illinois: Richard D. Irwin.

Seitz, Neil (1982). "Shareholder Goals, Firm Goals and Firm Financing Decisions", *Financial Management*, 11 (Autumn): 20–26.

Treynor, J.L. (1981). "The Financial Objective in the Widely Held Corporation", *Financial Analysts Journal*, 37 (Mar.–Apr.): 68–71.

2

TIME VALUE OF MONEY

OBJECTIVES

To explain the concept of time value of money in general

To show how the future value of cash flows is computed

To show how the present value of future cash flows is computed

The concept of the maximization of corporate wealth necessarily involves the study of the time value of money. This is because the benefits that a firm expects to receive from an investment are usually spread out over a period of time. Such benefits need to be translated into their present value so as to facilitate their comparison with the initial investment and thereby to ascertain whether the investment has really added something to corporate wealth.

The concept of time value of money is also relevant to the shareholders, who make present sacrifices in form dividend foregone for investment in the expectation of future benefits. They would thus like to know the present value of future benefits so as to find out whether these future benefits exceed their present sacrifice.

2.1 THE CONCEPT

The concept of time value of money deals with the fact that an amount of money received in the future is not as valuable as the same amount of money received in the present. This is because:

1. The future is uncertain;
2. Individuals prefer current to future consumption;
3. The opportunity exists to invest the amount received in the present at a specific rate of interest;
4. Inflationary trends are a common feature reducing the value of money in the future.

All this means that future benefits should include some compensation for waiting. In other words, the future benefits should be equal to the sum of the present benefits and an amount equivalent to the compensation for waiting. Suppose a person gets 5% per annum as interest on a savings bank deposit. He would be indifferent between the two options of getting Rs 100 today and receiving Rs 105 after a year. Here the sum:

(a) Rs 100 is the present value of the receipt.
(b) Rs 5 is the compensation for waiting.
(c) Rs 105 is the future value of the receipt.

The concept of time value of money deals with the fact that an amount of money received in the future is not as valuable as the same amount of money received in the present.

It can also be said that the future value is the sum of the present value compounded at a given rate of interest. The present value is therefore calculated by reverse compounding. It is the formula used to compute compound interest, and not the one used to compute simple interest, that is involved in computing the future value of a receipt. The reason for this is that it is not only the original amount that earns interest but also the earned interest that earns further interest.

2.2 COMPUTATION OF FUTURE VALUE

2.2.1 Future Value of a Single Amount

The future value of an amount at the end of Period 1 (A_1) will be equal to the product of the original value (P) and the rate of interest plus 1. This can be expressed in the form of an equation as follows:

$$A_1 = P(1 + r) \quad \text{...(2.1)}$$

Here the subscript denotes the end of the specific period.

EXAMPLE

If P is Rs 100 and r is 10%, A after a 1-year period will be:

Rs 100 × 1.10 = Rs 110.

Similarly the future value of the amount P at specific rate of interest r at the end of Period 2 will be:

$$A_2 = \{P(1 + r)\}(1 + r) \quad \text{...(2.2)}$$

EXAMPLE

Continuing on the basis of the above example, A after a 2-year period will be:

Rs 100 × 1.10^2 = Rs 121.

Again, the future value of an amount of money at the end of period n will be:

$$An = P(1 + r)n \quad \text{...(2.3)}$$

EXAMPLE

The future value of Rs 5,000, 10 years from now at 8% rate of interest will be:

$$A_{10} = \text{Rs } 5{,}000\ (1.08)^{10} = \text{Rs } 10{,}794.50.$$

Normally, it is difficult to raise $(1 + r)$ to the nth power. In order to overcome this difficulty, one uses numerical tables. The present value is multiplied by the compound factor (*CF*) given in the table in order to arrive at the future value $(P \times CF_{r,n})$.

As per the table given at the end of this book, the CF for 8% rate of interest for 10 years is 2.1589. On multiplying it by Rs 5,000, one gets the future value as follows:

$$\text{Rs } 5{,}000 \times 2.1589 = \text{Rs } 10{,}794.50.$$

2.2.2 Future Value of a Series of Payments

When a single amount is not involved; rather a series of receipts occurs over a specific period of time, the total future value of these receipts can be found out by adding up the individual future values at the same future time. If P_1, P_2, P_3 and so on are the receipts, their future value at Period n will be:

$$A_n = P_1(1 + r)^{n-1} + P_2(1 + r)^{n-2} + P_3(1 + r)^{n-3} + \ldots + P_{n-1}(1 + r) + P_n \qquad \text{...(2.4)}$$

EXAMPLE

The future value of a series of three annual receipts of Rs 1,000, Rs 500 and Rs 800 respectively at the end of the third year at 5% rate of interest will be:

$$A_3 = \text{Rs } 1{,}000\ (1.05)^2 + \text{Rs } 500\ (1.05) + \text{Rs } 800 = \text{Rs } 2{,}427.50.$$

2.2.3 Future Value in Case of Annuities

In the preceding sub-section, the size of receipts in different years was not uniform. But there are cases when the size of receipts over time is equal or uniform. Uniformity of cash flows represents a case of annuity. Annuity may be of two types:

1. Regular annuity where the cash flows, equal in size, occur at the end of each time period;
2. Annuity due where the uniform cash flows occur at the beginning of each period.

Irrespective of whether the cash flow occurs at the beginning or at the end of each period, *P* in Eq. 2.4 is equal and so it becomes a common factor. Eq. 2.4 can be re-written in cases of regular annuity as follows:

$$A_n = P\{(1 + r)^{n-1} + (1 + r)^{n-2} + \ldots + (1 + r) + 1\}$$

or

$$A_n = P\left[\frac{(1+r)^n - 1}{r}\right] \qquad \text{...(2.5)}$$

Here too, the difficulty of raising $(1 + r)$ to the *nth* power does arise if the value of n is large. In such cases, the amount of annuity is multiplied by the annuity compound factor (ACF). This can be expressed in the form of an equation as follows:

$$A_n = P(ACF_{r,n} - 1) \qquad \text{...(2.6)}$$

EXAMPLE

The future value of an equal annual investment of Rs 1,000 at the end of a 10-year period at 10% rate of interest will be:

$$\text{Rs } 1000\ [\{(1.10)^{10} - 1\}/0.10] = \text{Rs } 15{,}937.40$$

Alternatively, P multiplied by $ACF_{r,n}$ - 1 and then divided by r will be: Rs 1000 × 1.59374/0.10 = Rs 15,937.40.

In case of an annuity due where cash flows occur at the beginning of a particular period, the amount is invested for the year. As a result, in this case, Eq. 2.5 can be re-written as follows:

$$A_n = P\left[\frac{(1+r)^n - 1}{r}\right] \times (1+r) \qquad \text{...(2.7)}$$

EXAMPLE

The future value of equal annual investment of Rs 1,000 made at the beginning of each year for 10 years at 10% rate of interest will be:

$$\text{Rs } 1000\ [\{(1.10)^{10} - 1\}/0.10] \times 1.10 = \text{Rs } 17{,}531.14.$$

2.2.4 Frequency of Compounding

Normally, the interest rate is given in per annum terms and compounding is also done on an annual basis. But there are cases when compounding is done on a half-yearly or quarterly basis. In specific cases, it is even done monthly. If the frequency of compounding increases, which means that it is done more than once a year, the future value of the receipt will be greater. This is because the annual percentage yield (APY) is greater than the annual percentage rate (APR). The greater the frequency of compounding, the greater is the APY and the larger the future value of the receipt.

APY is the effective annual rate of interest. It is computed by compounding the periodic rate for the compounding frequency. This can be expressed in form of equation as follows:

$$APY = \left(1 + \frac{APR}{m}\right)^m - 1 \qquad \text{...(2.8)}$$

Where:

m = the number of compounding periods per year

EXAMPLE

If the annual interest rate is 12% and compounding is done on a monthly basis, the APY will be:

$$\{1 + (0.12/12)\}^{12} - 1 = 12.68\%.$$

2.3 COMPUTATION OF PRESENT VALUE OF CASH FLOWS

The present value shows today's value of a future sum of money. If today's investment of Rs 100 at 10% rate of interest brings in Rs 110 after a year, the latter is the future value and Rs 100 the present value. It means that if future value is found out through compounding, the present value can be calculated through the reverse of compounding. The process in different situations is shown hereunder.

2.3.1 Present Value of a Single Amount

The formula for determining the future value (A_1) of an amount of money (P) is given in Eq. 2.1. Given the future value of an amount (A_1) the formula for arriving at its present value (P) can be derived from Eq. 2.1 and written as follows:

$$P = \frac{A_1}{(1+r)} \qquad \text{...(2.9)}$$

The equation to arrive at P for Period n will be:

$$P = \frac{A_1}{(1+r)^n} \qquad \text{...(2.10)}$$

EXAMPLE

The present value of Rs 1000 to be received after 5 years at 10% rate of discount will be:

$$\text{Rs } 1000/(1.10)^5 = \text{Rs } 621$$

Alternatively, Rs 1000 can be multiplied by the present value factor ($PVF_{r,n}$) which is 0.621 in this case to arrive the present value:

$$\text{Rs } 1{,}000 \times 0.621 = \text{Rs } 621.$$

2.3.2 Present Value of a Series of Future Values

When a series of receipts occurs over a specific period of time, the present value of all the future values can be found out by adding up the present value of individual future values. If A_1, A_2, A_3 and so on are the receipts during different years, their present value will be:

$$P = A_1/(1 + r) + A_2/(1 + r)^2 + \dots + A_n/(1 + r)^n$$

Summing up the above equation, we get:

Where:

$$P = \sum_{t=1}^{n} \frac{A_t}{(1+r)^t} \qquad ...(2.11)$$

EXAMPLE

A_1, A_2 and A_3 are Rs 2,000, Rs 3,000 and Rs 4,000 respectively. Therefore, the present value at the discount rate of 5% will be:

$$P = \text{Rs } 2000/1.05 + \text{Rs } 3000/(1.05)^2 + \text{Rs } 4000/(1.05)^3 = \text{Rs } 8{,}081.$$

2.3.3 Present Value in Case of Annuity

In case of an annuity, the value of A is uniform and so the present value (P) of an annuity can be written in the form of an equation as follows:

$$P_A = A[1/(1+r) + 1/(1+r)^2 + 1/(1+r)^3 + ... + 1/(1+r)^n]$$

or

$$P_A = A\left[\frac{1-\frac{1}{(1+r)^n}}{r}\right] \qquad ...(2.12)$$

Alternatively, one can go for a tabular solution. In this process, the value of annuity is multiplied by the annuity discount factor. It can be shown as:

$$P_A = A(ADF_{r,n}) \qquad ...(2.13)$$

EXAMPLE

The present value of an investment yielding Rs 1,000 annually for 20 years at a discount rate of 8% will be:

$$\text{Rs } 1000\ [\{1 - (1/1 + r)^{20}\}/0.08\ ] = \text{Rs } 9{,}818.15$$

Alternatively,

$$\text{Rs } 1000\ (9.81815) = \text{Rs } 9{,}818.15.$$

If it is a case of annuity due which means that cash flows occur at the beginning of each period, the result will be multiplied by $(1 + r)$ and on the basis of above example, the present value will be:

$$\text{Rs } 9818.15 \times 1.08 = \text{Rs } 10{,}603.60.$$

2.3.4 Special Cases of Annuity

Perpetuity: There are some special cases of annuity. The first is perpetuity where annuity is infinite. In other words, a perpetuity assures the investor/owner of the funds, periodic cash flows over an infinite period of time (at least in theory). It is normally found in case of preference shares. In this case too, Eq. 2.12 applies, but with a difference. Since n approaches infinity, the term $\{1/(1 + r)\}^n$ approaches zero. As a result, the equation reduces to:

$$P_A = A[(1-0)/r] = A/r \qquad ...(2.14)$$

EXAMPLE

If a company offers an annual dividend of Rs 20 per share and the risk of investment justifies a rate of return of 14%, the present value of perpetuity annuity will be:

Rs 20/0.14 = Rs 142.86.

Deferred Annuity: The other special case of annuity is deferred annuity. It is regular annuity with the exception that the cash begins to flow only after the deferral period. If in a six-year annuity the deferral period is 2 years, cash flows will begin at the end of the third year. In this case, the present value of the cash flow during the deferral period will be subtracted from the present value of the cash flow for the entire period.

EXAMPLE

If the annual cash flow is Rs 500, the total period of annuity is 6 years and the deferral period is 2 years, the present value at a rate of discount of 10% will be:

$= 500\ (\text{ADF}_{10\%,\ 6+2\ \text{yrs}} - \text{ADF}_{10\%,\ 2\text{yrs}})$

$= 500\ (5.3349 - 1.73554) =$ Rs 1799.70.

2.3.5 Present Value of a Cash Flow with Growth Element

There may be a situation where the future cash flows grow at given rates. The growth element can be interpreted in two ways. The first is the arithmetic growth rate where the cash flows grow at a constant rupee value. The second is the compound growth rate where the cash flows grow at a constant percentage rate per period. The computation of the present value in these two cases differs slightly.

Arithmetic Growth Rate: In this case, the process of computing the present value begins with splitting the cash flows into two parts—one being the amount of annuity (without growth element) and the other being the growth value. The present value for both of them is computed separately and then they are added up. This can be expressed in the form of an equation as follows:

$$P_A = A\,(ADF_{r,n}) + G\,(GDF_{r,n}) \qquad ...(2.15)$$

Where:

$$GDF\ r, n = \frac{1}{r}\left[\sum_{t=1}^{n}\frac{1}{(1+r)^t} - n\left(\frac{1}{(1+r)^n}\right)\right]$$

EXAMPLE

An annuity stream for Rs 500 continues for a 5-year period. There is annual growth of Rs 60. The present value of the total cash flow involving a rate of discount of 10% will be:

$$P = \text{Rs } 500(3.7908) + 60[\,1/0.10\ \{3.7908 - 5(0.6209)\}\,]$$

$$= \text{Rs } 2{,}307.18$$

Compound Growth: In case of compound growth, cash flow grows at a certain percentage rate. Let A be the cash flow during Period 1, the cash flow during Period t would be $A(1 + g)^t$. Here g is the growth rate.

The present value is computed in a similar manner as fixed annuity but, at the same time, care is taken of the growth factor. The present value of an annuity with a growth factor can be expressed as an equation as follows:

$$P_{Ag} = \frac{A_t}{(r-g)}\left[1 - \left(\frac{1+g}{1+r}\right)^n\right] \quad ...(2.16)$$

EXAMPLE

A cash flow of Rs 500 grows for 4 years at the annual rate of 3%. The present value of this growing annuity if the discount rate is 10% will be:

$$P_{3,4} = \text{Rs } 500/(0.10 - 0.03)\ [1 - \{1.03)/(1.10)\}^4] = \text{Rs } 1{,}651.02$$

SUMMARY

An investment yields interest over the period for which it is made. Interest exists because of the preference for immediate consumption. It is because of this interest rate that money has a time value. The future value of an investment made today is equal to the sum of its present value and the interest compounded at regular intervals. The greater the number of compoundings in a year, the greater is the APY or the effective interest rate. The future value can be computed for a single investment, a series of investments of unequal amounts or for an annuity implying a uniform cash flow. The annuity may be a regular annuity, an annuity due, a perpetual annuity or a deferred annuity.

The calculation of the present value of an amount of future cash flow or a series of future cash flows is based on the reverse of compounding. However, in the case of perpetuity, the time period is infinite and there is no compounding of the discount rate.

When a cash flow is growing over time either by a fixed value or by a fixed percentage, the growth element is also taken into account for the purpose of discounting.

POINTS TO REMEMBER

1. Calculate the future value of a single amount.

$$A_n = P(1 + r)^n$$

2. Calculate the future value of a series of payments.

$$A_n = P_1(1 + r)^{n-1} + P_2(1 + r)^{n-2} + P_3(1 + r)^{n-3} + \ldots + P_{n-1}(1 + r) + P_n$$

3. Calculate the future value of a regular annuity.

$$A_n = P\left[\frac{(1+r)^n - 1}{r}\right]$$

4. Calculate the future value of an annuity due.

$$A_n = P\left[\frac{(1+r)^n - 1}{r}\right] \times (1+r)$$

5. Show how is frequency of compounding arrived at.

$$APY = \left(1 + \frac{APR}{m}\right)^m - 1$$

6. Calculate the present value of a single amount.

$$P = \frac{A_1}{(1+r)^n}$$

7. Calculate the present value of a series of future values.

$$P = \sum_{t=1}^{n} \frac{A_t}{(1+r)^t}$$

8. Calculate the present value in case of a regular annuity.

$$P_A = A\left[\frac{1-\frac{1}{(1+r)^n}}{r}\right]$$

9. Calculate the present value of perpetual annuity.

$$P_A = A[(1-0)/r] = A/r$$

10. Calculate the present value of cash flow with arithmetic growth rate.

$$P_A = A(ADF_{r,n}) + G\,(GDF_{r,n})$$

11. Calculate the present value of cash flow with compound growth rate.

$$P_{Ag} = \frac{A_t}{(r-g)}\left[1-\left(\frac{1+g}{1+r}\right)^n\right]$$

DESCRIPTIVE QUESTIONS

1. How do you find the future value of an amount invested today? Explain with the help of an example.
2. Why is it necessary to calculate the present value of an amount expected to be received in future? How is it calculated?
3. Explain the procedure for calculating the present value of:
   (a) regular annuity
   (b) annuity due
   (c) deferred annuity
4. Distinguish between annual percentage yield and annual percentage rate. Give an example in support of your explanation.

OBJECTIVE-TYPE QUESTIONS

1. Mark true or false.
   (a) Present value is multiplied by the compound factor to find the future value.
   (b) In case of regular annuity, cash flow occurs at the beginning of each time period.
   (c) In case of annuity due, cash flow occurs at the beginning of each time period.
   (d) Actual percentage rate and annual percentage yield are synonymous.
   (e) In case of deferred annuity, the present value of cash flow during the deferral period is subtracted from that for the entire period.

2. Choose the most suitable answer.
   (a) Computing future value involves:
      (i) simple interest rate formula
      (ii) compound interest rate formula
      (iii) the average of both the above
   (b) An annuity involves:
      (i) uniform cash flow during different periods
      (ii) different size of cash flows during different periods
      (iii) both of the above
   (c) Annuity due is a case in which:
      (i) uniform cash flows occur at the end of each period
      (ii) uniform cash flows occur at the beginning of each period
      (iii) uniform cash flows occur in the middle of each period
   (d) With increasing frequency of compounding:
      (i) annual percentage yield = annual percentage rate of interest
      (ii) annual percentage yield > annual percentage rate of interest
      (iii) annual percentage yield < annual percentage rate of interest
   (e) When cash flow grows at a constant percentage rate per period:
      (i) arithmetic growth rate factor is taken into account
      (ii) compound growth rate factor is taken into account
      (iii) none of the above

NUMERICAL PROBLEMS

1. Find out the future value of Rs 15,000 invested now for a period of 5 years using a time preference rate of 12%.
2. Compute the present value of Rs 60,000 to be received each year for 3 years from now using a discount rate of 14%.
3. A company promises to pay 6% interest annually, forever, on Rs 5,000 invested in one of its policies. Find out the present value of perpetuity annuity.
4. Find the present value of Rs 100 paid in Years 2, 4, 6, 8 and 10 assuming a 10% discount rate.
5. You have to choose between two savings accounts. One pays an annual rate of 6.10% compounded quarterly, whereas the other pays an annual rate of 6% compounded monthly. Which account will give you greater value?
6. At 10% annual interest, how long does it take Rs 10,000 to grow to become Rs 1,00,000. Find out the number of periods.
7. Find out the annual compound growth rate of an investment if Rs 232 increases to Rs 268 in 3 years.

8. Compare the future value in 2 years of Rs 100 to be invested today at 8% under the following schemes:
   (a) annual compounding
   (b) half-yearly compounding
   (c) quarterly compounding
9. What is the present value of a 7-year Rs 1,000 annuity if the first Rs 1,000 payment is made 4 years from today and discount rate is 10%.
10. Which of the perpetuities represent the largest present value:

Perpetuity	Annual amount (Rs)	Discount rate (%)
A	28,000	7
B	1,00,000	12
C	5,000	8

11. Mr. A is depositing Rs 4,000 in a recurring bank deposit that pays 9% p.a. compound interest. How much amount will he get at the end of the fifth year?
12. Mr. A deposits Rs 10,000 in a bank for 6 years. If the interest rate is 12% and the frequency of compounding is four times a year, what will be the size of deposit after 6 years?

SOLVED NUMERICAL PROBLEMS

1. A person saves Rs 10,000 every year for 18 years so that he will get a lumpsum amount thereafter to do a business. He expects that his savings should earn 8% interest. Find the size of the lumpsum amount.

Solution

Based on Eq. 2.5

Rs 10,000 x $\{(1.08^{18} - 1)/0.08\}$

= Rs 10,000 x 37.4502 = Rs 3,74,502.

2. A company has to replace a machine after 21 years for which it deposits Rs 30,000 every year in the beginning of the year. In all, there are 21 installments deposited at the rate of 5% p.a. Find the future value.

Solution

Based on Eq. 2.7

Rs 30,000 x $\{(1.05^{21} - 1)/0.05\}$ x 1.05

= Rs 30,000 x (2.7860/0.05) x 1.05

= Rs 11,25,180.

3. A shareholder receives dividend amounting to Rs 5000, Rs 5,200, Rs 5,500 and Rs 5,700 during next four years after which he sells the share. He deposits the entire amount of dividend to earn 10% interest. Find the amount of interest at the end of the fourth year.

Solution

Rs 5,000$(1.10)^3$ + 5,200$(1.10)^2$ + 5,500(1.10) + 5,700

= Rs 6,655 + 6,292 + 6,050 + 5,700 = Rs 24,697.

4. A person deposits Rs 5,000 for one year to earn 10% interest p.a.. Find the total amount if: (a) interest is compounded semi-annually, and (b) interest is compounded quarterly.

Solution

Based on Eq. 2.8

(a) interest is compounded semi-annually:

$\{1 + (0.10/2)\}^2 - 1$

$= 0.1025 = 10.25\%$

(b) interest is compounded quarterly:

$\{1 + (0.10/4)\}^4 - 1$

$= 0.1038 = 10.38\%$

5. A company is expecting to earn Rs 5,000, Rs 5,500, Rs 5,700 and Rs 6,000 during the next four years. What will be the present value of earning, given a discount rate of 10%?

Solution

Based on Eq. 2.11

Rs $5{,}000/1.10 + 5{,}500/1.10^2 + 5{,}700/1.10^3 + 6{,}000/1.10^4$

= Rs 4,545.45 + 4,545.45 + 4,282.49 + 4,098.08

= Rs 17,471.47

6. A security provides equal return amounting to Rs 10,000 per year for five years, given a required rate of return of 6%. Calculate the present value of return.

Solution

Based on Eq. 2.13

Rs 10,000 x 4.2124 = Rs 42,124

7. A seller offers you a deal that pays Rs 10,648 in 3 years for only Rs 8,000 that you pay today. Calculate the interest rate that your investment would earn.

Solution

Interpreting Eq. 2.9

Interest rate = $(10{,}648 / 8{,}000)^{1/3} - 1 = 0.10 = 10\%$

8. If a sewing machine company issues 8% preference shares of Rs 10 each paying a dividend of Rs 0.50 per share, what would be the current price of the share, given an interest rate of 8%?

Solution

Based on Eq. 2.14

Rs 0.50 / 0.08 = Rs 6.25

9. If an annuity payment for Rs 5,000 for 20 years is deferred by 2 years, meaning that the first payment will begin at the end of the third year, what would be the present value, given a discount rate of 10%?

Solution

Rs 5,000 $(ADF_{10\%,\ 22\ yrs.} - ADF_{10\%,\ 2yrs.})$

= Rs 5,000 (8.7715 – 1.7355) = Rs 35,180

10. If an annuity payment for Rs 5,000 goes for a 10-year period and the amount moves up by Rs 50 each, what would be the present value of the total payment including the growth factor, given a discount factor of 10%?

Solution

Based on Eq. 2.15

Rs 5,000 (6.1446) + 50 [1/0.10 {6.1446 – 10 (0.3855)}]

= Rs 30,723 + 1,144.80

= Rs 31,867.80

11. An annuity payment for Rs 10,000 for 4 years grows at 3% p.a. Find the present value, as shown in the book, given a discount rate of 10%.

Solution

Based on Eq. 2.16

$P_{3,4}$ = Rs {10,000/ (0.10 – 0.03)} x 1 – $(1.03/1.10)^4$

= Rs 1,42,857.14 x 0.231261

= Rs 33,037.29

12. If a house is expected to fetch a net rental of Rs 30,000 next year which is expected to increase by 5% every year. If the discount rate is 10%, find the present value of the rental stream.

Solution

Since $PV = \frac{C}{r - g}$

$\frac{30{,}000}{0.10 - 0.05}$ = Rs 6,00,000

CASE STUDY

ICICI Prudential Retirement Plan

ICICI Prudential has an insurance-cum-pension plan that covers not only risk but also provides pension after retirement.

How does the Plan work?

First, select a premium payment term that stretches over 3 to 5 years. The minimum amount of premium is Rs 1,00,000 for a three-year period or Rs 60,000 for five years. The vesting age lies between 50 and 80 years, subject to a minimum term of 10 years.

Second, when you pay the premium for 3 or 5 years, the amount is invested in different types of mutual fund schemes. The principal amount along with the earnings swells to a size that is sufficient for the payment of pension regularly.

Third, if you survive till the vesting age, you get pension. You do have an option to get up to one-third of the fund value as lumpsum. If you do not survive up to the beginning of the vesting age, the spouse/nominee receives the fund value. Alternatively, the fund value can be used to buy an annuity from ICICI Prudential.

Fourth, the payment of pension begins the moment you reach the age of 50. However, you have an option to defer this date till the age of 80 years.

Fifth, the amount of premium is invested in different types of schemes that contain various combinations of risk and return. The higher the risk, the greater is the return. The lower the risk, the smaller is the return. You are free to choose a particular combination and accordingly, your premium will be invested.

Sixth, you are free also to choose the frequency of pension payment. The annuity can be received monthly/ quarterly /half-yearly /yearly. You are free also to choose any of the following pension schemes:

(a) Life annuity
(b) Life annuity with return of purchase price
(c) Life annuity guaranteed for 5/10/15 years and for the life thereafter
(d) Joint life with or without return of purchase price

Illustration 1

Annual premium: Rs 10,00,000
Premium payment term: 3 years
Term: 15 years
Age at entry: 35 years

Return @ 6% p.a.		Return @ 10% p.a.	
Accumulated savings	Expected early annuity	Accumulated savings	Expected early annuity
Rs 56,34,422	Rs 4,84,043	Rs 94,71,548	Rs 8,13,683

Illustration 1I

Annual premium: Rs 5,00,000
Premium payment term: 5 years
Term: 15 years
Age at entry: 35 years

Return @ 6% p.a.		Return @ 10% p.a.	
Accumulated savings	Expected early annuity	Accumulated savings	Expected early annuity
Rs 45,65,962	Rs 3,92,253	Rs 74,15,988	Rs 6,37,094

The above are illustrative returns, net of all charges. The amount is subject to changes depending on changing behaviour of the financial market.

Source: icicibank.com

Questions:

1. Explain how the concept of future value works in this plan.
2. Can you find out what rate of interest rate is involved to make the accumulated value so big?

SELECT FURTHER READINGS

Osborn, R. (1957). *The Mathematics of Investment*. New York: Harper & Row.

Shao, Stephen P. and Lawrence P. Shao (1998). *Mathematics for Management and Finance*. Cincinnati: South Western Publishers, Part III.

3

CONCEPT OF RISK AND RETURN

OBJECTIVES

To describe the concept of returns from investment

To explain how returns are estimated based on the theory of probability

To describe the concept of risk

To show how risk is computed in case of a single investment/portfolio of investments

To analyse systematic/unsystematic risk in a Capital-Asset-Pricing Model (CAPM) framework

The returns from an investment cannot be thought of in isolation of the risk factor. Since the future is uncertain, there is always a chance that the returns will be either better or worse than anticipated. The larger the variation in returns, the greater the involvement of the risk factor.

The terms risk and uncertainty are often used synonymously. However, there is difference between the two. Uncertainty is the case when the decision-maker knows all the possible outcomes of a particular act, but does not have an idea of the probabilities of the outcomes. On the contrary, risk is related to a situation in which the decision-maker knows the probabilities of the various outcomes. In other words, risk is a quantifiable uncertainty.

The degree of risk may be lower for a firm whose finance manager is conservative. On the contrary, an aggressive finance manager is ready to bear even greater risk. The matter, however, does not end there. Risk needs to be measured in an objective way in order to know whether it justifies a specific rate of return. An investor requires a higher return from a risky project in order to compensate for the risk. The ultimate aim is to maximise the returns with a given level of risk or to minimise the risk with a given level of return. It is for this purpose that returns and risk need to be measured.

3.1 BASIC CONCEPTS OF RETURNS

3.1.1 Percentage Return

Return is the reward of making investment. If you buy a share of Rs 100 and get a dividend of Rs 12 at the end of the year, the return in rupee terms will be Rs 12. The percentage return will be:

$$12/100 = 0.12 \text{ or } 12\%$$

The percentage return in the form of dividend is also known as **dividend yield** which is simply the amount of dividend at the end of the year divided by the initial price of the share. In terms of an equation,

$$\text{Dividend yield} = D_t + 1/P_t \qquad \text{...(3.1)}$$

If you buy a share for Rs 100, the market price of share moves up to Rs 130 at the end of the year; the amount of increase is known as **capital gains**. Capital gain is also a type of return which will be in this case:

$$\text{Rs } (130 - 100)/100 = 0.30 = 30\%$$

In other words, capital gain is the change in the price of share divided by the initial price of the share. In terms of equation,

$$\text{Capital gains} = (P_t + 1 - P_t)/P_t \qquad \text{...(3.2)}$$

If dividend yield and capital gains occur at the same time, total return will be:

$$0.12 + 0.30 = 0.42 = 42\%$$

3.1.2 Average Return: Simple and Weighted Average

If you buy four shares of two different companies, the return in case of different companies will differ. In such cases you calculate the average return. The average may be a simple average. Alternatively, it may be an investment-weighted average.

If investment in Channel 1 gives 15% return and that in Channel 2 gives 12% return, the simple average return will be:

$$(0.15 + 0.12)/2 = 0.135 = 13.5\%$$

If 70% of the investment is made in Channel 1 and 30% investment is made in Channel 2, the weighted average investment will be:

$$\{(0.15 \times 0.7) + (0.12 \times 0.3)\}/2$$
$$= 0.105 + 0.036 = 0.141 = 14.1\%$$

3.1.3 Arithmetic and Geometric Mean

If the percentage return varies from year to year, it can be expressed in average terms. The average return is calculated normally on the basis of arithmetic mean. But the geometric mean can also be used in very specific cases. If one has to find out the average compound return per year over a specific period, the geometric mean will be used. But, on the other hand, if one has to know the return in an average year over a specific period, the use of the arithmetic mean is suggested.

The readers will find the calculation of arithmetic and geometric mean in any book on statistics. Yet a simple example can be presented here. If an investment has annual return of 10.0% in the first year, 12.0% in the second year and 5.0% in the third year,

Arithmetic mean will be: $(0.10 + 0.12 + 0.05)/3 = 0.09 = 9.0\%$.

Geometric mean will be: $(1.10 \times 1.12 \times 1.05)^{1/3} = 1.2936^{1/3} - 1 = 0.089599 = 8.96\%$.

3.1.4 The Concept of Probability

No finance manager knows in advance what is the actual return from an investment. He or she may base his/her decision of the actual outcomes on probabilities. Probabilities are merely numbers that represent the likelihood or chance of occurrence of various outcomes. For example, if an oil drilling operation has 60% chance of getting oil and 40% chance of not getting oil, one can say that getting oil has a 60% probability and not getting oil has a 40% probability. This means that the total probability always equals 100% or 1. A probability distribution thus describes the outcomes and their associated probabilities.

> The terms risk and uncertainty are often used synonymously. However, there is difference between the two. Uncertainty is the case when the decision-maker knows all the possible outcomes of a particular act, but does not have an idea of the probabilities of the outcomes. Risk is related to a situation in which the decision-maker knows the probabilities of the various outcomes. Risk is a quantifiable uncertainty.

A probability distribution may be either discrete or continuous. The former has only a finite number of outcomes, whereas in the case of a continuous distribution, outcomes are not finite. If one says that there is a 40% probability of earning Rs 400 and a 60% probability of earning Rs 600, it is a case of discrete distribution as the outcomes are finite. However, if one says that there is a 40% probability of earning between Rs 300 and Rs 500 and a 60% probability of earning between Rs 600 and Rs 800, it is a case of continuous probability distribution because the outcomes are not finite.

It is a fact that continuous distributions are a more realistic description of outcomes, but discrete distributions are normally used for practical applications. This is because discrete distributions are, first, simpler to use, and second, probability distributions are estimated on the basis of actual historical data that are usually finite numbers.

3.1.5 Expected Return from a Single Investment

Expected return (*A*) is the mean of probability distribution. It is the probability-weighted average of outcomes. It can be expressed in the form of an equation as follows:

$$\overline{A} = P_1 A_1 + P_2 A_2 + P_3 A_3 + \ldots + P_n A_n$$

Summing up, we get:

$$\overline{A} = \sum_{x=0}^{n} P_x A_x \qquad \text{...(3.3)}$$

EXAMPLE

If there is a 20% probability of an outcome of Rs 400, a 60% probability of an outcome of Rs 600 and a 20% probability of an outcome of Rs 900, the expected value will be:

$$\overline{A} = (0.2 \times 400) + (0.6 \times 600) + (0.2 \times 900) = \text{Rs } 620.$$

3.1.6 Expected Returns from International Investment

In case of international investment, the estimation of expected return also takes into account changes in the exchange rate. Therefore, the return from a security abroad in terms of home-country currency (HC) is calculated as follows:

$$1+R_{HC}=\left[1+\frac{S_1-S_0+I}{S_0}\right]\times 1+e \qquad \text{...(3.4)}$$

Where:

S_0 = host-country currency value of security during t_0
S_1 = host-country currency value of security during t_1
I = income from dividend/interest
e = the exchange rate changes.

EXAMPLE

The present value of security in terms of host-country currency is US $ 100 that goes up to US $ 102 after one year. The interest during the year is US $ 8. The US dollar appreciates by 3%. The return in terms of home-country currency, rupee will be:

R_{HC} = [{1 + (102 – 100 + 8)/100 } × 1.03] – 1 = 0.133 = 13.3%.

3.1.7 Portfolio Return

Portfolio return ($\overline{X}_p$) is the weighted average of the expected return from different securities existing in the portfolio. In a two-security portfolio model, $\overline{X}_p$ from Securities A and B can be expressed as follows:

$$\overline{X}_p=\overline{A}_A W_A+\overline{A}_B W_B \qquad \text{...(3.5)}$$

Where:

W is the relative share of investment in the two securities.

EXAMPLE

If Security A yields a 10% return and Security B a 12% return and if the amount of investment in these two securities is in the ratio of 60:40 respectively, the portfolio return will be:

$$\overline{X}_p = 0.10\times 0.6+0.12\times 0.4=0.108=10.8\%$$

3.2 CONCEPT AND MEASUREMENT OF RISK

3.2.1 Sources of Risk

In finance, risk is normally associated with the volatility of returns from investment. The greater the volatility of returns, the larger is the risk involved therein. There are a host of factors that lead to such volatility. They are:

1. Uncertainty in the future course of the economy in general;
2. Inflation;
3. Operating risk at the micro level;
4. Political risk.

The most important source of risk arises from uncertainty regarding the future course of the economy in general. For example, a boom is a condition of the economy in which production, profits and income tend to rise. On the contrary, a downtrend occurs in these same variables during a depression. These conditions are influenced by a host of factors the occurrence of which is not known to the decision-makers in advance. Again, there may be changes in the consumption pattern in general or there may be qualitative changes in commodities produced because of changes in technology. All of these influence future returns.

Inflation is another source of risk. The higher the rate of inflation, the lower the real value of returns. Moreover, inflation heightens uncertainty with regard to production cost as well as the price of the product. The firm may charge a higher price for its products and thus maintain the level of its profits, but then the consumption pattern may shift in favour of cheaper substitutes that may affect sales.

The firm may have to face various kinds of operating risks. Such risks may be high when the organisational linkages become weaker or the management's performance is poor. For example, if the management changes hands, the finance manager is not sure whether the new management will be better or equally efficient. If the new management turns out to be inefficient, the returns may be lower. Again, there may be labour problems that could have an adverse impact on productivity. Yet again, there may arise financial risk on account of sub-optimal leverage or due to the lack of sufficient liquidity.

Volatility in returns may also arise due to non-economic factors. Often political risk entails upon the performance of a firm. Political risk arises due to changes in the political structure of a country. Changes in governmental regulations may be another source of risk. Whatever be the reason, it does entail upon returns.

3.2.2 Risk in Case of a Single Investment

Risk represents the variance between actual returns or the *ex post* returns and the expected returns or the *ex ante* returns. After the computation of the expected value or the mean, it is necessary to measure the variance or the deviation of outcomes from the mean. The deviation is known as dispersion or the spread of probability distribution. There are various measures of dispersion, yet in finance it is traditionally measured by variance and the standard deviation.

Variance is a measure of dispersion of all possible outcomes around the mean. It is typically shown using the Greek letter, s2. It can be expressed in the form of an equation as follows:

$$\sigma^2(Var.) = P_1(A_1 - \overline{A})^2 + P_2(A_2 - \overline{A})^2 + \ldots + P_n(A_n - \overline{A})^n$$

Summing up, we get:

$$\sigma^2(Var.) = \sum_{x=0}^{n} P_x(A_x - \overline{A})^2 \quad ...(3.6)$$

Again, standard deviation (SD) is the square root of variance. Therefore SD is expressed as follows:

$$\sigma(SD) = (Var.)^{1/2} \quad ...(3.7)$$

EXAMPLE

There is a 20% probability of a boom in which case the returns may be Rs 800. There is a 20% probability a depression in which case returns may fall to Rs 400. But there is a 60% probability of a normal trend where the returns are expected to be Rs 600. Find out expected value, variance and standard deviation.

Expected Value:

$$(0.2 \times 400) + (0.6 \times 600) + (0.2 \times 800) = \text{Rs } 600.$$

Variance:

$$(0.2)\ (400 - 600)^2 + (0.6)\ (600 - 600)^2 + (0.2)\ (800 - 600)^2 = 16{,}000.$$

Standard Deviation:

$$(16000)^{1/2} = 126.49.$$

3.3 PORTFOLIO RISK

The preceding discussion shows how the risk of a particular investment is computed. The investor tries to reduce the risk involved in the existing portfolio through diversification. Diversification means simultaneous investment in different securities: which may be within the country or outside the country. But diversification will help reduce risk only when the co-variance/correlation of returns between the existing portfolio and the new portfolio is negative. This means that if returns in one set of investments is increasing, they are falling in the other set. If co-variance/correlation is positive it means that if returns in one set are increasing, they are increasing in the other set too, this means that diversification will raise the risk and, therefore, any diversification is futile. Again, if co-variance is zero or the returns from the two sets of investment are uncorrelated, it does not establish any linear relationship between the two sets of investment. Therefore, it is of great relevance to know what is meant by co-variance or correlation.

Co-variance is a statistical concept that relates movement in one set of variables to movement in other set of variables. The co-variance between two sets of returns, *A*1 and *A*2 can be written in the form of an equation as follows:

$$Cov(A_1, A_2) = \sum_{t=1}^{N} P_t(A_{1t} - \overline{A}_1)\ (A_{2t} - \overline{A}_2) \quad ...(3.8)$$

Similarly, correlation, which is denoted by the small Greek letter rho (r), serves the same purpose. The difference between co-variance and correlation is that while the former is sensitive to the particular units of measurement, correlation removes this sensitivity. Co-variance can take on any value, the correlation co-efficient can exist only between minus 1 and plus 1. The correlation co-efficient can be expressed as follows:

$$\rho_{1,2} = Cov\ A_1, A_2/\sigma_1\sigma_2 \quad ...(3.9)$$

After co-variance/correlation is established between the existing portfolio and the new investment, it is easy to measure the risk of the entire portfolio that includes both the existing portfolio and the new portfolio. Different sets of portfolio have their weight, w meaning how much of the total investment they represent. Portfolio risk (in terms of standard deviation) can be expressed as follows:

$$\sigma_p = [w_1^2 Var\ A_1 + w_2^2 Var\ A_2 + 2(w_1)\ (w_2)\ (Cov\ A_1, A_2)]^{1/2} \quad ...(3.10)$$

The portfolio risk can be shown with the following example.

EXAMPLE

Calculate the portfolio return and risk using the following data:

Probability of occurrence of returns	Existing portfolio	New portfolio
0.30	10%	8%
0.30	7%	12%
0.40	13%	7%

Expected Return:

Existing portfolio = 0.3 × 10.0 + 0.3 × 7.0 + 0.4 × 13.0 = 10.3%

New portfolio = 0.3 × 8.0 + 0.3 × 12.0 + 0.4 × 7 = 8.8%

Variance and Standard deviation:

Existing portfolio:

$$\sigma^2\ (Var.) = 0.3\ (10.0 - 10.3)^2 + 0.3(7.0 - 10.3)^2 + 0.4\ (13.0 - 10.3)^2$$
$$= 6.21.$$
$$\sigma\ (SD) = 2.49.$$

New portfolio:

$$\sigma^2\ (Var.) = 0.3\ (8.0 - 8.8)2 + 0.3(12.0 - 8.8)2 + 0.4(7.0 - 8.8)2$$
$$= 4.56.$$
$$\sigma\ (SD) = 2.14.$$

Co-variance A_1, A_2:

$$0.3(-0.3)\ (-0.8) + 0.3\ (-3.3)\ (3.2) + 0.4(2.7)\ (-1.8) = -5.040$$

Correlation co-efficient A_1, A_2: $\dfrac{-5.040}{2.49 - 2.14}$

$$= -0.9458$$

Portfolio return (assuming 70% investment on the existing portfolio and 30% on the new portfolio):

$$0.7 \times 10.3 + 0.3 \times 8.8 = 9.85\%$$

Portfolio risk in terms of variance:

$$(0.7)^2 (6.21) + (0.3)^2 (4.56) + 2(0.7)(0.3)(-5.040)$$

$$= 1.3365$$

Thus the above example shows that since the co-variance/correlation coefficient between the existing portfolio and the new portfolio is negative, diversification through investment in the new portfolio reduces the risk (in terms of variance) from 6.21 to 1.3365. In terms of standard deviation, it comes down from 2.49 to 1.1561.

3.4 THE CAPITAL-ASSET-PRICING MODEL (CAPM)

3.4.1 Systematic Risk versus Unsystematic Risk

The preceding section shows how portfolio risk can be reduced through diversification. However, diversification reduces only a particular type of risk. From this point of view, a particular asset or a portfolio of asset possesses two types of risk: first, the unsystematic risk that can be diversified away and; second, the systematic risk that cannot be diversified away through investment in domestic securities.

The unsystematic risk is firm-specific and so simultaneous investment in other securities may lower it. On the other hand, systematic risk is a macroeconomic risk, inherent in the performance of the economy as a whole. It is, therefore, similar to all the securities in the market. This is why it is also known as the market risk. It cannot be reduced through diversification and so it is the systematic risk that sets the expected or the required rate of return. Fig. 3.1 shows how the unsystematic risk is reduced through diversification or putting in more securities in the investment portfolio and also how the systematic risk remains unchanged.

The unsystematic risk is firm-specific and so simultaneous investment in other securities may lower it. On the other hand, systematic risk is a macroeconomic risk, inherent in the performance of the economy as a whole.

As per Fig. 3.1, when there are 12 assets in the investment portfolio, the risk includes both the components, viz., unsystematic risk and the market risk. But when diversification is introduced through adding more assets to the investment portfolio and when the number of assets in the portfolio reaches 30, the unsystematic risk is completely eliminated. The expected return comprises only market risk.

3.4.2 Measurement of Systematic Risk and Determinants of Beta

When one talks about the systematic risk, it is worth knowing how it is measured. One way to measure the systematic risk of an individual asset or a portfolio of assets is to compare

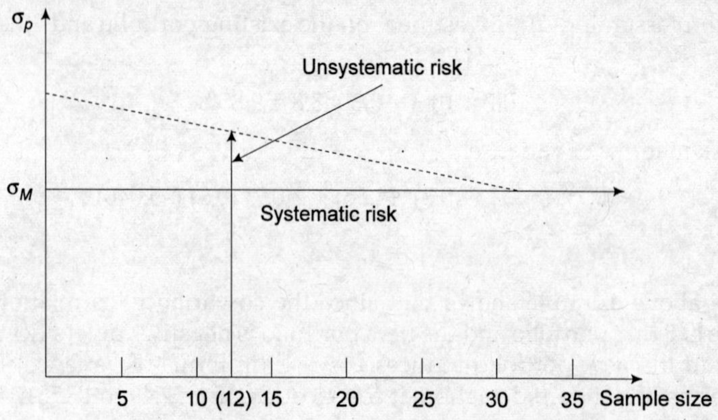

FIG. 3.1 Systematic risk and unsystematic risk

its returns over time with those of the market portfolio. The comparison reflects the asset exposure to the systematic risk factors.

An asset's systematic risk is denoted by a capital Greek letter, beta (b). It shows how an asset's returns vary with the market portfolio's returns, compared to the total risk of the market portfolio. It can be expressed in the form of an equation as follows:

$$\beta = \frac{cov A_1, A_M}{\sigma_M^2} \quad ...(3.11)$$

Where:

A_M = the market portfolio return

$\sigma^2{}_M$ = the total risk of the market portfolio.

Suppose cov (A_1, A_M) is 250 and σ^2_M is 225:

$\beta = 250/225 = 1.11$

The discussion of *beta* involves three situations. First, a beta being more than 1 means that the assets adding to the portfolio systematic risk have high co-variance with the market returns. Secondly, assets reducing portfolio systematic risk will have a low co-variance and a beta of less than 1. Thirdly, in case of assets neither increasing nor reducing the portfolio systematic risk, beta is equal to 1. Thus beta is a measure of relative risk compared to portfolio variance that measures absolute risk. Beta indicates the variability of an asset's returns relative to the market portfolio.

As far as determinants of beta are concerned, they are primarily:

1. Operating leverage
2. Financial leverage
3. Cyclicality of revenues

The operating leverage, which is discussed in Chapter 21, makes it clear that if the degree of operating leverage is large, the changes in the operating profits will be larger, making the venture riskier. Naturally, beta will be higher. The readers are suggested to go through Chapter 21.

Financial leverage means introduction of fixed-cost funds in the capital structure. Thus, when fixed-cost debt is brought into the capital structure, risk gets lower. In other words, the risk in an all-equity firm is higher than in a leveraged firm. Beta is thus higher in an all-equity firm. The readers are suggested to go through Chapter 14 for detailed discussion of financial leverage.

Lastly, higher cyclicality of revenues means that the range of expansion and contraction of revenues, respectively, during boom and depression is larger. The experiences show that the automobile industry has higher cyclicality of revenues than the utilities. Thus, automobile industry has a higher risk and higher beta than the utilities.

3.4.3 Beta and the Required Rate of Investment

Systematic risk can be avoided to a large extent through investment in risk-free securities. Literally speaking, there are no risk-free securities. Even government securities possess some amount of risk. But for all practical purposes, government securities are known as risk-free securities. In such a situation, if an investor invests in the market portfolio, he is prone to the systematic risk. Thus, he would like to invest in the market portfolio only when he gets a higher return than that from a risk-free investment. How much higher the required return should be or how much should be the risk premium, all depends upon the size of beta. The higher the beta, the larger will be the risk premium and the larger will be the required rate of return. The Capital Asset Pricing Model (CAPM) suggests that the total expected return of a security (A_1) should be the sum of the risk-free return (A_f) and its risk premium $\beta_1(\overline{A}_M - A_f)$. This can be expressed in the form of an equation as follows:

$$A_1 = A_f + \beta_1(\overline{A}_M - A_f) \qquad \text{...(3.12)}$$

EXAMPLE

If the risk-free rate of return is 8%, the rate of return on the market portfolio is 12%, variance of the market portfolio is 200 and co-variance between the particular asset and the market portfolio is 300, the required rate of return will be:

Applying Eq. 3.12, the systematic risk will be:

$$\beta = 300/200 = 1.5$$

Again, applying Eq. 3.13, the required rate of return will be:

$$A_1 = 8\% + 1.5\,(12\% - 8\%) = 14\%$$

3.4.4 Security Market Line

When the capital market is in equilibrium, Eq. 3.10 is called the security market line (SML) and at this point, the required rate of return equals the expected rate of return. It is a line joining the risk-free return from the risk-free investments and the risky return from the market securities. Fig. 3.2 shows that beta is zero with a risk-free return of 5%. The return on market portfolio is 12%. The required rate of return goes up to 12% with beta equal to 1. Again, the required rate of return moves further up to 15.5% with a beta equal to 1.5.

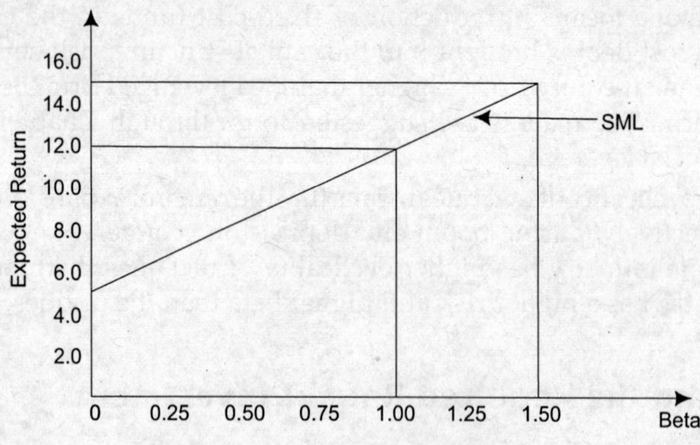

FIG. 3.2 Security Market Line (SML)

There may be a shift in the slope of the SML. The factors responsible for this shift are primarily:

1. Change in the inflationary expectations
2. Change in the risk aversion.

Changes in the inflationary expectations influence the risk-free interest rate insofar as the risk-free interest rate presents a combine of real interest rate and the inflationary expectations. With inflationary expectations being on the upward move, there would be an increase in the risk-free interest rate. With their downward move, risk-free interest rate would decline.

Again, risk aversion means that an investor requires an increased return for increased risk. The slope of the SML would be steeper if the degree of risk aversion is greater. It is because a higher level of return will be required for each level of risk as measured by beta.

Capital-Asset-Pricing Model (CAPM)

CAPM suggests the following:

1. Investors hold a risky investment portfolio only when it is well diversified so as to reduce unsystematic risk.
2. Expected returns are influenced by systematic risk that is measured by an asset's or a portfolio's beta. The higher the level of systematic risk, the greater is the expected return.
3. Expected returns have two components. The first is the risk-free rate and the second the risk premium.
4. An asset's risk premium is the reward for carrying systematic risk. It is equal to the product of market risk premium and the asset's beta.

3.4.5 Appraisal of CAPM

It is true that the CAPM developed by William Sharpe (1964) has important implications in corporate financial decisions and does have real-world applicability, but there are a few subsequent studies that show something more that has not been explained by CAPM. Fama and French (1992, 1993) find in their empirical study that the market capitalization size and market-to-book-value variables were a more significant influence on the average returns from shares. The influence of beta was minimal. However, they do agree that beta indicates the underlying minimum return that a risk-averse investor should expect to earn.

Again, there are some multifactor models based on the arbitrage pricing theory that believe that the returns from a security are sensitive not only to beta but a host of factors, such as changes in expected inflation, unanticipated changes in inflation, unanticipated changes in industrial production, unanticipated changes in the yield differential between low-rated and high-rated bonds, and unanticipated changes in yield differential between long-term bonds and short-term bonds (Roll and Ross, 1984; Chen, Roll and Ross, 1986). The discussion of the arbitrage pricing thoery lies outside the scope of this book.

SUMMARY

Returns from an investment are often fraught with risk, because the future is uncertain. Risk, unlike complete uncertainty, is measurable as the probabilities of various outcomes are known. The expected return is based on probabilities—discrete or continuous. It is the mean of probability distribution. In cases of international investment, it also takes into account changes in the exchange rate. Portfolio return is the weighted average of the expected returns from different securities existing in the portfolio.

Risk represents the variance between the probable returns and the expected return. Standard deviation is the square root of variance. Risk of a portfolio of assets depends on the co-variance/correlation of returns between the existing portfolio and the new asset. If the co-variance/correlation is negative, risk can be reduced through diversification of investment. But it is only the unsystematic risk that can be reduced in this way. Systematic risk, that is, macroeconomic or market risk denoted by beta is the major determinant of expected return. The higher the beta, the larger will be the risk premium and the greater will be the expected return.

POINTS TO REMEMBER

1. What is expected return?
   - It is the sum of probable returns where the total of probabilities is 1. In terms of an equation:

$$\overline{A} = \sum_{x=0}^{n} P_x A_x$$

2. What is portfolio return?
   - It is the weighted average of expected returns from different investments in the portfolio. In terms of an equation:

$$\overline{X}_P = \overline{A}_A W_A + \overline{A}_B W_B$$

3. What is risk? How is it measured?
   - Risk is volatility in returns. It is shown by variance or standard deviation. Standard deviation is the square root of variance. In terms of an equation:

$$\sigma^2 (Var.) = \sum_{x=0}^{n} P_x (A_x - \overline{A})^2$$

4. What is portfolio risk?
   - Portfolio risk is the weighted average of risk present in different investments in the portfolio. In terms of an equation:

$$\sigma_p = [w_1^2 \, Var\, A_1 + w_2^2 \, Var\, A_2 + 2(w_1)\,(w_2)\,(Cov\, A_1, A_2)]^{1/2}$$

5. What is co-variance?
   - It is the relationship between the movement of two sets of returns. In terms of an equation:

$$Cov(A_1, A_2) = \sum_{t=1}^{N} P_t (A_{1t} - \overline{A}_1)\,(A_{2t} - \overline{A}_2)$$

6. What is correlation co-efficient?
   - It is the co-variance divided by the product of standard deviation of two sets of returns. In form of an equation:

$$\rho_{1,2} = \frac{CovA_1, A_2}{\sigma_1 \sigma_2}$$

7. Distinguish between systematic and unsystematic risk.
   - Systematic risk, shown through beta, represents risk of the total market portfolio. Unsystematic risk is the firm-specific risk. While the latter can be reduced through diversification, the former cannot be.
8. What is Beta?

$$\beta = \frac{covA_1, A_M}{\sigma_M^2}$$

9. How is the required rate of return of a particular investment computed?

$$A_1 = A_f + \beta_1 (\overline{A}_M - A_f)$$

10. What is security market line?
    - It is the line joining the risk-free returns with the returns from risky investments in the market.

DESCRIPTIVE QUESTIONS

1. Distinguish between:
   (a) risk and uncertainty
   (b) discrete probability distribution and continuous probability distribution
   (c) variance and standard deviation
   (d) co-variance and correlation
   (e) systematic risk and unsystematic risk
2. How do you calculate the expected return of a single asset and a portfolio of assets? What factor is taken into account while computing the returns from an international investment?
3. How is risk of an asset measured? Is variance equal to standard deviation?
4. Explain the relationship between co-variance and correlation.
5. "Holding two or more assets is less risky than holing simply one asset". Explain.
6. Explain CAPM. Is it sufficient to explain variability in return from shares?

OBJECTIVE-TYPE QUESTIONS

1. Mark true or false.
   (a) When the capital market is in equilibrium, required rate of return and expected rate of return are equal.
   (b) Systematic risk reduces with diversification of investment within the country.
   (c) Unsystematic risk reduces with diversification of investment within the country.
   (d) CAPM suggests that total expected return of a security is the sum of risk-free return and its risk premium.
   (e) Beta of more than 1 suggests that assets adding to the portfolio systematic risk have high co-variance with the market returns.
   (f) Expected return from international investment does not take into account the changes in exchange rate.
2. Choose the most suitable answer.
   (a) Uncertainty is a case where:
      (i) the decision-maker does not know the probability of occurrence
      (ii) the decision-maker knows the probability of occurrence
      (iii) neither of the above
   (b) Variance as a measure of risk is:
      (i) the same as standard deviation
      (ii) the square of standard deviation
      (iii) the square-root of standard deviation

(c) Systematic risk is:
   (i) market risk
   (ii) firm-specific risk
   (iii) none of the two

(d) The larger the systematic risk:
   (i) the larger is the expected return
   (ii) the lower is the expected return
   (iii) the expected return remains unaltered

NUMERICAL PROBLEMS

1. Calculate the expected return from an investment based on the following probabilities:
   (a) 20% probability of earning 10%
   (b) 30% probability of earning 12%
   (c) 40% probability of earning 8%
   (d) 10% probability of earning 14%
2. If expected return from X, Y and Z is respectively 10.2%, 12% and 11% and investment in them is in the ratio of 40:40:20, find the portfolio return.
3. The probability of return from an investment is as follows:
   (a) 20% probability of earning Rs 600
   (b) 40% probability of earning Rs 800
   (c) 30% probability of earning Rs 500
   (d) 10% probability of earning Rs 1000

   Find the element of risk in the investment.
4. The probability of return from X and Y is as follows:

   For X
   (a) 20% probability of earning Rs 600
   (b) 40% probability of earning Rs 800
   (c) 30% probability of earning Rs 500
   (d) 10% probability of earning Rs 1000

   For Y
   (a) 20% probability of earning Rs 1000
   (b) 40% probability of earning Rs 400
   (c) 30% probability of earning Rs 900
   (d) 10% probability of earning Rs 1500

   The investment is in the ratio of 60:40 respectively in X and Y. Find out the portfolio return and risk.
5. Risk-free rate is 10%, market return is 13%, and beta is 1.50. Compute the required rate of return using CAPM.

6. The following is the scenario of returns from two channels of investment:

Scenario	Probability	Return	
		X	Y
1	0.3	0.10	0.08
2	0.4	0.16	0.15
3	0.3	0.12	0.20

Find out:

(a) expected return on each investment

(b) variance and standard deviation of X and Y

(c) co-variance and correlation coefficient between X and Y

(d) the expected return, variance and standard deviation of the total portfolio, if you create a total portfolio of 60% for X and 40% for Y

7. What would be the expected risk premium for a share with given market risk premium of 12% and beta of 1.3?

8. What would be the expected risk premium for a share with a given market risk premium being 20% higher than 12% last year and with no change is beta at 1.3?

9. If boom, normalcy and recession have respective probability of 30%, 50% and 20% and the earning during these three conditions is expected to be Rs 16, Rs 11 and Rs 6, respectively, find out the variance and the standard deviation.

10. Find out beta if the co-variance between two streams of return is 86 and the standard deviation of the return on the market portfolio is 10.66.

SOLVED NUMERICAL PROBLEMS

1. A company is expecting the following scenario of returns the next year. Find out the expected return.

Possible return %	Likelihood	Probability %
14	Normally likely	30
8	Most likely	50
3	Meagrely likely	18
–2	Least likely	2

Solution

Expected return = (0.14 x .30) + (0.08 x.50) + (0.03 x 0.18) + (–0.02 x 0.02)

= 0.042 + 0.040 + 0.0054 + –0.0004 = 0.087 = 8.7%

2. A company has the possible outcomes of cash flow given below:

Probability %	Cash flow Rs
40	2,00,000
30	5,00,000
30	3,00,000

Find the expected return and the variation in terms of standard deviation.

Solution

Expected return = (0.40 x 2,00,000) + (0.30 x 5,00,000) + (0.30 x 3,00,000)
= 80,000 + 1,50,000 + 90,000 = Rs 3,20,000

Std. dev = $\{0.40 (2,00,000 - 3,20,000)^2 + 0.30(5,00,000 - 3,20,000)^2 + 0.30(3,00,000 - 3,20,000)^2\}^{1/2}$
= $(5,76,00,00,000 + 9,72,00,00,000 + 12,00,00,000)^{1/2}$
= 1,24,899.95

3. Calculate co-variance between the two portfolios using the following data:

Probability %	*Return from Portfolio 1*	*Return from Portfolio 2*
0.40	10%	8%
0.40	8%	11%
0.20	12%	9%

Solution

Expected return:

Portfolio 1 = (0.4 x 0.1) + (0.4 x 0.08) + (0.2 x 0.12) = 0.096 = 9.6%

Portfolio 2 = (0.4 x 0.08) + (0.4 x 0.11) + (0.2 x 0.09) = 0.098 = 9.8%

Variance:

Portfolio 1 = $0.4(0.10 - 0.096)^2 + 0.4(0.08 - 0.096)^2 + 0.2(0.12 - 0.096)^2$
= 0.0000064 + 0.0001024 + 0.0001152 = 0.000224

Portfolio 2 = $0.4(0.08 - 0.098)^2 + 0.4(0.11 - 0.098)^2 + 0.2(0.09 - 0.098)^2$
= 0.0001296 + 0.0000576 + 0.0000128 = 0.0002

Co-variance = 0.4(0.004)(–0.018) + 0.4(–0.016)(0.012) + 0.2(0.024)(–0.008)
= (–0.0053665) + (–0.0000307) + (–0.0000384)
= –0.0054356

4. Find out the portfolio return and risk with help of the following data. The ratio of investment in the existing and the new portfolios is 60:40.

	Existing portfolio	*New portfolio*
Expected return	12%	12.5%
Variance	4.50	6.00
Co-variance	–0.2080	

Solution

Portfolio return = 0.60 x 0.12 + 0.40 x 0.125 = 0.122 = 12.2%

Portfolio risk = $(0.6)^2 (4.50) + (0.4)^2 (6.00) + 2(0.6)(0.4)(-0.2080)$
= 1.62 + 0.96 + (–0.09984)
= 2.48016

5. Find out the correlation co-efficient if the co-variance between Project X and Project Y is –0.2854 and the variance of the two projects is respectively 6.24 and 2.16.

Solution

Corr. Co-eff. XY = –0.2854 / ($\sqrt{6.24}$ x $\sqrt{6.16}$)

= –0.2854 / 3.671

= –0.07774

6. If the co-variance between the returns from Security X and from the market in general is 504 and the total risk in the market portfolio expressed in terms of standard deviation is 20, find the beta.

Solution

$504 / 20^2$

= 504 / 400 = 1.26

7. If beta is 1.26 in respect of Security X, risk-free return is 9% and the return from the market is 14%, find the required rate of return for Security X.

Solution

Based on Eq. 3.10

Required rate = 9% + (14% – 9%)1.26

= 15.3%

8. The risk-free rate of return of a firm is 8%. The expected rate of return on market portfolio is 14%. The expected growth rate of dividend of the firm is 7%. The latest dividend paid amounted to Rs 2 per share. The beta of the firm's equity stock is 1.2. Find out the equilibrium price of the firm's equity share.

Solution

Equilibrium price of equity share,

8 + 1.2 (13 – 8) = 14%

Taking into account the expected growth is dividend,

$$\frac{2.00(1.07)}{0.14 - 0.07}$$

Equilibrium price = Rs 30.57

Mini Case 1: Movement in the Select Share Prices and the BSE Indices

The following table shows the movement in the price of four individual shares over a period of five days from 24th October to 30th October 2007 and also in the BSE Sensex over the same period.

	October 2007				
	24th	25th	26th	29th	30th
BSE Sensex	18513	18771	19978	19784	19838
Patni Computers Rs	442.85	430.70	429.80	432.95	428.90
MTNL Rs	179.60	179.05	180.50	192.85	190.05
Bombay Rayon Rs	221.25	237.50	229.10	227.65	226.35
Jindal Steel Rs	7,485.55	7,928.55	8,382.29	8,884.79	9,459.35

Source: Business Standard/The Economic Times

The figures show the risk-return scenario of different securities as also of the market as a whole. It is easy to calculate from the figures the return and the risk involved in the individual shares. The market return and risk can also be computed. And then, one can calculate the co-variance between the individual securities and the market index.

Questions:

1. Calculate the average market return and risk in terms of standard deviation.
2. Calculate the return and risk of individual securities.
3. Calculate the co-variance between the individual securities and the market portfolio.
4. Calculate beta.

Mini Case 2: Stock Market Index in India during September 2010

The Indian secondary market is normally faced with volatile returns with the result that the returns vary every day and also the market possesses some amount of risk. The following table presents the stock market indices at BSE and NSE during the month of September 2010. There are some other indices, but the table shows only two major indices.

Date/September 2010	BSE Sensex	NSE S&PCNX Nifty
1	18206	5472
2	18238	5486
3	18221	5479
6	18560	5577
7	18645	5604
8	18667	5608
9	18800	5640
13	19208	5760
14	19347	5796
15	19502	5861
16	19418	5829

17	19595	5885
20	19906	5981
21	20002	6009
22	19942	5991
23	19861	5960
24	20045	6018
27	20117	6035
28	20105	6029
29	19956	5991
30	20069	6030

As far as return is concerned, it is the difference between the logarithm of the closing index of day $t + 1$ and day t.

The risk can be found out in terms of variances/standard deviation.

Questions:

1. Find out the average return during the month at both the exchanges.
2. Show which market has greater risk in terms of variations in the indices.
3. Are the indices in the two markets correlated?

REFERENCES

Chen, N., R. Roll and S.A. Ross (1986). "Economic Forces and the Stock Market", *Journal of Business*, 59 (July): 383–403.

Fama, E.F. and K.R. French (1992). "The Cross-section of Expected Stock Returns", *Journal of Finance*, 47 (2): 427–66.

______ (1993). "Common Risk Factors in the Returns on Stocks and Bonds", *Journal of Financial Economics*, 33 (Feb.): 3–56.

Roll, R. and S.A. Ross (1984). "The Arbitrage Pricing Theory Approach to Strategic Portfolio Planning", *Financial Analysts Journal*, 40 (May-June): 14–26.

Sharpe, William F. (1964). "Capital Asset Prices: A Theory of Market Equilibrium under Conditions of Risk", *Journal of Finance*, 19 (3): 425–42.

SELECT FURTHER READINGS

Black, F. (1993). "Estimating Expected Return", *Financial Analysts Journal*, 49 (5): 36–38.

______ (1993). "Return and Beta", *Journal of Portfolio Management*, 20 (1): 8–18.

Markowitz, H.M. (1991). "Foundations of Portfolio Theory", *Journal of Finance*, 46 (2): 469–78.

Wei, K.C.J. (1988). "An Asset-Pricing Theory Unifying the CAPM and APT", *Journal of Finance*, 43 (4): 881–92.

4

VALUATION OF THE FIRM

OBJECTIVES

To explain the various concepts of a firm's valuation
To show how the value of bonds is measured
To analyse the factors influencing bond valuation
To show how preference shares are valued
To explain the valuation of ordinary shares

The concept of valuation lies at the root of corporate financial decisions. Unless and until the finance manager is aware of the concept of valuation, it is difficult for him to evaluate whether the different financial decisions have actually added to the corporate wealth. Such an evaluation is significant not just for the finance manager. The other parties related to the company, viz., the shareholders and the creditors, would also like to know the value of the company insofar as it is an important motivation to their investment or lending. It is from this point of view that the present chapter deals with the concept of valuation.

The valuation of the firm, as discussed in Chapter 1, can be explained in two ways. First, is through the valuation of its assets and, second, through the estimation of the market value of the claim against its assets, or in other words, the market value of equity and debt. The value of total assets is the sum of the firm's productive assets and the value of wealth created by the firm through the use of productive assets. The amount of wealth created is nothing but the present value of future net proceeds of the firm's present and future assets. A detailed explanation of this given in Chapter 5. As far as the market value of equity and debt is concerned, the explanation is presented in this chapter.

4.1 VARIOUS CONCEPTS OF VALUE

There are various concepts of value. Each one of these concepts is significant in one way or the other. The approach to these concepts may be grouped under three heads. These are:

1. The asset approach that explains the book value, liquidation value, going-concern value and the replacement value;

2. The market value approach that explains the market value;
3. The capitalised earning approach that explains the intrinsic or real value of a firm.

4.1.1 Intrinsic Value

Let us begin with intrinsic value also known as real or fair value. The intrinsic value of a firm's asset represents the present value of its future earnings discounted at an appropriate or required rate of return. The value of securities is exactly analogous to the present value of assets. In other words, the value of securities depends upon the earnings and dividends as also on the capitalisation rate or the discount rate that represents the minimum rate expected by investors to buy or hold a security.

The capitalisation rate is equal to the risk-free rate of interest plus a risk premium. Government bonds are said to carry risk-free interest. The risk premium, as shown in Chapter 3, is the product of the risk premium in the market as a whole and the risk measure for the individual security. The former represents the difference between the return on the market and the risk-free rate, while the latter is measured by dividing the co-variance of the returns on the individual security with the returns on the market by the variance of the returns on the markets. The details of the calculation are given in Chapter 3. Thereafter, the future earnings of the assets or securities are discounted by the capitalisation rate in order to find out their intrinsic value.

4.1.2 Market Value

The market value is the price at which the assets or securities of a firm are sold in the market. In this respect, it may be noted that the assets have two market values. One is the liquidation value and the other is the going-concern value. In the latter, the goodwill of a firm is included insofar as the firm is sold as an operating concern; while in the former, it is only the asset that is sold exclusive of the goodwill and intangibles. Naturally, the going-concern value represents a higher market value and, therefore, the market value of a firm is represented by the going-concern value.

It is generally expected that the market price of a share is very close, or equal, to the intrinsic value. But in practice, this is seldom the case in the short run. In the short-run, there are a number of factors that cause share prices to fluctuate. However, in the long-run, the market value and the intrinsic value may be equal. This is because the intrinsic value determines the market price of a security.

4.1.3 Book Value

The book value is also known as the accounting value and it is ascertained from the balance sheet. The accounting value of an asset is equal to its original cost minus depreciation. While determining the book value of the assets as a whole, the intangibles are also included, although it is a common practice to amortize the intangibles.

The excess of assets over debt shows the accounting net worth of the enterprise or the book value of the owners' investment. The net worth is then divided by the number of equity shares outstanding to get the book value per share.

Book value is very simple to calculate. Moreover, it may be used in cases where assets are mostly in liquid form and their value is close to the accounting value. However, since book value represents a historical cost and does not provide a current picture, it fails to show the real worth of the enterprise.

4.1.4 Liquidation Value

The value realised from the sale of assets of a firm after it ceases to operate is termed liquidation value. The purchaser buys only the assets and not the organisation, therefore, the goodwill or the intangibles do not form a part of the liquidation value. When one deducts the amount of debt from this value, the remainder is the liquidating value of ownership in the enterprise.

This type of valuation is useful to the creditors who would like to know whether and to what extent they will be able to share in the liquidated assets of the enterprise. However, the value represents only the floor price that can be accepted in the event of sale of the assets and so it is generally far less then the real value of the firm.

4.1.5 Going-concern Value

The going-concern value is different from the liquidation value in the sense that the firm is sold as an operating concern and so it includes the goodwill and growth factor. It is because of this fact that the going-concern value is always higher than the liquidation value.

4.1.6 Replacement Value

Replacement value represents the cost of replacing the firm's assets in the current conditions. This means that the future life on an asset is deducted proportionately from the replacement cost. At the same time, the value of goodwill is taken into consideration. The replacement value has a limited applicability insofar as it depends upon historical cost and may not be relevant to the present and future period. Moreover, the computation of goodwill is a difficult task.

4.2 VALUATION OF BONDS OR DEBENTURES

A bond or debenture represents a long-term obligation for the money that the concern has borrowed. It has some distinctive features as compared to shares that are discussed in Chapter 15. However, for the convenience of the readers, an attempt is being made to acquaint them with a few terms that are frequently used.

The principal is the amount of borrowing in exchange for the bond. The coupon rate is the interest rate at which the money is borrowed. Coupon payment is the interest payment. The par value is the face value of the bond. It is the amount that is repaid at the end of the bond's life. The maturity date is the date on which the bond is fully repaid. When the entire face value of the bond is repaid on the maturity date, it is known as bullet repayment. But if the principal is repaid in instalments, the method of repayment is known as sinking fund. Last but not least, a call provision provides the issuer the right to pay off the bond prior to its maturity.

A bond's market value is its current price. The future cash payments to the holders thereof are contractual obligations in form of interest payments and repayment of principal at the time of maturity of the bond. So the present value of a bond is the present value of its promised future coupon and principal repayments. The appropriate discount rate or capitalisation rate or required rate of return may vary depending on the risk of default, which varies from case to case. Again, the value of a fixed-maturity bond may differ from that of a perpetual bond, which is why these two cases need separate discussion.

The present value of a bond is the present value of its promised future coupon and principal repayments.

4.2.1 Valuation of Bonds with Fixed Maturity

When the bond is issued for a fixed maturity, the value of the bond can be expressed as follows:

$$V_d = \frac{I_1}{(1+k_d)} + \frac{I_2}{(1+k_d)^2} + \ldots + \frac{I_n + M}{(1+k_d)^n} \qquad \ldots(4.1)$$

$$= \sum_{t=1}^{n} \frac{I_n + M_t}{(1+k_d)^t}$$

Where:

V_d = value of the bond or debenture
I = annual interest payment
K_d = capitalisation or discount rate
M = maturity value
n = number of years to maturity

EXAMPLE

If a 3-year-maturity bond pays Rs 50 as interest per annum and has a Rs 1,000 maturity value, its value at the time of issue at a discount rate of 4% will be:

$$V_d = \frac{50}{(1.04)} + \frac{50}{(1.04)^2} + \frac{50 + 1000}{(1.04)^3}$$

$$= \text{Rs } (48.10 + 46.25 + 933.45) = \text{Rs } 1027.80.$$

The valuation of a zero-coupon bond is not very different. Periodic interest is not payable in the case of zero-coupon bonds. Instead, such bonds are issued at a discount in order to attract investors. In other words, the discount provided at the time of issue serves the purpose of coupon. The value of such bonds at the time of issue is their issue price. At the end of the first year, the value will be equal to the product of the issue price and $(1 + K_d)$. where K_d is the discount rate. At the end of Year n, the value of the bond will be equal to the product of the issue price and $(1 + K_d)^n$ The value at the time of maturity will be equal to the maturity value.

EXAMPLE

If a 5-year-maturity Rs 1,000 zero-coupon bond is issued for Rs 747.30, its value at the end of the third year at 6% K_d will be:

$$V_d = \text{Rs } 747.30 \times (1 + 0.06)^3 = \text{Rs } 890.05$$

4.2.2 Perpetual Bonds

However, in case of perpetual bonds, or bonds with no maturity, which are rarely found in practice, the value of the bond would simply be the discounted value of the infinite stream of interest flows. The value of a perpetual bond can, therefore, be expressed as follows:

$$V_d = \frac{I_1}{(1+k_d)} + \frac{I_2}{(1+k_d)^2} + \ldots + \frac{I_n \infty}{(1+k_d)^n} \qquad \ldots(4.2)$$

$$= \frac{I}{k_d}$$

EXAMPLE

If I is Rs 50 and K_d is 4%, the value of bond will be:

$$V_d = \text{Rs } 50/0.04$$

$$= \text{Rs } 1250.$$

4.3 FACTORS INFLUENCING BOND VALUATION

4.3.1 Discount Rate versus Coupon Rate

The relationship between the discount rate and the coupon rate has an impact on the market value of a bond. If the coupon rate is equal to the required rate of return, the market value will be equal to the par value. The bond is then said to be selling at par.

EXAMPLE

If a 3-year-maturity bond pays Rs 50 as interest per annum and has a Rs 1,000 maturity value, its value at the time of issue at a discount rate of 5% will be:

$$V_d = (50/1.05) + (50/1.05^2) + (1050/1.05^3)$$

$$= \text{Rs } 47.62 + 45.35 + 907.03 = \text{Rs } 1000.$$

If the required rate of return or the discount rate is lower than the coupon rate, the market value of the bond would be greater than the par value. The bond is then said to be selling at premium.

EXAMPLE

If a 3-year-maturity bond pays Rs 50 as interest per annum and has a Rs 1,000 maturity value, its value at the time of issue at a discount rate of 4% will be:

$$V_d = \frac{50}{(1.04)} + \frac{50}{(1.04)^2} + \frac{50+1000}{(1.04)^3}$$

$$= \text{Rs } 48.10 + 46.25 + 933.45 = \text{Rs } 1027.80.$$

On the contrary, if the discount rate is greater than the coupon rate, the market value will be lower than the par value. The bond is then said to be selling at discount.

EXAMPLE

If a 3-year-maturity bond pays Rs 50 as interest per annum and has a Rs 1,000 maturity value, its value at the time of issue at a discount rate of 7% will be:

$$V_d = (50/1.07) + (50/1.07^2) + (1050/1.07^3)$$

$$= \text{Rs } 46.73 + 43.67 + 857.11 = \text{Rs } 947.51$$

4.3.2 Maturity and Value of Bonds

The preceding discussion shows that with a rise in discount rate, the value of the bond will be lower. But it is also the maturity that influences the value of a bond. In case of longer maturity, the shrinkage in the value will be larger than in case of shorter maturity even with a similar change in the discount rate. This means that longer maturity bonds are more prone to risk than those with shorter maturity. This fact will be clear from a simple example that is presented in Table 4.1. Suppose that two Rs 1000 bonds carry 5% discount rate, a maturity of 2 years and 5 years respectively and Rs 50 as annual interest charges. If the discount rate goes up to 8%, the fall in the present value of the bond having a longer maturity will be greater.

4.3.3 Yield to Maturity

The preceding discussion shows that the current market price of a bond depends on the coupon rate or the cash flow generated on this account on the one hand and the discount rate on the other. If a person buys a bond at its current market price and holds it till maturity, he would

Table 4.1

Annual Charge	*Maturity*	*Discount Factor*	*Present Value Rs*	*Change in Current Market Value Due To Change in Discount Rate (Rs)*
Rs 50	2 years	5% 8%	1000.00 946.47	 (–) 53.53
Rs 50	5 years	5% 8%	1000 880.24	 (–) 119.74

be interested in knowing the required rate of return. This rate is known as yield to maturity (YTM). In other words, YTM is the rate of return that a bondholder expects when purchasing a bond at its current market price and holding it till maturity. YTM is, simply, the bond's internal rate of return (IRR), meaning that, it is that discount rate which equates the present value of the bond's cash flow in the form of interest and repayment of principal to its current market price.

In Eq. 4.3, yield to maturity (YTM) is represented by r. It is the rate that equates the two sides of the equation.

$$B = \frac{CF_1}{(1 \quad r)} \quad \frac{CF_2}{(1 \quad r)^2} \cdots \frac{CF_n}{(1 \quad r)^n} \qquad ...(4.3)$$

Where:

B = the present market value of bond, and

CF = the cash flow inclusive of interest and principal during different time periods till maturity.

EXAMPLE

If a 2-year bond having a face value of Rs 1000 and coupon rate of 10% per annum has a present market value of Rs 1027.50, the yield to maturity computed on a trial-and-error basis, assuming yearly repayment of principal in equal instalments, will be:

$$1027.50 = (100 + 500)/1.0797 + (50 + 500)/1.0797^2$$
$$= 7.97\%$$

However, in case of a bullet bond, which is very much common and where principal is repaid in a lumpsum amount only on the maturity and not in instalments every year along with the interest payment, the cash flow each year (other than the final cash flow) will be inclusive of only interest payments and the final cash flow will include the interest and entire amount of principal. In such cases, the yield to maturity will be different.

EXAMPLE

Based on the above example, the yield to maturity will be:

$$1027.50 = 100/1.085 + 1100/1.085^2$$
$$= 8.50\%$$

Again, if bond is sold in the market after the issue, the buyer of the bond will pay the seller not only the market price of the bond but also the interest accrued for the fraction of the period. If a Rs 1000 bond is sold after 6 months of its issue, and if the coupon rate, as per the above example, is 10%, the interest accrued will be: 180/360 100 = Rs 50. The accrued interest is added to the market price of the bond while calculating the yield to maturity. Eq. 4.3 after taking into account the interest accrued can be re-written as follows:

$$B + if = \frac{CF_1}{(1+r)} + \frac{CF_2}{(1+r)^2} + \ldots + \frac{CF_n}{(1+r)^n} \qquad ...(4.4)$$

Where:

if = the interest accrued for the fraction of the period

If it is so, the yield to maturity will be different in this case.

Yet again, if interest payments are made quarterly or half-yearly instead of annually, yield to maturity will change because it has to include the compounding over the year. In this case, the cash flow has to be discounted at the rate, *R*, where:

$$(1 + R)^T = (1 + r) \qquad \text{...(4.5)}$$

Where:

T = the number of interest payments per annum

EXAMPLE

If interest payment is half-yearly and if R is equal to 5%, r will be:

$$(1 + 0.05)^2 = 10.25\%.$$

From Eq. 4.3, it is evident that YTM will be equal to the coupon rate if the bond is selling at par. If bond is selling at premium, YTM will be lower than the coupon rate. On the contrary, YTM will be higher than the coupon rate if the bond is selling at discount. Here it should be made clear that it is the market price of the bond that determines the YTM and not vice versa. The market price in turn is determined by the discount rate.

A Note on Yield Curve

Yield curve represents the relationship between a debt's remaining time to maturity and its yield to maturity, at any particular point of time. In other words, it presents the term structure of interest rates which means whether at a particular point of time, the short-term interest rate is higher/lower than, or equal to, the long-term interest rates.

If yield curve is *downward-sloping* or *inverted*, it means that the short-term interest rate is higher than the long-term interest rate. Long-term borrowing will be cheaper than the short-term borrowing. In practice, however, the inverted yield curve is only a rare possibility.

On the contrary, *upward-sloping yield curve* or *the normal yield curve* is a common phenomenon. It indicates that, at any point of time, the long-term interest rate is higher than the short-term interest rate, which means that the long-term borrowing is costlier than the short-term borrowing.

Again, a situation of *flat yield curve* cannot be negated. It occurs when the short-term and long-term interest rates are equal or similar. One can go either for short-term borrowings or for long-term borrowing without coughing more in terms of interest.

The concept and application of yield curve are thus very significant for the financing decision as to what should be the ratio between the short-term funds and the long-term funds to minimise the cost of financing. It is the influence of yield curve on financing decision that needs to be discussed at least at some length. The discussion is based on the following three theories:

1. Expectations theory;
2. Liquidity preference theory;
3. Market segmentation theory.

Firstly, the *expectations theory* suggests that the yield curve represents the investors' expectations about future interest rates and inflation. If the future rates of inflation are expected higher, the long-term interest rate will be higher. On the contrary, if higher inflation rate is expected in the immediate future, short-term interest rates will be higher. In other words, while increasing inflation expectations leads to an upward-sloping yield curve, decreasing inflation expectations leads to downward-sloping yield curve and, finally, an expectation for stable inflation leads to a flat yield curve.

Secondly, the *liquidity preference theory* explains that, first, investors perceive less risk in short-term securities on account of greater liquidity and so they accept even lower yield on them. Similarly, the borrowers pay a higher interest rate on long-term securities because they can lock the funds for a longer period. These preferences thus influence the yield curve.

Thirdly, the *market segmentation theory* explains that the borrowing/lending markets are segmented on the basis of maturity. The supply and demand of loans within each segment help determine the interest rate. The slope of the yield curve is determined by the prevailing rates in each market segment. If the interest rate is lower in the short-term market segment, the yield curve will be upward-sloping. Talking it the other way, higher interest rate in the long-term market segment means the upward-sloping yield curve. The opposite is the case if the short-term market segment has higher interest rate than in the long-term market segment.

4.3.4 Duration and the Bond Price

It is also the duration of the bond that influences its price. Duration is nothing but the weighted average maturity of a bond, where each date of interest plus instalment payment is weighted by the present value of cash flow. In form of an equation, duration (D) can be expressed as follows:

$$D = \sum_{t=1}^{n} t\,CF_t(1+r)^{-t}/B \qquad \text{...(4.6)}$$

EXAMPLE

Suppose a Rs 1000 bond has a coupon rate of 10% and a maturity of 2 years. The interest is paid annually. The principal is repaid on the maturity. The present market price of the bond is Rs 1027.50. The yield to maturity is 8.50%. The weighted average maturity will be calculated as follows:

(i) The sum of discounted value of cash flow at t_1 and t_2 = Rs 1027.50
(ii) The sum of the discounted cash flow as shown in (i) after being multiplied by t is = Rs 1960.97
(iii) The market price of the bond = Rs 1027.50
(iv) Duration = 1960.97/1027.50 = 1.9 years.

As it has already been stated, duration expresses the impact of changes in interest on the price of the bond, we can rearrange the first derivative of Eq. 4.6 with respect to (1 + r) and dividing by B, the present market value of the bond, we get:

$$(dB/B)/d(1+r)/(1+r) = -D \qquad \ldots(4.7)$$

EXAMPLE

Based on Eq. 4.7, if interest rate rises by 0.5% and if duration (D) is 1.9 years, the price of the bond will change by:

$$dB/B = -1.9 \times 0.005 = -0.0095 = -0.95\%$$

This clearly shows that the extent of change in the price of a bond as a sequel to a change in the interest rate depends upon the duration. The larger the duration, the greater will be the change in the price of the bond with the same percentage change in the rate of interest. For example, if the duration is 3 years, 0.5% increase in the interest rate will reduce the price of the bond by 1.5%.

4.3.5 Riskiness and the Value of Bond

The risk associated with a bond has an influence on its price. Different types of risk influence the value differently. The different types of risk are:

1. Interest rate risk
2. Reinvestment rate risk
3. Default risk

Interest rate risk arises when the value of a bond declines as a sequel to a rising interest rate. The larger the rise in interest rate, greater is the amount of risk and lower the value of bond.

On the contrary, a fall in interest rate may raise the value of the bond but lowers the income of the bondholder in the form of a reduced interest receipt. The reduction in income on account of a fall in the interest rate is known as reinvestment rate risk. Reinvestment risk is high in case of a callable bond or in case of a short-maturity bond. In a shorter maturity bond, the number of years of earning the older and higher interest rate are fewer, moreover, the funds are soon reinvested at a new and lower rate.

The default risk is no less important. The greater the possibility of default, the lower the repayment and lower the value of bond.

4.4 VALUATION OF PREFERENCE SHARES

The technique of valuing preference shares is not different from the valuation of bonds. Dividends are discounted by the required rate of return. The required rate of return is composed of the risk-free rate and a premium for risk. However, it may be noted that the risk premium in this case is greater than that in case of bonds, although less than that in case of equity shares. It is because dividend on preference shares is fixed, moreover, preference shareholders have a prior claim on both the income and assets of the firm vis-a-vis the equity shareholders, however this is subject to satisfaction of the claim of the debenture holders. The value of preference shares with a definite maturity can be expressed as follows:

$$V_p = \sum_{t=1}^{n} \frac{D_1}{(1+k_p)^t} + \frac{P_n}{(1+k_p)^n} \qquad ...(4.8)$$

Where:

V_p= the current price of the preference shares
P_n= the redemption value
D_t= the expected dividend in year t
K_p= is the discount rate applied to expected dividends on the preference shares
n= the maturity of preference shares

In practice, preference shares are normally irredeemable which means they have no maturity. So, Eq. 4.8 reduces to.

$$V_p = D/K_p \qquad ...(4.9)$$

EXAMPLE

if a preference share is expected to pay a Rs 6 dividend and the discount rate is 6%, the value of share with no maturity will be.

$$V_p = 6/0.06 = \text{Rs } 100.$$

4.5 VALUATION OF ORDINARY SHARES

The valuation of ordinary shares is not so easy as that of bonds and preference shares. The reason being that the dividend on ordinary shares is not known with certainty as is the case with dividend on preference shares or interest on debentures, which is known in advance. Moreover, the latter two are almost constant, whereas the dividend on ordinary shares is expected to grow.

The valuation of ordinary shares depends upon a host of factors, important among them being the system of dividends, expected price of the share when it is sold, current earnings and the flows resulting from future investment opportunities. This is why the techniques of the ordinary share valuation are either based on the earnings or on dividends or on the both. The value may differ accordingly, although, as Miller and Modigliani (1961) have found, these different valuation techniques yield almost similar results. We present here a very simplified version of the valuation techniques.

4.5.1 Single-period Analysis

Let us begin with a single-period analysis. Suppose an investor wants to buy one ordinary share and to hold it for 1 year after which he will sell it. In this case, his income at the end of the year will be the amount of dividend paid to him plus the price that he will be able to get by selling the share. This, in fact, will be the value of the share, which can be expressed as folows:

$$V_e = \frac{D_1 + P_1}{(1 + k_e)} \qquad ...(4.10)$$

Where:

V_e= the current price or intrinsic value of the share
D_1= is the expected dividend at the end of the year
P_1= is the expected price of the share at the year end
k_e= is the expected rate of return on the equity

EXAMPLE

If D_1 is Rs 1, P_1 is Rs 10, k_e is 15%, then the current price of share will be:

$$V_e = (1 + 10)/1.15 = \text{Rs } 9.57.$$

If the current price, which is the intrinsic value of the share, is more than the actual market price of the share, the investor will buy it. In the reverse case, he will not buy it, rather he will sell it if he has already owned it.

Putting Eq. 4.10 in a different way, we may say that by buying the share for Rs 9.57 and expecting Rs 1 as dividend and a sale price of Rs 10 after one year, the investor expects a rate of return equivalent to 15%. This expected rate of return is analogous to the internal rate of return (irr) (see, chapter 5 of this book) and so it equates the present value of the sum of the expected dividend and the expected sale price with the current share price. In terms of equation, the expected rate of return can be expressed as follows:

$$k_e = [(D_1 + P_1)/V_e] - 1 \qquad ...(4.11)$$

EXAMPLE

If a firm sells its equity share for Rs 9.57, with an expected dividend of Rs 1 and a sale price of Rs 10 after one year, the expected rate of return will be as follows:

$$k_e = (11/9.57) - 1$$
$$= 0.15 \text{ or } 15\%.$$

Here we would like to point out that the expected rate of return may not be equal to the required rate of return as the latter is composed of the risk-free rate plus the premium for risk. If the expected rate is more than the required rate, the investor will buy the share. On the contrary, if the expected rate is lower than the required rate, he will sell it if he has already owned it. If the two are equal, the share price will be supposed to be in equilibrium and the investor would be indifferent between buying or selling the share. It is suggested that the readers go through Appendix B of the present chapter for a detailed discussion of equilibrium in the share market.

4.5.2 Multi-period Analysis

In the multi-period context, the same technique of valuation for the ordinary share will be applied that has been applied in case of bonds or preference shares with perpetuity. We assume here that the investors do not contemplate selling their shares. Therefore so, the value of shares will be the present value of the expected future dividends, and can be expressed as follows:

$$V_e = \sum_{t=1}^{n} \frac{D_t}{(1+k_e)^t} \quad \text{...(4.12)}$$

However, D_t is normally not as constant as the interest on bonds or dividends on preference shares. D_t may be constant showing zero growth, it may grow at a constant rate, alternatively, it may be fluctuate randomly. These three possibilities—zero growth, constant growth and supernormal growth need to be discussed here.

Zero Growth: In the case of zero growth, D_1 is equal to D_2 and hence forth to D_∞.

Since $D_t = D_1$:

$$V_e = D_t / k_e \quad \text{...(4.13)}$$

Constant Growth: When dividend grows at a constant rate, dividend paid during the present period is multiplied by the growth factor for the specified period of time.

$$D_t = D_0 (1+g)^t \quad \text{...(4.14)}$$

Where:

D_0= the dividend already paid

g= growth rate in dividend

EXAMPLE

If a firm has just paid a dividend of Rs 2 and the investors expect a growth of 5% in dividend, the estimated dividend after a 5-year period will be.

$$2(1.05)^5 = \text{Rs } 2.55.$$

Interpreting Eq. 4.14, the current price of an ordinary share can be expressed as follows:

$$V_d = \frac{D_1}{(1+k_e)^1} + \frac{D_2}{(1+k_e)^2} + \frac{D_3}{(1+k_e)^3} + \ldots + \frac{D_n}{(1+k_e)^n}$$

$$= \frac{D_1(1+g)}{(1+k_e)} + \frac{D_2(1+g)^2}{(1+k_e)^2} + \frac{D_3(1+g)^3}{(1+k_e)^3} + \ldots + \frac{D_n(1+g)^n}{(1+k_e)^n}$$

$$= \sum_{t=1}^{n} \frac{D_0(1+g)^t}{(1+k_e)^t}$$

Since g is constant, the equation may be simplified as follows:

$$V_e = D_0\left[\frac{(1+g)}{(1+k_e)} + \frac{(1+g)^2}{(1+k_e)^2} + \dots + \frac{(1+g)^n}{(1+k_e)^n}\right] \qquad \text{...(4.15)}$$

Assuming that $n = \varpi$ and $K_e > g$, Eq. 4.15 may further be simplified as:

$$V_e = D_1/(k_e - g) \qquad \text{...(4.16)}$$

EXAMPLE

If the investors expect the firm to pay a dividend of Rs 1 next year and anticipate a growth of 5% in dividend per year for the foreseeable future, the current price of the share with a K_e of 10% will be:

1/(0.10–0.05) or Rs 20.

What Is *g*?

The g is a growth factor. No growth or zero growth means that the earning during the next year is the same as in the present year. It occurs when the net investment is not made or, in other words, when the total investment is equal to depreciation. It is a situation when plant and machinery is workable but no increase in earnings is expected because no additional investment over and above depreciation is made.

The question of any growth arises only when there is a net investment. Any net investment is possible when a part of earnings this year is not paid as dividend; it is retained and invested. In other words, growth is possible with retained earnings including, of course, a return on the retained earnings. This could be written as follows:

g = retention ratio × return on retained earnings

where the retention ratio is the ratio of retained earnings to total earnings.

The future earnings can be expected on the basis of the historical return on equity. So if historical ROE is 15%, on this basis, the earnings are expected to be Rs 1 million. If the retention ratio is 40%,

The retained earnings will be 0.40 × Rs 1,000,000 = Rs 400,000

Anticipated increase in earnings will be 0.15 × Rs 400,000 = Rs 60,000

The earning during one year from now will be Rs 1,060,000

The percentage growth in earnings (g) will be 0.06 = 6%

Supernormal or Non-constant Growth: It is not necessary that the rate of growth in dividend be always constant. Economic conditions may change and this may influence dividends. It may so happen that the dividends grow at a very high rate for 10 years but then the rate falls. In such cases, the value of a firm will be determined by summing up present value of dividends during the supernormal growth period and the value of the share price at the end of the supernormal growth period discounted back to the present.

This can be expressed in the form of an equation as follows:

$$D_0 = \sum_{t=1}^{n} \frac{D_0(1+g_s)^t}{(1+k_e)^t} + \left(\frac{(D_n+1)}{(k_e - g_n)}\right)\left(\frac{1}{(1+k_e)^n}\right) \qquad ...(4.17)$$

where:

g_s = the supernormal growth rate

g_n = the normal growth rate

EXAMPLE

A firm has a previous dividend (D_0) of Rs 1 and expects its dividend to increase phenomenally at 20% a year for 3 years and thereafter at 5% per annum indefinitely. In such case, the value of share with 10% required rate of return would be:

$$(1.09 + 1.19 + 1.30) + 40 \times 0.751 = \text{Rs } 33.62.$$

4.5.3 P/E Ratio Approach to Equity Valuation

P/E ratio has evolved as a common technique to value the equity shares. Under this technique, the estimated price of equity,

$$P_0 = E_1 \times P_0/E_1$$

where E_1 is the estimated earnings per share and P_0/E_1 is the justified price-earning ratio being equal to:

$$(1 - b)/r - ROE \times b$$

Here, b is ploughing-back ratio and r is the required rate of return.

The equation above shows that:

1. If $ROE > r$, an increase in b leads to an increase in *P/E*.
2. If $ROE = r$, an increase in b does not lead to any change in *P/E*.
3. If $ROE < r$, an increase in b leads to a decrease in *P/E*.
4. If r increases (consequent either upon the increase in interest rates or upon higher riskiness of the equity), equity price turns lower. It means that there is an inverse relationship between the interest rate and *P/E* ratio and also between higher riskiness and P/E ratio.
5. Highly liquid shares have high *P/E* ratio. It means that there is a direct relationship between the liquidity of the equity share and the price of the share.

SUMMARY

The value of a firm needs to be measured, and this value may be expressed in different ways. The intrinsic value of a firm's assets is the present value of its future earnings discounted at an appropriate rate of return. The market value is the price at which the assets or securities of a firm are sold in the market. The book value of an asset is equal to its original cost minus depreciation. Again, the value realised from the sale of assets of a firm after it ceases to work is known as the liquidation value, while the going-concern value includes the goodwill and the growth factors. Lastly, the replacement value is the cost of replacing the firm's assets in the current conditions.

The valuation of a firm includes the valuation of its assets and/or the securities. The valuation of any asset is determined on the basis of its earnings duly discounted to the present value. A bond's market value is its current price which is determined on the basis of interest, maturity, etc. The technique of valuing preference shares is not very different from the valuation of bonds. It is dividend divided by the required rate of return. However, the valuation of ordinary shares is not so easy, as the dividends thereof are uncertain. In a single-period framework, the value of share will be equal to dividend plus the market price of the share discounted by the required rate of return. In a multi-period context, however, it is assumed that the investors do not contemplate selling their shares and so the value of shares will be the present value of the expected future dividends. Although different results may be had in case of zero growth, constant growth and supernormal growth.

POINTS TO REMEMBER

1. What are the different concepts of a firm's value?
    - Intrinsic value meaning present value of future earnings
    - Market value at which a firm's assets are sold
    - Book value meaning original cost of assets minus depreciation
    - Liquidation value meaning sale value of the assets after the firm ceases to work
    - Going-concern value including also growth factor and goodwill
    - Replacement value meaning the cost of replacing assets in current conditions
2. How is a bond valued?

- The value of a fixed-interest/zero-coupon bond is the sum of the present value of the interest payment and the repayment of the principal during different periods discounted by the required rate of return. In terms of equation:

$$\sum_{t=1}^{n} \frac{I_n + M_t}{(1+k_d)^t}$$

- In a perpetual bond, a single-period interest is discounted by the required rate of return. In terms of equation:

$$I/K_d$$

3. What are the factors influencing the valuation of a bond?
   - Coupon rate vis-à-vis required rate of return
   - Maturity of the bond
   - Yield to maturity
   - Duration or the weighted average of maturity
   - Risk, such as interest rate risk, reinvestment rate risk and default risk
4. How is a preference share valued?
   - It is the dividend divided by the required rate of return. In terms of equation:

$$V_p = D/K_p$$

5. How is an ordinary share valued?
   - In a single period, it is the sum of dividend and the price expected to be obtained by selling the share discounted by the required rate of return. In form of an equation:

$$V_e = \frac{D_1 + P_1}{(1+k_e)}$$

   - In case of more than one period, the value of a share is the sum of the present value of expected dividend during different periods discounted by the expected rate of return. In form of an equation:

$$V_e = \sum_{t=1}^{n} \frac{D_t}{(1+k_e)^t}$$

   - In case of constant growth in dividend, growth factor is considered along with dividend before discounting. In form of equation:

$$V_e = D_1/(K_e - g)$$

   - In case of non-constant growth in dividend, the abnormal growth rate is considered separately from the normal growth rate. In form of an equation:

$$D_0 = \sum_{t=1}^{n} \frac{D_0(1+g_s)^t}{(1+k_e)^t} + \left(\frac{(D_n+1)}{(k_e - g_n)}\right)\left(\frac{1}{(1+k_e)^n}\right)$$

DESCRIPTIVE QUESTIONS

1. How do you compute the market price of: (a) a fixed-maturity bond; and (b) a perpetual bond?
2. Is it true to say that the value of the bond shrinks more in case of a longer maturity than in case of a shorter maturity with similar changes in the discount rate?
3. When will a bond sell at a premium? When will it sell for a discount? Explain it with suitable examples.
4. What do you mean by yield to maturity (YTM)? Explain the relationship between YTM and nominal interest rate.
5. Is it correct to say that with an increase in duration, the change in value of a bond will be larger with the same percentage change in the interest rate?
6. How do you compute the value of a preference share? Can a preference share be valued using the constant dividend growth model?
7. Do you agree that the computation of a bond's value is easier than that of an ordinary share?
8. How do you compute the value of an ordinary share with:
   (a) zero growth
   (b) constant growth rate
   (c) fluctuating growth rate

OBJECTIVE-TYPE QUESTIONS

1. Mark true or false.
   (a) The concept of intrinsic value is synonymous with the concept of book value.
   (b) Goodwill forms a part of the liquidation value.
   (c) The book value of an asset is equal to its original cost plus depreciation.
   (d) If the coupon rate of a bond is lower than the discount rate, its market value will be higher than its par value.
   (e) The larger the duration, the greater will be the rate of fall in the price of a bond with a given percentage of change in the interest rate.
   (f) The value of a share is equal to the present value of its expected future dividend.
2. Choose the most suitable answer.
   (a) Intrinsic value of a firm depends upon:
      (i) present value of its future earnings
      (ii) cost of its assets minus depreciation
      (iii) none of the above
   (b) Going-concern value is normally:
      (i) equal to liquidation value
      (ii) greater than liquidation value
      (iii) lower than the liquidation value

(c) Perpetual bonds have:
   (i) shorter maturity
   (ii) longer maturity
   (iii) no maturity

(d) Bonds will be selling at par, if:
   (i) discount rate = coupon rate
   (ii) discount rate < coupon rate
   (iii) discount rate > coupon rate

(e) Yield to maturity (YTM) is a bond's:
   (i) internal rate of return
   (ii) coupon rate
   (iii) market value

(f) The value of shares depends on:
   (i) dividend only
   (ii) earnings only
   (iii) both dividend and earnings

NUMERICAL PROBLEMS

1. What will be the market value of an 8%, Rs 1,000 par value bond with annual interest payment, where the required rate of return is 15%?
2. A company has a perpetual bond paying Rs 150 as annual interest. The current yield on this type of bond in the market is 13%. What would be the price of the bond?
3. Find out the yield of a 16%, Rs 1000 perpetual bond when the current price is Rs 1000.
4. A 3-year bond paying Rs 500 as interest p.a. has a maturity value of Rs 10,000. Find its value at the time of issue at a discount of 5%.
5. A Rs 1000 bond with 10-year maturity and a coupon rate of 8% has a yield to maturity of 9%. Find out the current market price of the bond.
6. A Rs 1000 bond with 10-year maturity and a coupon rate of 8% is selling at Rs 923. Find out YTM.
7. A company has paid Rs 1.50 as dividend per share. The dividend is expected to grow at 5% per annum for the next 3 years and then at 10% per annum. What is the expected dividend per share for each of the next 5 years?
8. Dividend at the end of the first year is Re 1 and it is expected to grow at a constant rate of 5% per annum. The required rate of return is 15%. Find out the value of the share.
9. The annual dividend of a preference share is Rs 5. the share sells for Rs 50. Find out the required rate of return.
10. Find the yield to maturity if bonds par value is Rs 1000; market price of the bond is Rs 1080; Coupon interest rate is 10%; maturity is 10 years and interest is paid annually.

11. Find out the current yield of a 10-year, 12% coupon bond, with a par value of Rs 1,000 which is selling at Rs 960.
12. The current dividend of an equity share of a company is Rs 4. The company is expected to enjoy a super-normal growth rate of 20% for a period of 6 years. After sixth year, the growth rate is expected to stabilise at 10%. Equity share holders require a return of 15%. Find out the intrinsic value of the equity share.

SOLVED NUMERICAL PROBLEMS

1. A company issues a 3-year zero-coupon bond with a face value of Rs 1,00,000. It is assumed that interest accrues twice a year. The investors wish to have a 5% return on investment. Find the issue value of the bond.

Solution

Effective interest rate = $\{1 + (0.05/2)^2\} - 1 = 0.050625 = 5.0625\%$

Issue value = Rs 1,00,000 / $(1+ 0.050625)^3$ = Rs 86,229.19

2. If a zero-coupon bond with a 5-year maturity is issued at Rs 13,611.66 and the investors' required rate of return is 8%, find the face value of the bond.

Solution

Rs 13,611.66 $(1.08)^5$ = Rs 20,000

3. A company issues a 5% Rs 1,00,000 bond with a 3-year maturity. The investors' required rate of return is 8%. Find the investors' intrinsic value of the bond if: (a) interest is paid annually and (b) interest is paid half-yearly.

Solution

(a) Annual payment of interest:

Rs $5{,}000/1.08 + 5{,}000/1.08^2 + 1{,}05{,}000/1.08^3$

= Rs 4,629.63 + 4,286.69 + 83,352.39 = Rs 92,268.71

(b) Half-yearly payment of interest:

Effective interest rate = $\{1 + (0.05/2)^2\} - 1 = 0.050625 = 5.0625\%$

Value of bond = Rs $5{,}062.50/1.08 + 5{,}062.50/1.08^2 + 1{,}05{,}062.50/1.08^3$

= Rs 4,687.50 + 4,340.28 + 83,402.00

= Rs 92,429.78

4. If a perpetual bond has a coupon rate of 5% and the interest payment amounts to Rs 50 annually, find the value of the bond.

Solution

Rs 50 / 0.05 = Rs 1,000

5. Find out the duration, if:
   (a) A 10% Rs 10,000 bond has 4-year maturity
   (b) The present market price of the bond is Rs 10,662.43
   (c) The yield to maturity is 8%
   (d) The principal is paid on maturity

Solution

The sum of the discounted value multiplied by t = Rs

$(1{,}000/1.08) \times 1 + (1{,}000/1.08^2) \times 2 + (1{,}000/1.08^3) \times 3 + (11{,}000/1.08^4) \times 4$

= Rs 925.23 + 1,714.68 + 2,381.50 + 32,341.31 = 37,363.41

Now Rs 37,363.41 / 10,662.43 = 3.50 years

6. Find the duration, if:
   (a) A 10% Rs 3,000 bond has a 3-year maturity
   (b) The present value of the bond is Rs 3,105.73
   (c) The yield to maturity is 8%
   (d) The installment of the principal is paid each year

Solution

The discounted value multiplied by t =

Rs $(1{,}300/1.08) \times 1 + (1{,}200/1.08^2) \times 2 + (1100/1.08^3) \times 3$

= Rs 1,203.70 + 2,057.61 + 2,619.65 = Rs 5,880.96

Now Rs 5,880.96 / 3,105.73 = 1.89 years

7. A company issues Rs 100 preference shares with Rs 10 as dividend per share per annum. The company's financial position is strong which means a perpetual dividend payment. If the investors require at least 12% return on their investment, find the value of share.

Solution

Rs 10 / 0.12 = Rs 83.33

8. If a company issues 10% Rs 10 preference shares and if the investors require only 8% return on their investment, find the intrinsic value of the share.

Solution

Rs 10/0.08 = Rs 125

Note: When required rate of return < dividend, the intrinsic value of share will be greater than the face value.

9. If a company is expected to pay dividend in the foreseeable future, say, the next three years at Rs 10, Rs 12, and Rs 12 per share of Rs 100 and the required rate of return is 11%, find the intrinsic value of share if a shareholder has contracted to sell the share for Rs 110 after the three-year period.

Solution

Intrinsic value = Rs $10/1.11 + 12/1.11^2 + 12/1.11^3 + 110/1.11^3$

= Rs 9.00 + 9.74 + 8.77 + 80.43 = Rs 107.94

10. A company being a matured one has witnessed 2% growth in dividend p.a. during the past. The growth rate in dividend is expected to be maintained. If the recent dividend has amounted to Rs 10 and if shareholders require 8% return, find the intrinsic value of the share.

Solution

Rs 10 /(0.08 – 0.02) = Rs 166.66

11. The recently paid dividend in a company is Rs 10 per share. The company expects growth in dividend of 15% p.a. for the next three years after which the growth in dividend stabilises at 3% p.a.. Find the value of the share, given a required rate of return of 18%.

Solution

Rs $\{10(1.15)\}/1.18 + \{10(1.15^2)\}/1.18^2 + \{10(1.15^3)\}/1.18^3$

$+ 10/(0.18 - 0.03) \times 1/1.18^3$

= Rs 9.75 + 9.50 + 9.26 = 40.58 = Rs 69.09

Mini Case 1

Energy Biscuits, producing varieties of biscuits, started functioning 10 years ago. There was then no other factory for biscuits in the region. It was one of the reasons that the firm earned huge amount of money.

The company had started with 50,000 shares of Rs 100 each. Presently, it likes to value its shares for the purpose of financial planning. This can be done in view of the trends in the biscuit industry as also the past performance of Energy Biscuits.

The share price and some other related financial variables of the competing firms in the industry are as follows:

	Firm EPS (Rs)	*DPS (Rs)*	*Share price (Rs)*	*ROE*	*Discount rate %*
Viva Biscuits	12.00	4.80	120	10.00	10.0
Ashok Food Products	7.00	2.10	80	8.75	10.0
Tasty Foods	17.50	8.75	140	12.50	14.0
Industry average	12.17	5.22	340	10.42	11.3

The last year, Energy Biscuits had an EPS of Rs 4.50. The dividend paid totalled Rs 53,500. The return on equity was 25%. The required rate of return was 15%.

Questions:

1. Find out the value of the shares of Energy Biscuits assuming that the company growth rate has not changed.
2. Does Energy Biscuits have the same price–earnings ratio as the industry average denotes?

Mini Case 2

Investment in Debentures by Prabhat Engineering

A company, Prabhat Engineering is planning to invest in the 8%, 25-year, Rs 1,000 debentures of Flex Engineering. The latter had issued those debentures 5 years ago. They are convertible into 50 equity shares and can be called any time at Rs 1,079.

It may be pointed out the current rate of inflation is 4.40 per cent and is likely to be 5.0 per cent annually. Thus inflation is a problem accompanied by the long maturity that is fraught with risk

Alternatively, Prabhat Engineering has access to make investment in another issue of debentures made by Rahul Engineering that have 10 per cent coupon, 10-year maturity, Rs 1,000 par value and a semi-annual interest payment.

In order to reach a decision whether to invest and where to invest, Prabhat Engineering goes for valuing the bond.

Questions:

1. If the market price of the equity share rises by Rs 25 per share after 3 years, will it be advisable for Flex Engineering to call the debentures?
2. Compare the two alternatives where Prabhat Engineering chould make investment.
3. If Prabhat Engineering goes for the first alternative and holds the debentures for 3 years, how much gain/loss will it experience in the value of debentures?

REFERENCE

Miller, M.H. and F. Modigliani (1961). "Dividend Policy, Growth and the Valuation of Shares", *Journal of Business*, 34 (Oct.): 411–33.

SELECT FURTHER READING

Fuller, R.J. and Chi-Cheng Hsia (1984). "A Simplified Common Stock Valuation Model", *Financial Analysts Journal*, 40 (Sept.-Oct.): 49–56.

APPENDIX A

Rating of Bonds

Bond rating means assigning of quality to the bonds. Rating is helpful in the marketability of the bonds and this in turn ensures the fund-raising ability of the firms. Rating also helps protect the interests of the investors insofar as they prefer to invest only in high-rated bonds, and do not fall prey to default risk. Sometimes investors do invest in low-rated bonds if the rate of return is high. Junk bonds are an apposite example of high-risk/high-yield bonds.

One can find bond rating institutions spread all over the globe. The rating institutions in the USA, Mood Investors Service, Standard and Poor's Corporation and Fitch Investors Service are well known throughout the world. In India, the Credit Rating and Information Services of India Ltd. (CRISIL), was set up in 1988. It currently rates the debt obligations of Indian companies, specifically, debentures and fixed deposit schemes, preference shares and short-term instruments like commercial paper. Such rating is now also done by two other institutions: ICRA and CARE.

As far as rating standards are concerned, the triple-and-double-A bonds are extremely safe. Single-A or triple-B bonds are also safe to large extent as they too come under the investment-grade securities. Risky bonds are those with a rating below this and carry a high probability of default.

Rating takes into account a number of qualitative and quantitative factors. Important among these are:

1. Mortgage provisions, or whether the bond is secured by a mortgage. Secured bonds have a high rating;
2. Subordination provision or whether the bond is subordinated to another debt instrument. A subordinated bonds have a low rating;
3. Guarantee provision, or whether the bond is guaranteed by a financially strong company. Presence of a guarantee ensures a high rating;
4. Operational and accounting standards maintained by the firm as reflected in various ratios.

APPENDIX B

Equilibrium in the Share Market

Conditions for, and the Restoration of, the Equilibrium

Equilibrium in the share market denotes a position when expected rate of return is equal to the required rate of return. The reader may note that the expected rate of return on an ordinary share is a rate that the shareholder expects to receive in the future. On the contrary, the required rate of return on an ordinary share is the rate that the shareholder considers acceptable. As discussed, in Chapter 3, the required rate of return is equal to the sum of the risk-free rate of return and the risk premium. The risk premium is equal to the product of beta (β) and the difference between the market rate of return and the rate of return on the security in question.

Let us assume a case where D_t is Rs 3, P_0 is Rs 30, expected growth in dividend is 5% per annum and required rate of return is 16%. In such a case, the expected rate of return will be:

$$\text{Rs } (3/30) + 0.05 = 0.15 = 15\%.$$

This is a case where expected rate of return is lower than the required rate of return. In this situation, shareholders will try to sell their shares. But there will hardly be any buyers for these share. As a consequence, the seller will have to reduce the price of the share. The cut in the price will continue till the expected rate of return equals the required rate of return. At Rs 27.27 or [3/(0.16 – 0.05)], the expected rate of return will be equal to the required rate of return. The market will then be in equilibrium.

On the contrary, if P_0 is Rs 25 with other variables unchanged, the expected rate of return will be higher than the required rate of return. Shareholders will begin buying shares. In the presence of a greater demand for the shares, their price will move up bringing down the expected rate of return. The price upsurge will take place till the two rates are equal and the share market is in equilibrium.

All this shows that if any of the variables, such as P_0, D_1 and g change, the equilibrium conditions in the market will change.

Efficient Market Hypothesis

Those who believe in market equilibrium base their views on the efficient market hypothesis (EMH). The EMH rests primarily on two facts. First, that the share market is in equilibrium. Second, that it is not possible for the investor to "beat the market". This is because shareholders have all the available information. However, the question here is whether all types of information are really available.

Fama (1970)[1], in his pioneering work in this area discusses three kinds of efficiency. They are:

1. Weak-form efficiency;
2. Semi-strong-form efficiency;
3. Strong-form efficiency.

The weak-form of EMH states that the information contained in the price movement in the past is completely reflected in the current market prices. It means that the current trend in share prices is of no use for selecting shares.

The semi-strong-form of EMH states that the current share market prices reflect all publicly available information. Investors may expect to earn the return predicted by security market line but not more than that insofar as they do not get information other than that which is publicly available. However, insiders in the companies can earn abnormal profits because they also possess information not publicly available.

The strong-form efficiency of EMH states that the current market price reflects both the publicly and privately available information, as a result of which the insiders too cannot earn abnormal profits in the share market.

Empirical studies show that strong-form efficiency is not found in the real world. Corporate officers, who are insiders, and also some prudent investors do have privately available information, they, therefore, perform better and reap some amount of abnormal profits. Nevertheless, the buy-and-sell activities of the investors bring market prices in equilibrium where the expected rate of return and the required rate of return are equal.

[1] Fama, E.F. (1970). "Efficient Capital Markets: A Review of Theory and Empirical Work", *Journal of Finance*, 15 (May): 384–87.

Part II

Long-term Investment Decision

Corporate financial activities begin with the selection of projects and the making of long-term investments. This process is known as capital budgeting. It involves intricate and well thought-out decisions, that help add to the corporate wealth. Part II deals with:

1. Principles of capital budgeting;
2. Capital budgeting in practice that is closer to the realities of the corporate world;
3. Cost of capital that represents the minimum required rate of return.

5

PRINCIPLES OF CAPITAL BUDGETING

OBJECTIVES

To describe the nature of capital budgeting and also the various steps taken in the process of capital budgeting

To explain the concept of cash flows

To show how the different segments of cash flow are computed

To explain various techniques – discounting and non-discounting – for project evaluation

Capital budgeting deals with the selection of proposals/projects for making long-term investments and their implementation. Its purpose is to yield positive cash inflows that can add to the corporate wealth. This requires a detailed study of the computation of cash flow, and how the cash flow is put into different evaluation criteria. The present chapter deals with these different aspects of capital budgeting.

5.1 NATURE OF CAPITAL BUDGETING

5.1.1 Meaning and Significance

Capital budgeting relates to long-term investment in fixed assets. Capital refers to long-term assets used in production. The budget is a plan detailing projected inflows and outflows of cash during a specific future period. It is different from an operating budget in that it usually involves a number of years, while an operating budget is confined to one fiscal year.

Capital budgeting decisions are significant for a firm. First, fixed assets account for a sizeable proportion of the firm's total assets and their life extends over a considerable number of years. If wrong decisions are taken, the amount of loss will be colossal. Second, long-term assets are usually specialised. This means that they are designed for a specific activity. If there is any mistake in judgement, they cannot normally be used for any other operation, as a result of which there may be huge wastage. Third, in order to maintain the value of corporate wealth, the management has to visualise the returns spread over the long life of the project. This visualisation necessitates capital budgeting. A system of capital budgeting is helpful in reaching logical investment decisions because

Capital budgeting deals with the selection of proposals/projects for making long-term investment.

the management is forced to estimate the probable cash commitments, their recovery and the time when they occur. Such estimates are often fraught with the possibility of error, yet such a plan is preferable to one without estimates. Last but not least, the system of capital budgeting forces co-ordination among different departments within a firm. The engineering, marketing, manufacturing and the finance departments—all provide necessary data for reaching an investment decision. Such team spirit helps a firm grow.

5.1.2 Types of Proposals

The proposals for which long-term investment decisions are taken can be grouped under the following heads:

1. Expansion proposals;
2. Replacement proposals;
3. Strategic proposals;
4. Safety and/or environmental proposals.

Expansion is the most common phenomenon. First, with economic growth, demand is bound to increase. Firms try to meet increased demand and expand their production and productive capacity. It is not only economic growth and increased demand that leads to expansion, internal factors can also often lead to expansion. For example, in order to reap economies of scale, firms expand their productive capacity. The expansion may also be aimed at producing a new product or catering to a new geographic area not currently in the range of supply.

Second, replacement is an unavoidable necessity. This is because the efficiency of machines and other capital equipment deteriorates over time. Moreover, technological improvements as a result of research and development make existing machines obsolete, requiring that they be replaced. Replacement may be of two kinds: like-for-like replacement that is caused by physical wear and tear; and replacement following obsolescence, normally caused by technological progress.

Third, strategic proposals are related to risk-reducing as well as welfare-improving investment. In a competitive business environment, every firm wishes to make its output best suited to consumers at the least possible cost. For this purpose, it makes long-term investments in research and development. The proposals involving investment in research and development are known as strategic proposals.

Fourth, proposals for investment in order to comply with governmental provisions, such as, labour laws, laws relating to the environment, etc., are known as safety/environmental proposals. This expenditure is called mandatory investment and such proposals are often non-revenue-generating projects.

5.1.3 Steps in Capital Budgeting Process

The process of capital budgeting involves a number of steps that follow in a set order. They are:

1. Identification of long-term goals;
2. Screening of proposals;

3. Project evaluation;
4. Project implementation;
5. Control;
6. Project audit.

Capital budgeting involves identification of long-term goals, screening of proposals, project evaluation, project implementation, control and project audit.

Identification of long-term goals: In the very beginning, the finance manager has to find out whether strategic or tactical investment will be more suitable for the firm from the viewpoint of its long-term goals. Entering a new product market involves strategic investment. Such proposals cannot be evaluated solely in terms of their impact on the cash flow. Intangible benefits that are in conformity with the firm's long-term goals should also be considered. On the contrary, tactical investments are those which primarily influence the firm's cash flow but do not necessarily change the character of the firm. Establishment of new facilities in an existing market for the purpose of manufacturing products related to the current product may be an example of a tactical investment proposal. Such investment proposals carry less risk as compared to the risk inherent in strategic proposals.

Screening of Proposals: When the manager is satisfied that the proposal conforms to the long-term goals of the firm, he or she proceeds on to the second phase, that of screening the proposal. The second phase is one in which the manager determines the impact of the proposal on the firm. In large firms, it is the project analysis division that looks for new ideas and qualitatively evaluates their potential impact on the firm's revenues and cost. It examines whether the proposal would reduce cost and/or expand revenue.

Project Evaluation: Once the proposal passes through the initial screening, detailed evaluation in quantitative terms begins. A detailed economic analysis using discounting/non-discounting cash flow techniques follows to find out whether the proposal is financially feasible. To be more specific, this phase comprises three activities:

1. Identification of the projects;
2. Estimation of cash flows;
3. Application of objective criteria to judge for acceptance/rejection.

While identifying projects, the finance manager must be able to distinguish between a proposal and a project. When two or more proposals are economically independent of one another such that the cash flow from one has no impact on the cash flow from the other, each proposal would be treated as a project and would be evaluated separately.

While identifying projects, the finance manager must be able to distinguish between a proposal and a project.

On the contrary, if two or more proposals are economically dependent meaning that the cash flow from one proposal has an impact on the cash flow from the other, they are collectively treated as a project and are evaluated collectively. From the viewpoint of economic dependence, proposals may be grouped as:

1. Complementary proposals;
2. Substitute proposals;
3. Mutually exclusive proposals.

If two proposals are complementary, the cash flow from the two proposals collectively would be larger than the sum of the individual cash flows from the two proposals. If a soft drink manufacturer adds snacks to its product line, the sale of soft drinks would be larger insofar as those eating snacks will demand for soft drinks.

If the two proposals are substitute proposals, the acceptance of one will reduce the cash flow from the other. For example, if a manufacturer of *gur* (molasses) decides to manufacture sugar, the cash inflow in the case of *gur* will tend to reduce as a result of the sale of sugar.

Proposals are mutually exclusive when the acceptance of one leads to the rejection of the other. If a manufacturer of sugar decides to either build a warehouse or to lease warehouse space in a business park, both alternatives are mutually exclusive, as taking up one means the rejection of the other.

When proposals are identified, the cash flow—inflow and outflow—is estimated over the lifetime of the project. Estimation of cash flow is discussed in the following section.

Again, when cash flows are estimated, they are put to different evaluation criteria so as to decide whether to accept or reject the proposal. The evaluation criteria are also discussed after the discussion regarding estimation of cash flow.

When the project is complete, the extent of success or failure and the reasons thereof are carefully studied.

Project Implementation: In this phase, the firm makes the required arrangements to take up the new project. This includes arrangement of capital, training of personnel and other relevant works.

Control: After the project is implemented, the firm monitors whether costs are incurred in accordance with the set standards. Minor deviations are managed, however, if deviations are very large, the project may be abandoned.

Project Audit: When the project is complete, the extent of success or failure and the reasons thereof are carefully studied. In this way the audit phase provides valuable information to the firm.

5.2 THE CONCEPT OF CASH FLOWS

5.2.1 Nature and Timing of Cash Flows

The long-term investment of funds, makes a demand on a part of the firm's current wealth, however, it also brings in funds and adds to the firm's stock of wealth in the future. While the former results in cash outflows from the firm, the latter is represented by cash inflows into the firm. Cash inflows thus include primarily revenue on account of additional sales or cash from the eventual sale of the assets, known as the salvage value. Cash outflows, on the other hand, occur on account of capital expenditures, other expenses, excluding depreciation, and payment of income tax.

Cash flow is related to different periods of time. It is trifurcated into initial cash flow, operating cash flow and terminal cash flow.

Cash flow is related to different periods of time. And accordingly, cash flow is trifurcated. The three parts are:

1. Initial cash flow;
2. Operating cash flow;
3. Terminal cash flow.

Initial Cash Flow: The initial cash flow takes place in the very beginning, that is during t_0. It includes:

1. Cash outflow in the form of gross investment for the purchase of assets, for example, land and building, plant and machinery, etc., and the installation and freight cost related to the assets;
2. The expenditure incurred for making machines operational. For example, if workers are trained so that they can successfully handle the new machinery, the expenditure incurred on their training is a part of the initial investment. Such expenditure is, however, subject to tax;
3. The opportunity cost of the assets. If a firm already has a plot of land and if the plot of land is used for the new project, the opportunity cost of the plot of land will be added to the initial investment;
4. Increase in net working capital. Investment in fixed assets leads to an increase in the amount of current assets required for enhancing the level of production. This increase in the net working capital is a part of initial capital outlay.

Operating Cash Flow: The operating cash flow takes place when the firm is in operation, that is during t_1 to t_n. It represents various revenues and cash expenses consequent upon the operation of the firm. When revenue exceeds cash expenses, there is a net inflow of cash. Net outflow occurs when cash expenses exceed revenue.

Terminal Cash Flow: Terminal cash flow represents salvage value or scrap value. It takes place when the life of the project comes to an end or during t_n. The salvage value is estimated on the basis of the cost of the asset and the accumulated amount of depreciation or the sale value of the used asset. The amount of clean-up and removal expenses, if any, is subtracted from this amount. Moreover, some amount of net working capital is released as a result of cessation of the operation. This amount is added to the salvage value.

When salvage value is uncertain, the finance manager makes various estimates of salvage value or terminal cash flow and computes the net present value (NPV) based on each possible outcome of the terminal cash flow. Alternatively, the *break-even salvage value,* which is the terminal cash flow necessary to achieve a zero NPV for the project is computed. The break-even salvage value or the break-even terminal cash flow is then compared with the estimated terminal cash flow. If the estimated terminal cash flow is less than the break-even salvage value, the investment proposal will be rejected. This is because in this case, NPV will be negative. On the contrary, if estimated terminal cash flow is more than the break-even salvage value, the proposal may be accepted.

For computing the break-even salvage value, the cash flow beginning from the first year to the nth year is segregated into the operating cash flow (OCF_t) and the terminal cash flow, (TCF_n): The break-even salvage value is derived as follows:

$$NPV = \sum_{t=1}^{n}\left(\frac{OCF_t}{(1+k)^t} + \frac{TCF_n}{(1+k)^n}\right) - I_0$$

$$\text{or } O = \sum_{t=1}^{n}\left(\frac{OCF_t}{(1+k)^t} + \frac{TCF_n}{(1+k)^n}\right) - I_0$$

$$\text{or } I_0 - \sum_{t=1}^{n} \frac{OCF_t}{(1+k)^t} = \frac{TCF_n}{(1+k)^n}$$

$$\text{or } TCF_n = \left[I_0 - \sum_{t=1}^{n} \frac{OCF_t}{(1+k)^t} \right] \times (1+k)^n \qquad ...(5.1)$$

EXAMPLE

Suppose the net cash inflow in a 3-year period, which is the lifespan of the project, is Rs 10,000, Rs 12,000 and Rs 13,000 respectively. The initial investment is Rs 20,000 and the discount rate is 10%. The break-even salvage value will be:

Rs [20,000 – {10,000/1.10 + 12,000/1.10^2 + 13,000/$1,10^3$}] x $(1.10)^3$

= Rs –11,680.

5.2.2 Factors Considered for Cash Flow Computation

There are particular ways in which the cash flow needs to be computed. These ways are as follows:

1. The cash flow should be computed on an after-tax basis;
2. The cash flow should exclude depreciation;
3. The cash flow should exclude financing cost;
4. The cash flow should be computed on an incremental basis.

Adjustment for Taxes: Cash expenditures lead to tax savings, and hence these expenditures have to be treated for taxes. However, for this purpose, one has to distinguish between the cash expenditure charged to profits in the current period and cash expenditure that is capitalised over a given number of years. While the former needs to be treated for taxes, expenditure that is capitalised need no such adjustment. If this is the basis for tax treatment, it will influence different forms of cash flow differently.

The cash expenditure meant for asset acquisition is not immediately charged to profits in the current period, and hence it is not subject to tax treatment. In case of replacement of an existing asset, tax is computed on the excess of its sale value over its book salvage value. It may be noted that the book salvage value of an asset is equal to the acquisition cost of the asset minus accumulated depreciation. If a machine is bought for Rs 1,10,000 and the amount of accumulated depreciation during its lifetime stands at Rs 1,00,000, its book salvage value would be Rs 10,000. This amount may differ from the cash salvage value insofar as the cash salvage value is the amount of cash received on account of the sale of asset. If the cash salvage value exceeds the book salvage value, the difference is treated as ordinary income and is taxed. This tax liability is added to the initial outlay.

As far as net operating cash flow is concerned, expenditures are immediately charged to profits in the current period, and hence they are estimated on an after-tax basis. The net operating cash flow after tax (CFAT) can be expressed as:

$$\text{CFAT} = (Revenue - Expenditure)\ (1 - T) \qquad ...(5.2)$$

As regards non-operating cash flow involving major repairs to machines on a less frequent basis, and the like, the adjustment for taxes depends again on whether the expenditure is charged immediately or capitalised. In the former case, expenditure is treated for tax.

Similarly, in the case of terminal cash flow, tax treatment, as discussed above, is required only when the cash salvage value is greater than the book salvage value. The tax is levied on the excess of the cash salvage value over the book salvage value. Again, tax adjustment is made also for clean-up and removal expenses associated with the worn-out machine. On the contrary, the release of net working capital is not treated for tax.

Exclusion of Depreciation: Depreciation is an allocation of the cost of fixed assets. Although, it involves an accounting entry as an expense, yet, it is a non-cash expense and hence does not constitute a part of the computation of the cash flow. In other words, depreciation has no direct bearing on the cash flow. It does, however, have an impact on the cash flow in the form of reduction of the tax liability. That is why depreciation is considered for the computation of after-tax cash flow in spite of the fact that it does not form a part of the cash flow.

EXAMPLE

A project involving Rs 50,000 as initial outlay generates Rs 20,000 annually. The operating expenses amount to Rs 10,000 and the amount of depreciation is Rs 5,000. The tax rate is 30%. Find out the cash flow after tax (CFAT).

Cash receipt	...	Rs 20,000
Less: Cash expenses plus depreciation	...	Rs 15,000
Taxable income	...	Rs 5,000
Less: Taxes	...	Rs 1,500
Net income after tax	...	Rs 3,500
Add: Depreciation	...	Rs 5,000
Net cash flow after tax	...	Rs 8,500

Exclusion of Financing Cost: Although, any form of capital has a cost, the cost of capital is not included while computing cash flow. This is because such costs are considered elsewhere while determining the required rate of return. If the financing cost is included in the calculation of cash flow, the problem of double counting would occur, and cash flow estimates would be misleading.

Incremental Cash Flow: Cash flow should be computed on an incremental basis. For determining the cash flow from an investment, one compares the firm's cash flow with, and without, that investment. The difference between the two is the additional cash flow on account of the investment. For example, if a firm's existing cash flow is Rs 10,000. And as a result of undertaking a new project, the cash flow moves up to Rs 15,000. The incremental cash flow in this respect would be Rs 5,000. Eq. 5.2 should then be re-written as follows:

$$\Delta \text{CFAT} = (\Delta Revenue - \Delta Expenditure)(1 - T) \quad ...(5.3)$$

A finance manager should be very particular while computing the incremental cash flow. An important question arises in this context, as to whether he/she should take into account the sunk cost. The sunk cost is a cash expenditure that has already been incurred and that cannot be recovered irrespective of whether the project is accepted or rejected. If a firm hired another firm for the site study for the project in question during the previous year, the amount spent for this purpose is a sunk cost and it cannot be a part of the cash flow.

The other question concerns opportunity cost. If a firm already possesses a plot of land and uses the land for the project in question, the return from the best alternative use of the plot of land would be considered for the determination of the cash flow.

Again, if the introduction of a new product through the new venture leads to a fall in the sale of existing products, the loss of revenue on this account should be considered for calculation of cash flow.

Important Guidelines for Computation of Cash Flows

1. Consider only those incomes and expenses that involve actual cash flows. So do not consider sunk cost and consider only those overheads that relate to the project in question.
2. Compute cash flows on an incremental basis, which means those cash flows that follow from the acceptance of the project.
3. Consider also the effects of possible downstream activities that normally generate cash flow in future years.
4. Consider additional net working capital requirements.
5. Consider the opportunity cost, if any.
6. Do not consider financing cost.
7. Calculate the cash flow on an after-tax basis.

5.2.3 Process of Computation

Taking into account the factors discussed in the preceding sub-section, the different segments of the cash flow—initial investment, operating cash flow and terminal cash flow—are computed in the following manner.

Initial Investment: Computation of initial investment can be expressed in the form of an equation as follows:

$$I_0 = -I - IE - E(1 - T) - \Delta W + S - T(S - B) \qquad ...(5.4)$$

where:

I = acquisition cost of asset
IE = installation expenses
E = expenses to make the machine operational
DW = increase in the net working capital
S = cash salvage value
B = book salvage value
T = tax rate

EXAMPLE

An old machine is replaced. It had been bought 4 years ago for Rs 1,20,000 and is now being sold for Rs 10,000. The accumulated depreciation amounts to Rs 1,12,000. The cost of the new machine is Rs 2,00,000. The installation cost amounts to Rs 4,000 and the training of personnel needed to make the machine operational is Rs 5,000. The increase in the net working capital amounts to Rs 3,000. The tax rate is 30%. The initial investment will be:

$$I_0 = \text{Rs } -2,00,000 - 4,000 - 5,000(1 - 0.30) - 3,000 + 10,000 - 0.30(10,000 - 8,000)$$
$$= \text{Rs } -2,01,100.$$

Net operating cash flow: The incremental operating cash flow after taxes, as discussed above, can be computed as follows:

$$\Delta\text{CFAT} = (\Delta\ Revenue - \Delta\ Expenditure - \Delta D)\ (1 - T) + \Delta D \qquad ...(5.5)$$

EXAMPLE

The incremental sales as a result of a new investment amounts to Rs 50,000. The incremental fixed and variable costs amount to Rs 20,000. The incremental depreciation amounts to Rs 5,000 at a flat rate. The tax rate is 30%. The incremental operating cash flow will be.

$$\text{Rs } (50,000 - 20,000 - 5,000)\ (1 - 0.30) + 5,000 = \text{Rs } 22,500.$$

Net salvage value: The net salvage value can be expressed as follows:

$$S - T\ (S - B) - (1 - T)\ RE + \Delta W \qquad ...(5.6)$$

Where:

RE = removal and clean-up expenses

EXAMPLE

A machine was bought for Rs 1,20,000. The accumulated depreciation is Rs 1,12,000. The machine is sold for Rs 15,000 which is the scrap value. The removal and clean-up expenses amount to Rs 500 and the net working capital release value is Rs 1,000. The tax rate is 30%. Find out the net salvage value.

$$\text{Rs } 15,000 - 0.30\ (15,000 - 8,000) - (1 - 0.30)\ 500 + 1000 = \text{Rs } 13,550.$$

5.3 PROJECT EVALUATION CRITERIA

After the cash flow is estimated in respect of a proposal/project, it is put to evaluation criteria in order to determine whether the proposal/project is to be accepted. Broadly, there are two types of evaluation criteria: First, where cash flow is discounted to the present value and, second, where it is not discounted. The commonly used discounting techniques are:

1. Net present value (NPV) method;
2. Discounted benefit-cost ratio method;
3. Internal rate of return (IRR) method;
4. Modified internal rate of return (MIRR) method.

The commonly used non-discounting techniques are:

1. Pay-back period method;
2. Accounting rate of return.

> It is reported that 10–20 per cent of the large US multinational firms use the accounting rate of return method. 28 per cent rely on pay-back period method. The rest use the discounting methods of capital budgeting.
>
> —*A. Buckley, Multinational Finance.*

5.3.1 NPV Rule

NPV is arrived at after subtracting the initial investment from the discounted value of the future cash flows where the discount rate is the firm's cost of capital. In terms of equation it can be expressed as follows:

$$NPV = \sum_{t=1}^{n} \frac{CF_t}{(1+k)^n} - I_0 \qquad ...(5.7)$$

where:

CF_t = expected after-tax cash flow from t_1 to t_n including both the operating cash flow and the terminal cash flow

I_o = initial investment

k = risk-adjusted discount rate

n = lifespan of the project.

EXAMPLE

A project involves an initial investment for Rs 50,00,000. The net cash inflow expected during the first, second and the third year is Rs 30,00,000, Rs 35,00,000 and Rs 20,00,000 respectively. At the end of the third year, the scrap value is indicated at Rs 10,00,000. The risk-adjusted discount rate is 10%. Calculate NPV.

$$30,00,000/1.10 + 35,00,000/(1.10)^2 + (20,00,000 + 10,00,000)/(1.10)^3 - 50,00,000 = \text{Rs } 28,73,778.$$

Therefore, as the NPV is positive the project would be accepted.

In this method, projects are accepted where the present value of net cash inflow during the lifespan of the project is greater than the initial investment. When NPV is positive, it means that some surplus accrues that raises the shareholders' wealth. When NPV is zero, it signifies that the project's cash flows are exactly sufficient to meet the initial investment and to provide the required rate of return on that capital. On the contrary, when NPV is negative, the proposal is rejected insofar as making an investment for the proposal will cause a drain on the resources.

There are cases when the cash flow is perpetual, perhaps with a constant growth rate in many cases. In such cases,

$$NPV = \frac{CF_t}{(k-g)} - I_0 \quad ...(5.8)$$

Let us take two examples. In both the cases, the initial investment is Rs 80,000, the annual cash flow is Rs 7,000 and the discount rate is 10%. But in one case, there is zero growth rate, while in the other, the growth rate is 5%. With zero growth rate,

NPV = Rs {7,000/ (0.10 – 0)} –80,000 = Rs –10,000

On the other hand, with 5% growth rate,

NPV = Rs {7,000/(0.10 – 0.05) – 80,000 = Rs 60,000.

In the first case, with negative NPV, the proposal will be rejected. But in the second case, with positive NPV, the proposal will be accepted.

5.3.2 Profitability Index

Profitability index (PI) shows the relationship between the net cash inflows and the initial investment. This means it shows the relative gains. It can be expressed in the form of an equation as follows:

$$PI = \sum_{t=1}^{n} \frac{CF_t}{(1+k)^n} / I_0 \quad ...(5.9)$$

EXAMPLE

Based on the example in the previous page, where initial investment is Rs 50,00,000 and the discounted value of operating and terminal cash flow is Rs 78,73,778,

PI = 78,73,778/50,00,000 = 1.57

Therefore, as the PI is more than 1, the project may be accepted.

5.3.3 Profitability Ratio versus NPV

The basic difference between the NPV and the PI is that while the former expresses the net benefit from a project in absolute terms, the latter measures it in relative terms. The result of the two methods is thus the same but there are times when they yield different results as regards ranking of proposals. To illustrate:

	Project A	*Project B*
Present value of net cash benefits	Rs 15,000	Rs 10,000
Initial cash outlay	Rs 10,000	Rs 6,000
NPV	Rs 5,000	Rs 4,000
Profitability Index	1.50	1.66

NPV is greater in Project A and, therefore, it is preferable to Project B. On the contrary, PI is greater in Project B which means that it is preferable to Project A. In such cases, NPV should be relied upon as it shows the absolute increase in corporate wealth.

In case of independent projects, with no capital rationing, both the projects will be accepted because NPV is positive and at the same time PI is more than 1. But in case of mutually exclusive projects, when one project is to be selected, Project A will be selected because it has higher NPV. If one relies on Project B with a higher PI, it would be wrong decision. The reason is that the selection of the project based on PI would contribute less to the corporate wealth.

Similarly, in case of capital rationing, the same problem would arise. With an available capital of Rs 10,000, PI will favour Project B, which contributes less to the corporate wealth. Again, it would be an erroneous decision.

5.3.4 IRR Rule

IRR is that discount rate which brings down the value of net cash inflows during the life of the project so that it is equal to the value of initial investment. It can be expressed in the form of equation as follows:

$$\sum_{t=1}^{n} \frac{CF_t}{(1+IRR)^n} - I_0 = 0 \qquad ...(5.10)$$

The project will be accepted if IRR is greater than the required rate of return.

The computation of IRR is not as easy as that of the NPV. This is because there is no fixed rate of discount. In such cases, trial-and-error method is normally used. However, one may base one's computation on the method of interpolation. If the future cash flows are constant or even, the computation is slightly easier. However, if cash flows are uneven, computation is not so easy.

In the case of even cash flows, the initial investment is divided by the annual cash flows. The result is located in the relevant annuity table on the line representing the number of years corresponding to economic life of the project. If this figure tallies exactly with the figure in the annuity table, the particular interest rate is the IRR. However, it usually falls between the two *ADF r, n*. In that case,

$$\text{IPR} = r_1 + [(P - I_0)]/\Delta P]\Delta r \qquad ...(5.11)$$

where:

$r1$ = the lower rate of discount
P = the calculated present value of future cash flows
I_0 = the initial investment
DP = the difference in calculated present value
Dr = the difference in interest rate

EXAMPLE

A proposal involves Rs 20,00,000. The annual cash flow is Rs 10,00,000 for 3 years. Find out the IRR.

Since the initial investment divided by the annuity is 2/1, one has to find out 2 in the annuity table. The annuity factor closest to 2 for 3 years is 1.9520 at 25% discount rate and 2.1065 at 20% discount rate. The annual cash flow will be multiplied by these two annuity factors and then a difference of the product from the initial outlay is found out. This is done as follows:

(a) At 20% discount rate: 10,00,000 × 2.1065 – 20,00,000 = 106.50
(b) At 25% discount rate: 10,00,000 × 1.9520 – 20,00,000 = –48.00

Since NPV is greater than 0 at 20% discount rate, one needs a higher discount rate to equate NPV to initial investment.
Using Eq. 5.9:

$$IRR = 20 + (106.50/154.50) \times 5 = 23.45\%$$

In case of unev en cash flow, the average of the cash flow is computed and then the same procedure applies. Although in this case, greater amount of trial-and-error work is needed.

If the required rate of return is 10%, the project would be accepted. This is because the IRR is greater than the required rate of return. The IRR on a project is its expected rate of return. If it is greater than the cost of funds used to finance the project, a surplus will accrue which will raise shareholders' wealth.

5.3.5 NPV versus IRR

The two methods—NPV and IRR—are commonly used for project evaluation. But the question is whether the two methods yield the same result. The answer depends on:

1. Type of projects;
2. Pattern of cash flow.

Independent Projects: If the projects are independent meaning that investment in one project has nothing to do with investment in others, the results of the two evaluation criteria will necessarily be the same. Both of them will lead to the same accept/reject decision. This is because when NPV is positive, IRR must be greater than the cost of capital. At zero NPV, the IRR will be equal to the cost of capital. And when NPV is negative, IRR is less than the cost of capital.

Mutually Exclusive Projects: In case of mutually exclusive projects where investment in one project means rejection of the other project, IRR and NPV may not yield the same accept/reject decision. In fact, there are two basic conditions that are responsible for such a conflicting result. They are:

1. Dissimilar size of the project;
2. Different timing of the cash flow in two projects.

When the size of two projects differs, the cost involved in them will also differs. The project with lower investment may have a larger IRR but a lower NPV. The larger project may have smaller IRR but a greater NPV. Suppose Project A has 30% IRR and Rs 500 as NPV. Project B has 20% IRR but Rs 800 as NPV. In such cases, if one bases one's decision on IRR, Project A will be considered. But if NPV is the basis, Project B will be accepted.

However, in such cases, an incremental approach is used. Suppose there are two proposals: Proposal A involving an initial investment of Rs 2,000 with an annual net cash inflow of Rs 610 for 5 years; and Proposal B having an initial outlay of Rs 3,000 with a net cash inflow of Rs 900 annually for 5 years. In the former IRR is 16%, while in the latter it is 15.2%. Proposal A will be accepted on the basis of higher IRR. However, in an incremental approach, it is found that the incremental outlay is Rs 1,000 and the incremental net cash inflow is Rs 290 per annum for 5 years. The incremental IRR would be 13.8% and Proposal B would be accepted. The only condition is that IRR should be higher than the cost of capital.

When the timing of the cash flow of two mutually exclusive projects differs, NPV and IRR will produce conflicting results. To illustrate:

		Proposal A	*Proposal B*
Initial investment		(–) Rs 9,000	(–) Rs 9,000
Net cash benefits: Year	1	Rs 3,000	Rs 6,000
	2	Rs 5,000	Rs 4,000
	3	Rs 6,000	Rs 3,000
NPV		Rs 2,367	Rs 2,014
IRR		22.5%	24%

Here, under the NPV rule, Proposal A is preferred, while as per IRR Proposal B is preferred. The reason for such a conflict is that NPV and IRR rest on different assumptions concerning the reinvestment of funds released from the project. The NPV rule implies reinvestment at a rate equivalent to the required rate of return used as a discount rate, while the IRR rule assumes that the funds are reinvested at IRR.

However, in such cases, the NPV rule is preferred in view of some limitations inherent in IRR. First, where projects of different lives are considered, the IRR rule will possibly inflate desirability of a short-life project insofar as IRR is a function of both time involved and the size of capital investment.

Second, IRR tends to be lower on projects with longer gestation period, even when NPV remains larger. This is because IRR ranks high in those projects where the bunch of benefits accrues early in the economic life of the protect.

Third, while computing IRR, there is possibility of more than one solution rate, inasmuch as IRR is a solution to a polynomial equation. If the polynomial is of the degree *n*, there will be *n* roots and *n* solution rates. Let us consider a simple example. Suppose initial investment is Rs 100. The net cash flow is Rs 320 during the first year and (-) Rs 240 during the second year. In this case, there will be two IRRs: 20% and 100%. It is difficult to arrive at a decision as to whether to accept or reject the proposal if the cost of capital is 25%.

Last but not least, in a changing cost of capital framework, the computation of IRR would not make an easy comparison, whereas the NPV rule incorporates into calculation such changes in the cost of capital.

Pattern of Cash Flow—Conventional versus Non-conventional: Normally, it is assumed that the pattern of the cash flow is conventional meaning that the initial investment represents cash outflow and the operating cash flow represents net cash inflow. But there are cases when the cash flow is non-conventional meaning that the initial cash flow represents cash inflow and the subsequent cash flow shows an outflow. When an insurance company receives a lump sum amount in the beginning and pays the insured person an annual instalment for the rest of his/her life, it represents a non-conventional cash flow and in such cases, NPV and IRR will produce conflicting results. In such cases, IRR is relied upon and the proposal is acceptable when the IRR is less than the cost of capital. The accept–reject norm is just the reverse of that in the case of a conventional cash flow pattern.

5.3.6 Modified IRR (MIRR)

In view of a few limitations, the IRR method has been modified (Shull, 1993). The modified IRR or the MIRR is the discount rate that equates the compounded value of the future cash flows to the initial investment. The compounded value of future cash flows means that the future cash flows are compounded by the firm's cost of capital. The compounded value is also known as the terminal value. It can be espresed in the form of an equation as follows:

$$I_0 = \sum_{t=0}^{n} \frac{CF_t (1+k)^{n-t}}{(1+MIRR)^n} \qquad \text{...(5.12)}$$

EXAMPLE

If the initial investment is Rs 1,000, the net cash inflow during the first, second and the third year Rs 500, Rs 400 and Rs 400 respectively, and the firm's cost of capital is 10%, find out the MIRR.

The terminal value = Rs 500 $(1 + 0.10)^2$ + 400 (1 + 0.10) + 400

= Rs 605 + 440 + 400 = Rs 1,445

Rs 1,000 = Rs 1,445/$(1 + \text{MIRR})^3$

= MIRR = 0.130549 or 13.05 %

MIRR is found to be a better evaluation technique than IRR. This is because it assumes that cash inflows are reinvested at the cost of capital which is closer to reality. This is the reason why MIRR is closer to the NPV rule.

Again, in case of mutually exclusive proposals, the accept–reject decision based on MIRR is not different from that based on NPV rule if the size of the investment and the life of the proposals are equal.

5.3.7 Pay-back Period

The pay-back period is defined as the expected number of years during which the original investment should be recovered. The management sets a target pay-back period on the basis of nature of the project and the industry norm. It then compares the actual pay-back period of the project with the target pay-back period. Finally, it takes the accept–reject decision on the basis of the comparison. A proposal is accepted if the actual pay-back period is lower than the target pay-back period, which implies that the initial investment is recovered within the target period.

EXAMPLE

Considering target pay-back period as two years, the cash flow of two proposals is as follows:

		Proposal A	*Proposal B*
Initial investment Rs		–2,000	Rs –2,000
Net cash benefits:	Year 1	Rs 1,200	Rs 1,200
	Year 2	Rs 800	Rs 400
	Year 3	—	Rs 300
	Year 4	—	Rs 300

Proposal A will be accepted as the investment is recovered within the target pay-back period despite the fact that the net cash benefits are greater in case of Proposal B. This is because this method does not consider net cash benefits beyond the target pay-back period.

Merits and Demerits: The pay-back period method is being used by many large companies because, firstly, it is simple and easy to use. Secondly, it is useful from the viewpoint of managerial control. The management is able to know within a short period of 2–3 years whether the cash flow assessed by the managers was correct. In other techniques, for example, NPV, it takes a longer period for the managers to know whether their cash flow assessment was actually realistic. Thirdly, this technique is used especially by small firms who believe in quick cash recovery because quick recovery enhances the possibility of reinvestment, if any.

However, the problems are there with the pay-back period method. It considers the cash flow only within the target pay-back period. If you look at the above example, Project A is accepted because the initial investment is recovered within the target pay-back period; and on this count, Project B is rejected despite Project B has large cash inflow. Thus, justice is not done to Project B.

The other objection to the pay-back period is that fixing of the target pay-back period is quite arbitrary. It is because there is no guide for choosing a pay-back cut-off date.

This method is unable to give a proper direction in case of projects with varying economic lives. Nevertheless, it is very simple from the viewpoint of computation, risk and liquidity.

Discounted Pay-back Period Method: It is a variant of the regular pay-back period method. In this case, it is the discounted value of the operating and terminal cash flow that is taken into account to find out whether the initial investment is recovered within the target pay-back period. Based on the example mentioned above, Proposal A will not be accepted because, assuming a discount rate of 10%, the discounted value of operating cash flow amounting to Rs (1,200/1.10) + Rs (800/1.21) will not be able to recover initial investment within the target pay-back period.

5.3.8 Accounting Rate of Return

The accounting rate of return or the average rate of return is the ratio of the average cash inflow to the average amount invested. In order to arrive at the average cash inflow, depreciation on the straight-line method is deducted from the gross profit.

EXAMPLE

Find out the average rate of return based on the following data:

Year	*Gross profit (Rs)*	*Depreciation (Rs)*	*Net profit (Rs)*	*Investment (Rs)*
1	2,000	5,332	(-) 3,332	13,334
2	6,000	5,332	668	8,000
3	10,000	5,332	4,668	2,666
Average			668	8,000

Accounting/Average rate of return = 668/8,000 = 0.0835 = 8.35%

A project is accepted if the average rate of return is higher than target rate of return which is set on the basis of the industry norm.

Sometimes the accounting rate of return is computed by dividing half of the total investment by the net profits. This is because the investment is supposed to depreciate during its service life and it has an average value of only half of its original value.

The method is a simple one. The only problem is that it does not consider the duration of the cash receipt. A receipt of Rs 1,000 annually for 10 years and of Rs 10,000 in the 10th year makes no difference according to this rule as the average is the same.

Investment Evaluation Criteria

1. NPV = PV of future cash flow - initial investment.
   Accept project of NPV is positive.
2. PI = PV of future cash flow divided by initial investment. Accept project if PI > 1.
3. IRR = Rate of discount equting PV of future cash flow to initial investment. Accept project if IRR > normal discount rate or the risk-adjusted cost of capital.
4. MIRR = Rate of discount equating the PV of the compounded value of future cash flows to initial investment Accept project if MIRR is greater than the risk-adjusted cost of capital.
5. Pay-back period = comparison of actual pay-back period with target pay - back period. Accept project if actual pay back period < target pay-back period.
6. Accouting Rate of Return (ARR) = Average net profit/Average investment
   Accept a project of ARR > the industry norm.

SUMMARY

The process of evaluation of proposals from the viewpoint of long-term investment is known as capital budgeting. It is significant from the viewpoint of maximising corporate wealth.

Proposals relate either to the expansion of existing activities or to replacement of assets or to some strategic activities, such as investment on research and development or to safety and the environment. The consecutive steps in this process are identification of long-term goals, screening of proposals, project evaluation, project implementation, control and project audit. The projects to be evaluated are either independent projects or dependent projects, such as complementary projects, substitute projects and mutually exclusive projects.

The entire evaluation is based on the cash inflow and the cash outflow. The cash flow is divided into initial cash flow, operating cash flow and terminal cash flow. It is computed on an after-tax basis and incremental basis. It does not include depreciation and the financing cost.

The evaluation criteria based on discounting of cash flow are NPV, discounted benefit-cost ratio, IRR and MIRR. The non-discounting methods are pay-back period and accounting rate of return. Projects are accepted when: NPV is positive; or IRR/MIRR is higher than the firm's cost of capital; or when the discounted benefit-cost ratio is greater than 1; or when the accounting rate of return is higher than target rate of return; or the initial investment is recovered within the target pay-back period.

POINTS TO REMEMBER

1. What are the different types of proposals?
   - Expansion proposals
   - Replacement proposals
   - Strategic proposals
   - Safety and/or environmental proposals
2. Distinguish between proposals and projects.
   - Two independent proposals with no influence on each other's cash flow can be treated as two projects. But two or more proposals influencing each other's cash flow are treated as complementary/substitute/mutually exclusive proposals.

3. What are different segments of cash flow?
   - Initial investment during t_0
   - Operating cash flow during t_1 to t_n
   - Terminal cash flow during t_n
4. What are the basic considerations for cash flow computation?
   - Taxes are considered.
   - Depreciation being non-cash flow expenditure is excluded.
   - Sunk cost is excluded.
   - Incremental approach is preferred.
5. Initial investment is arrived at:

$$I_0 = -I - IE - E(1 - T) - \Delta W + S - T(S - B)$$

6. Operating cash flow means:

$$\Delta \text{CFAT} = (\Delta\ Revenue - \Delta\ Expenditure - \Delta D)\ (1 - T) + \Delta D$$

7. Terminal cash flow means:

$$S - T(S - B) - (1 - T)RE + \Delta W$$

8. What is Net Present Value (NPV)?

$$NPV = \sum_{t=1}^{n}\left\{\frac{CF_t}{(1+k)^n}\right\} - I_0$$

9. What is Profitability Index (PI)?

$$PI = \sum_{t=1}^{n}\frac{CF_t}{(1+k)^n} / I_0$$

   Project is accepted if PI is more than 1.
10. What is Internal Rate of Return (IRR)?

$$\sum_{t=1}^{n}\frac{CF_t}{(1+IRR)^n} - I_0 = 0$$

   Project is accepted if IRR> cost of capital
11. What is Modified Internal Rate of Return (MIRR)?

$$I_0 = \sum_{t=0}^{n}\frac{CF_t(1+k)^{n-t}}{(1+MIRR)^n}$$

   Project is accepted if MIRR> cost of capital
12. What is Pay-back Period?
   - It is the period within which initial investment is recovered. Project is accepted if actual pay-back period < target pay-back period
13. What is accounting rate of return?
   - It is average net profit divided by average investment, expressed in percentage.

DESCRIPTIVE QUESTIONS

1. Explain the successive steps in the process of capital budgeting.
2. What are the ingredients of initial cash flow?
3. Does operating cash flow exclude: (i) depreciation; and (ii) financing cost? Give reasons in support of your argument.
4. How is terminal cash flow determined? Can a project be accepted if the break-even salvage value is greater than the actual salvage value?
5. What do you mean by sunk cost? Does it form a part of the cash flow?
6. Compare NPV and IRR. Do these two evaluation criteria yield similar results as far as ranking of projects is concerned? If not, what are the reasons behind this?
7. Compare NPV and Profitability Index. Which of the two is more reliable?

OBJECTIVE-TYPE QUESTIONS

1. Mark true or false.
   (i) Depreciation has no impact on the after-tax cash flow.
   (ii) Opportunity cost is a part of the cash flow computation.
   (iii) In the case of mutually exclusive proposals, acceptance of one means rejection of the other.
   (iv) When two proposals are substitutes, acceptance of one will reduce the cash flow from the other.
   (v) In complementary proposals, acceptance of one will reduce the cash flow from the other.
   (vi) A non-conventional cash flow pattern means cash outflow in the initial period and cash inflow during the subsequent period.
2. Choose the most suitable answer.
   (a) Mutually exclusive proposals are:
      (i) complementary in nature
      (ii) substitutes
      (iii) those where accepting one means rejecting the other
   (b) Cash flow should exclude depreciation, because:
      (i) depreciation is a non-cash expense
      (ii) depreciation extends over a number of years
      (iii) depreciation reduces the tax liability
   (c) Terminal cash flow is treated for tax when:
      (i) cash salvage value < the book salvage value
      (ii) cash salvage value = the book salvage value
      (iii) cash salvage value > the book salvage value
   (d) Profitability index shows benefits from the proposal in:
      (i) absolute terms

(ii) relative terms
(iii) both of the above

(e) The accept-reject result of NPV and IRR is the same if:
(i) projects are independent
(ii) projects are mutually exclusive
(iii) both of the two

NUMERICAL PROBLEMS

1. There are two investment projects, viz., X and Y. Each of them shows an initial investment of Rs 10,000. The discount rate is 12%. The cash flow in the first, second, third and fourth year is Rs 6500, Rs 3500, Rs 3000 and Rs 1000 respectively in Project X, and Rs 3500, Rs 3500, Rs 3500 and Rs 3000 respectively in Project Y.
   Calculate NPV, Profitability index, IRR and MIRR.
2. A project has the following cash flow:

Year	Amount (Rs)
1	–200
2	240
3	–70
4	290

   The discount rate is 10%. Find out the NPV. Do you think that IRR would be a suitable evaluation technique in this respect?
3. Calculate the initial investment if: the purchase price of the machine is Rs 20,000; installation expenditure is Rs 2,000; Rs 1,000 is spent to make the machine operational; net increase in working capital is Rs 500; cash salvage value is Rs 2,000; book salvage value is Rs 1,500; and the tax rate is 30%.
4. Calculate the operating cash flow if: the revenue from sales is Rs 50,000; Rs 30,000 is the operating cost including depreciation of Rs 7,000; and the tax rate is 30%.
5. Calculate the break-even salvage value if: the initial investment is Rs 50,000; the operating cash flow during each of the first, second and third year is uniform at Rs 20,000; and the discount rate is 10%.
6. Considering target pay-back period as 3 years, the cash flow of two proposals is as follows:

	Proposal A	*Proposal B*
Initial investment	–Rs 10,000	–Rs 10,000
Net cash benefits:Year 1	Rs 5,000	Rs 3,200
Year 2	Rs 4,800	Rs 3,000
Year 3	Rs 3,000	Rs 3,000
Year 4		Rs 2,500
Year 5		Rs 2,000

   Which of the two projects may be accepted?

7. A machine was bought for Rs 1,00,000. The accumulated depreciation is Rs 90,000. It is sold at a scrap value of Rs 16,000. The removal expenses are Rs 1,000, the net working capital release value is Rs 1,200 and the tax rate is 30%. Compute the net salvage value.
8. Find IRR if initial investment is Rs 2,00,000; cash inflow for 10 years in Rs 25,000 per year, and salvage value is Rs 50,000.
9. A firm is replacing the old machine by a more sophisticated new machine. The new machine costs Rs 4,00,000 inclusive of installation cost. The old machine is sold for Rs 2,80,000. Increase in working capital is Rs 17,000. Tax rate is 40%. Find the initial investment.
10. A project has an initial investment of Rs 10,900. The expected cash inflow during 4 years is Rs 6,000, Rs 2,000, Rs 1,000 and Rs. 5,000, respectively. Find out the IRR.

SOLVED NUMERICAL PROBLEMS

1. Calculate the initial investment cost of an expansion project, if:

Cost of machine:	Rs 10,00,000
Cost of transporting machine:	50,000
Other installation expenses:	20,000
Increase in net working capital:	60,000
Cost of training personnel:	20,000
Initial cost of advertisement:	20,000
Tax rate:	30%

Solution

(i) Installation of machine:	Rs 10,70,000
(ii) Training cost: 20000 × (1–0.30)	14,000
(iii) Increase in net working capital:	60,000
(iv) Initial advertising cost:	20,000
Total	11,64,000

2. A firm has to replace the existing machine. The cost of the new machine, transport and installation are respectively Rs 10,00,000; Rs 1,00,000 and Rs 20,000. The old machine which had been procured for Rs 9,70,000 is sold for Rs 80,000. The accumulated depreciation is Rs 9,00,000. The increase in net working capital amounts to Rs 1,00,000. Calculate the initial investment.

Solution

Cash outflow for replacement of machine:

Purchase price	Rs 10,00,000
Transportation	1,00,000
Installation cost	20,000
TotalRs 11,20,000	
Cash inflow after sale of old machine	Rs –80,000

(Cash salvage value – book salvage value) × Tax	
= 0.30(80,000 – 70,000)	3,000
Increase in net working capital	1,00,000
Initial investment	Rs 11,43,000

3. Calculate the operating cash flow if:

   The first year's sales are valued at Rs 1,00,000 which is expected to grow at 5% in the second year but to decline by 1% in the third year. The raw material cost is 40% of the sale value. The operating cost amounts to 20% of the sale value of which depreciation amounts to Rs 10,000 per annum. The interest amounts to Rs 5,000 p.a. Tax rate is 30%.

   Solution

	1st year	2nd year	3rd year
Sales	1,00,000	1,05,000	1,03,950
Less cost of goods	40,000	42,000	41,580
Gross margin	60,000	63,000	62,370
Less operating cost incl. dep.	20,000	21,000	20,790
Operating profit	40,000	42,000	41,580
Less taxes	12,000	12,600	12,474
Add depreciation	10,000	10,000	10,000
Operating cash flow	38,000	39,400	39,106

   Note: Interest payment is not considered insofar as it is considered for determining the discount factor.

4. The cost of machine, which is removed and sold as scrap, is Rs 5,00,000. The scrap value is Rs 50,000. The accumulated depreciation is Rs 4,80,000. The removal expenses amount to Rs 5,000. The release of net working capital amounts to Rs 7,000. Tax rate is 30%. Find the net salvage value.

   Solution

Scrap value	Rs 50,000
Less (cash salvage value – book salvage value)	
Tax rate = 0.30 (50,000 – 20,000)	9,000
Less removal expenses (1-Tax rate) = 5,000(1 – 0.30)	3,500
Add release of net working capital	7,000
NET SALVAGE VALUE	Rs 44,500

5. Calculate NPV with the following figures:

   Initial Investment: Rs 10,50,000

   Operating cash flow:

1st year	Rs 4,50,000
2nd year	Rs 6,00,000
3rd year	Rs 3,00,000
Terminal cash flow:	Rs 44,500
Discount factor:	10%

Solution

Present value:

Year 0 = Rs –10,50,000

Year 1 = 4,50,000/1.10 = 4,09,091

Year 2 = 6,00,000/1.10^2 = 4,95,868

Year 3 = (3,00,000 + 44,500)/1.10^3 = 2,58,828

NPV = Rs 4,09,091 + 4,95,868 + 2,58,828 – 10,50,000 = 1,13,787

Project may be accepted in view of positive NPV.

6. Based on the figures in Problem 5, find the Profitability Index.

Solution

PI = Rs (4,09,091 + 4,95,868 + 2,58,828) / 10,50,000 = 1.11

Since PI > 1, project may be accepted.

7. Based on the figures in Problem 5, find the IRR.

Solution

– 10,50,000 + (4,50,000/1.1625) + (6,00,000/1.1625^2) + 3,44,500/1.1625^3) = 0

Project may be accepted because IRR > discount rate.

8. Based on the figures in Problem 5, find the MIRR.

Solution

Rs 4,50,000 x 1.10^2 + 6,00,000 x 1.10 + 3,44,500

= Rs 5,44,500 + 6,60,000 + 3,44,500 = Rs 15,49,000

Now 10,50,000 = 15,49,000 / $(1+\text{MIRR})^3$

Or $(1+\text{MIRR})^3$ = 15,49,000 / 10,50,000

Or $(1+\text{MIRR})^3$ = 1.475238

Or (1+MIRR) = 1.1385

Or MIRR = 1.1385 – 1 = 0.1385 or 13.85%

9. There are two proposals. Their cash flow is hereunder:

Year	*Proposal A*	*Proposal B*
0	Rs –3,00,000	Rs –4,00,000
1	2,00,000	2,10,000
2	2,00,000	1,80,000
3	50,000	1,20,000
4	–	1,00,000

Find whether the proposals should be accepted if target pay-back period is 2 years.

Solution

Only Proposal A may be accepted as the initial investment is recovered during the target pay-back period. Proposal B cannot be accepted even if the total cash flow is larger.

10. A 4-year life project has a forecast of annual profit as:

Year	*Profit Rs*
1	3,00,000
2	3,50,000
3	4,00,000
4	3,75,000

If the average amount of investment taking into account the straight-line depreciation is Rs 12,50,000, find the accounting rate of return.

Solution

ARR = {(3,00,000 + 3,50,000 + 4,00,000 + 3,75,000) / 4} / 12,50,000

= 0.285 = 28.5%

Mini Case

The Geology Department of the Government has flashed news that in the hilly track of Madhya Pradesh, there is possibility for mining diamond. A company basically involved in diamond cutting likes to develop its backward linkage and so it is interested in diamond mining. It estimates that if mining is done at a particular rate per day, the operation will continue for the next 6 years, after which the stock of the mine will be finished.

The CEO of the company asks its finance officer to evaluate whether it is desirable for the company to undertake this project. The finance officer estimates the cost of opening of the mine at Rs 5.0 million at the present juncture and the annual operating expenditure for the 6-year period at Rs 0.5 million per annum. The closing of the mine and the reclamation of the area will need another Rs 1 million.

The finance officer expects an inflow of cash per annum as given below:

Year	*Rs*
1	975,000
2	1,750,000
3	1,800,000
4	2,100,000
5	1,145,000
6	546,000

Questions

1. Calculate the IRR and NPV.
2. Do you feel that on the basis of IRR and NPV, the company should go for mining?

REFERENCE

Shull, D.M. (1993). "Interpreting Rates of Return: A Modified Rate of Return Approach", *Financial Practice and Education*, 10 (Fall): 67–71.

SELECT FURTHER READINGS

Bierman, H. Jr. and S. Smidt (1993). *The Capital Budgeting Decision: Economic Analysis of Investment Projects*. New York: Macmillan.

Brick, I.E. and D.G. Weaver (1984). "A Comparison of Capital Budgeting Techniques in Identifying Profitable Investments", *Financial Management*, 13 (4): 29–39.

Schall, L.D.G. et al (1978). "Survey and Analysis of Capital Budgeting Methods", *Journal of Finance*, 33(2): 281–87.

Seitz, N. and M. Ellison (1998). *Capital Budgeting and Long-term Financing Decisions*. Fort Worth: Dryden.

6

CAPITAL BUDGETING IN PRACTICE

OBJECTIVES

- To discuss capital budgeting in a case when capital is rationed
- To discuss capital budgeting in inflationary conditions
- To use capital budgeting techniques when projects have unequal lives
- To include the conditions of risk in the project evaluation criteria
- To throw light on various aspects of managerial options and computation of cash flows in such scenarios
- To discuss capital budgeting process of multinational corporations.

The preceding chapter deals with the principles and techniques of capital budgeting. However, the problems concerning capital budgeting are not as simple and straightforward in real life. Practical realities introduce complexities that make the capital budgeting decision more challenging.

Complexities may manifest in a number of ways. The more important among these may be referred to here. First, are the conditions of capital rationing under which managers have to take a decision. Second, are the conditions of inflation that substantially influence the cash flow. Third, the lifetimes of the different projects to be evaluated may be different. Fourth, are the conditions of risk and uncertainty under which the future cash flow is estimated. Fifth, complexities may emerge when the cash flow tends to be quite different from that which was originally anticipated, as a result of which the managers may go either for expansion/contraction or for abandonment/postponement of the project. Sixth, complexities arise also when multinational corporations go for capital budgeing. The present chapter discusses the capital budgeting process under these conditions.

6.1 CAPITAL RATIONING

6.1.1 Conditions of Capital Rationing

Capital rationing indicates a situation in which funds for investment in a project are limited. The situation of capital rationing normally arises when a firm is not able to raise funds for the

Capital rationing is a situation in which funds for investment in a project are limited.

investment even if it wants to do so. But there are cases when a firm intentionally creates a capital rationing situation. If this is the case, the firm raises the discount rate, as a result of which many marginally NPV-positive proposals move to the reject zone and the available capital is utilised for only a limited number of proposals. Such a practice is however, not very common. The common practice, on the other hand, is to limit the availability of funds for the chosen proposals so that only a limited number of proposals are finally implemented.

Capital rationing may take two forms. One is "hard" capital rationing where the capital constraints are never violated. The other is "soft" capital rationing where capital constraints are rarely violated in very specific circumstances.

Capital constraints may be beneficial because a firm can manage the costs of asymmetric information related to getting additional funds for new projects. The argument is that when information is available to only a few participants, investors will raise the required rate of return to protect themselves. This would in turn lower the amount of funds obtained from selling new securities to outside investors. In the sequel, the firm tries to make the sale of new securities attractive.

However, the situation of capital rationing is sometimes not desirable. This is because if the firm is not in a position to take up the NPV-positive proposals, there arises an opportunity cost in form of an agency cost, where the shareholders and the managers will oppose each other on the choice of capital budgeting projects.

6.1.2 Capital Rationing and the Choice for a Proposal

It is true that in a situation of capital rationing, some proposals are not taken up even they satisfy the evaluation criteria. Thus in such a situation, it is crucial to select only those proposals out of the viable ones that are within the limits of the capital available and, at the same time, that bring in the highest possible net cash benefits for the firm.

The finance manager takes all the competing proposals and ranks them according to some criterion so that available capital may be allocated to the best projects. The literature on this subject discusses a number of approaches that include NPV technique, profitability index or the use of sophisticated programming techniques. Baumol, et al. (1985) suggest the use of linear programming. However, in actual practice, NPV and the profitability index are relied upon. The NPV technique is discussed here.

The NPV approach suggests that the projects be selected in such a manner that the combined NPV of the proposals should be the highest within the given amount of funds at the firm's disposal. However, in this case, the finance manager has to see that the entire funds are used even if he/she accepts a proposal with slightly lower NPV. Here the subscript denotes the end of the specific period.

EXAMPLE

From the figures below, find out which projects will be accepted if the capital limit is Rs 1,00,000.

Proposal	*Initial outlay (Rs)*	*NPV (Rs)*
A	50,000	40,000
B	40,000	10,000
C	50,000	20,000
D	60,000	5,000

In this example, there are four alternatives for project combination under the rationed capital availability. They are:

1. A + B
2. A + C
3. B + C
4. B + D

The combination of A and C will be accepted because:

1. It gives the maximum NPV.
2. It utilises the entire fund at the disposal of the firm.

6.2 CAPITAL BUDGETING UNDER INFLATIONARY CONDITIONS

Inflation is a common phenomenon. It has a direct impact on:

1. The cost structure in form of rising prices of input;
2. The revenue in form of higher prices of the output;
3. The required rate of return on account of higher cost of capital.

As a result, the treatment of the inflation factor is of much significance in the process of capital budgeting. However, if the same rate of inflation is found in case of all the three variables, the changes will cancel out one another and the NPV will remain unchanged. On the contrary, if these three variables are subjected to different rates of inflation, the impact on the NPV will definitely be visible.

When estimates of cash flow are inclusive of inflation, it is said to be stated in nominal terms. The exclusion of inflation states the cash flow in real terms. The nominal cash flow will be equal to the product of inflation rate and the real cash flow. This can be expressed in the form of an equation as follows:

$$CF_n = CF_r(1 + I) \qquad ...(6.1)$$

Where:

CF_n = nominal cash flow
CF_r = real cash flow
I = rate of inflation

EXAMPLE

If the cash flow is Rs 5,000 and the rate of inflation is 5%, the nominal cash flow will be:

$$CF_n = 5,000\ (1 + 0.05) = \text{Rs } 5250.$$

Similarly, the required rate of return inclusive of the inflation rate or the nominal required rate of return can be expressed as follows:

$$k = (1 + r)\,(1 + I) - 1 \qquad ...(6.2)$$

EXAMPLE

If the required rate of return is 10% and the rate of inflation is 5%, the inflation-inclusive required rate of return will be:

$$k = (1 + 0.10)\,(1 + 0.05) - 1 = 0.155 = 15.5\%$$

After combining Eq. 6.1 and Eq. 6.2, the NPV may be calculated as follows:

$$NPV_n = \frac{[\{CFIt(1 + I)t - CFOt(1 + I)t\}\,(1 - T) + Dt(T)]}{(1 + k)^t} - I_0 \qquad ...(6.3)$$

EXAMPLE

A project having a life of 3 years and an initial outlay for Rs 39,000 has Rs 20,000 per annum as cash outflow. The cash inflows are Rs 40,000, Rs 50,000 and Rs 30,000 respectively in the first, second and the third year. Depreciation of Rs 6,000 is allowed on the straight-line basis. The tax rate is 30% and the cost of capital is 10%. The inflation factor applying to cash inflow is 3%, 4% to cash outflow and 5% to the required rate of return. Find out the NPV_n.

NPV_r

	First year (Rs)	Second year (Rs)	Third year (Rs)
Expected cash inflow (Rs)	40,000	50,000	30,000
Expected cash outflow (Rs)	20,000	20,000	20,000
Net cash inflow (Rs)	20,000	30,000	10,000
Depreciation (Rs)	6,000	6,000	6,000
Pre-tax income (Rs)	14,000	24,000	4,000
After-tax income (Rs)	9,800	16,800	2,800
Depreciation (Rs)	6,000	6,000	6,000
Expected net cash inflow (Rs)	15,800	22,800	8,800

NPV_r = [(15,800/1.10) + (22,800/1.21) + (8,800/1.331)] – 39,000 = Rs 819.

NPV_n:

	First year (Rs)	Second year (Rs)	Third year (Rs)
Expected cash inflow (I = 3%) (Rs)	41,200	51,500	30,900
Expected cash outflow (I = 4%) (Rs)	20,800	20,800	20,800

Net cash inflow (Rs)	20,400	30,700	10,100
Less depreciation (Rs)	6,000	6,000	6,000
Pre-tax net income (Rs)	14,400	24,700	4,100
After-tax cash inflow (Rs)	10,080	17,290	2,870
Depreciation (Rs)	6,000	6,000	6,000
Expected net cash inflow (Rs)	16,080	23,290	8,870

Required rate of return as calculated above = 15.5%

$$NPV_n = [(16{,}080/1.155) + (23{,}290/1.334) + (8{,}870/1.541)] - 39{,}000$$
$$= \text{Rs } (-)\ 1{,}863.$$

Thus it is evident from the above example that inclusion of the inflation factor alters the NPV position. In fact, it has changed the very accept–reject decision. Without the inclusion of the inflation factor, the NPV is positive implying that the project should be accepted. With the inclusion of the inflation factor, NPV becomes negative implying that the project would be rejected. The right course of action would be that whenever inflation is anticipated, it should be taken into account for a correct investment decisions.

6.3 DECISION CONCERNING MUTUALLY EXCLUSIVE PROPOSALS WITH UNEQUAL LIVES

If a finance manager has to select only one of two proposals with varying economic lives, the traditional NPV rule may not yield an incorrect decision if the two proposals are independent. But in case of mutually exclusive proposals, the decision may be incorrect if the economic lives of the two proposals are different. Thus in such cases, the varying economic lives of the two proposals have to be made identical or comparable and then only the NPV rule needs to be applied. For this purpose, two types of methods are usually applied. They are:

1. Annualised NPV method
2. Replacement Chain method

6.3.1 Annualised NPV Method

In order to make the economic life comparable, the annualised NPV (ANPV) is computed. The proposal with greater ANPV is accepted. The computation of ANPVs is simple in the sense that the NPV is divided by the present value interest factor for an ordinary annuity of Re 1 for the respective time period and discount rate (*PVIFA r, n*). In form of an equation,

$$ANPV = NPV/PVIFA\ r, n \quad \text{...(6.4)}$$

EXAMPLE

Two mutually exclusive proposals, A and B, present the following cash flow to be discounted at 10%:

Year	Proposal A (Rs)	Proposal B (Rs)
0	–70,000	–84,000
1	30,000	34,000
2	32,000	31,000
3	38,000	26,000
4	–	20,000
5	–	15,000
6	–	10,000
NPV	12,267	20,680

Since:

$$ANPV = NPV/PVIFA\ r, n$$

$$ANPV \text{ for Proposal A} = 12267/PVIFA_{10,3} = 12267/2.4869 = \text{Rs } 4{,}933.$$

$$ANPV \text{ for Proposal B} = 20680/PVIFA_{10,6} = 20680/4.3553 = \text{Rs } 4{,}749$$

The traditional NPV rule suggests the acceptance of Proposal B as it has a greater NPV. This is, however, incorrect, because ANPV is higher with Proposal A and so Proposal A has to be accepted.

6.3.2 Replacement Chain Method

In this method, the proposal with shorter life is made to have a similar cash flow sequence in the extended period. Using the above example as a base, Proposal A will have Rs 30, 000, Rs 32,000 and Rs 38,000 cash inflow respectively during year 4, 5 and 6 assuming that the life of the two proposals becomes equal.

Based on the above example, the initial investment of Proposal A will be the same for the extended period, i.e., Rs 70,000. But since the initial investment for the extended period is made at the end of the third year, it will be brought down to its present value. It will be equal to Rs $70{,}000/(1.10)^3$ = Rs 52,592. The present value of the cash inflow during the extended period will be:

$$\text{Year 4: Rs } 30{,}000/1.10^4 = \text{Rs } 20{,}490$$

$$\text{Year 5: Rs } 32{,}000/1.10^5 = \text{Rs } 19{,}870$$

$$\text{Year 6: Rs } 38{,}000/1.10^6 = \text{Rs } 21{,}450$$

$$\text{Total} = \text{Rs } 61{,}810$$

Now the initial investment for the whole of the 6-year period will be equal to Rs (70,000 + 52,592) = Rs 1,22,592. On the other hand, the cash inflow for the respective period will amount to Rs (82,267 + 61,810) = Rs 144,077. All this means a NPV of Rs (1,44,077 –1,22,592) = Rs 21,485.

Since the NPV of Proposal A for the whole of 6-year period is greater than that of Proposal B, Proposal A should be accepted.

6.4 THE CONDITIONS OF RISK

In the preceding chapter, the capital budgeting techniques assumed the flow of cash with certainty meaning that the uncertainty or risk was not considered. Even if the risk was present, it was assumed that all the different capital projects had the same level of risk. However, in practice, risk in cash flow differs from one project to the other. And so, the risk factor needs to be incorporated in the capital budgeting analysis. The concept of risk and its measurement have already been discussed in Chapter 3. So, at this place, it is only the application of risk factor in the capital budgeting process that will be discussed.

6.4.1 Inclusion of Risk Factor in Cash Flow

There are two ways to incorporate the risk factor in the cash flow. While one is known as the certainty-equivalent approach, the other makes use of the risk-adjusted discount rate.

Certainty-Equivalent Approach: When the cash flow is uncertain, the certainty factor is introduced in the cash flow making it certain, it is then brought down to the present value through the use of the risk-free discount rate. Certainty equivalent (CE), often denoted by α is the specific percentage of estimated cash flow that the investor would be satisfied to receive for certain. In other words, it is derived on the assumption that there is equality between the estimated cash flow discounted by risk-adjusted discount rate, and the cash flow with certainty discounted by risk-free discount rate. The CE can be expressed in the form of an equation as follows:

There are two ways to incorporate the risk factor in the cash flow. While one is known as the certainty-equivalent approach, the other makes use of the risk-adjusted discount rate.

$$\alpha CF/(1 + rf)^t = CF/(1 + r)^t$$

Rearranging the equation, one finds:

$$\alpha = \frac{(1+rf)^t}{(1+r)^t} \qquad \text{...(6.5)}$$

EXAMPLE

Find out the CE for the first three years if the risk-free discount rate is 9% and the risk included discount rate is 15%.

Year 1 : 1.09/1.15 = 0.9478

Year 2 : $(1 + 0.09)^2/(1 + 0.15)^2 = 0.8984$

Year 3 : $(1 + 0.09)^3/(1 + 0.15)^3 = 0.8515$

After the CE is arrived at, it is included in the cash flow or the numerator of the NPV rule. The CE cash flow is discounted by the risk-free rate.

EXAMPLE

Assuming the CE factor as computed above, a project has a 3-year life with an initial investment of Rs 2,000 and a cash inflow of Rs 1,000 during the first and the second year and Rs 2,000 during the third year. The NPV will be:

$$(0.9478 \times 1{,}000/1.09) + (0.8984 \times 1{,}000/1.09^2) + (0.8515 \times 2{,}000/1.09^3) - 2{,}000 = \text{Rs } 1{,}041.$$

Risk-adjusted Discount Rate (RADR) In this case, the risk factor is included not in the cash flow but in the discount rate or the denominator of the NPV rule. The risk factor takes into account both the systematic and unsystematic risk that has already been discussed in Chapter 3. The greater the risk, the larger the RADR. At the same time, the risk factor grows with futurity with the result that RADR increases in every subsequent year.

EXAMPLE

Assuming the initial investment and the net cash inflow as in the above example, if the risk-adjusted discount rate is 15%, 16% and 17% respectively in the first three years, the NPV will be:

$$(1{,}000/1.15) + (1{,}000/1.16^2) + (2{,}000/1.17^3) - 2{,}000 = \text{Rs. } 862.$$

The two methods—the CE approach and the RADR—should yield the same result (Mao, 1976). However, there are theoretical differences between the two. RADR lumps together the risk-free interest rate and the risk premium that is not justified. This is because the time value of money and the risk factor are two different things. If one adds risk premium to the discount rate, it leads to compounding of risk over time. The CE approach avoids this problem. It first eliminates risk from the cash flow and then discounts the cash flow at the risk-free rate. Nevertheless, because of complexities in the determination of CE, RADR is frequently used.

The Computational Steps	
Certainty-Equivalent Approach	Risk-Adjusted Discount Rate
• Multiplying the cash flow by certainty-equivalent coefficient • Discounting the cash flow by risk-free interest rate • Applying the normal decision criteria	• Adjusting the discount rate for risk • Discounting the cash flow by risk-adjusted discount rate • Applying the normal decision criteria

6.4.2 Risk Analysis Based on Portfolio Approach

Two or more proposals may be compared on the basis of NPV incorporating either the CE factor or the RADR. This, however, is insufficient. Selection of projects should be made keeping in view the impact on the return–risk pattern of the entire portfolio of investment. This is because the very purpose of the investment decision is to maximise the overall returns with a given level of risk or to minimise the risk with a given level of returns.

In order to achieve this objective, those projects are selected that have a high returns–risk ratio. Suppose there are two projects with the same rate of returns but with differing sizes of risk. A firm will select that project which involves lower risk. In this manner it lowers the risk with a given level of return. However, if there is a third project with a higher rate of return and similar risk, it would be selected insofar as the selection will help raise returns with a given level of risk. Thus different projects are evaluated on the basis of returns–risk ratio. The one with the greatest ratio is selected.

Eiteman, *et al.* (1995) have suggested that this ratio is found out through dividing the difference between the returns from the project and the risk-free returns by the risk factor. Thus the returns/risk ratio can be expressed in the form of an equation as follows:

$$\text{Return/risk ratio} = \frac{(R_p - R_f)}{\sigma} \qquad \text{...(6.6)}$$

However, the selection is not so simple as it appears to be. A project with very low risk may raise the risk of the total portfolio of investment. On the other hand, a project with very high risk may lower the risk of the total portfolio of investment. Here the total portfolio means the existing portfolio plus the new portfolio of investment. All this depends on how the returns from the existing portfolio and those from the new portfolio are correlated. In case of negative correlation, the risk of the total portfolio drops as a sequel to the acceptance of the new project. On the contrary, risk of the total portfolio increases if the returns are positively correlated. Thus while selecting the new project, correlation co-efficient needs to be taken into account.

6.4.3 Sensitivity Analysis

Sensitivity analysis is a risk analysis technique where key variables are changed and the impact of such changes on the NPV is found out. The first step is to find out the base-case that indicates the most likely case of the revenue and the various types of cost. The second step is to estimate the probable deviation. The deviations may be from both sides. For example, they may be (-) 10% or (+) 10%. After estimating the possible deviations, their impact on the cash flow is established. For example, if there is the most likelihood that 300 units are expected to be sold at Rs 5 per unit, the base-case revenue will be Rs 1,500. If the deviation is (-) 10% in the units to be sold, the revenue will drop to Rs 1,350. If there is 10% deviation in the number of units to be sold, the revenue will rise to Rs 1,650. Similarly, there may be so many possible deviations not only in the number of units to be sold but also in the various costs, as a consequence of which, the figures of revenue and cost will change and the NPV will also change.

When one is comparing two projects, the project having less steep changes in the revenue and cost variables will be supposed as less risky project and will be preferred on this account.

It is a fact that sensitivity analysis reflects the risk scenario, but it cannot be relied upon fully. It is because the estimates made by different managers estimating the deviations in the cash flow may themselves vary widely. Moreover, the factors responsible for the deviations may not be the same for the managers who estimate the deviations.

6.4.4 Scenario Analysis

Despite the fact that sensitivity analysis is commonly used, it suffers from a few limitations. If there is a zero probability of high or low sales price and input costs, the project will be treated as the least risky in spite of its sensitivity to these variables. In such cases, the sensitivity analysis needs to be extended to deal with the probability distributions of the inputs. Such extensions are found in case of scenario analysis insofar as it considers the probabilities of changes in more than one key variable at a particular point of time. The scenario analysis is a risk analysis technique where "good" and "bad" sets of financial situations are compared with the base-case situation. The worst-case and the best-case scenarios are normally defined as having a 25% probability of conditions being bad or good respectively and with a 50% probability of the base-case. If the project is expected to present a case of high sale price and sales volume along with lower cost compared to that of the base-case scenario, it will result in high NPV and represent the best-case scenario. On the contrary, lower sales revenue with high cost represents the worst-case scenario.

6.4.5 Monte Carlo Simulation

Monte Carlo simulation is one of the methods, apart from sensitivity analysis and scenario analysis, which may be used for the risky proposals. Sensitivity analysis helps to find effects of change of only one variable at a time. In scenario analysis, we may consider the effect of a limited number of possible combinations of variables. Monte Carlo simulation helps to consider all possible combinations of project outcomes and is, thus, a better method to understand and model uncertainties in the capital budgeting process.

Simulation means imitating or duplicating the features, appearance and characteristics of a real system. Simulation is a technique of problem solving based upon experimentation performed on a model of a real-world system. It tries to imitate the features of a real-world situation with a mathematical model that does not affect operations. It is an appropriate technique where it is not feasible to experiment on the system itself or where direct analytical techniques cannot handle the complexities involved in the real system. It may be used to experiment with new situations about which we have little or no information, so as to prepare for what may happen. We try to imitate possible new situations mathematically, study their properties and draw conclusions and make action decisions based on the results of the simulation.

Simulation models are relatively straightforward and flexible to accommodate several changes in the problem scenario. It allows what-if questions so that a manager can try out several policy decisions within a matter of minutes. It allows us to study the interactive effects of individual components or variables to determine which are important. Time compression is possible with simulation. The effects of ordering, advertising and other policies over many months can be obtained by simulation model in short time. It also allows for inclusion of real-world complications that most other decision models cannot permit. Simulation can be a useful tool where a model of the project may be built to gain better understanding of the project and see how outcomes would be affected by altering the scope of the project or the distribution of any of its variables.

When a problem contains elements that exhibit chance or probability in their behaviour, Monte Carlo simulation can be applied. The process attempts to randomly generate values for the unknown variable in the model. In the first step, a probability distribution is established for random variables. The values from the probability distribution are simulated using random numbers. The process may be replicated for a number of trials. The process takes its name from the famous European casino and helps to analyse projects in the same way as one might analyse gambling strategies.

Monte Carlo simulation can be applied in capital budgeting through five basic steps:

1. *Develop a model for the project.* The cash flows may be modelled as a function of revenues, costs, depreciation and tax rate. Revenues may be seen as a function of market size, market share and unit price. Costs are a function of market size, market share, variable unit cost and fixed cost. For each variable, for example, market size, we try to estimate the expected value and the forecast error and write in terms of an equation for each of the coming years that are considered during the life of the project. So the complete model will have a set of equations for each variable.
2. *Specify a probability distribution for each variable in the model.* The probabilities may be estimated from historical data or experience. These help in incorporating the possible errors in forecast data.
3. *Simulate the cash flow.* The computer draws one outcome. This step generates the cash flow for each year from a single outcome.
4. *Repeat the procedure.* We are interested in the distribution of cash flow each year across many outcomes. Step 3 may be repeated a number of times to understand the yearly cash flow from many different outcomes. The computer may be called to generate millions of outcomes. This gives a distribution of cash flow for each future year against the number of outcomes considered. This is the main output of Monte Carlo simulation.
5. *Calculate NPV.* The distribution of cash flows for each year may be used to calculate the expected cash flows for each future year. Then the NPV of the project may be calculated by discounting these expected cash flows at an appropriate rate.

Monte Carlo simulation thus provides a complete analysis of the capital budgeting. However, even if the method is in vogue for about more than 35 years, and the software is available that can handle large volumes of data and can give quick results, few firms actually use it. It may be because of the difficulty in developing the mathematical model and specifying the interactions between variables in the model (Balakrishnan et al., 2007).

6.5 MANAGERIAL OPTIONS AND THE CASH FLOW

The traditional capital budgeting theory does not deal with the actions to be taken after the project has been accepted and subsequently implemented. However, in real life, there is every possibility of changes in the cash flow from that originally anticipated. If the project does not perform well after two years, it may be abandoned. Again, if it performs well but the demand suddenly falls, the productive capacity will need contraction. On the contrary, the demand may suddenly rise needing expansion in the productive capacity. Again in other cases, investment is postponed just to have more information from the market. The efforts of the managers to respond to these changing circumstances are known as the managerial options. The managerial options usually relate to:

The efforts of the managers to respond to possible changes in the cash flow from that originally anticipated are known as managerial options.

1. Options to expand or to contract;
2. Options to abandon;
3. Options to postpone.

These options are also known as strategic options insofar as they are often related to large, strategic projects rather than the routine maintenance projects. They are sometimes also known as real options as they influence the real assets. These options form a part of the capital budgeting analysis insofar as they do influence the cash flow.

Let us discuss, for instance, postponement. In this case, option value is decomposed into the value of options if exercised today and the value of waiting. Investing today is the intrinsic value and waiting for a specific period represents time value. Suppose a petroleum exploration company has to undertake a project. If it invests today, considering that perpetual cash flow begins in one year, the NPV of investing today would be expressed as follows:

$$NPV_0 = \frac{(P-V)Q}{r} - I_o \qquad \text{...(6.7)}$$

If it waits for one year before making any investment, the NPV at time $t = 0$ will be expressed as follows:

$$NPV_0 = \frac{\frac{(P-V)Q}{R}}{(1+R)} - I_o \qquad \text{...(6.8)}$$

EXAMPLE

If initial investment is Rs 5 lakh, risk-free interest rate is 10%, the expected price level of oil is Rs 10 per barrel and the variable cost is Rs 4 per barrel, expected production is 1,00,000 barrels a year, the NPV of investing today will be:

[{(10 – 4)1,00,000 }/0.10] – 50,00,000 = Rs 10,00,000

EXAMPLE

On the contrary, if the company waits for a year because price of oil is expected to go up to Rs 15 per barrel, the NPV after a 1-year wait will be:

$$[\{(15 - 4)1,00,000\}/0.10]/1.10 - 50,00,000 = \text{Rs } 50,00,000$$

Here NPV for the "wait" option is higher. So the company should postpone the investment for a year. The value of the option to postpone the investment can be viewed as managerial flexibility. It is because of this flexibility that the company gains more. However, if the price of oil per barrel shrinks unexpectedly to a lower value, the company will not make any investment after a year. It can be analogised with the out-of-money option when the option buyer does not exercise the option.

Let us switch over to the abandonment option. Suppose a firm finds that it is not feasible to operate profitably. It decides to abandon the project and sells the assets. If the firm is engaged in extraction and refining of oil and if the cost rises unexpectedly to Rs 8 per barrel (with a price per barrel being Rs 10), the NPV of abandonment today will be:

$$[\{(10 - 8)\ 1,00,000\}/0.10] - 50,00,000 = \text{Rs } (-)\ 30,00,000$$

The company will abandon the project in view of the negative NPV. But if price of oil is expected to rise by 100% after a year, the project will not be abandoned. Rather the company shall wait and watch for the price rise. If it rises as per expectations, it will continue to operate. If the price does not rise after a year, the project will finally be abandoned.

If demand goes up suddenly and the company raises its production level, it will find out the option value of expansion. It will expand the level of operation if the NPV is greater than in case of no expansion.

Again, if demand falls suddenly, the company will find out the NPV of contracted level of production. If it is greater than in case of no contraction, it will go for contraction in the level of operation. The reader should try to compute the NPV in different scenarios and then conclude what would be the firm's real option.

6.5.1 The Decision-tree Approach

Sometimes cash flow is estimated under different managerial options with the help of decision-tree approach. A decision tree is a graphic presentation of the relationship of the present decision with future events and decisions. The sequence of events is shown in a format that resembles the branches of a tree.

The first step in constructing a decision tree is to define a proposal. It may be concerning either a new product or an old product entering a new market. It may also be an abandonment option or a continuation option, expansion option or no-expansion option, etc.

Second, various alternatives are identified. For example, if a firm is launching a new product, it must chalk out the demand possibilities and on that basis it identifies different alternatives—whether to have a large factory or a medium-size one or only a small plant. Each of the alternatives will have varying consequences on the cash flow.

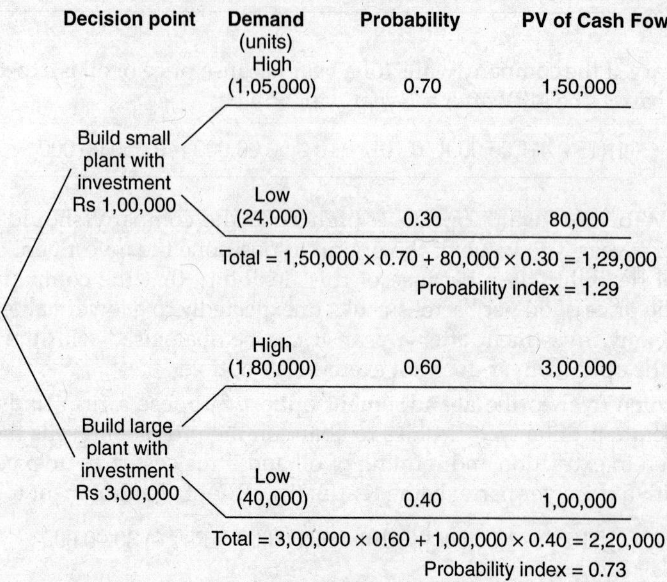

FIG. 6.1 Decision tree—small versus large plant

The third step is to lay out the decision tree showing the different alternatives through different branches. And finally, the estimates of cash flow with probabilities in each branch are made. The results of the different branches are calculated that show desirability of a particular alternative over the others.

In order to illustrate this approach, let us assume that a firm is going to introduce a new product. There are two alternatives regarding the size of plant. The first is that the firm sets up a small plant that will be suitable for low or medium-size demand for the product. In this case, cash flow will remain small. The second alternative is to build a big plant in order to cater to a greater demand for the product. However, if demand is not as high as is expected, the cash inflow will be small as compared to the investment in construction of a big plant. These comparative pictures can be presented through a decision tree. The profitability index of both the alternatives will help in taking a correct decision.

Again, if in view of high demand conditions, the firm expands the size of its small plant. This possibility may also be examined, of course, with multiple decision points that should begin at the end of the high-demand branch of the small plant. However, the present illustration gives only a simple presentation and does not examine the expansion possibilities.

The profitability index in case of the small plant is greater, it should be preferred to the large-size plant.

6.6 INTERNATIONAL CAPITAL BUDGETING

When a firm investments in a project abroad, it also applies the techniques of project evaluation. Capital budgeting among the multinational firms is a common feature. They apply the same evaluation criteria that have been discussed in the preceding chapter. However, they have to face a few problems in this context. First, the tax rate in different countries is different. Projects may be feasible taking into account low tax rates in the host country, but may not be feasible with a high tax rate in the home country. Second, changes in the exchange rate may put the project into the unfeasible zone from the parent's point of view, if not from the viewpoint of the subsidiary. What is more important is that the same cash flow may be cash inflow from the parent's angle, but cash outflow from the subsidiary's viewpoint. If subsidiary pays royalty or dividend to the parent, such problems arise. There are a number of cases of this type where such problems do arise. However, the ethics of corporate financial management are clear on this issue. It is the global profit that helps move a firm across national boundaries. Therefore, it is from the viewpoint of the parent company that a particular cash flow should be treated as either an inflow or an outflow. Nevertheless, to make the investment decision more transparent and more reliable the cash flow from the viewpoint of the subsidiary is also computed. Both results are then compared and finally the investment decision is taken. Here we discuss both viewpoints.

6.6.1 Parent's Perspective and the Cash flow

Initial Investment: Let us first take the case of initial investment. If the entire project cost is met by the parent company, the entire amount of initial investment is treated as a cash outflow. In some cases, the project is partly financed by the subsidiary itself through local borrowing. However, such borrowings of the subsidiary do not form a part of the initial cash outflow.

Again, in some cases, the subsidiary makes additional investment for expansion out of the retained earnings. At the first instance, there is apparently no flow of cash from the parent company to the subsidiary. But it should be treated as an opportunity cost insofar as in absence of retention of earnings, these funds would have been remitted to the parent company rather than invested in the project in question. Thus the investment out of retained earnings should be treated as cash outflow from the parent's perspective.

Yet again, the issue of blocked funds is very pertinent in this respect. Sometimes the host government imposes exchange controls and does not allow any cash to flow to the parent company. These funds are known as blocked funds. Thus that part of the cash inflow of the subsidiary which is represented by blocked funds is not treated as a cash inflow from the parent's perspective. Suppose the incremental cash inflow of the project is Rs 2 crore, out of which the host government allows only Rs 1.5 crore to flow to the parent company. In this case, a sum of Rs 1.5 crore will be treated as the cash inflow. But if the blocked funds are invested in some new project, that amount is treated as an investment by the parent company and is recorded as a cash outflow.

Last but not least, if the host government provides subsidised initial establishment for the subsidiary, the gain on this account should not form a part of the initial investment of the parent company.

EXAMPLE

A project of the subsidiary costs Rs 15.5 crore. The parent company makes an initial investment of Rs 10.0 crore. A sum of Rs 2 crore is invested out of the blocked funds.

Another sum of Rs 2 crore is taken out of the retained earnings. The rest of the project cost, that is, a sum of Rs 1 crore is met by the subsidiary out of local borrowing. At the same time, the host government provides some subsidised establishment for the project that brings in a gain of Rs 0.5 crore. Thus in this case, the cash outflow recorded for initial investment from the parent's perspective will be:

10 + 2 + 2 = Rs 14.0 crore.

It may be mentioned here that the initial investment outflow out of blocked funds and retained earnings and the gain on account of the subsidised establishment are shown at the spot exchange rate.

Operating Cash Flow: Besides the initial investment, the operating cash flow also needs some adjustment. As a normal practice, the revenue generated through the sale of the subsidiary's product in the local market as well as in other countries is shown as the operating cash inflow from the parent's perspective. It is, however, subject to downward adjustment for the lost income on sales previously realised through the parent company's export to these markets. On the contrary, if the operation in the subsidiary leads to import of components and raw material from the parent company, the value of such import will be added to revenue.

EXAMPLE

A subsidiary is fetching Rs 1.5 crore through the sale of its product in the local market and a sum of Rs 0.3 crore through export to third countries. But this sale replaces the parent company's export to these markets by Rs 0.7 crore. Again, the subsidiary imports components from the parent company worth Rs 0.2 crore. The total operating cash inflow on account of sales will be:

Rs 1.5 + 0.3 + 0.2 – 0.7 = 1.3 crore.

The operating cash flow is influenced by some other factors too. First, if the subsidiary pays royalty to the parent company worth Rs 0.3 crore, the operating cash inflow in the above example will rise to Rs 1.6 crore. However, if the parent company faces loss on account of diseconomies of scale due to shifting of production to the host country to the extent of Rs 0.1 crore, the operating revenue will come down to Rs 1.5 crore.

Second, the operating cash flow is influenced by transfer pricing when the parent company or any other unit of the firm charges arbitrary prices for intra-firm movement of intermediate goods. It may be noted here that transfer pricing is adopted either for a better working capital management or for reducing the overall tax burden of the company through shifting of the before-tax profit to a country with lower tax rates. If transfer pricing lowers the overall tax burden of the company and thereby increases the revenue of the parent company, the additional revenue or saving should be treated as a cash inflow. However, it may be noted that such inflows are discounted at a higher rate because they involve greater risk.

Third, if the host government offers incentives, they should be included in the capital budgeting decision. For example, if the host government offers tax incentives or provides loan at a subsidised rate, the amount of gain on this account should be added to the operating cash inflow.

Fourth, when the subsidiary makes local borrowings for meeting a part of the initial investment and pays interest on such borrowings, the amount of interest payment is deducted from the operating cash inflow. Had it been domestic capital budgeting, the interest payment on such borrowing would not have formed a part of cash flow insofar as financing cost is included in the discount rate. But in case of international capital budgeting, the cash remitted to the parent company will stand overstated if interest payments are not treated as cash outflow for the subsidiary. This is why it is necessary that the investment made by the subsidiary out of local borrowings is separated from the investment made by the parent. The present value of cash flow received by the parent company should take into consideration the interest paid by the subsidiary on local borrowing and then only it should be compared with the initial investment made by the parent company.

the operating cash flow is influenced by transfer pricing when the parent company or any other unit of the firm charges arbitrary prices for intra-firm movement of intermediate goods.

Fifth, it is the inflation rate differential that needs to be taken into account. Inflation influences both the cost and revenue streams of the project. If the inflation rate is higher in the host country and if the import from the parent company constitutes a significant portion of the input of the subsidiary, the cost will not move up very much. But if the inputs are obtained locally, the cost will move up a great deal. Again, as far as revenue is concerned, it will move up if there is no competition from a foreign supplier and if the demand for the product is price-inelastic. So the computation of cash flow relies on the inflation forecast in the host country and its possible effects. However, if the inflation is quite volatile from year to year, as it is found in many developing countries, it is difficult to make an accurate forecast.

Sixth, it is the exchange rate fluctuation that influences the size of cash flow. It is a fact that the changes in the exchange rate are tagged with the changes in the rate of inflation. But there are other factors that also cause exchange rate fluctuations. It is difficult to predict the behaviour of all those factors. Nevertheless, the cash flow computation process incorporates different scenarios of exchange rate movements. From the parent company's point of view, appreciation in the currency of the host country will be favourable and will increase the size of the cash inflow in terms of the home-country currency. A joint effect of inflation and exchange rate changes may produce a partial offsetting effect on the net cash flows of the subsidiary. But if the rate of inflation is expected to be lower in future helping the value of the host country's currency appreciate, the subsidiary may locally invest the amount of its payments to the parent company till the strengthening of the currency. The accumulated earning of the parent company will be larger after the appreciation of the host country's currency.

the computation of cash flow relies on the inflation forecast in the host country and its possible effects.

Terminal Cash Flow: Besides adjustments in the initial investment and in the operating cash flow, some adjustments have to be made for the salvage value that influences the terminal cash flow. First, if there is a provision in the foreign collaboration agreement for the reversion of the project to the host government after a certain period of time, on the payment of a specific amount, that specific amount is treated as the terminal cash inflow.

Second, if the first condition is not present, the net cash flow generated in the terminal year is multiplied by a specific number of years and the product is treated as the terminal cash inflow.

Third, if the project is dismantled in the terminal year, the scrap value is treated as the terminal cash inflow.

Fourth, when salvage value is uncertain, the parent company makes various estimates of the salvage value or terminal cash flow and computes the NPV based on each possible outcome of the terminal cash flow. Alternatively, it computes the *break-even salvage value* (discussed in the preceding chapter) which is then compared with the estimated terminal cash flow. If the estimated terminal cash flow is less than the break-even salvage value, the investment proposal will be rejected. This is because in this case, the NPV will be negative. On the contrary, if the parent company assesses that the subsidiary would sell for more than the break-even salvage value, it will incorporate this assessment into its accept–reject decision.

6.6.2 Parent–Subsidiary Perspective

The very rationale of this argument is that if a project's NPV is positive, it is bound to add to the corporate wealth of the firm as a whole. Under this approach, two NPVs are computed. One is the NPV from the parent's perspective (NPV_P) and the other is the NPV from the viewpoint of the project itself that is known as the subsidiary's perspective (NPV_S). Finally, acceptance/rejection decision of the project is based on the NPV of both of them.

In order to find out the NPV_P, the following successive steps are taken:

1. Estimate the cash flow in the host-country currency;
2. Estimate the future spot exchange rate on the basis of available forward rates;
3. Convert the host-currency cash flow into the home-country currency;
4. Find NPV in home-country currency using the home-country discount rate.

Here the cash inflow represents all cash flowing towards the parent unit as has been explained earlier. Cash outflow will represent cash flowing out of the parent unit.

Similarly, to find out the NPV_S, the following steps are taken:

1. Estimate the cash flow in host-country currency;
2. Identify the host-country discount rate;
3. Discount the host-currency cash flow at the host-country discount rate;
4. Convert the resultant NPV into the home-country currency at the spot exchange rate.

In this case, the cash inflow represents the earnings of the project in the host-country currency irrespective of the whether cash moves towards, or away from, the parent unit.

These two methods assume an all-equity capital structure and so, if parity conditions exist in the real world, the results from the two approaches will be the same. But in the real world, debt is normally included in the capital structure in order to lower the cost of capital; moreover, parity conditions do not exist. Naturally, the results from the two approaches will differ. The possible results will be:

1. NPV_P and NPV_S both being negative. In such case, project cannot be accepted.

2. NPV_P and NPV_S both being positive. In such case, project can be accepted.
3. $NPV_P > 0 > NPV_S$. The project is attractive from the viewpoint of the parent unit but not attractive from the subsidiary's viewpoint. In such a case, project may be accepted but there will be chances of a loss in the value in terms of the host-country currency.
4. $NPV_P < 0 < NPV_S$. The project being attractive from the subsidiary's perspective is unattractive from the parent's perspective. The project may be accepted but its usefulness to the parent unit is doubtful.

SUMMARY

Capital budgeting techniques need some adjustments in order to be closer to real life situations. In the real world, the size of funds available for investment is often limited. In such cases, the finance manager selects the proposal/ proposals in a way that helps fully utilise the available resources, and at the same time, maximises the NPV or the profitability index.

Again, the inflationary trend is a common phenomenon. In order to incorporate the inflation factor, the cash flow as well as the discount rate is adjusted for inflation and then only the NPV is found out.

When two proposals have unequal lives, it becomes difficult to have a comparable picture of NPV or IRR. In such cases, the annualised NPV is found out. Alternatively, the economic life of the shorter-life proposal is extended assuming an analogous cash flow stream in order to match the life of the other proposal and then the NPV for the extended life is computed.

It is a fact that the future cash flow is not known with certainty. There is always the factor of risk. The risk factor is incorporated either in the numerator or in the denominator of the NPV rule. In the former, the cash flow is multiplied by the certainty equivalent factor. In the latter, risk is incorporated in the discount factor.

The capital budgeting regime extends even after the project is implemented. Considering the demand for the product, the firm may need expansion or postponement or even abandonment of the project. These are managerial options and that influences the process of capital budgeting. Usually, a decision-tree approach is followed in such cases in order to arrive at a decision.

Last but not least, capital budgeting technique is adopted also by multinational firms. Cash flow computation needs some adjustment in this case as it is the interests of the parent company that is the primary consideration.

POINTS TO REMEMBER

1. What is capital rationing? What is the process of accepting a project in such cases?
   - Limited availability of resources for investment is capital rationing.
   - For accepting projects, the finance manager tries to utilise the entire available funds and, at the same time, to maximise the NPV.
2. Explain the process of capital budgeting under inflationary conditions.
   - Cash inflow, cash outflow and discount factor – all are treated for inflation and then NPV is calculated on the basis of treated figures.
3. How is NPV of two mutually exclusive proposals with unequal lives calculated?
   - There are two methods – one is annualised NPV method and the other is replacement chain method.
   - In the first, the annualised NPV of the two proposals is compared. In the second, the cash flow of the shorter-life proposal is extended comparable to the longer-life one and then the NPV is found.
4. How is risk factor included in capital budgeting process?
   - Risk is either included in the numerator of the NPV rule through multiplying the cash flow by certainty-equivalent factor, or in the denominator of the NPV rule through letting the discount rate include the risk factor.
   - It is also included through the sensitivity analysis where key variables, such as cash flows and discount rate are changed assuming varied conditions and then NPV is calculated.
   - It is also included through the scenario analysis which is an extension of the sensitivity analysis.
5. What are managerial options?
   - They are options after the project is accepted. They are related either to expand/contract the size of the project or to postpone or abandon the project depending upon the possible changes in the key variables.
6. What is decision-tree approach?
   - It is a graphic presentation relating present decision with future events to arrive at decision.
7. What is the process of international capital budgeting?
   - In cases of multinational investment, cash flow is treated as inflow/outflow either from the viewpoint of the parent or from the viewpoint of subsidiary. And then NPV is calculated.

DESCRIPTIVE QUESTIONS

1. Define capital rationing. How does a finance manager select proposals when the situation of capital rationing exists?

2. What are the two approaches that are adopted while dealing with proposals with unequal lives?
3. Distinguish between certainty equivalent factor and the risk-adjusted discount rate as a tool for analysing the risk factor.
4. Does inflation influence the size of NPV? Explain with the help of a simple example.
5. What do you mean by managerial options? In what way are they relevant to capital budgeting?
6. Explain the decision-tree approach for evaluating investment proposals.
7. Explain the main issues involved in the computation of cash flows in the context of multinational capital budgeting.

OBJECTIVE-TYPE QUESTIONS

1. Mark true or false.
   (i) Nominal required rate of return is the product of real required rate of return and the inflation rate.
   (ii) Hard capital rationing position means a situation where capital constraints are never violated.
   (iii) Certainty equivalent approach means adjustment of risk factor in the denominator of the NPV rule.
   (iv) Managerial options are also known as real options as they influence the real assets.
   (v) Return-risk ratio is the key factor in selecting an investment portfolio.
2. Choose the most suitable answer.
   (a) In "soft" form of capital rationing, capital constraints are:
      (i) never violated
      (ii) often violated
      (iii) rarely violated in very specific cases
   (b) Differing economic life of proposals matters if:
      (i) proposals are independent
      (ii) proposals are mutually exclusive
      (iii) both of the above
   (c) Certainty-equivalent approach considers risk factor in:
      (i) the numerator of NPV formula
      (ii) the denominator of NPV formula
      (iii) both of the above
   (d) Blocked fund of the parent company lies normally in:
      (i) the home country
      (ii) the host country
      (iii) a third country where no restrictions on transfer exist

NUMERICAL PROBLEMS

1. There are three projects. Project X has Rs 150 as the initial investment, Rs 60 as NPV and 1.40 as profitability index. The respective figures for Project Y are Rs 300, Rs 105 and 1.35 and for Project Z are Rs 200, Rs 100 and 1.50.
   (a) Which two projects should be selected if there is no capital rationing?
   (b) Which two projects should be selected if there is capital rationing of Rs 450?
2. A machine costing Rs 1,50,000 has a life of 4 years. Incremental pre-tax net cash inflow is Rs 80,000 per annum. Tax rate is 30%. Inflation rate is expected to average 5% and the cost of capital in real terms is 8%. Compute NPV in real and nominal terms.
3. A firm is considering two mutually exclusive projects. Both of them have an initial investment of Rs 20,000. Project X has a life of 2 years with after-tax cash flow of Rs 10,000 and Rs 7,000 at the end of the first and the second year respectively. Project Y has an expected life of 4 years with an after-tax cash flow of Rs 8,000 annually. The firm's cost of capital is 10%.. Find out NPV if the project can be repeated and there is no anticipation of any change in the cash flow stream.
4. Proposal A has a life of 2 years with annual cash inflow of Rs 6,000. Project B has a life of 4 years with annual cash inflow of Rs 4,000. Initial investment in both the cases is Rs 10,000. Discount rate is 10%. Which of the two will be accepted using the annualised NPV rule?
5. Find out the certainty equivalent factor for a period of 3 years if risk-free interest rate is 10% and the risk-adjusted discount rate is 15%.
6. A manufacturer decides to set up a project and starts production with an initial investment of Rs 1,00,000. The sale price of the product is Rs 10 with a variable cost of Rs 4. As much as 10,000 units are to be produced. The manufacturer may start production now. But he would like to postpone it for two years insofar as he expects a rise in the sale price to Rs 12 after two years. What should be the appropriate option?
7. Calculate the operating cash flow in the context of multinational capital budgeting from the viewpoint of the parent unit on the basis of the following data:
   (a) Sales in the domestic market = Rs 1 crore
   (b) Export = Rs 0.4 crore
   (c) Replacement of parent's export = Rs 0.2 crore
   (d) Parent's export of components to subsidiary = Rs 0.3 crore
   (e) Royalty payment by subsidiary = Rs 5 lakh
   (f) Dividend flow to the parent = Rs 5 lakh
8. The required initial investment and the NPV of different projects are given here. Find out which projects need to be taken up if the capital is rationed at Rs 2,50,000

Project	*Initial Investment (Rs)*	*NPV (Rs)*
A	1,00,000	20,000
B	2,75,000	30,000
C	50,000	18,000
D	2,00,000	30,000
E	1,00,000	16,000

9. The initial investment in a project is Rs 5,00,000. The cash inflow during the first, the second and the third years is Rs 3,00,000, Rs 2,00,000 and Rs. 2,00,000, respectively. The certainly equivalent coefficient for 3 years is 0.90, 0.85 and 0.82, respectively. If the risk-free interest is 5%, calculate the NPV.

SOLVED NUMERICAL PROBLEMS

1. A firm with rationed funds for Rs 1,20,000 has in view 5 projects with varying NPV and IRR. Find out which of the projects will be taken up, with a given discount rate of 10%.

Project	*Initial Investment Rs*	*NPV Rs*	*IRR%*
A	50,000	2,275	15
B	45,000	1,820	14
C	55,000	1,280	13
D	25,000	460	12
E	80,000	–800	8

Solution

A + B + D are three projects that make use of the entire funds in hand, although the total NPV is not the maximum. The NPV can be maximised with A + B + C but in this case, funds are not sufficient. Thus the first alternative is the only way out under the conditions of capital rationing.

2. There are two proposals with unequal lives. The cash flow and NPV with 10% discount rate are as follows:

Cash flow Rs	*Proposal A*	*Proposal B*
Year 0	–50,000	–50,000
Year 1	40,000	30,000
Year 2	40,000	30,000
Year 3		30,000
Year 4		30,000
NPV	19,420	45,094

Solution

(a) Replacement chain method:
NPV for Proposal A

	Cash flow Rs	*Present value Rs*
Year 1	40,000	36,364
Year 2	40,000	33,056
Year 3	40,000	30,052
Year 4	40,000	27,320
Total		1,26,792

Initial investment = Rs 50,000 + 50,000/1.10^2
= 91,322

NPV of Proposal A = Rs 1,26,792 – 91,322 = Rs 35,470

Here Proposal B with greater NPV will be accepted.

(b) Annualised NPV method:

ANPV Proposal A = Rs 19,420 / 1.7355 = Rs 11,190

ANPV Proposal B = Rs 45,094 /3.1699 = Rs 14,226

Proposal B with higher ANPV will be accepted.

3. The net cash flow of a project in the first, second and the third year is respectively Rs 30,000, Rs 32,000 and Rs 35,000. The cash flow is subject to an inflation rate of 3% and the discount factor of 10% is subject to a 5% inflation rate. Calculate NPV with and without inflation-adjustment, with a given initial investment for Rs 50,000.

Solution

	Without inflation		*With inflation*	
	Cash flow	*Present value*	*Cash flow*	*Present value*
Year 0	–50,000	–50,000	–50,000	–50,000
Year 1	30,000	27,272	30,900	19,871
Year 2	32,000	26,446	32,960	13,631
Year 3	35,000	26,296	36,050	9,588
NPV		30,014		–6,910

Note: Cash flow during Year 1 to Year 3 has been multiplied by 1.03 and the discount factor has been multiplied by 1.05.

Thus during inflationary scenario, the project cannot be accepted in view of negative NPV.

4. The risk-free discount factor is 10%. The risk-added discount rate is 15%. Find out the certainty-equivalent factor for a three-year cash flow of a risky project.

Solution

Year 1: 1.10 / 1.15 = 0.9565

Year 2: 1.10^2 / 1.15^2 = 0.9149

Year 3: 1.10^3 /1.15^3 = 0.8751

5. If the cash flow during the first, second and the third year is respectively Rs 30,000, Rs 35,000 and Rs 29,000 with a given initial investment of Rs 50,000,the risk-free discount rate is 10% and the risk-adjusted discount rate is 14%,calculate the NPV.

Solution

Certainty-equivalent factor:

Year 1: 1.10 / 1.14 = 0.9649

Year 2: 1.10^2 / 1.14^2 = 0.9311

Year 3: 1.10^3 /1.14^3 = 0.8984

NPV = Rs

–50,000 + (30,000 x 0.9649)/1.10 + (35,000 x 0.9311)/1.10^2 + (29,000 x 0.8984)/ 1.10^3

= Rs –50,000 + 26,315 + 26,933 + 19,575 = Rs 22,823

6. A project has an initial investment of Rs 1,00,000. The risk-free interest is 10%. The expected price of the product is Rs 10 per unit and the expected variable cost is Rs 6 per unit. The expected output is 6,000 units. Find the NPV of investing today.

Solution

NPV = Rs {6,000 x (10 – 6)}/ 0.10 – 1,00,000 = Rs 1,40,000

7. Based on the figures in Problem 6, if the price of the product is expected to move up to Rs 16 per unit in view of risen demand for 8,000 units and if the cost of input has to squeeze to Rs 3 in view of tariff cut, would it be advisable to postpone the investment by one year?

Solution

NPV_1 = Rs [{8,000 x (16 – 3)}/0.10] /1.10 – 1,00,000 = Rs 8,45,455

Since PV moves up more than six-fold after one year, it is advisable to postpone the investment by one year.

8. Based on figures in Problem 6, if restrictions on import raise the variable cost to Rs 8.50 after 2 years, demand falls to 3,000 units and the price per unit falls to Rs 9, what should be the option before the investor?

Solution

NPV_2 = Rs [{3,000 x (9 – 8.50)}/ 0.10] / 1.10^2 – 1,00,000 = Rs –87,603

Postponement cannot be justified

Mini Case

Vinoy Ahuja completed an aeronautical engineering course. But he did not opt for any job. Rather he thought of airline business. The business was helicopter services transporting persons and goods in the hilly areas of Arunachal Pradesh.

Before actually starting operations, he calculated the initial investment of Rs 350 million and made various estimates for the next 6 years; the details of which are as follows:

Rs Million						
Year	2012	2013	2014	2015	2016	2017
Expected distance (km)	50,000	50,000	50,000	50,000	50,000	50,000
Cash inflow	240	240	240	240	240	240
Variable expenses	102	102	102	102	102	102
Fixed expenses	50	50	50	50	50	50
Terminal cash flow						180
Net cash flow	88	88	88	88	88	88

The estimates were of his own. This is why he preferred to consult a financial analyst. The financial analyst utilised the concept of scenario analysis based on the level of income, weather in the region during different months and a number of other factors. According to him, the probability of optimistic, pessimistic and normal scenario was 30%, 30% and 40%, respectively. It was also estimated that in case of optimistic scenario, the revenue could increase by 15%, but under the pessimistic scenario, it could go down by 10% during all the years. Depending on the scenarios, the value of net cash inflow changed. Truly speaking, the inclusion of the scenario was a better course of action as it was closer to reality.

Questions:

1. Calculate the NPV of the project under different scenarios.
2. Should Ahuja go for the project?
3. Ahuja may change the price of transportation per km; if he does it, explain the impact of changes in the rate on the sensitivity of the project.

REFERENCES

Balakrishnan, N., B. Render and R.M. Stair (2007). *Managerial Decision Modeling with Spreadsheets*, 2nd Edition. Delhi: Pearson Education.

Baumol, W.J. *et al.* (1985). "Investment and Discount Rates under Capital Rationing: A Programming Approach", *The Economic Journal*, 75 (June): 317–29.

Eiteman, D.K. *et al.* (1995). *Multinational Business Finance*. Reading, Mass.: Addison-Wesley.

SELECT FURTHER READINGS

Butler, J.S. and B. Schachter (1989). "The Investment Decision: Estimation of Risk and Risk-adjusted Discount Rates", *Financial Management*, 18 (4): 13–22.

Dixit, A. and R.S. Pindyck (1995). "The Options Approach to Capital Investment", *Harvard Business Review*, 73 (May–June): 105–115.

Hertz, D.B. (1964). "Risk Analysis in Capital Investment", *Harvard Business Review*, 42 (Jan–Feb): 95–105.

Rappaport, A. and R.A. Taggart, Jr. (1982). "Evaluation of Capital Expenditure Proposals under Inflation", *Financial Management*, 11 (1): 5–13.

Sick, G.A. (1986). "A Certainty-Equivalent Approach to Capital Budgeting", *Financial Management*, 15 (4): 23–32.

7

COST OF CAPITAL

OBJECTIVES

To highlight the significance of computation of cost of capital
To show how cost of debt is computed
To show how cost of preference shares is computed
To analyse the different techniques of computation of cost of equity shares
To explain the concept of weighted average cost of capital
To explain the significance of marginal cost of capital

Any discussion on capital budgeting is not complete in the absence of a discussion of the cost of capital. This is because cost of capital acts as a cut-off rate or minimum rate of return required from an investment. An investment can bring gains only when its rate of return is greater than the cut-off rate. The present chapter, therefore, focuses on the computation of cost of different forms of capital and then, on that basis, the computation of the weighted average cost of capital.

Cost of capital acts as a cut-off rate or the minimum rate of return required from an investment.

7.1 SIGNIFICANCE OF COST OF CAPITAL

The concept of the cost of capital is significant not only for capital budgeting. It is also indispensable in other areas of financial management. In the context of capital budgeting, cost of capital forms the basis of the discount rate, that is, the rate at which future cash flows are discounted (brought down) to the present value for comparison with the initial investment and for arriving at the net present value (NPV). It is the cost of capital with which the internal rate of return (irr) is compared. A project adds to the corporate wealth if it has a positive npv, or if the irr exceeds the cost of capital.

The concept of the cost of capital is also used for designing the firm's capital structure. Debt and equity are combined in varying proportions in order to bring the cost to a minimum. Again, the cost of capital forms the basis for evaluating the financial performance of the top management. Yet again, for raising funds from the market, for financing the current assets with a mix of short-term loans and long-term capital, and for apportioning the after-tax profits between retained earnings and dividend, the evaluation of the cost of capital plays an important role.

7.2 COMPUTATION OF THE COST OF CAPITAL

Since there are different forms of capital in a firm's capital structure, the cost for each type of capital is measured exclusively, then, along with their respective weights, all these costs are combined to arrive at the weighted average cost of capital.

7.2.1 Cost of Debt

The cost of debt (K_d) is the interest rate mentioned in the instrument subject to the adjustment for taxes. Cost of debt can be expressed in the form of an equation as follows:

$$K_d = I(1 - T) \qquad \text{...(7.1)}$$

Where:

I = the interest rate

T = the tax rate

EXAMPLE

If a firm has debentures carrying 5% coupon and if the tax rate is 30%, the cost of debt will be:

$$K_d = 0.05\,(1 - 0.30) = 0.035 = 3.5\%$$

Cost of New Debt: When a new debenture is issued, it involves some amount of floatation cost. Taking into consideration this cost, the cost of debt will be higher. The cost of new debt can be expressed in the form of an equation as follows:

$$K_d\ New = \frac{I + \left(\frac{P - NP}{N}\right)}{\left(\frac{P + NP}{2}\right)} \qquad \text{...(7.2)}$$

Where:

P = par value of debentures

NP = net proceeds

N = number of maturity years

EXAMPLE

A company issues 10-year debentures for Rs 1,00,000 with 5% coupon. The floatation cost is Rs 2,000 and the tax rate is 30%. The cost of debt will be:

$$5{,}000 + [(1{,}00{,}000 - 98{,}000)/10]/(1{,}00{,}000 + 98{,}000)/2$$
$$= 5{,}200/99{,}000 = 0.0525$$

Adjusting the cost for taxes, we get:

$$0.0525\ (1 - 0.30) = 0.0\ 3675 = 3.675\%$$

Adjustment for Premium/Discount: A new issue of debentures often comes out at a premium/discount, depending upon the firm's performance. In either of the cases, net proceeds differ from the face value of the bonds. Naturally, the same formula is applicable which is used in case of floatation cost.

EXAMPLE

Let us suppose that a 10-year debenture having a face value of Rs 100 is sold at Rs 90 with 5% coupon, K_d with 30% tax rate will be:

$$\frac{[5 + (100 - 90)/10]}{(100 + 90)/2}$$

$$= 0.063\ (1 - 0.30) = 0.0441 = 4.41\%$$

High Interest Rates Pinch India Inc.

The high interest rate regime is now pinching the corporate houses. Interest cost of 496 major corporate entities has gone up by 7.9 per cent in the first half of 2007-08 over the corresponding period of the previous year to touch Rs 12,759 crore and to account for over 18 per cent of the sales revenue. Among 223 of such companies, the interest cost climbed up faster than the growth in sales. The top 5 companies shelling out huge interest charges are: Indian Oil (Rs 671 crore), Reliance Industries (Rs 552 crore), NTPC (Rs 524 crore), Power Grid (Rs 374 crore) and Tata Steel (Rs 282 crore). —*Financial Express, 25.11. 2007.*

7.2.2 Cost of Preference Share Capital

Despite the fact that dividend on preference shares is not legally binding on the firm as opposed to interest on debt which is legally binding on the firm, the computation of the cost of preference shares is similar to that of the cost of debt. The only difference is that dividend is paid to the preference shareholders after taxes have been charged and is, therefore, not tax-deductible. This means that there is no need for tax adjustment in case of the cost of preference shares. The result is that the cost of preference shares is often higher than the cost of debt. The cost of preference shares can be expressed in the form of an equation as follows:

$$Kp = DP/P \qquad ...(7.3)$$

Where:

P = the par value of preference shares on a per share basis

DP = the expected dividend on a per share basis

EXAMPLE

The cost of a Rs 100 per preference share with a 6% coupon will be:

6/100 = 0.06 or 6%.

Similarly, a new issue of preference shares requires adjustment for floatation cost, as is done in the case of new debt. Adjustment for premiums and discounts is made in a similar manner.

EXAMPLE

If 6% Rs 100 par preference shares are actually sold at Rs 90 per share, the effective cost will be:

6/90 or .0667 or 6.67%.

7.2.3 Cost of Equity Shares

The computation of the cost of equity share capital is not as easy as the computation of cost of debt or preference share capital. This is because there is no fixed contractual obligation for payment of dividend to the equity shareholders. The equity shareholders only have expectations as to what would be the size of future dividends. Determination of expected value is thus a difficult process. Nevertheless, various techniques have been developed to measure the cost equity shares. Those that are commonly used are explained here.

Historical Rate of Return: This technique is based on the historical rate of return. This method assumes that the equity shareholders earn on an average what they expect to earn. That is why the previous figures are collected, say, for 5 to 10 years preceding the computation year, and on that basis, cost is computed.

EXAMPLE

The price of an equity share for the last 3 years has been Rs 100 and Rs 8 is paid as dividend each year. The average rate of return for an equity shareholder would be:

8/100 or 8% per year.

The cost of the equity share would thus be 8%.

The process is very simple but unsound in practical terms. In fact, the assumption of this method, that there would be no significant change either in investor's expectations as to the future performance of the firm or in the investor's attitude towards risk, does not hold good. Therefore, other methods are preferred. These are explained hereafter.

Use of Current Price of Shares: This method estimates the investors' expectations for the future dividend on the basis of the current price of the shares. The current price of an equity share, *P*, is equal to the present value of expected dividends, *D*, given the risk-adjusted rate, *ke*, required by investors. Therefore, the current price of an equity share can be expressed as follows:

$$P = \frac{D_1}{(1 + ke)} + \frac{D_2}{(1 + ke)^2} + \frac{D_3}{(1 + ke)^3} + \ldots + \frac{D_n}{(1 + ke)^n} \qquad \ldots(7.4)$$

We may know the cost of equity share capital, K_e, if we know the current price of shares, P, and the value of future dividend, D. That is:

$$Ke = \frac{D}{P} \qquad \text{...(7.5)}$$

Here the estimation of D is made on the basis of past records.

EXAMPLE

If the dividend per share has been Rs 6 during the last 10 years and the current price of share is Rs 60, then:

$$K_e = 6/60 \text{ or } 10\%.$$

However, in the normal course, the investors expect a growing rate of dividend per share, particularly when this has been a phenomenon in the past. As a result, a growth factor has to be included in the computation of K_e. If dividends are expected to grow at a compound rate of g per annum and if D_1 is the dividend expected the next year, then K_e can be expressed as follows:

$$K_e = \frac{D_1}{P} + g \qquad \text{...(7.6)}$$

EXAMPLE

The price of a share is Rs 50, dividend pay-out is 50%, the earning per share is Rs 8 and the growth factor is 5%, the cost of the share will be:

$$4/50 + 0.05 = 13\%$$

As far as the cost of new shares is concerned, this is computed after the adjustment of floatation cost in the same way as is done for preference shares. That means, floatation cost is deducted from the market value of shares.

EXAMPLE

A firm has Rs 5 as EPS with 50% dividend pay-out ratio. Public offering is considered at Rs 80 on which floatation cost comes to Rs 5 per share. K_e would be:

$$[2.50/(80 - 5)] + 0.05 = 8.33\%$$

***Ke* on the basis of Security Market Line:** Friend and Blume (1970) estimate the cost of equity shares using Beta as a measure of risk. According to them the cost of equity shares can be expressed as follows:

$$K_e = K_r + (K_m - K_r)\, Beta_e \qquad \text{...(7.7)}$$

Where:

K_r = the risk-free rate of interest;

K_m = the expected rate of return (average) on the portfolio of all securities in the market

$Beta_e$ = the product of shares' standard deviation, *SDe*, and their correlation with the market portfolio divided by the standard deviation of rate of return on the market portfolio

As per Eq. 7.7, the return required by an investor on an equity share depends on its risk measured by Beta, the risk-free rate, and the average rate of return on all securities in the market. The estimate of Beta is made from past rates of return since the historical Beta is often close to the true Beta. Beta being equal to 1 indicates that the risk present in the equity shares is equal to that found in the total portfolio in the market. Beta being higher than 1 reveals that risk present in the equity shares is higher than that of the total portfolio in the market. Now the risk-free rate of interest is that interest rate which is found in case of Class I securities. Similarly, the average market rate can be found on the basis of historical average rates of return on a large sample of securities. If all the three variables are estimated, it is easy to estimate *Ke*.

EXAMPLE

If risk-free rate is 10%, K_m is 15% and Beta is 0.8, *Ke* will be:

$$10\% + (15\% - 10\%)\ (0.8) = 14\%$$

***Ke* on the basis of K_d:** The above methods are applicable only where historical figures are available, that is, when the firm has already been paying dividend. But in the absence of the historical figures, the cost of equity shares is computed on the basis of interest rate on debentures, that is, K_d. In practice K_e is higher than K_d. So the highest rate of interest paid by the firm is taken into account and K_e is fixed at a point higher than it. It is generally 4 or 5% higher than K_d. Thus it is a very simple method and can be used when other methods cannot be used easily.

7.2.4 Cost of Retained Earnings

Retained earnings form a part of the capital structure. It is not, however, necessary to calculate a separate cost of retained earnings. This is because the cost is included in the cost of existing equity shares. Since the equity shares have claims against both the share value and the retained earnings, a separate cost of retained earnings does not exist.

7.3 WEIGHTED AVERAGE COST OF CAPITAL

7.3.1 The Measurement

In the computation of the weighted average cost of capital, the first step is to measure the cost of different forms of capital. This has already been explained. The second step is to determine the weight to be assigned to the different costs. Various methods are adopted to determine this weight. One method is to base the weight on the existing proportions of various forms of capital in the firm's balance sheet. The other is to base these weights on the proportions in which the current capital budget is expected to be financed. Still another method is to base the weights on the current proportions of the market value of the firm's outstanding securities.

The last option, that is, basing the weights on the market value of the firm's outstanding securities is preferable to other options because it is known to the finance manager at the time of the investment decision being made; and moreover, the cost of capital is based on the market price of securities which shows the investor's assessment of business and financial risk. Therefore, if the market value of debt, preference shares and equity shares is respectively Rs 4,00,000, Rs 1,00,000 and Rs 5,00,000, their respective proportion will be 40% or 0.4, 10% or 0.1 and 50% or 0.5.

Finally, after the weight is determined, the cost of different forms of capital is multiplied by their respective weights in order to arrive at the weighted average cost of capital, K_o. In other words,

$$K_o = K_d W_d + K_p W_p + K_e W_e \qquad ...(7.8)$$

EXAMPLE

Calculate the weighted average cost of capital when the capital structure shows:

(a) Existing debt of Rs 5,00,000 at 10% for 6 years (tax rate is 30%);
(b) New debt of Rs 3,00,000 at 8% for 10 years with a floating cost of Rs 20,000;
(c) Preference shares Rs 1,00,000 (1000 shares) with 6% coupon rate;
(d) Existing equity shares (40,000 shares) with a market price of Rs 15 per share, EPS of Rs 4, growth rate of 5% and the dividend pay-out ratio of 50%; and
(e) Proposed equity shares (10,000 shares) to be sold at Rs 13, with Rs 20,000 as floatation cost.

Solution

Cost of Different Forms of Capital

Existing debt: 0.10 (1 – 0.30) = 0.07 or 7%

New Debt: {24,000 + [(3,00,000 – 2,80,000)/10]}/(3,00,000 + 2,80,000)/2
= 0. 08965 (1 – 0.3) = 0.062755 or 6.28%

Preference shares: 6/100 = 0.06 or 6%

Existing equity shares: 2/15 + .05 = 0.1833 or 18.33%

New equity shares: 2/11 + .05 = 0.2138 or 23.18%

Proportions

	Value (Rs)	Weight
Existing debt	5,00,000	0.31
New debt	3,00,000	0.18
Preference shares	1,00,000	0.06
Existing common shares	6,00,000	0.36
New common shares	1,50,000	0.09
Total	16,50,000	1.00

Weighted Average Cost of Capital

	Cost	Weight	Cost × weight
K_d (old)	0.0700	0.31	0.0217
K_d (new)	0.0628	0.18	0.0113
Kp	0.0600	0.06	0.0036
K_e (existing)	0.1833	0.36	0.0660
K_e (new)	0.2318	0.09	0.0209
			0.1235
			= 12.35%

7.3.2 The Influencing Factors

There are two types of factors influencing the weighted average cost of capital. One is internal which is within the control of the enterprise. The other is external lying beyond the control of the enterprise. In all they are as follows:

1. Internal factors
   (a) Capital structure policy
   (b) Dividend policy
2. External factors
   (a) Tax rates
   (b) Interest rates
   (c) Market risk premium

Interest is tax-deductible and so the cost of debt is lower than the cost of equity. If a firm has higher proportions of debt in its capital structure, the weighted average cost of capital will be lower. Similarly, a company distributes less dividend and reinvests the profits in highly profitable avenues, and the weighted average cost of capital will be higher than when the funds are borrowed at lower cost to finance the new project. Thus, it is the capital structure policy as well as the dividend policy that influences the weighted average cost of capital.

The tax rates have direct impact on the cost of debt. With the same coupon rate, the effective cost of debt with higher tax rate will be lower. On the contrary, higher interest rate makes the debt costlier. Again, the market risk premium affects the cost of equity as it indicates the perceived riskiness of equity and the investor's aversion to risk.

7.4 MARGINAL COST OF CAPITAL

The weighted average cost of capital or the average cost of capital indicates to large extent the historical cost of capital. It is very relevant for comparing the actual cost of funds with some pre-determined standards of cost of capital. However, while making capital budgeting decisions, the firm is in need of additional funds that represent the cut-off rate, and not the historical cost of additional funds raised for making investments.

The computation of marginal cost of capital involves the process of calculating the cost of different types of additional capital required. Then marginal weight is assigned to each of them which is computed on the basis of the proportion of different types of additional capital required. Here it must be made clear that for calculating marginal weight, there is no question of any choice for the market value of additional capital as against the book value.

The marginal cost of capital may be equal to the average cost of capital to the extent:

(i) the proportion of additional capital does not change; and

(ii) the cost of the components remains constant.

However, in practice, it is not necessary that the additional capital be raised in the same proportion as the existing capital. The optimum of capital structure may differ. At the same time, it is not essential that additional capital be raised at constant cost. In the chapter discussing capital structure, it is evident that an increase in the amount of equity capital raises the cost of equity after a certain point. The cost of debt too rises after some time. The moment such changes occur, there takes place a break in the weighted marginal cost of capital (MCC) schedule and the MCC curve rises leaving behind the average cost of capital. The returns on the project must be higher than the MCC in order for the value of the firm to increase.

SUMMARY

The analysis of the cost of capital is of immense significance in many areas of business finance, more particularly for making investment decisions. This is because it acts as a cut-off rate or minimum acceptable rate of return from an investment. This implies that the cost of capital must be lower than the rate of return from an investment, so as to raise the value of the firm.

Since a firm utilizes different forms of capital, it is required to compute weighted average cost of capital. To this end, the cost of different forms of capital is first computed, and then they are combined along with their respective weights. The cost of existing debt is simply the coupon rate adjusted for taxes, while the cost of new debt needs also to be adjusted for floatation cost. Similar adjustments are made when debentures are issued either at a premium or at a discount.

The computation of the cost of preference shares does not need adjustment for taxes as dividend on preference shares is not tax-deductible. It is equal to expected dividend on a per share basis divided by the par value of preference share on a per share basis. Adjustment for premium or discount is made in a manner similar to that used in case of the cost of debentures.

The computation of the cost of equity shares is more difficult as there is no fixed contractual obligation for the payment of dividends to shareholders. The simplest way to determine the cost of equity shares is to base it on the historical rate of return. However, as this method fails to take into account the investors' expectations of the future performance of the firm, it is not generally used. The second method, however, takes into account the investors' expectations for the future dividend on the basis of current price of shares. The third method of computing the cost of equity uses Beta as a measure of risk. The cost is equal to the risk-free rate of interest plus the difference between the expected rate of return on total portfolio in the market and the risk-free rate multiplied by Beta. These three methods are useful in case of an existing venture. However, in case of new ventures where different variables are not available, cost of equity shares is fixed at a point higher than the highest rate of interest. Cost of retained earnings need not to be calculated as it is included in the cost of equity shares.

After the costs of different forms of capital are determined, respective weights are assigned to them, preferably on the basis of the current proportions of the market value of the firm's outstanding securities. In other words, cost of each component of capital is multiplied by its weight, and the product is summed up which shows the weighted average cost of capital.

When the firm raises additional funds for investment in a new project, what matters is the weighted cost of capital of the additional funds or the weighted marginal cost of capital.

POINTS TO REMEMBER

1. What is cost of capital?
   - It is the weighted average of cost of different forms of capital – equity share capital, preference share capital and debt.
2. How is cost of debt calculated?
   - Interest x (1 – tax rate)
3. How do you calculate the cost of new debt which includes floatation cost?

$$K_d\ New = \frac{I + \left(\frac{P - NP}{N}\right)}{\left(\frac{P + NP}{2}\right)}$$

4. How do you calculate the cost of preference share capital?

$$Kp = DP/P$$

5. What are the basis for calculating the cost of equity share capital?
   - Historical rate of return
   - Current price of shares considering also the expected growth in dividend
   - Security market line comprising both the systematic and unsystematic risk
   - Cost of debt
6. How do you calculate the cost of equity share capital based on MPS and growth in dividend?

$$K_e = \frac{D_1}{P} + g$$

7. How do you calculate the cost of equity share capital based on security market line?

$$K_e = K_r + (K_m - K_r)\ Beta_e$$

8. How is cost of retained earnings calculated?
   - Cost of retained earnings is included in the cost of equity. A separate cost of retained earnings does not exist.
9. Point out the significance of marginal cost of capital.
   - The cost of capital may change if additional funds are raised at varying cost or the proportion of different forms of capital changes changing in turn their respective weight. Under these circumstances, marginal cost of capital will be different from the average cost of capital.

DESCRIPTIVE QUESTIONS

1. How do you calculate the after-tax cost of debt? Does it increase with a decrease in tax rate?
2. How do you treat the floatation cost while computing the cost of either debt, or preference share or equity share capital?
3. Does the cost of debt change when debentures are sold either at premium or at a discount?
4. How do you compute the cost of preference shares? Is it true that the cost of preference shares is higher than the cost of debt?
5. Explain the different ways in which the cost of equity shares is computed.
6. What is the weighted average cost of capital? When is the marginal cost different from the average cost of capital?

OBJECTIVE-TYPE QUESTIONS

1. Mark true or false.
   (a) The cost of retained earnings is separately calculated.
   (b) The dividend on preference shares is adjusted for taxes to arrive at their cost.
   (c) Beta of less than one lowers the cost of equity shares.

(d) Marginal cost of capital is always equal to the average cost of capital.
(e) The cost of a share is higher if it sells at premium.
(f) The interest rate on debentures may be the basis for ascertaining the cost of equity shares.

2. Choose the most suitable answer.
(a) Cost of new debt incorporates:
  (i) floatation cost
  (ii) no floatation cost
  (iii) only a part of floatation cost
(b) Cost of preference shares is:
  (i) treated for taxes
  (ii) not treated for taxes
  (iii) only occasionally treated for taxes
(c) Cost of equity shares is influenced by:
  (i) growth rate of dividend only
  (ii) growth rate of earnings only
  (iii) both of the above
(d) If the cost of funds for the new project is higher,
  (i) marginal cost of capital = average cost of capital
  (ii) marginal cost of capital > average cost of capital
  (iii) marginal cost of capital < average cost of capital

NUMERICAL PROBLEMS

1. Compute the after-tax cost of debt if:
(a) Interest rate is 12% and tax rate is 30%.
(b) Interest rate is 10% and tax rate is 35%.

2. A company issues 10-year debenture for Rs 1,00,000 with 8% coupon. The floatation cost is Rs 3,000 and the tax rate is 30%. Find the cost of debt.

3. A firm's expected dividend at the year-end is Rs 3.50. Growth rate in dividend is 6%. The share sells at Rs 35. The price of each new share net of floatation cost is Rs 32.
(a) Find out the cost of equity shares.
(b) What is the floatation cost?
(c) What is the cost of the new issue?

4. A firm plans to issue some Rs 100 par preference share with a 10% dividend. The market price of each share is Rs 98 which is further lower at Rs 96 net of the floatation cost. Find out the cost of share with floatation cost and without floatation cost.

5. A company sells its ordinary share for Rs 25. The expected dividend at the year-end is Rs 2.50. Growth rate in dividend is 7%. Its bonds earn 12% interest. The company's

beta is 1.5. The risk-free rate is 9%. The average return on the market is 13%. Find out the cost of ordinary share taking into account:

(a) the growth factor;
(b) CAPM; and
(c) the bond yield.

6. Find out the weighted average cost of capital when debt-equity ratio is 60:40. The pre-tax cost of debt is 12% with a tax rate of 30%. The cost of equity share is 16%.
7. The market price of a company's equity share is Rs 50. Dividend is Rs 4 per share and the growth rate in dividend is 5%. If the company issues new equity share, the share is sold at a discount of Rs 3 because of tough competition in the market. Floatation cost is Rs 2.50 per share. Find the cost of the new equity share.
8. A 10% preference share, which is expected to sell at Rs 87, is issued involving a floatation cost of Rs 5 per share. Find the cost of the new preference share.
9. A company has equity shares of Rs 10 each, the market price of which is Rs 56. A constant growth of 5% is expected and a dividend of Rs 3.60 per share has been paid. Find out the cost of equity share.
10. A company expects a 16% return on its equity share. The risk-free interest on government securities is 9% and the shares' beta factor is 1.40. Calculate the cost of equity based on CAPM.

SOLVED NUMERICAL PROBLEMS

1. A company has issued only recently Rs 100 preference shares with an annual dividend of 10%. They are redeemable preference shares with a maturity of 10 years. Find the cost if floatation cost amounts to Rs 4 per share.

Solution

$K_p = \{10 + (4/10)\}/\{(100 + 96)/2\} = 0.1061 = 10.61\%$

2. A company issues 10% Rs 100 debentures. The floatation cost is Rs 4. Tax rate is 30%. Debentures are redeemable after 5 years at a premium of Rs 3. The difference between the redemption value and the net amount realised is to be written off during the life time of the debentures. Find the cost of debt.

Solution

$K_d = [\{10 \times (1 - 0.30)\} + \{(103 - 96)/5\} \times \{1 - 0.30)] / (103 + 96)/2$

$= 0.0802 = 8.02\%$

3. The market price of a company's equity share is Rs 220. The expected dividend per share is Rs 20 which is expected to grow at a constant rate of 6% p.a. Find the cost of equity share capital.

Solution

$K_e = (20/220) + 0.06 = 0.1509 = 15.09\%$

4. Find the cost of equity if the risk-free rate is 8%, the expected return on the market securities is 15% and beta is 1.2.

Solution

$K_e = 0.08 + (0.15 - 0.08)\ 1.2$

$= 0.08 + 0.084 = 0.164$

$= 16.4\%$

5. The capital structure of a company has the following components:

10,000 shares of Rs 100 each	=	Rs 10,00,000
10% 1,000 preference shares of Rs 100 each	=	1,00,000
12% debentures	=	9,00,000

The current market price of equity share is Rs 140. The expected dividend is Rs 20 which is to grow at 5% p.a. Tax rate is 30%. Find the weighted average cost of capital.

Solution

Weight = Equity share capital 50%; Preference share capital 5%; Debt 45%

$K_e = 20/140 + 0.05 = 0.1928 = 19.28\%$

WACC = 0.5 x 0.1928 + 0.05 x 0.10 + 0.45 x 0.12(1 – 0.30)

= 0.0964 + 0.005 + 0.0378

= 0.1392 =13.92%

6. A company has a gearing ratio of 30%. The cost of equity is 20% and the cost of debt is 14%. If the corporate tax rate is 30%, calculate WACC.

Solution

WACC = (20% x 0.70) + [{14% (1 – 0.30)} x 0.30]

= 14% + 2.94%= 16.94%

Mini Case

Aman Industries, a producer of automobile spares, is planning to diversify its production structure. In this context, it likes to evaluate the weighted average cost of capital required for the new line of production. The latest balance sheet of the company shows the various liabilities and assets as follows:

Liabilities	*Amount (million Rs)*	*Assets*	*Amount (million Rs)*
Equity capital	700	Fixed assets	1400
Reserves	600	Investments	200
Debentures	900	Current assets	800
Current liabilities and provisions	200		
Total	2400	Total	2400

The existing debentures have a par value of Rs 100, selling in the market at Rs 112. They have a coupon of 10% and a maturity of 8 years. The shares are selling at Rs 80 per share. The preceding year's dividend was Rs 2.50 per share with an expected growth rate of 5%. Tax rate is 30%.

The company is going to raise Rs 200 million for the new project. The debt-equity ratio will be 1:1.

Questions:

1. Find out the cost of debt and the cost of equity.
2. Find the existing weighted average cost of capital.
3. Do you think that the weighted average cost of capital for the new project will be different from the present one?

REFERENCE

Friend, I. and M. Blume (1970). "Measurement of Portfolio Performance under Uncertainty", *American Economic Review*, 60: 561–75.

SELECT FURTHER READINGS

Arditti, F.D. and H. Levy (1977). "The Weighted Average Cost of Capital as a Cut-off Rate: A Critical Analysis of the Classical Textbook Weighted Average", *Financial Management*, 6 (Fall): 24–34.

Pratt, S.P. (1998). *Cost of Capital: Estimates and Applications:* New York: John Wiley & Sons.

Part III

Working Capital Management

Selection of a project and investment in fixed assets is not enough. A firm has to make investment in current assets so as to facilitate actual operation. The management of current assets and their financing form the subject-matter of this part of the book. To be precise, it incorporates the discussion on:

1. Working capital policy;
2. Management of cash and near-cash assets;
3. Management of accounts receivable;
4. Inventory management;
5. Sources of short-term finance.

8

WORKING CAPITAL POLICY

OBJECTIVES

To describe what working capital actually means

To assess the factors influencing the size of current assets/working capital both in absolute terms and in relation to the fixed assets

To explain how current assets are financed—whether by short-term funds or by long-term funds or by both

The working capital provides the firm with liquidity, which is essential for the efficacious use of the fixed assets and, thereby, for achieving the expected rate of return. Any error in working capital decision may entail upon the desired liquidity and, thereby, on the efficient use of the fixed assets. It would not help gear up the firm to maximise corporate wealth. The emphasis in the present chapter thus lies on the concept of working capital, and on the major issues that are involved in its management. The major issues are, first, what the size of current assets should be and, second, how they should be financed.

8.1 CONCEPT OF WORKING CAPITAL

8.1.1 Gross and Net Working Capital

A firm's balance sheet shows both liabilities and assets. The liabilities are either current liabilities or long-term liabilities. Similarly, the assets are either fixed assets like plant and machinery, land and building, etc., or the current assets. The current assets are represented by:

1. Cash in hand and at bank;
2. Near-cash assets or short-term marketable securities in which the surplus cash is invested;
3. Accounts receivable which include sundry debtors or credit sales and the amount the firm has paid in advance to the supplier of the inputs;
4. Inventory including raw material, semi-finished goods and finished goods.

The current assets are also known as the circulating assets because cash takes the form of other current assets that, in the end, again take the form of cash. The operating cycle discussed subsequently at some length in this chapter is thus complete. Similar operating cycles continue as long as the firm remains in operation. The operating cycle normally takes less than a year. Therefore, a year is the period that demarcates between fixed assets and current assets. However, Park and Gladson (1963) are of the view that the one year temporal standard explaining currentness of assets is simply arbitrary, because the operating cycle may be as short as two or three months in the case of the food-processing industry, and as long as two to three years in the ship-building industry. Thus the term, natural business year should be used, instead of one year.

The operating cycle normally takes less than a year. Therefore, a year is the period that demarcates between fixed assets and current

The term, working capital is frequently used in a gross sense. The gross working capital refers to the total amount of current assets. However, the term, net working capital, is also frequently used. The net working capital is the amount shown by the difference between the current assets and the current liabilities. A positive net working capital denotes a position where the current assets are greater than the current liabilities. Excess of current liabilities over the current assets denotes a position of negative net working capital. The rationale behind the concept of net working capital is that it shows the ability of the current assets to pay for the current liabilities. It is for this reason that the current ratio and the quick ratio are computed to show the firm's liquidity position (Walker, 1974).

Gross Working capital or the current assets	–	Current liabilities	=	Net working capital

8.1.2 Permanent and Variable Working Capital

Originally when the size of firms was small and their operation substantially dependent on agriculture, the concept of permanent working capital was lacking. Firms would borrow funds for purchase of raw material, process the same and sell it, repaying the loan from the sale proceeds. So the amount of current assets, which was one time the largest, fell almost to zero at other points of time.

When the size of firms grew, and the production and financing cycle became a continuous phenomenon, a certain volume of current assets had to be maintained throughout the year, this came to be known as permanent working capital. However, in continuous operations too, seasonal variations were marked as far as the requirements for current assets were concerned. During periods of peak demand, the amount of current assets rose over and above the stable volume or the permanent volume. In periods of normal demand, the amount of current assets came down to the permanent level. For example, in a firm manufacturing woollen blankets, the demand for the blankets grows during the winter season and during this period the amount of current assets grows beyond the normal level. The amount by which the current assets rise over the permanent

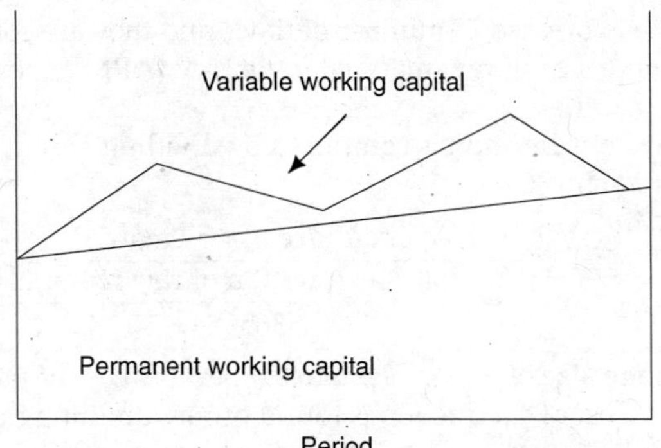

FIG. 8.1 Permanent and variable working capital

or normal level is known as the variable working capital. Figure 8.1 shows permanent and variable working capital

8.2 SIZE OF CURRENT ASSETS

The issue of the size of the current assets primarily involves two questions. First, how the size can be assessed? Second, whether the size is optimal in relation to the fixed assets? These two questions need some explanation here.

8.2.1 Assessment of the Size: The Concept of Operating Cycle

The desired size of the current assets is assessed on the basis of the length of the operating cycle.

The desired size of the current assets is assessed on the basis of the length of the operating cycle. Besides the use of cash for routine expenses, it is also used to acquire raw material. Once the raw material is converted into the finished product it is sold on credit creating accounts receivable. Accounts receivables are collected after a specific period of time thus again taking the form of cash. The movement of cash into different forms of current assets ultimately once more taking on the form of cash is known as operating cycle. The longer the operating cycle (involving larger number of days) the larger is the size of current assets inasmuch as cash is tagged for a longer period of time. This is because, in a going concern, fresh doses of investment are made in the current assets in order to ensure continuity of operations. If the operating cycle is longer, the number of fresh doses of investment would be larger and the total amount of the current assets would naturally be greater.

The concept of operating cycle may be explained at greater length. It is the sum of the inventory conversion period (ICP) and the debtors conversion period (DCP). The inventory conversion period is the sum of raw material conversion period (RMCP), work-in-progress conversion period (WIPCP) and finished goods conversion period (FGCP).

In other words:

$$\text{Operating cycle} = (\text{RMCP} + \text{WIPCP} + \text{FGCP}) + \text{DCP} \quad ...(8.1)$$

All the periods are expressed in number of days, and they are computed as follows:

1. RMCP = Average size of raw material inventory (ARMI)/per day consumption of raw material

   Where per day consumption is computed by dividing annual consumption of raw material (ACRM) by 365

$$\text{RMCP} = \frac{\text{Average size of raw matrial}}{\dfrac{\text{Annual consumption of raw material}}{365}} \qquad \text{...(8.2)}$$

2. WIPCP = Average size of work-in-progress/per day cost of production

   Where per day cost of production is found out by dividing the annual cost of production by 365

$$\text{WIPCP} = \frac{\text{Average size of work-in-progress}}{\dfrac{\text{Annual cost of finished goods produced}}{365}} \qquad \text{...(8.3)}$$

3. $$\text{FGCP} = \frac{\text{Average size of finished goods}}{\dfrac{\text{Annual cost of goods sold}}{365}} \qquad \text{...(8.4)}$$

   Where per day cost of goods sold is equal to annual sales at cost divided by 365

4. $$\text{DCP} = \frac{\text{Average Recievables}}{\dfrac{\text{Credit Sales}}{365}} \qquad \text{...(8.5)}$$

   Where per day credit sale is equal to annual credit sales divided by 365

The total number of days computed in this way reveals the length of the operating cycle.

Inventary conversion period	+	Debtor conversion period	=	Gross operating cycle	–	Payables deferral period
			=	Net operating cycle or Cash conversion period		

However, the operating cycle discussed so far is the gross operating cycle. The operating cycle can be expressed also in terms of net operating cycle that is also known as the cash conversion cycle. The cash conversion cycle is arrived at after the payables deferral period (PDP) is subtracted from the gross operating cycle. The basic rationale is that if debtors cause an increase in the length of the operating cycle and thereby the need for cash, the trade credits shorten this length and reduce the need for cash. The payables deferral (PDP) period can be expressed as follows:

$$\text{PDP} = \frac{\text{Creditors}}{\dfrac{\text{Credit Purchase}}{365}} \qquad \text{...(8.6)}$$

EXAMPLE

The following are the figures on the basis of which you have to compute the length of the gross operating cycle and the cash conversion period:

raw material inventory–Rs 8,00,000; raw material consumption–Rs 40,00,000; work-in-process inventory–Rs 3,60,000; cost of production–Rs 54,00,000; finished goods inventory–Rs 6,50,000; cost of goods sold–Rs 52,00,000; credit sales–Rs 49,50,000; debtors–Rs 9,00,000; creditors–Rs 5,00,000 and credit purchases–Rs 45,00,000.

$$\begin{aligned}
\text{RMCP} &= 8{,}00{,}000 \times 365/40{,}00{,}000 = 73 \text{ days}\\
\text{WIPCP} &= 3{,}60{,}000 \times 365/54{,}00{,}000 = 24.3 \text{ days}\\
\text{FGCP} &= 6{,}50{,}000 \times 365/52{,}00{,}000 = 45.6 \text{ days}\\
\text{DCP} &= 9{,}00{,}000 \times 365/49{,}50{,}000 = 66.4 \text{ days}\\
\text{Gross operating cycle} &= 73 + 24.3 + 45.6 + 66.4 = 209.3 \text{ days}\\
\text{PDP} &= 5{,}00{,}000 \times 365/45{,}00{,}000 = 40.5 \text{ days}
\end{aligned}$$

Cash conversion period = 209.3 - 40.5 = 168.8 days

8.2.2 Ratio between Current Assets and Fixed Assets: Liquidity versus Profitability

A firm needs both fixed assets and current assets in order to support a specific level of output. Again, with the same amount of fixed assets, the amount of current assets may be different depending upon a host of factors. The most important is the trade-off between the risk and return or the trade-off between the liquidity and profitability. It is such a trade-off that tends to optimise the size of the current assets in relation to the fixed assets. Optimisation lies at the core of the working capital management. This is because there are inherent dangers in cases where the size of the current assets is either in excess of or less than the optimal size. If it exceeds the optimal size, sufficient liquidity is generated in the firm but the cost of holding and financing current assets grows large enough to bring down the profits. Chances of mishandling, theft and wastage of inventory may also increase. It may also lead to complacency among the managers that may cause a fall in managerial efficiency. Again, excessive working capital may manifest itself in a liberal credit policy accompanied by greater incidence of losses caused by bad debts. All this entails upon the return from investment. On the contrary, inadequate working capital leads to illiquidity causing interruptions in the production process. Sometimes it is difficult for the firm to undertake even profitable projects for want of sufficient working capital. It also affects sales as the firm finds itself incapable of providing liberal credit.

Current Asset Scenario in Indian Manufacturing Companies

Component	2000–01	2001–02	2002–03	2003–04	2004–05	2005–06
Cash (Rs crore)	29,587	32,614	37,412	55,881	77,211	1,03,432
Receivables (Rs crore)	1,76,801	1,71,360	1,74,681	1,88,100	2,11,092	2,32,525
Inventory (Rs crore)	1,33,351	1,31,099	1,44,106	1,57,381	1,87,975	2,19,642
Total current assets (Rs crore)	3,39,739	3,35,073	3,56,199	4,01,362	4,76,278	5,55,599
Current ass./total assets %	40.39	37.54	38.48	39.52	41.88	42.55
No. of companies	4,719	4,588	4,476	4,549	4,323	3,732

Source: *RBI Bulletin, July 2007.*

Thus in order to optimise the level of current assets or the gross working capital, the finance manager makes a trade-off between liquidity and profitability or, in other words, between risk and return. This is illustrated in Fig. 8.2 where the liquidity position improves with the growth in the size of the current assets, but at the same time, profitability tends to decline. The optimum position is indicated at that point where the liquidity curve and the profitability curve intersect each other.

However, in real life, the size of current assets is often more than the optimal size or less than it. This is due to the psyche of different finance managers which varies greatly. A conservative manager prefers liquidity to profitability and, hence, may prefer to maintain a greater amount of the current assets than what the optimal level requires. On the contrary, an aggressive manager emphasising on profitability and may do with even a lower amount of current assets than the optimal size. Table 8.1 shows how with a decreasing amount of current assets or current assets/fixed assets ratio, the return on investment rises. Suppose a firm has fixed assets worth Rs 50,000, and the amount of current assets is valued at Rs 50,000. The operating profit is 10% of the sales valued at Rs 1,50,000. In case an aggressive policy is followed, the amount of current assets is reduced to Rs 40,000. As a result, return on investment goes up to 16.66% with an operating profit of Rs 15,000. On the other hand, if the amount of current assets is increased to Rs 60,000

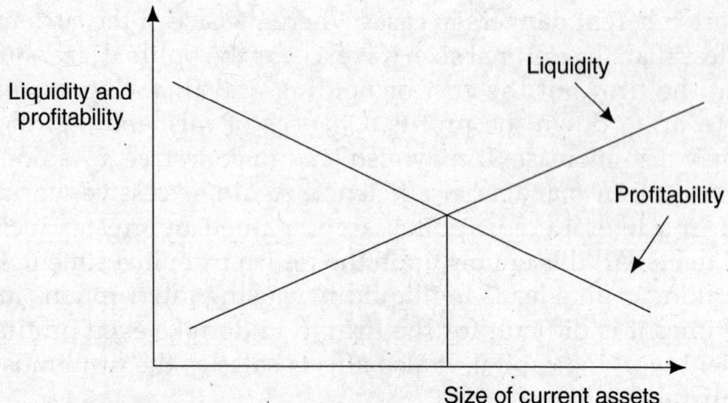

FIG. 8.2 Optimum size of working capital

TABLE 8.1 Return on Investment under Changing Working Capital Policy

Items	*Average policy*	*Conservative policy*	*Aggressive policy*
Sales (Rs)	1,50,000	1,50,000	1,50,000
EBIT (Rs)	15,000	15,000	15,000
Current Assets (Rs)	50,000	60,000	40,000
Fixed assets (Rs)	50,000	50,000	50,000
Total assets (Rs)	1,00,000	1,10,000	90,000
Current assets/fixed assets ratio	1:1	1.20:1	0.8:1
Return on investment (EBIT/Assets) (%)	15.0	13.64	16.66

under a conservative policy framework, the return on investment falls to 13.64% with the same amount of operating profit.

8.2.3 Other Factors Influencing the Size of Current Assets

It has already been pointed out that the size of current assets depends on the length of the operating cycle and also on the trade-off between liquidity and profitability. It has also been mentioned how the psyche of the finance managers brings about deviations from the optimal size of the current assets. Nevertheless, there are other factors that influence the size of current assets. This is the reason why the current assets/fixed assets ratio varies widely between different industries and between different firms. The more important of these factors are explained here. They are as follows:

1. **Size and Nature of Business:** The larger the scale of the firm, the greater is the need for the current assets, although the need for current assets grows at a decreasing rate with an increase in the scale of operations. Again, the nature of operation is also an important factor. For example, trading and financial firms require more of current assets, while some of the public utility services require large fixed assets. The Water Supply Board in New Delhi has more fixed assets in form of overhead tanks and pipelines, on the contrary, a wholesaler has only a little amount of fixed assets in form of his small shop.

2. **Seasonal and Cyclical Factors**: These two factors influence the size of working capital differently. Seasonal factors, such as variations in demand for a firm's output during different months of the year, influence mainly the variable working capital. During the peak season, the amount of current assets expands, while it contracts during the slack season. On the other hand, cyclical factors primarily influence the permanent working capital. The boom is characterised by an upward trend in production that necessitates a greater amount of working capital. The case is just the reverse in the case of a depression. Sometimes when a boom or depression continues for a long period, fixed assets too require marginal change and this is reflected in a change in the current assets/fixed assets ratio.

Seasonal factors, such as variations in demand for a firm's output during different months of the year, influence mainly the variable working capital.

3. **Easy Access to Finance:** If a firm gives more importance to the retention of profits or it has easy access to sources of finance to meet its working capital requirements, it will definitely invest less in current assets. This is because profitability can be

increased without jeopardising liquidity. If access to the sources of finance is not easy, a conservative policy is more appropriate.

4. **Operational Efficiency:** If a firm maintains high operational efficiency, resources would be used more efficiently and even a lower amount of current assets would serve the purpose. Operational efficiency depends upon the efficiency of labour, quality of labour, quality of machines and the efficiency of the managers optimising the overhead costs.
5. **Operational Policy:** A liberal operational policy requires more of current assets. For example, a liberal credit policy helps increase the amount of bills receivable, and a liberal inventory policy leads to greater size of inventory. A strict operational policy, however, would help keep the current assets within reasonable limits.

8.3 FINANCING OF CURRENT ASSETS

Apart from the size of current assets, the other significant issue in the management of working capital is how these current assets should be financed. There is no problem in financing the fixed assets as they are financed through long-term funds. In case of the current assets, however, any such decision is not easy, because current assets are financed out of both short-term funds (current liabilities) and long-term funds. It is crucial as to what should be the mix of short-term funds and long-term funds for the purpose of financing the current assets. The use of short-term funds is advocated on the grounds that they are less costly than the long-term funds, and their use will have a favourable impact on profitability. On the other hand, the use of long-term funds is favoured on the grounds that they provide liquidity for a longer period of time. Thus, again, it is a question of a trade-off between liquidity and profitability. The mix of long-term and short-term funds should possess a desired amount of both profitability and liquidity.

As far as the mix of long-term and short-term funds is concerned, three approaches can be mentioned here. They are as follows:

1. Matching approach
2. Conservative approach
3. Aggressive approach

> Apart from the size of current assets, the other significant issue in the management of working capital is how these current assets should be financed.

The matching approach suggests that permanent part of the working capital should be financed with long-term funds and the variable part of the working capital should be financed with short-term funds. Permanent working capital it exists for a comparatively longer period of time and it is thus difficult to finance with short-term funds as they have a shorter maturity.

When the management is conservative, it does not like to expose itself to greater risk. It finances the permanent current assets as well as a part of the variable current assets with long-term funds. This, however, makes the financing pattern less flexible. During the slack period, when the need for variable current assets ebbs to zero, funds remain idle as they cannot be repaid easily. Again, long-term funds are often costly and this entail upon the firm's profitability.

TABLE 8.2 Return from Investment in Changing Working Capital Financing Policy

Item	*Matching approach*	*Conservative approach*	*Aggressive approach*
Current assets (Rs)	50,000	50,000	50,000
Fixed assets (Rs)	50,000	50,000	50,000
Total assets (Rs)	1,00,000	1,00,000	1,00,000
Short-term credit at 10%	25,000	10,000	40,000
Long-term credit at 12%	25,000	40,000	10,000
Current ratio	2:1	5:1	5:4
EBIT (Rs)	15,000	15,000	15,000
Less: Interest	5,500	5,800	5,200
EBT (Rs)	9,500	9,200	9,800
Taxes @ 30% (Rs)	2,850	2,760	2,940
NIAT (Rs)	6,650	6,440	6,860
Return on equity assuming debt ratio of 50%	13.30	12.88	13.72

Sometimes the firm's management is aggressive, in which case it may make greater use of short-term funds and finance variable current assets and also a part of the permanent current assets with these short-term funds. Such funds are not only less costly but are more flexible and adaptable to the changing need for current assets. On the other hand, this policy carries greater risk of getting funds at fluctuating interest rates that is a normal feature for such funds. Sometimes non-availability of funds or the problem of repaying them within a short span of time may force the firm into bankruptcy.

Table 8.2 presents a comparative picture of these different approaches and their impact on the return on equity.

Table 8.2 shows that while the conservative approach yields lower return on equity, the aggressive approach helps increase the return on equity. The impact of the matching approach lies between the two. The finance manager makes a trade-off between risk and return. Less liquid assets, such as inventory is financed preferably through long-term funds. Highly liquid assets, such as cash are brought in from the sources of short-term funds. In practice, however, the industry norm is followed. Minor changes are made according to convenience.

SUMMARY

Working capital refers to the current assets. When the term, net working capital is used, it specifically means current assets less current liabilities. Again, that part of working capital which is maintained throughout the year is known as permanent working capital. The other part that fluctuates at different periods during the year is known as variable working capital.

The management of working capital involves two major issues. One is related to the size of current assets. The size of the current assets is ascertained on the basis of the operating cycle, yet it is optimised through a trade-off between maintenance of liquidity and profitability. However, the size often varies from that which is optimal, depending upon the psyche of the finance manager, primarily, towards the taking of risk and also certain other factors, such as, nature of business, cyclical and seasonal factors, operational policy and efficiency, etc.

The other issue related to the management of working capital is how the current assets should be financed. Any one of the approaches—matching, conservative and aggressive—is followed depending upon the preference of the finance manager. Matching approach means financing the permanent current assets with long-term funds and the variable part with short-term funds. Conservatism means financing also a part of variable current assets with long-term funds. An aggressive policy favours financing also a part of the permanent current assets with short-term funds. Each of these approaches has its merits, however, in practice, the industry norm is widely followed.

POINTS TO REMEMBER

1. Distinguish between gross working capital and net working capital.
    - While gross working capital means current assets, net working capital is equal to current assets minus current liabilities.
2. Distinguish between permanent and variable current assets. What is their significance?
    - The size of working capital maintained round the year is permanent working capital. Variable working capital arises during peak months/days to meet the additional demand.
    - The conservative finance manager finances permanent and also a part of the variable current assets with long-term capital in order to avoid risk. The aggressive manager, on the other hand, finances variable current assets and also a part of permanent current assets with short-term funds, thus takes risk and increases profitability. The matching approach lying between the two extremes suggests for financing permanent part of current assets with long-term funds and the variable part with short-term funds.
3. What are the factors determining the size of current assets?
    - Length of the operating cycle
    - Trade-off between profitability and liquidity
    - Other factors, such as size and nature of business, seasonal and cyclical factors, easy access to sources of finance, operational efficiency and operational policy.

4. What is operating cycle? What are its components?
   - The movement of cash into different forms of current assets ultimately once more taking the form of cash is the operating cycle.
   - Operating cycle is the sum of inventory conversion period and debtors' conversion period.
   - Inventory conversion period is the sum of raw material conversion period, work-in-progress conversion period and finished goods conversion period.
   - Operating cycle minus payables deferral period is known as net operating cycle or the cash conversion cycle.

DESCRIPTIVE QUESTIONS

1. Distinguish between:
   (a) gross working capital and net working capital;
   (b) permanent working capital and variable working capital.
2. What do you mean by operating cycle? How do you calculate its different segments?
3. The varying ratio between fixed assets and current assets has an impact on profitability/liquidity of a firm. Discuss.
4. Mention the factors influencing the size of current assets in a firm.
5. Current assets are financed through a mix of short-term and long-term funds. Discuss the statement and explain various approaches in this context.

OBJECTIVE-TYPE QUESTIONS

1. Mark true or false.
   (a) Net working capital means current liabilities.
   (b) Gross working capital means total current assets.
   (c) In public utility services like an electricity distribution company, the ratio of current assets to fixed assets is large.
   (d) The more liberal the terms of credit offered to the customers, the shorter is the operating cycle.
   (e) An aggressive approach to current asset financing is to finance a part of the variable current assets with long-term funds.
   (f) Liquidity rises with an increase in the size of the current assets.
2. Choose the most suitable answer.
   (a) Net working capital means:
      (i) current assets + current liabilities
      (ii) current assets - current liabilities
      (iii) current assets only

(b) Operating cycle includes:
  (i) inventory conversion period + debtors conversion period
  (ii) inventory conversion period – debtors conversion period
  (iii) inventory conversion period only

(c) An aggressive approach to current asset financing leads to:
  (i) greater profitability
  (ii) lower profitability
  (iii) no impact on profitability

(d) Variable current asset/permanent current asset ratio is normally:
  (i) very high
  (ii) very low
  (iii) constant throughout the year

(e) The longer the operating cycle:
  (i) the larger the size of current assets
  (ii) the smaller the size of the current assets
  (iii) the size of current assets remain unchanged

NUMERICAL PROBLEMS

1. Find out the raw material conversion period if the average size of raw material inventory amounts to Rs 5,00,000 and the annual consumption of raw material amounts to Rs 20,00,000.
2. Calculate the work-in-progress conversion period if the average size of work-in-progress is Rs 2,00,000 and the annual cost of production is Rs 10,00,000.
3. Calculate the finished goods conversion period if the average size of the finished goods is Rs 5,00,000 and the annual sales value Rs 25,00,000.
4. Calculate the debtors conversion period if the annual credit sales amount to Rs 50,00,000 and the average size of receivables amount to Rs 10,00,000.
5. The following are the figures on the basis of which you have to compute the length of the gross operating cycle and net operating cycle:

   raw material inventory–Rs 9,00,000; raw material consumption–Rs 45,00,000; work-in-process inventory–Rs 3,50,000; cost of production–Rs 51,00,000; finished goods inventory–Rs 6,00,000; cost of goods sold–Rs 52,00,000; credit sales–Rs 48,00,000; and debtors–Rs 7,00,000, creditors–Rs 9,00,000; and credit purchases–Rs 45,00,000.
6. The following are the figures on the basis of which you have to compute the size of gross working capital and net working capital:

   bills payable–Rs 20,000; short-term bank loans–Rs 10,000; other short-term credits–Rs 7,000; cash–Rs 15,000; bills receivable–Rs 28,000; short-term marketable securities–Rs 3,000; raw material–Rs 10,000; semi-finished goods–Rs 10,000; and finished goods–Rs 6,000.
7. A company having current assets of Rs 25 lakh, fixed assets of Rs 15 lakh, annual sales of Rs 1 crore and EBIT of 12% plans to double the level of current assets in order to

ensure greater liquidity. The new current asset is to be financed by equity. Find the asset turnover ratio and return on investment under the original plan and after the current asset expansion.

8. A Company maintains permanent current assets for Rs 1,20,000. Its variable current assets vary between zero and Rs 5,00,000 with an average of Rs 1,50,000. Short terms funds are available at 10% interest rate and long-term funds are available at 15% interest rate. Find out the total cost of financing the current assets on the assumption that the company follows a matching approach—financing permanent current assets with-long term funds and the variable part with short-term funds.
9. A firm has fixed assets of Rs 3,00,000 and current assets of Rs 2,00,000. Earning before tax is Rs 90,000. Find out the return on capital employed if the current asset is reduced by 20%.

SOLVED NUMERICAL PROBLEMS

1. Calculate cash conversion period from the financial variables given hereunder:

Rs lakh

	FY 2005–06	*As on March 2005*	*As on March 2006*
Sales	7,936		
Cost of goods	7,036		
Inventory		940	936
B/R		942	962
B/P		608	606

Solution

Inventory conversion period:

{(940 + 936)/2 / (7,036/365) = 48.7 days

B/R conversion period:

{(942 + 962)/2}/(7,936/365) = 43.8 days

Payables conversion period:

{(608+606)/2}/(7,036/365) = 31.5 days

Cash conversion period:

48.7 + 43.8 – 31.5 = 61 days

2. Find the average conversion period with the help of the following data:

Gross operating cycle = 88 days
Net operating cycle = 65 days
Raw material storage period = 45 days
Work-in-progress conversion period = 4 days
Finished goods storage period = 25 days

Solution

88 – (45 + 4 + 25) = 14 days

3. Calculate the finished goods conversion period if:

Finished goods opening stock Rs lakh	525
Finished goods closing stock	850
Cost of production	8,000
Administrative expenses	2,250
Excise duty	3,000

Solution

Average stock of finished goods

Rs (525 + 850)/2 = Rs 687.5 lakh

Cost of goods sold

Rs 525 + 8,000 + 2,250 + 3,000 – 850 = Rs 12,928 lakh

Daily average = 12,925/365 Rs 35.41 lakh

Finished goods conversion period = 687.5/35.41 = 19.42 days

4. If average stock of work-in-progress is Rs 60 lakh and the average conversion period is 4 days, find the annual cost of production.

Solution

Interpreting Eq. 8.3

Average daily cost of production = 60/4 = Rs 15 lakh

Annual cost of production = Rs 15 x 365 = Rs 5,475 lakh

5. Calculate inventory conversion period if:

Raw material inventory Rs lakh	10,00,000
Raw material consumption	50,00,000
Work-in-progress inventory	4,00,000
Cost of production	56,00,000
Finished goods inventory	8,00,000
Cost of goods sold	48,00,000

Solution

RMCP = (10,00,000 x 365)/50,00,000 = 73 days

WIPCP = (4,00,000 x 365)/56,00,000 = 26.1 days

FGCP = (8,00,000 x 365)/48,00,000 = 60.8 days

Inventory conversion period = 73.0 + 26.1 + 60.8 = 159.9 days

6. Find the ratio between short-term funds and long-term funds under:

   (a) Aggressive approach assuming the manager encroaches upon 10% of the permanent current assets with short-term funds

   (b) Conservative approach if the manager encroaches upon 20% of the variable current assets with long-term funds

   (c) Matching approach

   The size of funds is as follows:

   Permanent current assets amount to Rs 12,00,000

   Variable current assets 3,00,000

Solution

Aggressive approach:

Short-term funds for variable current assets + 10% of permanent current assets

= Rs 3,00,000 + 10% of 12,00,000 = 4,20,000

Long-term funds for permanent current assets = 12,00,000 – 1,20,000

= 10,80,000

Short-term fund/long-term fund ratio = 4,20,000/10,80,000

Conservative approach:

Long-term funds for permanent current assets + 20% of variable current assets

= 12,00,000 + 20% of Rs 3,00,000 = 12,60,000

Short-term funds for variable current assets

= Rs 3,00,000 - 60,000 = 2,40,000

Short-term fund/long-term fund ratio = 2,40,000/12,60,000

Matching approach:

Short-term funds/long-term funds ratio = 3,00,000/12,00,000

7. Profitability in terms of return on capital can be improved through changes in the size of current assets. Thus, if the size of fixed assets is Rs 20,00,000, the size of current assets is Rs 30,00,000 and the earning before tax is Rs 9,00,000, how far can the current assets be reduced to raise profitability to 20%?

Solution

Before any change in current assets, the return on capital is:

$$\frac{9{,}00{,}000}{50{,}00{,}000} = 0.18 = 18\%$$

If the return on capital is to be raised to 20%

$$\frac{9{,}00{,}000}{x} = 0.20$$

or $$\frac{9{,}00{,}000}{0.20} = \text{x}$$

or x = Rs 45,000, which means that current assets have to be reduced to Rs 25,000.

CASE STUDY

Varying Current Assets Composition in Indian Manufacturing, Food Products and Electronics Industries

The current assets/total assets ratio as well as the composition of current assets varies from one industry to the other depending upon a host of factors, of which the nature of operation is an important one. This fact leads us to study the current asset composition of three different groups of industries – manufacturing in general, food products and electronics. The major segments of the current assets of these different industries are presented here for a three-year period.

Current Assets Position in Different Industries during FYs 2003–06

Rs crores

Industry	Year	Cash & near cash assets	B/R	Inventory	Total current assets	Current assets/total assets ratio %	Current liabilities
Manufacturing	2003–04	55,881	1,88,100	1,57,281	4,01,262	39.51	3,25,294
	2004–05	77,211	2,11,092	1,87,975	4,76,278	41.88	3,69,095
	2005–06	1,03,432	2,32,525	2,19,642	5,55,599	42.55	4,10,044
Food products	2003–04	3,564	8,429	13,874	25,867	47.20	14,649
	2004–05	3,086	9,468	13,748	26,302	45.15	15,290
	2005–06	3,508	9,277	13,206	25,991	42.75	15,556
Electronics	2003–04	5,202	12,088	6,386	20,976	48.70	15,234
	2004–05	3,626	13,012	7,047	23,685	54.50	14,646
	2005–06	5,667	13,576	6,909	26,152	54.64	15,292

Based on CMIE figures.

A detailed analysis shows that there is not only year-wise variation, but also the variation is manifest in the three industries with regard to the stress on maintaining current assets as a part of the total assets. Besides, there is variation in the share of different components in the total current assets. The current ratio too is not an exception. It too varies from industry to industry.

Questions:

1. How much does current asset/fixed asset ratio vary among different sets of industries and what does this variation indicate?
2. How far do different industries care for maintaining liquidity? Base your answer on the current ratios.
3. What is the possible reason behind larger share of receivables than those of inventory in some cases?
4. What is the possible reason behind larger share of inventory than those of receivables in some cases?

REFERENCE

Park, C. and J.W. Gladson (1963). *Working Capital*. New York: Macmillan.

SELECT FURTHER READINGS

Kallberg, J.G. and K. Parkinson (1984), *Current Asset Management*, New York: Wiley Interscience.

Vander Weide, J.H. ands. F. Maier (1985), *Managing Corporate Liquidity: An Intoduction to Working Capital Management*, New York: Wiley.

9

MANAGEMENT OF CASH AND NEAR-CASH ASSETS

OBJECTIVES

To describe the motives behind holding of cash in a firm

To ascertain the cash requirements of a firm during a particular period

To discuss how the cash need is optimised through accelerating cash inflows and controlling disbursements

To determine the optimal ratio between cash and near-cash assets

To discuss cash management in international firms whose operations are spread out over a number of countries

Cash is the most liquid form of current assets. It is crucial if the firm is to operate on a continuous basis. This is why a firm's cash balance, that is, cash in hand and demand deposits with the bank, must not be so low as to cause an interruption in its operations, and, thereby, retard return on investment. But at the same time, if the cash balance is very large, a good part of it will remain idle affecting in turn the return on equity. Therefore, effective cash management is imperative. Effective cash management requires the following steps:

1. Cash planning projecting the requirements for the cash balance
2. Toning up the procedure of cash flows
3. Determination of the ratio between cash and near-cash assets

9.1 CASH PLANNING

9.1.1 Motives behind Holding Cash

Cash planning involves to a large extent ascertaining the cash requirement. However, before ascertaining the cash requirement, there arises the question as to why firms need to hold cash. The motives behind the holding of cash are as follows:

1. Transaction motive
2. Precautionary motive

3. Speculative motive
4. Motives of exploiting potential investment opportunities
5. Compensating balance requirements

A firm needs cash for transaction purposes. This means that cash is needed to buy raw materials, to pay wages and salaries and to meet many other expenses. The satisfaction of these needs results in a continuous outflow from the cash balance. But, at the same time, sales leads to a cash inflow. Had the inflows and outflows of cash been simultaneous and of equal magnitude, there would not have been any need for holding cash. But, in practice, there is always a time lag between cash outflows and the inflows depending on the length of the operating cycle. This lag makes it imperative to hold cash for transaction purposes.

The time lag between cash outflows and the inflows depends on the length of the operating cycle. This lag makes it imperative to hold cash for transaction purposes.

A firm also holds cash for meeting any exigencies that may arise. Such a motive is called a precautionary motive. It may so happen that a major customer suddenly becomes incapable of paying a bill. It is also possible that the supplier of the input suddenly eliminates credit. The need for a cash balance arises in all such cases. Such needs are unforeseen and it is very difficult for the firm to forecast them. But since they are not of a continuous nature, the cash balance for this purpose is held in form of near-cash assets where the investment earns a specific rate of return. Whenever the need arises, near-cash assets are converted into cash.

When prices change more frequently, the managers are found either leading or lagging purchases of raw material. If prices are to fall in the near future, they need to hold cash so that they may buy the inputs immediately at a low price. The motive behind such holdings is nothing but speculative.

Again, a firm holds cash in order to exploit potential investment opportunities which may suddenly arise. If cash is available with the firm, it may exploit such opportunities to bring in ample profits. But since such opportunities are occasional, cash for this purpose is held in form of near-cash assets.

Yet again, the bank where a firm maintains its account, asks it to maintain a minimum balance that acts as a guarantee and on which the bank normally does not pay interest. It may be mentioned that this balance, termed as compensating balance, does not improve firm's liquidity insofar as the firm cannot write cheques against it. Nevertheless, it forms a part of the firm's cash holding.

9.1.2 Ascertaining Cash Requirements

It has already been mentioned that cash planning essentially involves the estimation of the firm's cash requirements. Now the question is how this is done. The estimation is related to the cash required for transaction purposes, as the holdings governed by other motives are found in form of near-cash assets. This is normally done through the preparation of a cash budget, although the adjusted net income method is also relied upon for this purpose.

Cash Budget: A cash budget indicates various inflows and outflows of cash and the net position of cash during a particular period, say, a week, a fortnight, a month and so on. Table 9.1 shows how a cash budget is prepared showing the cash position during different months.

Table 9.1 Cash Budget

Item	*January*	*February*	*March*	*April*
A. Cash receipts (Rs)				
Cash sales	10,000	10,000	12,000	15,000
Credit sales	20,000	30,000	28,000	35,000
Total sales	30,000	40,000	40,000	50,000
Collections:				
Net 30 (60%)		12,000	18,000	16,800
Net 60 (40%)			8,000	12,000
Total receipts (A)	10,000	22,000	38,000	43,800
B. Cash payments (Rs)				
Purchases @ 60% of sales	18,000	24,000	24,000	30,000
Administrative exp	5,000	5,000	5,000	5,000
Interest	250	250	250	250
Taxes			1,000	
Total payments (B)	23,250	29,250	30,250	35,250
Net cash balance (A-B)	(13,250)	(7,250)	7,750	8,550

It is clear from Table 9.1 that during the first two months, the firm is running in deficit and so it requires borrowing at least to the extent shown as net cash balance. This borrowing will meet the transaction demand. Additional funds need to be borrowed for cash holdings under precautionary, speculative and other motives. The third and the fourth month show a positive cash balance that may be used for repayment of the borrowings or should be held in form of near-cash assets. Whenever required, the near-cash assets can be converted into cash. Here it may be pointed out that cash budget is only a rough estimate. Its proximity to accuracy depends on the extent to which accurate forecasts are made.

Adjusted Net Income Method: The contents of the adjusted net income forecast resemble the cash-flow statement where sources and uses of cash are presented. It projects a firm's need for cash at a future date and shows how far the firm is able to generate the desired funds internally.

Sensitivity Analysis: Whatever the figures of cash inflow or outflow or the sources and uses of cash are presented, they are the estimated ones. If the estimates are wrong, the whole exercise is futile. It is thus suggested that there should be at least three scenarios of forecast—optimistic, normal and pessimistic. And ultimately, all these figures should be put to a sensitivity analysis.

9.2 MANAGING CASH INFLOWS AND OUTFLOWS

After the cash requirements are assessed, the finance manager then strives to make do with a minimum level of cash. If the time lag between the cash inflows and cash outflows is significantly reduced, the cash requirement will definitely be lower. To this end, the finance manager expedites cash collection or cash inflows and controls disbursements or cash outflows.

9.2.1 The Concept of Float

Float represents the difference between the cash balance appearing in the bank records and that appearing in the firm's books. Positive float occurs when the firm makes payment. Negative float exists when payments made by the firm's customers are not credited to its bank account.

The process of accelerating cash collection and controlling disbursements is essentially related to the concept of float. Float represents the difference between the cash balance appearing in the bank records and that appearing in the firm's books. It may be either negative or positive. A negative float occurs when the firm receives payment. On the other hand, a positive float occurs when the firm makes payments. This means that a negative float exists when the customer has made payments for goods purchased to the firm but the amount does not stand credited to the firm's bank account. This is because there are different kinds of delays with respect to the crediting of the amount to the firm's bank account. If a customer posts the cheque for the payment, the firm may receive the cheque after, say, two days. This is known as a mailing delay. When the firm's office gets the cheque and if the office machinery is lax, the cheque is deposited with the bank not on the same day but the next day. This is known as a processing delay. Again, if the cheque is drawn on some other bank, the firm's banker may decide to get the cheque cleared before it credits the firm's account. This is nothing but a clearing delay. These delays create a float. In other words, a negative float is the sum of the mailing delay, processing delay and clearing delay. Thus, whenever one talks about the acceleration of the cash collection, the objective is to minimise the negative float so as to improve the cash holding without much delay as well as to reduce the cost of the float as far as is possible.

The of cost of float is the opportunity cost in terms of interest foregone on the uncredited amount of cash.

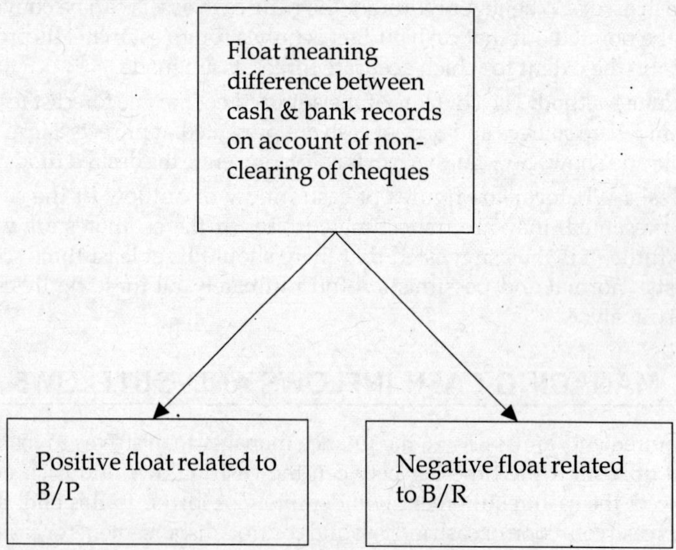

EXAMPLE

A firm receives a cheque of Rs 1000 on a particular day but the amount is credited only after four days. If the interest rate is 10%, the cost of float on this single transaction will be:

$$\text{Rs } 1000 \times 0.10 \times 4/365 = \text{Rs } 1.10.$$

9.2.2 Instruments of Cash Collection

In India, the instruments frequently used for cash collection are as follows:

1. Cheques
2. Drafts
3. Documentary bills
4. Trade bills
5. Letter of credit

Cheques are the instrument most frequently used for cash collection. This is because it is least cumbersome to issue cheques. Normally the amount of a cheque is credited after the cheque is cleared. But the cheques are also discounted at a very low charge. The only problem is that they sometimes bounce and also the clearing time for outstation cheques is very long.

Drafts are preferable to cheques insofar as they are subject to only local clearing and the clearing delay is minimum. But drafts are a costlier mode for those who make the payment.

The acceptance of documentary bill means that the drawee pays the amount after a specific period of time. The bills may be discounted by the drawer even before maturity after paying a nominal discounting charge. Trade bills carry no charge except for the stamp duty. But the procedure is relatively cumbersome. Moreover, the buyers sometimes do not adhere to the due date discipline.

Letters of credit assure the supplier that the goods will be released only after payment or acceptance of the bill. But they involves a number of charges, such as opening charges, negotiation charges, etc.

9.2.3 Ways to Accelerate Cash Collections

There are different ways of accelerating cash collection. They are as follows:

1. Creation of a wholly-owned collection centre;
2. Contracting out of the collection centres;
3. Appointing banks as collection agents;
4. Lock-box system;
5. Use of pre-authorised cheques;
6. Electronic funds transfer;
7. Netting of payments.

Creation of Wholly-owned Collection Centres: Under this method, a firm sets up its own collection centres in the cities where there are the majority of its customers. Customers mail their payments to these offices. The office receives the payments, processes them and records the transactions in the books of accounts. It then deposits the cheques with the designated bank and transmits payment to the central office. The benefit of this system is that the firm has full control over the collection process. Moreover, the collection centres perform additional functions too, such as collecting information about the changing creditworthiness of the customers in their respective areas.

Contracting out of Collection Centres: Sometimes the establishment cost of its own collection centres being large, the firm comes to an agreement with certain local firms that offer cash collection services. This procedure saves the establishment cost, but it is difficult to say how far the local firm will be interested in the collection of cheques.

Appointing Banks as Collection Agents: The firm may appoint a bank as its collection agent and inform the customers of that area to deposit cheques with the said bank. Normally, these banks are the branches of the bank with which the central office of the firm maintains its account. This reduces the clearing delay to a large extent. The problem, however, is that the firm has to meet the compensating balance requirements with all such branches and that entails upon the firm's liquidity. So this option is advantageous only when:

Opportunity cost savings on the float reduced > (compensating balance requirements + increased cost of bank charges + increase in administrative cost)

Lock-Box System: In this system customers mail their payments to a post-office box located in their region, from where the local bank collects the cheques and deposits them in the firm's account. The bank charges fees for collecting cheques but such charges account for only a fraction of the total amount of collection.

Sometimes the customers do not deposit cheques to the lock-box of their own region. Instead they mail their cheques to the lock-box of another zone if such practice result in cost savings.

Pre-authorised Cheques: Customers deposit with the supplier pre-signed cheques. The date of the cheque corresponds to the date when payment is due. The supplier deposits the cheque on the appointed date and the amount is credited to his account. It is highly convenient from the viewpoint of the supplier as the cheques are often credited even before the goods arrive at the customer's end.

Electronic Funds Transfer: Under this system, customer sends an electronic payment through the banking ACH system to the supplier's bank. The amount is credited immediately and the float is greatly reduced. At the international level, the Society for Worldwide Inter-bank Financial Telecommunication (SWIFT) system operates, this has reduced the float to the minimum possible level.

Netting of Payments: In cases of two-way payments where both parties have to receive payments from each other, the number of transactions and the amount involved

Chart 9.1 Functioning of the Lock-box System

therein can be significantly reduced through netting of payments. Naturally, the float involved in these transactions will also be reduced. Netting means that only the net amount is payable. Suppose A has to pay Rs 10 to B, and B has to pay Rs 3 to A. In a case of netting, A will pay B only Rs 7. Two transactions have thus been reduced to one and the amount involved has been reduced from Rs 10 to Rs 7. Netting may be bilateral when only two parties are involved. It may also be multilateral when more than two parties are involved.

Netting means that only the net amount is payable. Netting may be bilateral when only two parties are involved. It may also be multilateral when more than two parties are involved.

9.2.4 Controlling Disbursements

The firm should make full use of the credit period allowed to it. It may delay payment if it does not entail upon its creditworthiness or it does not involve any payment of interest. The instruments of payment are the same as the instruments of collection and so there is always the possibility of a positive float. The finance manager can estimate the size of float and can invest this amount during the float period in order to earn a return.

In order to delay the payments, the normal practice is to write a cheque on a distant bank, to call the recipient to verify the accounts, especially if large amount of money is involved, and to mail the cheque from a post-office located outside the area.

9.3 INVESTMENT OF SURPLUS CASH IN NEAR-CASH ASSETS

9.3.1 Determination of Ratio between Cash and Near-Cash Assets

It has already been pointed out that the funds for precautionary and speculative purposes are normally held in form of near-cash assets. Whenever required, they are converted into cash. The funds for transaction purposes are held in form of cash as they are required for day-to-day expenses. However, there is every possibility that the amount of cash is in excess of the actual requirements during a particular period, say, a week or a fortnight or a month. In such cases, the excess cash is invested in marketable securities for that period. The benefit of such investment is that the cash is not lying idle and the firm earns a specific return. But the problem is that the making of such investment or disinvestment in order to get the cash back involves a transaction cost or conversion cost. If on the other hand, no such investment is made, such conversion cost does not arise, but there exists an opportunity cost in terms of interest foregone. Thus the optimal balance of cash/near-cash assets, or in other words, the optimal ratio between cash and near-cash assets lies at a point where the sum of the opportunity cost and the conversion cost is the minimum. Fig. 9.1 shows that the opportunity cost rises and the conversion cost declines with an increase in the cash balance. The total cost declines in the beginning but then tends to rise. At Point E, it is the lowest and at this point the size of the cash balance shown by OM represents the optimal size. It means that any amount of cash beyond this point should be invested in the near-cash assets. As a natural corollary, optimal ratio between the cash and the near-cash assets is automatically determined.

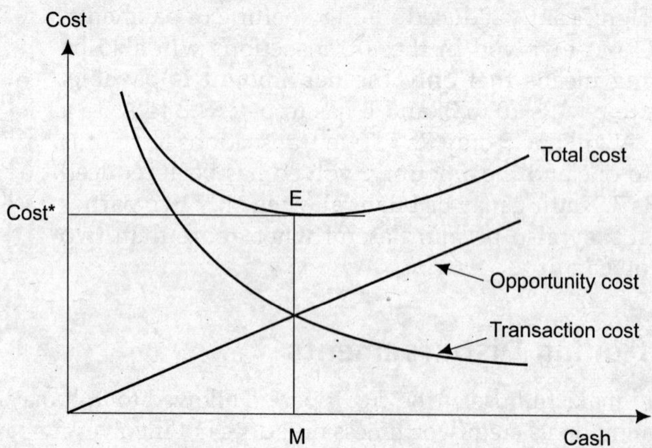

FIG. 9.1 Optimal balance of cash/near-cash assets

9.3.2 Optimal Cash Balance under Conditions of Certainty: Baumol Model

William J. Baumol (1952) developed a model showing how the optimal cash balance is determined. The model assumes that a firm's cash balance behaves over time in a saw-tooth manner, similarly, as in case of inventory meaning that the cash needs are known with certainty, the pattern of the payments is uniform, the opportunity cost is known and it does not fluctuates over time, and also the transaction cost is uniform.

Figure 9.2 shows how the level of cash tends to decline with its continuous use from its peak during t_0. The moment it reaches zero during t_1, fresh cash receipts take place through selling of securities and the level goes again to the peak in the beginning of the period t_1. Similar process takes place during the subsequent periods.

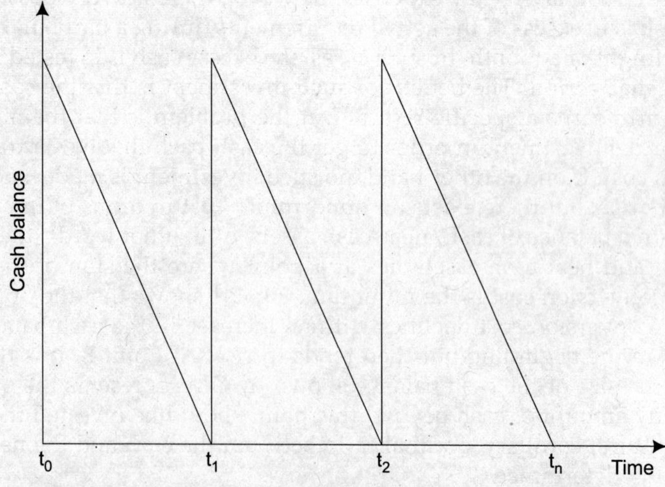

FIG. 9.2 Optimal level of cash and near-cash asset holding

The optimal level of cash during a particular period will be determined at a point where the sum of the conversion cost and the opportunity cost is the minimum. This is found when the conversion/transaction cost and the opportunity cost are equal. Mathematically, the optimal cash balance *O* will be equal to:

$$tT/O = iO/2$$

or $$2tT = iO^2$$

or $$O^2 = \frac{2tT}{i}$$

or $$O^2 = \sqrt{\frac{2tT}{i}} \qquad \text{... (9.1)}$$

Where:

t = transaction cost or conversion cost

T = total level of cash requirements during a particular period

i = opportunity cost in terms of interest foregone

EXAMPLE

A firm disburses Rs 20 lakh every year. The conversion charge is Rs 40 per conversion. The current risk-free interest rate is 10%. Therefore, the optimal cash balance (OCL) will be:

$$\text{OCL} = \text{Rs}\ \{(2 \times 20{,}00{,}000 \times 40)/0.10\}^{1/2} = \text{Rs}\ 40{,}000$$

9.3.3 Optimal Cash Balance under Uncertainty: The Miller-Orr Model

Baumol assumes the cash flow with certainty which is far from the real life situation. But the Miller-Orr model (1966) allows for a random variation in the cash flow. It assumes that the net cash flow is normally distributed with a zero value of mean and a standard deviation. It mentions the upper and lower limits of variation and also a return point. When the cash flow touches the upper limit, the finance manager buys marketable securities so that the cash level drops and attains the return point. On the other hand, when the level of cash touches the lower limit, the finance manager converts some of the marketable securities into cash in order to raise the cash level and attains the return point. The movement in cash balance is depicted in Fig. 9.3.

The difference between the upper limit and the lower limit depends on conversion cost, interest rate and the standard deviation of the net cash flows. This difference can be expressed as follows:

$$D = (3/4 \times t \times Var/i\,)^{1/3} \qquad \text{... (9.2)}$$

Where:

var = the cash flow variance.

i = interest rate per day

The upper limit (UL) = Lower limit (LL) + 3D ... (9.3)

Return point (RP) = LL + D ... (9.4)

Average cash balance = LL + 4/3D ... (9.5)

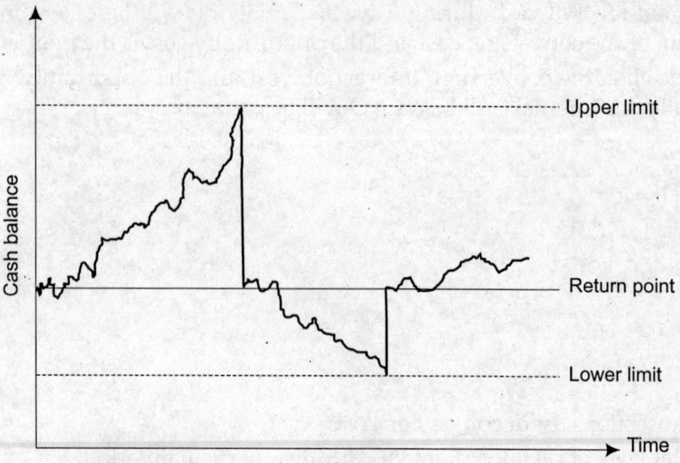

FIG. 9.3 Cash balances with the Miller-Orr model

i is interpreted in one day's interest rate or annual interest rate divided by 365. Sometimes the one-day interest rate is found out on the basis of compound interest rate formula but normally, the simple interest rate formula is used.

EXAMPLE

A firm maintains a minimum cash balance of Rs 10,000. Standard deviation of the daily cash flow is Rs 2,000. The annual interest rate is 10%. The conversion cost is Rs 40 per transaction. Find out the upper limit, return point and average cash balance.

$$D = \{3/4 \times 40 \times 40{,}00{,}000/(0.10/365)\}^{1/3}$$
$$= \text{Rs } 7{,}594$$

$$\text{Upper limit} = 10{,}000 + (3 \times 7594) = \text{Rs } 32{,}782$$
$$\text{Return point} = 10{,}000 + 7{,}594 = \text{Rs } 17{,}594$$
$$\text{Average cash balance} = 10{,}000 + (7{,}594 \times 4/3) = \text{Rs } 20{,}125$$

All this means that the moment the firm's cash balance touches Rs 32,782, the finance manager will convert part of the cash into marketable securities so that the cash component drops to Rs 17,594. Again, if the level of cash touches the lower limit of Rs 10,000, marketable securities will be converted into cash so as to achieve a cash balance of Rs 17,594.

9.3.4 Selection of Near-Cash Assets

Features of the Securities: A firm should select those securities that give high return and possess low risk. The higher the risk, the greater the chance of the emergence of the problem of illiquidity. Thus there should be a trade-off between profitability and liquidity.

Again, the maturity of the securities should coincide with the period of additional cash requirements. If this is the case, there would be no problem in meeting cash requirements.

Yet again, the securities must be easily marketable, so that, whenever necessary, they can be sold to obtain cash. This is all because liquidity reigns supreme in working capital management.

Form of the Securities: There are a few short-term investment instruments that have the feature of safety, shorter maturities and easy marketability. More common among of them are:

1. Treasury bills: These are short-term government securities and are, therefore, safe. In India, they are sold at discount and are redeemed at par on maturity. They can be bought at any given time.
2. Certificates of deposit: It is the bank that issues certificates of deposit. They are analogous to short-term fixed deposits. They are negotiable instruments and so carry enough of liquidity.
3. Commercial paper: These are issued by highly-rated companies asking for short-term funds with a maturity of 3 months to 1 year. They are explained at some length in Chapter 12.
4. Bank deposits: Banks accept short-term fixed deposits ranging from 30 days to 45 days. They may even be for longer maturities.
5. Inter-corporate deposits: It is frequently found that a company deposits its excess cash with another company. Risk is high in such cases and so inter-corporate deposits are normally found among companies of the same ownership.
6. Money market mutual funds: They have recently emerged in India. Unit Trust of India, Industrial Development Bank of India, etc., have started such schemes. They focus on short-term marketable securities and have a normal lock-in period of 30 days.

9.4 CASH MANAGEMENT IN INTERNATIONAL FIRMS

Cash management in an international firm is comparatively a more complex task. This is because the intra-firm transfer of funds is a common feature. The tax rate and interest rate vary between countries. Exchange rate is subject to frequent changes. Political, legal, economic and other features of the environment in different host countries are not fully known to the parent unit. And above all, the host government often places restrictions on the transfer of funds across the national boundaries.

Against this background, it is worthwhile to explain, first, the intra-firm transfer of funds in the face of restrictions; and second, the investment of surplus cash at a particular international location.

9.4.1 Intra-firm Transfer of Funds in Presence of Exchange Control

In presence of exchange control, a multinational enterprise adopts the following methods for transferring cash from one unit to other. They are as follows:

1. Transfer pricing;
2. Parallel loans;
3. Leads and lags;

4. Changes in the rates of royalty and other fees;
5. Changes in dividend pay-out ratio;
6. Use of blocked funds.

Transfer Pricing: Transfer pricing is nothing but under-invoicing and over-invoicing of export and import so that funds could be transferred under the garb of such practices. For example, if an Indian firm has to transfer funds from India to its subsidiary in the USA, it will under-invoice its export to the subsidiary and/or over-invoice its import from the subsidiary.

Transfer pricing is nothing but under-invoicing and over-invoicing of export and import so that funds can be transferred under the garb of such practices.

Parallel Loans: A parallel loan is often known as back-to-back loan or credit swap loan. Under this arrangement, the amount of the loan moves within the country but it serves the purpose of cross-border loan. At the same time, such loans are not exposed to the changes in exchange rate because the funds do not move across national borders. Suppose a US company (parent company) has a subsidiary in India. At the same time, an Indian company (parent company) has a subsidiary in the USA. Suppose further that the US parent company has to lend US $1000 to its subsidiary in India for a specific period. The Indian parent company too has to lend to its subsidiary in the USA a similar amount for the same maturity. In such cases, to avoid restrictions on transfer, the Indian parent company will lend the above amount converted into rupees at the spot exchange rate to the US subsidiary. Simultaneously, the US parent company will lend a similar amount in terms of US dollars to the Indian subsidiary. On the expiry of the specified period, the two loans will be repaid to the respective lenders.

Leads and Lags: Leading means shortening of credit terms in number of days, while lagging means extending or enlarging of the days of credit. Shortening of the period of credit causes greater flow of cash from the purchaser (importer) to the seller (exporter). Lagging, on the other hand, causes flow of cash from exporter to importer. Suppose Unit A regularly supplies raw material to Unit B worth Rs 20 lakh a month on 90-day credit. The average size of receivables will be Rs 60 lakh. Suppose further that Rs 40 lakh of cash has to be transferred from B to A, there will be a leading of the credit terms to 30 days. This will reduce the size of receivables to Rs 20 lakh and it will result in the flow of cash worth Rs 40 lakh from B to A. If, on the other hand, a sum of Rs 60 lakh has to be transferred from A to B, the terms of credit will be lagged to 180 days. The average size of receivables will move up to Rs 1.2 crore. It will represent a cash flow of Rs 60 lakh from A to B during the 3-month period. Leads and lags are practised in face of exchange control insofar as the governments are less likely to interfere with the payment terms. However, benefit from this process cannot be thought of in isolation of the borrowing and the lending rate.

As in the case of royalty, an increase in the dividend pay-out ratio helps the subsidiary transfer funds to the parent company. The lowering of the ratio leads to a reverse flow.

Changes in the Rate of Royalty and Other Fees: The rate of royalty and other fees are fixed by an agreement between the parent company and its subsidiary. But when possible, the parent company makes changes in these rates for the purpose of transfer of liquidity. If the subsidiary is cash-surplus and it has to remit the surplus to the parent company, the latter will raise the rate of royalty and other fees. On the contrary, the rates will be lowered if the subsidiary is cash-deficit. The lowering of rates will help the subsidiary to conserve cash. However, host governments do not usually like such changes.

Changes in the Dividend Pay-out Ratio: As in the case of royalty, an increase in the dividend pay-out ratio helps the subsidiary transfer funds to the parent company. The lowering of the ratio leads to a reverse flow. This is a very common method as around one-half of total remittances to US firms by their affiliates is represented by such payments.

However, in view of uniformity in the dividend pay-out ratio in line with that of the parent company, any wide deviation in this ratio is not possible. Moreover, liquidity transfer through changes in the dividend pay-out ratio depends to a considerable extent on the cost of alternative sources of funds. This ratio can easily and preferably be raised if the cost of borrowing is lower than the opportunity cost of the cash balance in the host country. Again, changes in the ratio depend also upon the differential between the tax rate on dividend pay-out and the tax rate on retained earnings. If the latter is higher, the parent company will prefer to raise the dividend pay-out ratio. Nevertheless, strict controls on dividend flow exercised by host governments come in the way of this practice. Additionally, some firms relishing the idea of dividend stability do not permit abrupt changes in the dividend pay-out ratio.

Use of Blocked Funds: If there exist blocked funds in a host country as a sequel to restrictions on the transfer of funds, it is the motive of the parent company to use that amount either in that host country itself or in any other country through transfer pricing, leading and lagging, use of fronting loans, creation of unrelated export, etc.

Here it may be explained that a fronting loan is a parent to affiliate loan channelled via a financial intermediary, usually an international bank. Suppose for the moment that a US subsidiary in India has blocked funds which cannot be transferred to US parent on account of exchange control prevalent in India. Now the US parent would like to use this fund. If it prefers to use a fronting loan, it will authorise an international bank that has an office in India to make a loan for that amount to the US subsidiary in India. In fact, it will simply front for the parent. After the lapse of a specified period, the subsidiary will repay the loan to the international bank and the repaid amount will be passed on to the parent. Here the bank will be interested in this function insofar as the interest paid by the bank on the deposit will be lower than the interest received on account of loan.

If there exist blocked funds in a host country as a sequel to restrictions on the transfer of funds, it is the motive of the parent company to use that amount either in that host country itself or in any other country through transfer pricing, leading and lagging, use of fronting loans, creation of unrelated export, etc.

Creation of unrelated export is another method. Since the creation of additional export needs some amount of additional investment that will come out of blocked funds, the parent company emphasises on the creation of additional export by the subsidiary. Again, the additional export may be a barter deal in which the US subsidiary in India in our example may normally export those items that are not in demand abroad. This way the barter deal will not affect India's export to the general currency area, and, at the same time, the blocked funds will be utilised for making exports.

Again, if blockage is only temporary, it is better to invest the blocked funds in the money market of the host country itself. If the money market is not well developed, the subsidiary can invest the blocked funds in certain industries. If this channel too is not possible, the blocked funds can be used to purchase an asset, the value of which can rise with an increase in the inflation rate.

9.4.2 Investment of Surplus Cash

As far as investment of surplus cash is concerned, it is necessary to examine whether the process should be centralised; and secondly, which country the funds should be invested in.

> The process of centralisation of surplus cash can take two forms: first, the centralised control of the parent company over the surplus cash of different units; second, the actual movement of cash to a centralised pool.

The process of centralisation of surplus cash can take two forms. First, the centralised control of the parent company over the surplus cash of different units. In this case, cash does not actually move to a centralised pool, but its movement to a cash-deficit unit or for investment in near-cash assets is strictly guided by the parent company. Second, is the actual movement of cash to a centralised pool. Any investment in near-cash assets takes place only out of the centralised pool. Since the working capital management among different units of a multinational enterprise is designed to maximise the benefit of the firm as a whole, it is always better to have centralisation of decision. In case of centralisation, the funds of the firm are invested in the most desirable way so as to avoid the weaknesses of some of the host-country currencies. Whenever any unit falls into liquidity distress, funds are immediately rushed to it.

However, when a central pool is maintained, some precautions should be taken. First, each of the units should have smooth cash collection and disbursement procedures. Second, each of them should be aware of the quantum of cash inflow and cash outflow at a particular point of time. Third, the system of movement of cash to and from the pool should not face any restrictions. Fourth, the information system must be substantially improved.

The centralised pool may be located either in the host country or in the home country or in a third country where the currency is strong, the money market is developed, the tax rate is low and political and legal climate is congenial.

SUMMARY

The very objective behind the management of cash is to determine the optimal level of cash holding so that the cost of holding does not mount, and at the same time, it meets the different purposes for which cash is held. The motives behind cash holding are transaction motive, precautionary motive, speculative motive, exploitation of investment opportunities and compensating balance requirements.

The first step in the management of cash is to assess the size of cash requirements for which cash budget is normally prepared. However, the finance manager tries to do with the minimum possible level of cash and to this end he or she accelerates cash collection through reducing negative float and controls the disbursement procedure.

The finance manager tries to determine the optimal level of cash so that the excess cash at a particular point of time may be invested in short-term marketable securities or near-cash assets so as to earn a specific rate of return. This level is determined through a trade-off between conversion cost and opportunity cost in terms of interest foregone. Baumol has presented an inventory model for cash that takes into account the transaction cost and the opportunity cost. However, since cash forecasts cannot be made with certainty, the Miller—Orr model suggests a range, that is, an upper limit, a lower limit and a return point between which the cash balance moves and an optimal balance between cash and near-cash assets is maintained.

Whenever excess cash is invested in form of treasury bills, commercial papers, certificates of deposit, bank deposits, inter-corporate deposits, etc., care is taken that the investment is safe, that it possesses easy marketability and that its maturity coincides with the need for cash.

An international firm too follows the same rules. But the cash management in this case is complex, especially in view of the varying exchange rate, tax rate, interest rate and political, legal and economic environment. It adopts various techniques to help transfer funds across countries when restrictions on transfer exist. It also takes care in which countries it will invest the surplus cash.

POINTS TO REMEMBER

1. What are the different aspects/stages of cash management?
   - Cash planning in order to know about cash requirements
   - Expediting cash inflows and delaying cash outflows
   - Investment of surplus cash in near-cash assets or short-term marketable securities
2. What are the steps in cash planning?
   - To determine how much cash will be required during a period for transaction, precautionary, speculative and other purposes
   - To prepare proforma cash budget showing inflow and outflow of cash and the net requirements
3. How is cash inflow expedited?
   - It is through shortening of the negative float that can be done through:
     - Creation of a wholly-owned collection centre
     - Contracting out of the collection centres
     - Appointing banks as a collection agent
     - Creating lock-box system
     - Use of pre-authorised cheques
     - Electronic transfer of funds
     - Netting of payments

4. What is float? Distinguish between negative float and positive float.
    - Float represents the difference between cash balance shown by bank records and that appearing in the firm's records.
    - Negative float arises when payments by the debtors do not appear in the bank's records.
    - Positive float arises when payments made by the firm to the supplier are not shown by the bank records.
5. What is the optimal size of cash invested in near-cash assets?
    - Under the conditions of certainty, it is where the opportunity cost and transaction cost are equal making the total cost minimum.
    - Under the conditions of uncertainty, the cash level moves between a lower limit and an upper limit. The residue is invested in near-cash assets.
6. What are the common forms of near-cash assets?
    - Treasury bills
    - Certificates of deposit
    - Commercial papers
    - Bank and inter-corporate deposits
    - Money market mutual funds
7. What are the ways of intra-firm transfer of funds in an MNC?
    - Transfer pricing
    - Parallel loan
    - Changes in dividend pay-out and royalty rates
    - Use of blocked funds

DESCRIPTIVE QUESTIONS

1. What are the motives that influence the holding of cash in a firm?
2. Explain with an example how cash requirements in a particular period are assessed.
3. What is float in the context of cash management? Explain positive and negative float.
4. Name some common instruments for cash collection. What are the ways in which cash collection is accelerated?
5. The determination of the ratio between cash and near-cash assets is based on a trade-off between opportunity cost and conversion cost. Discuss.
6. Explain the Baumol model for cash level determination.
7. How is the Miller-Orr model different from the Baumol model? How do you determine the upper limit, point of return and the average cash level under the Miller-Orr model?
8. Name some short-term marketable securities. Explain the criteria adopted in their selection.
9. What are the different modes of intra-firm transfer of funds in the presence of restrictions imposed by the host government?

OBJECTIVE-TYPE QUESTIONS

1. Mark true or false.
   (a) Cash required for precautionary purposes is normally held in form of near-cash assets.
   (b) Negative float occurs when a firm makes payment.
   (c) Float is normally the sum of mailing, processing and clearing delays expressed in number of days.
   (d) A firm can invest the cash meant for payment during the positive float.
   (e) Baumol explains the cash holding principle under conditions of certainty.
   (f) Intra-firm transfer of funds is common among multinational firms.
2. Choose the most suitable answer.
   (a) Size of cash holding under precautionary motive is:
      (i) almost fixed
      (ii) variable
      (iii) highly variable
   (b) Float exists when:
      (i) cash balance in the cash book differs from that with the bank
      (ii) company floats shares in the market
      (iii) none of the above
   (c) Negative float will occur when:
      (i) firms receive payment
      (ii) firms make payment
      (iii) both of the above
   (d) Netting:
      (i) reduces transaction cost
      (ii) increases transaction cost
      (iii) has no impact on transaction cost
   (e) Leading means:
      (i) shortening the period of credit
      (ii) lengthening the credit period
      (iii) neither of the above
   (f) Centralised cash pool is located in a country where:
      (i) tax rate is very high
      (ii) tax rate is very low
      (iii) political instability is a big problem
   (g) Fronting loan:
      (i) is a parent to affiliate loan channelled through a financial intermediary
      (ii) is an inter-firm loan
      (iii) none of the above

NUMERICAL PROBLEMS

1. A firm disburses Rs 30 lakh every year. Conversion charge is Rs 50 per conversion. The current risk-free interest rate is 9%. Find out the optimal cash balance using Baumol model.
2. A firm maintains a minimum cash balance of Rs 20,000. Standard deviation of the daily cash flow is Rs 2,500. The annual interest rate is 9%. The conversion cost is Rs 50 per transaction. Find out the upper limit, return point and average cash balance using the Miller—Orr technique.
3. Everyday a company receives an average of Rs 50,000 in the form of cheques. As per the practice, the cheques are deposited with the banker only twice a week: Wednesday and Friday. If the interest rate on bank overdraft is 16%, find out the weekly cost of float.
4. A firm sells goods of Rs 1,00,000 every month. 20% of the sale is made on cash terms, 40% on net 30 and the rest 40% on net 60. If the sale begins in January, find out the cash balance with the firm on the sale account during January, February and March.
5. A company has a collection of Rs 5,00,000 per day. Mailing and processing delay account for 6 days. If a lock-box system is introduced, delay is reduced to 3 days but the annual cost of the lock-box system comes to Rs 50,000. Find:
   (a) how much cash is released on account of shortening of mailing and processing delay.
   (b) what will be annual benefit on account of lock-box system if the released amount is invested at 10% p.a.
6. The annual disbursements in a company amounts to Rs 30,00,000. The conversion charge for converting surplus cash into marketable securities is Rs 30 per conversion. The risk-free interest is 10%. Find the optimal cash balance as per Baumol's model.
7. Find out the size of cash required each time to restore balance to minimum cash if the cash inflow is Rs 30 crore, the return on marketable securities is 8% and the transfer cost from securities to cash is Rs 125 each time a transfer occurs.

SOLVED NUMERICAL PROBLEMS

1. A firm sells its final products for Rs 2,00,000 per month, 80% of which is sold on net 30 terms. The cost of material accounts for 60% of the sale value and the operating cost amounts to 10% of the sale value: The firm has to make interest payment of Rs 10,000 every month. Find the monthly cash requirements of the firm.

Solution

Proforma Cash Budget

	Month 1	*Month 2*	*Month 3*
Revenue			
Month 1 Sales	40,000	1,60,000	–
Month 2 Sales	–	40,000	1,60,000
Month 3 Sales	–	–	40,000
Total cash inflow	40,000	2,00,000	2,00,000
Expenses			
Cost of goods	1,20,000	1,20,000	1,20,000
Operating expenses	20,000	20,000	20,000
Interest payment	10,000	10,000	10,000
Total cash outflow	1,50,000	1,50,000	1,50,000
Cash required/surplus	1,10,000 (Required)	50,000 (Surplus)	50,000(Surplus)

Surplus cash may be invested in near-cash assets.

2. A firm expects that the adoption of lock-box system will shorten the cash collection by 3 days. Credit sales amount to Rs 7,20,00,000 per year billed on a continuous basis. The cost of lock-box system is Rs 50,000. The opportunity cost of funds is 15%. Find the gain/loss of the lock-box system.

Solution

Cash released through the lock-box system
= (7,20,00,000 /360) x 3 = Rs 6,00,000
Savings = Rs 6,00,000 x 0.15 = Rs 90,000
Cost of lock-box system = Rs 50000
Net savings = Rs 90,000 – 50,000 = Rs 40,000

3. An electronic transfer of funds saves 3 days' time of float. The daily interest rate is 0.025%. The cost of electronic transfer is Rs 8. Find how large the amount of transfer should be to justify the additional cost of electronic transfer.

Solution

Break-even level for the funds to be transferred =
Funds to be transferred/(Interest saving x no. of days)
= Rs 8/(0.00025 x 3) = Rs 10,667

4. Find out the optimal cash balance if a firm pays out Rs 1,00,000 per month. The investment in marketable securities gives 8% p.a. but the transaction cost is Rs 20 per transaction.

Solution

Based on Eq. 9.1,

Optimal cash balance = $\sqrt{}$ (2 × 1,00,000 × 12 × 20) / 0.08

= $\sqrt{}$ Rs 60,00,00,000

= Rs 24,495

5. A company requires Rs 50 lakh to cover its transaction requirements during a year. It holds marketable securities of an equivalent amount that yield 20%. The transaction cost is Rs 200 per transaction. If the optimal size of conversion of securities into cash is Rs 1 lakh, calculate the total transaction and opportunity cost for the optimal size.

Solution

No. of transactions =. 50,00,000/1,00,000 = 50

Total transaction cost = Rs 200 x 50 = Rs 10,000

Opportunity cost = Rs 1,00,000 x 0.20/2 = Rs 10,000

Total cost (opportunity and transaction costs) = Rs 10,000 + 10,000 = Rs 20,000

6. A company writes cheques for Rs 20,000 per day on an average. The cheque takes 5 days to be cleared. On the other hand, the company receives Rs 22,000 per day on an average. Float in this case is 3 days. Calculate negative and positive floats. What would be the annual saving if the negative float reduces to 1 day, with interest rate being 6%?

Solution

Positive float = Rs 20,000 x 5	=	Rs 1,00,000
Less Negative float = Rs 22,000 x 3	=	Rs 66,000
Net float		Rs 34,000

Annual interest earnings when negative float reduces to one day

= Rs 22,000 x 2 x 0.06 = Rs 2,640

7. Find the average cash balance based on Miller—Orr model, if a firm maintains a minimum cash balance of Rs 5,000, variance of daily cash balance is Rs 1,000, conversion cost is Rs 20, and the interest rate per annum is 10%.

Solution

Based on Eq. 9.2,

D = $\{(3/4 \times 20 \times 1000)/(0.10/365)\}^{1/3}$

= Rs 379.7055

Average cash balance = Rs 5,000 + (379.7055 x 4/3) = Rs 5506.27

Mini Case

Bhushan Cosmetics was established 15 years ago. In the beginning, it was limited to mail-order business but now it is carrying out full-fledged business over a well-spread geographic area. In view of a very big area where its customers are spread-over, it is in a mood to restructure its cash collection policy.

Presently, it has 20 lock box centres. Each centre handles Rs. 60,000 of collection per day. The collections are invested in short-term marketable securities every day at the collection centre banks. After every 15 days, the invested amount is wire-transferred to the head office. The income from the investment is 0.012 per cent per day and the wire transfer cost is 0.15 per cent of the amount transferred.

Bhushan Industries is considering setting up a concentration banking centre which will accept daily collections from the lock-box centres that will be passed on to the head office through clearing. The clearing delay is one day. The cleared funds will be deposited in a short-term account yielding 0.015 per cent a day. Each clearing transfer costs Rs. 150. The finance manager has to decide whether the new alternative is useful.

Questions:

1. Find the size of total net cash flow from the existing lock box system.
2. Do you advocate for the new collection system based on concentration banking?

REFERENCES

Baumol, W.J. (1952). "The Transactions Demand for Cash: An Inventory Theoretic Approach", *Quarterly Journal of Economics*, 66 (Nov.): 545–56.

Miller, M.H. and D. Orr (1966). "A Model for the Demand for Money by Firms", *Quarterly Journal of Economics*, 80 (Aug.): 413–35.

SELECT FURTHER READINGS

Finnerty, J.E. ed. (1993). *Planning Cash Flow*. New York: AMACOM Books.

Gallinger, G.W. and P.B. Healey (1991). *Liquidity Analysis and Management*. Reading M.A.: Addison-Wesley.

Vander Weide, J. and S.F. Maier (1985). *Managing Corporate Liquidity*. New York: John Wiley & Sons.

10

MANAGEMENT OF ACCOUNTS RECEIVABLE

OBJECTIVES

To assess the benefits and costs of maintaining accounts receivable

To show how the credit policy of a firm is designed

To show how customers are selected to whom credit facilities are to be granted

To explain how the credit level is monitored and controlled

> In accounting terms, accounts receivable are known as sundry debtors. But, in finance, sundry debtors are only a part of total accounts receivable.

A large part of the goods produced by a firm are sold on credit. As a result, accounts receivable emerge. They exist until they are converted into cash, that is, until the supplier of the goods receives payment for them. In accounting terms, accounts receivable are known as sundry debtors. However, the two terms are not entirely the same. Accounts receivable come into existence even when a firm makes advance payments to the supplier of the inputs in order to ensure their timely and uninterrupted supply. Sundry debtors are only a major part of the total accounts receivable.

In the past, credit sales were secured by bills of exchange or promissory notes, but now this practice has been largely discontinued. Rather, credit sales are made on "open accounts" which do not require any formal bill or note. Whatever may be the practice, the present chapter discusses the major aspects of accounts receivable.

10.1 BENEFITS AND COSTS OF ACCOUNTS RECEIVABLE

10.1.1 Benefits

Cash sales are free from bad debt losses, yet firms rely more on the credit-sale system as it possesses many advantages. These are as follows:

Greater Sales and Profitability: Credit sales help boost the volume of sales and help improve the firm's competitiveness in the market. This in turn leads to higher profitability. There are many reasons for greater sales. First, the buyers prefer to buy on credit terms as this improves their liquidity. Second, there are certain marginal customers who can buy only on credit terms. They can only make payments after they resell the goods and, thereby, get cash to make payments. Third, the price of the products in the hands of the consumers is lower because of the time value of money. This is why customers tend to cluster where they can buy goods on the most liberal terms of credit.

Absorbing Fluctuations in Demand: Credit sales bring about not only greater sales but also absorb the shocks of fluctuations in demand. When demand for a product shrinks, the firm makes the terms of the credit liberal. It is thus able to sell a larger amount of goods and maintains the demand for the product at the earlier level.

Providing Liquidity to the Firm: Accounts receivable provide liquidity to the firm, especially, when there is sudden drop in liquidity. When there is a desired amount of liquidity, the firm can lend a part of its liquid resources directly to its customers in the form of trade credit for a specific period. During the period of shortage of liquidity, it can ask for repayment of credit. In cases where the firm draws bills of exchange, the bill can be discounted with the bank and the liquidity needs can be met.

Effecting Price Discrimination: Accounts receivable are a tool for price discrimination. Since the credit term has an impact on the price of the product, the firm can use different credit terms for different market segments. In markets where the demand for the product is established, credit term may not be very liberal. On the other hand, in newly discovered markets where the firm has to enlarge its share, credit terms may be liberal.

> Cash sales are free from bad debt losses, yet firms rely more on the credit-sale system as it possesses many advantages.

Encouraging Intermediaries: In a country like India where the fund requirements of market intermediaries are crucial and the banks do not attach importance to them, trade credit acts as an incentive to these intermediaries. The intermediary—wholesaler or retailer—is able to sell the products of a manufacturer offering liberal credit terms faster. This is because the products are available to him on credit terms.

10.1.2 Costs

Benefits from the receivables are only one side of the coin. Finance managers cannot continue either increasing the size of the credit sales or making the terms of credit more liberal indefinitely, insofar as the costs will begin outweigh the benefits. The costs are many; they are the financing cost, administrative cost, collection cost and bad debt losses.

Financing Cost: Accounts receivable tie up a part of the firm's financial resources. These financial resources may be either owner's capital or the creditor's capital. In both the cases, there exists cost of funds that is calculated on the basis of their marginal increase or decrease caused by the changes in the size of receivables. Suppose a firm has Rs 50,000 in debt financed at the rate of 10% and a part of this amount is financing Rs 20,000 receivables with the net 30 term. If the average size shrinks to Rs 15,000 in the wake of the firm's stringent credit policy, a part of the funds would be untied, as a result, there would be a saving in the financing cost to the extent of 0.10 × (20,000 – 15,000) = Rs 500. If, on the other hand, the average size of receivables swells to Rs 30,000 as a sequel to a liberal credit policy, the additional financing cost would be equal to 0.10 × (30,000 – 20,000) = Rs 1,000

Here it would be relevant to know how the average size of receivables is calculated on different credit terms. Average size of receivables (AR) can be calculated as follows:

AR = Sales/Accounts receivable turnover

Where:

Accounts receivable turnover = 360/average collection period

Where:

Average collection period = net period + % of late payment x net period ...(10.1)

EXAMPLE

A net 30 term accounts for a sale of Rs 20,00,000. There are 20% of the customers who do not make payments in time. Find out the average collection period and the average size of receivables.

Average collection period = 30 + 20/100 × 30 = 36 days

Average size of receivables = 20,00,000/360 × 36 = Rs 2,00,000.

Again, if the credit term is 2/10 net 30 and 70% of the customers avail of the discount, the average collection period will be computed as follows:

% taking discount × discount period + % not taking discount × (net period + % of late payment × net period)

And on this basis, the average collection period will be equal to:

(0.7 × 10) + 0.3 (30 + 0.2 × 30) = 18 days

Average size of receivables = 20,00,000/360 × 18 = Rs 1,00,000.

After the calculation of the average size of receivables, it would be easy to know how much funds are additionally tied up with them and what is the financing cost.

Administrative Cost: Maintenance of receivables requires the employment of personnel, some office space to keep records, expenses on account of correspondence and investigation of the creditworthiness of the customers. Administrative expenses grow with the growing size of receivables, although not proportionately.

Collection Cost: If the bills are not paid in time, the firm has to make efforts for their collection first through correspondence and then through agents. It is found that if receivables rise by a fixed percentage, collection cost would change by the same percentage. For example, if collection cost amounts to Rs 2,000 with receivables of Rs 1,00,000, ratio of collection cost is 2%. After a liberal credit policy raises the size of receivables to Rs 1,50,000, the collection cost should mount to Rs 3,000.

Bad Debt Losses: Bad debt losses occur even after serious collection efforts, inasmuch as there are always some high-risk customers. The more liberal the credit policy, the greater are the bad debt losses. Normally, such losses rise at a faster rate than the rate of increase in the size of receivables.

10.2 CREDIT POLICY

10.2.1 Optimising the Term of Credit

Whether the credit policy is tight or liberal depends upon what the term of the credit is. A credit term with longer period for making payments is supposed to be liberal. For example, a net 60 credit term is more liberal than a net 30 credit term. It also depends on whether the term includes any discount if payment is made by a section of the customers at any time earlier than the stipulated date. For example, a credit term of 2/10 net 30 means that the amount is to be paid within 30 days, but a customer will be entitled to a 2% discount if he or she pays the amount within 10 days.

Maximising the Value of the Firm: A firm cannot go on liberalising its credit policy indefinitely. This is because benefits would cease to accrue and costs would escalate with the size of receivables becoming unmanageable. So the question is uptil which point should the credit policy be liberalised. If the goal of managing accounts receivable is to enhance the value of the corporate wealth, the firm has to see that:

1. The incremental profit on account of changes in the credit terms should be positive; or
2. Expected return from additional investment in receivables must be higher than the required rate of return.

As far as the incremental profit is concerned, it depends on the increased revenue on account of increased sales vis-à-vis different costs involved in the increased size of receivables. Since the fixed costs are by definition fixed within a relevant range of production, it is, therefore, the variable costs that are considered for the purpose of computation. The variable costs are normally the cost of raw material, collection expenses, financing cost and the bad debt losses related to the additional credit sales. These costs are deducted from the additional sale amount in order to reach the incremental profit. Incremental profit can be expressed as follows:

$$P = s - (sv + sc + sb + ivt \times s/365) \qquad ...(10.2)$$

Where:

P = incremental profit
s = additional sales due to liberal credit policy
v = variable cost of sales in percentage
c = additional collection cost in percentage terms
b = additional bad debt losses in percentage terms
i = opportunity of cost of capital in percentage terms
t = credit period

EXAMPLE

A company relaxes the credit period to 90 days, as a result of which sales revenue increases by Rs 5000; collection cost increases by 3%; bad debt increases by 2%; opportunity cost of capital is 20%; and variable cost is 80%. Find out the incremental profit.

$$P = 5000 - \{(5000 \times 0.8) + (5000 \times 0.03) + (5000 \times 0.02) + 0.20 \times 0.80 \times 90 \times 5000/365\}$$
$$= \text{Rs } 553$$

Now the expected rate of return (ERR) can be expressed as follows:

$$ERR = \Delta \text{ Operating profit after tax} / \Delta \text{ Investment in accounts receivables} \quad ...(10.3)$$

As far as the increase in investment in accounts receivable is concerned, it depends upon the increase in the average size of receivables, the computation of which has already been explained in the preceding section. On the other hand, the operating profit after tax is found out by subtracting the variable cost of material and the variable operating expenses from the additional sale revenue and then subjecting the balance to the tax rate. Fixed operating costs are not included as they are fixed within a relevant range.

Similarly, the required rate of return will be the risk-adjusted cost of capital. Here risk adjustment is necessary in view of the fact that the element of risk increases with an increase in the size of receivables.

When the three variables, viz., additional investment in accounts receivable, additional operating profit and the required rate of return are computed, it is easy to know whether liberalisation in credit terms has added to the corporate wealth.

EXAMPLE

Liberalisation in credit policy raises the average size of receivables by Rs 50,000 and the operating profits by Rs 20,000. Tax rate is 35% and required rate of return is 20%. Find out whether liberalisation in the credit policy is justified.

Expected rate of return.

$$ERR = \{20{,}000\ (1 - 0.35)\}/50{,}000 = 0.26 = 26\%$$

Here ERR > required rate of return, So the liberalisation in the credit policy is justified on account of enhancing the corporate wealth.

A particular credit term will be an optimal one when the ERR exceeds the required rate of return by the largest margin.

Proforma Income Statement: The other way to determine the optimal credit term is to prepare a proforma income statement for each possible term of credit. Table 10.1 incorporates such a statement where sale amounts as well different costs vary with the changing credit terms. The optimal credit term is 2/10 net 60 where the net profit is the largest. Nevertheless, the finance manager should compare the profit forecast with the growth prospects and take into account other vital variables before taking a final decision regarding the credit term.

10.2.2 Changes in Credit Standard

The above discussion shows how the optimal credit policy is determined. However, it will not be irrelevant if we discuss here the impact of the changes in the credit standards. It has already been mentioned that any liberalisation in the terms of credit leads to an increase in the amount of sales and the average size of receivables, but, at the same time, causes an increase in the costs related to the receivables. In this respect, Dyl (1977) is of opinion that a change in the credit standard and a change in the period of credit have varying consequences. Relaxation in credit standards implies that credit is also being extended to

Table 10.1 Proforma Income Statement with Varying Credit Terms

Items	*No credit (Rs)*	*Net 30 (Rs)*	*2/10 net 30 (Rs)*	*Net 60 (Rs)*	*2/10 net 60 (Rs)*
Sales	1,50,000	2,00,000	2,00,000	2,50,000	2,50,000
Cost of goods (50–60%)	90,000	1,20,000	1,20,000	1,25,000	1,25,000
Gross margin	60,000	80,000	80,000	1,25,000	1,25,000
Administrative cost	15,000	20,000	20,000	25,000	25,000
Collection cost	–	6,000	5,000	12,000	10,000
Bad debt losses		8,000	7,000	20,000	18,000
Discounts taken			2,800		3,500
EBIT	45,000	46,000	45,200	68,000	68,500
Interest	5,000	5,000	5,000	5,000	5,000
Financing cost	(5,000)	(500)	(1,500)	2,500	347
EBT	45,000	41,500	41,700	60,500	63,153
Taxes @ 35%	15,750	14,525	14,595	21,175	22,104
Net profit	29,250	26,975	27,105	39,325	41,049

Note: Financing cost is based on the example given in the preceding section.

high-risk customers. Naturally, the new customers coming into the fold of the new credit policy may cause an increase in bad debt losses, despite, the existing customers maintaining their payment schedule. On the other hand, when the credit period is relaxed, the existing customers also delay their payment schedule with the result that the average collection period elongates and in turn the average size of receivables swells. Bad debt losses in this case are not expected to rise because even the marginal customers get sufficient time to make payments. However, there is limit to making the credit standard and the credit period more liberal. It can be done only till costs remain confined within meaningful limits.

10.2.3 Discount Policy

The discount policy is also relevant to the design of an optimal credit policy. There are two types of discount extended to the customers: the trade discount and the cash discount. Trade discount is a percentage cut in the list price that in effect lowers the price of the product and helps increase sales, provided the price elasticity of demand of the product is greater than unity. It is the cash discount, however, that expedites collection. The credit term often possesses cash discount meaning that the customers will get discount at specific percentage rate if they make payments at any time earlier than the stipulated date. There is always a specific section of customers that likes to avail of this discount and for that reason makes payments earlier.

Trade discount is a percentage cut in the list price that in effect lowers the price of the product and helps increase sales, Cash discount, however expedites collection.

Cash discount has several different impacts. First, that the volume of sales increases. Once those who avail of the discount get the product at a cheaper rate, as a result of which their, demand for it increases. The normal law of demand applies in this case, and with an increases in sales profits increase.

Second, sales increase without a corresponding increase in bad debt losses. This is because many of the marginal customers, who are more risk-prone, prefer to avail of the cash discount and thus make payments earlier.

Third, the average collection period tends to be lower in view of the fact that a section of the customers make early payments in order to avail of the discount. The lower the average collection period, the smaller the average size of receivables and the lower the amount of cash tagged with the receivables. If the cash tagged with the receivables is lower, the cost of financing the receivables will also be lower. This means that there will be saving in the financing cost.

EXAMPLE

Annual sale is Rs 10,00,000. The existing credit term is net 30. The firm introduces a discount of 2% if payment is made within 10 days. The opportunity cost or the cost of capital is 20%. Find out the average size of receivables and thereby the saving in the financing cost.

Average collection period assuming that 20% of the customers do not pay within 30 days and 70% of the customers avail of the discount will be:

Net 30 = 30 + 20/100 × 30 = 36 days

2/10 net 30 = (0.7 × 10) + 0.3 (30 + 0.2 × 30) = 18 days

Average size of receivables:

Net 30 = 10,00,000 × 36/365 = Rs 98,630

2/10 net 30 = 10,00,000 × 18/365 = Rs 49,315

Assuming cost of capital @ 20%, saving of financing cost will be:

(98,630 – 49,315) × 0.20 = Rs 9,863.

However, there is limit to the extent to which the discount rate can be raised. This is because the demand for the product may not be price-elastic beyond a certain range. First, the loss of revenue on account of the offering discount may be greater than the increase in revenue on account the expanded sales. Second, with a rising discount rate, the percentage of customers availing of discount may not rise, because their payment schedule depends on their liquidity position. A higher discount rate may not tempt them in absence of greater liquidity support. In view of these limitations, a firm should optimise its discount policy at the point where the present value of the cash inflows is maximum.

10.3 SELECTION OF CUSTOMERS

Apart from the formulation of a general credit policy for the firm, it is equally important to know to whom and to what extent credit facilities are to be offered. A firm takes the following steps in selecting its customers:

1. Collecting necessary information
2. Analysis of the information
3. Fixation of the credit limit

10.3.1 Collecting Necessary Information

For extending credit to a customer, the firm must ensure that the financial background and the payment habits of the customer are good enough to honour bills. To this end, it needs to collect the necessary information about the customer. However, the process of collecting information suffers from two problems. First, collecting credit information involves expenses as well as time. Thus the finance manager must be alert that this cost does not exceed the profitability of extending credit. At the same time, the time consumed should not be so long as to lose a particular customer.

The other problem manifests in the lack of proper agencies for this purpose. In advanced countries, there are credit bureau organisations that furnish comprehensive information about the customer. But in developing countries, however, this is a problem. Banks are not confident about disclosing certain facts. Sometimes customers give trade references, but the lack of complete honesty and seriousness on the part of the referees cannot be ruled out.

In absence of proper sources of information, a firm tries to avail of the financial statements of the customer's firm on the basis of which various ratios are computed to show the operating and financial structure of the customer firm. The ratios that are normally looked into are the fixed asset turnover ratio, return on investment, equity debt ratio, finished goods inventory turnover ratio, receivable turnover ratio, current ratio, etc. If the financial structure and the operating structure are both strong, there is nothing to worry about. However, in the event of one of the two not being strong, the finance manager must first ensure the operating structure is strong. This is because a continuously weak operating structure tends to impair the financial structure.

10.3.2 Analysis of the Information

On the basis of the collected information, the firm analyses the information and takes a decision as to whom it should extend the credit facilities. There are two ways in which the information is analysed. One is the subjective analysis through the risk-class approach, and the other is the quantitative approach.

Risk-class Approach: A firm may adopt a risk-class approach grouping customers in different classes from the point of extending credit facilities. Different risk-classes are created on the basis of the financial position and payment behaviour of the customer and separate policies are framed for each class. When a customer applies for credit, he or she is placed in one of the classes that has been created. It eliminates the need to make exclusive decisions every time a customer applies for the credit. This system is quite flexible. A customer can be put in a different class if his financial position or payment behaviour changes. Table 10.2 presents different classes.

Table 10.2 Risk-class Approach to Receivables Management

Risk-class	*Description of the customer*	*Credit policy*
1	Sound financial position and good past record of payment	Liberal credit
2	Sound financial position but past record not available	Specified credit
3	Sound financial position but past record not good	Restricted credit
4	Financial position not sound but good records of payment	Very restricted credit
5	High-risk as well as financially weak firms	No credit

Quantitative Approach: The quantitative approach involves cost-benefit analysis or discriminant analysis. In this context, we may refer to the credit-scoring model of Altman (1970) who used multiple discriminant analysis to select customers to whom credit can be provided. He relied upon a few ratios, such as working capital to total assets, retained earnings to total assets, earnings before interest and tax (EBIT) to total assets, market value of equity to book value of debt and the asset turnover ratio. He then weighted different ratios and the weighted sum was taken as the overall index. According to him, the customers securing 1.81 or less were classified as bankrupt and should not be provided credit. Those scoring 2.99 and above were treated as healthy customers and should be provided credit. Those falling between the two limits were marginal customers and here the element of subjectivity had a role to play in decisions as to whether they should be extended credit. One can take into account fixed asset turnover ratio, return on investment and gross profit ratio to appraise the operating structure and a few more ratios for the appraisal of the financial structure, such as equity-debt ratio, equity-short-term debt ratio, current ratio, finished goods inventory turnover ratio, debt-service coverage ratio, receivables turnover ratio and creditors turnover ratio. He also calculates the moving averages in order to discern the trend in the ratio. He then weights different ratios and finally reaches a score to show whether the application for credit facilities should be rejected or accepted or forwarded to a higher authority for a further probe.

The credit extension decision based on the credit-scoring models can be explained with the help of an example. For example, let the score be based on four financial variables expressed in terms of percentage, viz., net working capital/sales (X_1), debt/assets (X_2), assets/sales (X_3), and net profit margin (X_4), and let them be assigned weights. Positive weight means that a higher value results in a higher credit score. Negative weight means that a higher ratio reduces the credit score. It means that the total score (S) along with a given weight can be expressed as follows:

$$S = w_1X_1 + w_2X_2 + w_3X_3 + w_4X_4 \quad ...(10.4)$$

EXAMPLE

If there are two customers whose ratios are as follows:

Financial ratios with weight (%)	Customer 1	Customer 2
$0.6\ X_1$	14	8
$-0.3\ X_2$	40	50
$0.1\ X_3$	110	108
$0.6\ X_4$	11	10

Customer 1 credit score $= (0.6 \times 14) - (0.3 \times 40) + (0.1 \times 110) + (0.6 \times 11)$
$= 14.0$

Customer 2 credit score $= (0.6 \times 8) - (0.3 \times 50) + (0.1 \times 108) + (0.6 \times 10)$
$= 6.6$

If the demarcating line is represented by a score of 10, Customer 1 will get credit, while Customer 2 will not be given credit.

10.3.3 Fixation of the Credit Limit

After it is decided that a particular customer will be provided credit facilities, a limit is fixed to the amount of credit that can be extended. The limit differs from one customer to the other. The maximum limit represents the maximum risk exposure that the firm will allow itself to undergo on a particular account. The line for a particular customer is fixed normally at a lower level than the maximum. It is fixed as per his normal buying pattern. Suppose a particular customer's purchase amounts to Rs 20,000 a month, the amount of credit may be set at this level. However, if his past performance with respect to payment has not been very regular, credit line is fixed with reference to the outstanding amount. It is because of this reason that the customers' accounts are periodically checked and the line of credit revised either upward or downward.

10.4 MONITORING AND CONTROL OF CREDIT

Monitoring of credit is done at the customer's level as well as at the aggregate level. At the customer's level, the objective is to expedite collection so as to reduce bad debt losses. At the aggregate level, the objective is to examine whether the accounts receivable move exactly in conformity with the laid down policies.

10.4.1 Monitoring at the Customer's Level

Collection from a customers should be looked after by an exclusive department, known as the credit department. Customers should be classified on the basis of size of receivables. Different classes of customers should be treated differently. If the collection is not made within the prescribed time period, the customer should be reminded over the telephone. If this does not work, a letter should follow. If the letter is ineffective, collection agents should be sent to retrieve the payment. If the payment is not received even after these steps have been taken, further credit should not be extended and the officer incharge of the customer's firm at the highest level should be contacted. In the end, if all these steps prove ineffective, legal action may be taken. However, the credit manager should always bear in mind that the costs involved in the process of collection should not exceed the benefits of a stringent collection policy. Here it may be pointed out that the benefits involved in early collection are the resultant reduction of the average collection period and the average size of the receivables, which in turn reduces the financing cost and bad debt losses. Similarly, the costs involved are the collection cost and a fall in sales as the result of a stringent credit policy.

10.4.2 Monitoring at the Aggregate Level

Monitoring credit at the aggregate level is done in a number of ways. These are as follows:

1. Preparation of a receivables ageing schedule;
2. Computation of average age of accounts receivables;
3. Preparation of percentage cash flow matrix.

Receivables ageing schedule: An ageing schedule is a table that shows the amount of receivables outstanding as also their share in the total amount of receivables falling into

Table 10.3 Ageing Schedule—31 March, 2002

Age (days)	*Amount*	*% share*
0–30	25,000	50.0
31–60	12,000	24.0
61–90	13,000	26.0
Over 90	0	0
Total	50,000	100.0

different age classifications, such as, 0–30 days, 31–60 days and over 60 days or other similar classifications. Table 10.3 shows an example of ageing schedule.

The aging schedule depends upon the terms of the credit, the payment habits of the customers and the recent trends in the sales. If sales increase in the current month or the customers pay early, the receivables in the youngest class will increase. But if the period of credit is long, the amount of receivables in the youngest age group will be lower as the customers would want to reap benefit of the longer credit term.

Average Age of Accounts Receivables: The average age of receivables can be computed on the basis of Table 10.3 assuming the mid-point of each age class as the average number of days of that class. The mid-point is multiplied by the relative percentage of outstanding credit of that age group.

EXAMPLE

If the average number of days is 15 for 0–30 days class, 45 for 31–60 days class, and 75 for 61–90 days class. The average age of receivables will be:

$$0.50 \times 15 + 0.24 \times 45 + 0.26 \times 75 = 37.8 \text{ days}$$

Percentage Cash Flow Matrix: The cash flow matrix shows whether collection is slowing down, staying at the same level or improving. On this basis, appropriate action can be taken to improve the situation. Table 10.4 shows such a matrix.

Table 10.4 Cash Flow as Percentage of Month's Sales

	Jan.	*Feb.*	*Mar.*	*Apr.*	*May*	*June*	*July*	*Total*
Jan.	20	20	40	20				100
Feb.		20	20	40	20			100
Mar.			20	20	20	20	20	100
Apr.				20	20	20	20	80
May					20	20	20	60
June						20	20	40
July							10	10

The matrix shows that the total collection has been on a decreasing trend since April. At the same time, the collections are stretched from four months during the first two months to five months and more during the subsequent months. It means that the management must take steps to improve collection.

10.4.3 Factoring

Since collection activities have greater impact on the liquidity of the firm, factoring maintains a close relevance to accounts receivable management as it expedites collection. This is because factoring is a process where a firm sells its receivables for cash to another firm that specialises in their collection and administration. The factor buys the client's receivables and controls the credit and collects it at maturity. The normal practice is that the seller of the goods informs the factor about the customer's order. The factor evaluates the customer's creditworthiness and approves the deal. After the approval by the factor, the seller dispatches the consignment and informs the factor and also asks the customer to make payments directly to the factor. Once the factor has approved the deal, it means that it has purchased the accounts receivable and will provide coverage for any bad debt loss.

This way the entire responsibility of credit monitoring and collection shifts to the factor. The factor provides full credit administration services and makes every effort to collect the funds at the maturity. It also extends cash to the client against book debts. In developed countries, the factor also provides ancillary services, such as, financial counselling, collecting information about prospective customers, providing facilities for opening letters of credit by the client, etc.

> Factoring is a process where a firm sells its receivables for cash to another firm that specialises in their collection and administration. The factor buys the client's receivables and controls the credit and collects it at maturity.

It should be mentioned here, that factoring is a broader term incorporating also bill discounting. In bill discounting, the seller draws a bill on the purchaser and gets it discounted from a bank. In this case, the drawer of the bill has to face a bad debt loss because the bills discounting is always with recourse. Factoring, however, covers all types of book debt whether or not bills have actually been drawn in their context. Moreover, bad debt losses are borne by the factor.

Forms of Factoring: Broadly speaking, there are four forms of factoring. First, is the full service non-recourse factoring. In this case, the factor buys the client's entire book debt, administers it, collects the payment and bears the bad debt loss. It makes advances to the client to the extent of 80–90% of the book debt immediately after buying it. This type of factoring is also known as old-line factoring and it is popular in the USA.

The second type of factoring is known as full service recourse factoring. In this case, risk of bad debt lies with the client. Therefore, if the client has obtained any advance from the factor against the book debt, it will have to refund the amount in case of uncollected debt. In this case, the factoring charges are lower than in the first case.

The third is bulk/agency factoring. The administration of book debt is done by the client itself. The factor simply provides an advance against the book debt either with recourse or without recourse. Clients having an efficient administration system opt for factoring for the purpose of funds.

The fourth one is the non-notification factoring. In this case, the identity of the factor is kept confidential. The factor performs functions in the name of a sales company to which the client sells its book debt. This type of factoring is often found in the UK.

Factoring Cost: The factor charges commission for its services. The charges are expressed in terms of a specific percentage of full net face value of receivables factored. The rate varies normally between 2.5% and 3% based on the volume and quality of book debt and also on the fact whether factoring is with recourse or without recourse.

Thus whenever a firm avails of the services of a factor, it needs to compare the cost of this service with its benefits. Its decision to opt for the service is final only when the benefits exceed the cost. The benefits manifest themselves in the form of saving of collection cost and protection from losses on account bad debts. The costs manifest themselves in the form of factoring commission and interest on advances against book debt. If the ratio between net cost of factoring and net advances received is lower than the interest rate on other short-term funds, factoring is advisable.

Factoring in India: Factoring in India is of recent origin. It was the Vaghul Committee that had recommended the introduction of factoring services in India. It was followed by the report of the Kalyanasundaram Committee that also suggested this kind of initiative. As a result, the RBI advised banks to introduce factoring through the creation of subsidiaries. In 1991, SBI Factors and Commercial Services Ltd. was promoted, which now extends factoring services.

Benefits of Factoring

1. The time needed for administering collection is saved, as a result of which the firm can concentrate on improving production and sales.
2. The factoring charges may be there, but that is more than compensated by savings on account of administrative expenditure.
3. Factoring helps improve the current ratio of the firm. Naturally, it enjoys a higher credit rating.
4. The factor services include various kinds of collection services, and from this viewpoint, they are preferable to general receivable financing by banks.

EXAMPLE

Average level of receivables is Rs 50,000. The factor charges 2% commission and provides advances up to 80% of the receivables for 90 days at 18% interest rate. Find out the net cost of factoring or the effective rate of advances provided by the factor.

1. Factor commission = 0.02 × 50,000 = Rs 1,000
2. Net advance available = (0.8 × 50,000) – 1,000 – (0.18 × 39,000 × 90/365)
   = Rs 37,269
3. Annual cost of factoring = (1000 × 365/90) + (0.18 × 39,000)
   = Rs 11,075
4. Assuming saving in the administrative cost, collection cost and bad debt loss as Rs 3,500,

Net cost of factoring = 11,075 – 3,500
= Rs 7,575
or
7,575/37,269 = 0.2033
= 20.33%

10.4.4 Forfaiting

Forfaiting is an extension of factoring in the area of international trade. An exporter discounts the bills with an agency known as a forfaitor. Forfaiting in India was initiated by Exim Bank and even today it is a nodal agency. A few other commercial banks have already started forfaiting.

After the export deal is finalised, the exporter intimates the forfaitor who in turn makes an appraisal of the deal. After being satisfied, it quotes the discount rate and then the deal is signed. The forfaitor may present the bill on the due date or may discount the bill in the secondary market. The cost of forfaiting is the sum of financing charges, commitment fee and the Exim Bank fee. Presently, the financing charges are normally the London Inter-Bank Offered Rate (LIBOR) + 50 – 14 basis points (b.p.) The commitment fee depends upon the usance period and varies in the range of 13 – 15 b.p.

It is true that factoring and forfaiting have the same purpose of easing the collection process. But the two are different on a few counts:

1. Factoring is used on a continual basis for ongoing open account sales. Forfaiting is related normally to a single transaction.
2. Factoring is available for credit sales involving only up to a period of 6 months. Forfaiting is available for longer period.
3. Factoring is a continual arrangement between the factor and the client which automatically involves that the sales are routed through the factor. Forfaiting covers individual transaction.
4. Collection is the duty of the factor. The forfaitor collects only forfeited debt.
5. The forfaitor charges only discount rate, whereas the factor charges administration cost, collection cost and information providing charges, etc.
6. Forfaiting is found normally in case of international trade. Factoring is common in domestic sales.
7. Forfaiting is always "without recourse", whereas factoring may involve "with recourse" or "without recourse" financing.

SUMMARY

Credit sales lead to the creation of accounts receivable. Receivables lead to greater sale and profitability, help absorb any fluctuations in demand, provide greater liquidity, act as a tool for price discrimination and encourage intermediaries. But they have costs too, in form of administrative cost, financial cost, collection cost and bad debt losses.

A firm's credit policy should be such that helps maximise corporate wealth. It can be determined through a cost-benefit analysis or through preparing a proforma income statement. However, deviations can be made to suit the firm's overall strategy. Any change in the credit standard or the period of the credit or in the discount policy must ensure that benefits exceed the costs.

Customers to whom credit facilities are to be provided are selected after gathering information about them and analysing the information either through subjective tools or through quantitative tools. Finally, the credit limit is fixed.

Receivables management involves their monitoring and control both at the customer's level and at the aggregate level. At the customer's level, a proper collection policy should be developed. At the aggregate level, they can be monitored through the maintenance of receivables ageing schedule, through computation of the average age of receivables and through percentage cash flow matrix. Collection can be improved through factoring or forfaiting.

POINTS TO REMEMBER

1. What are the benefits of the credit sale/maintaining accounts receivable?
   - Greater sales leading to greater profitability
   - Absorption of fluctuation in demand
   - Providing liquidity to the firm
   - Effective tool for price discrimination
   - Encouragement to intermediaries
2. What are the costs of maintaining accounts receivable?
   - Financing cost or the interest cost during the period when cash is tagged with receivables
   - Administrative cost
   - Collection cost
   - Bad debt losses
3. How do you optimise the terms of the credit?
   - A particular credit term is optimal when:
     (i) Net profit calculated through proforma income statement is the highest
     (ii) Expected rate of return, meaning the incremental tax-adjusted operating profit divided by the additional investment in the receivables is the highest
4. What are the different steps in extending credit to a customer?
   - Collection of information about the customers

- Analysing the information based on financial ratios and putting customers in different risk classes
- Fixing the credit limit based on the analysis

5. How are receivables/credit sales monitored/controlled?
    - Monitoring at the customer's level through energising the collection methods
    - Monitoring credit at the firm's level through:
        (i) preparation and analysis of receivables aging schedule
        (ii) preparation and analysis of percentage cash flow matrix
    - Maintaining receivables within desired limit through factoring and forfaiting

DESCRIPTIVE QUESTIONS

1. Explain the benefits and costs of maintaining receivables.
2. How is the term of credit optimised? Is this to do with maximisation of the corporate wealth?
3. Mention the impact of the changes in the credit standard/period of the credit.
4. How far do the changes in discount policy influence the credit policy?
5. What are the sources of information on which the credit policy is based?
6. Explain the procedure adopted for selecting a customer to whom credit facilities are provided.
7. How is credit monitored at the customer's level? How is credit monitored at the aggregate level?
8. Write a note on factoring. Is it different from forfaiting?

OBJECTIVE-TYPE QUESTIONS

1. Mark true or false.
    (a) Average size of receivables is the product of sales and accounts receivable turnover.
    (b) Relaxation of credit standard means extending credit facilities to higher-risk customers.
    (c) Ageing schedule shows the size of outstanding receivables in different age classes.
    (d) Forfaiting is a practice normally found in international trade.
    (e) Factoring may be only on a recourse basis.
2. Choose the most suitable answer.
    (a) Average size of receivables is equal to:
        (i) sales × receivables turnover
        (ii) sales/receivables turnover
        (iii) sales + receivables turnover

(b) Optimum credit term exists when:
   (i) average rate of return > required rate of return by the largest margin
   (ii) average rate of return = required rate of return
   (iii) average rate of return < required rate of return by the largest margin

(c) Ageing schedule depends on:
   (i) terms of credit only
   (ii) amount of the credit only
   (iii) both terms and amount of credit

(d) Provision of discount:
   (i) raises the average collection period
   (ii) lessens the average collection period
   (iii) has no impact on average collection period

(e) Factoring is a process in which:
   (i) bills are sold for cash before maturity
   (ii) bills are sold for cash on maturity
   (iii) neither of the above

NUMERICAL PROBLEMS

1. A net 30 term accounts for a sale of Rs 10,00,000. There are 30% of the customers who do not make payments within time. Find out the average collection period and the average size of receivables. Will there be change in the average size of the receivables if the credit term is 2/10 net 30 and 70% of the customers avail of the discount?
2. A company relaxes its credit period from 60 to 90 days, as a result of which sales revenue increases by Rs 15,000; collection cost increases by 3%; bad debt increases by 2%; opportunity cost of capital is 12%; and variable cost is 80%. Find out the incremental profit.
3. Liberalisation in credit policy raises the average size of receivables by Rs 30,000 and the operating profits by Rs 15,000. Tax rate is 30% and required rate of return is 12%. Do you suggest liberalisation of the credit policy?
4. Annual sale on net 30 credit term is Rs 20,00,000. The firm introduces a discount of 2% if payment is made within 10 days. The opportunity cost of capital is 20%. Find out the average size of receivables and thereby the saving in the financing cost if 20% of the customers do not pay within 30 days and 70% of the customers avail of the discount.
5. If the size of outstanding receivables is Rs 15,000 in 0–30 days class, Rs 12,000 in 31–60 days class and Rs 8,000 in 61–90 days class, find the average age of receivables.
6. If average level of receivables is Rs 40,000. The factor charges 2% commission and provides advances up to 75% of the receivables for 90 days at 12% interest rate. Find the net cost of factoring or the effective rate of advances provided by the factor.

7. Find the average age of the receivables based on the following table:

   Ageing Schedule on 31.3.2008

Age (days)	*Amount Rs*	*% Share*
0–30	3,00,000	0.50
31–60	1,00,000	0.17
61–90	2,00,000	0.33

8. The annual credit sale of a firm is Rs 12,80,000. The debtor amounts to Rs 1,60,000. Find out the average collection period.
9. A company sells for Rs 60,00,000. The debtor amounts to Rs 5,30,000. Find out the debtor's turnover in terms of the number of days.

SOLVED NUMERICAL PROBLEMS

1. Find out the average size of receivables if the goods are sold for Rs 10,00,000 on a net 60 credit term with an assumption that 20% of the customers do not pay within the prescribed time. Will there be any change in the average size if the terms of credit change to 2/10 net 60 with an assumption that 60% of the customers avail the discount?

   Solution

   Case I:

   Average collection period = 60 + 0.20 x 60 = 72 days

   Average size of receivables = Rs (10,00,000/360) x 72 = Rs 2,00,000

   Case II:

   Average collection period = (0.6 x 10) + 0.4 (60 + 0.2 x 60)

   = 6 + 28.8 = 35 days

   Average size of receivables = Rs (10,00,000 / 360) x 35 = Rs 97,222.22

2. A firm sells 25,000 units at an average price of Rs 200 per unit. The variable cost is 80 per cent of the sale price. The credit term is 1/10 net 30. One-tenth of the customers avail the discount and the average collection period is 28 days. Administrative cost is Rs 20,000. Collection cost/sales and bad debt/sales ratios are 2% each. To increase the level of sales, credit term is changed as 2/10 net 30 as a result of which the sales are expected to be 50,000 units. The administrative cost, collection cost ratio and bad debt ratio are expected to be unchanged. The cost of funds is 10%. Tax rate is 30%. Find the net benefit of the changed credit terms.

   Solution

   Average size of receivables:

   Case I: Rs (50,00,000 /360) x 28 = Rs 3,88,889

   Case II: Rs (1,00,00,000 /360) x 28 = Rs 7,77,778

   Financing cost:

   Case I: Rs 3,88,889 x 0.10 = Rs 38,889

   Case II: Rs 7,77,778 x 0.10 = 77,778

Net Benefit:

	Case I	*Case II*
Revenue (sales)	50,00,000	1,00,00,000
Less variable cost	40,00,000	80,00,000
Net revenue	10,00,000	20,00,000
Less financing cost	38,889	77,778
Less administrative cost	20,000	20,000
Less collection cost	1,00,000	2,00,000
Less bad debt losses	1,00,000	2,00,000
Profit before tax	7,41,111	15,02,222
Less tax @ 30%	2,22,333	4,50,667
Net profit after tax	5,18,778	10,51,555

Net benefit of liberal term = Rs 10,51,555 – 5,18,778 = Rs 5,32,777

3. If the liberalisation of credit terms helps increase the average size of receivables by Rs 5,00,000 and the net operating profit by Rs 1,00,000, find whether liberalisation is justified, with a given tax rate of 30% and the required rate of return of 20%.

Solution

Expected Rate of Return = Rs {1,00,000 (1 – 0.30)}/5,00,000 = 0.14 = 14%

Liberalisation is not justified because ERR < required rate of return.

4. Find the average age of the receivables, if

Outstanding period (days)	*Outstanding amount of receivables (Rs)*
0–25	2,00,000
26–35	1,00,000
36–45	50,000
46–60	30,000
61–70	20,000
Total	4,00,000

Again, if the target age of receivables is 30 days, does it mean that the firm is pursuing a sound credit policy?

Solution

Outstanding period (days)	*Outstanding amount of receivables (Rs)*	*% of total receivables*
0–25	2,00,000	50.0
26–35	1,00,000	25.0
36–45	50,000	12.5
46–60	30,000	7.5
61–70	20,000	5.0
	4,00,000	100.0

0.5 x 12.5 + 0.25 x 30.5 + 0.125 x 40.5 + 0.075 x 52.5 + 0.05 x 65

= 26.13 days

The actual average age of receivables < target age of receivables which means that the firm is pursuing a sound receivables policy.

5. Find the net cost of factoring if average size of receivables amounts to Rs 1,00,000; and the factor charges 2% commission and provides advances up to 75% of the receivables for 90 days at 15% interest rate. On the other hand, factoring saves administrative and collection cost and also bad debt losses which are expected to be Rs 5,000.

Solution

Factor's commission = 0.02 x Rs 1,00,000 = Rs 2,000

Net advance available = Rs (0.75 x 1,00,000) – 2000 – (0.15 x 73,000 x 90/360)

= Rs 75,000 – 2,000 – 2,737.50

= Rs 70,262.50

Annual cost of factoring = (2,000 x 360/90) + (0.15 x 73,000)

= Rs 8,000 + 10,950

= Rs 18,950

Net cost of factoring = Rs 18,950 – 5,000 = Rs 13,950

Net cost in percentage terms, 13,950 / 70,262.50 = 0.1985 = 19.85%

6. A firm's current sale is Rs 10,00,000, It plans to introduce a cash discount policy of 2/10 net 30. As a consequence, the average collection period is expected to reduce by 10 days and 80% of the customers are expected to opt for discount. If the required rate of return on investment in B/R is 20%, find out whether the new policy should be introduced.

Solution

a) Prior to introduction of cash discount policy, the size of B/R

$$\text{Rs } 10{,}00{,}000 \times \frac{30 \; days}{360 \; days} = Rs \; 83{,}333$$

b) After the introduction of the discount policy, the size of B/R

$$\text{Rs } 10{,}00{,}000 \times \frac{20}{360} = Rs \; 55{,}555$$

c) Decrease in investment in B/R = Rs 27,778

d) Saving in cost of funds:

$$\text{Rs } 27{,}778 \times \frac{20}{100} = Rs \; 5{,}556$$

e) Cost of extending discount:

$$\text{Rs } 10{,}00{,}000 \times \frac{80}{100} \times \frac{2}{100} = Rs \; 16{,}000$$

f) Net loss on introduction of cash discount:

Rs 16,000 - 5,556 = Rs 10,444

The discount policy should not be introduced.

Mini Case 1
Managing Receivables by a Delhi-based Shoe Manufacturer

A small shoe manufacturer of Delhi operates on a very narrow margin of profit in order to survive a keen competition in the market. He has no problem on the count of operating cost, such as cost of material, labour cost and other overheads insofar as he is able to get raw material of desired quality at reasonable cost. The labour force is highly efficient. He buys raw material at net 90 terms of credit which is a liberal term of credit. But he is facing problems on account of customers whom he provides net 60 term of credit. Around 20% of his customers are stretching the payment beyond 60 days. So the average life of credit sale gets longer which raises the financing cost. Collection cost is as high as 4.0 per cent of the credit sales and bad debt loss is also sizeable at 2.0 per cent of the credit sale.

The manufacturer plans to improve his return on investment. He can make the credit term still liberal for a greater sale. But that will raise the financing cost of credit. In face of high cost of funds, it will erode his profitability more than the profit on the enhanced sale. On the contrary, if he tightens the term of credit, he will lose sales that will lower the asset turnover and thereby the return on investment.

Presently, the financial figures are as follows:

1. Sales Rs 2,00,000
2. Total asset Rs 1,20,000
3. Operating profit Rs 20,000
4. Cost of funds 16%

If he liberalises the term of credit to 90 days, sales may go up by 10%. The collection cost may go up by 0.50%. A greater amount of cash will be tagged with the receivables. Under these circumstances, he is to find a solution.

Questions:

1. Find what should be the optimal term of credit.
2. Should he provide 2% discount if customers pay within 10 days?
3. What measures should he take to cut the average age of receivables?
4. Should he liberalise the credit term to net 90?
5. What measures can be taken to prune collection cost and bad debt losses?

Mini Case 2

Arvind Juicer and Mixer sells 80% of its product on credit terms after due scrutiny of the customers' financial soundness and their past history of payment. This means that cash sales are limited in view of the risky customers. The term of credit is net 30; however, to boost up the sales, the company provides 2% discount if payment is made within the first 10 days. It may be mentioned that 80% of the credit-availing customers are availing cash discount.

The sales amount is Rs 2 million. The contribution margin ratio is 25%. Tax rate is 30%. Post-tax cost of capital is 12%. The average collection period is 11 days in case of 2/10 net 30 and 16 days in case of net 30 terms.

If the company liberalises the credit policy to net 60, sales are expected to rise to Rs 2.2 million. But the collection cost rises from 2% to 3% and bad debt losses are expected to move up from 1.5% to 3%. The administrative cost is not expected to change.

In this context, the finance manager has to find out whether there should be change in the credit standard from net 30 to net 60.

Questions:

1. Prepare a pro forma income statement on the basis of the present variables and the expected changes.
2. Find whether the new credit standard of net 60 should be followed.

REFERENCES

Altman, I.E. (1970). "Corporate Bankruptcy Prediction and Its Implications for Commercial Loan Evaluation", *The Journal of Commercial Bank Lending*, (Jan.): 8–22.

Dyl, E.A. (1977). "Another Look at the Evaluation of Investment in Accounts Receivable", *Financial Management*, 6 (Winter): 23–34.

SELECT FURTHER READINGS

Mavrovitis, B.P. (1994). *Cashflow, Credit and Collection*. Chicago, Ill: Probus Publishing Co.

Mian, S.L. and C.W. Smith Jr. (1992). "Accounts Receivable Management Policy: Theory and Evidence", *Journal of Finance*, 47 (1): 169–200.

Scherr, F.C. (1996). "Optimal Trade Credit Limits", *Financial Management*, 25 (1): 71–85.

11

INVENTORY MANAGEMENT

OBJECTIVES

To delineate the costs and benefits of holding inventory

To explain the goals of inventory management in terms of classification of inventory and determination of economic order quantity, re-order point and safety level of stock

To explain what JIT system of inventory management actually means

Inventory, as you know, means raw material, semi-finished goods and finished goods. It accounts for the largest segment of investment in the current assets; and so, its proper management is of utmost significance. The management of inventory involves primarily:

1. Its classification based on its value, volume and importance
2. Determination of an economic size of order
3. Decision of the re-order point
4. Establishing a safety level of stock

The present chapter discusses the above issues; although, in the beginning, the benefits and costs of maintaining inventory will be mentioned.

11.1 BENEFITS AND COST OF MAINTAINING INVENTORY

11.1.1 Benefits

Maintaining a desired level of inventory has the following benefits:

1. It meets the transaction, precautionary and speculative needs of the operation.
2. It helps reduce cost of operation.

Meeting transaction needs means meeting normal requirements for raw material on a day-to-day basis that ensures smooth operation. If raw material falls short on a particular day, the operation will be interrupted causing uncertainty in output. The customers may shift to some other supplier which will ultimately entail upon sales and profitability.

Again, as far as the precautionary motive behind maintaining inventory is concerned, it is to guard against the risk of unpredictable changes in the forces of demand and supply. If a supplier of raw material stops supplying the input, operations will come to a halt. But if the firm maintains a certain level of raw material against such contingencies, it may be possible for it to tide over such a situation.

Yet again, it is also a speculative motive that induces a firm to hold inventory. If there is price change in favour of the firm's product, the firm will reap the benefits of this only when it has a sufficient stock of inventory enabling to sell larger amounts of the product and reap the benefits of the price change.

Last but not least, a firm holds larger amount of inventory also because the purchase of larger volumes of raw material is often cheaper. At the same time, a larger order size tends to reduce the order cost.

The benefit of maintaining inventory is that it meets the transaction needs, precautionary needs and speculative needs of the operations.

11.1.2 Costs

Holding inventory is beneficial from the viewpoint of maintaining continued operation, however, it also has costs. These costs do not necessarily move in one direction with the growing size of inventory and so their management is crucial in order to minimise the total cost. These costs are as follows:

1. Material cost
2. Order cost
3. Holding cost
4. Financing cost
5. Stock-out cost

The first is material cost that includes the cost of goods purchased, transportation and handling cost. It increases with the size of inventories. The second is the order cost which is incurred while placing orders for raw material. The larger the size of inventories, the lower is the number of orders placed and the lower is the order cost. The third is the holding cost or carrying cost that represents the expenditure on account of storing the goods. It includes: (a) the storage cost involved in the operation of a warehouse, (b) insurance which is required against hazards of various kinds, e.g., fire, theft, etc., and (c) obsolescence and spoilage that includes the cost of being unable to sell the goods because of changes in the pattern of demand and as a result of damage during storage. The larger the size of inventory, the greater is the holding cost. The fourth type of cost is the cost of funds tied up in inventory. If inventory is financed with debt or the firm's general funds, there is financing cost. The larger the size of inventory, the greater is the financing cost. Lastly, there is stock-out cost. It is an implicit cost arising out of lost sales due to shortage of supply. It may manifest in loss of profit on account of lost sale and the cost of losing goodwill.

11.2 GOAL OF INVENTORY MANAGEMENT

Since inventory management is fraught with both costs and benefits, a finance manager must make a trade-off between the two so as to maximise the value of the firm. To be precise, he or she must take into account four important points. They are as follows:

1. Inventories should be grouped according to their importance and special care should be taken of more important items;

Break-up of Inventory among 1,377 private limited companies in India

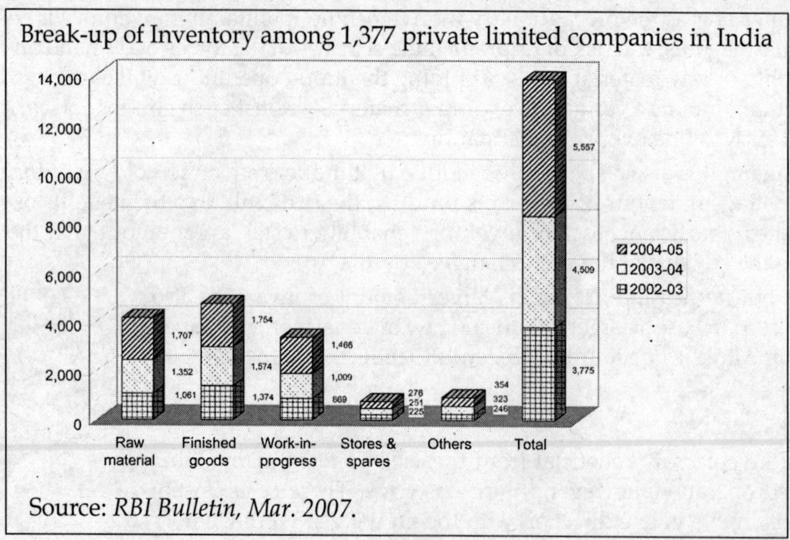

Source: *RBI Bulletin, Mar. 2007.*

2. The size of the order for inventories should be economic so as to minimise the total cost;
3. The re-order point needs to be determined so that the firm may not run out of necessary raw material;
4. A proper level of safety stock must be maintained.

11.2.1 Classification of Inventories

Items of inventory differ in their importance. Certain items are high-cost, others have a high margin of profit, while still others are bottleneck items. The rest may command lesser importance. The more important the items are, the more intensive care must be taken of them. A firm should therefore be selective in its approach in order to control investment in various types of inventories. This analytical approach is known as the ABC approach. It is also known as control by importance and exception (CIE) or as proportional value analysis (PVA). The highest value items are grouped as A-class items, next in importance as B-class items and the rest as C-class items. The above classification is illustrated in Table 11.1.

TABLE 11.1 ABC Analysis

	Quantity				*Cost*				
Item	*Units*	*% of total*	*Cumulative %*		*Unit cost*	*Total cost*	*% of total*	*Cumulative %*	
1	60	6			50	3000	19		
2	140	14	20	20	40	5600	35	54	54
3	150	15			20	3000	19		
4	200	20	35	55	10	2000	13	32	86
5	200	20			6	1200	8		
6	250	25	45	100	4	1000	6	14	100
Total	1000					15800			

All this shows that A-class items accounting for 20% of the total volume (nos.) account for 54% of the total value. B-class items accounting for the other 35% of the volume account for 32% of the value. This means that 55% of the items account for 86% of the value of inventories. The remaining 14% of the value is represented by almost one-half of the items, say 45%. On this basis, handling care should differ for different classes of items.

11.2.2 Economic Order Quantity (EOQ)

The size of the order must be economic. If it is larger than economic size, holding cost of inventory will be larger. On the contrary, if it is lower than the economic size, this would raise the order cost. What should then be the economic size of the orders placed for inventory? One of the earliest exercises was carried out in 1915 when P.W. Harris developed the economic-lot-size equation that minimised the sum of inventory holding cost and re-order cost. At present, there exists ample literature on this subject.

It is very easy to determine the economic order quantity (EOQ) in case of known demand where a specific quantum of goods is to be supplied at a uniform rate. But it becomes a little more complex when the size of demand is not precisely known.

EOQ in Case of Known Demand: In case of known demand, the stock is not allowed to become negative and the lead time is assumed to be zero. In such a situation, the average stock is equal to $R/2$ where R is the EOQ. The total stock-holding cost or the carrying cost c over a certain period of time T will be $R/2 \times cT$. The number of R or the EOQ at a time to meet the total demand Q is Q/R, and the total order cost a for total number of orders will be aQ/R. This means that the total cost incurred during a period, T will be equal to:

$$aQ/R + cTR/2 \qquad ...(11.1)$$

With an increase in the size of order, there will be a lesser number of orders and the order cost aQ/R will tend to be lower. On the other hand, the carrying cost $cTR/2$ will tend to rise. The total cost will be the minimum where these two types cost are equal. Fig 11.1 shows how these two costs behave and when the total cost is minimal.

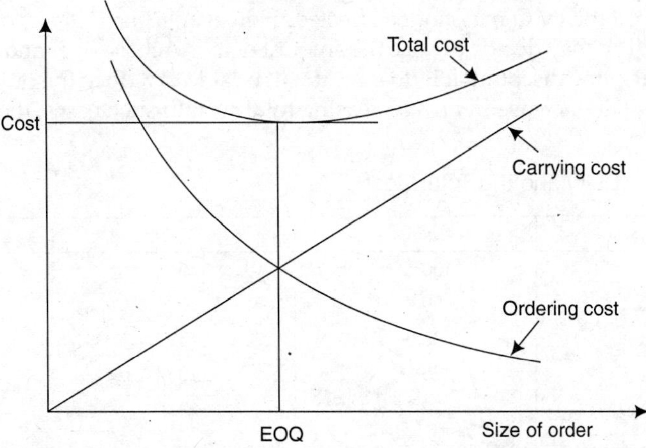

FIG. 11.1 Behaviour of cost with varying size of order

In form of equation, total cost will be minimum when:

$$aQ/R = cTR/2$$

or

$$2aQ/R^2 = cT$$

or

$$R^2 = 2aQ/cT$$

or

$$R = \sqrt{2aq/cT} \qquad \text{...(11.2)}$$

EXAMPLE

Total demand for a commodity is 100 tonnes in time *T*. The carrying cost is Rs 10 per tonne of stock during the time, *T* and the order cost is Rs 1 per order. Find out the EOQ.

$$\text{EOQ} = \sqrt{(2 \times 1 \times 100)/10} = \sqrt{20} = 4.472 \text{ tonnes}$$

The concept of EOQ based on the above example, can be explained in a tabular form.

Given the EOQ as 4.472 tonnes, the number of orders during T will be:

$$100/4.472 = 22.36 \text{ or } 23.$$

And if T is equal to one year, the inventory of a particular order will last for:

$$365/100 \times 4.472 = 16.32 \text{ days.}$$

EOQ with Quantity Discounts: When the suppliers offer a price discount on a prescribed minimum quantity of sale in order to attract the customers, the practice may influence the EOQ. If the EOQ is higher than the minimum prescribed amount eligible for discount, the decision on the EOQ may not be affected. However, if the EOQ is lower than the said amount, the firm may decide to raise the amount of its purchase over and above the EOQ in order to avail of the discount. If it does so, it will be able to reduce the purchase cost but the carrying cost will increase in turn increasing total cost. In such cases, the finance manager

TABLE 11.2 EOQ and the Total Cost

R (Tonnes)	*aQ/R*	*CTR/2*	*aQ/R + cTR/2*
1	100	5	105
2	50	10	60
3	33.3	15	48.3
4	25	20	45
4.472	**22.37**	**22.37**	**44.74**
5	20	25	45
6	16.6	30	46.6

has to make trade-off between the purchase cost and the carrying cost so as to minimise the total cost. In this case total cost will be:

Total cost = order cost + carrying cost – price discount ...(11.3)

EXAMPLE

Based on the last example, EOQ is 4.472 tonnes. But the supplier provides discount at the rate of Re 0.10 each tonne, if the purchase amount is at least 8 tonnes. Should the firm place an order for 8 tonnes in order to get the discount?

1. Number of orders = 100/8 = 12.5 or 13.
1. Order cost based on the above example = 13 × Re 1 = Rs 13.
4. Carrying cost based on the above example = 8/2 × Rs 10 = Rs 40
5. Price discounts = Re 0.10 × 100 = Rs 10
6. Using Eq. 11.3., total cost = 13 + 40 – 10 = Rs 43
7. The total cost of 8-tonne order (Rs 43) < the total cost of EOQ (Rs 44.74)

Hence, it is advisable to increase the size of order to 8 tonnes.

Inflation and EOQ: Inflation is a normal phenomenon. If it is a constant price increase, there is no problem. But if it is large, some modifications are required in the EOQ model. The firm buys in addition to the EOQ in the anticipation of large inflation so as to secure the goods at lower cost. This type of buying may be termed as *anticipatory buying*. The carrying cost increases in the sequel. Moreover, the inflation pushes up the interest rate that gives further rise to the carrying cost. However, the risen carrying cost on the above two counts is compensated in varying proportions by the low cost of buying. The management has to see that the size of anticipatory buying should be confined to a point where the increase in the transaction cost should not be higher than benefit on account of lower cost of buying.

EOQ under Uncertain Demand Conditions: The EOQ model explained above is based on known demand. However, in real life, demand is not known with certainty in advance. Firms protect themselves from uncertainty by maintaining a safety stock which is also known as the buffer inventory. If demand suddenly increase and there is no safety stock, firms may experience a stock-out resulting in a loss of goodwill. This may then result in lost sales. Even if orders are not cancelled by the customers, there does exist back-order cost. Thus under the conditions of uncertain demand annual inventory cost will be expressed as follows:

Annual inventory cost = order cost + holding cost + stock-out cost ...(11.4)

A larger safety stock reduces the expected stock-out cost but increases the handling/carrying cost because the average inventory level includes also the safety level of stock. Thus there is again a trade-off between the carrying cost and the stock-out cost so as to minimise the total inventory cost. As long as the expected stock-out cost declines faster than the increase in the carrying cost, increase in safety stock is justified.

11.2.3 Determination of Re-order Point

There is always a time lag between the time of placing an order for inventory and its actual delivery. This time lag is known as the lead time. If the lead time is zero, a firm can make an order for the EOQ when the stock of inventory touches zero. If, however, there is lead time equal to 3 days, the order will be placed three days in advance of the stock level touching zero. If a firm maintains a safety level of stock of 2 days in order to protect itself from the stock-out cost, the order should be placed 5 days in advance of the inventory stock touching zero. The time so preceding should be equal to the sum of lead time and the number of days for which safety stock will last. Again, if the usage rate of inventory is higher, the order has to be placed at a much earlier point of time. This is because the stock of inventory touches the safety level of stock in a shorter period of time. However, the point of time the order is placed should be determined carefully so that it should not be either too late or too early. If it is earlier than the optimum point, the carrying cost of inventories will unnecessarily rise. On the contrary, if it is late, the stock of inventory may decline beyond the safety level with the resultant possibility of a stock-out. The situation can well be explained in Fig 11.2.

In Fig 11.2, The y-axis shows the stock of inventory and the x-axis shows time. The stock of inventory moves in a saw-tooth pattern. In the beginning when EOQ reaches the store, the quantum of stock is at its highest. With its use, the level of stock declines and if no orders are placed again, it reaches zero level at the end of the period. After the stock comes to zero level, a fresh lot of EOQ reaches the store. However, as the firm does not allow the inventory to fall below the safety level, it must place an order for the inventory at Point S.

Re-order point is determined on the basis of lead time, day of safety level of stock and the usage rate.

The above explanation assumes that the moment an order is placed the goods reach the store. Lead time is, however, a common phenomenon, the firm must, therefore, place the new order at Point B so that by the time the stock touches the safety level, the order has reached the store. Again, if the usage rate is higher, the new order will be placed earlier at Point E.

Thus on the basis of the lead time *L*, days of safety level of stock, *D*, and the usage rate *U*, the re-order point is determined. The re-order point can be expressed as follows:

$$ROP = UL + UD \quad ...(11.5)$$

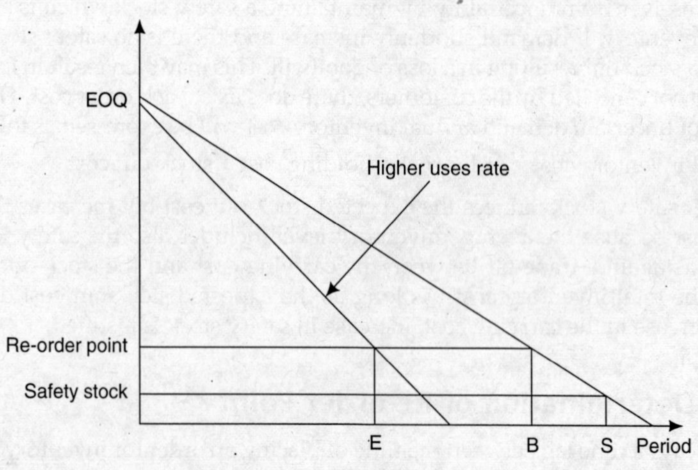

FIG. 11.2 Re-order point

EXAMPLE

If usage rate per day is 100 units, lead time is 5 days and safety level is equal to 6 days of sales, the re-order point will be:

$$ROP = 100 \times 5 + 100 \times 6 = 1{,}100 \text{ units}$$

In other words, a fresh order will be placed when the stock level comes down to 1100 units.

11.2.4 Safety Level of Stock

Safety stock is considered as a static reservoir, not involved in day-to-day turnover of stock. The actual items themselves are not retained as quality may deteriorate, but each item taken out of safety stock is replaced.

There are two types of safety stock models—one is the two-bin model and the other is the cyclical review model. The term, two-bin originates from the idea that the stock is stored in two bins and when the first bin is empty, a replacement order is made and until this arrives, the customers are served from the second bin. The cyclical review method is found when a variable quantity is ordered at fixed intervals of time.

The safety stock is generally expressed in terms of the number of days sales and is calculated by multiplying the usage rate times the number of days the firms like to hold the inventory as a protection against shortages. The number of days varies according to the conservative, aggressive or moderate attitude of the finance manager.

The safety stock is generally expressed in terms of the number of days.

Banks and Fabrycky (1987) have developed a model to incorporate the stock-out cost and on this basis, they try to determine the safety level of stock. They express the safety level of stock as follows:

$$S = [cTR\,(p - u)]/(cT + E)p \qquad ...(11.6)$$

Where:

p = rate of production per day
u = rate of demand per day
E = stock-out cost per unit per annum

EXAMPLE

Based on the earlier figures where R is 4.472 tonnes, holding cost is Rs 10 per tonne, p is 0.300 tonne, u is 0.274 tonne and E is Re 0.50, the safety level of stock will be:

$$S = \{4.472 \times 10 \times (0.300 - 0.274)\}/10.50 \times 0.300$$

$$= 1.16272/3.15 = 0.369 \text{ tonne}$$

11.3 JUST-IN-TIME INVENTORY SYSTEM

The just-in-time (JIT) inventory system was first adopted in Toyota factory in Japan and it was known in the very beginning as *kanban* system. The rationale behind the JIT inventory just-in-time (JIT) inventory system is that raw material arrives at the firm exactly when it is required for the production process.

system is that it reduces the carrying cost significantly inasmuch as raw material arrives at the firm exactly when it is required for the production process. JIT involves reducing the number of suppliers, streamlining the purchase procedure, redesigning the plant lay-out and proper control over production.

The suppliers should be few and well-chosen. The relationship with them should be close and well-regulated so that they supply defect-free, high quality inputs. This ensures the manufacture of high quality products as well as a reduction in pre-storage inspection cost.

As already stated, JIT ensures tuning of the consumption of raw material with its delivery time. If this is the case, the need for maintaining safety stocks can be avoided both at the suppliers and at the buyer's end.

In order to make JIT successful, the supplier must be educated to cooperate. They must, of course, be in the close proximity to ensure timely delivery of the material. In many cases, the supplier maintains a warehouse in the buyer's premises. Procedures need to be evolved in order to reduce the moving time with a view to reducing the inventory build-up along the moving line. The lay-out of the factory should be so designed as to minimise the distance over which the materials are moved. The material delivery process should be also improved. However, the most important feature is the need to revamp the entire organisational structure to pursue the common goal of making JIT a success.

However, if there is breakdown in the supply of inventory, the result may be catastrophic. There are many such examples. In General Motors, which was adopting the JIT system, the supply chain was broken in 1996 due to strike. The production was stopped. The loss was heavy.

SUMMARY

Maintaining inventory is beneficial as it meets the transaction, precautionary and speculative needs of the operation. But it also involves costs in the form of cost of material, order cost, carrying cost, financing cost and stock-out cost.

The goal of inventory management is to make the best use of inventory through its classification on the basis of its importance. Greater care is taken of more important items. The firm has to determine an economic order quantity through a trade-off between the carrying cost and the order cost so that the total cost is minimised. When suppliers offer quantity discounts, a firm may raise the size of its order over and above the EOQ if the benefits of discount reduce the total cost below the level warranted by the EOQ. Again, in cases of uncertain demand, the firm maintains a safety stock in order to protect itself from the stock-out cost. Safety stock depends inter alia on the production per day, demand per day and the stock-out cost.

The determination of a re-order point is also important. It is done on the basis of the safety level of stock, usage rate and the lead time.

The JIT inventory system reduces the inventory cost significantly insofar as the inputs arrive at the firm only when they are required for the production process.

POINTS TO REMEMBER

1. What are the benefits of holding inventory?
   - It meets the transaction needs, precautionary needs and the speculative needs of the operation.
2. What are the costs of holding inventory?
   - The costs having direct relationship with holding of inventory, are material cost, holding cost and financing cost.
   - The costs having inverse relationship with holding of inventory are order cost and stock-out cost.
3. What is ABC analysis?
   - Classification of inventory based on its importance and cost.
4. What is EOQ?
   - The size of a particular order where the order cost equals the holding cost of the average size of inventory or, in other words, the total cost is the minimum. In terms of equation,

$$EOQ = \sqrt{2aq/cT}$$

5. At what point of time, the subsequent order is placed?
   - When the existing order quantity of inventory falls to a point that accommodates the lead time and safety level of stock. In terms of equation,

Re-order point = Usage rate x lead time + usage rate x days of safety stock

6. How do you assess the safety level of stock?
   - Safety level of stock, normally expressed in terms of number of days, depends upon the usage rate and the number of days for which safety stock is maintained. Taking into account also the stock-out cost, it may be equal to:

$$S = [cTR\,(p - u)]/(cT + E)p$$

7. What is just-in-time inventory system?
   - Raw material reaches the firm exactly when it is required meaning that it does not require holding of inventory.

DESCRIPTIVE QUESTIONS

1. Explain the benefits and cost of maintaining inventory.
2. Explain the purpose and nature of ABC analysis.
3. What is EOQ? How is it determined when demand is known?
4. Does EOQ change with quantity discounts, and when demand is uncertain?
5. How is the re-order point determined?
6. What is safety level of stock? How is it computed?
7. Write a note on the JIT inventory system.

OBJECTIVE-TYPE QUESTIONS

1. Mark true or false.
   (a) Carrying cost and the order cost move in the same direction.
   (b) Lead time is large in case of JIT inventory system.
   (c) Safety level of stock is normally expressed in terms of amount of the raw material.
   (d) Stock-out cost is an implicit cost arising out of lost sales due to shortage of supply.
   (e) Inventory does not include semi-finished goods.
2. Choose the most suitable answer.
   (a) The larger the size of inventory:
      (i) the greater is the order cost
      (ii) the lower is the order cost
      (iii) the order cost remains unchanged
   (b) Holding cost:
      (i) increases with growing inventory
      (ii) decreases with growing inventory
      (iii) remains unchanged with growing inventory
   (c) Economic order quantity represents a point where:
      (i) order cost = holding cost
      (ii) order cost = total cost
      (iii) total cost tends to decline
   (d) Determination of re-order point depends upon:
      (i) lead time only
      (ii) usage rate only
      (iii) both of the above
   (e) JIT involves:
      (i) large carrying cost
      (ii) no carrying cost
      (iii) no order cost

NUMERICAL PROBLEMS

1. Total demand for a commodity is 1000 tonnes in time T. The carrying cost is Rs 20 per tonne of stock during time T, and the order cost is Rs 2 per order. Find out:
   (a) The EOQ and the number of orders. How long will a particular order of inventory last?
   (b) The EOQ if the order cost comes down to Re 1.
2. If total demand during a year is 50,000 tonnes, EOQ is 780 tonnes, how long will a particular order last?
3. EOQ is 14.1421 tonnes with a total demand for the stock being 1000 tonnes, order cost being Rs 2 per order and carrying cost being Rs 20 per tonne. The supplier provides discount at the rate of Re 0.10 each tonne if the purchase amount is at least 20 tonnes. Should the firm place an order for 20 tonnes in order to avail of the discount?
4. Based on the figures in the earlier problem where R was 14.1421 tonnes, holding cost is Rs 20 per tonne, rate of production per day 0.950 tonne, rate of demand per day 0.675 tonne and stock-out cost per unit per annum Re 0.50. Find the safety level of stock.
5. If usage rate is 0.950 tonne per day, lead time is 5 days and the safety level of stock is maintained for 5 days, find out the re-order point.
6. If annual consumption of raw material is 1100 units. Order cost is Rs 150 per order. Find the carrying cost per unit, if the EOQ is 40.62 units.
7. A firm uses 400 units of component every month for Rs 40 per unit. The order cost is Rs 100 and carrying cost is 15% of the value of the stock. Find out the EOQ.

SOLVED NUMERICAL PROBLEMS

1. A firm uses 1,100 units of a raw material per annum, the price of which is Rs 1,500 per unit. The order cost per order is Rs 150 and the carrying cost of the inventory is Rs 200 per unit. Find the EOQ and the number of orders that are to be made during the year.

   Solution

   Based on Eq. 11.2,

   $$EOQ = \sqrt{(2 \times 1,100 \times 150)/200} = 41 \text{ units}$$

   No. of orders during the year = 1,100/41 = 26.8 or 27

2. A factory uses 40,000 tonnes of raw material priced at Rs 50 per tonne. The holding cost is Rs 10 per tonne of inventory. The order cost is Rs 200 per order. Find the EOQ. Will this EOQ be maintained if the supplier introduces 5% discount if the order lot is 2000 tonnes or more?

   Solution

   (a) EOQ without discount $= \sqrt{(2 \times 40000 \times 200)/10}$
   $= 1,264.97$ tonnes

No. of orders = 40,000/1,264.97 = 31.62 or 32

Order cost = Rs 200 × 32 = Rs 6,400

Carrying cost = Rs 10/2 × 1,264.97 = 6,325

Total cost = Rs 6,400 + 6,325 = Rs 12,725

(b) EOQ with discount:

No. of orders = 40,000/2000 = 20

Order cost = Rs 200 × 20 = Rs 4,000

Carrying cost = Rs 10/2 × 2,000 = Rs 10,000

Price discount = 40000 × 0.05 = Rs 2,000

Total cost = 4,000 + 10,000 – 2,000 = Rs 12,000

Since total cost without discount > total cost with discount, discount may be availed. In this case, there will be deviation from the EOQ.

3. Find out the total demand for the commodity if the order cost is Rs 60 per order, the carrying cost is Rs 50 for an EOQ of 10 tonnes.

Solution

Based on Eq. 11.2

Q = (50 × 10 × 10)/(2 × 60) = 5,000/120 = 416.7 tonnes

4. If the usage rate per day is 50 units, lead time is 5 days and the safety level of stock is equal to 5 days of sales, find the re-order point.

Solution

ROP = 500 × 5 + 500 × 5 = 5,000 units.

The moment the order lot will fall to 5,000 units, a fresh order for raw material will be placed.

5. If usage rate is 500 units of raw material per day, safety stock is equal to 5 days of sales, re-order point is represented by 3500 units, find out the lead time in number of days.

Solution

UL = 3,500 – 5 × 500 = 1,000 units

or L = 1,000/500 = 2 days

6. The size of order is 500 tonnes. Holding cost is Rs 20 per tonne. Production per day is 0.500 tonnes. Demand per day is 0.450 tonnes. Stock-out cost per unit per annum is Re 1. Find the safety level of stock.

Solution

Based on Eq. 11.6,

S = {500 × 20 × (0.500 – 0.450)}/{(20 + 1) × 0.500}

= 47.62 tonnes

7. The minimum and maximum weekly consumption of raw material in a company is 25 and 75 units, respectively. The reorder quantity is 300 units, and the lead time lies between 4 and 6 weeks. Find out the reorder level and average reorder period.

Solution

Reorder level = Maximum use per week × maximum reorder period

Or 75 × 6 = 450 units

Average reorder period = (4 weeks + 6 weeks)/2 = 5 weeks

Mini Case

SPL Idols manufactures idols and allied products. It requires casts to manufacture its products because it does not produce any cast itself. After make-or-buy analysis, it was preferred to buy casts. So it buys casts from a foundry. The castings are used throughout the year.

In a year, 50,000 castings are bought at a rate of Rs 900 per cast. The holding cost is a bit high because adequate temperature needs to be maintained for the castings. The holding cost is thus Rs 350 per casting. The order cost is Rs 900 per order. The lead time is 6 days but sometimes it goes up to even 10 days. On the basis of the experience, it has been found that 70% of the orders involve 6 days lead time, 20% of the deliveries involve 8 days lead time and the rest 10% of the deliveries take 10 days in transporting castings from foundry to its own plant.

The firm assumes 15% risk in terms of out-of-stock. Again, in a highly competitive market, the firm tries to reduce the ordering cost and the carrying cost, both. It reconstructs its godown to lower the carrying cost. The carrying cost comes down to Rs 250 per unit. It also re-engineers the ordering mechanism and is able to reduce the ordering cost to Rs 850.

Questions:

1. Find out the new EOQ. How much is it different from the old EOQ?
2. Considering the stock-out cost, what will be the safely level of stock and the reorder point?

REFERENCE

Banks, J. and W.J. Fabrycky (1987). *Procurement and Inventory Systems Analysis*. Englewood Cliffs: Prentice-Hall.

SELECT FURTHER READINGS

Attila, C. and M.C. Lovell, eds. (1988). *The Economics of Inventory Management*. Amsterdam: Elsevier Science Publishers.

Tersine, R.J. (1994). *Principles of Inventory and Materials Management*. Englewood Cliffs: Prentice-Hall.

12

SOURCES OF SHORT-TERM FINANCE

OBJECTIVES

To analyse trade credit as a source of short-term funds

To focus on short-term funds financing by commercial banks, and the norms in this respect in India

To describe commercial papers as an instrument for short-term funds

After the discussion of the current assets, it is worthwhile to discuss how they are financed. It has already been mentioned that the current assets are financed partly with short-term funds and partly with long-term funds. However, the discussion in the present chapter is limited to the short-term funds or the current liabilities as they are an essential part of the net working capital.

There are two classes of short-term funds: spontaneous and negotiated. Trade credits are the most important form of spontaneous financing: Negotiated funds are largely obtained from commercial banks and through the issue of notes and commercial papers.

Broadly speaking, there are two classes of short-term funds: spontaneous and negotiated. The former refers to those sources of funds that come up automatically in the normal course of business and do not require many formal arrangements on the part of the firm to avail of them. Trade credits are the most important form of spontaneous financing, although various accruals on account of wages, taxes and interest payments also form a part of this type of funds. On the contrary, negotiated funds are largely obtained from commercial banks and through the issue of notes and commercial papers.

12.1 TRADE CREDIT

12.1.1 Nature of Trade Credit

Trade credit or accounts payable is the mirror image of accounts receivable or the sundry debtors. It emerges when a firm purchases raw material on credit. Trade credit is a source of finance in the sense that it finances purchases during the period of the credit. When a firm buys material on credit instead of paying cash, this frees funds that can be used elsewhere in the same manner as if the funds had been borrowed. Trade credit is thus, the act of obtaining funds by delaying payments to the supplier.

The volume of trade credit depends upon the quantum of purchases and the period for which credit is available. For example, if a firm buys goods worth *Rs* 500 per day on a net 30 term, the amount of trade credit will be Rs 500 × 30 = Rs 15,000.

Trade credit emerges when a firm purchases raw material on credit. The volume depends upon the quantum of purchases and the period for which credit is available.

The nature of trade credit varies from one firm to the other. One form of trade credit does not carry instruments effecting transaction. It is known as open account. The supplier checks the creditworthiness of the buyer and after being confident, extends credit. But the supplier may find fall into trouble if the buyer does not make the payments.

On the other hand, there is another form of trade credit that requires instruments, such as, promissory notes or bills of exchange. If the supplier needs immediate payment, he gets the bill of exchange discounted by any commercial bank. If the buyer has high credit rating, the bill can be sold. The instrument minimises the risk of bad debt losses but dishonour of the instrument cannot be ruled out.

12.1.2 Benefits and Costs of Trade Credit

Trade credits are preferred to other sources of short-term funds. There are primarily three reasons for this. First, they are easily available. Except in cases of firms that are financially very weak, they are easily available without any formal negotiation or arrangement.

Secondly, these credits are highly flexible. Their size increases or decreases in conformity with the level of operation. With an increase in sales, the size of purchase increases and the volume of trade credit expands. When sales shrink, trade credit automatically shrinks.

Lastly, trade credit carries fewer restrictions. In case of negotiated funds, the lender often puts restrictions on the use of the funds. In case of trade credit, however, there are no such restrictions. Moreover, late payment of bills is a common practice, whereas, late payment of negotiated funds can lead to severe consequences.

Trade credits are preferred to other sources of short-term funds. There are primarily three reasons for this. First, they are easily available. Secondly, these credits are highly flexible. Lastly, trade credit carries fewer restrictions.

Trade credits do have benefits, but, at the same time, they also carry costs. These costs are either implicit or explicit. Implicit costs are difficult to quantify. The cost of paying late in form of reduced credit-standing of the firm is an example of an implicit cost. Similarly, an implicit cost also exists when the supplier charges a higher price in order to pass on the cost of credit to the buyer. On the other hand, explicit costs are easy to quantify. When the buyer does not avail of the discount provided by the supplier, the cost of foregoing discount is an explicit cost.

Let us quantify the cost of foregoing discount. When the supplier provides no discount, the credit term is simply net 30 or net 60, in such cases there is no cost of foregoing discount. Similarly, the cost does not exist when the terms of the credit are 2/10 net 30 and the buyer makes a payment for Rs 98 within 10 days. The cost does, however, exist when the buyer does not avail of the discount and makes the payment within 30 days. This is because the buyer does not only pay Rs 98 but also Rs 2 that can be analogised with interest payment on the principal amounting to Rs 98. In other words, the buyer is borrowing Rs 98 for 30 – 10 = 20 days and paying an interest of Rs 2. When the amount of interest, principal and the number of days is known, the interest rate can easily be calculated. There are two ways to calculate interest. While one is the simple interest rate method, the other is the compound interest rate method. In a single case, it is normally the simple interest rate method that is followed. But if it is a continual phenomenon all year round, the compound interest rate method is followed. Let us first explain the simple interest rate method. The simple effective annual interest rate,

$$k = \{C/(100\% - CD)\} \text{ x } 365/N \qquad (12.1)$$

Where CD = cash discount

N = number of days for which payment can be delayed by giving up the cash discount

EXAMPLE

In the above example, CD = 2%, N = 20 days. So:

$$k = (2\%/98\%) \times 365/20 = 37.24\%$$

Again, based on the compound interest rate method, the effective annual interest rate, the effective annual interest rate on trade credit can be expressed as follows:

$$k = [1 + \{(\text{discount }\%/(100 - \text{discount }\%)\}]^{\{365/(\text{days to pay} - \text{discount period})\}} - 1 \qquad ...(12.2)$$

EXAMPLE

Based on the above figures the effective annual rate of interest on trade credit will be:

$$k = [1 + \{(0.02/0.98)\}]^{\{365/(30 - 10)\}} - 1$$
$$= (1.020408)^{18.25} - 1 = 0.4458 = 44.58\%$$

Now the question is whether the firm should avail of trade credit if bank loans are available at a lower interest rate. The answer taking into account the explicit cost is that they should not. Nevertheless, trade credit is preferred. This is because it possesses certain merits as discussed above that are not possessed by other sources of short-term funds.

12.1.3 Stretching of Accounts Payable

Sometimes the buyer stretches the payment even beyond the due date. This is tantamount to an increase in the positive float. The longer the time before payment, the lower is the present value of such payments and the higher is the value of the firm. However, stretching of payment entails upon the buyers creditworthiness, and sometimes manifests in the worsening of relations between the buyer and the supplier. Moreover, when the supplier imposes a penal interest rate during the stretched period, the benefits of this practice are eroded. The larger the penal rate, the greater is the possibility of a positive net cost of stretching accounts payable.

EXAMPLE

Assume three possibilities with a credit term of 2/10 net 30, opportunity cost of capital at 15% p.a. (0.0411% per day) and with Rs 10,000 being the average invoice value of the order:

1. The buyer does not stretch the payment and pays within 30 days;
2. The buyer stretches the payment by 10 days and makes payment within 40 days but does not pay any penal interest rate;
3. The buyer stretches the payment by 10 days and pays 2% penal interest rate.

Find out the present value of payment in these three different cases.

Case 1: Rs 10,000/(1 + 30 (0.000411) = Rs 9,878.20

Case 2: Rs 10,000/(1 + 40 (0.000411) = Rs 9,838.26

Case 3: Rs 10,000 × {(1 + 0.02)/(1 + 40 × 0.000411)} = Rs 10,003.50

It is evident from the above example that stretching the payment by 10 days is the best option if it does not involve any penal interest rate. The finance manager has to examine every possibility and then select the one where the present value of payment is the minimum.

12.2 BANK FINANCE

12.2.1 Nature of Bank Finance

Commercial banks have a significant role to play in meeting the short-term financial needs of the corporate sector. Trade credit meets only a limited part of this need. The gap is, therefore, largely met by the commercial banks.

Broadly speaking, there are two forms of bank credit. First, is unsecured credit that is not covered by collateral securities. The other is secured credit that is backed by collateral—which may be receivables or even inventory. Again, the credit is provided either as a single loan or as a line of credit. A single loan is normally provided for a specific purpose. The firm signs a promissory note to document its indebtedness and repays the loan within the stipulated period.

On the other hand, a line of credit is more common. When a borrower approaches the bank at short intervals, the process would be cumbersome if he is required every time by the bank to go through the necessary formalities. This is why the bank fixes an upper limit within which the borrower can draw any amount. The upper limit is fixed considering the fund requirements and the financial position of the borrower as also the safety factor.

The amount of borrowing from the bank can be drawn in a number of ways. They are as follows:

1. Overdraft
2. Cash credit
3. Purchase or discounting of bills
4. Letter of credit
5. Working capital loan

First, overdraft facilities allow the borrower to draw in excess of the balance lying in his current account but within the limit fixed. Interest is charged on the daily balance subject to some minimum charges. Second, cash credit is to large extent similar to an overdraft. Its limit is fixed on the basis of the security of current assets. Third, under the purchase or discounting of bills, a borrower can obtain funds against the bills. Fourth, the letter of credit arrangement is used in case of foreign suppliers. The bank opens a letter of credit account in the name of the customer. It pays the amount to the supplier and after the credit period is over, collects the payment from the customer. Last, when the borrower needs additional amounts over and above the fixed credit limit, the bank provides funds in the form of a demand loan. In such cases, the rate of interest is higher.

The various modes of security that a bank may require are as follows:

1. Hypothecation
2. Pledge
3. Mortgage
4. Lien

In case of hypothecation, the security is a moveable property, usually inventory. The property is not handed over to the bank. The hypothecation is simply a charge against property for the amount of debt. On the contrary, under a pledge, the security is transferred to the possession of the bank. In the event of default, the bank can sell the goods under security. Mortgage is different from the above two in the sense that it involves the transfer of immoveable property. The possession of the property lies in the hands of the borrower but the title lies in the hands of the lender. Lastly, lien is the right of the lender to retain property of the borrower until the amount borrowed is repaid.

12.2.2 Effective Interest Rate

The effective interest is the amount of interest divided by the amount of the loan that the borrower gets for use expressed as percentage. In cases where interest is paid on maturity, the entire loan amount is taken into account for the calculation of the effective rate. However, when the interest is collected up front, the amount of interest is divided by the net amount of loan received.

EXAMPLE

If loan amount is Rs 1000 and the amount of interest is Rs 100, find out the effective interest rate:

(a) when interest is paid on the maturity; and
(b) interest is collected up front:

1. when interest is paid on the maturity:
   100/1000 = 0.10 or 10%
2. when interest is collected up front:
   100/(1000 – 100) = 0.1111 or 11.11%

Again, if compensating balance requirements are imposed by the bank, the borrower will be required to maintain a minimum balance in his account with the bank, this amount is deducted from the amount of the loan.

EXAMPLE

If the compensating balance is Rs 50 and the interest is paid on maturity, the effective rate will be:

$$100/(1000 - 50) = 0.1053 \text{ or } 10.53\%$$

12.2.3 Bank Financing Norms in India

Prior to the nationalisation of commercial banks in India, bank lending was not properly in tune with the working capital requirements of the corporate sector. Statistics reveal that during 1950s and the first half of 1960s, bank lending had grown over 7.7-fold as compared to only a 6.7-fold increase in current assets in the manufacturing and processing industry. Because of easy availability of bank credit, the corporate sector did not use it properly. The Dehejia Committee reported this anomaly and recommended a few measures in 1969. However, long before the Dehejia Committee recommendations were fully implemented, demand for bank credit rose very high in 1974 despite, a stagnation in industrial production. Many banks had, therefore, to freeze credit limits. The Reserve Bank of India appointed a committee under the chairmanship of P.L. Tandon in July 1974 to suggest guidelines for the allocation and use of bank credits.

Tandon Committee Recommendations: The Committee found several weaknesses of the working capital financing system. These were as follows:

1. Bank credit flowed on the basis of demand for it by the borrowers and not on the basis of credit planning of the banks;
2. The quantum of bank credit was dependent on the security available and not on the level of operations of the borrowing firm;
3. The bank credit was treated as the first source of finance and not as supplementary to the other sources of finance.

In view of the perusal of the existing situation, the committee was of the view that the banks should only supplement the borrowers' resources meant for carrying an acceptable level of current assets. The acceptable level was the level of current assets conforming strictly to the production plan, economic ordering level, lead time and the safety factor. At the same time, supplementing of the borrowers' resources means that a part of the resources was to be met by the borrowers themselves out of their long-term capital.

The Committee has suggested three ways of bank financing. These were as follows:

1. A quarter of the working capital gap is to be met by the borrower and the rest by the bank. The working capital gap means the difference between the current assets and the current liabilities excluding the bank borrowing. Suppose the current assets amount to Rs 100. The current liabilities excluding bank credit are Rs 20. The working capital gap will be Rs 80. Now the borrower has to contribute Rs 20 and the remaining Rs 60 can be extended by the bank. The current ratio will naturally be 100:80.
2. The other alternative is that the borrower has to contribute to the extent of 25% of the current assets. In this case, with current assets of Rs 100 and current liabilities of Rs 20, the borrower's contribution will be Rs 25. Now the bank will extend only Rs (100 – 20 – 25) = Rs 55. The current ratio will thus be 100:75.

3. Still another alternative was for the borrower to contribute the entire amount of core assets and also 25% of the current assets net of core assets. The core assets were defined as 25% of the current assets. If the current assets amount to Rs 100, the core assets would amount to Rs 25 and the borrower would contribute Rs [25 + 0.25 (100 – 25)] = Rs 44 out of long-term capital. With the current liabilities being Rs 20, the bank credit would be Rs [100 – (20 + 44)] = Rs 36. The current ratio would be further strengthened to 100:56.

The committee's view was that the third alternative was ideal, and that the first two should be relied upon only as stop-gap arrangements. In order to restrict bank credit, the committee suggested that the fixed part of the working capital requirements should be met through demand loans and the variable part through cash credit, a part of which may be by way of bills. However, a rational restructuring of bank credit would only be possible when the bank had the necessary information about the borrower. For this reason the Committee emphasised the periodic submission of operating and financial statements by the borrower.

The Tandon committee's view was that the third alternative was ideal, and that the first two should be relied upon only as stop-gap arrangements.

The RBI considered the main recommendations of the Tandon Committee. At the same time, however, it constituted a Committee of Direction in 1975 for an on-going review of, and modifications to, the Tandon Committee recommendations. Accordingly, banks were advised to relax the current ratio norm of the borrower under specific conditions.

Chore Committee Recommendations: The recommendations of the Chore Committee appointed in 1979 were not very different from those of the Tandon Committee. The committee stressed the second method of financing as suggested by Tandon Committee. In cases of borrowers experiencing financial hardship, the bank could lend additional funds. Such excess lending should, however, be segregated and treated as a working capital loan carrying a higher interest rate, normally, 2% above the cash credit rate. The committee also suggested the submission of a monthly cash budget by the borrower so that the bank could differentiate between the normal month and peak month requirements for funds. Last but not least, it suggested discouraging the borrowers seeking ad hoc limits over and above the sanctioned limit. This it suggested would be possible achieved by charging a higher interest rate on the additional funds.

Commercial Bank Finances for Corporate Working Capital: With the growth of the corporate sector in the Indian economy, the funds flowing from the commercial banks for meeting their working capital needs has increased from year to year. The following table provides a bird's-eye view of these flows.

Rs Crore

At March-end	Bills purchased & discounted	Cash credit & overdraft
2004	47,926	3,00.413
2005	62,642	3,48,556
2006	1,03,657	5,65,001
2007	1,24,424	7,12,866

Source: *Reserve Bank of India, Report on Trends and Progress of Banking in India for 2004–05 & 2006–07*

Liberalised Lending Policy since 1997–98: The Reserve Bank of India has now given freedom to commercial banks to make their own assessment of the working capital needs and to evolve suitable internal guidelines for evaluating working capital projections made by the borrowers. The turnover method of working capital financing of small-scale borrowers has been made more flexible. Under this method, one-quarter of the projected turnover of a borrowing unit is considered as its working capital requirement, of which 80 per cent is normally provided by the bank. The banks are free to set the upper limit in this case. As regards export credit, the provision for the margin requirements has been done away with. Again, the banks can raise the loan component of the working capital finance to 100 per cent. The banks form a consortium and go for a syndicated lending if the amount of lending is big. However, they follow the exposure norms for individual and group borrowers as prescribed by the Reserve Bank.

12.3 OTHER SOURCES OF SHORT-TERM FUNDS

Besides bank finances, there are also other sources of short-term funds, such as, issue of commercial paper, factoring, forfaiting, inter-corporate deposits, etc. Factoring and forfaiting have been discussed in Chapter 10. The present chapter discusses commercial paper.

12.3.1 Commercial Papers

Commercial paper (CP) originated in the USA on the pattern of short-term notes which meant that a company in need of short-term funds could issue CP. It is now common in developed and developing countries. There are of course differences in the procedure of issue in different countries.

In India, the issue of CP came into being after the Vaghul Committee recommendations of 1987.

In India, the issue of CP came into being after the Vaghul Committee recommendations of 1987. Here a banking company cannot issue CP. CP is issued in the form of usance promissory notes. The maturity lies between 15 days and less than one year. It is only blue-chip companies that can raise funds through the issue of CP. It is issued in the multiples of Rs 5 lakh but the minimum amount to be invested by a single investor in the primary market must be at least Rs 10 lakh. The CP cannot be underwritten, nor it can be co-accepted. It can also be issued to non-resident Indians (NRIs) but only on a non-repatriation basis.

CP is issued at a discount. The discount serves the purpose of an interest rate. Moreover, there are certain costs in the issue that are to be taken into account while computing the effective interest rate. The effective interest rate can be expressed on follows:

$$\text{EIR} = (\text{Total financing cost/net cash from the issue}) \times (365/\text{days of maturity}) \quad ...(12.3)$$

EXAMPLE

The issue cost of *CP* for Rs 10,00,000 is 1%. The discount is 10% and the maturity is 180 days. Find out the EIR.

The net amount received by the issuer = 10,00,000 – (1,00,000 + 10,000) = 8,90,000

$$(1{,}10{,}000/8{,}90{,}000) \times (365/180) = 0.2506 = 25.06\%$$

12.3.2 Public Deposits

The working capital requirements are also met through unsecured public deposits. The term of such deposits normally varies between 6 months and 3 years. The ceiling on the interest rates was dismantled in 1996, although longer term carries higher interest rates.

Such deposits are governed by the Companies (Acceptance of Deposits) Amendment Rules 1978, as per which such deposits cannot exceed one-quarter of share capital and free reserves and a company accepting deposits needs to disclose its financial performance.

The companies prefer to accept such deposits because neither restrictive covenants are involved nor cumbrous procedures are there. Moreover, they do not involve the collaterals.

12.3.3 Intercorporate Deposits

A company gets deposits from other companies. The term varies from 1 day to 6 months. The 1-day deposit is normally known as call deposits. The other short-term deposits are accepted by those companies that have to tide over the disruption in production, causing illiquidity for some time. However, too much of secrecy is maintained in this regard by both the depositors and the borrowers.

SUMMARY

Short-term financing is either spontaneous or negotiated. Trade credit emerging out of credit purchases is the most significant form of spontaneous source of funds. Trade credit is either in the form of an open transaction or it carries an instrument effecting it. This form of financing does have benefits, but, at the same time, it involves certain implicit and explicit costs. Payments can be stretched only to an extent where the cost of stretching does not exceed the benefits from it.

Among the sources of negotiated financing, banks are the most important source. Bank credit is either unsecured or against collateral. There are different modes of collateral, such as hypothecation, pledge, mortgage and lien. Bank credit takes the form of overdraft, cash credit, discounting of bills, letters of credit and working capital loan. The effective interest rate depends on whether interest is paid up-front or at maturity or if there is an amount involved as compensating balance requirements.

The banks in India follow norms for providing working capital funds. The norms are as per those suggested by the Tandon Committee as far back as in 1970s. They have, however, been modified as per the suggestions of the Chore Committee.

Among the other sources of short-term funds is the issue of CP. It involves costs in form of discount provided at the time of offer and the other costs associated with the issue. These costs do matter in determining the effective interest rate.

POINTS TO REMEMBER

1. What are the different forms of short-term funds to finance the current assets?
   - Spontaneous funds known as trade credit. They emerge when a firm buys raw material on credit terms.
   - Negotiated funds that take the form of short-term loans either from banks or from other sources.
2. Why do firms prefer trade credit?
   - It is easily available.
   - It is highly flexible.
   - It carries fewer restrictions.
3. Can the payment be stretched beyond the due date?
   - It can be if the present value of payment is lower than in the case of no stretch.
4. What are the different forms of bank finances?
   - Overdraft
   - Cash credit
   - Purchase/discounting of bills
   - Letter of credit
   - Working capital loan
5. What are the different modes of security against bank loan?
   - Hypothecation
   - Pledge
   - Mortgage
   - Lien
6. What are the factors considered while computing effective interest rate on bank loan?
   - Whether interest is paid on maturity or it is paid upfront.
   - Compensating balance requirements of the banks, if any.
7. Comment on the norms related to bank finances for working capital.
   - Since 1997–98, banks are free to assess the working capital needs of a firm and to evolve suitable guidelines.
8. What is commercial paper?
   - It is an instrument in form of usance promissory note issued by companies to get short-term funds

DESCRIPTIVE QUESTIONS

1. What is trade credit? What are its benefits and costs?
2. How far can the payment on trade credit be stretched?
3. What are the different forms of bank credit? Explain different modes in which collateral is placed.
4. How do you calculate the effective interest rate on bank credit?
5. Explain the norms suggested by Tandon Committee for providing bank credit. How did the recommendations of Chore Committee bring modifications to then existing norms?
6. Write a note on commercial paper (CP) as a source of short-term finance.

OBJECTIVE-TYPE QUESTIONS

1. Mark true or false.
   (a) Trade credit represents a non-negotiated, spontaneous flow of funds.
   (b) Open account involves writing of instruments effecting transaction.
   (c) In case of 2/10 net 60, the firm has an explicit cost if it avails of the discount.
   (d) In case of 2/10 net 60, the firm has explicit cost if it does not make payment within 60 days.
   (e) Mortgage involves transfer of raw material to the lender.
   (f) Cash credit and overdraft is the same mode of lending.
2. Choose the most suitable answer.
   (a) An increase in the size of operation helps:
      (i) increase the size of trade credit
      (ii) decrease the size of trade credit
      (iii) create no change in trade credit
   (b) The size of overdraft depends on:
      (i) value of security of current assets
      (ii) value of security of fixed assets
      (iii) neither of the above
   (c) Mortgage involves:
      (i) moveables as collateral
      (ii) immoveables as collateral
      (iii) no collateral
   (d) In the first alternative under the Tandon Committee norms, the current ratio is:
      (i) 100/80
      (ii) 100/75
      (iii) 100/56

(e) Commercial paper is issued by:
   (i) any company
   (ii) only blue-chip companies
   (iii) only government companies

NUMERICAL PROBLEMS

1. Find the effective annual interest rate on trade credit if the credit term is 3/10 net 30, and the firm does not avail of the discount facility.
2. Assume a credit term of 3/10 net 30, opportunity cost of capital at 12% p.a., and Rs 20,000 being the average invoice value of the order. Should the buyer stretch the payment by 10 days and pay 2% penal interest rate?
3. The issue cost of CP for Rs 10,00,000 is 2%. The discount is 12% and the maturity is 180 days. Find out the EIR.
4. A company raises Rs 10,00,000 by issuing CP for 120 days. It is sold at 10% discount. Stamp duty and other charges account for 2% of the value. Calculate the effective cost of CP.
5. With current assets of Rs 5,000, current liabilities of Rs 1,000 and a borrower's contribution of being Rs 1,250, find the amount of bank lending as per the second norm suggested by the Tandon Committee.
6. If loan amount is Rs 5,000 and the amount of interest is Rs 500, find the effective interest rate:
   (a) when interest is paid on the maturity;
   (b) when interest is collected up front.
7. Based on Tandon Committee recommendation, how much will a bank lend under the second method of lending if total current asset is Rs 60,000, current asset other than bank borrowing is Rs 15,000 and core current asset is Rs 7,500?

SOLVED NUMERICAL PROBLEMS

1. Find out the effective annual interest rate if sale is made on a credit term of 2/10 net 60 and the payment is not made within 10 days.

Solution

(a) As per the simple interest rate method mentioned in Eq. 12.1,
Effective Annual Interest Rate = $(2\%/98\%) \times 365/50 = 14.90\%$

(b) As per the compound interest rate method mentioned in Eq. 12.2,
Effective Annual Interest Rate = $\{1 + (0.02/0.98)\}^{365/50} - 1 = 0.1589 = 15.89\%$

2. Company A buys components from Company B on credit terms of 2/10 net 35. In a subsequent deal, the former requests the latter to raise the discount percentage to 3 without any change in the credit period. Company B raises the discount to 3% and also changes the credit period, as a result of which the cost of not paying within the credit period rises three-fold. Find the new credit period.

Solution

Cost of trade credit = (0.02/0.98) × (365/35) = 0.2128 = 21.28%

Raised cost of credit = 21.28% × 3 = 63.84%

Changed period of credit:

$$(0.03/0.97) \times \{365/(x - 10)\} = 63.84\%$$
$$\text{or } x = (10.95/0.619) + 10$$
$$\text{or } x = 27.69 \text{ or } 28 \text{ days}$$

3. A firm buys raw material for Rs 50,000 on a credit term of 2/10 net 30. It has to opt for one of two alternatives. One is to pay within 30 days. The other is to stretch the payment by 20 days more or to 50 days and to pay a penal interest rate of 1%. Find which one of the two alternatives will be more suitable with a given opportunity cost of capital at 15% p.a.

Solution

Interest rate per day = 0.15/365 = 0.0004109

Present value of payment:

(a) when payment is made within 30 days:
Rs 50,000/(1 + 30 × 0.0004109) = Rs 49,391.16

(b) when payment is made within 50 days along with penal interest rate:
Rs 50,000 × {(1 + 0.01)/(1 + 50 × 0.0004109)} = Rs 49,483.36

The present value of the payment is lower in case the payment is made within 30 days. So this alternative is preferred.

4. Find the effective interest rate of a bank loan if the loan amount is Rs 50,000; the compensating balance is Rs 1,000 and the rate of interest is 15% p.a.

Solution

Interest payment = 0.15 × Rs 50,000 = Rs 7,500

Effective interest rate = 7,500/(50,000 – 1,000) = 0.15306 = 15.31%

If interest is collected upfront:

Effective interest rate = 7,500/(50,000 – 1,000 – 7,500) = 0.1807 = 18.07%

5. The face value of a commercial paper is Rs 5,00,000. The issue cost is 1%. The discount rate is 10% and the maturity is 180 days. Find the effective interest rate.

Solution

Effective interest rate = {(Int. + Cost of issue)/Net amount} × 365/180
= (55,000/4,45,000) × 365/180 = 0.2506 = 25.06%

SELECT FURTHER READINGS

Gallinger, G.W. and P.B. Healey (1991). *Liquidity Analysis and Management*. Reading MA: Addison-Wesley.

Gupta, L.C., ed. (1988). *Banking and Working Capital Finance*. New Delhi: Macmillan.

Part IV

Long-term Financing and Dividend Decisions

After determining the size of the fixed and current assets, funds are then raised to finance these assets. The raising of funds involves a few issues, such as the size of funds, their sources and what should be the ratio between the different types of funds. Again, as far as the sources of funds are concerned, the choice of internal sources or retained earnings cannot be overlooked. The size of retained earnings depends inter alia on the firm's dividend policy and, therefore, dividend decisions are related to the financing decisions.

The present part discusses these issues. The discussion is divided into the following chapters:

1. Capitalisation
2. Capital Structure
3. Corporate Securities
4. Term Loans and Leases
5. Dividend theories and policies

13

CAPITALISATION

OBJECTIVES

To explain the concept of capitalisation
To discuss the meaning, causes and effects of over-capitalisation
To discuss the meaning, causes and effects of under-capitalisation
To focus on the ways designed to achieve optimal capitalisation

The financing decision in a firm involves two basic issues. The first is concerned with the amount of capital employed in a firm which is often referred to as capitalisation. The other is related to the proportion in which different forms of capital make up the firm's capital structure. The present chapter deals with the first of these issues. The discussion of the second will find place in the next chapter.

13.1 SIGNIFICANCE AND BASES OF CAPITALISATION

13.1.1 Meaning of Capitalisation

The term, capitalisation refers to the magnitude of capital employed in a firm. This includes both long-term and short-term capital. Any financing decision in respect of capitalisation is of much significance to the firm. This is because any deviation from optimum capitalisation may lead to unhealthy environment, and come in the way of maximisation of the value of the firm. If the size of the capital is more than optimal, a part of it will remain idle, this will entail on the profitability of operations. If it is less than optimal, this will affect liquidity. This is why an estimate of the firm's capital requirements must be made very carefully, after a thorough study of the cost of the assets and the earning capacity of the firm.

13.1.2 Bases of Capitalisation

There are two bases for estimating the firm's capital requirements. One basis is the cost of the assets and the other the earnings of the firm. The cost theory of capitalisation suggests that the

If the size of the capital is more than optimal, a part of it will remain idle, this will entail on the profitability of operations. If it is less than optimal, this will affect liquidity. This is why an estimate of the firm's capital requirements must be made very carefully.

amount of capital in a firm should be equal to the value of its assets. The assets include both fixed and current assets as also certain intangible ones, such as, promotional and organisational expenses, goodwill, patent, etc. If all of them taken together value Rs 1,00,000, the funds to be raised from different sources should be equal to Rs 1,00,000.

The cost theory of capitalisation seems to be logical insofar as the amount of funds collected in the firm depends on the value of assets. In fact, the very purpose of fund collection is to invest it in different forms of assets. Nevertheless, this theory does not provide a sufficient basis for capitalisation in a firm with fluctuating earnings. When the market price of shares fluctuates, discrepancy may appear between the value of the firm's assets and the value of its shares.

This limitation of the cost theory has led to the acceptance of the earning theory. The earning theory of capitalisation suggests that a firm should be capitalised on the basis of the expected earnings and the rate at which earnings are capitalised. If a firm expects a net annual earning of Rs 5,000, and if the minimum acceptable rate of return, which is the basis of the capitalisation rate, is 10%, the amount of capital in the firm should be equal to Rs 5,000 x 100/10 = Rs 50,000.

Here it may be pointed out that the earnings for this purpose represent the future annual net income. Estimates of future annual income are made on the basis of historical profit. The only care that needs to be taken is that the period representing the historical income should be a normal one without having any significant trend for either a boom or a depression. At the same time, any expansion that may increase the volume of sales and thereby the earnings has to be taken into consideration. Moreover, only the operational income and not the non-recurring gains should enter the net annual earnings. Otherwise, the entire computation would be meaningless.

The capitalisation rate refers to the minimum acceptable rate of return. It is the reciprocal of average price-earning ratio or in other words, earning per share divided by market price of share.

After the determination of future net annual income, it is necessary to know the capitalisation rate. The capitalisation rate refers to the minimum acceptable rate of return that is more specifically the cost of capital. It can easily be estimated by way of compiling the rate of return among a large sample of similar firms. In actual practice, the reciprocal of average price-earning ratio is the capitalisation rate where the price-earning ratio is computed by dividing the market price of share by earning per share. Its reciprocal, earning per share divided by market price of share, is the capitalisation rate. If the market price of share is Rs 50 and the earning per share is Rs 5, the capitalisation rate would be (5/50)100 or 10%. The capitalisation rate of 10% means a price-earning ratio of 10/1. Now the future net annual income is multiplied by the price-earning ratio in order to determine capitalisation. To repeat the earlier example, an annual earning of Rs 5,000 with a capitalisation rate of 10% would necessitate Rs 50,000 as the firm's capital.

The earning theory has an edge over the cost theory insofar as the capitalisation is determined in the light of the firm's earning capacity. No discrepancy arises between the value of shares and the value of assets. However, its accuracy depends on the accurate estimate of the future earnings and of the capitalisation rate, in the absence of which results would be misleading. This is why the earning theory is preferably adopted in a going concern where estimates of future income can be made at least with some accuracy on the basis of the past ones. In the case of new enterprises, where historical profit does not stand as a guide to future income, the cost theory is preferred.

13.2 OVER-CAPITALISATION

Despite careful study of different variables in order to determine capitalisation, there is always a possibility of deviation from the optimum capitalisation point. This may result either in over-capitalisation or in under-capitalisation, both of which are harmful to a firm.

13.2.1 Meaning of Over-capitalisation

Over-capitalisation is a state of affairs when firm's capital is too large to be justified by its earnings. In other words, the amount of capital in the firm is too large to earn, on an average, a rate of return that is common among similar firms. Suppose the average annual earning in a firm is Rs 20,000. When the rate of return in similar firms is 10%, the amount of capital that is justified by its earnings should be Rs 20,000 x 100/10 or Rs 2,00,000. If the amount of capital raised is Rs 2,50,000, the rate of return would fall to $(20{,}000/2{,}50{,}000) \times 100$ or 8%. Since this rate is less than the going rate, the firm is said to be over-capitalised.

Over-capitalisation is a state of affairs when the amount of capital in the firm is too large to earn, on an average, a rate of return that is common among similar firms.

13.2.2 Causes of Over-capitalisation

Since over-capitalisation indicates reduced earning capacity of the assets, any factor that causes the book value of assets rise or that causes a diminution in the net earnings, may lead to a state of over-capitalisation. For example, when a partnership firm is converted into a corporate form of organisation or when a private limited company is converted into a public limited company, assets are generally transferred at an inflated price that in turn leads to an increase in the book value of assets. If increased book value of assets is not matched by a corresponding rise in earnings, over-capitalisation tends to occur.

Similarly, when firms are set up during a boom in the economy, the assets are bought at a higher price. This is not a feature that will cause much concern during the boom when earnings are high. However, the moment a depression sets in, earnings fall far below what is necessary to justify the existence of huge investments in assets, the result is a situation of over-capitalisation.

Again, there may be the expectation of higher earnings in the initial stage of setting up a firm, followed by the creation of larger assets which are later not matched by actual earnings, which may be especially true in the earlier stages of operation. The result is again over-capitalisation.

On the other hand, certain factors may lead to a shrinkage in the firm's net earnings, for example, an uneconomical production process leading to higher production cost, a higher rate of interest and taxation, a defective dividend and depreciation policy, etc., may also cause a disparity between capital employed in the firm and the earnings generated. Again, the result is over-capitalisation.

13.2.3 Effects of Over-capitalisation

Since earning per share in cases of over-capitalisation remains low, the market price of the shares falls. Sometimes, the market price of the shares is less than their par value, this may also cause a slump in the real value of shares, sometimes below their book value. It may be stated here that while the book value represents the value arrived at after dividing the sum of capital stock and the surpluses by the number of outstanding shares, the real value of shares is the value arrived at after dividing the capitalised value of the firm's assets by the number of outstanding shares. Because of decline in the real value of shares, the creditworthiness of the firm is affected. Lenders hesitate to lend funds to the firm that often jeopardises liquidity and whose operational efficiency falls. The firm often declares high dividend in order to regain lost confidence and pays dividend out of surpluses. This further worsens its financial position.

> Over-capitalisation affects not only the financial position of the firm but also the interests of its shareholders. The price of their shares on the stock exchange ebbs.

Over-capitalisation affects not only the financial position of the firm but also the interests of its shareholders. The price of their shares on the stock exchange ebbs, which in turn adversely effects their capital gains. The value of their shares as a collateral security diminishes. Moreover, they have to be satisfied with a lower amount of dividend.

Last but not least, society in general bears the brunt of an over-capitalised firm. Consumers get inferior products or products at higher prices. Liquidation may result if situation does not improve and this may lead to the retrenchment of the firm's labour force. The process of capital formation is hampered, and, as a chain reaction, development activity in the economy in general slows down.

13.3 UNDER-CAPITALISATION

13.3.1 Meaning and Causes of Under-capitalisation

Under-capitalisation is the exact opposite of over-capitalisation, meaning that the value of assets is small in relation to the firm's earnings. Naturally, the real value of the firm's shares is higher than their book value and the market price of shares is higher than their par value.

Under-capitalisation generally occurs in a firm which is incorporated during a depression. This is because assets are acquired at lower prices, but during the following boom, the earnings increase. The result is that the rate of return increases rapidly. The other reason for such firms becoming under-capitalised is that during a depression earnings are lower, but when a recovery sets in, earnings rise rapidly, with a corresponding rise in the average rate of return.

Moreover, the other factors like a conservative dividend policy which allows for larger reinvestment of profits and thereby higher earnings, lower rates of interest and taxation that maintains the net income at a higher level and, over and above these, operational efficiency – all of these factors can lead to under-capitalisation.

13.3.2 Impact of Under-capitalisation

Under-capitalisation is the exact opposite of over-capitalisation meaning that the value of assets is small in relation to the firm's earnings. Naturally, the real value of the firm's shares is higher than their book value and the market price of shares is higher than their par value.

Since the rate of return increases in a situation of under-capitalisation, this is not an economic problem. To the contrary, rather, it enhances the firm's creditworthiness in the capital market. However, high earnings may attract competitors who may give the under-capitalised firm a tough fight.

This is not all. In an under-capitalised situation, the firm's share prices register wide oscillations and speculators may take undue advantage of such a situation. Greater speculation in respect of the firm's shares on the stock exchange is not regarded a healthy sign for the under-capitalised firm.

Again, higher profits may lead to demands for higher wages and this may push up the cost of the product. The production process would become uneconomical, and the firm may lose its competitiveness in the market.

Unlike a situation of over-capitalisation, under-capitalisation is advantageous to the shareholders, because they get a higher rate of dividend. They also get higher capital gains from their shares on the stock exchange, and they are in a position to get higher loans against shares, as the value of shares as collateral security rises.

Apart from the shareholders, society as a whole benefit from an under-capitalised firm, as consumers get cheaper and better quality products. Moreover, a higher rate of return acts as booster to the economic activity in the country.

13.4 WAY TO OPTIMUM CAPITALISATION

under-capitalisation is a lesser evil than over-capitalisation.

The preceding discussion makes it clear that under-capitalisation is a lesser evil than over-capitalisation. So, whenever either of the two appears, the firm should try to remedy the situation and attain optimum capitalisation. There are two ways in which the problem can be tackled. One is the capital re-organisation, while the other is the maintenance of desired earnings.

13.4.1 Re-organisation of Capital

Re-organisation of capital includes several measures. Important among these are:

1. Redemption of high interest debt and of high dividend preference shares;
2. Changes in the par value of shares;
3. Changes in the number of shares including the capitalisation of the surpluses of the firm.

Redemption of High-interest Bonds and High-dividend Preference Shares: This is a method followed in cases of over-capitalisation. If high-coupon debentures and high-dividend preference shares are redeemed and converted into new low-cost issues, the servicing cost can be reduced and the net earnings can be raised. A couple of difficulties can, however, arise in this process. The first is that it is difficult to issue bonds or preference shares at a rate of interest or dividend lower than the prevailing market rate, and if they are issued, the investors would not want to invest in them. The second is that a large

The number of outstanding shares may be increased by issuing bonus shares so that the intensity of under-capitalisation may be eased. This is because the procedure reduces the earning per share.

sum of money would be needed for the redemption procedure. Redemption cannot, therefore, be suggested when a firm's financial position is weak.

Changes in the Par Value of Shares: In cases of over-capitalisation, the par value of shares may be reduced. This helps the firm obscure the real state of affairs without any change in its total liability. For example, if a company is capitalised at Rs 1,00,000 with 5,000 ordinary shares of Rs 20 each, its annual earning is Rs 10,000, and its earning per share is Rs 2 and the return on capital employed is 10%. If the par value of its shares is reduced by 50% and the same amount is transferred to a surplus account, the total of liabilities side of the balance sheet will not change, but there will be a 100% increase in the return on its equity shares.

In case of under-capitalisation, the par value of shares is reduced by stock split, that is, by increasing the number of shares. If the company splits 5,000 share into 10,000 shares, the par value of shares will come down to Re 10. The earning per share is reduced to Re 1, however, in this case the shareholders will not have any cause for worry because their total earnings remain the same as they now own two shares in the place of one.

Increase in the Number of Outstanding Shares: The number of outstanding shares may be increased by issuing bonus shares so that the intensity of under-capitalisation may be eased. This is because the procedure reduces the earning per share.

13.4.2 Maintenance of Desired Earnings

In cases of over-capitalisation, a higher rate of return can be ensured by increasing:

1. Profit margin
2. Asset turnover

The profit margin can be increased either by curtailing unnecessary expenses and optimising the use of resources or by increasing the revenue or sales. Similarly, asset turn over can be increased by either increasing sales or optimising the size of assets.

In cases of under-capitalisation, the firm can check the rate of return from growing beyond a limit. For this, expansion schemes should be undertaken or labour welfare schemes adopted. These methods would certainly be able to maintain a proper balance between the amount of capital and the earnings.

SUMMARY

Capitalisation, which denotes the amount of long-term and short-term capital employed in a firm, is an important issue involved in the financing decision. It is true that the amount of capital is determined on the basis of the cost of various assets, but at the same time, the amount of capital must justify the earnings of the firm. In case the magnitude of capital exceeds this limit so that a part of capital remains unemployed, the return on investment falls below the normal rate in the industry and the firm is said to be over-capitalised. This is often caused by factors that cause inflation of the book value of assets on the one hand, and shrinkage in the earnings, on the other. However, this lowers the value of the corporate wealth, and at the same time, adversely affects the interests of all parties related to the firm.

If, on the contrary, a firm is under-capitalised, the rate of return on investment rises. However, the firm's operation may be marred by the lack of the funds, and, at the same time, demand for higher wages in view of a higher rate of return, may create difficulties for the firm.

Thus, over-capitalisation and under-capitalisation are both undesirable, although, the latter is the lesser evil. A firm should not prefer either of the situation and should try to remedy these situations if and when they arise. The remedies may be either re-organisation of capital either through redemption of costly securities or through changes in the par value of shares or even through changes in the number of shares including the capitalisation of surpluses. At the same time, it should try to maintain the rate of return by increasing the profit margin and asset turnover. The ultimate motive is to attain a state of optimum capitalisation.

POINTS TO REMEMBER

1. What is capitalisation?
   - Capitalisation means magnitude of capital employed in a firm. It is based on the size and value of assets and also on the capitalisation rate.
2. What is over-capitalisation? When does it arise?
   - Over-capitalisation exists when poor earnings do not justify large amount of capital.
   - It emerges when assets are bought at higher prices; when firm set up during boom faces depression; and when earnings drop.
3. What are the effects of over-capitalisation?
   - Weak financial position
   - Fallen market value of shares
   - Poor quality/higher price of products

4. What is under-capitalisation? When does it arise?
   - Under-capitalisation means value of assets being small in relation to the firm's earnings
   - It occurs (a) when firms are set up during depression, (b) when conservative dividend policy is followed and (c) when operational efficiency is higher.
5. What are the effects of under-capitalisation?
   - Market value of shares > par value
6. How is optimal capitalisation achieved?
   - Through re-organisation of capital
     - Redemption of debt/high-dividend preference shares
     - Changes in the par value of shares
     - Increase in the number of outstanding shares
   - Maintenance of desired earnings either through raising profit margin or through raising asset turnover or through both.

DESCRIPTIVE QUESTIONS

1. What do you mean by over-capitalisation? What are its causes?
1. What do you mean by over-capitalisation? What are its causes?
2. Explain under-capitalisation and the factors behind its emergence.
3. "Over-capitalisation and under-capitalisation, are both unhealthy signs for a firm". Discuss. Can they be remedied?

OBJECTIVE-TYPE QUESTIONS

1. Mark true or false.
   (a) Capitalisation rate is the reciprocal of average price-earning ratio.
   (b) The lower the asset turnover, the higher is the rate of return on investment.
   (c) Over-capitalisation exists when the real value of shares is higher than their book value.
   (d) Under-capitalisation exists when the market price of shares is higher than their par value.
   (e) Share split reduces the earnings of the shareholders.
2. Choose the most suitable answer.
   (a) Capitalisation includes:
      (i) long-term capital only
      (ii) short-term capital only
      (iii) both of the above

(b) Cost theory suggests that the amount of capital should be equal to:
   (i) value of total assets
   (ii) value of fixed assets only
   (iii) value of fixed assets minus value of current assets

(c) Capitalisation rate is:
   (i) the minimum acceptable rate of return
   (ii) the rate at which capital is available
   (iii) the average rate of return

(d) Share split:
   (i) raises the value of each share
   (ii) lowers the value of each share
   (iii) keeps the value of each share unchanged

(e) Redemption of high-interest bonds is a remedy for:
   (i) over-capitalisation
   (ii) under-capitalisation
   (iii) both of the above

NUMERICAL PROBLEMS

1. The market price of a share is Rs 50, EPS is Rs 10, and net profit is Rs 20,000. Indicate optimal capitalisation.
2. If the market price of total assets is Rs 1,00,000, what should be the consolidated amount of debt and equity? Indicate this on the basis of the cost theory of capitalisation.
3. A company with a capital of Rs 7,00,000 earns Rs 50,000 a year, while the return on investment in that industry as a whole is 10%. Can it be called a situation of over-capitalisation? If it is over-capitalisation, indicate the amount by which profits need to be raised.

SOLVED NUMERICAL PROBLEMS

1. A company has a capital of Rs 10,00,000. The value of its assets amounts to Rs 10,00,000. Its earnings amount to Rs 90,000. The rate of return in the industry is 10%. Does it show optimal capitalisation?

   Solution

   As per the cost theory, capitalisation is optimal insofar as the capital is equal to the cost of the assets.

   But as per the earning theory, its earnings based on industry norms should be equal to:

   Rs 10,00,000 × 0.10 = Rs 1,00,000

   Since its actual earnings < the required earnings, the company stands over-capitalised.

2. The market price of the share of a company is Rs 100. The EPS is Rs 10. The net profit is Rs 50,000. Find the optimal capitalisation.

Solution

EPS = 10/100 = 10%

Amount of capital with Rs 50,000 net profit = Rs 50,000 × 100/10
= Rs 5,00,000

SELECT FURTHER READING

Gerstenberg, C.W. (1956). *Financial Organisation and Management of Business*. Englewood Cliffs: Prentice-Hall.

14

CAPITAL STRUCTURE

OBJECTIVES

To explain the concept of capital structure

To discuss the views supporting the theory that capital structure has no relevance to the value of a firm

To explain the impact of capital structure on the risk and return aspect of the shareholders based on the view that capital structure influences the value of a firm

To analyse the features of optimal capital structure and the process of attaining it

It is not only the size of capital which is significant, but, more importantly, it is the ratio between the owners' capital and the borrowed capital that is crucial from the viewpoint of maximisation of corporate wealth. The present chapter discusses the issue of capital structure and examines whether capital structure is really significant to the maximisation of corporate wealth. If so, it examines whether an optimal capital structure exists.

14.1 THE BASIC ISSUE

Capital structure represents the ratio between different forms of capital. Broadly speaking, there are two types of capital: the owner's fund or share capital; and the borrowed fund. The borrowed fund is also known as the fixed-cost fund insofar as the amount of interest is fixed. The dividend on preference shares is also fixed but such shares represent the owners' fund. On the contrary, the dividend on the equity shares is not fixed, and so the equity share capital is not a fixed-cost capital.

Mixing fixed-cost capital with the equity share capital is known as financial leverage. The process is known also as trading on equity as the equity capital forms the basis for raising the borrowed funds.

In this context, there are two important questions. The first is whether the entire capital of the firm should represent only equity capital or it should represent a mixture of equity capital and the borrowed funds. In other words, the question is whether a firm

Capital structure represents the ratio between different forms of capital.

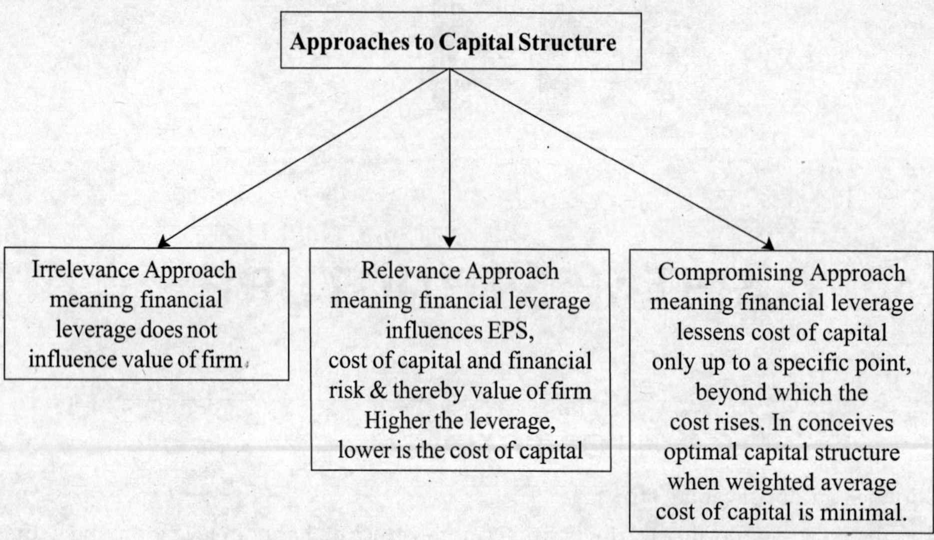

Debt to Equity of the Select FDI Companies %.

Industry	2002–03	2003–04	2004–05
Tea plantation	7.0	5.4	5.8
Food products & beverages	9.5	1.8	1.7
Chemicals & chemical products	26.1	21.3	21.0
Rubber & plastic products	59.3	57.7	54.4
Machines & machine tools	20.1	14.4	11.2
Electrical machinery	24.3	17.6	17.0
Motor vehicles & transport equipment	22.5	16.9	19.7
Wholesale & retail trade	21.4	35.9	40.5
Computer & related activities	0.6	0.5	0.9
Country			
UK	25.2	17.6	23.2
USA	14.8	13.3	19.4
Germany	13.5	10.4	8.9
Switzerland	25.4	21.0	17.7
Japan	23.6	19.4	17.3
France	34.3	22.5	21.5
The Netherlands	11.2	8.6	9.7
Mauritius	119.0	105.4	95.1
All companies	51.7	43.3	41.4

Source:RBI data base.

should opt for financial leverage. The views on this are divergent. One view suggests that financial leverage is irrelevant insofar as its presence or absence has no impact on corporate wealth. Another view is that leverage does have an impact on the earning per share, the risk aspect and on the cost of capital and, thereby, on the value of the corporate wealth. These two divergent views need a detailed discussion.

The second question is closely related to the first. It is that, if leverage leads to an increase in the value of corporate wealth, is it then desirable to have a very high degree of leverage? This raises yet another question, that of whether an optimal capital structure really exists; and if it does, then, what are the other factors, apart from taxes, that influence its optimality. These issues are of great significance to a firm.

14.2 THE IRRELEVANCE APPROACH

Those who believe in perfect market conditions are of the view that the issue of capital structure is irrelevant, implying that any change in capital structure has no influence on the value of corporate wealth. For the first time, it was Durand (1952) who explained the capital structure theory which is known as the net operating income (NOI) approach. His theory can be explained with the help of a simple example. Suppose a company has 100,000 shares of Rs 10 each. The expected level of net operating income or the operating profit is Rs 100,000. The dividend pay-out ratio is 100%. This means that the dividend or the cost of equity capital,

K_e = Rs 100,000/1,000,000 = 0.10 = 10%

If the NOI is capitalised at the rate of 10%, the value of equity would be Rs 1,000,000. Apart from Durand, Modigliani and Miller (1958) were of the opinion that the introduction of debt in the capital structure does not lead to any change in the value of the firm. The reasons they argue are two-fold. Firstly, the shareholders opt for the arbitrage process, which results in any financial leverage having no influence on total cash flow, and ultimately the value of corporate wealth remains unchanged. Secondly, financial leverage does not bring about changes in the cost of capital, and, as a result, the value of the firm remains unchanged. These views are explained at great length by Modigliani and Miller (1958). Therefore, the reader must be acquainted here with the Modigliani-Miller (M-M) hypothesis.

14.2.1 The Arbitrage Process

At the very outset, the M-M hypothesis assumes that:

1. The firm pays no taxes;
2. There is no transaction cost. This means that investors borrow and lend money at the same interest rate, and, as a result, the firm and its investors buy and sell securities at zero cost;
3. Investors have the same expectations as to the firm's future earnings and risk, therefore, they treat different firms similarly;
4. Future financing decisions do not affect the firm's investment in assets.

Considering the above assumptions, let us assume that there are two firms. Firm U is unleveraged meaning that the entire capital is made up of equity share capital. On the other hand, Firm L is leveraged, meaning that its capital represents a debt-equity mix. Let us further assume, for the time being, that Firm L has a higher market value on account of its being leveraged.

The M-M hypothesis suggests that the difference in market value between the two firms cannot persist, because the shareholders will indulge in a process of arbitrage or home-made leverage, buying the low-value shares and selling the high-value shares. The shareholders of Firm L will realise a greater return on their shares without any increase in their investment or in their risk perspective. The arbitrage process will occur as follows:

1. The shareholders will sell their shares in Firm L;
2. They will borrow and create their own personal leverage to duplicate Firm L's capital structure; and
3. They will use all the resultant cash to purchase shares in Firm U.

The selling of Firm L's shares and the purchase of Firm U's shares will continue till the market value of the shares of both firms is equal. When the value of two firms is equalised, the process of arbitrage ceases.

EXAMPLE

The following are the financial statements of an unleveraged firm and a leveraged firm:

	Unleveraged firm (Rs)	Leveraged firm (Leverage ratio = 50%) (Rs)
Operating income	50,000	50,000
Interest income (12%)	0	18,000
Net income	50,000	32,000
Market value of equity	2,50,000	1,50,000
Market value of debt		1,50,000
Total market value	2,50,000	3,00,000

Suppose an equity shareholder owns 1% shares of the leveraged firm. As per the M-M hypothesis, he will sell these shares at the market value of Rs 1,500. Subsequently, he will borrow an identical amount, i.e., Rs 1,500 at 12% rate of interest. This creates a personal leverage ratio of 50%, which is exactly similar to the firm's capital structure. Finally, with the entire amount of Rs 3,000, he will purchase the shares of the unleveraged firm which will be equal to (3,000/250,000) = 1.2% shares of the unleveraged firm.

Prior to the three-step arbitrage, the investor's share of return in the leveraged company's net income was Rs 320. After arbitrage, it is Rs 600 (equal to 1.2% of the expected net income of the unleveraged company) minus an interest charge of Rs 180 (12% of Rs 1,500) or Rs 420. The investor, without adding any fund, has an investment with an identical amount of leverage that earns (420 – 320) = Rs 100 more on account of arbitrage.

Lured by profit, he will continue selling shares of the leveraged company and buying shares of the unleveraged company until the market value of the two firms becomes equal.

14.2.2 Leverage and the Cost of Capital

Considering the same assumptions mentioned in the preceding sub-section, the M-M hypothesis suggests that the cost of capital or the cost of equity capital for an unleveraged firm is equal to its expected level of operating income [$E(EBIT)$] divided by its assets. This can be expressed in the form of an equation as follows:

$$K_U = E(EBIT)/Assets \quad ...(14.1)$$

Since the value of assets is entirely represented by equity share capital, one can substitute the total assets in Eq. 14.1 by equity. The equation will thus be written as follows:

$$K_U = E(EBIT)/Equity \quad ...(14.2)$$

However, in case of a leveraged firm, the cost of equity possesses not only the business risk found in the unleveraged firm but also a risk premium that is required to compensate the shareholders for the firm's financial risk. Thus the cost of equity capital of a leveraged firm can be expressed as follows:

$$K_{eL} = k_U + (k_{eU} - k_d)\,(D/E) \quad ...(14.3)$$

And the weighted average cost of capital ($WACC$) of the leveraged firm can be expressed as follows:

$$WACC = k_d\left(\frac{D}{D+E}\right) + k_d\left(\frac{E}{D+E}\right) \quad ...(14.4)$$

Rearranging Eq. 14.4, we have:

$$K_{eL} = WACC + D/E\,(WACC - k_d) \quad ...(14.5)$$

As a result, with an increase in debt or with a growing leverage ratio, the cost of equity capital in a leveraged firm will rise reflecting the financial risk borne by the shareholders. Any rise in the cost of equity capital will fully negate the lowering of WACC on account of lower cost of debt. The WACC will remain constant. In other words, any change in capital structure will not influence the WACC. This state of affairs is shown in Fig. 14.1.

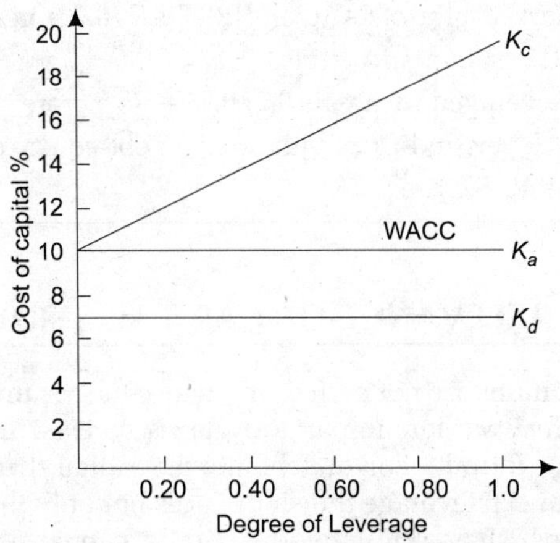

FIG. 14.1 Leverage and the cost of capital

EXAMPLE

Find out the WACC of a firm when:

(a) its capital structure is all-equity and the cost of equity is 14%;

(b) the capital structure has a debt-equity ratio of 50:50 and the cost of debt is 10%.

(a) WACC of the unleveraged firm is:

$$\text{WACC} = w_d k_d + w_e k_e$$
$$= 0(0.10) + 1(0.14) = 0.14 = 14\%.$$

(b) WACC of lthe leveraged firm:

(i) $k_d = 0.10 = 10\%$

(ii) $K_{eL} = k_U + (k_{eU} - k_d)\ (D/E) = 0.14 + (0.14 - 0.10)\ (1.0) = 0.18 = 18\%$

(iii) WACC = (0.5) (0.10) + (0.5) (0.18) = 0.14 = 14%

14.2.3 Value of the Firm

Since the WACC of the leveraged firm is always equal to the cost of capital of the unleveraged firm, the value of the leveraged firm will be equal to the value of the unleveraged firm. Based on Eq. 14.2 to Eq. 14.4 the value of a leveraged firm can be expressed as follows:

$$V_L = V_u = \frac{E(EBIT)}{WACC} = \frac{E(EBIT)}{k_u} \quad ...(14.6)$$

EXAMPLE

Suppose a firm has a market value of Rs 5 crore. EBIT is Rs 0.7 crore. On the basis of Eq. 14.6:

(i) Unleveraged cost of equity = 14%

(ii) Value of unleveraged firm = Rs 0.7/0.14 = Rs 5 crore

(iii) Value of the leveraged firm with 50 : 50 debt-equity and 10% cost of debt = Rs 0.7/0.14 = Rs 5 crore

14.3 RELEVANCE OF CAPITAL STRUCTURE

In real life, market conditions are not perfect and hence the assumptions of the irrelevance approach are far from reality. More importantly, taxes do exist. Interest payments are tax deductible and hence the introduction of debt into the capital structure lowers the WACC. The introduction of financial leverage thus influences not only the WACC but also has an impact on the earning per share (EPS). In other words, capital structure is of relevance to the financial managers.

14.3.1 Financial Leverage and EPS

The greater the leverage, the higher the EPS. This is because the average cost of capital declines, which in turn increases the earnings-share ratio. The effect can be shown with the help of a simple example.

EXAMPLE

There are three firms each with Rs 50,000 worth of assets. To finance these assets, Firm A sells 5,000 ordinary shares of Rs 10 each; Firm B sells 3,000 ordinary shares and fills up the gap with 10% debentures for Rs 20,000; and Firm C sells only 1,000 shares and fills up the gap with Rs 40,000 debentures. The rate of return on investment is 20%. The tax rate is 30%. Find out the EPS in these three cases.

	Firm A (Rs)	Firm B (Rs)	Firm C (Rs)
Equity	50,000	30,000	10,000
Debt	–	20,000	40,000
Total assets	50,000	50,000	50,000
EBIT	10,000	10,000	10,000
Interest	–	2,000	4,000
EBT	10,000	8,000	6,000
Taxes @ 30%	3,000	2,400	1,800
Net income after taxes	7,000	5,600	4,200
Shares outstanding	5,000	3,000	1,000
EPS	1.40	1.87	4.20
Return on equity (%)	14.0%	18.67%	42.0%

With rising leverage, the earning per share increases from Rs 1.40 to Rs 1.87 and then to Rs 4.20

However, a direct relationship between increase in leverage ratio and increase in EPS or, in other words, the favourable impact of leverage on EPS depends on:

1. The return on investment (ROI) compared to the rate of interest on the borrowed capital;
2. The magnitude of financial risk to which the shareholders are exposed in the wake of leverage.

ROI vis-à-vis Interest Rate: Leverage raises EPS only when the return on investment is greater than the interest rate on debt. If the two are equal, the EPS will remain constant irrespective of leverage. On the contrary, if return on investment is less than the interest rate, leverage will push down the EPS. The varying impact is illustrated in the following example.

EXAMPLE

There are three cases with varying interest rates. In one case, it is 5%, which is less than the rate of return. In another case, it is 10%, which is equal to the rate of return, and in yet another case, it is 15%, which is higher than the rate of return.

	Case A: No debt (Rs)	Case B: 5% debt (Rs)	Case C: 10% debt (Rs)	Case D: 15% debt (Rs)
Equity	50,000	30,000	30,000	30,000
Debt		20,000	20,000	20,000
Total assets	50,000	50,000	50,000	50,000
EBIT (10%)	5,000	5,000	5,000	5,000
Interest		1,000	2,000	3,000
EBT	5,000	4,000	3,000	2,000
Taxes (30%)	1,500	1,200	900	600
Post-tax income	3,500	2,800	2,100	1,400
EPS	0.70	0.93	0.70	0.47
Return on equity (%)	7.0%	9.3%	7.0%	4.7%

Summing up:

(a) ROI > interest rate on debt = Increase in EPS = Favourable leverage

(b) ROI < interest rate on debt = Decrease in EPS = Unfavourable leverage

(c) ROI = interest rate on debt = Constant EPS = No leverage effect

Leverage and Financial Risk: The favourable impact of leverage on EPS cannot be thought of in isolation of the financial risk that the shareholders have to face as a result of oscillation in the EPS with changing economic fortunes of the firm. The readers are well aware of the fact that the financial risk is manifest in form of variation in EPS. The larger the variation or, to be precise, the larger the standard deviation, the greater is the risk. If a firm goes for a very high leverage ratio, any downtrend in the firm's economic fortunes may cause the EPS move into negative zone, and, as a result, the firm will not be able to pay fixed interest charges, ultimately facing liquidation.

The following example involving three cases presents here the varying amount of risk in the sequel of varying degree of leverage with a given amount of variation in ROI.

EXAMPLE

A firm with an asset for Rs 50,000 has varying return on investment of 5% during depression, 10% during normal period and of 15% during boom. There are three scenarios. Case I presents no leverage, Case II presents 40 % debt, and Case III presents 60% debt. The tax rate is 30%. Find the extent of financial risk in these three scenarios.

Case I: No Debt

	5% ROI (Rs)	10% ROI (Rs)	15% ROI (Rs)
Equity	50,000	50,000	50,000
Debt	–	–	–
Total assets	50,000	50,000	50,000
EBIT/EBT	2,500	5,000	7,500
Taxes	750	1,500	2,250
After-tax net income	1,750	3,500	5,250
EPS	0.35	0.70	1.05
Return on equity (%)	3.5%	7.0%	10.5%

Case II: 40% Debt

	5% ROI (Rs)	10% ROI (Rs)	15% ROI (Rs)
Equity	30,000	30,000	30,000
Debt	20,000	20,000	20,000
Total assets	50,000	50,000	50,000
EBIT	2,500	5,000	7,500
Interest	2,000	2,000	2,000
EBT	500	3,000	5,500
Tax	150	900	1,650
Post-tax income	350	2,100	3,850
EPS	0.12	0.70	1.28
Return on equity (%)	1.2%	7.0%	12.8%

Case III: 60% Debt

	5% ROI (Rs)	10% ROI (Rs)	15% ROI (Rs)
Equity	20,000	20,000	20,000
Debt	30,000	30,000	30,000
Total assets	50,000	50,000	50,000
EBIT	2,500	5,000	7,500
Interest	3,000	3,000	3,000
EBT	(500)	2,000	4,500
Tax	–	600	1,350
Post-tax income	(500)	1,400	3,150
EPS	(–0.25)	0.70	1.58
Return on equity (%)	Negative	7.0%	15.8%

It is evident from the three tables that with a given variation in the return on investment, growing leverage ratio leads to a greater variation in the EPS. This means that the greater the leverage ratio, the higher is the financial risk borne by the shareholders. The variation in the EPS can be measured in terms of standard deviation.

14.3.2 Financial Leverage and Cost of Capital

Interest payment is tax-deductible. Therefore, so, when taxes exist, interest is adjusted for tax. As a result, the effective cost of debt is lower than the coupon rate. It is because of the adjustment for taxes that the cost of debt is much lower than the cost of equity. Thus when debt is introduced into the capital structure or when lower-cost capital is combined with the equity capital, WACC is bound to be lower.

In other words, when there is no debt in the capital structure, the cost of capital will be equal to cost of equity. When debt is introduced, WACC will tend to decline and it will continue declining with a growing degree of leverage. At 100% leverage, when the capital structure represents only debt, cost of capital will be equal to cost of debt. It is this phenomenon that is depicted in Fig. 14.2.

> **Reliance on Debt Getting Lower**
> Resource mobilisation through debt/bond on private placement by corporates has witnessed a dip of around 8.0 per cent during the first half of 2007-08. During this period, 59 companies raised debt resources on private placement basis to the tune of Rs 48,164 crore compared to Rs 52,220 crore mobilised during the corresponding period of 2006-07. Among public sector units, the drop was marked to the extent of 98 per cent – from Rs 4,068 crores to a meagre sum of Rs 100 crore. In case of financial institutions, the fall occurred from Rs 1,140 crore to Rs 73 crore that is around 94 per cent.
>
> – *Financial Express, 1.12.2007*

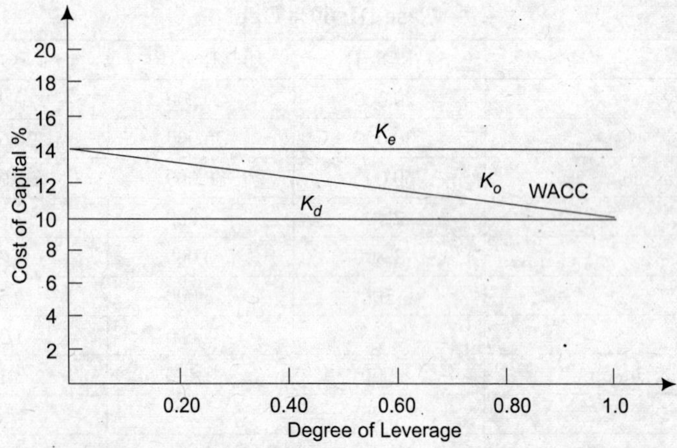

FIG. 14.2 Leverage and declining WACC

EXAMPLE

In a firm, which is unleveraged, the cost of equity is 14%. Subsequently, it introduces 10% debt into its capital structure. The tax rate is 30%. Find out the WACC with:

(a) debt-equity ratio of 1:1;

(b) a debt-equity ratio of 3:2.

(a) WACC with debt-equity ratio of 1:1:

$$(0.5)(0.14) + (0.5)(0.10)(1 - 0.30) = 0.105 = 10.5\%$$

(b) WACC with debt-equity ratio of 3:2:

$$(0.4)(0.14) + (0.6)(0.10)(1 - 0.30) = 0.098 = 9.8\%$$

14.3.3 Value of Leveraged and Unleveraged Firm in Presence of Taxes

It is the existence of tax that brings about a difference in the value of a leveraged firm and an unleveraged firm. The difference is equal to the product of the tax rate and the amount of debt. The value of an unleveraged firm in presence of taxes can be expressed as follows:

$$V_u = \frac{E(EBIT) \times (1 - T)}{k_u} \qquad ...(14.7)$$

On the other hand, the value of a leveraged firm can be expressed as follows:

$$V_L = V_u + T.D \qquad ...(14.8)$$

EXAMPLE

If, expected EBIT in a company is Rs 0.7 crore or 20% of total capital employed, the cost of equity is 14%, and the prevailing interest rate on debt is 10%. Find the value of the firm where:

(a) tax rate is zero with no leverage

(b) tax rate is 30% with no leverage

(c) tax rate is 30% with a leverage of 1:1

(a) Value of Unleveraged firm with no taxes:

Rs 0.7 crore/0.14 = Rs 5 crore

(b) Value of unleveraged firm with 30% tax:

[Rs 0.7 crore (1 – 0.30)]/0.14 = Rs 3.5 crore

(c) Value of leveraged firm with 30% tax:

Rs 3.5 crore + 0.3 (1.75) = Rs 4.025 crore

All this shows that in presence of taxes, the value of a leveraged firm is greater than that of an unleveraged firm. Although this situation is close to reality, yet, it fails to recognise that, with growing debt, the financial risk perceived by the shareholders rises and they thus require a higher premium for the growing risk.

14.3.4 Views of Modigliani and Miller in Presence of Taxes

The M-M hypothesis in a world of taxes is in conformity with the view that with growing leverage, WACC tends to decline. However, it suggests that if the leverage ratio rises, the financial risk borne by the shareholders also rises (Modigliani and Miller, 1963). As a result, WACC does not fall sharply but at a very slow rate.

The WACC does not fall as sharply as that shown in sub-section 14.3.2. This phenomenon is depicted by Fig. 14.3.

Again, since WACC tends to fall with growing leverage, the value of an unleveraged firm differs from that of a leveraged firm. Modigliani and Miller explain that the cost of equity in an unleveraged firm, in presence of taxes, is to be adjusted for taxes. Hence Eq. 14.2 will be presented as:

$$k_{eU} = \frac{EBIT(1-T)}{E_U} \qquad \text{...(14.9)}$$

Since the entire capital is made up of equity, $K_{eU} = K_U$ and the value of unleveraged firm,

$$V_U = \frac{EBIT(1-T)}{k_{eU}} \qquad \text{...(14.10)}$$

On the other hand, in a leveraged firm, the cost of equity will be equal to the after-tax cash flow accruing to shareholders divided by the value of equity. In form of an equation,

$$K_{eL} = \frac{EBIT - I(1-T)}{E_L} \qquad \text{...(14.11)}$$

And then, the WACC for the leveraged firm,

$$k_L = k_d \text{x} \left(\frac{D_L}{D_L + E_L}\right)(1-T) + k_{eL} \text{x} \left(\frac{E_L}{D_L + E_L}\right) \qquad \text{...(14.12)}$$

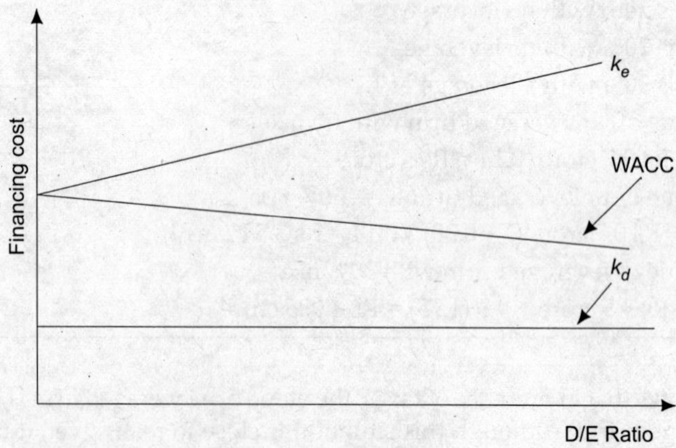

FIG. 14.3 M-M hypothesis in the world of taxes

The value of the leveraged firm,

$$V_L = \frac{EBIT(1-T)}{k_{eU}} + \frac{k_d DLT}{k_d} \qquad ...(14.13)$$

EXAMPLE

EBIT is Rs 2,000. Cost of equity in an unleveraged firm is 10%. Tax rate is 30%. The firm issues debt for Rs 10,000 at 8% interest rate. Find: V_U, E_L, E_L, K_{eL} and WACC or K_L.

V_U = {Rs 2,000 (1–0.3)}/0.10 = Rs 14,000

V_L = Rs 14,000+(10,000 x 0.3) = Rs 17,000

E_L = Rs 17,000 – 10,000 = Rs 7,000

K_{eL} = [{2,000 – (10,000 x 0.08)} 1 – 0.3] / 7,000 = 0.12 = 12.0%

K_L = {0.08(10,000 / 17,000) (1 – 0.3)} + 0.12 (7,000 / 17,000) = 0.0823528 = 8.24%

14.4 DETERMINATION OF OPTIMAL CAPITAL STRUCTURE

14.4.1 The Lowest WACC

The preceding section makes it clear that with growing leverage WACC tends to decline. The question, therefore, arises as to whether the firm should have a very high degree of leverage. The question arises because a high degree of leverage raises the financial risk of the shareholders. It may also raise the financial risk of the bondholders insofar as in times of lean profits, it will be difficult for the firm to make interest payments. Thus, there will be a point beyond which leverage is not desirable. This point should be treated as the optimal capital structure.

> WACC presents an approximating V-shape or a saucer-shape curve. The point at which the WACC is minimum represents optimal capital structure.

It was Ezra Solomon (1963) who explained the concept of optimal capital structure more elaborately. Her approach is known as a compromising approach. She divides the debt-equity relationship into three stages. In the first stage, with moderate leverage, k_e either remains constant or rises very slowly with a rise in financial risk. Even if k_e rises, this rise does not completely offset the benefits accruing from the use of cheaper debt and, as a result, WACC tends to decline. The second stage begins when the rise in k_e offsets the benefits accruing from the use of cheaper debt, the result is that WACC begins to rise. Still further with growing leverage, the situation reaches the third stage when k_d also rises with growing risk to be borne by the bondholders. This causes WACC to rise at a faster rate. The overall result is that the WACC presents an approximating V-shape or a saucer-shape curve. The point at which the WACC is minimum represents optimal capital structure. The shape of the WACC may be shown in Fig. 14.4.

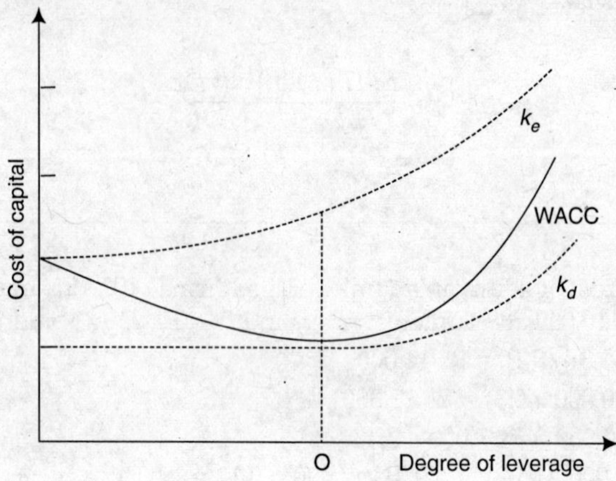

FIG. 14.4 Cost of capital under compromising

EXAMPLE

1. A company has a capital of Rs 5,00,000 with an equity capitalisation rate of 15% with no taxes. The finance manager likes to introduce financial leverage for which he has the following information:

Debt Rs	Interest rate %	Equity capitalisation rate for a given level of debt %
–	–	15.0
1,00,000	8.0	15.5
2,00,000	8.0	16.0
3,00,000	9.0	17.5
4,00,000	9.0	18.5
5,00,000	9.5	19.0
6,00,000	9.5	22.0

Solution:

Weighted average cost of capital at varying levels of debt/equity ratios:

Debt/equity	K_dW_d	K_eW_e	$K_o = K_dW_d + K_eW_e$
0	0.0000	0.1500	0.1500
1,00,000/9,00,000	0.0080	0.1395	0.1475
2,00,000/8,00,000	0.0160	0.1280	0.1440
3,00,000/7,00,000	0.0270	0.1225	0.1495
4,00,000/6,00,000	0.0360	0.1110	0.1470
5,00,000/5,00,000	0.0475	0.0950	0.1425
6,00,000/4,00,000	0.0570	0.0880	0.1450

At 1/1 debt-equity ratio, the capital structure will be optimal insofar as this point of leverage represents lowest weighted average cost of capital.

14.4.2 Corporate Income Tax and Personal Income Tax

The discussion of tax lowering WACC and raising the value of corporate wealth is so far limited to corporate income tax only. It was Miller (1977) who suggested the incorporation of personal income tax into the leverage effect insofar as the shareholders and bondholders have to pay taxes on dividend and interest respectively. A firm needs to minimise its total tax burden—both corporate income tax and personal income tax while deciding about the leverage.

In practice, bondholders and shareholders are treated differently as far as taxes are concerned. In India, dividend in the hands of shareholders is exempt from taxes. Capital gains are favourably treated for taxes. The shareholders can postpone payment of capital gains tax by postponing the sale of the shares. As a result, the personal income tax is often higher for the bondholders than it is for shareholders. This situation reduces the advantage of corporate borrowing and thereby reduces the value of the firm.

14.4.3 Bankruptcy and Agency Costs

It is true that the existence of taxes lowers the WACC and it is one factor that influences the optimality of the capital structure. But, on the other hand, there are some costs associated with debt that limit any further doses of leverage. One such cost is known as bankruptcy cost. When the degree of financial leverage increases, the probability that a firm will be unable to meet its financial obligations also increases. Any continuance of this problem may lead to financial distress, default and ultimately bankruptcy.

> Bankruptcy costs are both direct and indirect. Direct costs are accounting and legal fees, re-organisation cost and other administrative expenses. The indirect costs are less tangible, such as lost sales, lost profit, higher cost of credit, etc.

Bankruptcy costs are both direct and indirect. Direct costs are accounting and legal fees, re-organisation cost and other administrative expenses. The indirect costs are less tangible, such as lost sales, lost profit, higher cost of credit, etc. The greater the probability of default, the higher will be the present value of the bankruptcy cost and the lower the value of the firm. The empirical evidence of Altman (1984) reveals that the present value of the bankruptcy cost accounts for 11 to 17% of the value of the firms. If this is the case, the tax advantage can easily be outweighed by the bankruptcy cost and the optimality of capital structure can easily be influenced.

Apart from the bankruptcy cost, it is also the agency cost that erodes the tax advantage. Agency cost denotes a situation of conflicting interest between the shareholders and the bondholders, the cost normally being borne by the bondholders. An example will make clear the nature of agency cost. Suppose the bondholders lend money to the firm assuming that the firm will invest the same in a low-risk project. However, if the firm invests the borrowed fund in a risky project, the required rate of return on loans will be higher and the present value of loan will be lower. It is believed that with an increase in leverage ratio, the

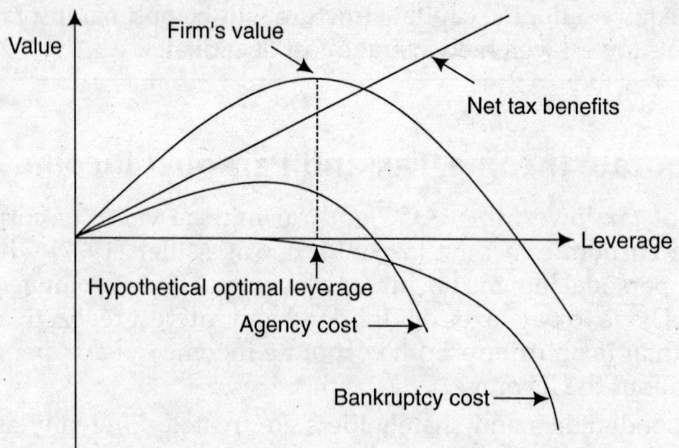

FIG. 14.5 Bankruptcy and agency costs and the value of the firm

agency cost will rise and erode the tax advantages, accordingly the optimality of the capital structure will be influenced.

It is now clear that the bankruptcy and agency costs act in a direction opposite to that of the tax advantages and, thus, lower the value of the firm. The value of the levered firm can thus be expressed as follows:

$$VL = VU + PV(TD) - PV(c) - PV(a) \qquad ...(14.14)$$

Where:

$PV(TD)$ = the present value of tax advantages of debt
$PV(c)$ = the present value of bankruptcy cost
$PV(a)$ = the present value of agency cost

The influence of the tax advantages and bankruptcy and agency costs on the value of the firm can be seen in Fig. 14.5.

14.4.4 The Pecking Order Hypothesis: A Critique of an Optimal Leverage

> Pecking order hypothesis suggests that there is no optimal leverage ratio as such. Firms have a financing "pecking order" and accordingly, they use different forms of funds.

The transaction cost involved in external financing is yet another factor influencing a firm in the extent to which it will prefer debt in the capital structure. In the pecking order hypothesis, firms prefer using internally generated funds as these do not involve any transaction cost. New debt is their second choice. Debt-equity mix instruments, such as convertible debentures are their third choice. External equity is the last choice. Again, a large-size issue involves a proportionately lower transaction cost than small-size frequent issues to meet financial needs. In short, the pecking order hypothesis suggests that there is no optimal leverage ratio as such. Firms have a financing "pecking order" and accordingly, they use different forms of funds. This hypothesis also suggests that the firms with high profitability should have a low leverage ratio insofar as they prefer using internal funds to borrowing (Baskin, 1989).

14.4.5 Process of Attaining Optimal Capital Structure

With the aim of maximising the firm's value, the managers consider the benefits and costs of borrowing and try to achieve the optimal point of the capital structure. However, the rate of adjustment varies from one firm to the other depending upon the firm-specific and macroeconomic environment. The adjustment may be quicker, or it may be gradual. The steps involved are mentioned hereunder.

For Quick Increase in Leverage:

1. Borrowing money and buy-back of shares;
2. Debt-equity swap;
3. Selling a portion of assets and using the proceeds for repurchase of shares.

For Quick Decrease in Leverage:

1. Issue of equity and pay-off of a part of the debt;
2. Asking lenders to accept equity in lieu of the debt.

Increasing Leverage Gradually:

1. Financing new projects only with debt;
2. Repurchase of shares if new projects have negative NPV.

Decreasing Leverage Gradually:

1. Greater stress on internal financing;
2. Paying-off of outstanding debt if good projects are not in hand.

14.5 FEATURES OF A SOUND CAPITAL STRUCTURE

The preceding section has thrown a good deal of light on the attainment of an optimal capital structure. Based on this discussion, the features of a sound capital structure can be delineated as follows:

1. Perfect trade-off between risk and return;
2. Minimum cost of capital;
3. Sufficiency of cash flow to service debt;
4. Maintenance of industry norm;
5. Flexibility.

Leverage raises the return on equity and thereby the value of the firm. However, at the same time, it tends to inflate the debt to an unmanageable extent, increasing in turn the financial risk to be borne by the shareholders. Thus a sound capital structure permits leverage only to that extent that represents a perfect trade-off between risk and return.

Second, the capital structure in order to be sound should have the minimum cost of capital. It has already been mentioned that both the relevance approach and the irrelevance approach in a world of corporate taxes support the view that consistent use of leverage leads to a decline in the weighted average cost of capital. However, when a firm considers a target debt ratio beyond which financial risk appears unmanageable, these two approaches analogise with the traditional approach and confirm that only a moderate use of leverage minimises the cost of capital, and is compatible with a sound capital structure.

Third, a sound capital structure should take into account the cash flows that form the basis for servicing debt. In other words, leverage should be used only to the extent that the cash flows are available to service debt. Otherwise, inability of the firm to service debt may lead it into liquidation. During a boom, the problem of debt servicing does not usually arise. During a recession, however, when cash flows are scanty, debt servicing may pose a problem. Thus the capital structure decision must take into account the probability of shrinkage in cash flows during times of recession and accordingly, debt should be relied upon to that extent only.

Fourth, the capital structure of a firm should conform to industry norms. This means that the debt-equity ratio of a firm should not vary widely from the industry average. This is relevant in the sense that whenever the lenders lend to a firm, they analyse the debt-equity ratio of the firm against the background of the industry norm. In fact, any major deviation from the industry average makes the firm conspicuous.

Fifth, a sound capital structure must be significantly flexible so as to be attuned to changes in macroeconomic conditions. Flexibility means that the firm is in a position to raise funds easily and, at the same time, redeem its securities without much difficulty whenever it does not require the given amount of capital. Flexibility depends upon a number of factors, important among these being:

(a) Flexibility in service charges;
(b) Restrictive clauses in loan agreements;
(c) Process of redemption;
(d) The debt capacity.

As far as rigidity of service charges is concerned, debt is at the top. Interest has to be paid irrespective of whether the firm has earned profit. Preference shares carry fixed dividend but it is payable only when there is profit. Ordinary shares are highly flexible as dividend is neither a compulsion nor fixed. This means that capital structure should have large component of ordinary share capital.

Similarly, restrictive clauses in the loan agreement restricting purchase of certain kinds of assets, distribution of cash dividend, etc., create problems and come in the way of flexibility. A firm should minimise such clauses, for this it would be better if it relied less on debt.

Again, there should be easy terms for redemption of debt. Firms redeem debentures and bonds when their capital requirements shrink. The softer the terms, the easier is the redemption.

Last but not least, a firm should not make use of its entire debt capacity or the target debt ratio. This is because when the firm needs additional funds, it can issue debentures. This implies that that the actual debt ratio should lie at a point earlier than the target debt ratio. This will serve to maintain flexibility in the capital structure.

SUMMARY

The introduction of borrowed funds in the capital structure is known as financial leverage. One view is that the financial leverage does not influence the value of corporate wealth insofar as the shareholders indulge in an arbitrage process of selling and buying their shares on the one hand and, on the other, the cost of capital remains unaffected, although, in presence of taxes, leverage raises the value of the firm.

The other view is that leverage tends to lower the cost of capital and raises the eps, thereby, raising the value of the firm. Raising of the value of the firm through financial leverage does not mean that this process should go on indefinitely. After a specific point, leverage will raise the financial risk of the equity shareholders and then, if the process is continued, it will also raise the risk borne by the creditors. This means that cost of capital, which earlier fell with leverage, will start increasing. Optimal leverage thus exists at a point where the weighted average cost of capital is the lowest. However, the personal income tax, agency cost and bankruptcy cost and also transaction cost influence the optimality to some extent.

The process of attaining optimality involves, among other things, borrowing money and buy-back of shares, debt-equity swap, issue of equity and pay-off of debt, greater stress on internal financing, etc.

A sound capital structure has some distinctive features, such as perfect trade-off between risk and return, minimal cost of capital, sufficiency of cash flow to service debt, flexibility and maintenance of industry norms.

POINTS TO REMEMBER

1. What is financial leverage?
   - Mixing fixed-cost capital with equity is known as financial leverage.
   - A firm may have either all-equity/unleveraged capital structure or a leveraged capital structure meaning a combination of debt and equity.
2. What is irrelevance approach to capital structure?
   - Irrelevance approach, propounded by Modigliani and Miller, suggests that in a perfect capital market with no taxes, introduction of debt in the capital structure does not change either value of the firm or the cost of capital.

3. Does the irrelevance approach exist in presence of taxes?
   - Modigliani and Miller feel that in presence of taxes, financial leverage lowers the cost of capital.
4. Does financial leverage influence EPS and cost of capital in real life?
   - Financial leverage, mainly because taxes exist in real life, lowers WACC and raises EPS but tends to increase the financial risk.
5. What is optimal capital structure?
   - WACC tends to be lower with growing leverage, but beyond a point, any further dose of leverage raises WACC in view of growing risk to be borne by equity shareholders and also by debenture holders. Thus optimal capital structure lies at a point where WACC is the lowest.
6. What are the factors influencing the capital structure optimality?
   - Since dividend and interest are subject to tax, optimal capital structure should have the least burden of taxes.
   - Bankruptcy cost too rises with growing debt. Such costs should be minimal.
   - Agency cost too grows with growing leverage insofar as large interest payment erodes dividend. The conflict arises between the shareholders and creditors. Agency cost may be avoided.
7. What is "pecking order" hypothesis?
   - Firms have a financing "pecking order" and so they attach less importance to those funds having large transaction cost. In other words, firms with large profitability should rely less on debt.
8. What are the ways to achieve optimal capital structure?
   - To increase debt through greater borrowing/buy-back of shares, debt- equity swap, financing new projects only with debt, repurchase of shares, etc.
   - To lower debt through issue of equity, paying off of a part of debt, greater stress on internal financing, etc.
9. What are the features of a sound capital structure?
   - Perfect trade-off between risk and return
   - Minimum WACC
   - Sufficiency of cash to service debt
   - Maintenance of industry norm
   - Flexibility

DESCRIPTIVE QUESTIONS

1. What do you mean by financial leverage? Mention the features of a sound capital structure.
2. Explain the M-M hypothesis indicating that financial leverage does not have an influence on the value of the corporate wealth. Is this true when taxes exist?
3. Does EPS improve in the wake of financial leverage? Explain.

4. "Financial leverage reduces the WACC but at the same time gives rise to financial risk borne by the shareholders". Discuss.
5. Can the capital structure be an optimal one? Explain and discuss the ways in which to achieve the optimal situation.
6. Are the personal income tax, agency cost and bankruptcy cost relevant in the context of optimising the capital structure?

OBJECTIVE-TYPE QUESTIONS

1. Mark true or false.
   (a) Financial leverage and trading on equity carry different meanings.
   (b) The M-M hypothesis indicates that in presence of taxes, financial leverage raises the value of corporate wealth.
   (c) Financial leverage reduces the eps if the interest rate is lower than the rate of return on investment.
   (d) Optimal capital structure exists when WACC is minimum.
   (e) Under the pecking order hypothesis, firms prefer to use internally generated funds.
2. Choose the most suitable answer:
   (a) M-M theory suggests that changing leverage ratio does not influence the value of a firm because of:
      (i) the arbitrage process
      (ii) no change in the WACC
      (iii) both of the above
   (b) If WACC, according to M-M hypothesis, remains unchanged with leverage, it is because:
      (i) the cost of debt tends to decline
      (ii) the cost of equity tends to rise
      (iii) both of the above
   (c) Leverage causes a rise in the EPS when:
      (i) return on investment = cost of debt
      (ii) return on investment > cost of debt
      (iii) return on investment < cost of debt
   (d) The value of levered firm > the value of an unlevered firm by:
      (i) amount of tax + amount of debt
      (ii) tax rate x amount of debt
      (iii) neither of the above
   (e) Capital structure is optimal when:
      (i) WACC tends to decline
      (ii) WACC is the lowest
      (iii) Cash is sufficient to meet debt

NUMERICAL PROBLEMS

1. Find the value of the firm on the basis of the M-M hypothesis when the cost of equity is 15%, cost of debt is 10%, and expected operating profit is Rs 5,000 in the following cases:
   (a) capital structure is all-equity with no taxes.
   (b) capital structure is all-equity with 30% taxes.
   (c) Captial structure with Rs 20,000 debt and with tax rate of 30%.
2. A company has operating income of Rs 50,000. It has Rs 1,00,000 of debt carrying 10% interest rate. The equity capitalisation rate is 20%. Indicate the market value of the firm assuming no taxes.
3. Firm A being a levered one has 10% Rs 4,00,000 debentures. Firm B is an unlevered firm. both firms earn 20% operating profit on their assets valued at Rs 10,00,000. The tax rate is 30% and equity capitalisation rate is 20%. Calculate wacc for the two firms.
4. A company likes to invest Rs 20,00,000 and maintains its capital structure at its book value. Expected EBIT is Rs 3,20,000. In order to have an optimal capital structure, indicate the debt-equity ratio based on:
   (a) M-M approach,
   (b) traditional approach.
5. The amount of capital is Rs 1,00,000, EBIT is 20%, the tax rate is 30%, and the interest rate is 10%. Find the return on equity if:
   (i) capital is all-equity
   (ii) debt-equity ratio is 60:40
6. A company's present capital structure consists of Rs 2,50,000, 14% debt and 2000 equity share. Tax rate is 30%. Calculate the earning per share if EBIT is Rs 80,000.
7. A company has Rs 2,50,000 of debt and Rs 4,00,000 as the market value of equity. Beta for share is 0.95. Market premium is 5%. Risk-free interest rate is 9%. Interest on debenture is 10%. Tax rate is 30%. Find the weighted average cost of capital.
8. If a company has 1,00,000 equity shares of Rs 100 each and 10% debentures for Rs 1,40,00,000. The market price of share is Rs 240 per share. The return on equity share is 20%. Find the cost of equity capital, based on M-M approach.
9. EBIT in a firm is Rs 4,00,000, tax rate is 30%, the required rate of return on equity in the absence of borrowing is 15% and personal tax rate is zero. Find out the value of the firm with no leverage under M-M hypothesis.

SOLVED NUMERICAL PROBLEMS

1. Find out the leverage ratio if the capital structure has Rs 4,00,000 equity and Rs 1,60,000 debt.

Solution

Leverage ratio = Debt/(equity + debt)

1,60,000/(4,00,000 + 1,60,000) = 0.2857 = 28.57%

2. A company has 5,000 shares of Rs 100 each. It goes for capital restructuring and issues debentures for Rs 2,00,000 to buy back the shares. If the interest rate on debentures is 10% with no tax, find: (a) the leverage ratio after restructuring, and (b) EPS with an EBIT of Rs 1,20,000.

Solution

(a) Equity = Rs 5,00,000 – 2,00,000 = Rs 3,00,000
Debt = Rs 2,00,000
Leverage ratio = 2,00,000/(3,00,000 + 2,00,000) = 0.40 = 40%

(b) EBIT = Rs 1,20,000
Less interest @ 10% = Rs 20,000
EBT/NIAT = Rs 1,00,000
EPS = Rs 1,00,000/3,000 = Rs 33.33

3. A firm has a total capital of Rs 3,00,000 comprising of Rs 2,00,000 equity and Rs 1,00,000 debt. Debt involves 8% interest rate. Tax rate is 30%. The cost of equity is 15%. Find the weighted average cost of capital.

Again, if the firm restructures the debt-equity ratio of 1:4 with the same amount of total capital, find the changed weighted average cost of capital.

Solution

(a) When D/E ratio is 1:2
Cost of equity = 0.15 × 2/3 = 0.10 = 10%
Cost of debt = 0.08(1– 0.30) × 1/3 = 0.01867 = 1.87%
WACC = 10.00% + 1.87% = 11.87%

(b) When D/E ratio is 1:4
Cost of equity = 0.15 × 4/5 = 0.12 = 12%
Cost of debt = 0.08(1 – 0.30) × 1/5 = 0.0112 = 1.12%
WACC = 12% + 1.12% = 13.12%

This shows that with a reduced leverage ratio, WACC has moved up.

4. A company has 10,000 shares of Rs 100 each, selling at Rs 120 each. It has also 10% Rs 12,00,000 debt. The operating profit is Rs 2,40,000. The required rate of return on equity is 20%. Find out WACC under the M-M approach assuming (a) no tax, and (b) tax rate is 30%.

Solution

(a) When there is no tax:
K_{eL} = 0.20 + (0.20 – 0.10) (12,00,000/12,00,000)
= 0.30 = 30.0%
WACC = (0.10 × 12,00,000/24,00,000) + (0.30 × 12,00,000/24,00,000)
= 0.05 + 0.15 = 0.20 = 20.0%

(b) In case of 30% tax rate:
K_{eU} = {2,40,000 (1– 0.30)/12,00,000} = 0.14 = 14.0%
K_{eL} = {(2,40,000 – 1,20,000)(1 – 0.30)}/12,00,000 = 0.07 = 7.0%
WACC = {0.10 × 12,00,000/24,00,000 (1 – 0.30)} + (0.07 × 12,00,000/24,00,000)
= 0.035 + 0.035 = 0.07 = 7.0%

5. A company has all-equity capital structure. Its EBIT amounts to Rs 40,000. The cost of equity is 15%. Find the value of the firm assuming (a) no taxes, and (b) 30% tax rate.

Solution

(a) When there is no tax:

Rs 40,000/0.15 = Rs 2,66,667

(b) In case of taxes:

Rs 40,000 (1 – 0.30)/0.15 = Rs 1,86,667

6. A company has Rs 2,00,000 equity and 10% Rs 1,00,000 debt in its capital structure. EBIT is Rs 40,000. The cost of equity is 15%. Find the value of the firm when tax rate is 30%.

Solution

Since VL = VU + DT

VL = Rs {40,000 (1 – 0.30)/0.15} + 1,00,000 × 0.30

Rs 1,86,667 + 30,000 = Rs 2,16,667

7. A company has a capital of Rs 10,00,000 with an equity capitalisation rate of 14% with no taxes. The finance manager likes to introduce financial leverage for which he has the following information:

Debt Rs	*Interest rate %*	*Equity capitalisation rate for a given level of debt %*
–	–	14.0
1,00,000	8.0	15.0
2,00,000	8.0	16.0
3,00,000	9.0	17.0
4,00,000	9.0	17.5
5,00,000	9.5	18.0
6,00,000	9.5	20.0
7,00,000	10.5	24.0

Find (a) equity capitalisation rate based on M-M approach, and (b) the amount of debt that denotes the optimal capital structure.

Solution

(a) M-M View:

Debt Rs	K_d	K_o	*Debt/equity*	$K_e = K_o + (K_o - K_d)D/E$
–	–	0.14	–	0.1400
1,00,000	0.080	0.14	1,00,000/9,00,000	0.1467
2,00,000	0.080	0.14	2,00,000/8,00,000	0.1550
3,00,000	0.090	0.14	3,00,000/7,00,000	0.1614
4,00,000	0.090	0.14	4,00,000/6,00,000	0.1733
5,00,000	0.095	0.14	5,00,000/5,00,000	0.1850
6,00,000	0.095	0.14	6,00,000/4,00,000	0.2075
7,00,000	0.105	0.14	7,00,000/3,00,000	0.2217

The M-M approach assumes that leverage does not influence the weighted average cost of capital. Rather it is the cost of equity that rises with growing degree of leverage.

(b) Optimal capital structure based on Ezra Solomon's view:

Debt/equity	K_dW_d	K_eW_e	$K_o = K_dW_d + K_eW_e$
0	0.0000	0.140	0.1400
1,00,000/9,00,000	0.0080	0.135	0.1430
2,00,000/8,00,000	0.0160	0.128	0.1440
3,00,000/7,00,000	0.0270	0.119	0.1460
4,00,000/6,00,000	0.0360	0.105	0.1410
5,00,000/5,00,000	0.0475	0.090	0.1375
6,00,000/4,00,000	0.0570	0.080	0.1370
7,00,000/3,00,000	0.0735	0.072	0.1455

At a debt/equity ratio of 6/4, the weighted average cost of capital is the minimum. Thus at this point of leverage lies the optimal capital structure.

8. An unleveraged company has a total market value of Rs 15,00,000. It decides to go for financial leverage to have a positive present value of tax benefit equal to 20% of the market value of debt. But it fears that if it borrows beyond Rs 5 lakh, there would be bankruptcy cost, agency cost and also the risk borne by the creditors would rise progressively. To be specific, the present value of these costs would be 5% on a borrowing of Rs 10 lakh, 10% on a borrowing of Rs 12 lakh and 20% on a borrowing of Rs 15 lakh. Can you think of an optimal capital structure in such cases?

Solution

Rs lakh

Debt	*Value of firm with no leverage*	*PV of tax benefit*	*Bankruptcy + agency + increased interest costs*	*Value of the firm*
0	15	0.0	0.0	15.0
5	15	1.0	0.0	16.0
10	15	2.0	0.5	16.5
12	15	2.4	1.2	16.2
15	15	3.0	3.0	15.0

The optimal size of debt is Rs 10 lakh because at this point of leverage, the value of the firm is the highest.

Mini Case

Bharti Electronics manufactures select electronic items. In order to finance its operations, it employs both equity capital and debt. The operational position and how it is financed is clear from the latest financial statements given as follows:

Income Statement

	(million Rs)
Revenue	6000
Variable cost	3600
Marginal contribution	2400
Fixed operating cost	1200
EBIT	1200
Interest	300
EBT	900
Tax at 30%	270
Net income	630

Balance Sheet

Liabilities	Amount (million Rs)	Assets	Amount (million Rs)
Share capital (120 million shares)	1200	Net fixed assets	3000
Reserves	2000	Net current assets	2000
Debt	1800		
Total	5000	Total	5000

The firm plans to diversify operations that will require funds amounting to Rs 1000 million. After the expansion is complete, additional revenue is expected to be Rs 2000 million annually. The variable cost of the new project will be at the same rate as the existing one. The fixed cost will be Rs 600 million.

In order to finance the expansion, the firm is to make a public issue of equity shares at Rs 105 per share. The floatation cost is expected to be Rs 5. Alternatively, it may raise funds from the issue of debentures at an interest rate of 8%.

Questions:

1. Do the two ways of raising funds to finance the new project impact the leverage ratio?
2. Calculate the EPS under the two ways of financing.

REFERENCES

Altman, E.I. (1984). "A Further Empirical Investigation of the Bankruptcy Cost Question", *Journal of Finance*, 39 (Sept.): 1067-89.

Baskin, J. (1989). "An Empirical Investigation of the Pecking Order Hypothesis", *Financial Management*, 18 (1): 26–35.

Durand, D. (1952). "Cost of Debt and Equity Funds for Business: Trends and Problem in Measurement", *Conference on Research in Business Finance*. New York: NBER, pp. 235–47.

Miller, M.H. (1977). "Debt and Taxes", *Journal of Finance*, 32 (2): 261–75.

Modigliani, F. and M.H. Miller (1956). "The Cost of Capital, Corporation Finance and the Theory of Investment", *American Economic Review*, 48 (June): 261–97.

______ (1963). "Corporate Income Taxes and the Cost of Capital: A Correction", *American Economic Review*, 53 (June): 433–43.

Solomon, E. (1963). "Leverage and the Cost of Capital", *Journal of Finance*, 18 (May): 319–32.

SELECT FURTHER READINGS

Bradley, M. et al. (1984). "On the Existence of an Optimal Capital Structure: Theory and Evidence", *Journal of Finance*, 39 (3): 857–78.

Harris, M. and A. Raviv (1991). "The Theory of Capital Structure", *Journal of Finance*, 46 (1): 297–356.

Titman, S. (1988). The Determinants of Capital Structure Choice", *Journal of Finance*, 43 (1): 1–19.

15

CORPORATE SECURITIES

OBJECTIVES

To focus on the main features of equity shares in general and in particular on the pre-emptive rights of the equity shareholders

To discuss the features of preference shares

To discuss the features of debentures and also the economic size of their issue

To explain the process of retirement of debt

To describe warrants and their usefulness

To explain international equities and international bonds

After the discussion of the optimal mix of share capital and borrowed capital, it is worth discussing how the share capital and the borrowed capital are raised. Share capital is primarily raised through the sale of ordinary shares, also known as equity shares. Sometimes it is also raised through the sale of preference shares. Borrowed capital is primarily raised through the sale of debentures. The present chapter thus focuses on these corporate securities, viz., ordinary shares, preference shares and debentures that represent the lion's share of the long-term funds in a company. Warrants and international securities will also be discussed at some length.

15.1 EQUITY SHARES

Section 2 (46) of the Indian Companies Act, 1956 defines a share as "a share in the share capital". A company, other than that one limited by guarantee, has got the statutory right to raise capital through the issue of shares. As mentioned earlier, there are two kinds of shares: ordinary or equity shares and preference shares.

15.1.1 Features of the Equity Shares

Permanent Capital Base: The equity shares represent a company's permanent capital base, that is, the capital that is returned to the shareholders only after the company's lifetime comes to an end or it goes into liquidation. However, it is not certain what amount the shareholders will get at such time. In fact, the shareholders are paid an amount only after meeting all claims. If the value of assets is insufficient to meet the claims in the wake of liquidation, the shareholders will not receive anything.

> Section 2 (46) of the Indian Companies Act, 1956 defines a share as "a share in the share capital". A company, other than that one limited by guarantee, has got the statutory right to raise capital through the issue of shares. As mentioned earlier, there are two kinds of shares: ordinary or equity shares and preference shares.

No Fixed Dividend: The amount of dividend on equity shares is not fixed insofar as it is the residual amount left after the retention of earnings and payment of dividend to the preference shareholders. Moreover, the equity shareholders cannot force the company to pay them dividend even if its earnings are sufficient. The company has full discretion over this issue.

Voting Rights: Since the equity shareholders are the owners of the company, they have the right to vote at the company's meetings and for important decisions and thereby to exercise control over the management of the enterprise. An equity shareholder possesses one vote for each of the shares he/she owns. If the shareholder is not able to be present at the company's meetings, he/she may vote by proxy.

Basis for Raising Borrowed Capital: With a given leverage ratio, more borrowed capital can be raised with a rise in the equity share capital. This means that these shares form the basis for raising debt.

Public Issue or Private Placement: Equity shares are sold to the public through a prospectus published in the newspaper. A new company issues shares at par. However, a company with a good record can issue shares at a premium. These issues are normally underwritten by underwriters, that are usually banks, financial institutions and brokers. The underwriters provide a guarantee that if the shares are not fully purchased by the public, they will purchase them instead.

In the case of private placement, shares are sold to a few select investors, for example, LICI, UTI, IDBI, etc. Private placement is often found when the size of the issue is small. It involves less cost, less time is involved in raising the funds.

15.1.2 How Do Companies Issue New Shares?

Forms of Offering: It has already been explained that the companies issue equity shares to get the required funds. The issue can be made either by a newly floated company or by an existing one. In case of the former, the issue is known as the "initial public offering" (IPO). In the latter case, it is known as "further issues" or "follow-on public offers" (FPOs). Again, the FPOs can be made in two ways. While one is the general cash offer which involves new as well as the existing investors, the other is known as the rights offer in case of which the shares are allotted only to the existing shareholders on a pro rata basis. The rights issue is discussed at some length in the subsequent subsection.

The offer is made normally through prospectus. A prospectus is a statement issued by a company to the public, inviting them for subscription. It contains the necessary financial information about the company. The management of the public issues is normally looked after by the merchant bankers that are either the commercial banks, development financial corporations or some other financial institutions. Besides, some other agencies are also involved. They are, for example, underwriters, brokers, advertising agencies, legal advisors and registrar to the issues. The role of the underwriters needs to be referred to here at least at some length.

The Underwriter: The underwriter underwrites the securities and thereby shares the risk relating to the issue. In order to minimise such risks, it makes every effort to help sell the issue. The practice is that the underwriters buy the shares at a lower than the offer price. The difference between the underwriter's buying price and the offer price is called spread or discount. The spread or discount acts as a basic compensation received by the underwriter for taking the risk. Sometimes the underwriter gets shares or warrants in lieu of cash.

The Offer Price: The determination of the offer price for IPOs is not very easy. If it is too high, the entire issue will turn unsuccessful in view of lack of demand. If, on the other hand, it is too low, the existing shareholders may experience an opportunity loss. Thus, in order to get a more realistic offer price, the SEBI has encouraged a process, known as "book-building process", for the issues beginning from 1995 in India. Book building is simply a process of price discovery based on the market-based demand and price determination. The potential buyers state how many shares they are prepared to buy at a given price. The price is determined on the basis of the feedback from the investors with the result that the issuing company finds the highest market clearing price from high-quality investors. The other advantage of the book-building process is that the demand for the issue is approximately known even before the issue is closed and so the issue may be deferred if the demand at a particular point is lacking.

The process of book-building: It is divided into two parts: one is related to placement and the other is related to the public issue. As per the SEBI rules, a maximum of three-fourths of the issue may be offered to eligible non-resident Indians and institutional investors. The rest one-quarter is identified as the "net offer to the public". The issue price for the placement and the public offering remains the same.

The prospectus holds all required information. It contains the name of the book runner and the price band within which the securities are offered for subscription. The price is determined within this band and then the prospectus is filed with the Registrar of Companies. Individual investors are considered for whom at least 15% of the shares are reserved for allocation.

SEBI Regulations

- A company appoints intermediaries to the issue, such as merchant bankers, registrar and brokers.
- In large issue, more than one merchant bank can be appointed but their limits must be indicated and the details need to be conveyed to the SEBI.
- The prospectus is filed with SEBI at least 3 weeks prior to its filing with the Registrar of Company.
- The stock exchange is also informed for the listing of the securities.
- Road show may be arranged in order to attract the potential investors.
- SEBI approves registration. The issue price is agreed upon between the book runner and the company.

- The subscription list is kept open for 3--10 days. The maximum number of days for infrastructure companies may be 21.
- It is the merchant banker that manages for the allotment of shares, refunds and the investors' grievances, if any. It also ensures that the underwriters, if any, honour their commitments within 60 days of the closure of the issue.
- As per the Green-shoe Option that was introduced in August 2003, a company may appoint one of the issue managers as stabilisation agent to see that the post-listing price of its shares is stabilised.

(Based on www.sebi.govt.in)

Private Placement: Prospectus is not issued in case of private placement. Private placement means direct sale of shares by a company to the institutional investor, such as LIC, UTI, GIC, SFCs, pension and insurance funds and financial intermediaries. This mode of issue is preferred because it involves greater speed and lower cost of issue and maintains confidentiality. However, the new companies that are not well known in the financial market do not find placement an easy way to access funds.

The Cost of New Issues: The new issues involve cost, both direct and indirect. The direct costs are apparently the legal fees, filing fees and the taxes. The underwriting fee is also a cost since the underwriters pay the company a lower price that the price offered to the public.

The indirect cost is an implicit cost in form of the time and energy consumed in the process of the issue. Sometimes the offer price drops abnormally in case of the secondary offering. This is also an implicit cost.

15.1.3 Pre-emptive Rights of Equity Shareholders

Equity shareholders enjoy pre-emptive rights under which they have the right to preserve their proportionate ownership in the company. When a company issues additional equity shares, it first has to offer them to the existing equity shareholders so that they are given the opportunity of maintaining their pro rata share in the company. With pre-emptive rights, the control of the existing shareholders is protected as they can maintain their proportionate voting power. The gain to the company in this case is that it is able to save on floatation costs, although, the standby underwriting arrangements do exist in many cases.

With pre-emptive rights, the control of the existing shareholders is protected as they can maintain their proportionate voting power.

The State Bank of India is offering rights shares of shareholders in the ratio of one rights share for every five shares held. The rights shares with a face value of Rs 10 will be offered at Rs 2462.25.

The Bank has fixed February 4, 2008 as the record date for the purpose of the rights issue.

This way, a sum of Rs 16,736.31 crore will be raised from the existing shareholders, including GDR holders, at Rs 1590 per equity share of Rs 10 each.

– *The Financial Express, 15.1.2008.*

Whenever a company issues additional shares, it informs its existing equity shareholders about the number of issues, the subscription price per share and the expiry date of the offering. It also gives them the option to buying such shares for which it establishes a date of record. If a shareholder buys the share before that date, he/she is said to utilise the pre-emptive right. In this case, the share is said to sell with rights-on. On the other hand, after this date, the shares are traded without the rights attached. In this case, the shares are said to sell ex-rights.

From the finance manager's point of view, the following questions are important:

1. How many rights will be required to buy a share in the new issue?
2. What is the value of each right?
3. What effect will the rights offering have on the price of the existing shares?

Rights Required for a New Share: The number of new shares depends upon how much capital has to be raised and what is the subscription price. It can be expressed as follows:

Number of new shares = Funds to be raised/subscription price ...(15.1)

EXAMPLE

A company already has 4,00,000 shares, the market price of which is Rs 60 each. In order to raise additional capital of for Rs 20,00,000, it has decided to issue new shares at a subscription price of Rs 40 per share. Find out the number of new shares.

The number of new shares = 20,00,000/40 = 50,000 shares.

Once the number of new shares has been determined, one can compute how many rights are required to buy a new share. This is computed by dividing the number of rights issued by the number of new shares. This can be expressed as follows:

Number of rights per new share

= Number of rights issued/Number of new shares ...(15.2)

As per the above example:

4,00,000 rights/50,000 shares = 8 rights per new share

If a shareholder owns 4,000 shares or 1% of the total number of shares, he will have 4,000 rights as one share equals one right. On this basis, he would be able to buy 500 or (4,000/8) shares of the new issue. Now this particular shareholder has 4,500 shares in the total number of 4,50,000 shares. In other words, it means that his 1% share in the total number of shares is not disturbed even after buying the new shares. This is his pre-emptive right.

Value of Rights: When the new shares are issued, the existing shareholders get three options. These are as follows:

1. They can exercise their pre-emptive rights and subscribe to the additional shares within the date of record.
2. They can sell the additional shares insofar as the shares are transferable.
3. They can simply do nothing and let the allotment expire.

If the shareholder exercises the first option, he/she would then have to pay for the new shares the subscription price plus the number of rights required per new share. Taking into account the above example, the cost of one new share would be, Rs 40 + 8 rights.

It may be noted that the value of rights-on shares is very close to the market price of the existing shares. If a shareholder sells the shares well within the date of record, the new buyer will pay the rights-on price.

In the case of the second option, if the shareholder sells the new share on a date very close to the date of record, it is normally not possible to change the shareholder's name in the company's register. In this case, the share is sold ex-rights. The rights may subsequently be transferred to the new buyer.

In the third option, the existing shareholder loses his rights. If he sells these new shares, he will sell them ex-rights. This is why the value of the ex-right shares is often less than the value of the rights-on shares, unless large gains are expected to be reaped by the company in the near future. The value of an ex-rights share can be expressed as follows:

$$Px = Wo\,Po + Ws\,Ps \qquad \ldots(15.3)$$

where:

P_o = the price of rights-on shares

P_s = the subscription price

W_o = the number of old shares per number of total shares

W_s = the number of new shares per number of total shares

EXAMPLE

P_s = Rs 40; P_o = Rs 60; W_o = 1:1.125; and W_s = 1:9. Find out the value of the ex-rights shares and also the value of one right.

P_x = (1/1.125) 60 + (1/9) 40 = Rs 57.78.

On this basis, the value of one right will be:

Rs (57.78 – 40)/8 = Rs 2.22.

An alternative formula is also used for computing the value of ex-rights shares. Here the value of ex-rights share is expressed as follows:

$$P_x = \frac{(P_o N + Ps)}{N+1} \qquad \ldots(15.4)$$

Where:

N = the number of rights required to buy a new share

EXAMPLE

Based on the earlier example the value of the ex-rights share will be:

P_x = Rs (60 8 + 40)/(8 + 1) = Rs 57.78.

Effects on Shareholder's Position: At the very first glance, it seems that a rights issue leads to a diminution in the share price on an ex-rights date and lessens the shareholders' wealth. This is, however, not actually true. The shareholders are not put to any loss unless they go for the third option, that is they let the option expire. If they exercise the right or they sell the right, their wealth remains the same. This is because the subscription price plus the value of rights is equal to the current value of original wealth.

EXAMPLE

A shareholder possesses 4,000 shares having a market value of Rs 60 per share and 8 rights are required to buy one new share. Subscription price is Rs 40. The ex-rights price of the share is Rs 57.78 and the value of right is Rs 2.22. Based on the this fact, the current value of his original wealth under the three options mentioned above will be as follows:

Option I: When the shareholder exercises his pre-emptive rights	Rs
Owns 4,500 shares @ Rs 57.78	2,60,000
Less: investment cost @ Rs 40 each for the new 500 shares	20,000
Current value of original wealth	2,40,000
Option II: The shareholder sells the rights:	Rs
Owns 4,000 shares @ Rs 57.78	2,31,120
Add: value of sold rights @ Rs 2.22 per right for 4,000 rights	8,880
Current value of original wealth	2,40,000
Option III: The shareholder does not use the rights:	Rs
Owns 4,000 shares @ Rs 57.78 per share Rs	2,31,120

15.2 PREFERENCE SHARES

15.2.1 Features of Preference Shares

Preference share capital also represents owner's wealth. Like equity shares, the preference shares also too represent a permanent capital base. But they differ from equity shares, on a few counts.

Preference shareholders have a prior claim on the company's assets in the event of liquidation.

1. A particular type of the preference share, known as redeemable preference share may be, as its name suggests, redeemed by the company during its lifetime as per the terms of the issue, although the shareholders cannot force the company to go for redemption. The Indian Companies Act, 1956, provides that these share, prior to redemption, should be fully paid-up. The company will make the redemption payment to the shareholders either out of profits or out of the proceeds of a fresh issue or out of the sale proceeds of an asset.

2. Preference shareholders have a prior claim on the company's assets in the event of liquidation. However, they can share in these assets only if something remains after meeting various claims.
3. The preference shareholders have a prior claim on the dividend. The equity shareholders have a share in dividend only after it has been paid to the preference shareholders.
4. The rate of dividend given to the preference shareholders is fixed. This means that such shares are less risky than the equity shares. However, in a particular kind of preference share, known as a participating preference share, the shareholders get a fixed rate of dividend, and they additionally participate along with the equity shareholders in the remaining dividend.
5. When a company does not distribute dividend, the preference shareholders, like the equity shareholders, do not get any dividend. However, in the case of a particular kind of preference share, known as a cumulative preference share, the shareholders are entitled to a fixed rate of dividend. The dividend for a particular year is carried forward from year to year till it is finally paid.
6. Some of the preference shares are convertible, meaning that they are converted into equity shares as per the terms specified in the agreement. When there is a bullish trend in the market, the convertible preference shareholders convert their shares into equity shares in order to increase their wealth.
7. Preference shares do not normally carry voting rights. However, in specific cases, they acquire the right to vote. Under Sec. 87 of the Indian Companies Act, 1956, the preference shareholders do vote on resolutions concerning the winding up of the company or the reduction or repayment of share capital, etc.

15.3 DEBENTURES

15.3.1 Significance of Debentures

Debentures are no less significant than the shares. They represent borrowed capital. The holders debentures are known as the creditors of the company. In fact, a debenture is a written instrument through which a company acknowledges a debt due to the holder and promises to repay it after a specified period of time along with the interest payable at regular intervals. It may be mentioned that the terms, bonds and debentures are used synonymously, although, in the USA, bonds refer to debt having lien on specific asset and debentures are unsecured bonds.

Debentures are popular the world over. The reason being that the effective cost of debentures is lower. It is for this reason that share capital is supplemented with debt. Moreover, firms prefer to issue debentures as they do not give their holders any control over the management of the firm.

However, a company cannot issue debentures indefinitely. This is because their increased use increases the financial risk borne by the shareholders. Furthermore, since debentures represent a fixed-cost fund, they are not suitable for a firm that has unstable earnings.

> Bonds can be grouped into either secured bonds having lien on specific assets or unsecured bonds having no such lien.

During lean years, it may be very difficult for the company to pay the fixed rate of interest due on debentures.

Debentures are issued only after the approval of the board of directors. A registration statement is prepared that includes essentially an **indenture or a deed of trust**. An indenture is a written agreement between the debenture issuing company and a trust company appointed by the former to protect the interest of the debenture holders. The document includes the basic terms of the debentures, the description of the security, sinking fund arrangement, call provision, if any, and the protective covenants. The call provision allows the company to repurchase the debentures at a predetermined price over a specific period. The sinking fund arrangement is concerned with the repaying of the debentures. Protective covenant, especially if it is a negative covenant, limits the company to act in certain areas. For example, it may limit the amount of dividend to be paid or to raise any additional loan. It can restrict the company to pledge any asset to other lenders. It can prohibit any merger with another firm.

15.3.2 Features of Debentures

Sometimes company securities are pledged for the bond issue. Such bonds are known as collateral trust bonds and are rarely issued. Again, bonds are sometimes secured by equipment purchased on a credit basis. These are known as equipment trust bonds. These types of bonds are not popular in India.

Retirement Provisions: Although in certain cases, there are irredeemable debentures that last the entire lifetime of the company, yet, in majority of the cases, debentures have a fixed life, after which they are retired. The process of retirement is explained in a subsequent section of this chapter.

Priority Claim to Income: Debenture-holders have a prior claim on the firm's income. Unlike the shareholders, they can force the company to pay them the interest due. For this reason, they can ask the company to restrict dividend payments.

Fixed Rate of Interest: The interest rate is fixed. Its amount cannot vary with any variation in the company's earnings. In this way it is similar to the dividend on preference shares, which is paid at a fixed rate.

Prior Claim to Assets: In cases of liquidation or re-organisation, debenture-holders have a prior claim on the company's assets. They get the amount of their principal along with any unpaid interest. From this point of view, bonds can be grouped into either secured bonds having lien on specific assets or unsecured bonds having no such lien. In the event of liquidation, the secured bond-holders receive payment out of the specific asset, only then do the unsecured creditors get paid.

Secured bonds generally have a pledge on specific assets, usually fixed assets. They are also known as mortgage bonds. If company's tangibles are mortgaged for bonds, it is called a blanket mortgage. A blanket mortgage often carries an "after-acquired" clause which means that any real property acquired after the bond issue serves as a security to the loan. However, such a provision can be negated by the issue of a "closed-end" mortgage bond.

Sometimes company securities are pledged for the bond issue. Such bonds are known as collateral trust bonds and are rarely issued. Again, bonds are sometimes secured by equipment purchased on a credit basis. These are known as equipment trust bonds. These types of bonds are not popular in India.

Absence of Control: The debenture-holders do not possess voting rights. However, in the event of default in payment of interest due to them they can assume control over the affairs of the company.

15.3.3 Economic Size of the Issue of Debentures

The preceding chapter shows that there is always a target amount of debt in order to attain an optimal capital structure. The question, however, is whether the entire targeted amount of debentures should be issued at one point of time or whether they should be issued in lots. If the latter option is decided on, the company should determine an economic size of the lot, so that the total cost related to the issue is minimised.

The costs involved will be as follows:

1. carrying cost
2. floatation cost

If the size of the issue is greater than the economic size, floatation cost will be lower but carrying cost will be higher. Even if the excess of debt funds is invested in short-term securities, carrying cost will exist insofar as the rate of return on short-term investment is often lower than the interest rate on debentures. On the other hand, if the size of the issue is lower than the economic size, carrying cost will be lower but the floatation cost will be higher. The total cost will be the minimum at a point when these two costs are equal.

The floatation cost is both fixed and variable. While fixed cost is manifest in form of legal fees, registration and accounting cost, etc., the variable cost includes underwriting cost. The total floatation cost can be expressed as follows:

$$FD/S \quad \text{...(15.5)}$$

where:

F = the fixed floatation cost per issue of debt

D = the total amount of debt to be raised during an interval

D/S = the number of issues during the interval

Similarly, the carrying cost may be expressed as follows:

$$(S/2)\,(L - B) \quad \text{...(15.6)}$$

where:

$S/2$ = the average investment in short-term securities

L = the interest rate on debt

B = the rate of return on temporary investment

For the total cost to be minimum, the two costs, i.e., the flotation cost and the carrying cost, should be equal. The equality can be expressed as follows:

$$FD/S = S\,(L - B)/2$$

$$S^2 = 2FD/(L - B)$$

or

$$S = [2FD/(L - B)]^{1/2} \quad \text{...(15.7)}$$

EXAMPLE

A firm needs Rs 10 lakh in the form of debt over a 5-year period. If the floatation cost is Rs 500, the interest on debt 12%, and the return on investment 10%, the optimal size of the debenture issue will be:

Here the carrying cost over the 5-year period is (12% – 10%) 5 or 10%

The optimal issue size = Rs $[(2 \quad 500 \quad 10{,}00{,}000)/0.1]^{1/2}$ = Rs 3,16,230

The firm has to issue this economic size of debt every 18.97 or (3,16,230/10,00,000 60 months) months.

15.3.4 Retirement of Debt

Debentures have retirement features meaning that the principal amount has to be paid back to the holder thereof after maturity. There are three ways to retire debt:

1. Redemption
2. Refunding
3. Conversion

In case of refunding, the existing bond is exchanged for a new bond under a special privilege accorded to the holders thereof in the indenture, and after a mutual agreement between the firm and the creditors. Normally this is done at maturity, in special cases, however, this may be done even before maturity when the bonds incorporate call features.

Redemption: Redemption means paying back the principal to the debenture-holder. There are two methods of redemption. One is through the creation of a sinking fund. The other is through buy-back provisions. A sinking fund provision helps in the orderly repayment of debentures at maturity without entailing upon the firm's liquidity position. Under this arrangement, the company makes a periodic cash payment to a trustee who administers the sinking fund created for the repayment of debt. Sometimes a part of the earnings every year is allocated for this purpose, and the allocated amount is invested in government bonds that are in turn liquidated at the time of redemption.

The buy-back provision enables a company to redeem debentures even before maturity. A price is specified that may be higher than the par value of debentures. The excess of the price over the par value is known as the buy-back premium which is around 5% of the par values in India.

Refunding: In case of refunding, the existing bond is exchanged for a new bond under a special privilege accorded to the holders thereof in the indenture, and after a mutual agreement between the firm and the creditors. Normally this is done at maturity, in special cases, however, this may be done even before maturity when the bonds incorporate call features providing the firm an option of buying back the bonds at a stated price prior to maturity.

The question arises as to why a company should want to opt go for refunding. Refunding generally occurs when the interest rate tends to decline. The new bonds carry lower interest rate than the old bonds. However, the company should opt for refunding only when the net present value (npv) of the resulting cash flow is positive.

Calculation of the npv is the same as that explained in Chapter 5. Here the initial investment represents the difference between the cash flowing out on the purchase of old debt and the cash flowing in on account of new debt issued. These cash flows also include the floatation cost of the new bonds and the call premium on the old bonds.

The operating cash inflow is equal to the sum of the saving on account of interest payment and the tax benefit from the amortisation of the floatation cost. The annual operating cash flow is discounted to the present value. The discount rate is equal to the current after-tax market interest rate on the firm's debt.

After the initial investment and the present value of operating cash flow are computed, NPV is automatically arrived at. Refunding is suggested if the NPV is positive.

EXAMPLE

A firm has 12% 20-year Rs 10 lakh debentures. The debentures were issued 5 years ago involving a floatation cost of Rs 25,000. The floatation cost is being charged off for tax purposes as an expense at the rate of Rs 1250 annually flat for 20 years. The debentures incorporate call features with a premium of Rs 60,000. Now the firm is considering a new issue of 10% 15-year Rs 10 lakh debentures that will involve a floatation cost of Rs 30,000. the tax rate is 30%. Calculate the NPV of the refunding operation.

Initial Outlay:	Rs
Face value of old debentures	10,00,000
Add: after-tax call premium [Rs 60,000 × (1 – 0.30)	42,000
Less: tax benefit from write-off of the unamortized floatation cost [(25,000 – 6,250) (1 – 0.30)]	(13,130)
Less: value of new debentures minus floatation cost	(9,70,000)
Total	58,870

Present Value of Operating Cash Benefits	Rs
Interest cost saving (annual):	
After-tax interest expense on old debt [10,00,000 × 0.12 (1 – 0.30)]	84,000
Less: after-tax inter new debt [10,00,000 × 0.10 (1 – 0.30)]	(70,000)
Add: benefits from amortisation of floatation cost:	
Annual: Rs 30,000/15 years = Rs 2,000 This is greater than that on old debt by Rs 750 and so will be treated for tax. Rs 750 (1 – 0.30)	525
Total	14,525

Discount Rate

Since the new debentures carry 10% interest rate, the after-tax discount rate will be [0.10 (1 – 0.30)] = 7%

Present value factor for 15 years annually at 7% for Rs 14,525

= Rs 14,525 9.108 = Rs 1,32,294

NPV of refunding operation

Rs 1,32,294 – 58,870 = Rs 73,424

Refunding is suggested because NPV is positive.

Conversion: Conversion means converting bonds or debentures into equity shares. Convertible bonds possess this feature. It is done at the discretion of the debenture-holders. The conversion takes place at a fixed price that is known as the conversion price. Conversion ratio is the number of equity shares received per convertible debenture or par value of convertible debenture divided by the conversion price.

EXAMPLE

The conversion price of the equity share is Rs 50 per Rs 1,000 convertible debenture. Find out the conversion ratio.

Conversion ratio = 1,000/50 = 20.

The valuation of a convertible debenture depends on the market price of an ordinary share and the conversion ratio. In other words the conversion value can be expressed as follows:

$$\text{Conversion value} = \text{Share price} \times \text{Conversion ratio} \qquad ...(15.8)$$

If the conversion ratio is 20, and the market price of ordinary share is Rs 60, the conversion value of Rs 1,000 debenture will be Rs 1200.

Now the question is whether conversion is beneficial to the shareholders or for the firm. Conversion appears to lower earning per share (eps) insofar as there is addition to the number of equity shares. However, the exact position depends upon the magnitude of the interest payment on debt and the number of shares to be added to the stock. It is because the larger the interest payment, the lower is the net profit and lower is the EPS.

Again, as far as the firm is concerned, it is beneficial to issue convertible debentures as they carry a lower interest rate than general debentures. The investors are attracted to convertible debentures even with lower coupon rate because they get a chance to participate in the equity in the future. Moreover, when the money market is tight, convertible debentures are easily sold out. Last but not least, convertible debentures reduce the floatation cost. This is because without incurring any floatation cost, the firm gets equity capital.

15.4 WARRANTS

15.4.1 Features of Warrants

A warrant is a certificate, normally issued along with a debt instrument, in which a company gives the holder the right to buy a specific number of ordinary shares for a particular price for a specified length of period. The issue of warrants is very common in the USA and many other countries. It is however rare in India. It was Deepak Fertilisers and Petrochemicals Corporation of India that issued warrants for the first time in India in 1987.

Warrants have a number of features. More importantly, they have exercise price at which their holder can buy the issuing firm's ordinary shares. Similarly, the exercise ratio means the number of shares bought per warrant. Warrants have an expiry date on which the option to buy ordinary shares expires.

15.4.2 Valuation of a Warrant

The theoretical value of a warrant depends on the market value of ordinary shares, the exercise price, and the exercise ratio. It can be expressed as follows:

Warrant's value = (Share price – Exercise price) × Exercise ratio ...(15.9)

EXAMPLE

If the market price of share is Rs 60, the exercise price is Rs 50 and the exercise ratio 1, find the value of the warrant.

Warrant's value = (60 – 50) × 1 = Rs 10

The market value of warrant may be lower/higher than its theoretical value. If the market price of share is lower than the exercise price, the warrant cannot be sold and hence its theoretical value will be zero. On the contrary, if it is higher than the exercise price, the warrant would be called selling at premium. The extent of premium is equal to the difference between the warrant's market value and its theoretical value divided by the theoretical value.

> The DCM Shriram is a company formed after DCM Ltd. was restructured in 1990. Its Board decided on 19.11.2007 to issue 7,00,000 preferential warrants to its promoters, that is to raise the promoter's post-conversion stake by an estimated 10 per cent or to 42.54 per cent. Each warrant is to be converted into three shares at different points of time over the next one and a half years. It is believed that the purpose of this issue is to get funds for working capital, especially after the company incurred a loss of Rs 7.4 crore in the first half of FY 2007-08 on a turnover of Rs 283 crore. —Based on report published in *Business Standard*, 22.11.2007 and *Hindustan Times*, 22.11.2007.

15.4.3 Usefulness of Warrants

A debenture issued along with a warrant normally carries a lower rate of interest. This is because the investors buy the debenture in the expectation that they will be participating in the equity. It is advantageous for the firm because it gets additional capital at lower interest.

When warrants are exchanged for ordinary shares, their holders pay some cash besides the warrant. In such cases, the firm gets additional cash. Thus issue of warrants improves liquidity.

Issue of warrant keeps equity at a comparatively low level with the result that there is every possibility of an improvement in the EPS.

15.5 INTERNATIONAL SECURITIES

15.5.1 International Equities

When companies need foreign exchange, they issue international equities and international bonds. While issuing international equity, the company does its basic homework and gets approval from the regulatory authorities. It deposits the shares to be issued with the custodian bank located in the domestic country. The custodian bank is appointed by the depository in consultation with the share-issuing company.

An American depository issues American depository receipts (ADRs), while a depository in the international financial market outside the USA issues global depository receipts (GDRs).

The custodian bank asks the depository located in a foreign country to issue depository receipts in lieu of the shares held. The ratio between the number of shares and the number of depository receipts is decided well before the actual issue. In fact, the fixing of the issue price or the ratio between the depository receipts and the shares depends upon a host of economic variables. Generally, the issues are priced at a discount insofar as the eps drops in proportion to the increase in capital. The market price of a depository receipt in international market is largely dependent upon earnings potential, industry fundamentals and macroeconomic fundamentals.

The depository, which is a bank or financial institution situated in an international financial centre, functions as a link between the issuing company and the investor. On receiving information from the issuing company about the launch, the depository issues depository receipts. An American depository will issues American depository receipts (ADRs), while a depository in the international financial market outside the USA will issues global depository receipts (GDRs).

Indian firms listed on the US stock exchanges raised their total market capitalisation from $121 billion in the beginning of 2007 to $140 billion by December 7 the same year. While a few were gainers, the other few were losers. ICICI Bank recorded a gain of $9.9 billion followed by mining giant Sterlite Industries that gained $7.3 billion and HDFC Bank making a gain of $6.7 billion. The other gainers were VSNL, Satyam and MTNL. On the contrary, the losers were Infosys, Wipro and Patni Computers. The biggest loss was recorded by Infosys amounting to $5.6 billion. —*Financial Express, 10.12.2007.*

When GDRs are purchased by investors, the proceeds flow from the depository to the custodian bank and from the custodian bank to the issuing company. The company enters the name of the investor in its register of shareholders. The investor has the right to surrender GDRs and to receive back the investment. For their surrender, the investor deposits the GDRs with the depository who in turn informs the custodian who issues the share certificates in exchange for the GDRs. The proceeds from the sale of shares are converted into foreign exchange for the purpose of making payments to the foreign investors. It may be noted here that once the GDRs are surrendered in exchange for shares, these shares cannot be converted back into GDR.

Again, investors can sell the GDR back in the issuing company's domestic capital market. In order to discourage this practice, the issuer introduces a clause, known as a lock-in period during which this practice is prohibited.

GDRs are traded on the stock exchange after they have been listed there. There are also international clearing houses, such as Euro-clear and CEDEL that ease the settlement of transactions.

Since GDR investors keep changing from time to time, they do not seem very interested in voting rights even though these cannot be denied to them. There are different procedures followed in this respect. One is that the issuing company and the overseas depository enter an agreement where a depository can vote either with the majority voters or according to the wishes of the management. In another procedure, it is implicit that the depository votes in the same proportion as the rest of the shareholders. Again, there is yet another alternative where the depository votes in accordance with the instructions of a nominee of the management.

GDR investors keep changing from time to time, they do not seem very interested in voting rights even though these cannot be denied to them.

15.5.2 International Bonds

International bonds are classified as foreign bonds and Euro bonds. There is difference between the two. In the case of foreign bond, the issuer selects a foreign financial market where the bonds are issued in the currency of that very country. If an Indian company issues bonds in New York, usa, and the bond is denominated in US dollars, it will be called a foreign bond. On the contrary, Euro bonds are denominated in a currency other than the currency of the country where the bonds are issued. If an Indian company's Euro bond is denominated in US dollars, the bonds will be issued in any country other than the USA.

Again, foreign bonds are normally subject to governmental regulations in the country where they are issued. For example, in the case of Yankee bonds (the bonds issued in the USA) the regulatory thrust lies on disclosures. In certain European countries, the thrust lies on resource allocation and monetary control. Samurai bonds (bonds issued in Japan) involved minimum credit-rating requirements prior to 1996. But the Euro bonds are free from the rules and regulations of the country in which they are issued. The reason being that the currency of denomination is not the currency of that country and so it does not have a direct impact on the balance of payments.

Euro bonds are free from the rules and regulations of the country in which they are issued.

International bonds are either straight bonds carrying a fixed rate of interest or floating rate notes carrying a variable interest rate depending upon the London Inter-Bank Offered Rate (LIBOR). Sometimes cocktail bonds are issued involving more than one currency.

There are different stages involved in the issue of international bonds. First, a company does the necessary desired homework under the guidance of a lead manager which may be either a commercial bank or an investment bank and takes approval from the monetary authorities of the country.

The second stage begins when the issue is launched. Investors look at the credit-rating of the issuer as well as its underwriter(s). This is why the lead manager along with the co-managers helps in the credit-rating of the issuer by a well-recognised credit-rating institution. At the same time, it functions as an underwriter and charges an underwriting fee.

The third stage begins after the underwriting process is complete. This stage includes the process of selling the bonds. More often, the lead manager functions as a selling group and for that it charges commission at varying rates.

The investors, on the other end, are individuals, or institutions, such as, investment trusts, banks and companies. They often purchase the bond through their buying agents. There are also trustees involved, who are usually a bank appointed by the issuer. Their duty is to protect the interests of the investors, especially in case of default by the borrower. Sometimes the lead manager acts as a trustee. Last but not least, there are listing institutions. They enlist the bonds for secondary marketing. The secondary market for international bonds is mainly an over-the-counter market, although, the bonds are listed with the stock exchanges.

It may be noted that the entire procedure of the international bond issue is completed within a specified time span. After the press release of the prospectus, it takes 27 days. The first 12 days are spent on a sales campaign which is known as the offering period. On the 12th day, the underwriting agreement is signed which is known as the pricing day. During the following 15 days, the bonds are sold and delivered and the necessary payments are made.

SUMMARY

Corporate securities—shares and debentures—are the traditional sources of funds for a company. The shares are either equity or preference shares. Equity shareholders are the last claimants for dividend and for a share of the company's assets after liquidation. They do, however, possess voting rights. They also have pre-emptive rights to buy new issues, if any.

Preference shareholders have a prior claim on dividend and assets as compared to the equity shareholders. The rate of dividend they receive is fixed. They have voting powers only in special cases. In some cases, preference shares are redeemed. In other cases, the holders of preference shares additionally participate in dividend along with the equity shareholders. In all, both the equity and preference shares are a permanent source of funds.

Debentures represent debt. They carry a fixed rate of interest and a fixed maturity after which debt is retired. The retirement takes place either through redemption, through refunding or through conversion. The debenture-holders have a prior claim on the company's assets in the event of liquidation as compared to the shareholders.

Sometimes, warrants conferring the option of buying ordinary shares at a later date are issued along with debt instruments. This is done to make the debt issue more attractive.

When companies require foreign exchange, they issue international equities and international bonds.

POINTS TO REMEMBER

1. What are the different kinds of corporate securities that help obtain funds from the market?
   - Equity shares
   - Preference shares
   - Debentures
   - Warrants
2. What are the features of equity shares?
   - Permanent capital base
   - No fixed dividend
   - Voting rights
   - Basis for raising borrowed capital
   - Public issue or private placement or both
3. What are pre-emptive rights of equity shareholders?
   - Additional shares, when issued, are first offered to the existing equity shareholders in proportion of their shareholding. It is their pre-emptive right.
4. How are preference shares different from equity shares?
   - Preference shares may be redeemed.
   - Preference shares have a prior claim on company's assets and on dividend.
   - Preference shares have fixed dividend
   - Preference shares may have cumulative dividend.
   - Preference shares have limited voting rights only in specific cases.
5. What are the features of a debenture?
   - Retirement provisions
   - Prior claim to income and assets
   - Fixed rate of interest
   - Absence of voting rights
6. How is the optimal size of the issue of debentures determined?
   - It lies at a point where the carrying cost and the floatation cost are equal or, in other words, the total cost relating to the issue is the minimum.
7. What are the ways to retire debt?
   - Redemption or paying back the principal to the debenture-holders
   - Refunding or exchanging the existing debenture for a new debenture
   - Conversion into equity shares
8. What is a warrant? How is it valued?
   - It is an instrument normally issued along with a debt instrument, as per which the holder gets the right to buy specific number of ordinary shares.
   - Its value = (share price – exercise price) x exercise ratio.

9. What are international securities?
    - Companies convert their shares into American/global depository receipts that are issued in the international financial market.
    - Companies also issue foreign currency convertible bonds in the international financial market.

DESCRIPTIVE QUESTIONS

1. Explain the broad features of equity shares.
2. What do you mean by pre-emptive rights of equity shareholders? How do you find the value of these rights?
3. What are the options a shareholder enjoys when rights issues are declared? Do the different options have the same impact on the value of the shareholder's wealth?
4. Distinguish between preference shares and equity shares.
5. Explain the broad features of debentures. How do you plan for an economic size of the debenture issue?
6. How is debt retired? When is refunding suggested? Explain with the help of an example.
7. What do you mean by warrants? How are they valued?
8. How are international equities and international bonds issued?

OBJECTIVE-TYPE QUESTIONS

1. Mark true or false.
    (a) Preference shares have no fixed dividend.
    (b) Private placement of shares is normally found in the case of small-size issues.
    (c) Pre-emptive rights protect a shareholder, maintaining his share in the total amount of share capital.
    (d) Floatation cost is only variable and not fixed in nature.
    (e) Refunding is a means of retiring debt.
    (f) Debt can be retired also through converting it into equity shares.
    (g) Euro bonds are denominated in the currency of the country in which they are issued.
    (h) The value of a warrant may be negative.
2. Choose the most suitable answer.
    (a) Shareholders can get back their capital:
        (i) during the lifetime of the company
        (ii) only after the liquidation of the company
        (iii) not even after liquidation

(b) Voting rights are enjoyed by:
   (i) equity shareholders
   (ii) bond-holders
   (iii) preference shareholders on all occasions

(c) Dividend is a fixed amount in the case of:
   (i) equity shares
   (ii) preference shares
   (iii) bonds

(d) Pre-emptive right of equity shareholders means:
   (i) they have the right to sell the shares
   (ii) they have right to maintain their proportionate share in ownership
   (iii) the right to vote on major decisions

(e) Redemption of debentures means:
   (i) paying back the principal to the debenture-holder
   (ii) exchange of old debenture for a new one
   (iii) conversion of debenture into equity share

(f) Warrants assure the holder of getting:
   (i) ordinary shares in the company
   (ii) debentures of the company
   (iii) none of the above

NUMERICAL PROBLEMS

1. A company already has 5,00,000 shares, the market price of which is Rs 60 per share. In order to raise additional capital of Rs 10,00,000, it has decided to issue new shares at a subscription price of Rs 50 per share. Find out the number of rights per new share.
2. When the subscription price is Rs 40, price of rights-on share is Rs 60, the number of old shares per number of total shares is 1:1.125, and the number of new shares per number of total share is 1:9. Find the value of ex-rights shares and also the value of one right.
3. A shareholder possesses 5,000 shares having a market value of Rs 50 per share and 10 rights are required to buy one new share. The subscription price is Rs 40. The ex-rights price of the share is Rs 46 and the value of right is Rs 4. Find the current value of his original wealth under three options:
   (a) he exercises his pre-emptive rights and subscribes to the additional shares within the date of record;
   (b) he sells the additional shares; or
   (c) he simply does nothing and the allotment expires.
4. A firm needs Rs 5,00,000 in the form of debt over a 5-year period. If the floatation cost is Rs 500, interest on debt is 12%, and return on investment is 11%, find the optimal size of the debenture issue.

5. A firm has 15% 20-year Rs 5,00,000 debentures. The debentures were issued 5 years ago involving a floatation cost of Rs 20,000. The floatation cost is being charged off for tax purposes as an expense at the rate of Rs 1000 annually flat for 20 years. The debentures incorporate call features with a premium of Rs 50,000. The firm is now considering a new issue of 10% 15-year Rs 50,000 debentures that will involve a floatation cost of Rs 5,000. The tax rate is30 %. Suggest whether the company should opt for a refunding operation.

SOLVED NUMERICAL PROBLEMS

1. Company A sells Rs 100 preference shares at a dividend of Rs 12. If it were to sell debentures, interest rate cost would be 13%. Tax rate is 30%. Find (a) the after-tax cost of each of the financing method, and (b) the after-tax return if you invest in these instruments.

   Solution

   Cost:

   Preference shares = 12/100 = 0.12 = 12%

   Debentures = 13% (1 – 0.30) = 0.091 = 9.1%

   Return from investment:

   Debt = 13% (1 – 0.30) = 9.1%

   Preference shares assuming 50% tax exemption

   = 12% {1 – (0.5 0.3)} = 0.1020 = 10.20%

2. The market value of a share of a company is Rs 140. The company has issued rights shares. The existing shareholders are allowed to subscribe for one additional share at a price of Rs 120 for each 9 rights held. Compute the theoretical value of the following:
   (i) A right when shares are selling "rights-on"
   (ii) Value of one share if it goes "ex-rights"
   (iii) A right when the share sells "ex-rights" and the actual market price moves to Rs 138.

   Solution

   (i) A right when shares are selling "rights-on"
   = Rs (140 – 120)/(9 + 1) = Rs 2

   (ii) Value of one share if it goes "ex-rights"
   = Rs (140 9+120)/(9 + 1) = Rs 138

   (iii) A right when the share sells "ex-rights" and the actual market price moves to Rs 138.
   = Rs (138 – 120)/9 = Rs 2

3. A company needs Rs 5,00,000 to finance a new project over a period of three years. The floatation cost per issue lot of debentures is Rs 1,000 and the interest on debt is 15% p.a. The return from the new project is 12%. Find the optimal size of the issue of debentures.

Solution

Based on Eq. 15.7,

Optimal size of issue = Rs [{(2 1,000 500,000)/{(0.15– 0.12)3}]$^{1/2}$

= (1,00,00,00,000/0.09) $^{1/2}$

= $\sqrt{11111111111}$ = Rs 1,05, 409

No of issue lots = Rs 5,00,000/1,05,409 = 4.74 or 5

4. A company has outstanding a Rs 1,000 debenture that is convertible into ordinary share at Rs 62.50 per share. The market price of the share is Rs 65. Find the conversion ratio, the conversion value and gain to the holder of debenture after conversion.

Solution

Conversion ratio = Rs 1,000/62.50 =16.

Conversion value = Rs 65 16 = Rs 1,040

Gain to the debenture-holder = Rs 1,040 – 1,000 = Rs 40

5. A company has just sold a Rs 1,000, 20-year, 12% convertible debenture. The interest is paid every year at the year-end but the principal is paid at maturity. Had it not been a convertible debenture, it could have been sold with a 16% coupon. Find the value of the convertible debenture.

Solution

Year	*Payment Rs*	*PVIF at 16%*	*Present value Rs*
1 – 20	120 p.a.	6.259	751.08
20	1,000	0.051	51.00
			802.08

The value of the convertible debenture = Rs 802.08

6. A company has outstanding warrants that are exercisable at Rs 50 per share. The holders of warrants are entitled to purchase 3 ordinary shares. The market price of the ordinary share is Rs 60 per share. Find the theoretical value of warrant.

Solution

Theoretical value of warrant = (MPS – exercise price) shares per warrant

= (60 – 50) 3 = Rs 30

7. A firm has 14% 10-year, Rs 5,00,000 debentures. They were issued five years ago involving a floatation cost of Rs 20,000. The debentures have call features with a premium of Rs 50,000. Now the firm is issuing 10% 8-year, Rs 5 lakh debentures involving a floatation cost of Rs 25,000. Tax rate is 30%. Is refunding a viable option?

Solution

Initial outlay:

Face value of old debentures	Rs 5,00,000
Add after-tax call premium = Rs 50,000 (1 – 0.30)	35,000
Less after-tax floatation cost Rs 20,000(1 – 0.30)	14,000
Less value of new debentures net of floatation cost	4,75,000
Total	46,000

Present value of operating cash benefits:

Annual interest cost saving Rs 5,00,000 0.04 (1 – 0.30)	14,000
Excess of floatation cost p.a. treated for tax =	
{(25000/8) – (20000/10)}(1 – 0.30)	788
Total	14,788

After-tax discount rate (new debentures) = 10% (1 – 0.30) = 7%

PVF 7%, 8 yrs for Rs 14,788

= Rs 14,788 × 5.9713 = Rs 88,303.58

NPV of refunding operation = Rs 88,303.58 – 46,000 = Rs 42303.58

Refunding is viable since NPV is positive.

Study Topic: Trends in the Primary Market for Corporate Securities during September 2010

During September 2010, a sum of Rs 48,024 million was mobilised in the primary market through 18 issues compared to Rs 10,497 million through 6 issues mobilised during August 2010. Segregating this figure into IPO, FPO and rights issues, it was Rs 40,730 million, Rs 515 million and Rs 6780 million, respectively. The cumulative amount mobilised during April to September 2010 stood at Rs 187.412 billion through 44 issues compared to Rs 177.595 million through 29 issues during the corresponding period of FY 2009–10.

The rights issues pertained to State Bank of Mysore and Rohit Ferro Tech. Ltd. The former issued 10,800,000 shares of Rs 10 each at Rs 540. The latter issued 15,793,178 shares of Rs 10 each at Rs 60.

In September 2010, seven listed companies both at BSE and NSE raised Rs 22,270 million through QIP channel compared to Rs 43,420 million raised by three companies during August 2010.

Again, there were 16 preferential allotments for Rs 35,430 million listed at BSE and NSE during September 2010 compared to 31 allotments for Rs 34,170 million in August 2010.

Last but not least, in the corporate debt market, Rs 157,390 million was raised through 120 issues by way of private placement listed at BSE and NSE during September 2010 compared to Rs 133,800 million through 76 issues in August 2010.
Based on: *SEBI Bulletin*, October 2010.

Questions:

1. In what ways the funds are raised in the primary market for securities?
2. Why are the rights issues so small compared to issues through IPO?
3. Present an overall picture of funds-raising in the Indian primary market for corporate securities.

CASE STUDY

Preferential Allotment of Shares or Warrants

In recent years, in the sequel of regulatory ease, preferential allotment of shares and warrants has become a common practice. The preferential allotment is a tool to infuse fresh equity in the corporate unit. It is by way of issuing shares or warrants at a given price to promoter or promoter group or a person acting in concert or institutional players. This is done when the unit needs additional funds to grab any lucrative investment opportunity. If the investment makes a good return, it is natural that the share prices will soar up for the benefit of the company.

During the first half of 1990s, the regulations were rigid on this count. After the preferential allotment, the allottee had to go through a mandatory open offer to the public which the allottee did not take in good spirit. It was only after the Bhagwati Committee recommendations that the rules were made liberal since 1997. It is found that the promoters, especially of foreign companies allot equity shares to themselves at comparatively lower prices than those prevailing in the market and then selling those shares in the market at market rates, ultimately reaping huge profits.

However, the SEBI has issued guidelines to curb such profiteering. The price at which the preferential allotment is made must conform to an average of weekly high and low of the closing prices of the related shares during past fortnight. The company has to let the SEBI know about the details of the number of shares and about the allottee.

The preferential allotment, apart from helping in funds-raising, transfuses confidence in the general investors. The issue price functions as a benchmark for them. It is true that such issues lead to lowering of earning per share and of return on the net worth and thus impair the share prices. But, on the other hand, it has experience of better performance and rising profits among a number of companies.

There is, of course, some difference between shares and warrants. Warrants take time for their conversion into shares and so there is a time lag for better results. However, to shorten the time lag related to fund-raising, SEBI guidelines make it mandatory for the allottee to make an upfront payment of at least 10 per cent of the total amount.

Let us see now the performance of the following five companies going for preferential allotment.

Rs crore

Company	Date of allotment	Pre-allotment		Post-allotment		% change		Allotment price Rs	MPS Rs on 20.11.2007
		Sales	EBIT	Sales	EBIT	Sales	EBIT		
Bhushan Steel	05/2006	3,050	385	3,856	593	26.4	53.9	156.05	1,028.60
Apollo Tyres	10/2006	3,375	228	3,486	413	3.3	81.6	323.19	40.40
JK Lakshmi	09/2006	803	182	1,026	341	27.8	87.0	147.75	185.70
Jyoti Structures	05/2006	738	77	1,025	126	38.9	64.2	625.10	1,386.75
EMCO	10/2006	508	60	753	99	48.3	64.8	630.17	1,388.75

Source: *Financial Express*, 25.11.2007

It is obvious that all the five companies listed in the table showed upward jump in sales volume and operating profit. The share price in the market too soared up except in one case.

Questions:

1. What is preferential allotment?
2. What are the broad rules in this context?
3. Do you agree that such allotments have yielded good performance results?

SELECT FURTHER READINGS

Easterbrook, F.H. and D.R. Fischel (1985). "Limited Liability and the Corporation", *University of Chicago Law Review*, (Winter): 89–117.

Fooladi, R. and G.S. Roberts (1986). "On Preferred Stock", *Journal of Financial Research*, 9 (Winter): 319–24.

Ofer, A.R. *et al* (1977). "Bond Refunding: A Clarifying Analysis", *Journal of Finance*, 32 (March): 21–30.

Shelton, J.P. (1967), "The Relation of the Price of a Warrant to the Price of its Associated Stock", *Financial Analysts Journal*, 4 (May-June): 143–51.

16

TERM LOANS AND LEASES

OBJECTIVES

To explain the features of term loans and their amortisation schedule
To explain various forms of lease and its advantages and disadvantages
To examine whether leasing of an asset is preferable to its purchase

The issue of shares and debentures meets, to a great extent, the firm's needs for long-term funds. Yet the significance of term loans and leases is no less significant. In view of certain specific advantages that they are widely used for meeting long-term fund requirements. The present chapter thus deals with the term loans and leases.

16.1 TERM LOANS

16.1.1 Basic Characteristics

Although term loans and debentures, both represent debt, yet they vary in their characteristics. In particular, term loans have five basic characteristics that distinguish them from debentures. These characteristics are as follows:

1. Fixed maturity
2. Direct negotiation with the lender
3. Tie up with collateral
4. Restrictive covenants
5. Fixed repayment schedule

First, they have a fixed maturity within which the entire loan must be repaid along with the interest. It is their maturity that distinguishes long-term loans from intermediate and short-term loans. The first few months or the first few years represent a grace period during which repayment of the principal does not commence.

Second, term loans require direct negotiation with the lender. This is private placement as against the bonds that are publicly placed. Sometimes when the amount of loan is very large, more than one lender participates in the lending. Even then, however, the feature of direct negotiation will subsist.

Third, barring a few exceptional cases, term loans require that the borrower provide collateral, which may either be in form of current assets or fixed assets. The amount of the loan is normally lower than the value of the collateral. This is because the lender maintains a margin of safety. In the case of small firms whose credit-rating is not very high, and when large-scale fluctuation is expected in the value of collateral, the margin of safety will be large in order to ensure the lender greater security.

A lender often adds restrictive covenants to the loan agreement in order to make lending safer.

Fourth, the lender often adds restrictive covenants to the loan agreement in order to make lending safer. For example, the borrower has to submit periodically financial statements to the lender, with a view to keeping the latter informed of its financial position. Other restrictions are, for example, asset control provision, liquidity control provision, cash flow control provision and control of the management in general. In case of the asset control provision, it is specified that the borrower has to maintain a certain minimum of net working capital and/or it cannot sell a part of its fixed assets without the consent of the lender. The liability control provision specifies that the borrower cannot issue bonds or pledge the assets against a new loan without the consent of the original lender. Cash flow control provision provides that the borrower cannot declare dividend or repay loans beyond a certain limit. If these restrictions do not work properly, the lender appoints a person on the management of the borrowing firm to supervise them. However, the stringency of the restrictions depends upon the strength of the borrower. If the borrower is not strong, the lender will dictate its own terms to the extent possible.

Fifth, term loans have a fixed repayment schedule. Except for a very few cases where loans are repaid in lumpsum amounts at maturity, normally termed balloon repayment, in a majority of the cases repayment is through instalments. The instalments are for the most part annual, they may, however, be semi-annual, quarterly or even monthly. The instalment includes both principal and interest.

16.1.2 Amortisation Schedule

Repayment schedules are of two kinds. In the first case, the instalment of principal remains constant. The interest is paid on the remaining balance of the loan and so the amount of instalment (inclusive of principal and interest) gets smaller with each successive instalment paid. For example, if a firm borrows Rs 10,000 for 5 years at 10% rate of interest, the repayment schedule can be shown in Table 16.1.

However, in the other form of repayment schedule, the total amount of instalment (inclusive of principal and interest) remains constant, the interest segment tends to decline with every successive instalment insofar as it is charged on the remaining balance of the loan. On the contrary, each successive instalment of the principal goes on inflating. This is because it represents the difference between the amount of instalment payment and the amount of interest. The instalment, I can be calculated as follows:

$$I = P / \sum_{t=1}^{n} 1/(1+r)^t \qquad \ldots(16.1)$$

Table 16.1 *Amortisation Schedule of Loan (All Amounts in Rs)*

End of the period	Instalment of principal	Interest	Instalment payment	Balance of principal
0	–	–	–	10,000
1	2,000	1000	3000	8,000
2	2,000	800	2800	6,000
3	2,000	600	2600	4,000
4	2,000	400	2400	2,000
5	2,000	200	2200	0

Where:

P = the principal amount

r = the interest rate

EXAMPLE

A loan of Rs 10,000 is negotiated at 10% interest and is to be repaid in five annual instalments. Find the amount of annual instalment.

$$I = \text{Rs } 10{,}000/3.791 = \text{Rs } 2{,}637.83$$

This is inclusive of instalment of principal and interest payment.

The instalment of principal will be equal to the amount of instalment minus the interest paid, where interest will be calculated on the remaining balance of loan.

At the end of the first year, the amount of interest will be 10% of Rs 10,000 or Rs 1,000. Therefore, the amount of the instalment of principal will be: Rs 2,637.83 – 1,000 = Rs 1,637.83

The details are shown in Table 16.1.

16.1.3 Advantages of Term Loans

Since term loans represent borrowed capital, they have all the merits of borrowed capital. Over and above this, they also have the merits of directly negotiated debt. Placement is faster, and this guards against any deterioration of conditions in the general capital market.

Table 16.2 *Term Loan Amortisation Schedule—Based on the above Example (All amounts in Rs)*

End of the period	Instalment payment	Interest	Instalment of principal	Balance
0	–	–	–	10,000.00
1	2637.83	1000.00	1637.83	8362.17
2	2637.83	836.22	1801.61	6560.56
3	2637.83	656.06	1981.77	4578.79
4	2637.83	457.88	2179.95	2398.84
5	2637.83	239.88	2397.95	0.89

Floatation cost is lower, and a very close relationship is found between the lender and the borrower that provides the borrower greater access to the lender in case of a difficult financial situation.

Again, in case of term loans, the firm matches up the maturity of assets with that of the loans. For example, if the firm has to buy an asset with a life of 10 years, it will negotiate for a 10-year loan. In this way it can ease its financial position.

Yet again, term loans are helpful to those firms that have limited access to the general bond market.

However, regular servicing of a loan and the accompanying restrictions must be judged against the benefits of a term loan.

16.2 NATURE AND FORMS OF LEASE

A lease is a rental agreement where a series of fixed payment is made for the use of an asset over a period of time. Since it provides an alternative to outright purchase of an asset for use, leasing has become an important source of intermediate and long-term financing. In this process, a firm acquires the economic use of an asset for a specific period of time. this firm is known as the lessee. On the other hand, the asset owner is known as a lessor. The lessee pays the lessor lease rent for the use of the asset.

Broadly speaking, there are two types of leases.

1. Operating lease
2. Financial lease

These distinguishing features of these two types of lease are as enumerated below.

16.2.1 Operating Lease

An operating lease is cancellable by the lessee even before the expiry of its term. The lessor in this case provides services and maintenance of the asset. The payment made by the lessee may not necessarily provide in full for the recovery of the value of the asset. An apposite example of an operating lease is a lease for telephone services.

An operating lease is cancellable by the lessee even before the expiry of its term. The lessor in this case provides services and maintenance of the asset. The payment made by the lessee may not necessarily provide in full for the recovery of the value of the asset.

16.2.2 Financial Lease

A financial lease cannot be cancelled by the lessee before the expiry of the term. Moreover, it is not obligatory for the lessor to provide maintenance. The asset is fully amortised over the life of the lease. It is for this reason that a financial lease is treated as a source of financing. Financial leases may be of three kinds. They are as follows:

1. Direct lease
2. Leveraged lease
3. Sale and lease-back arrangement

In case of direct lease, the lessor buys the asset afresh from the manufacturer and leases it to the lessee. Sometimes the manufacturer or vendor and the lessor are the same person.

(a) Direct lease

Funds
Lease payment
Manufacturer
Lessor
User
Asset
Use of asset
Equity
Funds
Financial markets

(b) Leveraged lease

Funds
Lease payment
Manufacturer
Lessor
User
Asset
Use of asset
Funds
Debt (perhaps) equity
Financial markets

(c) Sale and lease back arrangement

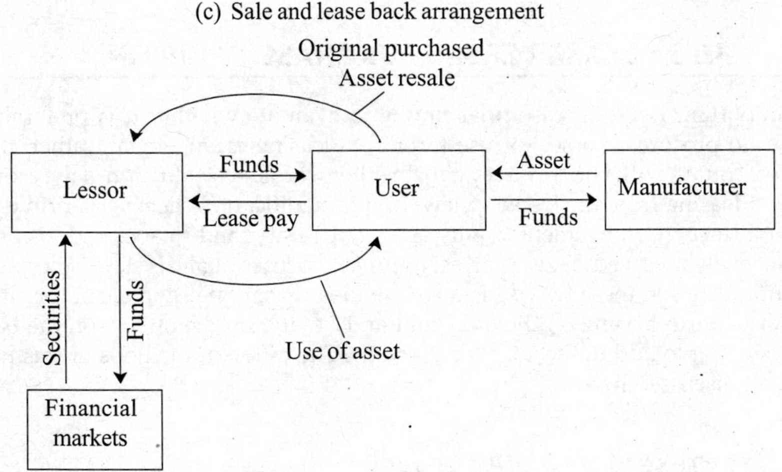

FIG. 16.1 Flows of Assets and Funds in Different Types Leases of Financial

Leveraged lease resembles a direct lease, except that a third party known as the lender is involved. The lender lends to the lessor who buys the asset with the borrowed money and leases it out to the lessee.

A financial lease cannot be cancelled by the lessee before the expiry of the term. The asset is fully amortized over the life of the lease.

Under the sale and lease-back arrangement, lessor buys the asset from the lessee and immediately leases it back to the lessee. The lessee thus gets back the asset for use that it was using earlier and, at the same time, gets cash from the sale of the assets to meet some other requirements.

16.2.3 Straight and Modified Lease

Based on the scope for modification in the terms of the lease agreement, such agreements can be classified as a straight lease or a modified lease. In a straight lease, the conditions of the agreement cannot be modified. A straight lease obligates a firm to make a series of identical payments over the life of the lease. The annual payment will be equal to the cost of the asset divided by the present value factor. Let the cost of the asset be Rs 1,00,000 with a 5-year lease period. With a 10% yield, the present value of annuity would be 3.791 and the annual payment will be:

$$\text{Rs } 1{,}00{,}000/3.791 = \text{Rs } 26{,}378$$

In case of a modified lease, the rental may be changed. The lessee may get the right to purchase the asset at a declining price after each year of the lease period.

16.3 LEASE VERSUS PURCHASE DECISION

The most important issue in lease financing is to evaluate whether it is preferable for a lessee firm to procure an asset for use through a leasing arrangement, rather, than to purchase it (of course, with borrowed capital). In other words, an evaluation of the economic desirability of leasing from the lessee's viewpoint is significant. Whenever a firm decides in favour of a leasing arrangement, the investment decision and financing decision both are simultaneously involved. Thus a correct approach to lease analysis should be based on the interaction between these two decisions. The idea is that one should opt for either of the two alternatives—leasing on the one hand and buying on the other—on the basis of whether it is going to add to the corporate wealth. The different methods of this kind of evaluation are discussed here.

16.3.1 Net Present Value Approach

The analyst computes the net present value (npv) of the two alternatives. The process is to:

1. To compute NPV of the buy alternative;.
2. To compute NPV of the leasing alternative;
3. To opt for the alternative with higher positive NPV

The NPV of the purchase alternative will be computed in a manner similar to that discussed in Chapter 5. It is suggested that the readers refer to Eq. 5.6. Initial investment will be the cost of the asset. Operating cash flow will be the net cash inflow resulting from the use of the asset. The terminal cash flow will normally be the salvage value of the asset.

The NPV of the lease alternative should be computed in a similar manner. The only difference is that the amount of after-tax cash flow takes into account the lease payments. In terms of an equation, cash flow during a particular period can be expressed as follows:

$$CF_t = (R - L - OC)(1 - T) \quad ...(16.2)$$

Where:

R = revenue

L = lease payment

OC = operating cost

T = tax rate

In this case, the initial investment is zero insofar as the asset is not purchased and the first rental is paid at the end of the first year. The discount rate is normally higher than in the buy alternative insofar as a lease plan by definition uses lease financing.

After the NPV of the two alternatives is computed, they are compared. The alternative with higher positive NPV is chosen.

EXAMPLE

A firm needs an asset that costs Rs 6,000. The salvage value at the end of the third year is expected to be Rs 600. The annual revenue is expected to be Rs 4,000 and the annual operating cost to be Rs 1,000. The discount rate is 10%. The tax rate is 30%. If the firm leases the asset instead of buying it, it has to pay an annual rental of Rs 2,500 on the condition that it would be payable at the end of the first, second and the third year. In this case, the annual operating expenses should be Rs 800 and the discount rate would be 12%.

(a) *Buy Alternative:*

Initial investment = Rs 6,000

Operating cash flow per annum = (Revenue – operating expenses – Depreciation) $(1 - T)$ + Depreciation

= Rs (4,000 – 1000 – 1,800) (1 – 0.30) + 1,800 = Rs 2,640

Terminal cash flow = Rs 600

Applying the NPV Rule:

$$NPV = 2640/1.10 + 2640/1.21 + 2640/1.33 - 6000 = \text{Rs } 1{,}018$$

(b) *Lease Alternative:*

In this case, the question of an initial investment on account of purchase of the asset, depreciation related to the asset and its salvage value does not arise. However, lease rental and operating cash flow are tax deductible.

Operating cash flow = Rs (4000 – 2500 – 800) (1 – 0.30) = Rs 490

Applying the NPV rule:

$$NPV = 490/1.12 + 490/1.25 + 490/1.41 = \text{Rs } 1177$$

Since the NPV of lease alternative is higher than that of the buy alternative, leasing and not buying should be the right course of action.

16.3.2 Net Advantage of Leasing (NAL) Approach

NAL represents the cost saving on account of leasing over normal purchase financing. Lease versus buy decision based on this approach involves three steps. They are as follows:

1. Computation of NPV (P), that is, NPV of the purchase option;
2. Computation of NAL;
3. Comparison of NAL with the NPV (P).

Three possibilities exist after such comparison. They are as follows:

1. NPV (P) is positive and NAL is negative. In such cases, the firm should opt for the purchase option;
2. NPV (P) and NAL are both positive. In such cases, the firm should opt for the lease option,
3. NPV (P) is negative and NAL is positive and large enough to offset the negative NPV (P). The firm should opt for leasing.

In form of an equation, net advantage of leasing (nal) can be expressed as follows:

$$\text{NAL} = I_0 - \sum_{t=1}^{n} \frac{O_t(1-T) + R_t(1-T) + I_t.T + \Delta I_t.T + D_t.T}{(1+r)^t} - \frac{V_n}{(1+k)^n} \qquad ...(16.3)$$

Where:

O_t = operating cost in period t
T = the marginal tax rate
R_t = annual lease rental
I_t = tax-deductible interest expense forfeited in period t if the firm opts for leasing
ΔI_t = the interest on debt to be repaid in the event of the lease of the asset
D_t = the depreciation during period t
V_n = the expected after-tax salvage value of the asset
r = the discount rate which is equal to interest rate on borrowed funds
k = after-tax cost of capital of the firm.

This approach is fairly similar to the NPV approach, except that it also takes into account the interest tax shelters lost on account of leasing the asset. These tax shelters are lost or foregone because the firm does not use normal debt financing, and, at the same time, the firm uses more than its target debt ratio allotment when lease financing is equal to 100% of the asset's purchase price. Since salvage value in difficult to predict, it is discounted at a higher rate, say, at the firm's cost of capital.

EXAMPLE

A firm needs an asset that costs Rs 6,000. The salvage value at the end of the third year is expected to be Rs 600. The annual revenue is expected to be Rs 4,000 and the annual operating cost Rs 1,000. The discount rate is 8%. The tax rate is 30%. If the firm leases the assets instead of buying it, it has to pay an annual rental of Rs 2,500 on the condition that it would be payable at the end of the first, second and third year. In this case, the annual operating expenses would be Rs 800. The after-tax, firm's cost of capital in 10%.

As per Eq. 16.2:

$O_t\,(1 - T)$ = Rs (800 × 0.7) = Rs 560

$R_t(1 - T)$ = Rs (2500 × 0.7) = Rs 1750

D.T = Rs (1800 × 0.3) = Rs 540

$I_t.\,T + \Delta I_t.T$ = (assuming 8% interest rate)

First year: Rs (6000 × 0.08 × 0.3 + 0) = Rs 144

Second year: Rs (4000 × 0.08 × 0.3) + 48 = Rs 144

Third year: Rs (2000 × 0.08 × 0.3) + 48 = Rs 96

Operating cash flow Combining $O_t(1 - t)$, $R_t(1 - T)$, $I_t.T + \Delta I_t.T$ and $D.T$:

First year: Rs [– (560 + 1750 + 540 + 144)]/1.08 = – Rs 2772

Second year: Rs [– (560 + 1750 + 540 + 144)]/1.08^2 = – Rs 2567

Third year: Rs [– (560 + 1750 + 540 + 96)]/1.08^3 = – Rs 2339

Total operating cash flow = – Rs 7678

Terminal cash flow: Rs – 600/1.10^3 = – Rs 451

Initial Investment: Rs 6000

NAL: – Rs 2129

Since NAL is negative, the firm should pursue the purchase option.

16.3.3 Internal Rate of Return (IRR) Method

Based on the IRR technique, a firm should opt for leasing if the after-tax cost of lease is lower than the after-tax cost of debt financing. The after-tax cost of leasing resembles IRR insofar as it is that rate of discount, which equates the present value of lease payments net of tax shields together with the tax shield for depreciation, with the cost of asset. In other words, the after-tax cost of leasing can be determined through solving the following equation for *r*:

$$I_0 - \sum_{t=1}^{n} \frac{R_t}{(1+r)^t} + \sum_{t=1}^{n} \frac{T(R_t - D_t)}{(1+r)^t} = 0 \qquad ...(16.4)$$

EXAMPLE

A firm needs an asset that costs Rs 6,000. The salvage value at the end of the third year is expected to be Rs 600. The annual revenue is expected to be Rs 4,000 and the annual operating cost to be Rs 1,000. The discount rate is 8%. The tax rate is 30%. If the firm leases the asset instead of buying it, it would have to pay annual rentals of Rs 2,500 on the condition that it would be payable at the end of the first, second and the third year. In this case, the annual operating expenses should be Rs 800.

Solving the following equation for IRR we get

$$\{6000 - [(2500 + 210)/(1 + IRR) + (25\,00 + 210)/(1 + IRR)^2 + (2500 + 210)/(1 + IRR)^3]\} = 0$$

$$IRR = 16\%$$

The IRR is 16% as compared to the after-tax cost of debt which is being 5.60%. Since the cost of leasing is higher than the cost of debt, the purchase of the asset, and not leasing, should be preferred.

16.3.4 The Lessor's Viewpoint

The loss/profit of the lessor is the mirror image of the loss/profit of the lessee. In other words, the loss of the lessee is a gain for the lessor, and a gain for the lessee is a loss for the lessor of the same amount, provided the tax rate, borrowing rate and other costs are analogous for both of them. A simple example will make this phenomenon clear. Suppose a lessee opts for leasing a machine that costs Rs 30,000. The present value of the cash outflow on account of annual rental, etc., during the 5-year period of the lease is Rs 32,370. Since the lessee does not buy the machine, he has saved the initial investment. The NPV will be: Rs (30,000 – 32,370) = Rs – 2,370. The lessee loses this amount. On the contrary, the lessor buys the machine with an initial cash outflow of Rs 30,000. The present value of the cash inflow on account of rental, etc., will be Rs 32,370. The NPV will be: Rs (– 30,000 + 32,370) = Rs 2,370. The lessor gains by this amount.

However, leasing can be made gainful for both the lessor and lessee through tax rate and borrowing rate differentials between them.

16.4 ADVANTAGES AND DISADVANTAGES OF LEASING

16.4.1 Advantages

A growing tendency to favour leasing testifies to the fact that it carries specific advantages. The first advantage is that it helps conserve working capital. This is because leasing does not require a lumpsum outflow of funds in the form of the purchase price of the asset. Cash is thus retained in the business, and can be used for other important purposes.

The second advantage is that lease financing is highly flexible. A lease can be easily negotiated without the approval of the corporate capital budgeting committee and with little documentation. Moreover, the rental payment schedule can be designed to coincide with the cash cycle or the revenue generated from the asset.

The third advantage is that lease financing is highly convenient. There is no need to prepare a subsidiary fixed asset schedule for tax purposes. Neither does the management have to bother about the maintenance of the real estate business. The human resources at their disposal can thus be utilised elsewhere.

Fourth, it is often argued that leasing allows a firm to avoid the risk of obsolescence. The reason being that the lessor normally provides the lessee with better service in order to maintain the resale value of the asset.

Fifth, even firms with a poor credit rating can manage to secure assets through leasing when they do not get funds from other sources to buy the asset. In other words, a lease eases the availability of credit.

Sixth, the tax shield generated by the lease payment is often larger than that generated by depreciation on an asset that has been purchased. The firm gets an added advantage of savings on account of taxes.

Last but not least, leasing does not carry restrictive covenants that are found in the case of term loans. Restrictive covenants are imposed by the lender in order to make better use of the loan and to protect its own interests.

16.4.2 Disadvantages

Despite a number of advantages, lease financing also involves a few disadvantages. First, the cost of leasing is often higher than that of debt. This is because the lessor passes on the cost relating to inventory, overheads and the risk of obsolescence, to the lessee. However, it depends on how far the lease market is competitive and how far tax savings reduces the cost.

Second, a lease does not provide the lessee with a title to the residual value of the asset. In the case of plant and machinery, the residual value is not very significant, however, in the case of real estate, it is large with the result that the lessee does not reap such benefits.

Third, leasing curtails the lessee's freedom as far as the use of the asset is concerned. It is often found that inferior quality of inputs are used.

SUMMARY

Term loans and leases are an important source of intermediate and long-term financing. Term loans are distinctive: insofar as they have a fixed maturity; they are directly negotiated with the lender; they need collateral; and they have a repayment schedule. Debt maturity can easily be matched with the maturity of the assets. However, restrictive covenants are often derogatory.

The amortisation schedule may be of two kinds. In one, the amount of instalment declines over time as the interest is charged on the remaining balance of the principal. In the other, the amount of the instalment remains the same throughout.

Leasing provides an alternative to buying an asset, it can, therefore, be considered a source of financing. The financial lease arrangement, other than the operating lease arrangement, is either a sale and lease-back arrangement or a direct or leveraged lease. Again, a lease can either be a straight one or modified one depending upon the scope for modification in the lease agreement.

The decision whether a lessee firm should buy an asset or should acquire it on lease depends on: first, the NPV from the two alternatives; second, on the net advantage of leasing (nal); and third, on the IRR of leasing compared with the after-tax cost of debt.

Leasing has various advantages, such as conservation of working capital, flexibility, convenience, avoidance of risk of obsolescence, greater tax shield and absence of restrictive covenants. The disadvantages manifest in higher rentals, absence of ownership of the asset in question, etc.

POINTS TO REMEMBER

1. What are the basic features of term loans?
   - Fixed maturity
   - Direct negotiation with the lender
   - Tie-up with collateral
   - Restrictive covenants
   - Fixed repayment schedule
2. What are the different kinds of amortization schedule?
   - In the first case, repayment of the principal is periodic and its size is constant. The size of instalment varies because of varying interest payment.
   - In the other case, repayment of the principal is made at the maturity in a lumpsum. Interest payment is periodic.
   - Still in the other case, the size of instalment is constant, the size of principal rises, but the size of interest payment declines.
3. What are the different kinds of leases?
   - Operating lease where lessor provides services and maintenance of the asset. The lessee can cancel the lease even before expiry of the lease period.
   - Financial lease involves no cancellation before expiry, nor maintenance of the asset. The asset is fully amortized over the life of the lease.
4. What are the different kinds of a financial lease?
   - Direct lease
   - Leveraged lease
   - Sale and lease back arrangement
5. How do you decide for lease versus buy?
   - Leasing when NPV of lease alternative > NPV of buying alternative
   - Leasing when NAL is > 0
   - Leasing when IRR of leasing < tax-adjusted cost of debt with which asset is bought

6. What are the advantages of leasing?
   - Conservation of cash
   - Flexibility
   - Convenience
   - Avoidance of obsolescence risk
   - Easy availability of credit
   - Absence of restrictive covenants
7. What are the disadvantages of leasing?
   - The cost of leasing is often higher than that of debt.
   - Lessee does not get the residual value of the asset.
   - Absence of freedom regarding use of the asset.

DESCRIPTIVE QUESTIONS

1. Describe the features of term loans as distinct from debentures.
2. Explain the different types of amortisation schedule of a term loan with the help of a simple example.
3. Distinguish between:
   (a) an operating and a financial lease; and
   (b) a sale and lease-back arrangement, direct lease and leveraged lease.
4. Discuss the NPV approach to the lease versus buy decision.
5. What do you mean by NAL? Explain it with the help of a simple example.
6. Examine the IRR method as applicable to the lease versus buy decision.
7. The gain/loss of the lessor is the mirror image of gain/loss of the lessee. Discuss.
8. Enumerate the advantages and disadvantages of leasing.

OBJECTIVE-TYPE QUESTIONS

1. Mark true or false.
   (a) In cases where the size of the instalment payment is constant or equal, the amount of principal decreases with successive instalments.
   (b) Floatation costs are often large in the case of term loans as compared to debenture issues.
   (c) An operating lease is cancellable by the lessee even before maturity.
   (d) A financial lease is cancellable by the lessee even before maturity.
   (e) In the case of financial lease, it is not obligatory on the part of the lessor to provide maintenance for the asset in question.

(f) In the case of a leveraged lease, the lender is also a party to the lease arrangement.
(g) The terms of the lease agreement are modified in the case of a straight lease.
(h) Both lessor and lessee can benefit from leasing if the tax rate is different for each.
(i) NAL represents a cost saving resulting from leasing.

2. Choose the most suitable answer.
   (a) Leasing should be preferred if:
      (i) NPV (P) is positive and NAL is negative.
      (ii) NAL is positive and NPV(P) is negative.
      (iii) Neither of the above.
   (b) Leasing should be preferred if:
      (i) NPV of the buy alternative > NPV of the leasing alternative
      (ii) NPV of the buy alternative < NPV of the leasing alternative
      (iii) NPV of the buy alternative = NPV of the leasing alternative
   (c) Leveraged lease is a form of:
      (i) operating lease
      (ii) financial lease
      (iii) both of the above
   (d) Balloon repayment means:
      (i) repayment of the principal at maturity
      (ii) repayment of the principal in instalments
      (iii) neither of the above
   (e) With no tax rate differential:
      (i) lessor gains when lessee loses
      (ii) lessor gains when lessee gains
      (iii) lessor loses when lessee loses.

NUMERICAL PROBLEMS

1. Find out the annual lease payment if purchase price is Rs 50,000, implicit interest rate is 12% and the period of lease is 5 years.
2. Find the implicit interest rate if purchase price is Rs 2,00,000, annual lease payment is Rs 43,431 and lease period is 5 years.
3. Find the purchase price if the implicit interest rate is 12%, lease period is 5 years and annual lease payment is Rs 20,000.
4. A company leases a machine on a payment of Rs 10,000 per annum for a period of 4 years. The payment is made at the beginning of the year. Calculate the cost of leasing.
5. ABC Company is considering leasing a computer that costs Rs 1,00,000. The 4-year agreement involves Rs 23,000 as annual rental payable at the end of the year, and the annual operating expenses amount to Rs 3,000. If the company purchases the computer,

straight-line depreciation is charged taking into account an estimated salvage value of Rs 20,000. The annual revenue is Rs 7,000 and the annual operating cost is Rs 3,000. Interest rate on debt is 12% and the cost of capital is 20%. Find out: (i) NAL, and (ii) IRR of the lease when tax rate is 30%.

6. A loan of Rs 1,00,000 carrying 12% interest rate has to be repaid in 10 equal annual instalment (principal+interest). Prepare a repayment schedule showing both the interest and principal.
7. Find the annual equal instalment of a loan repayment if the amount of loan is Rs 20,000; maturity is 4 years and interest rate is 10%.

SOLVED NUMERICAL PROBLEMS

1. A person borrows Rs 10,000 for 4 years at 10% interest rate. Find the annual equal instalments that he has to pay.

Solution

Since present value interest factor from an annuity corresponding to 10% and 4 years,

PVIFA 10%, 4 years = 3.1699

Annual instalment = Rs 10,000/3.1699 = Rs 3,154.67

Instalment payment schedule

Year	*Total instalment*	*Interest*	*Principal*	*Year-end Principal*
0	–	–	–	Rs 10,000
1	3,154.67	1,000	2,154.67	7,845.33
2	3,154.67	784.53	2,370.14	5,475.19
3	3,154.67	547.52	2,607.15	2,868.04
4	3,154.67	286.80	2,867.87	0.00

2. A person borrows Rs 10,000 for 4 years at 10% interest rate. Find the size of total instalments when principal is repaid in equal instalment annually.

Solution

Repayment Schedule

Year	*Total instalment*	*Interest*	*Principal*	*Year-end Principal*
0	–	–	–	Rs 10,000
1	3,500	1,000	2,500	7,500
2	3,250	750	2,500	5,000
3	3,000	500	2,500	2,500
4	2,750	250	2,500	0.00

3. A person borrows Rs 10,000 for 4 years at 10% interest rate. Find the size of total instalments when principal is repaid at maturity.

Solution

Repayment Schedule

Year	*Total instalment*	*Interest*	*Principal*	*Year-end Principal*
0	–	–	–	Rs 10,000
1	1,000	1,000	–	10,000
2	1,000	1,000	–	10,000
3	1,000	1,000	–	10,000
4	11,000	1,000	10,000	Nil

4. A firm has to acquire a machine that will last for 4 years. Its purchase price is Rs 50,000 with no salvage value. A straight-line method of depreciation is followed. Tax rate is 30%. If the firm borrows to buy the machine, it has to pay 14% interest. If it goes for leasing the machine for a period of 4 years, annual rental will be Rs 15,000. Which of the two should be preferred?

Solution

Purchase Option:

Schedule of loan repayment (Based on the process in Problem 1) Rs

Year	*Instalment*	*Interest*	*Principal*	*Balance*
0	–	–	–	50,000
1	17,160	7,000	10,160	39,840
2	17,160	5,578	11,582	28,258
3	17,160	3,956	13,204	15,054
4	17,160	2,108	15,054	–

After-tax cash flows (Rs)

Year	*Instalment*	*Interest tax shield*	*Depreciation tax shield*	*Tax-adjusted loan repayment*
1	– 17,160	2,100	3,750	– 11,310
2	– 17,160	1,673	3,750	– 11,737
3	– 17,160	1,187	3,750	– 12,223
4	– 17,160	632	3,750	– 12,778

Tax-adjusted discount rate = 14% (1 –0.30) = 9.8%

Present value = Rs $(-11{,}310/1.098) + (-11{,}737/1.098^2) + (-12{,}223/1.098^3) + (-12778/1.098^4)$

= Rs – 38,060

Lease Option:

After-tax lease payment = Rs 15,000 (1 – 0.30) = Rs 10,500

Present value = Rs $(-10{,}500/1.098) + (-10{,}500/1.098^2) + (-10{,}500/1.098^3) + (-10{,}500/1.098^4)$ = Rs – 33,428

Lease to be preferred since present value of outflow is lower in case of lease.

5. A person needs a computer for a 3-year period that costs Rs 50,000. He has an option either to buy it or to lease it. The lease rental is Rs 20,000 annually. As per tax rules, he cannot claim depreciation, nor can he deduct interest on personal borrowing from his income. The borrowing rate is 14%. Find whether he should buy the computer or lease it.

   Solution

   Lease Option:

   Present value of lease payment = Rs(– 20,000/1.14) + (– 20,000/1.14^2) + (– 20,000 /1.14^3) = Rs – 46,433

   Loan Option:

   Instalment Rs 50,000/2.3216 = Rs 21,537

   PV of loan repayment = Rs – 21,537/1.14 + (– 21,537/1.14^2) + (– 21,537/1.14^3) = Rs 50,000

   PV of lease payment is less than loan repayment. Hence lease should be preferred.

6. A firm needs an asset that costs Rs 60,000. Interest rate on borrowing is 12%. Tax rate is 30%. Lease rental is Rs 24,000 annually. Find whether to lease or to buy the asset.

   Solution

   Based on Eq. 16.4,

   Annual depreciation = Rs 60,000/3 = Rs 20,000

   Rental + (Rental – Depreciation) Tax rate = Rs 24,000 + (24,000 – 20,000)0.30 = Rs 24,000 + 1,200 = 25,200

   Rs – 60,000 + 25,200/(1+IRR) + 25,200/(1+IRR)^2 + 25,200/(1+IRR)^3

   = IRR = 12.5%

   Since IRR of leasing > tax-adjusted interest rate, purchase, and not leasing, should be preferred.

7. A firm needs an asset that costs Rs 60,000. Interest rate on borrowing is 12%. Tax rate is 30%. Discount rate is 10%. Lease rental is Rs 24,000 annually. Find whether to lease or to buy the asset.

   Solution

   Based on Eq. 16.3,

   Tax-adjusted lease rental = Rs 24,000 × (1 – 0.30) = Rs 16,800

   Tax shield of depreciation = Rs 20,000 × 0.30 = Rs 6,000

   Interest: Year 1 = Rs 60,000 × 0.12 × 0.30 = Rs 2,160

   Year 2 = Rs 40,000 3 0.12 3 0.30 = Rs 1,440

   Year 3 = Rs 20,000 × 0.12 x 0.30 = Rs 720

   Operating cash flow: Year 1 = {– (16,800 + 6,000 + 2,160)}/1.10

   Year 2 = {– (16,800 + 6,000 + 1,440)}/1.102

   Year 3 = {– (16,800 + 6,000 + 720)}/1.103

   Rs 60,000 – 22,690 – 20,033 – 17,671 = – 395

   Since NAL is negative, purchase option should be preferred.

8. The cost of a machine is Rs 10,000. If it is procured on lease, the annual rental amounts to Rs 2,330 for 5 years. If it is purchased with borrowing, the interest rate is 10% with a tax rate of 30%. Find out whether lease is to be preferred.

   Solution:

   After-tax cost of discount = 0.10 (1 – 0.30) = 0.7 = 7%

   At 7% discount rate, the NPV of lease = Rs 10,000 – Rs 2,330 × 4.1002 = Rs 446.53

   Since the net present value of incremental cash flow from leasing relative to purchase is positive, lease can be preferred. Here, 4.1002 is the present value of annuity for 5 years/7% discount rate.

Mini Case

Sumeet Computers is planning to manufacture keyboards. The keyboard needs a microphone, which the firm can easily produce. But there is a problem that in view of fast-changing technology, the price of the microphone-manufacturing equipment is expected to fall drastically. During past 3 years, it fell from Rs 4 million to Rs 5,00,000. This is the reason that Sumeet Computers does not like to purchase the microphone-manufacturing equipment. It finds out an alternative of leasing the equipment. The lease contract involves three annual payments of Rs 1.5 million due at the beginning of the year. There is also involved a security money of Rs 250,000 that will be returned at the expiry of the lease. The firm has the option of buying the equipment at the expiry of the lease either at the fair market value or at a fixed price. There is also a provision that the lease can be cancelled in the midway. The company can issue bonds with a yield of 11%. The tax rate is 30%.

Questions:

1. Should the company lease the equipment rather than buying it?
2. What will be the value of the lease if it is cancelled in the midway?

SELECT FURTHER READINGS

Middleton, J.W. (1968). "Term Lending–Practical and Profitable", *Journal of Commercial Bank Lending*, 50 (Aug.): 26–35.

Mukherjee, T.K. (1991). "A Survey of Corporate Leasing Analysis", *Financial Management*, 20 (3): 96–107.

Schall, L.D. (1987). "Analytic Issues in Lease vs. Purchase Decisions", *Financial Management*, 16 (2): 17–20.

17

DIVIDEND THEORIES AND POLICY

OBJECTIVES

To make an appraisal of various theories of dividend

To explain the factors influencing the dividend policy of a firm

To focus on the stability of dividend payment

To explain bonus shares and the relevant statutory provisions in India

To describe share split, reverse split, and repurchase of shares

It is a common practice among the firms to allocate a part of their net profits for dividend payments and to retain the other part within the firm with a view to making investments. The retained profit is thus a source of financing. Since such funds are generated out of the firm's operations, they are known as an internal source of financing quite at par with some non-cash charges, such as, depreciation that form a part of internal financing.

Retention of earnings depends upon the firm's dividend policy. If the dividend policy is liberal, the size of retained earnings will be lower. However, if the firm depends more on internal financing, its dividend policy must be conservative so as to make a larger amount of funds available for making investments. Thus framing an optimal dividend policy is significant in order to meet the investment needs of a firm on the one hand, and to meet the dividend expectations of the shareholders on the other. An optimal dividend policy is also significant in view of the fact that like any other financial decision, the objective of the dividend decision is to maximise corporate wealth. However, the shape of an optimal dividend policy has been a subject of debate. The present chapter explains the different views on this subject and also the procedures of dividend payment.

17.1 THEORIES OF DIVIDEND

The theories explaining dividend policy are divergent. The divergence is related to the very assumption of perfect capital market, vis-à-vis, imperfect market conditions. It is also related to whether dividend payments have any relevance to maximising the shareholders' wealth.

Based on these divergent views, the theories of dividend can be put into three groups. They are as follows:

1. Dividend irrelevance approach explaining that the payment or otherwise of dividend has the same impact on the firm's value, and therefore the shareholders are indifferent between dividend payment and retention of earnings. This theory has been propounded by Miller and Modigliani.
2. Dividend irrelevance approach preferring retention of earnings. The residual theory of dividend can be grouped under this head.
3. Dividend relevance approach showing that dividend payment influences the value of shareholders' wealth. The smoothened residual theory of dividend, Walter's theory, Gordon's theory, etc., explain the preference for dividend payment.

17.1.1 Dividend Irrelevance—Miller-Modigliani (M-M) Approach

The most significant proponents of the dividend irrelevance hypothesis are Miller and Modigliani (1961). They assume a perfect capital market where, more importantly, all investors are rational and have identical beliefs; information is available to all; and, at the same time, transaction costs and taxes do not exist. Under these conditions, distribution of dividend or otherwise has the same impact on the shareholders' wealth. As a consequence, the shareholders are indifferent between the payment of dividend and the retention of earnings.

The two authors assume four situations. In all the four situations, the value of the shareholders' wealth remains the same. The four situations are as follows:

1. The firm retains the entire earnings and does not declare dividend. The value of shares during $t + 1$, taking into account the capitalisation rate for a specific class of risk, will be:

$$P_{t+1} = P_t(1 + \rho) - D_{t+1} \qquad ...(17.1)$$

Where:

ρ = the capitalisation rate

EXAMPLE

If each share of a firm is selling at Rs 100, and the firm is thinking of declaring a dividend of Rs 5 at the end of the first year, but ultimately it does not declare dividend. The value of shareholder's wealth in the case of a shareholder possessing one share at the end of the first year, assuming a capitalisation rate of 10%, will be:

Rs [100 (1.10) – 0] = Rs 110.

2. The firm possesses the required cash to pay dividend. If dividend is paid out of cash, money is transferred from one form, a claim on the company, to the other form, that is, cash in the shareholders' hand. The value of shareholders' wealth will remain the same, that is, equal to the sum of the value of their shares and the amount of cash dividend they receive.

EXAMPLE

On the basis of the above example, the value of the share at the end of the first year will be:

Rs [100 (1.10) – 5] = Rs 105.

In the case of a shareholder possessing one share the value of the shareholder's wealth will be:

the value of one share + the value of cash dividend he or she receives

Rs (105 + 5) = Rs 110.

3. If the firm does not possess sufficient cash to pay dividend, it issues shares in lieu of cash and allots these shares to the existing shareholders. The shareholders' wealth remains the same because they get either cash or shares of the same value.
4. If the company issues new shares in lieu of cash payment dividend, but the shareholders need cash, then, in such cases, the shareholders would sell their newly issued shares either in full or in part to some new investors and get cash. In this case too, the shareholders' wealth remains the same. It is the sum of the value of the existing and new shares and the cash received from the new investors in exchange for the shares. The transaction involving the sale of shares by the existing shareholders to the new investors is known as a "homemade dividend".

If the firm does not possess sufficient cash to pay dividend, it issues shares in lieu of cash and allots these shares to the existing shareholders. The shareholders' wealth remains the same because they get either cash or shares of the same value.

17.1.2 Miller-Modigliani Hypothesis in Imperfect Market

In real life, the capital market is not perfect, and taxes do have a role to play. Moreover, transaction cost exists when the shareholders sell any part of the shares they receive in lieu of cash dividend. Again, information is not equally available to all participants in the capital market. If capital market is imperfect, the dividend irrelevance theory does not hold good. Here some of the features of the imperfect capital market are mentioned as a result of which shareholders are not indifferent between getting cash dividend and the retention of earnings.

Existence of Taxes: If the tax rate on dividend is greater than the tax rate on capital gains, shareholders would prefer the reinvestment of the earned profit to getting a cash dividend. Moreover, the capital gains tax timing provisions further lower the incidence of tax, and thus the preference of the shareholders for not receiving cash dividend will be greater. This is because in such cases where tax on capital gains is lower than tax on dividend, distribution of dividend in form of cash lowers shareholders' wealth.

Existence of Transaction Cost: Lower tax rate on capital gains motivates shareholders against cash dividend. However, if a large transaction cost is involved in the sale of shares by the shareholders, they would prefer cash dividend. Taking the earlier example, if the shareholder sells the share for cash and if the transaction cost is Rs 2, he will get only Rs 108 in place of Rs 110 as per the earlier example.

Rationality in the Market: The M-M hypothesis assumes that firms act rationally while selling additional shares at the current market price. However, the capital issue authorities normally exercise

The M-M hypothesis assumes that firms act rationally while selling additional shares at the current market price. However, the capital issue authorities normally exercise control over the prices.

control over the prices. Again, it is expected that the firms behave rationally while investing retained earnings, and that they invest up to a point where internal rate of return (IRR) is higher than the cost of capital. This, however, is usually not the case. There are market-imposed constraints. If the market constraints do not permit the firm to make profitable investments, the shareholders would prefer dividend to retention of earnings.

Existence of Uncertainty: If there is high degree of uncertainty, share prices tend to fluctuate. If the share prices increase, shareholders would prefer retention of earnings. However, when there is a possibility of falling prices, the shareholders would prefer dividend.

17.1.3 Residual Theory of Dividends

The residual theory states that the dividend decision is primarily a financing decision. It means that the profits should first be retained within the firm for meeting investment needs. If any amount remains after this, then that amount may be distributed as dividend. In other words, this theory does not assume the dividend decision as being very relevant to the maximisation of shareholders' wealth.

The argument is based on the rationale that internal financing is more convenient than the external financing. The cost of debt is undoubtedly lower than the cost of equity capital. However, there is a target debt-equity ratio beyond which debt financing is not justified. Thus if a new investment has to be financed, the firm prefers to use retained earnings instead. If the size of investment in a particular period is equal to the earnings, there will be no funds left for dividend distribution. Dividend is possible only when the magnitude of investment is lower than the earnings.

The residual theory of dividend is followed in actual practice. Higgins (1972) has found in an empirical study that dividends vary positively with earnings but negatively with investment.

17.1.4 "Smoothened" Residual Theory of Dividend

The residual dividend theory has yet another version. It is known as the "smoothened" residual theory of dividend. This revised version is suggested on two grounds. One being that the original version of the residual theory of dividend leads to large-scale volatility in dividend payment depending upon the changing magnitude of earnings vis-à-vis investment needs. If the market does not like volatility, this will affect the share price, especially, when dividend payment are rolled back. Second, the revised version does not reject the relevance of the dividend payments outright, as stability in dividend payment conveys useful information to the market.

This is why it suggests that the amount of the dividend should be set at a constant local currency value along with a certain element of growth. The set dividend should be such that, over a long period of time, it represents an amount equal to earnings minus new investment. In other words, this theory is a compromise between stability of dividend payment along with an element of growth and the expected investment needs. How the dividend amount will be set taking into account the growth element is dealt with in the following section explaining stability in dividend.

Lintner's (1956) partial adjustment model is to a great extent similar to the smoothened residual theory of dividend. He believes that a firm should have a desired level of dividends that is based on its expected level of earnings. When earnings vary, the firm will adjust its dividends to reflect its new level of earnings, this does not happen suddenly but is effected over a long-spread period.

Lintner's perception can be explained in form of an equation. Actual change in dividend,

$$D_1 - D_0 = s \cdot (tE_1 - D_0) \qquad \text{...(17.2)}$$

where s is the speed of changes in the dividend and t is the target payout ratio.

The value of s varies between 0 and 1. The former means no change in dividend. The latter means that the actual change in dividend is equal to the target change in dividend.

17.1.5 Walter's Model of Dividend Policy

James E. Walter (1963) is an advocate of the dividend relevance theory. This theory states that the retention of earnings and dividend payment influence shareholders' wealth differently. He assumes three cases that are presented hereunder:

1. When the return on new investment is greater than the market capitalisation rate, it is the retention of earnings and their investment that will raise the value of shares;
2. When the return on new investment is equal to the market capitalisation rate, both the retention of earnings and dividend payment will have the same impact on the value of shares;
3. When the return on new investment is lower than the market capitalisation rate, it is the dividend payment, and not the retention of earnings, that will raise the value of shares.

Walter's dividend relevance theory states that the retention of earnings and dividend payment influence shareholders' wealth differently.

Walter develops a model where the market price of a share is expressed as follows:

$$P = \{D + A/\rho(E - D)\}/\rho \qquad \text{...(17.3)}$$

Where:

D = the dividend per share
E = the earning per share
A = the return on investment
ρ = the market capitalization rate

EXAMPLE

Basing on Eq. 17.3, if A is 12%, ρ is 10%, E is Rs 4 and D is Rs 2, the value of share will be:

$$P = \{2 + 0.12/0.10\,(4 - 2)\}/0.10 = \text{Rs } 44.$$

If A drops to 10%, the market value of shares will slip to:

$$P = \{2 + 0.10/0.10\,(4 - 2)\}/0.10 = \text{Rs } 40.$$

Again, if A drops to 8%, the market value of shares will be lower at:

$$P = \{2 + 0.08/0.10\ (4 - 2)\}/0.10 = \text{Rs } 36.$$

This shows that:

1. When $A = \rho$, the value of shares is Rs 40.
2. When $A > \rho$, the value of shares goes up to Rs 44.
3. When $A < \rho$, the value of shares declines to Rs 36.

It suggests that the retention of earnings/dividend policy does have an impact on the shareholders' wealth. But the retention of earnings leads to an increase in the share price only when the rate of return is greater than the capitalisation rate. If the case is just the reverse meaning that the rate of return is lower than the capitalisation rate, it is suggested that dividend be distributed rather than making investment of the retained earnings in order to maintain/increase the shareholders' wealth.

Walter's model is simple. It does not, however, incorporate the complexities of the real world. For example, it does not conceive of external financing through debt or fresh equity. It believes that a new investment is financed only through the retained earnings. Second, it assumes a constant market capitalisation rate. In real life, however, this changes depending on the risk element. Third, this theory assumes the rate of return remains constant with a growing amount of investment. However, the rate of return tends to decrease with a growing amount of investment.

17.1.6 Dividend Relevance—Gordon's Dividend Capitalisation Model

Assuming no financial leverage, absence of taxes, no external financing, constant return, constant cost of capital and constant retention ratio, Gordon (1962), is of the view that the market price of a share is equal to the present value of an infinite stream of dividends to be received by the shareholders. Here the future dividend is inclusive of the growth element g that is equal to the product of the retention ratio b and the rate of return r. In form of an equation, the price of share can be expressed as follows:

$$P_0 = D(1 + g)/(1 + k) + D(1 + g)^2/(1 + k)^2 + ... + D(1 + g)^n/(1 + k)^n$$

Or $$P = \sum_{t=1}^{n} \frac{D(1+g)^t}{(1+k)^t} \qquad \text{...(17.4)}$$

Solving Eq. 17.4, we get:

$$P_0 = \frac{D_1}{k-g}$$

Substituting $EPS_1\,(1 - b)$ for D_1 and br for g, Eq. 17.4 can be re-written as follows:

$$P_0 = \frac{EPS_1\,(1-b)}{(k-br)} \qquad \text{...(17.5)}$$

EXAMPLE

The rate of return is 10%. The discount rate is 10%. EPS is Rs 5. The retention ratio is 50%. The market value of share will be:

$$\text{Rs } [5\ (1 - 0.5)/(0.10 - 0.05)] = \text{Rs } 50.$$

Being an advocate of the dividend relevance hypothesis, Gordon is of the view that the value of share changes with a change in the retention ratio/dividend ratio. However, such changes are effected only when the rate of return is lower/higher than the discount rate. Equality between the two rates does not cause any change in the value of shares even when there is change in the retention ratio. When $r > k$, an increase in the retention ratio leads to an increase in the share prices. On the contrary, when $r < k$, an increase in the retention ratio lowers the share prices.

EXAMPLE

A. When r > k: Assuming r = 12%, k = 10% and EPS = Rs 10

(i) Dividend pay-out ratio = 30% meaning that the retention ratio is 70% and $g = (0.7 \times 0.12) = 0.084$

$$P = \text{Rs } \{[10\ (1 - 0.7)]/(0.10 - 0.084)\} = \text{Rs } 187.50$$

(ii) Dividend pay-out ratio = 60% meaning that the retention ratio is 40% and $g = (0.4 \times 0.12) = 0.048$

$$P = \text{Rs } \{[10\ (1 - 0.4)]/(0.10 - 0.048)\} = \text{Rs } 115.38$$

B. When $r < k$: Assuming $r = 8\%$, $k = 10\%$ and *EPS* Rs 10

(i) Dividend pay-out ratio = 30% meaning that the retention ratio is 70% and $g = (0.7 \times 0.08) = 0.056$

$$P = \text{Rs } \{[10\ (1 - 0.7)]/(0.10 - 0.056)]\} = \text{Rs } 68.18$$

(ii) Dividend pay-out ratio = 60% meaning that the retention ratio is 40% and $g = (0.4 \times 0.08) = 0.032$

$$P = \text{Rs } \{[10\ (1 - 0.4)]/(0.10 - 0.032)\} = \text{Rs } 88.24$$

However, when simplifying the assumptions to fit more to the conditions of uncertainty, Gordon believes that the share prices change with varying dividend/ retention ratio even when $r = k$. It is because of growing uncertainty that dividend occurring in the distant future is discounted at a greater rate than that occurring in the immediate future. Krishman (1969) explains this phenomenon at greater length, and opines that a the bird in hand is better than two in the bush. The rational investors prefer to avoid uncertainty and would be willing to pay a higher price for a share that is going to pay higher current dividend.

17.1.7 Dividend Preference Theory—Ezra Solomon's Approach

Dividend preference theory is supported by Ezra Solomon (1963). The author prefers dividend pay-out to the retention of earnings, because a high rate of dividend pay-out ratio helps increase the price of shares. The reasons given are as follows:

Dividend preference theory is supported by Ezra Solomon who prefers dividend pay-out to the retention of earnings, because a high rate of dividend pay-out ratio helps increase the price of shares.

1. Dividend payment provides first-hand information to investors about a firm's profitability. Naturally firms with higher current dividend enjoy the confidence of the shareholders and a higher price for their shares;
2. There is always a group of low-income shareholders that need stable and regular cash dividend for the purpose of supplementing their income;
3. Current dividend payments resolve uncertainty in the minds of investors. This is because retention of earnings and its positive impact on the share prices in the future cannot be precisely estimated under conditions of uncertainty.

From the arguments provided by different authors, one can come to the conclusion that both retention of earnings and pay-out of dividend are crucial for a firm. The ratio between the two depends upon a host of factors that ultimately shape the dividend policy. These factors are explained in the following section.

17.2 FACTORS INFLUENCING THE DIVIDEND POLICY

The framing of a dividend policy is primarily influenced by four factors, these are: the preference of the shareholders for getting dividend as well as for exercising control over the firm; financial requirements of the firm; legal and financial constraints; and the macroeconomic environment in the country. These factors need some explanation.

17.2.1 Expectations of the Shareholders

Normally shareholders prefer current dividend insofar as the future is uncertain and dividend payment generates confidence among them. This means that a firm should maintain a higher dividend pay-out. However, the preference for higher dividend is not equally applicable to different kinds of shareholders.

Shareholders belonging to higher income brackets prefer capital gains to dividends as the tax rate applicable to capital gains is lower than the tax rate applicable to dividend received. This means that they prefer retention of earnings and their investment.

On the contrary, shareholders belonging to lower-income brackets, and who lead a retired life, prefer dividend to the retention of earnings. This is because they supplement their income with the dividend they receive.

Institutional investors, who buy large blocks of shares and hold them for relatively a long period of time, are more interested in profits. They, therefore, prefer high dividend pay-out. Again, the amount of the dividend a firm is going to declare depends upon the choices of the different groups of the shareholders. In a closely held company, their choice is easily known. In widely held companies, however, this is not easy. In practice, dividend pay-out depends upon the choice of the dominant shareholders.

17.2.2 Financial Requirements of the Firm

The financial requirements of a firm influence its dividend policy. This is why a growing firm, which needs funds for growth, pays lower dividend and retains a larger part of its earnings. On the contrary, a mature firm pays large dividend, inasmuch as it does not require a larger amount of funds for further investment.

Even a growing firm may pay large dividends if it is able to get funds from other sources with a minimum of effort and at a lower cost. However, if the firm has no easy access to sources of funds or it gets funds at greater cost, it will rely more on internally generated funds and pay lower dividend.

Again, if the directors of a company decide to conserve cash either for maintaining liquidity in the firm or for repaying debt or for any other purpose, the firm does not declare large dividend despite large earnings.

Last but not least, if profitable investment opportunities exist before the firm, it will prefer retention of earnings for making investments. If this is not the case, the firm will prefer large dividend payments. Dividend payments will be larger even if the shareholders have profitable investment opportunities instead of the firm.

17.2.3 Legal and Financial Constraints

The management of a firm is not completely free to frame dividend policy in view of the legal and financial constraints. In many countries, the law of the land limits the amount of cash dividend. It does not permit cash dividend to exceed current net income plus cumulative retained earnings with a view to protecting the interests of the preference shareholders and the creditors. In India, the Companies Act provides that dividend shall be declared and paid only out of the profits—current and past, and after providing for depreciation.

Sometimes, lenders impose restrictions on the payment of dividend beyond a specific limit in order to protect their own interests. They prefer the firm to retain sufficient funds necessary to repay the debt due to them.

It is also the liquidity position of the firm that influences the size of dividend. The greater the liquidity, the bigger the size of dividend. It may be noted here that greater earnings do not necessarily mean greater liquidity. A liberal dividend policy will exist only when earnings and liquidity, both are satisfactory.

17.2.4 General Economic Conditions

If the general economic conditions in the country are buoyant, the rate of asset expansion will be higher. It will necessitate large funds for making investments. The dividend pay-out will certainly be lower. However, the buoyant economic conditions are often associated with a hopeful capital market from where the funds can be easily obtained. In such cases, the dividend pay-out may be large.

On the contrary, during an economic downtrend, when profitability and liquidity both move downward, the firm lays emphasis on conserving cash. The result is that the dividend pay-out is lower.

Again, if inflationary pressures are acute, dividend payment is largely constrained; because the funds generated out of depreciation are generally not adequate to replace assets or maintain the capital intact. It is but natural for the firm to retain a larger share of its earnings and to lower the dividend pay-out.

17.3 STABILITY OF DIVIDEND PAYMENTS

17.3.1 Meaning of Stable Dividend

It is a normal practice among the firms to make stable dividend payments. The question, however, is what stability actually means. Stability is often interpreted in three ways. They are as follows:

1. Constant dividend per share;
2. Stable dividend pay-out ratio;
3. Low Constant dividend per share plus extra dividend in times of greater earnings.

Constant dividend per share: If the dividend policy involves constant dividend per share, this implies a constancy in the size of dividend. If a company pays Rs 5 as dividend in the current year, the amount will be the same in years to come in spite of changes in the earnings per share (EPS). However, if there is a consistent upward trend in the EPS, the firm slowly and gradually revises the size of dividend upward so that the revision does not mar the very purpose of stability. Since the dividend is adjusted slowly to changes in corporate income, the following model can be constructed to study the dividend behaviour of the firm. The model is as follows:

$$D - D_{-1} = a + c(rP - D_{-1}) + u \qquad \text{...(17.6)}$$

Where:

D = current dividend

D_{-1} = the lagged dividend

P = profits

a = a positive term to allow for the firm's reluctance to cut dividends

r = target pay-out ratio

c = speed of adjustment co-efficient

u = error factor (unexpected)

If a firm adopts a policy of pursuing a target pay-out ratio r which is applied to current earnings P, dividends are adjusted fully each year to achieve the targeted level rP and then they would change by $(rP - D_{-1})$ during the period t over t_{-1}. However, the management's conservative bias against a big upward revision in order to maintain stability leads dividends to move only a fraction of the way, given the speed of adjustment co-efficient c.

Stable Dividend Pay-out Ratio: If the policy of a firm is to maintain a fixed ratio between dividend and EPS, the amount of dividend is bound to fluctuate with a fluctuation in the

EPS. For instance, if a firm maintains a dividend pay-out ratio of 40% and if the EPS is Rs 4, the amount of dividend will be Rs 1.60. If the earning goes up next year to Rs 6, the dividend amount too will rise to Rs 2.40.

This type of stability is often preferred by those firms that link their dividend policy with their ability to pay dividend. On the contrary, the shareholders, especially, those who supplement their regular income with the dividend they receive, would not prefer this type of stability because they are more interested in a fixed amount of dividend.

Low Dividend Amount plus Extra dividend: Occasionally, firms follow a policy of low regular dividend but extra dividend when EPS is greater. This policy is a compromise between the first two types. Since the amount of dividend is low, there is no problem in dividend distribution even when earnings are low. It is beneficial for those shareholders who prefer stable dividend.

Profit After Tax and Dividend Payment among 1,377 Private Limited Companies

Rs lakh

	2001–02	2002–03	2003–04	2004–05
Profit after tax	956.64	939.15	1,315.90	1,622.42
Dividend: of which	468.10	259.73	296.94	398.93
Div. on ord. shares	462.61	257.64	293.98	397.68
Div. on pref. shares	5.48	2.09	2.95	1.26
Profits retained	488.54	679.42	1,018.96	1,223.49
Dividend pay-out ratio	48.93	27.66	22.56	24.59

Source: *RBI Bulletin, January 2006 and March 2007*

17.3.2 Significance of Stable Dividend

A stable dividend policy is not only in the interest of the shareholders, it also acts in the interest of the company. From the viewpoint of the shareholders, stable dividend, first, resolves uncertainty; and, second, meets the desire for current income. Resolution of uncertainty means that the shareholders know in advance how much dividend they are going to receive. If they know the amount in advance, they can plan their personal budget accordingly.

Again, if there is a group of shareholders that have invested with the expectation that the dividend will meet the gap between their income and expenditure. If the amount of dividend is stable, the gap is easily met and they can easily manage their expenditure.

From the viewpoint of the company, stable dividend is preferable, inasmuch as it reflects a sound financial position. This is why the share price of a firm with stable dividend is often greater than that of a firm with fluctuating dividend payment.

This is not all, stable dividend enhances the creditworthiness of a firm with the result that it can raise funds from the market more easily. Stability in dividend attracts not only the equity shareholders but also preference shareholders and debenture-holders. This is because it creates faith in the company.

17.4 BONUS SHARES

Usually dividend is paid in form of cash. Cash dividend is liked by those shareholders who attach greater importance to supplementing their current income with dividends. When cash dividend is paid, reserves fall to a corresponding extent, and this may endanger the cash position of the firm. Thus in view of the limitations of cash dividend, dividend is also paid in form of shares, these are known as bonus shares in India and stock dividend in many other countries.

17.4.1 Impact of the Bonus Issue

Let us begin with an example how the face of the balance sheet changes after the issue of bonus shares but the company's net worth as well as the shareholders' wealth remain unchanged. Suppose Company A has 10,000 shares of Rs 1 each, selling at Rs 50 each. It means that the market value of equity is Rs 5,00,000. With a 10% bonus share, a shareholder receives one additional share for each 10 shares owned by him. The total number of outstanding shares rises to 11,000 after the issue of bonus shares.

Prior to the issue of bonus shares, the shape of the balance sheet was as follows:

Ordinary shares (10,000 shares × Rs 1)	Rs 10,000
Capital in excess of par value	2,00,000
Retained earnings	2,50,000
Total owners' equity	4,60,000

When 1,000 bonus shares are issued, there will be 11,000 shares outstanding. Retained earnings will reduce to Rs 2,00,000 or Rs 2,50,000 – (1,000 × 50). The capital in excess of par value will change to Rs 2,49,000. Here, one finds that despite changes in the size of different components, the owner's equity remains the same. To be more precise:

Impact on the Company's Net Worth: It is a fact that the issue of bonus shares raises the number of outstanding shares, however, since it represents a shift in the value from reserves to paid-up share capital, the net worth of the company remains unaltered.

Impact on the Shareholders' Wealth: As far as the shareholders are concerned, bonus shares do not have any impact on their wealth insofar as the EPS and the market price of the share falls proportionately to the bonus share issue. Nevertheless, the issue of bonus shares is advantageous for the company as well as its shareholders.

17.4.2 Merits and Demerits

It is advantageous for the company because dividends can be announced also in cases when the company is facing financial stringency. The dividend is paid without jeopardising the company's cash position. Sometimes creditors place restriction on the payment of large cash dividends. In such cases, the issue of the bonus shares is the only way out. Again, as we have discussed earlier, retention of earnings and the payment of dividend do not go hand-in-hand. But if they do occur simultaneously, it is only possible in the case of bonus shares. Dividends are paid and at the same time cash is conserved for making investment in profitable channels.

The shareholders prefer bonus shares because the tax rate on personal income (in the case of receipt of cash dividend) is often higher than capital gains tax (receipt on account of the sale of the shares).

However, administration of the bonus issue is often costly. Again, the adjustment of the eps and the price-earning ratio is often difficult, especially when the size of the issue is small. When the eps is not adjusted properly, there may be malalignment between measured growth in eps and true growth, and the price-earning ratio may be distorted.

17.4.3 Bonus Share Issue in India

Bonus shares are issued in India to supplement cash dividend and not as a substitute for cash dividend. Moreover, there are a few conditions that have to be fulfilled while issuing bonus shares. These are as follows:

1. The shares should be fully paid-up;
2. The company should not have defaulted on any payment of statutory dues to its employees, and on term loans to financial institutions;
3. Bonus shares are issued out of share premium and free reserves (not the capital reserves arising out of the revaluation of assets);
4. 30% of the previous 3 years' average pre-tax profits should be greater than, or at least equal to, one-tenth of the increased share capital;
5. The reserves remaining after the issue of bonus shares should be greater than, or at least equal to, 40% of increased paid-up capital.

17.5 SHARE SPLIT AND REVERSE SPLIT

17.5.1 Share Split

Share split means the breaking of a share into two or more parts. If the value of a share is Rs 100 and it is split into two parts, there will be two shares of Rs 50 each in lieu of one share of Rs 100. The shareholders will possess twice the number of shares and earning and dividend per share will be halved after the split but their total wealth will remain unchanged.

Share split is done when the market price of share is very large and it is beyond the reach of general investors. In such conditions, the marketability of the share is reduced. Thus in order to improve the marketability of the shares, they are split so that the lower-income investors can purchase them.

> Share split means the breaking of a share into two or more parts.

17.5.2 Reverse Split

Reverse split is the exact opposite of a share split. If two shares of Rs 50 are converted into one share of Rs 100, this is known as a reverse split. The shareholders possess, in this case, half the number of shares after the reverse split but their earnings and dividend per share is doubled. In all their wealth remains unchanged.

Reverse split is adopted when the market price of a share is very low. It is done in order to improve the image of the company. However, it gives out a negative signal in the market, that the company is not doing well and that its share prices have fallen.

17.6 REPURCHASE OF SHARES

17.6.1 Modes of Share Repurchase

Companies often buy-back their issued shares from the shareholders. So repurchase is nothing but the buy-back of the shares. There are different modes of the repurchase. They are as follows:

1. Self-tender offer at a fixed price;
2. Self-tender offer within a price range;
3. Open market purchase.

In case of fixed-price, self-tender offer, the company makes a formal offer to shareholders to buy-back a certain number of shares at a specified price. The quoted price is higher than the market price in order to attract the shareholders.

Alternatively, the company may make a formal offer to shareholders to buy-back the shares quoting a floor and a ceiling price. The minimum price is higher than the market price. The shareholders quote a price within the specified range. Then the company arrays the prices from low to high and determines the lowest price at which the shares can actually be bought back. This method is different from the fixed-price tender as the company does not know in advance the eventual purchase price.

As far as the open-market purchase is concerned, the company buys its shares on the open market in the normal manner through a share broker. In this case, the company has to disclose why it is going to buy-back the shares and has to abide by the rules fixed by the governmental authorities in this respect.

17.6.2 Purpose of the Share Buy-back

Buy-back of shares by companies has become normal practice. The factors encouraging such practice are many. It would be worthwhile here to explain a couple of them.

Repurchase as a Financing Decision: Shares are bought back when the debt-equity ratio is low, and when the company would like to raise the ratio of debt in order to lower its average cost of capital. In such cases debt securities are issued and with the debt proceeds, the company buys-back the shares. Buy-back of shares is important in such cases because in its absence, the conditions of over-capitalisation may emerge.

Repurchase as an Alternative to Dividend: A company either distributes dividend or buys back its shares only when it has sufficient cash. Therefore, the question arises as to whether these two options are alternatives to each other. The answer is in the affirmative if it one does not take into account the capital gains tax or the transaction cost involved in this respect. When repurchases are made, the number of outstanding shares falls. With the same amount of earnings, the EPS rises. With a rise in EPS, the share price rises. The extent of rise in the share prices represents the amount that is to be paid as dividend. The difference is only that while in case of a rise in the share prices, capital gains tax is applicable, personal income tax is applicable in case of the receipt of dividend. If the rates of capital gains tax are lower than the rates of personal income tax, repurchases are preferable to dividend. The following example shows how the rise in the share price represents the dividend.

EXAMPLE

A company has 10,000 shares of Rs 20 each. It expects a total earning of Rs 40,000, half of which it plans to distribute as dividend. This means that the eps is Rs 4 and the dividend per share, if distributed, is Rs 2. If the company plans to repurchase 1,000 shares through a tender offer at a price of Rs 22 per share, the increase in the share price as a sequel to repurchase wil be equal to the amount of dividend.

The EPS being Rs 4, the P/E ratio will be: 20/4 = 5.
The EPS after repurchase of 1,000 shares = 40,000/9,000 = Rs 4.44
Expected MPS after repurchase = Rs 5 $\times$ 4.44 = Rs 22.20.

Thus the capital gains on account of repurchase is almost equal to the amount of dividend.

Share-option Plan for the Employees: Sometimes a company provides its employees with a share-option plan. If this is its objective, it buys-back some shares for its employees. It encourages employees' participation in the management and at the same time avoids any over-capitalisation.

Return of Surplus Cash to Shareholders: If a company has surplus cash, buy-back of shares helps it transmit the surplus cash to the shareholders, although, this purpose is not very significant.

17.6.3 Advantages and Disadvantages of Share Buy-back

Share buy-back has many advantages. At the same time, it has disadvantages too. The readers should note them.

Advantages

- It gives a positive signal to the investors that the shares of the company are undervalued. The signal boosts up the demand for the share which in turn helps raise its price at the stock exchange. It has been found that the share price performance in the long term is better after a buy-back.
- Buy-back is preferable also from the viewpoint of tax considerations. It is because the tax rate on capital gains is often lower than the personal income tax.
- In case of buy-back, the number of outstanding shares is reduced. And at the same time, the amount of cash on the asset side reduces. As a result, return on assets increases along with an increase in the return on equity. The company gets a better image in the market.
- When a cash surplus position exists for short period, the company does not like to distribute the surplus as dividend because it attaches importance to stable dividend. Surplus cash is passed on to the shareholders through buy-back of shares. In other words, share buy-back helps maintain stability in dividend.
- Buy-back of shares is also advisable when there is surplus cash but no profitable investment opportunities exist.
- Sometimes creditors put restrictions on the distribution of dividend as per the restrictive covenants. In such cases, buy-back of shares is suggested through which the surplus cash is passed on to the shareholders.

Disadvantages

- When shareholders prefer dividend in order to supplement their regular income, repurchase of shares cannot be advocated because they do not serve the interest of the shareholders.
- When shares are not actively traded, any repurchase on a large scale tends to reduce the share price after the process of repurchase is complete.

17.6.4 Share Buy-back in India

The buy-back of shares is allowed in India. But till 1998, it was done through reduction of capital under Section 100 of the Indian Companies Act or as a scheme of arrangement under Section 391. In both the cases, the Government's approval was mandatory. In 1998, the Companies Act introduced three new sections—77A, 77AA and 77B facilitating companies buy-back of their own securities with effect from 31 October 1998. Certain modalities were also prescribed for this purpose. The major provisions are:

1. Buy-back of securities is permitted only out of:
   (a) free reserves, such as dividend equalisation reserves, investment allowance reserves, debenture redemption reserves, export profit reserves, etc.
   (b) securities premium
   (c) proceeds of any shares and other specified securities, not being the proceeds of the same kind of shares issued earlier. This means that proceeds of an earlier issue of preference shares may be used for buying back equity shares and vice versa.
2. Buy-back of equity shares in any financial year shall not exceed 25% of its paid-up equity capital in that financial year.
3. Buy-back should not lead to a rise in the ratio of debt owed by the company to more than twice of the sum of the capital and free reserves.

The new buy-back scheme incorporates that the company has to appoint a merchant banker and to announce publically about the offer at least 7 days in advance. The announcement has to be conveyed to SEBI indicating the details, especially the name of the brokers and the stock exchange where the buy-back process would be adopted. Again the process has to be completed within 12 months of the offer.

The scheme was made more transparent in 2002 as per which a special resolution has to be passed in the general meeting of the shareholders. A declaration of solvency has to be filed with the SEBI and the Registrar of Companies. The bought-back shares have to be destroyed. The company cannot make any new issue within the next 2 years except for issue of bonus shares. In fact, the purpose of the transparent rules was to protect the interest of the small investors.

SUMMARY

The usual practice in a company is to apportion a part of the profit for dividend payment and to retain the other part for investment in profitable channels. Determination of the ratio between dividend payment and retention of earnings is very important.

There are different views in this respect. M-M hypothesis suggests that dividend payment or no dividend payment has the same impact on the value of a firm. The shareholders are therefore indifferent towards dividend. However, in imperfect market conditions, where taxes and transaction cost exist, shareholders prefer cash dividend. Residual theory prefers retention of earnings; however, smoothened residual theory suggests that retention should be preferred only after constant dividend payment. Walter believes that retention/dividend ratio influences shareholder' wealth. It raises share prices only when return from investment is greater than the capitalisation rate. Gordon and Ezra Solomon are in favour of dividend payment as it has a positive impact on share prices. There are certain factors that influence dividend payment, such as, shareholders' expectation, financial requirements, legal and other constraints, etc.

Dividend should be stable. It is normally paid in cash form. Sometimes, however, it is also in form of shares that are known as bonus shares.

Share split means breaking of shares in two or more parts. Reverse split is just the opposite. Sometimes shares are repurchased or bought back. There are specific rules in India regarding this.

POINTS TO REMEMBER

1. What are the different groups of dividend theories?
   - Dividend or retained earnings have the same impact. Thus dividend is not relevant. Modigliani-Miller approach falls under this group.
   - Retention of earnings is important. So dividend is not relevant. Residual Theory of Dividend falls under this group.
   - Dividend is relevant because it raises the value of the firm. Smoothened Residual Theory, Walter's Theory, Gordon's Theory, etc. come under this group.
2. What is M-M approach?
   - In perfect conditions, dividend payment or no-dividend have the same influence on the value of shares. But if the market is imperfect, meaning that there are taxes, transaction cost, irrationality and uncertainty, dividend or no-dividend have varying influence on the value of shares.
3. What is Residual Theory of Dividend?
   - Dividend should be paid only after the need for reinvestment is met.
4. What is Smoothened Residual Theory of Dividend?
   - It gives importance to both stable dividend and reinvestment of profit.

5. What do you mean by Walter's Model of Dividend?
   - Reinvest first if return on investment > capitalisation rate.
   - Pay dividend first if return on investment < capitalisation rate.
   - Indifferent between dividend and retention if return on investment = capitalisation rate.
6. What is the view of Gordon on dividend payment?
   - Value of share depends on the dividend ratio/retention ratio
7. What is Ezra Solomon's view on dividend?
   - Dividend is important because:
   - It gives first hand information about the firm.
   - It is a supplement to income of low-income persons.
   - It resolves uncertainty.
8. What are the factors influencing the dividend policy?
   - Expectations of the shareholders
   - Financial requirements of the firm
   - Legal and financial constraints
   - General economic conditions
9. How is stability of dividend judged?
   - Constant dividend per share
   - Stable dividend pay-out ratio
   - Constant dividend plus extra payment
10. Why is stable dividend significant?
    - It resolves uncertainty and serves as a regular income among shareholders.
    - It reflects sound financial position and thereby creditworthiness of the company.
11. Comment on the issue of bonus shares.
    - Dividend distributed in form of share is known as bonus share.
    - It raises the number of outstanding shares. EPS and MPS fall.
    - Administration of bonus shares is often costly.
    - It leads to conservation of cash.
    - It does not add to the tax burden of the shareholders.
    - The Indian Companies Act regulates the issue of bonus shares.
12. What is share split and reverse split?
    - Breaking of shares in two or more parts is share split. Just the other way, combining of two or more shares is known as reverse split.
13. What do you mean by repurchase of shares? What is its purpose?
    - Buying back of shares by the company is known as share repurchase. It is done either through self-tender offer at a fixed price/within a price range or through open market purchase.
    - The purpose is to attain a desired debt-equity ratio and/or to raise earning per share that may be treated as an alternative to dividend payment.
    - The Indian Companies Act permits buy-back under specific conditions.

DESCRIPTIVE QUESTIONS

1. Examine M-M's dividend irrelevance approach. Is it applicable to imperfect market conditions?
2. Comment on the residual theory of dividend. Can it be smoothened?
3. Discuss Walter's theory of dividend.
4. Present the arguments given by Solomon for dividend payment, and enumerate the factors influencing dividend.
5. What do you mean by stability of dividend payment? Explain its significance.
6. Comment on the issue of bonus shares. Mention the specific provisions prevalent in India in this respect.
7. Distinguish between share split and reverse split.
8. What do you mean by share buy-back? Is it related to the dividend policy? Comment on the Indian scenario in this respect.

OBJECTIVE-TYPE QUESTIONS

1. Mark true or false.
   (a) Shareholders prefer cash dividend when tax rate on dividend is greater than tax rate on capital gains.
   (b) Transaction cost involved in the sale of shares motivates shareholders to get cash dividend.
   (c) According to Walter, retention of earnings helps increase share prices only when return from investment is greater than capitalisation rate.
   (d) Lower-income shareholders normally prefer retention of earnings in order to meet their consumption budget.
   (e) Stable dividend does not mean a fixed dividend pay-out ratio.
   (f) Reverse split means breaking the share into two or more parts.
   (g) Bonus shares are issued when cash has to be conserved in the enterprise.
2. Choose the most suitable answer.
   (a) M-M theory in perfect market suggests that dividend payment:
      (i) has a positive impact on the value of a firm
      (ii) has a negative impact on the value of a firm
      (iii) as no impact on the value of a firm
   (b) The residual theory of dividend is applicable only when:
      (i) the cost of retained earning is lower than the cost of debt
      (ii) the cost of retained earning is greater than the cost of debt
      (iii) the cost of retained earning is equal to the cost of debt

(c) Stable dividend means:
  (i) constant dividend per share
  (ii) constant dividend pay-out ratio
  (iii) both of the above

(d) Bonus shares are issued in India:
  (i) as a substitute for cash dividend
  (ii) to supplement cash dividend
  (iii) both of the above

(e) According to Gordon, the value of a share changes with:
  (i) changes in retention/dividend ratio
  (ii) even in the stability of retention/dividend ratio
  (iii) both of the above

NUMERICAL PROBLEMS

1. A company earns 12% against a required rate of return of 10%. The EPS is Rs 8 with a 50% dividend pay-out ratio. Find the value of its share using:
   (a) Walter's model; and
   (b) Gordon's model.
2. EPS is Rs 10. Capitalisation rate is 12.5%. IRR is 15%. Determine the pay-out ratio and the price of shares at this pay-out ratio based on Walter's theory.
3. If a share is selling for Rs 150. the company is to declare dividend for Rs 10 per share. The capitalisation rate is 10%. Find the shareholders' wealth in case of dividend/no dividend.
4. A company has Rs 50,000 shares. Its earnings and investment requirements are as follows:

Year	Earnings (Rs)	Investment (Rs)
1	50,000	60,000
2	50,000	55,000
3	50,000	30,000
4	50,000	20,000

   Find dividend per share based on the residual theory of dividend.
5. A company's EPS is as follows:

Year	Amount (Rs)
1	2.00
2	2.20
3	1.80
4	2.30
5	2.10

Determine dividend per share based on:

(a) the constant dividend pay-out ratio of 40%; and

(b) a regular dividend of Rs 1 plus extra dividend to be closer to 40%

6. After a 4-for-1 share split, a company pays a dividend of Rs 1.10 per new share that represents a 10% increase over pre-split dividend. Find the pre-split dividend per share.
7. A company with 50:50 debt-equity ratio earns a net income of Rs 50,000. What will be the pay-out ratio based on residual dividend theory, if it has two independent projects under consideration, each of them requiring Rs 40,000 and one with 15% cost of capital and 20% IRR, while the other has 8% cost of capital and 10% IRR.
8. A company with 1,00,000 equity shares earns Rs 4,00,000. The market price of a share is Rs 50. It plans to repurchase 20% of its shares in the open market. The repurchase is not expected to alter either the net income or P/E ratio. Find the post-repurchase price of share.
9. If earning per share is Rs 10 and cost of capital is 10%, find the MPS with given rate of return of 15% and divident pay-out ratio of 40%. Base your answer on Walter's model of dividend
10. If EPS is Rs 10, cost of capital is 10%, rate of return is 15%, dividend pay-out ratio is 40%, find the MPS, based on Gordon's model of dividend.

SOLVED NUMERICAL PROBLEMS

1. Find the dividend pay-out ratio if EPS is Rs 10 and the amount of dividend is Rs 4.

Solution

DPR = 4/10 = 0.40 = 40%

2. A company has 10,000 shares of Rs 100 each. The capitalisation rate is 12%. Income before tax is Rs 1,50,000. Tax rate is 30%. Dividend pay-out ratio is 60%. The company has to take up a project costing Rs 4,00,000. Find MPS at the end of the current year and the number of shares to be issued for financing the new project if (a) dividend is paid, and (b) if dividend is not paid. Base the answer on M-M approach.

Solution

Net income = Rs 1,50,000(1 – 0.30) = Rs 1,05,000

Dividend = Rs 1,05,000 × 0.6 = Rs 63,000

Dividend per share = Rs 63,000/10,000 = Rs 6.30

MPS_1 when dividend is paid = Rs 100 × 1.12 – 6.30 = Rs 105.70

Additional investment required = Rs 4,00,000 – 1,05,000 – 63,000

= Rs 2,32,000

No. of shares to be issued additionally = Rs 2,32,000/105.70 = 2,195

MPS_1 when dividend is not paid = Rs 105.70 + 6.30 = Rs 112

Additional investment required = Rs 4,00,000 – 1,05,000

= Rs 2,95,000

No. of shares to be issued additionally = Rs 2,95,000/112 = 2,634

3. A company has operating profit of Rs 10,00,000. The capital structure is all-equity with 1,00,000 shares outstanding. The tax rate is 30%. The company has a viable project in hand that costs Rs 6,00,000. Based on the Residual Theory of Dividend, find the EPS and dividend per share.

Solution

Net profit = Rs 10,00,000 × (1 – 0.30) = Rs 7,00,000

Profit after financing of the new project = Rs 7,00,000 – 6,00,000 = Rs 1,00,000

EPS = Rs 7,00,000/1,00,000 = Rs 7

Dividend per share = 1,00,000/1,00,000 = Re 1

4. The recently paid dividend of a firm is Rs 2. The current EPS is Rs 10. The cost of equity capital is 15%. MPS is Rs 60. Based on Walter's Theory of Dividend, find out the MPS if EPS is Rs 12 and the dividend pay-out ratio is 40%.

Solution

Based on Eq. 17.3,

Dividend = Rs 12 × 0.4 = Rs 4.80

Return on investment = 12/60 = 0.2 = 20%

P = [4.80 + 0.2/0.15(12.00 – 4.80)]/0.15 = Rs 96

5. A company has: EBIT = Rs 4,00,000; Tax rate = 30%; Dividend pay-out ratio = 40%; No. of outstanding shares = 1,00,000; Equity capitalisation rate = 15%; and ROI = 12%. Find the MPS based on Gordon's Theory of Dividend.

Solution

Net profit = Rs 4,00,000 × (1 – 0.30) = Rs 2,80,000

Earning per share = Rs 2,80,000/1,00,000 = Rs 2.80

Dividend paid = Rs 2,80,000 × 0.4 = Rs 1,12,000

Dividend per share = 1,12,000/1,00,000 = Rs 1.12

Retention ratio = 1 – 0.40 = 0.60 = 60%

P = {2.80 (1 – 0.60)}/{0.15 – (0.60 × 0.12)

= 1.12/0.078 = Rs 14.36

6. A company has 1,000 shares. MPS is Rs 20. The firm has either to pay Re 1 per share as dividend or repurchase shares for Rs 1,000. Earning is Rs 2,000 with no tax. Find:

(a) MPS in case of either of the alternatives

(b) EPS under each alternative

(c) P/E ratio in each alternative

Solution

If dividend is paid:

(a) MPS = Rs 20

(b) EPS = Rs 2000/1000 = Rs 2

(c) P/E ratio = Rs 20,000/2,000 = 10

If shares are repurchased:

(a) MPS = Rs 20

(b) No. of shares bought = 1,000/20 = 50 shares

(c) Remaining shares = 1,000 – 50 = 950

(d) EPS = Rs 2,000/950 = Rs 2.105

(e) P/E ratio = Rs 20/2.105 = 9.5

7. A company has the following figures of EPS during past five years:

Year	*EPS (Rs)*
2000	1.80
2001	2.00
2002	2.20
2003	1.70
2004	3.00

Determine the annual dividend per share under the following conditions:

(a) Stable dividend pay-out ratio of 50%

(b) A regular dividend of Re 1 and extra dividend to match with the stable dividend pay-out ratio

(c) A stable dividend amount but that can be raised to a DPR of 40%-60%. The dividend amount should be approximately equal to 40%

Solution

Rs

Year	*Scheme A*	*Scheme B*	*Scheme C*
2000	0.90	1.00	0.72
2001	1.00	1.00	0.80
2002	1.10	1.10	0.88
2003	0.85	1.00	0.68
2004	1.50	1.50	1.20

8. A firm having an extra cash for Rs 1,000 has two options. One is that it can invest in treasury bills having a yield of 10%. The other option is that it can distribute this amount as dividend to shareholders who can invest the dividend the same way. Suppose the corporate tax is 32%, the personal income tax is 30% and the tax on dividend is 15%. Find out how much cash the investors will have after 3 years under these two different policies.

Solution

A. If the dividend is paid now, the shareholders will get Rs 1,000 (1 – 0.15) = Rs 850

B. Considering personal income tax, the return from treasury bills = 0.10 (1 – 0.30) = 0.07%

C. The shareholders, in 3 years, will have Rs 850 × $(1.07)^3$ = Rs 1,047.14

Alternatively, if the firm invests that amount in treasury bills instead of giving dividend, the after-tax interest rate will be: 0.10 (1 – 0.32) = 0.068 or 6.8%

After 3 years, the firm will have: Rs 1,000 × $(1.068)^3$ = Rs 1,218.19

If these amounts are then paid as dividend, the shareholders will get:

Rs 1218.19 × (1 – 0.15) = Rs 1035.46

It implies that cash paid to shareholders is greater if the firm pays dividend now.

Mini Case

Patni Computer Systems Ltd. (PCSL) was incorporated in 1978 first as a private limited company. In 1995, it was converted into a public company. The original activities were computer time rental, resale of imported computer hardware and software exports. Subsequently, it began manufacturing computer hardware. During 2000s, the company emerged as a major IT service company.

As its income statement shows, its net earnings have grown fast during a past few years. From Rs 1944.1 million at the end of 2005, the net earnings recorded an increase to Rs 5427.3 million at the end of 2009 which is slightly less than threefold. But the dividend paid to the shareholders did not increase at the same rate. The dividend pay-out ratio increased in the earlier years, but was found declining during 2009.

Rs Million

Year	2005	2006	2007	2008	2009
Net income	1944.1	2057.6	3868.3	3891.5	5427.3
Dividend	344.5	414.8	418.2	384.5	387.4
Div. Pay-out ratio	17.72	20.16	10.81	9.88	7.14

Dividend pay-out ratio does not indicate any focus on stability. In terms of the absolute amount of dividend payment, some amount of stability is, of course, indicated.

From the trend, it is also clear that the company is giving greater focus on retention of earnings than giving more care for the payment of dividend.

Questions:

1. Explain the concept of stability in dividend payment based on the trend found in case of PCSL.
2. Which of the theories of the dividend payment is greatly evident from the trend of PCSL's dividend payment?

REFERENCES

Gordon, M.J. (1962). *The Investment, Financing and Valuation of Corporation*. Boston: Richard D. Irwin.

Higgins, R.C. (1972). "Corporate Dividend-Saving Decision", *Journal of Financial and Quantitative Analysis*, 7 (March): 272–79.

Krishman, J.E. (1933). *Principles of Investment*. Englewood Cliffs: McGraw-Hill.

Lintner, J. (1956). "Distribution of Income of Corporations among Dividends, Retained Earnings and Taxes", *American Economic Review*, 46 (May): 97–113.

Miller, M.H. and F. Modigliani (1961). "Dividend Policy. Growth and the Valuation of Shares", *Journal of Business*, 34 (October): 411–33.

Solomon, E. (1963). *The Theory of Financial Management*. Columbia: Columbia University Press.

Walter, J.E. (1963). "Dividend Policy: Its Influence on the Value of the Enterprise", *Journal of Finance*, 18 (May): 280–91.

SELECT FURTHER READINGS

Asquith, P. and D.W. Mullins, Jr. (1983). "The Impact of Initiating Dividend Payments on Shareholders' Wealth". *Journal of Business*, 56 (Jan.): 77–96.

Baker, H.K., et al. (1995). "The Stock Distribution Puzzle: A Synthesis of the Literature on Stock Splits and Stock Dividends", *Financial Practice and Education*, 5 (Spring/ Summer): 24–37.

______ (1985). "A Survey of Management Views on Dividend Policy", *Financial Management*, 14 (3): 78–84.

Ofer, A.R. and A.V. Thakor (1987). "A Theory of Stock Price Responses to Alternative

Corporate Cash Disbursement Methods: Stock Repurchases and Dividends", *Journal of Finance*, 42 (2): 365–94.

Part V

Financial Analysis Planning and Forecasting

After funds are raised to meet long-term investment and working capital requirements and the firm begins operation, the role of financial analysis becomes significant. The analysis helps evaluate how far operations have added to corporate wealth, and also the financial position of the firm. The analysis is supplemented with forecasts of the future sales and other variables, and also the required financial planning to meet the desired goal. These issues are discussed in the present part of the book. The chapters included in this part are as follows:

1. Financial Statements
2. Financial Ratio Analysis
3. Break-even Analysis
4. Leverage
5. Financial Forecasting

18

FINANCIAL STATEMENTS

OBJECTIVES

To acquaint the readers with financial statements and the purpose for which they are prepared

To explain how an income statement is prepared

To show how a balance sheet is prepared

To describe the sources and uses of funds that form the basis for a funds-flow statement

To delineate the sources and uses of cash for preparing a cash-flow statement

Financial statements that present an organised collection of financial data, consistence with accounting norms, form the basis of financial analysis and planning. They help convey an understanding of certain very significant aspects of a firm's finances, e.g., the various inflows and outflows of cash ultimately resulting in profits (or losses) during a particular fiscal period, the financial position as on a particular date, that is, the value of the assets the firm owns and its liabilities, as also the sources and uses of the funds. Some important financial statements that will be discussed here are the income statement, balance sheet, funds-flow statement and cash-flow statement.

18.1 INCOME STATEMENT

An income statement is the presentation of a firm's activities during a given fiscal period, normally one year. It shows firm's revenues and expenses along with interest and taxes and their impact on its net income. This statement can be presented in different ways. One is the accounting form where the income statement is known as the profit and loss account. There are two sides. On the right hand, revenues are shown, and on the left, expenses are shown. The excess of revenue over expenses is called profit, and the excess of expenses over revenue is a loss.

> An income statement is the presentation of a firm's activities during a given fiscal period, normally one year. It shows firm's revenues and expenses along with interest and taxes and their impact on its net income.

The other form of the income statement is the managerial format where the revenue and expenses are not shown on two different sides.

Rather, different types of expenses are deducted from the revenue showing different forms of profit.

The marginal-analysis format is not very different from the managerial format. The only difference is that operating expenses are divided in the marginal-analysis format between variable cost and fixed cost. The details of the managerial format and the marginal-analysis format are explained hereunder.

Audited Financial Results of Automotive Axles Limited for the year ended 30th September, 2007

		Rupees in Million
Description	Current year ended 30 Sept 2007 (Audited)	Previous year ended 30 Sept 2006 (Audited)
01. Sales/Income from Operations	6,989.14	5,279.23
02. Other Income	8.58	5.06
03. Exchange Fluctuation	49.32	(14.73)
Total Income (1+2+3)	7,047.04	5,269.57
04. Total Expenditure	5,981.93	4,427.99
(a) (Increase)/Decrease in Stock-in-Trade	(54.53)	(49.15)
(b) Consumption of Raw-materials	4,232.18	3,109.27
(c) Employee Cost	266.84	225.03
(d) Excise Duty	872.53	661.69
(e) Other Expenditure	664.92	481.15
05. Interest	75.21	56.32
06. Depreciation & amortisation of expenses	170.90	136.91
07. Profit before Tax (1+2+3–7–8–6)	819.01	648.35
08. Provision for Tax	282.73	214.86
(a) Current Tax	245.70	189.16
(b) Deferred Tax-Liability/(Assets)	35.43	23.40
(c) Fringe Benefit Tax	1.60	2.30
09. Net Profit (7–8)	536.27	433.49
10. Paid-up Equity Share Capital (Face Value Rs 10)	151.12	151.12
11. Reserves excluding Revaluation Reserves (As per the Balance Sheet of the Previous accounting year) to be given in Col. (5)	–	800.32
12. Basic & diluted EPS for the period, for the year to date & for the previous accountign year (not-annualized) Rupees per Share	35.49	28.69

13. Aggregate of Non-Promoter Shareholding - Number of Shares	4,376,894	4,376,894
- % of Shareholding	28.96	28.96
14. Investors Complaints	Un-Resolved at the end of Quarter Nil	

18.1.1 Managerial Format

Table 18.1 illustrates the managerial format of the income statement that begins with the firm's revenue, a lion's share of which is accounted for by sales. Here sales mean net sales. The value of the items returned or the value of the discount is deducted from gross sales. The other forms of revenue are commonly royalty income and income in form of interest and dividend from securities. These different types of revenue may be stated separately in the income statement. Similarly, cash sales and

Table 18.1 *Income Statement of ABC Co. for the Year Ended ... (Managerial Format)*

	Amount (Rs)
Total revenues	....
Less: Cost of good sold	....
Gross Margin	....
Less: Operating expenses	
General and Administrative	....
Selling	....
Lease payments	....
Total operating expenses	....
Operating Income(EBIT)	....
Less: Interest	....
Earning before taxes(EBT)	....
Less: Taxes	....
Net income after taxes(NIAT)	....
Dividends	....
Increase in retained earnings	....

credit sales may be shown separately. Otherwise, it is assumed that the entire sales have been made on credit terms.

The cost of goods sold is deducted from the revenue. This cost represents an accounting allocation of the cost of raw materials, wages, overheads and other similar expenses. It consists of both fixed and variable costs. Profitable operations imply an excess of revenue over the cost of goods sold. This excess is known as the gross margin.

The next item in the income statement is represented by operating expenses. These expenses are administrative and general expenses as well as distribution expenses to be deducted from the gross margin. The gross margin minus operating expenses is known as the operating income. It is also known as earning before income and taxes (EBIT). A positive EBIT indicates that operations have been profitable, although, it is not the ultimate measure of profit.

In order to arrive at the net income, interest and then taxes have to be deducted from the operating profit. Borrowing is common and therefore interest is also deducted from the operating income. The remainder is earning before taxes (EBT). When taxes are deducted from the earning before taxes, one arrives at the net income or net profit that is also known as net income after taxes (NIAT). The computation of net profit is of utmost significance insofar as it is the ultimate profit either to be distributed among the shareholders or to be retained with the firm for the further investment.

While preparing the income statement, care is taken to include only those revenues or expenses that concern the current fiscal period. Expenses relating to the previous year or the income received in advance must be excluded. Similarly, outstanding expenses and incomes not received are added back respectively to expenses and income. Again, during the year, some losses may occur. If they are accidental and heavy, only a part of the loss is charged to the income statement, the balance is carried forward to be charged off in future years. However, if the loss has resulted from trading operations, the whole of it is charged to the current year's income.

18.1.2 Marginal-Analysis Format

Table 18.2 shows an income statement prepared in a different format based on marginal-analysis. In this case, the entire cost relating to operations is divided into variable and fixed costs. The variable cost changes directly with changes in output, while fixed cost is fixed, and does not vary within a relevant range. In fact, the finance manager is more interested in dividing the operating cost in this way as this serves the purpose of profit planning. When fixed cost is known, a firm is able to plan for the magnitude of output essential for covering total cost, and also for a desired amount of profit. A detailed discussion of this issue can be found in Chapter 20.

In marginal-analysis format, variable costs are deducted from the revenue and the remainder is known as marginal contribution. Marginal contribution is the profit available to the firm to cover fixed costs, interest and taxes. Fixed costs are deducted from the marginal contribution. The remainder is known as the operating income. Operating income, as discussed above, is a measure of profit from operations. Interest and then taxes are deducted from the operating income in a similar way as shown in, Table 18.2, in order to arrive at the net profit or net income after taxes.

Table 18.2 *Income Statement of ABC Co. for the Year Ending … (Marginal-Analysis Format)*

	Amount (Rs)
Total revenues	....
Less: Variable costs	....
Marginal contribution	....
Less: Fixed cost	....
Operating Income (EBIT)	....
Less: Interest charges	....
Earning before taxes (EBT)	....
Less: Taxes	....
Net income after taxes (NIAT)	....
Dividends	....
Retained earnings	....

EXAMPLE

Find out the net income after taxes with the help of the following figures; Sales: Rs 4,50,000; cost of goods sold: Rs 2,60,000, other variable costs: Rs 40,000; fixed cost: Rs 30,000; interest on debt: Rs 15,000; taxes paid @ 30%.

Solution:	Amount (Rs)
Revenue from sales	4,50,000
Less: Cost of goods sold….	(2,60,000)
Marginal contribution	1,90,000
Less: Other variable costs…	(40,000)
Less: Fixed cost..	(30,000)
Operating profit	1,20,000
Less: Interest	(15,000)
EBT	1,05,000
Less: Taxes..	(31,500)
NIAT	73,500

18.2 BALANCE SHEET

A balance sheet indicates a firm's financial position as on a particular date, usually on the last day of a particular fiscal period. In particular, it shows the assets of the firm and how the assets are financed by different types of capital. The assets are displayed on one side, and the sources of the assets or the liabilities are displayed on the other.

As a natural corollary, a balance sheet measures a firm's liquidity and profitability. It measures liquidity in the sense that it shows whether the firm is able to pay its debts in a short-run scenario. Similarly, solvency means the firm's ability to meet all its long-term and short-term debt.

The assets and liabilities are displayed in a particular order, say, order of performance. Table 18.4 shows how they are displayed.

18.2.1 Assets

Table 18.3 shows the assets and the liabilities. On the side of the assets, there are fixed assets shown at full cost less depreciation written off. Additions to fixed assets are also shown separately. Plant and machinery and land and building are common examples of fixed assets.

Similarly, investments are duly classified and shown at cost price. If the market price differs from the cost price, this should be indicated by way of additional information. Moreover, it is necessary to disclose the method of valuation of the investments.

Current assets, different from the fixed assets, are convertible into cash within one accounting year. Daily operations are conducted with these assets. The largest share of current assets is represented by inventory that includes raw material, semi-finished goods and finished goods. Besides inventory, the current assets represent debtors, short-term

Table 18.3 *Balance Sheet of ABC Co. as on ...*

Liabilities	*Amount (Rs)*	*Assets*	*Amount (Rs)*
Share Capital:		Fixed Assets:	
Authorised	....	Land & building,	
Issued	....	Plant & machinery	....
Subscribed	....	(net of depreciation)	
Paid-up	....	Construction work-in-progress	....
Reserves and Surpluses	....	Investment (at cost)	....
Secured loans	....	Current Assets:	
Unsecured loans	....	Inventories	....
Deferred payment credits	....	Accounts receivable	....
Current liabilities and provisions	....	Short-term marketable Securities	....
		Cash	....
		Miscellaneous expenditure	....
	....		....

marketable securities, and the cash balance. These assets have already been discussed in the chapters dealing with working capital management.

Sometimes, as is the practice, certain losses are shown on the asset side, although they do not actually constitute assets. Examples are, losses on account of issue of shares and debentures, expenses concerning the formation of the company, etc. They are thus known as fictitious assets and are shown on the asset side just to balance the assets with liabilities.

> Goodwill is the most important of the intangible assets. Goodwill arises when a company acquires another company for a price in excess of the fair market value of the net identifiable assets.

Goodwill is the most important of the intangible assets. Goodwill arises when a company acquires another company for a price in excess of the fair market value of the net identifiable assets. Certain expenses are sometimes paid in advance. They are shown on the assets side.

18.2.2 Liabilities

Share capital and reserves are shown on the liabilities side of the balance sheet. Share capital may take different forms. The first is the authorised capital, also called nominal capital. Nominal capital is the total amount of share capital that a company can have as per its Memorandum of Association. Second is the issued capital which equals the face value of shares allotted by a company. Third is the subscribed capital, it is represented by the value of shares taken up by the public. If the whole of the issued shares are subscribed to, the issued and the subscribed capital will be equal. Fourth is the paid-up capital, normally a company asks its shareholders to pay up the value of the shares that they hold in different instalments. The paid-up capital is the sum of instalments paid by the shareholders.

The ordinary and the preference share capital are shown separately, while the number of bonus shares issued in lieu of profits payable to shareholders is disclosed by way of note.

Reserves too form a part of equity capital as they are the part of profits retained with the firm either for a particular purpose or for general purposes. General-purpose reserves are maintained in order to meet contingencies that may arise, while specific reserves are meant for a specific purpose. For example, dividend equalisation reserves are meant for use in paying dividend so that the payment of uniform rate of dividend can be maintained. Debenture reduction reserves and plant replacement reserves are some other examples of specific reserves.

Besides the above, there are borrowings by way of issue of debentures, or borrowings from financial institutions or banks. Secured loans and unsecured loans are shown separately. Moreover, any interest accrued and due on loans is added to the loan amount.

The shares and debentures represent long-term funds. On the other hand, current liabilities represent short-term funds which are repayable in the normal course of business, for example, bills payable or deferred payment credits and other short-term credits. Again, there are contingent liabilities which become liabilities on the occurrence of a certain event. For example, if a company enters into an agreement to construct a building, it has to pay the settled price after the completion of the building. A note is given in the balance sheet in case of contingent liabilities.

Here, it may be mentioned that the funds presented on the liabilities side represent investments either by outsiders or by the owners of the company. While the latter is known as owners' equity, the former is known simply as liabilities. Since the total of the assets side of the balance sheet is equal to that of the liabilities side, total assets are equal to the sum of total liabilities and the owners' equity. In other words:

Total assets = Total liabilities + Owners' equity

EXAMPLE

Find out the amount of debt—both short-term and long-term, if assets amount to Rs 4,58,000 and the owners' equity amounts to Rs 2,60,000.

Rs 4,58,000 – 2,60,000 = Rs 1,98,000

18.2.3 Limitations of the Balance Sheet

Although the balance sheet acquaints the analyst with the financial position of a firm, and is very useful when used along with the income statement, in computing various ratios regarding the firm's profitability and liquidity and other vital ratios, it has certain limitations. The most significant of these limitations is that it provides no explanation of how different balances have occurred. The balance sheet does not show the movement of funds in a given fiscal period.

Moreover, it does not show the various accounting techniques used to prepare it. Some of the accounting methods used are standard ones; however, certain variances are permitted which can greatly change the amounts reported in certain accounts.

Yet again, some of the assumptions on the basis of which the balance sheet is prepared are not known. For example, assumptions as to when obligations have been incurred or when revenues have accrued may have marked effects on the figures of different accounts in the balance sheet. Nevertheless, despite these limitations the usefulness of the balance sheet cannot be denied.

18.2.4 Complementarity between Income Statement and Balance Sheet

It is true that the purpose of the income statement and the balance sheet is different. While the former indicates the income and expenditure during a specific period, the latter presents the financial strength - assets and liabilities - on a particular date, normally the year-end. But it does not mean that the two are not complementary. They are complementary on the following counts:

1. Balance sheet cannot be prepared without preparing the income statement. The picture of equity cannot be complete unless and until the profit/loss of the company is taken into account. Similarly, the income statement cannot be drawn in absence of the balance sheet. The amount of interest is arrived at only on the basis of debt mentioned in the balance sheet. There are many such examples that show the interdependence of the two statements.
2. The balance sheet serves as a link between the income statements of the two consecutive years. For example, the capital incomes and expenditures of one

accounting year are carried forward to the next year only through the balance sheet. This type of interdependence between the two financial statements is often known as the link relationship.

18.2.5 Comparative Financial Statements

The financial statements of companies are published in the newspaper that often shows the financial performance in two consecutive financial years. The purpose is to show whether certain financial variable has improved/deteriorated during the period. For example, if the amount of sales is Rs 40 million and Rs 42 million, respectively, during FY 2008–09 and FY 2009–10, it means that the sales have improved by 5.0% during 1-year period. Similarly, other variables of the income statement and the balance sheet can be analysed. In some cases, there may be improvement. In others, there may be deterioration. The variation can be shown in absolute terms, but normally, it is shown in percentage terms.

EXAMPLE

Analyse the performance of the company on the basis of the comparative balance sheet given below:

Rs. million

Liabilities			Assets		
At the year-end	2009	2010	At the year-end	2009	2010
Share capital	40.0	40.0	Fixed assets	45.0	44.0
Reserves	30.0	33.0	Debtor	20.0	25.0
Debentures	35.0	38.5	Bank	20.0	12.5
			Inventory	20.0	30.0
Total	105.0	111.5		105.0	111.5

Solution

Rs. Mill.

	2009	2010	Absolute change	% Change
Share capital	40.0	40.0	No change	No change
Reserves	30.0	33.0	3.0	10.0
Debentures	35.0	38.5	3.5	10.0
Total liabilities	105.0	111.5	6.5	6.2
Fixed assets	45.0	44.0	(1.0)	- 2.2
Debtors	20.0	25.0	5.0	25.0
Bank	20.0	12.5	(7.5)	–37.5
Inventory	20.0	30.0	10.0	50.0
Total assets	105.0	111.5	6.5	6.2

1. Total assets/liabilities have increased by 6.2% in 2010 over 2009. The followings are the reasons for this increase:
   (a) Reserves have increased because there have emerged profits from the operations and a part of, or the whole of, the profit stands retained.
   (b) The company has gone to the debt market for additional funds for financing the operation.
   (c) Fixed assets have reduced marginally either on account of sale of a specific part. But, on the other hand, current assets have increased. The reason may be partly increased credit sale and partly the unsold goods.

18.3 FUNDS-FLOW STATEMENT

Funds mean working capital, that represents the difference between current assets and current liabilities. All flows of funds pass through working capital. This means that every transaction has an effect on the firm's working capital position.

The limitations of the income statement and the balance sheet highlight the importance of the funds-flow statement. This is because in the first two statements, one does not know from where the firm has received funds and where it has spent these funds. Therefore, a situation may arise when a firm has earned net profits but does not have money in the bank for meeting various claims. The reasons for this would not be evident either from its income statement or from its balance sheet. It is only a funds-flow statement that can reveal the reality of the situation.

Funds mean working capital, this working capital represents the difference between current assets and current liabilities. All flows of funds pass through working capital. This means that every transaction has an effect on the firm's working capital position. An example illustrates this is as follows, an increase in profits increases the cash balance and hence the working capital. Similarly, an increase in long-term liability or any decrease in fixed assets increases the cash balance and hence the working capital. If, on the other hand, fixed assets are purchased or the debentures are redeemed, the cash balance will be eroded to that extent, and this will have an effect on the working capital. Therefore, the funds-flow statement shows the movement of funds into, or out of, the current asset account of the firm.

The movement of funds, as we have just pointed out, has two aspects: one relates to the sources of funds and the other to the uses of funds. The former supply funds to the working capital and enhance its position. The latter, on the other hand, consume funds and erode the working capital position. The sources and the uses of funds are stated hereunder.

18.3.1 Sources of Funds

The sources of funds that contribute to the working capital pool are as follows:

1. Sale of fixed assets;
2. Sale of shares;
3. Long-term borrowings;
4. Funds from operation.

The sale value of fixed assets including profits, if any, is one of the sources of funds. If such profits have been included in the sale value, they are not included in the profit figures. The reason being that this would lead to double counting.

Similarly, loans raised including any premium or net of discount are considered as sources of funds. However, loans in form of supplies or services of a non-current nature do not constitute sources of funds.

Again, the full amount collected from the issue of shares is treated as a source of funds. This means that the amount of premium or discount, if any, is taken into account for this purpose. However, the issue of shares out of reserves in the form of bonus shares or those for supply of machinery, etc., which do not involve the working capital, are not treated as a source of funds.

The most important source of funds is profit from the firm's operation. The profit from operations means the net profit after taxes plus the non-cash expenses. Non-cash expenses, such as depreciation, write-off of preliminary expenses, or share issue expenses etc., reduce income but do not cause any outflow of funds from the operation, they are therefore added to the net income after taxes.

18.3.2 Uses of Funds

The uses of funds which cause an outflow from the working capital pool, are as follows:

1. Purchase of fixed assets;
2. Repayment of capital;
3. Make-up of losses;
4. Acquisition of investments;
5. Payment of dividends.

Acquisition of fixed assets causes an outflow of funds from the working capital pool. While bringing this effect to the funds-flow statement, double counting must be avoided. Gross changes in fixed assets through adding depreciation for the period to net fixed assets at the ending financial statement date, and subtract from this amount the net fixed assets at the beginning financial statement date, should be computed. In other words, gross changes in the fixed assets, ΔGFA, should be computed. This can be expressed as follows in the form of an equation.

$$\Delta GFA = (D + NFA_t) - NFA_{t-1} \quad ...(18.1)$$

Where:

D = depreciation for the current period

NFA_t = the net fixed assets at the ending financial statement date

NFA_{t-1} = the net fixed assets at the beginning financial statement date.

If the gross changes in the fixed assets are positive, as usually is the case, the state of affairs represents a use of funds. If negative, it represents a source of funds.

A company redeems the redeemable preference shares. Moreover, equity shares can also be paid back as per the procedures laid down in the Indian Companies Act, 1956. Similarly, loans are repaid or debentures are redeemed. Sometimes, premium is paid on the redemption of debentures or on the preference shares. All these cause an outflow of funds, and should therefore be treated as uses of funds.

Again, if the firm is operating at a loss, an outflow of funds will be there to the extent of net loss minus the non-cash expenses like depreciation, etc. Besides this, the outflow of funds takes place on account of acquisition of long-term investments and the payment of cash dividend.

18.3.3 Preparation of a Funds-flow Statement

The various sources and uses of funds can be spotted from the income statement of the current year and two balance sheets—one pertaining to the beginning of the period and the other to the end of the period. Suppose a funds-flow statement has to be prepared for the year 2003, it would be based on the income statement for the year 2003 along with two balance sheets—one as on the 31 December 2002 and the other as on the 31 December 2003. The sources should be written on one side and the uses, on the other. The difference of the two sides will show the changes in the working capital position. If the balance of the source side is larger, this will show an increase in the working capital. Excess of the uses side over the sources side shows a decrease in the working capital. An illustration may reveal the nature of the funds-flow statement.

EXAMPLE

From the following income statement and the balance sheets, prepare a funds-flow statement:

The Income Statement for the Year Ended 31 December 2003 shows:

	Amount (Rs)	Amount (Rs)
Profit before depreciation		15,000.00
Less: Depreciation	5,000	
Taxation	5,000	
Dividend	500	
Transfer to reserves	3,500	14,000.00
Balance of Profit and Loss (P & L) A/c		1,000.00

The Balance Sheet as on 31 December, 2002 and 31 December, 2003 is as follows:

Liabilities	As on 31.12.02 (Rs)	As on 31.12.03 (Rs)	Assets	As on 31.12.02 (Rs)	As on 31.12.03 (Rs)
Share capital	25,000	30,000	Fixed assets	40,000	42,500
Reserves	15,000	18,500	Current assets:		
P & L A/c	–	1,000	Stock	10,000	15,000
Secured loans	9,000	14,000	Debtors	15,000	21,000
Current liabilities			Cash	2,500	4,000
& provisions	18,500	19,000			
	67,500	82,500		67,500	82,500

Solution

Funds-flow Statement

Sources	Amount (Rs)	Uses	Amount (Rs)
Funds from operations	10,000	Purchase of fixed assets	7,500
Issue of share capital	5,000	Payment of dividend	500
Secured loans	5,000	Increase in working capital	12,000
	20,000		20,000

18.4 CASH-FLOW STATEMENT

A cash-flow statement is to a large extent similar to a funds-flow statement. The only difference is that a cash-flow statement shows the position of the cash balance in a firm (including cash at bank), whereas the funds-flow statement indicates the changes in the working capital as a whole. Cash is only a part of working capital, and so any change in the working capital does not necessarily indicate a changes in the cash balance. It is possible for there to be an increase in working capital, with the cash position either deteriorating, or not satisfactory from the viewpoint of liquidity. If, for example, sales have been larger but bills stand uncollected, the working capital would be larger without any increase in cash. It is for this very reason that the firms prepare a cash-flow statement in addition to a funds-flow statement.

18.4.1 Sources and Uses of Cash

All the sources and uses of funds are respectively the sources and uses of cash. In addition, in the cash-flow statement, changes in the current assets other than cash and those in the current liabilities are also considered as sources and uses of cash. Increase in current liabilities, and, at the same time, any decrease in current assets other than cash improve the cash position. On the other hand, repayment of current liabilities and purchases of inventories or increase in uncollected bills weaken the cash balance..

Moreover, as far as funds from operations are concerned, they do not add to cash in entirety. They influence the cash position only to the extent that cash is collected from the customers minus cash paid for the cost and expenses. If at all, the entire sales are made on cash terms and all the expenses are met in cash, the funds flow and the cash flow will be identical. This is however, seldom the case. When one considers the operational flow for the cash-flow statement, accrued and prepaid items are offset from the operational funds-flow.

18.4.2 Preparation of Cash-flow Statement

A cash-flow statement is prepared in a manner similar to that in which the funds-flow statement is prepared. It means that the income statement and the two balance sheets form the basis for its preparation. Sources of cash are displayed on the one side and the uses on the other. The opening balance of cash is written on the source side, and the closing balance of cash is arrived at on the uses side. An illustration of a cash-flow statement is presented here in order to give the reader a better grasp of its preparation.

EXAMPLE

ABC Co. Ltd has to prepare a cash-flow statement for the year ended 31 December, 2003 from the details given below:

Balance Sheet of ABC Co. Ltd as on 31 December 2002 and 31 December 2003

Liabilities	As on 31.12.02 (Rs)	As on 31.12.03 (Rs)	Assets	As on 31.12.02 (Rs)	As on 31.12.03 (Rs)
Share capital	40,000	40,000	Fixed assets (gross)	60,000	92,500
Reserves & surplus	30,000	55,000	Depreciation	(17,500)	(27,500)
Long-term loans	20,000	30,000	Inventory	40,000	35,000
Current liabilities & provisions	15,000	26,000	Accounts Receivable	20,000	34,000
Dividend provision	....	8,000	Cash	2,500	25,000
	1,05,000	1,59,000		1,05,000	1,59,000

The Income Statement for ABC Co. Ltd for the Year Ended 31 December 2003 shows the following information:

	Amount (Rs)
Sales	1,45,000
Cost of Sales	99,000
Tax provision	12,500
Dividend provided	8,000

Solution

Cash-flow Statement for the Year Ended 31 December 2003

Sources	Amount (Rs)	Uses	Amount (Rs)
Balance of cash (opening)	2,500	Purchase of fixed assets	32,500
Operational cash-flow	43,000	Increase in accounts receivable	14,000
Long-term loans	10,000	Closing balance of cash	25,000
Increase in current liabilities	11,000		
Decrease in inventory	5,000		
	71,500		71,500

Note: Operational cash flow is equal to

		Amount (Rs)
Funds from operations	....	33,000
Add: Depreciation	....	10,000
		43,000

The funds from operations are derived as follows:

		Amount (Rs)
Sales	....	1,45,000
Less: Cost of sales	....	99,500
		45,500
Less: Taxes	....	12,500
Net profit after taxes	....	33,000

Difference between Funds-flow Statement and Cash-flow Statement

1. Funds-flow statement shows working capital position. Cash-flow statement shows the position of cash only.
2. Funds-flow statement is prepared on the accrual basis of accounting. Cash flow statement is prepared on cash basis of accounting.
3. The net funds flowing from operation are not separately shown in a funds-flow statement. In cash flow statement, funds flowing from operations are shown separately.
4. Cash flow statement is a useful tool for short-term liquidity analysis. Funds flow statement is more relevant for long-term and medium-term financial analysis.

SUMMARY

Financial statements show, among other things, the various outflows and inflows of cash and profits as also the financial position of a firm. This is why they are very important for financial analysis and planning. The income statement is one such statement, which shows the firm's income and expense and the resulting profits during a particular fiscal period. Various measures of profit, such as gross profit, operating profit, earning before taxes and the net income after taxes are evident from the income statement.

The other important financial statement is the balance sheet, which shows the firm's various liabilities and assets as on a particular date, generally the closing day of the fiscal period. However, the balance sheet does not show the movement of funds during a particular fiscal period. That is why the above two statements are often supplemented with a funds-flow statement. Such a statement shows the different sources of funds during a given period and how they are put to different uses thus effecting the working capital of the firm. This statement is prepared on the basis of the income statement and two successive balance sheets—one prepared at the beginning of the period and the other at the end of the period. The sources of funds are normally the sale of fixed assets, sale of shares, long-term borrowings and the funds from operation. The uses of funds, on the other hand, are the repayment of capital, make-up of losses, purchases of fixed assets, acquisition of investments and the payment of dividends.

Apart from the funds-flow statement, a cash-flow statement is often prepared as it shows the changes in a firm's cash position. The sources and uses of funds are the sources and uses of cash. In addition, changes in the current assets other than cash and those in the current liabilities are also treated as sources and uses of cash. The sources are recorded on the one side and the uses, on the other, in both the cash-flow and the funds-flow statement.

POINTS TO REMEMBER

1. What is an income statement? Distinguish between its managerial format and the marginal-analysis format.
   - Income statement presents the income and expenditure of a firm during a particular financial period.
   - Managerial format shows net income at different stages – after deducting the cost of raw material, operating expenses, interest and taxes.
   - Marginal-analysis format shows similarly the net income at different stages but divides the cost of goods and the operating cost as variable and fixed expenses.
2. What is a balance sheet? What are its limitations?
   - Balance sheet shows a firm's assets and liabilities on a particular date, normally the last day of the financial year.
   - It does not show the movement of funds during the fiscal period, nor does it reveal the accounting technique used to prepare it.
3. What is a funds-flow statement? What are the sources and uses of funds?
   - It incorporates all forms of the movement of funds that either add to the working capital or erode the working capital ultimately showing the position of working capital in a firm.
   - The sources of funds that add to the working capital are: sale of fixed assets, sale of shares, long-term borrowings, and funds from operation.
   - The uses of funds that erode working capital are: purchase of fixed assets, repayment of capital, make-up of losses, acquisition of investment and payment of dividend.
4. What is a cash-flow statement? What are the sources and uses of cash?
   - It shows the position of cash in a firm through incorporating the sources and uses of cash. The sources and uses of cash are all the sources and uses of working capital. Additionally, the sources are the increase in current liabilities/decrease in current assets other than cash. The uses are the increase in current assets other than cash/decrease in current liabilities.

DESCRIPTIVE QUESTIONS

1. Show how revenue and expenses are presented in an income statement.
2. What are the different items that appear on the assets side of a balance sheet?
3. Distinguish between owners' equity and liabilities.
4. Comment on the usefulness of a funds-flow statement. What are the sources and uses of funds?
5. How is a cash-flow statement different from a funds-flow statement? What are the sources and uses of cash?

OBJECTIVE-TYPE QUESTIONS

1. Mark true or false.
   (a) Current assets do not include inventory.
   (b) Inventory means raw material and not finished goods.
   (c) Retained earnings are a part of equity.
   (d) Bills payable are a part of current liabilities.
   (e) EBIT shows whether the firm's operations have been successful.
   (f) The margin of contribution means revenue minus variable costs.
   (g) The value of total assets may not be equal to the sum of total liabilities and shareholders' equity.
   (h) Goodwill is a tangible asset.
   (i) Increase in long-term liabilities leads to an increase in the cash balance.
   (j) Loans in form of supplies or services of non-current nature constitute the sources of funds.
2. Choose the most suitable answer.
   (a) In a cash-flow statement, sources and uses of cash are represented by:
      (i) changes in the cash position
      (ii) changes in current assets other than cash
      (iii) both of the above
   (b) Sources and uses of funds can be spotted from:
      (i) the income statement alone
      (ii) the balance sheet alone
      (iii) both of the above
   (c) Outflow of funds takes place on account of:
      (i) acquisition of long-term investments
      (ii) payment of cash dividend
      (iii) both of the above

(d) Issue of shares out of reserves is treated as:
   (i) a sources of funds
   (ii) uses of funds
   (iii) neither of the above

(e) Contingent liabilities are those which:
   (i) are repayable in the normal course of business
   (ii) arise on the occurrence of a certain event
   (iii) both of the above

(f) Costs are divided into fixed and variable cost in:
   (i) a managerial format of income statement
   (ii) a marginal-analysis format of income statement
   (iii) both of the above

NUMERICAL PROBLEMS

1. Find out the operating profit if: sales are Rs 5,50,000; cost of goods sold is Rs 2,70,000; other variable costs are Rs 45,000; fixed operating cost is Rs 40,000; and interest payments amount to Rs 20,000.
2. Find out the net income after taxes if marginal contribution is Rs 2,00,000; operating cost is Rs 40,000; interest paid is Rs 10,000 and tax rate is 30%.
3. If a balance sheet shows owners' equity at Rs 3,50,000, debt at 3,00,000 and current assets at Rs 4,00,000, find the amount of fixed assets.
4. Calculate funds from operations if pre-tax profit is Rs 60,000; tax rate is 30%; depreciation is Rs 10,000 and share issue expenses are Rs 5,000.
5. Find out the changes in cash position if decrease in marketable securities is Rs 10,000; increase in bills receivable is Rs 50,000; decrease in inventories is Rs 20,000; increase in provisions is Rs 15,000; increase in short-term loans is Rs 25,000 and decrease in bills payable is Rs 18,000.
6. The following is the balance sheet of ABC Co. as on 31 December 2002 and 31 December 2003

Item	*Liabilities (Rs)*		*Item*	*Assets (Rs)*	
	31.12.2002	31.12.2003		31.12.2002	31.12.2003
Share capital	5,000	5,000	Fixed assets (net)	8,500	10,000
Reserves	4,250	5,000	Inventories	3,400	3,500
Loan	3,000	3,300	Debtors	3,600	3,300
Creditors	3,750	4,000	Cash	300	350
			Other assets	200	150
Total	16,000	17,300	Total	16,000	17,300

During 2003, the income statement was as follows:

Net sales: Rs 20,400; cost of goods sold: Rs 13,600; stocks: Rs 10,100; wages: Rs 2,100; other manufacturing expenses: Rs 1,400; gross profit: Rs 6,800; depreciation: Rs 1,100; general operating expenses: Rs 2,300; operating profit: Rs 3,400; non-operating surplus: Rs 250; EBIT: Rs 3,650; interest: Rs 700; EBT: Rs 2,950; tax: Rs 1,300; net profit: Rs 1,650; dividend: Rs 900 and retained earnings: Rs 750.

Prepare a funds-flow statement and a cash-flow statement.

7. A company's net earning is Rs 3,70,000, out of which dividend for Rs 40,000 is given to the preference shareholders. Again, a sum of Rs 1,20,000 is transferred to reserves. Find the EPS and DPS with a given 1,00,000 shares outstanding.
8. Prepare an income statement if the firm has a gross sale of Rs 3,00,000. The cost of goods accounts for 60% of the sale value. The operating cost accounts for 20% of the gross sale value. The interest was paid amounting to Rs 15,000. The tax rate is 30%.

SOLVED NUMERICAL PROBLEMS

1. Prepare income statement and find out the changes in EBIT and net income in 2007–08 over 2006–07 on the basis of the following details:

   Sales during 2006–07 amounted to Rs 4,00,000 that increased by 20% in the following year. The cost of goods accounted for 60% of the sale value during 2006–07 which, on account of economy measures, slumped to 55% in the following year. Operating expenses too fell from 10% to 8% of the sale value. But the amount of interest payment rose from Rs 25,000 to Rs 30,000 in 2007–08. Tax rate was constant at 30%.

Solution

Income Statement

	2006–07	*2007–08*
Revenue from sales	4,00,000	4,80,000
Less cost of goods	2,40,000	2,64,000
Margin of contribution	1,60,000	2,16,000
Less operating expenses	40,000	38,400
Operating profit	1,20,000	1,77,600
Less interest payment	25,000	30,000
Earnings before taxes	95,000	1,47,600
Less taxes @ 30%	28,500	44,280
Net income after taxes	66,500	1,03,320

Increase in EBIT = Rs 1,77,600/1,20,000 = 48%

Increase in net income = Rs 1,03,320 /66,500 = 55.37%

2. Prepare balance sheet as on 31.3.2008 from the following figures:

	Debit Rs	*Credit Rs*
Equity capital (face value= Rs 50 per share)		5,00,000
Calls in arrear	500	
Land & Build.	2,75,000	
Plant & mach.	2,62,500	
Furniture	25,000	
General reserves		1,05,000
Loan from financial corporation		75,000
Stock	1,25,000	
Provision for taxation		34,000
B/R	1,00,000	
Advances	21,350	
Proposed dividend		30,000
Profit		50,000
Cash	1,38,500	
Preliminary expenses	6,650	
Unsecured loan		60,500
Creditors		1,00,000
Total	9,54,500	9,54,500

Note: 1. Rs 2,850 paid to auditors.

2. 2,000 equity shares were issued not for cash.

3. B/R for Rs 26,000 are due for more than 6 months.

4. The cost of fixed assets:

Land & Building:	Rs 2,00,000
Plant & mach.	3,50,000
Furniture	31,250

5. Loan for Rs 75,000 was inclusive of Rs 3,750 as interest accrued but not due.

6. B/R for Rs 1,37,500 have been discounted

7. The contract for erection of machinery for Rs 75,000 is still incomplete.

Solution

B/S as on 31.3.2008

Liabilities	*Amount Rs*	*Assets*	*Amount Rs*
Share capital 5,00,000		Fixed assets:	
Less calls in arrear 500	4,99,500		
Reserves	1,05,000	Land & Build.	2,75,000
Profit	50,000	Plant & Mach.	2,62,500
Loan 75,000			
Less hypoth. 3,750	71,250	Furniture	25,000

Unsecured loan	60,500	Current assets:	
Sundry creditors	1,00,000	Inventory	1,25,000
Int. accrued but not due	3,750	B/R	1,00,000
Provision for taxes	34,000	Cash	1,38,500
Proposed dividend	30,000	Loans & Adv. not written off	21,350
		Misc. expenses	6,650
Total	9,54,000	Total	9,54,000

3. Calculate funds from operations from the following figures:
   1. Expenses paid & outstanding — Rs 6,00,000
   2. Depreciation — 1,40,000
   3. Loss from sale of machine — 8,000
   4. Discount paid — 400
   5. Goodwill — 40,000
   6. Other expenses — 6,68,400
   7. Gain from sale of land — 1,20,000
   8. Net profit — 2,31,600

Solution

		Amount Rs
Net profit		2,31,600
Add:		
Depreciation	1,40,000	
Loss on sale of mach.	8,000	
Discount	400	
Goodwill	40,000	1,88,400
Less gain from sale of land		(1,20,000)
Funds from operation		3,00,000

4. From the following B/S, prepare a funds-flow statement:

Liabilities	*Mar. 2007*	*Mar. 2008*	*Assets*	*Mar. 2007*	*Mar. 2008*
Capital	1,60,000	1,70,000	Land & Build.	1,00,000	1,00,000
Profits	29,000	49,000	Plant & mach.	48,000	68,000
Creditors	18,000	10,000	Stock	18,000	14,000
Mortgage	–	10,000	Investment	33,000	39,000
			Cash	8,000	18,000
Total	2,07,000	2,39,000	Total	2,07,000	2,39,000

Solution

Funds-flow Statement during 2007–08

Sources of funds	*Amount Rs*	*Uses of funds*	*Amount Rs*
Profits	20,000	Purchase of plant & mach.	20,000
Additional share capital	10,000		
Mortgage	10,000	Net increase in working capital	20,000

5. Prepare a cash-flow statement from the following B/S and income statement:

B/S as on.

Liabilities Rs	Mar. 2007	Mar. 2008	Assets Rs	Mar. 2007	Mar. 2008
Creditors	33,000	39,000	Cash	4,500	6,000
Div. payable	1,000	–	Marketable securities	1,000	500
Tax payable	1,500	2,500	B/R	47,500	39,500
Debt	37,500	21,000	Prov. for debt	(1,500)	(1,000)
Share capital	13,000	13,000	Inventory	51,500	46,000
Profits	84,000	78,000	Prepaid exp.	3,000	2,500
			Land	34,500	33,000
			Plant	86,000	78,000
			Prov. for depr.	(56,500)	(51,000)
Total	1,70,000	1,53,500	Total	1,70,000	1,53,500

Income Statement for the year ending March 2008

	Amount Rs
Revenue from sale	3,00,000
Less cost of goods	2,50,000
Gross margin	50,000
Less operating expenses	33,000
EBIT	17,000
Less interest payment	2,000
EBT	15,000
Add compensation	2,500
Less taxes	8,500
Net income	9,000

Note: Dividend declared was Rs 3000, MPS was Rs 7.25. Land was acquired for Rs 500. For acquiring equipment, only Rs 3,000 was paid in cash form.

Solution

		Amount Rs
Operating profit before changes in working capital		
EBIT	17,000	
Dep.	5,500	
Provision for doubtful debt	500	23,000
Less: Increase in debtor	8,000	
Increase in inventory	5,500	
Increase in prepaid exp.	500	
Decrease in creditors	6,000	20,000
Cash generated from operations		3,000
Less: taxes		9,500
Purchase of land	1,500	
Purchase of equip.	3,000	
Dividend & interest	4,000	
Add: Compensation received	2,500	
Proceeds from long-term borrowing	11,500	
Net decrease in cash		1,000

CASE STUDY

Dabur India Ltd. is basically an ayurvedic medicine manufacturing firm having its registered office in New Delhi. Over the years, it diversified its operations covering cosmetics and food products. On the 1st of April 2007, it merged with its subsidiary, Dabur Foods Limited. Again, its wholly-owned subsidiary. H&B Stores Ltd. was created during FY 2007–08. The Board has proposed the final dividend of 75% or Re 0.75 per equity share having a face value of Re 1 per share for FY 2007–08 amounting to Rs 64.80 crores (excluding tax on dividend) which has already been paid as interim dividend. With this, the pay-out ratio is 47.86% (including tax on dividend).

The following is the audited financial result for the year ended March 2007 and March 2008. It covers both the consolidated details and the stand-alone ones.

Dabur (Consolidated) Year ended		Particulars	Rs crores Dabur (Stand-alone) Year ended	
31.3.2007	31.3.2008		31.3.2007	31.3.2008
2080.25	2396.29	Gross sales	1637.36	2117.79
37.11	35.22	Less excise duty	36.93	34.39
2043.14	2361.07	Net sales	1600.43	2083.40
25.91	34.01	Other incomes	16.51	27.91
2069.05	2395.08	Total income	1616.94	2111.31

Dabur (Consolidated) Year ended		Particulars	Rs crores Dabur (Stand-alone) Year ended	
1734.18	1993.84	Total expenditure	1328.29	1717.58
15.38	16.80	Interest and financial charges	4.43	8.55
319.40	384.44	Profit before tax	284.22	365.18
37.23	50.65	Taxes	32.14	48.41
282.17	333.79	Net profit after taxes from ordinary activities	252.08	316.77
–	–	Extra-ordinary items	–	–
282.17	333.79	Net profit after taxes	252.08	316.77
1.33	0.98	Provision for taxes for earlier years	0.13	0.86
280.84	332.81	Net profit	251.95	315.91
0.87	0.13	Minority interest	–	–
28.71	332.94	Net profit after adjustment for minority interest	251.95	315.91
86.29	86.40	Paid-up equity share capital	86.29	86.40
393.28	531.17	Reserves excluding revaluation reserves	316.90	441.92
3.27	3.85	Basic EPS (Rs)	2.93	3.66
3.24	3.83	Diluted EPS (Rs)	2.90	3.64
		Public shareholding:		
		No. of shares	226041835	252188500
		Percentage of shareholding	26.20	29.19

Based on the reports published in Mint, 7.5.2008.

Questions:

1. Find out the operating profit. Does it show an increase in FY 2007–08 over the previous financial year?
2. How do you arrive at the EPS? Distinguish between basic EPS and diluted EPS.
3. How do you calculate the percentage of shareholding mentioned in the last row of the table?
4. Explain minority interest.

SELECT FURTHER READING

Harrington, D.R. (1998). *Corporate Financial Analysis*. Cincinnati, O.H.: South Western Publishers.

19

FINANCIAL RATIO ANALYSIS

OBJECTIVES

To highlight the significance of financial ratio analysis
To explain and compute different types of liquidity ratios
To explain and compute profitability ratios
To elucidate and calculate ownership ratios
To pinpoint the limitations to ratio analysis

Once the financial statements are prepared, the figures therein must then be interpreted. The relationship between two sets of figures is established and on that basis, the necessary inference is drawn so as to bring about changes if necessary in the financial policy. The present chapter discusses this process which is also known as the financial ratio analysis.

19.1 SIGNIFICANCE OF RATIO ANALYSIS

The relationship between two items of financial data expressed in the form of a ratio and then interpreted with a view to evaluating the financial condition and performance of a firm, form the basis of financial ratio analysis. Any evaluation of this type is not only necessary for the management, but also necessary for outsiders who are interested in the performance of the firm. For example, creditors are interested in the firm's ability to meet their claims, they would therefore need to evaluate the firm's liquidity. Security analysts would be interested in the evaluation of the firm as an investment prospect. They would evaluate with the help of ratio analysis the desirability of the firm's shares and debentures as an investment and the other information reflecting upon the firm's operating efficiency and financial strength.

Inside the firm, the managers are concerned with financial planning and control. They need to maintain a proper balance between profitability and liquidity and thereby allow smooth operation of the firm. They are also interested in protecting the interests of the creditors and the investors. This is why they evaluate from time-to-time the firm's liquidity and profitability positions as also the return on equity using financial ratio analysis.

It may be pointed out here that it is not only the present financial condition of a firm that can be evaluated with the help of the ratio analysis. A financial analyst can foresee or predict the future and thereby help check the firm from running into liquidation. This is because the ratios for a certain period can well show the trend leading to liquidation. If these ratios show a worsening trend, efforts can be made to check the same. The study of Altman (1986) shows that only five ratios, such as, working capital to total assets, market value of equity to book value of total debt, retained earnings to total assets, operating profit to total assets and sales to total assets, can do the best combined job in predicting bankruptcy. In short, with ratio analysis, the firm's management is able to diagnose the factors leading to bankruptcy or any adverse trend. If precisely diagnosed, a remedy would not be difficult.

19.2 TYPES OF FINANCIAL RATIOS

Ratios reveal many financial dimensions of a firm. So different types of ratios are computed depending upon the purposes for which they are computed. Broadly speaking, financial ratios that are normally computed on the figures presented in the income statement and the balance sheet can be grouped under three heads:

1. Liquidity ratios that examine whether the funds with the firm are adequate to avoid insolvency;
2. Profitability ratios that measure the efficiency of operations;
3. Ownership ratios that help evaluate the activities and policies of the firm that influence the market price of its equity shares.

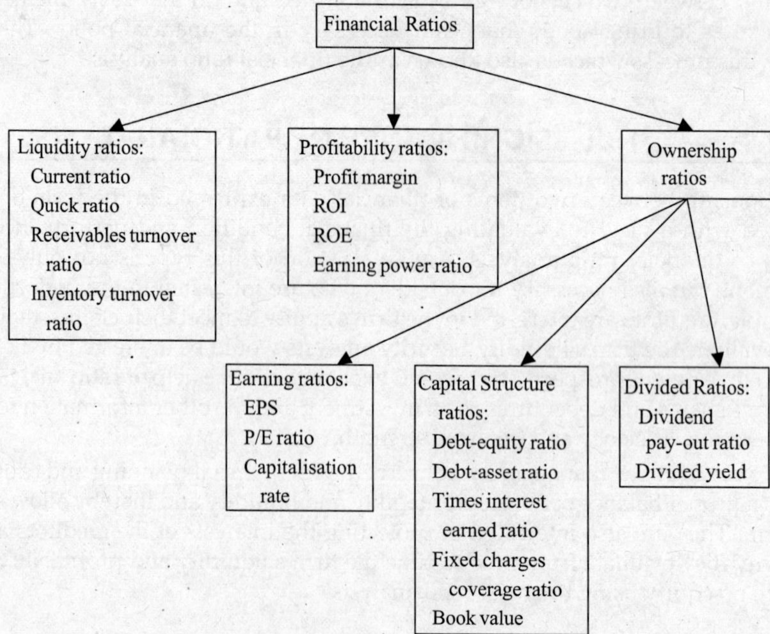

19.2.1 Liquidity Ratios

The current ratio indicates the relationship between total current assets and total current liabilities.

Liquidity ratios that reveal the firm's liquidity position are normally the current ratio, quick ratio, receivables ratio and inventory turnover ratio.

Current Ratio: The current ratio indicates the relationship between total current assets and the total current liabilities in a firm. It can be computed as follows:

Current Ratio = Current Assets/Current Liabilities

or

Current Ratio = (Cash + near cash assets + receivables + inventories)/ accounts payable and other short-term liabilities ...(19.1)

A high current ratio means that the firm is able to pay future bills, whereas, a low ratio indicates the firm's inability to make such payments. At the same time, a high ratio indicates an excess of current assets which means the firm's inability to properly utilise its resources. It is thus very difficult to quantify an optimal current ratio. It differs from one firm to the other and from one industry to the other. However, a 2:1 ratio is generally acceptable for most of the firms.

Quick Ratio: The liquidity of a firm can be measured more precisely by excluding inventories from the current assets. The reason for this is that inventories are not as liquid as other current assets. Liquidity can thus be better revealed if one excludes inventory from the current assets. The quick ratio, or acid test ratio as it is sometimes called, measures the firm's liquidity after excluding inventory. It can be computed as follows:

Quick Ratio = (Cash + near cash assets + receivables)/Current liabilities

or

Quick ratio = (Current assets – inventory)/Current Liabilities ...(19.2)

Since inventory is excluded, a quick ratio of 1:1 is normally accepted as optimal. Any deviation indicates either insufficient liquidity or greater liquidity or the inability of the firm to properly utilise its resources.

Receivables Ratio: The current ratio and the quick ratio measure overall liquidity. However, to measure the liquidity of receivables alone, two ratios are computed. They are as follows:

1. Average collection period ratio;
2. Receivable turnover ratio.

The average collection period is the average number of days for which receivables are outstanding. It is the average time that is taken to convert receivables into cash.

The average collection period is the average number of days for which receivables are outstanding. It is the average time that is taken to convert receivables into cash. It can be computed as follows:

Average collection period = Receivables × Days in a year/ Annual credit sales ...(19.3)

A high average collection period means that it takes a longer time for credit to take the form of cash. This would mean lower liquidity. On the other hand, a low ratio means greater liquidity of receivables.

The receivables turnover ratio shows the relationship between the size of firm's sales and the magnitude of uncollected bills. It can be computed as follows:

Receivables turnover ratio = Annual credit sales/Receivables ...(19.4)

If the receivables turnover ratio is low, it means that there is a large balance of receivables in view of a slow collection rate. This in turn indicates a lower degree of liquidity of receivables. A high ratio would indicate greater liquidity of receivables.

Inventory Turnover Ratio: Similar to the case of receivables, liquidity of inventory is measured by the inventory turnover ratio. It can be computed as follows:

Inventory Turnover Ratio = Cost of goods sold/Inventories ...(19.5)

Maintenance of an optimal amount of inventory saves the firm from two opposing dangers. One is running out of goods to sell which is apparent in the case of a high inventory turnover. The other is unwarranted heavy investment in inventories which manifests in a low inventory turnover.

19.2.2 Profitability Ratios

It has already been pointed out that the profitability ratios indicate a firm's efficiency of operation. These ratios are therefore shown either in relation to sales or in relation to assets. In addition to this, these ratios are sometimes linked through a ratio of sales to assets, or a ratio of net profit to net worth.

Profit Margin: Profit margin is arrived at after dividing profits by sales. Since there are different measures of profit, there are different variants of this ratio. They are as follows:

1. Gross profit margin which means gross profit (sales minus cost of goods sold) divided by sales,
2. Profit margin which means operating profit divided by sales, and
3. Net profit margin that means net profits after taxes divided by sales.

Profitability ratios indicate a firm's efficiency of operation. These ratios are therefore shown either in relation to sales or in relation to assets. These ratios are sometimes linked through a ratio of sales to assets, or a ratio of net profit to net worth.

If these ratios are computed jointly, we may have a deeper vision into the operation of a firm. For example, if the net profit margin declines without any diminution in the gross profit margin, this shows that the administrative or distribution expenses or high tax rate is the cause of lower net profits. If, on the other hand, the gross profit margin falls faster than the net profit margin, it indicates that the cost of producing goods is increasing very fast relative to sales.

Return on Investment (ROI): ROI is a product of profit margin and assets turnover. The profit margin, as discussed above, is computed by dividing the operating profit by sales. The asset turnover is the ratio between sales and the total assets. Combining these two ratios, ROI can be computed as follows:

$$ROI = \text{Profit Margin} \times \text{Assets Turnover}$$

or $$ROI = (EBIT/Sales) \times (Sales/Assets)$$

or $$ROI = EBIT/Assets \qquad ...(19.6)$$

If, for example, assets turnover is 3 and the profit margin is 6% the ROI would be 18%. The ROI measures the ability of the management to earn a return on resources. Firms using their assets efficiently have a relatively high return and vice versa.

Return on Equity: The return on equity helps in analysing the ability of a firm to realise an adequate return on capital invested by the equity shareholders. In order to compute this ratio, the net income after taxes (NIAT) is divided by total equity. Return on equity, (ROE) can be computed as follows:

$$ROE = NIAT/Equity \quad ...(19.7)$$

In the case of firms having preference share capital, dividend on preference shares is deducted from the NIAT and then NIAT is divided by total equity. Total equity means net worth minus par value of preference shares. In other words ROE is computed in this case as follows:

$$ROE = (NIAT - \text{Dividend on preference shares}) / (\text{Net worth} - \text{par value of preference shares}) \quad ...(19.8)$$

Earning Power Ratio: The earning power ratio measures the efficiency of a firm in achieving an after-tax return on resources. This ratio is computed by dividing the NIAT by total assets. It is computed as follows:

$$\text{Earning Power Ratio} = NIAT/Assets \quad ...(19.9)$$

It establishes a relationship between the book value of assets and the after-tax profits. If a firm utilises its assets efficiently, its earning power ratio will be higher than that of similar firms.

19.2.3 Ownership Ratios

Ownership ratios assist the shareholders in analysing their present and future investment in a company through changes in the value of their holdings. These ratios may be grouped under three heads. They are as follows:

1. Earning ratios that reveal the earnings of a firm;
2. Capital structure ratios that indicate the proportion-mix of various forms of capital;
3. Dividend ratios that reflect the adequacy of dividend paid.

> Ownership ratios assist the shareholders in analysing their present and future investment in a company through changes in the value of their holdings.

Earning Ratios: Earning ratios provide information on the earnings of a firm and how the earnings affect the price of its equity shares. These ratios can be grouped under three heads as follows:

1. Earning per share (EPS);
2. Price-earnings ratio(P/E Ratio); and
3. Capitalisation rate.

EPS is calculated by dividing earnings available to the equity shareholders by the number of shares outstanding. It can be computed as follows:

$$EPS = \text{Net earnings for equity shareholders/Number of equity shares outstanding} \quad ...(19.10)$$

Investors are more concerned with year-to-year comparison of EPS that reveals the trend of a company's performance. A rising trend in EPS tends to increase their wealth.

The P/E earnings ratio is computed by dividing the market price of the share by EPS. The P/E ratio can be computed as follows:

$$P/E \text{ Ratio} = \text{Market price of share}/EPS \quad ...(19.11)$$

This ratio considers after-tax profits and the market price of the shares and in this way links EPS to activity in the market. If a share has a low price-earnings multiple, this would mean that the share is undervalued. On the other hand, a high multiple denotes overvalued shares. However, this ratio is used as a going-concern method of valuing shares.

Capitalisation rate is the reciprocal of the P/E ratio. The capitalisation rate can be computed as follows:

$$CR = EPS/Market\ price\ of\ share \quad ...(19.12)$$

To make this clear with the help of an example, if the P/E ratio is 5/1, the capitalisation rate would be 1/5 or 20%. This means that the firm earns 20% on the value of the equity shares.

Capital Structure Ratios: The purpose of the capital structure ratios is to identify the sources of funds, that is the proportion-mix of debt and equity. These ratios also measure the extent of firm's total debt burden as well as the financial risk borne by the equity-holders as also the creditors. The inclusion of debt in the capital structure up to a certain point lowers the cost of capital without increasing financial risk. Beyond that point, debt raises financial risk and thereby the cost of capital. This is because the payment of interest is an expense and that increases phenomenally with an increase in the debt component, with the result that the magnitude of returns on equity falls considerably. The company can even experience bankruptcy with a very high debt-equity ratio. A higher proportion of debt is also a matter of concern to the creditors insofar as it may entail upon the firm's capacity to meet its fixed charge obligations, that is, interest payments. The creditors fear that the regularity of their interest receipts would be jeopardised. Capital structure ratios include the following ratios:

> The purpose of the capital structure ratios is to identify the sources of funds, that is the proportion-mix of debt and equity.

1. Debt-equity ratio;
2. Debt-asset ratio;
3. Times interest earned ratio;
4. Fixed-charges coverage ratio;
5. Book value.

The debt-equity ratio is computed by dividing the total debt including also short-term debt by total equity. As a general guideline, debt should not exceed 60% of total capital. This means that the debt-equity ratio can go up to 60/40 or 1.5/1.

When the amount of debt is expressed in relation to the total assets, this is known as the debt-asset ratio. For computing this ratio, total debt is divided by total assets. The debt-asset ratio is often simply referred to as the debt ratio. It has a definite relationship with the debt-equity ratio. For example, a debt/equity of 60:40 or 1.5:1 means a debt ratio of 60:100 or 0.6:1. This is because the amount of assets is equal to the sum of debt and equity.

The times interest earned ratio is equal to the operating profit divided by interest. This ratio reflects the firm's ability to pay annual interest on its debt out of its earnings. If this ratio is 1, this means that the entire operating profit is consumed by the interest payment and nothing is left for the shareholders. It is for this reason that this ratio should greatly exceed 1.

The fixed-charges coverage ratio is equal to income available to meet fixed charges divided by fixed charges, where fixed charges being a contractual obligation includes all fixed outlays including interest paid, sinking fund contribution and lease payments. This ratio indicates the amount of income a firm possesses in order to pay for all fixed charges. The minimum acceptable ratio in the normal course of business is 3.5:1.

Last, book value is equal to equity divided by the number of equity shares outstanding.

Capital Structure Ratios

1. Debt-equity ratio = Total debt/Total equity
2. Debt-asset ratio = Total debt/Total assets
3. Times interest earned ratio = EBIT/Interest
4. Fixed-charges coverage ratio = (EBIT + lease payments and other incomes)/ (Interest + lease payments + before-tax sinking fund contribution)
5. Book value = Equity/Number of equity shares outstanding

Dividend Ratios: A firm maintains a balance between the payment of dividend and retention of earnings. If the amount of dividend is insufficient, its shares may not be attractive to the investors. On the other hand, if sufficient funds are not retained, the firm may run into illiquidity. The dividend ratio reveals the position and policy of a firm in relation to dividend and retention of earnings.

Dividend ratios are either dividend pay-out or dividend yield. Dividend pay-out is calculated by dividing dividend per share by EPS. If EPS is Rs 5, and the amount of dividend paid per share is Rs 2 the dividend pay-out ratio would be (2/5 × 100) or 40%. There is no guideline as to what should be the normal dividend pay-out ratio. It depends upon the common rate found in the industry as well as the existence of profitable opportunities in which profits can be invested. A detailed discussion on this is found in Chapter 17 dealing with dividend decisions.

Dividend yield is the ratio of dividend per share to the market price per share. This indicates the current rate of return to the investors, particularly those who desire dividends as a source of income.

19.3 APPLICATION OF RATIOS

19.3.1 Financial Statements

Since the computation of various ratios involves two types of corporate financial statements—the income statement and the balance sheet—they are shown hereunder, on the basis of which these ratios will be computed.

Table 19.1 *Income Statement of ABC Co. for the year Ending, 31 December, 2003*

	Amount (Rs)	Amount (Rs)
Net sales		27,00,000
Less: Cost of goods sold		22,00,000
Gross margin		5,00,000
Less: Administrative expenses	1,50,000	
Selling expenses	1,15,000	
Lease payments	10,000	2,75,000
Operating Income (EBIT)		2,25,000
Add: Revenues on account of interest and royalty		1,500
Operating Income plus other incomes...		2,26,500
Less: Interest payment		26,500
Net Income before taxes(NIBT)...		2,00,000
Less: Taxes @ 30%		60,000
Net income (NIAT)...		1,40,000
Dividends		50,000
Increase in retained earnings		90,000

Table 19.2 *Balance Sheet of ABC Co. as on 31 December, 2003*

Liabilities	*Amount (Rs)*	*Assets*	*Amount (Rs)*
Accounts payable	75,000	Cash	35,000
Bank loans (15%)	1,00,000	Marketable securities	15,000
Accruals	10,000	Bills receivable	2,25,000
Tax payable	40,000	Inventory	1,75,000
Total current liabilities	2,25,000	Total current assets	4,50,000
Mortgage bonds (10%)	75,000	Gross plant and equipment	10,50,000
Debentures (10%)	2,00,000	Allowance for depreciation	2,50,000
Equity shares of Rs 10 each	2,50,000	Net plant and equipment	8,00,000
Retained earnings	5,00,000		
Total	12,50,000		12,50,000

Note: The amount of before-tax sinking fund contribution is Rs 12,500

19.3.2 Computation of the Ratios

A. Liquidity Ratios

1. Current Ratio = (4,50,000/2,25,000) = 2/1
2. Quick Ratio = (4,50,000 – 1,75,000)/2,25,000 = 1.22/1
3. Average collection period = 2,25,000 360/27,00,000 = 30 days
4. Receivable turnover ratio = 27,00,000/2,25,000 = 12/1
5. Inventory turnover = 22,00,000/1,75,000 = 12.57/1
   (Generally the average of the closing and opening inventories is taken)

B. Profitability Ratios:

1. Profit margin = 2,25,000/27,00,000 = 8.33%
2. Gross profit margin = 5,00,000/27,00,000 = 18.52%
3. Net profit margin = 1,40,000/27,00,000 = 5.19%
4. Return on investment = 2,25,000/12,50,000 = 18%
5. Return on equity = 1,40,000/7,50,000 = 18.67%
6. Earning power = 1,40,000/12,50,000 = 11.2%

C. Ownership Ratios:

1. *Earning Ratios:*
   (i) Earning per share (EPS) = 1,40,000/25,000 = Rs 5.6
   (ii) P/E ratio = Rs 11.20/5.6 = 2/1 (assuming market price of share as Rs 11.20)
   (iii) Capitalisation rate = Rs 5.6/11.20 = 0.5 or 50%
2. *Capital Structure Ratios:*
   (i) Debt/Equity ratio = 5,00,000/7,50,000 = 5/7.50 or 66.66%
   (ii) Debt-asset ratio = 5,00,000/12,50,000 = 5/12.50 = 40%
   (iii) Times interest earned ratio = 2,25,000/26,500 = 8.49/1
   (iv) Fixed-charges coverage ratio = (2,25,000 + 10,000 + 1,500)/(26,500 + 10,000 + 12,500) = 4.83/1
   (v) Book value of share = Rs 7,50,000/25,000 = Rs 30 per share
3. *Dividend Ratios:*
   (i) Dividend pay-out ratio = Rs 2/5.56 = 35.97%
   (ii) Dividend yield = Rs 2/11.20 = 17.99%

19.4 USES OF RATIO ANALYSIS

The first few lines of the present chapter have pointed out the usefulness of the financial ratios to those who manage a firm as well as to those who are related to it in any way, such as, creditors, investors, financial analysts and so on. In order to avoid duplication, it is discussed here how the different ratios should be used in order to arrive at any conclusion. In fact, any ratio per se cannot be a perfect indicator of a firm's performance or financial position unless it is viewed against, or in comparison to some norm. In the generality of cases, the norm is the industry average. For example, if the current ratio in a particular industry is, on an average, 2:1, a firm having current ratio of 2:1 would be said to be conforming to this norm. Any deviation on either side would mean either illiquidity or a more than desired level of liquidity. The reason behind this type of intra-industry comparison is that different firms in the same industry have financial ratios more or less in common. However, if a majority of firms in the industry are facing illiquidity, any comparison of the current ratio of the firm with the industry average would be a misleading one.

Sometimes a particular ratio of a firm is compared with a similar ratio of another firm in some other industry or industries. This is known as an inter-industry comparison which indicates variations between different industries.

When a financial analyst or a creditor or an investor looks into the financial ratios of a firm, he or she must ensure the reliability of the norm against which the ratios are viewed, and, at the same time, he or she should view the ratios in totality.

Sometimes a particular ratio of a firm is compared with a similar ratio of another firm in some other industry or industries. This is known as an inter-industry comparison which indicates variations between different industries. It is, however, very difficult to say whether a particular firm is doing well or is lagging behind, as firms in different industries operate under varying settings.

Sometimes when a trend is to be found out, whether, it is moving upward or downward with respect to profitability or liquidity or in some other financial aspects during a period of time, the ratios are compared on an inter-period or time-series basis. For example, if a firm's profit margin is 20% in 1985 as against 18% in 1984 and 15% in 1983, its profitability trend is said to be an upward one.

Here it would be relevant to mention that the different financial ratios of a firm are interrelated and must therefore be evaluated together and not individually. For example, a low current ratio does not matter much in the long-run if the debt ratio is low because the firm can safely raise long-term debt to finance its current assets and thereby repay its short-term liabilities. Similarly, a lower profit margin does not matter much if the firm has reduced prices with a view to raising its sales volume because in such case the yield on investment would be quite high even with a lower profit margin. This type of inter-relationship must be taken into account.

In short, whenever, a financial analyst or a creditor or an investor looks into the financial ratios of a firm, he or she must ensure the reliability of the norm against which the ratios are viewed, and, at the same time, he or she should view the ratios in totality.

19.5 LIMITATIONS OF FINANCIAL RATIO ANALYSIS

Those who use financial ratio analysis for decision-making purposes must also be aware of its limitations. This analysis cannot be a true guide to a firm's performance as it does not help the analyst go deep into operational intricacies. For example, if a firm does not maintain a sound depreciation policy and declares large profits, high profitability ratios would simply be deceptive. With any breakdown of machines, the production process would be severely interrupted and the profitability ratio would unexpectedly show a sharp decline.

Again, the prices of the output as well as of the current assets change frequently which may produce distortions in accounting measures of performance and financial position.

Yet again, reliability of the norms against which the ratios are viewed, is often doubtful. Unless the norm is reliable, any inference drawn on the basis of ratios may be misleading. Thus, those, who interpret the ratios, must supplement the financial ratio analysis with other tools to check its reliability.

The published industry averages are simply approximations. They are not very exact. Nor are they representative sample of the firms in an industry. Even in an industry, accounting norms differ among different firms and so it is difficult to find out a particular ratio well applicable to different firms.

Last but not least, many firms experience seasonality in their operations. The month-end inventory balance of a particular month may not be interpreted equally for different firms. So on all these counts, the ratios cannot be a true guide.

SUMMARY

Financial ratios, representing the relationship between two sets of financial data, are the indicators of a firm's performance and provide vital information in which the management, the creditors, the investors and financial analysts in general are interested. The firm's ratios are compared with the industry norm, with those of similar firms in other industry or industries or on a time-series basis. This comparison makes deviations clear and the management adopts financial measures accordingly.

There are broadly three types of ratios: the liquidity ratio which indicates the liquidity position in a firm and manifests in various forms, e.g., current ratio, quick ratio, receivables ratio and inventory turnover ratio, the profitability ratio which gives information about profitability and is manifest in the profit margin, return on investment, return on equity and earning power ratio; and the ownership ratio. The ownership ratios are either earning ratios showing eps, p/e ratio and the capitalisation rate, or the capital structure ratio showing debt-equity ratio, debt-asset ratio, times interest earned ratio, fixed-charges coverage ratio and the book value of shares. The ownership ratios are apparent also in form of dividend ratios which reflect on the adequacy of dividends paid. Dividend ratios are either dividend pay-out ratio or the dividend yield.

Despite the usefulness of ratio analysis, there are certain limitations to it. Nevertheless, if proper care is taken, it is very useful for financial analysis and planning.

POINTS TO REMEMBER

1. What are the different types of financial ratios?
   - Liquidity ratios
   - Profitability ratios
   - Ownership ratios

2. What are the different liquidity ratios?
   - Current ratio = current asset/current liabilities
   - Quick ratio = (current asset – inventory)/current liabilities
   - Receivables turnover ratio = Annual credit sales/receivables
   - Inventory turnover ratio = Cost of goods sold/inventory
3. Name the profitability ratios.
   - Profit margin = operating profit/sales
   - Return on investment = (operating profit/sales) × (sales/assets)
   - Return on equity = Net earnings/total equity
   - Earning power ratio = Net earnings/assets
4. Name the ownership ratios.
   - Earning per share = Net profit for equity-holders/No. of outstanding equity shares
   - Price/earning ratio = MPS/EPS
   - Capitalisation rate = EPS/MPS
   - Debt-equity ratio = Total debt/total equity
   - Debt-asset ratio = Total debt/asset
   - Times interest earned ratio = EBIT/interest
   - Fixed-charges coverage ratio = (EBIT + other incomes)/(Interest + other payments)
   - Book value = Equity/No. of equity shares outstanding
   - Dividend pay-out ratio = DPS/EPS
   - Dividend yield = DPS/MPS
5. How are ratios used?
   - Comparison of ratios on a time-series basis
   - Inter-firm comparison
   - Inter-industry comparison

DESCRIPTIVE QUESTIONS

1. Describe the significance of financial ratio analysis. In what ways are ratios used for financial analysis? What are the limitations it is subject to?
2. How do you interpret liquidity in a firm? Which ratios are used for assessing liquidity?
3. How do you assess profitability in a firm? Is ROI a better guide than the return on equity for this purpose?
4. What do you mean by ownership ratio? Discuss its various forms. Is the debt-equity ratio a good measure of a firm's solvency?

OBJECTIVE-TYPE QUESTIONS

1. Mark true or false.
   (a) ROI is the net profit divided by sales.
   (b) Quick ratio is the ratio between current assets and current liabilities.
   (c) Inventory turnover ratio is equal to inventory divided by the cost of goods sold.
   (d) Asset turnover ratio is sales divided by assets.
   (e) Return on equity is the net profit divided by equity.
   (f) Capitalisation rate is the reciprocal of the P/E ratio.
   (g) A firm's ability to pay interest on its debt can be reflected through time interest earned ratio.
   (h) Equity divided by the number of outstanding shares is book value.
   (i) Dividend yield is the ratio of dividend per share to the market price of a share.
   (j) Dividend pay-out ratio is the share of the dividend in the net earning.
2. Choose the most suitable answer.
   (a) Ratios are compared:
      (i) intra-industry
      (ii) inter-industry
      (iii) both of the above
   (b) Capitalisation rate is equal to:
      (i) EPS/market price per share
      (ii) market price per share/EPS
      (iii) neither of the above
   (c) ROI is:
      (i) the product of profit margin and asset turnover
      (ii) the profit margin per share
      (iii) both of the above
   (d) Manageable size of debt is reflected through:
      (i) debt-equity ratio
      (ii) debt-asset ratio
      (iii) both of the above
   (e) Current ratio is:
      (i) current liabilities divided by current assets
      (ii) current assets divided by current liabilities
      (iii) Current assets net of inventory divided by current liabilities

NUMERICAL PROBLEMS

1. The following are the income statement and balance sheet of XYZ Co. Income Statement of XYZ Co. for the Year Ending 31 December, 2003.

	Amount (Rs)	Amount (Rs)
Net sales		30,00,000
Less: Cost of goods sold		21,00,000
Gross margin		9,00,000
Less: Administrative expenses	1,00,000	
Selling expenses	95,000	
Lease payments	15,000	2,10,000
Operating Income (EBIT)		6,90,000
Add: Revenues on account of interest and royalty		1,500
Operating Income plus other incomes...		6,91,500
Less: Interest payment		27,500
Net Income before taxes(NIBT)		6,64,000
Less: Taxes @ 30%		1,99,000
Net income (NIAT)		4,65,000
Dividends		46,500
Increase in retained earnings		4,18,500

Balance Sheet of XYZ Co. as on 31 December, 2003

Liabilities	Amount (Rs)	Assets	Amount (Rs)
Accounts payable	50,000	Cash	30,000
Bank loans (15%)	1,25,000	Marketable securities	15,000
Accruals	10,000	Bills Receivables	2,20,000
Tax payable	40,000	Inventory	1,70,000
Total current liabilities	2,25,000	Total current assets	4,35,000
Mortgage bonds (10%)	50,000	Gross plant and equipment	9,50,000
Debentures (10%)	2,25,000	Allowance for depreciation	2,00,000
Equity shares of Rs 10 each	2,50,000	Net plant and equipment	8,50,000
Retained earnings	5,35,000		
Total	12,85,000		12,85,000

Note: The amount to sinking fund contribution is Rs 10,700

Calculate:

(a) current ratio;

(b) quick ratio;

(c) receivable turnover ratio;

(d) inventory turnover ratio;

(e) profit margin;

(f) ROI;

(g) return on equity;
(h) EPS;
(i) capitalisation rate;
(j) debt-equity ratio;
(k) debt-asset ratio;
(l) book value;
(m) dividend yield.

2. If current assets amount to Rs 2,00,000 and the current ratio is 2:1, what is the size of inventory to have a quick ratio of 1.25:1?
3. If the debt/asset ratio is 3:5 and if debt amounts to Rs 3,00,000, what would be the size of owners' equity?
4. If operating profit is Rs 50,000, profit margin is 25% and assets amount to Rs 1,00,000, what would be the asset turnover ratio?
5. If the market price of a share is Rs 60, EPS is Rs 12, dividend per share is Rs 3, compute:
   (a) capitalisation rate;
   (b) dividend pay-out ratio;
   (c) dividend yield.
6. If net profit is Rs 50,000, sales is Rs 2,00,000, and the asset turnover ratio is 2:1, find out the earning power ratio.
7. If the assets to sales ratio or the capital intensity ratio is 0.5 and if the firm plans to achieve a sales target of Rs 2,00,000, what should be size of total assets required to achieve the sales target?
8. If the size of total assets is Rs 2,00,000 and if the net profit is Rs 20,000, find out the earning power ratio. If earning power ratio has to be improved to 25%, what should be the size of net profit assuming that there is no change in the amount of assets?

SOLVED NUMERICAL PROBLEMS

1. A firm has current assets for Rs 1,25,000 including an inventory for Rs 63,000. The current liabilities, on the other hand, amount to Rs 68,000. Find out the current ratio and the quick ratio, with a given industry norm of 2/1 and 1/1 respectively.

Solution

(a) Current ratio = current assets/current liabilities

= Rs 1,25,000/68,000 = 1.84/1

(b) Quick ratio = (current assets – inventory)/current liabilities

= (1,25,000 – 63,000)/68,000 = 0.91/1

Both these ratios are below the industry norm indicating liquidity lower than desired.

2. A firm has equity and debt in its capital structure amounting to Rs 2,00,000 and Rs 3,00,000 respectively. The sale amounts to Rs 8,00,000. The cost of material and

the operating cost amount to Rs 5,60,000. Find (a) profit margin, and (b) return on investment.

Solution

Operating profit = Rs 8,00,000 – 5,60,000 = Rs 2,40,000

Asset = Debt + equity

= Rs 2,00,000 + 3,00,000 = Rs 5,00,000

(a) Profit margin = Operating profit/sales

= Rs 2,40,000/8,00,000 = 0.30 or 30%

(b) Return on investment = (operating profit/sales) × (sales/assets)

= (2,40,000/8,00,000) × (8,00,000/5,00,000) = 0.48 = 48%

3. A firm has equity and debt in its capital structure amounting to Rs 2,00,000 and Rs 3,00,000 respectively. The operating profit is Rs 2,40,000. The interest payment on debt amounts to Rs 30,000. The tax rate is 30%. Find the earning power ratio.

Solution

Assets = Debt + Equity

or Rs 2,00,000 + 3,00,000 = Rs 5,00,000

Net profit = Operating profit – interest payment - taxes

= Rs 2,40,000 – 30,000 – 0.30 of Rs 2,10,000 = Rs 1,47,000

Earning power ratio = Net profit after taxes/Assets

= Rs 1,47,000/5,00,000 = 0.294 = 29.4%

4. A firm has equity and debt in its capital structure amounting respectively to Rs 2,00,000 divided in 20,000 shares of Rs 10 each and Rs 3,00,000. The market price of a share is Rs 50. The operating profit is Rs 2,40,000. The interest payment on debt amounts to Rs 30,000. The tax rate is 30%. Find (a) earning per share, (b) P/E ratio, and (c) capitalisation rate.

Solution

Net profit = Rs (2,40,000 – 30,000)(1 – 0.30) = Rs 1,47,000

(a) EPS = Net earning/Number of outstanding shares

Rs 1,47,000/20,000 = Rs 7.35

(b) P/E ratio = Market price of share/EPS

= Rs 50/7.35 = 6.80/1

(c) Capitalisation rate = EPS/MPS

= 7.35/50 = 0.147 = 14.7%

5. A firm has equity and debt in its capital structure amounting respectively to Rs 2,00,000 divided in 20,000 shares of Rs 10 each and Rs 3,00,000. Find out the debt/equity ratio and debt/asset ratio.

Solution

Debt/ equity ratio = Debt/equity

= 3,00,000/2,00,000 = 3/2

Debt/ asset ratio = Debt/asset

= 3,00,000/5,00,000 = 0.60/1

6. A firm has an equity capital of Rs 2,00,000 divided into 20,000 shares. The market price per share is Rs 50. Its net profit amounts to Rs 1,50,000. It has a dividend pay-out ratio of 60%. Find (a) dividend per share, and (b) dividend yield.

Solution

Earning per share = Net profit/No. of outstanding shares
= 1,50,000/20,000 = Rs 7.50

(a) At 60% dividend pay-out ratio,
Dividend per share = Rs 7.50 × 0.60 = Rs 4.50

(b) Dividend yield = Dividend per share/Market price of share
= Rs 4.50/50 = 0.09 = 9%

7. A firm has a share capital of Rs 2,00,000 divided in 20,000 equity shares. Besides, the reserves amount to Rs 3,00,000. The shares are selling at a premium of Rs 20. Find (a) par value of shares, (b) book value of shares, and (c) the market price of a share.

Solution

(a) Par value of shares = Rs 2,00,000/20,000 shares = Rs 10 per share

(b) Book value of a share = Total equity = share capital + reserves
= Rs 2,00,000 + 3,00,000 = Rs 5,00,000
= Rs 5,00,000/20,000 = Rs 25

(c) Market value of a share = Par value + premium/discount
= Rs 20 + 20 = Rs 40

CASE STUDY

Financial Analysis of Apollo Tools Pvt. Ltd.

The following are the income statement and balance sheet of Apollo Tools Pvt. Ltd.

Income Statement for FY 2005–06

	2005–06 Rs
Sales revenue	25,67,000
Less cost of goods sold	17,11,000
Gross profit	8,56,000
Less operating expenses	
Selling expenses	1,08,000
Administrative expenses	1,87,000
Depreciation	2,58,000
Total operating expenses	5,53,000
Operating Profit	3,03,000
Less interest paid	91,000
EBT	2,12,000
Less taxes @ 30%	63,600

	2005–06 Rs
NPAT	1,48,400
Less dividend on preference shares	10,000
Earnings available to equity shareholders	1,38,000
EPS (10,000 shares)	13.80
DPS (40% dividend pay-out ratio)	5.52

Balance Sheet as on 31 March 2006

Liabilities	Amount Rs	Assets		Amount Rs
Current liabilities	6,16,000	Current assets		
Long-term debt	11,65,250	Cash	1,25,000	
10%, 1000 Preference shares	1,00,000	B/R	7,05,556	
10,000 Ordinary shares	10,00,000	Inventory	7,00,625	15,31,181
Retained earnings	3,00,000	Fixed assets	21,50,069	
		Less dep	5,00,000	16,50,069
Total	31,81,250	Total		31,81,250

Questions:

1. Calculate the company's profitability ratios.
2. Assess the liquidity position of the company.
3. Summarise the firm's overall financial position on the basis of different ratios.

REFERENCE

Altman, Edward I. (1986). "Financial Ratios, Discriminant Analysis and the Prediction of Corporate Bankruptcy", *Journal of Finance*, 23 (Sept.): 589–609.

SELECT FURTHER READINGS

Benishay, H. (1971). "Economic Informationin Financial Ratio Analysis", *Accounting and Business Research*, 2 (Spring): 123–29.

Chen, K.H. and T.A. Shimerda (1991). "An Empirical Analysis of Useful Financial Ratios", *Financial Management*, 10 (Spring): 51–59.

20

BREAK-EVEN ANALYSIS

OBJECTIVES

To highlight the concept of break-even analysis

To explain the determination of break-even point in case of a single commodity/mix of commodities

To evaluate the use of the break-even analysis for profit planning

To pinpoint the limitations to the break-even analysis

Finance managers interpret financial ratios for policy measures. But, at the same time, they also plan the profit. The process of profit planning is a two-step one. The first step is to have an idea of the break-even output, where revenue is able to recover the total cost. When this point is established, the second step begins when the finance manager designs the costs, volume and price so as to plan the profit. The present chapter discusses these issues.

20.1 SIGNIFICANCE OF BREAK-EVEN ANALYSIS

When a firm begins operations, it plans for sales that will yield desired profits. It may so happen that in course of the operations the sales volume contracts due to reduction in demand. Contrarily, a rise in demand for the product may demand an increase in sales. Similarly, the cost may rise due to rise in the prices of raw material. It may also decrease as a result of cost-controlling measures. A firm may have to reduce the price of the goods produced in the face of keen competition in the market. Whichever may be the case, it is very important for the management to know the relationship between cost, output, and profits so that it can consider pricing and cost structure changes for achieving greater profitability.

While determining the size of output, the finance manager has to ensure that, first, it covers the total cost including both fixed and the variable costs, and second, that it yields the desired amount of profit. Had there been no fixed cost, the question of covering the cost would not have posed a problem. Let us assume for a moment that there exists only variable cost in a pen-manufacturing firm, and that it is Rs 1.20 per pen as compared to a sale price of Rs 2.00 per pen.

A profit of Re 0.80 per pen would be reaped. It does not matter how many pens the firm must manufacture in order to cover the cost. The operation is profitable at any point of output. However, in real life, it is not only variable costs that exist; fixed cost is also an essential part of the total cost, and it remains unchanged over a relevant range of output. If the fixed cost in the firm amounts to Rs 400, it will remain Rs 400 whether the firm is manufacturing a single pen or thousands of pens (which is the relevant range). In such cases, if the firm manufactures and sells, say, 200 pens, the variable cost would be Rs (200 × 1.20) or Rs 240 and combining it with the fixed cost of Rs 400, the total cost would be Rs 640. The revenue, on the other hand, would be only Rs (200 × 2.00) or Rs 400. The firm will therefore incur a loss of Rs 240. The cost would be covered only if the firm produces 500 pens. In that case, the variable cost would be Rs 600 and adding to it the fixed cost of Rs 400, the total cost would be Rs 1000. At the same time, the revenue would be Rs (500 × 2.00) or Rs 1000. The entire cost would be covered but the operation would not yield profits. The profits will arise if the firm manufactures and sells more than 500 pens.

> While determining the size of output, the finance manager has to ensure that, first, it covers the total cost including both fixed and the variable costs, and second, that it yields the desired amount of profit.

The above example showing the relationship between the cost, output, and profits is a very simple one. In fact, the finance manager may have to face many complex situations with changes in the cost structure, prices and the output. However, break-even analysis comes to the rescue of the finance manger since this analysis deals with the relationship between cost, output and profits and it explains how profit varies with changes in the sales volume or with changes in cost and price. With this analytical tool, the finance manager compares profits from different levels of output under different cost and price structures and thereby selects the best strategy for investment or marketing.

20.2 DETERMINATION OF BREAK-EVEN POINT

The most important step in the break-even analysis is the determination of the break-even point (BEP). BEP refers to that level of operation at which a firm makes neither profit nor loss. It refers to a zero level of profit where the revenue equals the cost.

20.2.1 Graphical Presentation

The BEP can be depicted on a graph (See Fig. 20.1). Rupees are shown on the vertical axis or y-axis and units of output on the horizontal axis or x-axis. By its very nature the fixed cost is constant, and that is why it is shown with a straight horizontal line. The variable cost is zero at the zero level of production but it changes directly with the number of units produced. That is why its curve starts from the vertex and moves upward with an increase in output. The curve representing the total cost combines in it both fixed and the variable costs. The revenue curve, on the other hand, is shown diagonally beginning at the vertex and rising more quickly than the total cost. It is but natural that the revenue per unit of production will be more than

> BEP refers to that level of operation at which a firm makes neither profit nor loss. It refers to a zero level of profit where the revenue equals the cost.

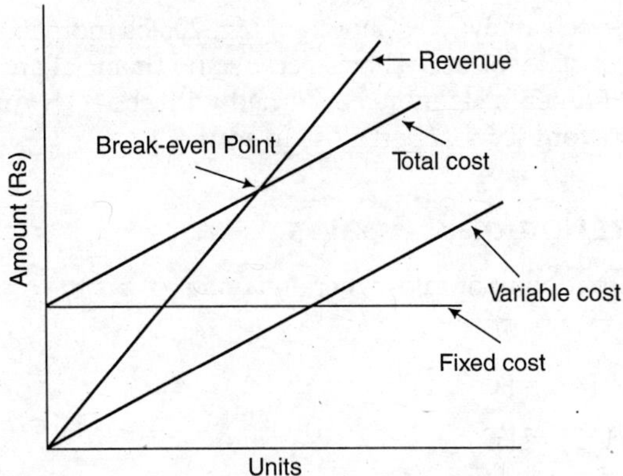

FIG. 20.1 Break-even point

the variable cost per unit. The break-even point lies where total cost is equal to the total revenue and represents a sales level of 500 units. Beyond this point, with sales of more than 500 units, profits will accrue to the firm. This means that the firm will incur losses at any level of sales prior to the BEP.

In Fig. 20.1, we find a linear relationship or straight-line relationship. But reality is more close to a non-linear relationship where increased sales can be obtained only when sale price is reduced, or where average variable cost per unit falls over limited range of output. In Fig. 20.2, the total cost curve meets the revenue curve twice. First, at the lower break-even point where it intersects the revenue curve from above, and, second, at the higher break-even point where it intersects the revenue curve from below. Thus it shows two loss zones—one prior to Point A and the other after Point B. The sales level with the maximum profit is also indicated in this Figure.

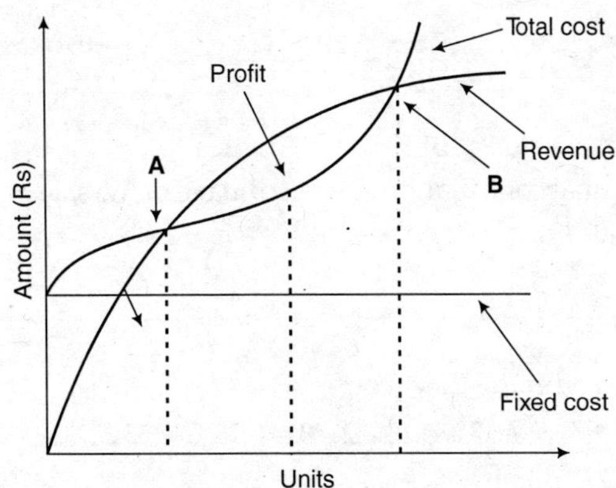

FIG. 20.2 Non-linear break-even analysis

Non-linear break-even analysis as shown in Fig. 20:2 is more logical. However, linear analysis is more appropriate for use. This is because no financial analyst is interested in a high or low extreme. Rather, he is more concerned with the relevant range within which the linear functions are for the most part close to accuracy.

20.2.2 Computation of BEP Sales

Since BEP represents that point of sales where revenue equals the cost:

$$P.Q = FC + VC.Q$$

or $$P.Q - VC.Q = FC$$

or $$Q(P - VC) = FC$$

or $$Q = FC/(P - VC) \quad \text{(at the break-even } Q\text{)} \qquad ...(20.1)$$

Here:

P = the sales price per unit
Q = the quantity produced and sold
FC = the fixed cost
VC = the variable cost per unit

EXAMPLE

A firm has a fixed cost of Rs 20,000, the variable cost per unit of output is Rs 2, and the selling price is Rs 3 per unit. Therefore its BEP will be:

$$20{,}000/(3 - 2) = 20{,}000 \text{ units}$$

In terms of sales value, it would be Rs (20,000 × 3) or Rs 60,000.

However, to calculate the BEP in terms of sales value, there is another formula which is as follows:

$$S_{bep} = FC/MC\% \qquad ...(20.2)$$

Where:

S_{bep} = rupee sales value at BEP
$MC\%$ = the marginal contribution as a percentage of the sale price which is computed as $(P - VC)/P$.

EXAMPLE

Based on the above example. S_{bep} will be:

$$MC\% = (3 - 2)/3 = 0.33\% = 33\%.$$

Therefore:

$$S_{bep} = \text{Rs } (20{,}000/0.33) = \text{Rs } 60{,}000$$

20.3 BREAK-EVEN POINT AND PROFIT PLANNING

After BEP is determined, the finance manager plans for profits. This can be done in three ways. They are as follows:

1. Increasing the sales volume;
2. Increasing the sales price;
3. Decreasing the cost, both fixed and variable.

20.3.1 Increase in Sales Volume

Since the volume of sales over and above the BEP allows a firm to reap profits, the firm, in normal course, plans to achieve a level of output and sales at a point beyond the BEP. It depends upon a couple of factors. One is the amount of profits the firm would like to earn; and the other is a certain margin of safety that the firm likes to maintain in view of the fact that a reduced level of activity as a result of reduction in demand may not put the firm to loss.

Let us first explain how the output is determined with a given level of profit. For this purpose, planned profit is added to the fixed cost and then the total amount is divided by the contribution margin percentage.

Sales along with a given profit = (*FC* + *Profit*)/*MC*% ...(20.3)

EXAMPLE

A firm plans to earn Rs 20,000 with a fixed cost of Rs 20,000 and a 33.3% contribution margin. Find out the size of sales.

Sales = Rs [(20,000 + 20,000)/0.33] = Rs 1,20,000

If the sale price per unit is Rs 3, the size of output or sales would be (1,20,000/3) = 40,000 units.

The margin of safety which is the difference between actual sales and the BEP sales would thus be Rs (1,20,000 – 60,000), or Rs 60,000, or expressing it in terms of the percentage of sales, it would be 50%.

> The margin of safety is the difference between actual sales and the BEP sales expressed in terms of the percentage of sales.

Interpreting these facts in another way, it can be said that the break-even analysis helps us to ascertain the profit with changing levels of output. Interpreting Eq. 20.3, we find that:

Profit = (*Sales* × *MC*%) – *FC* ...(20.4)

EXAMPLE

On the basis of the above data, the amount of profits at a sales level of Rs 1,50,000 can easily be computed.

Profit = Rs [(1,50,000 × 0.33) – 20,000] = Rs 30,000

20.3.2 Increase in Sale Price

It is not only the increase in the volume of sales beyond the BEP that leads to the emergence of profits. The firm can also reap profits by increasing the price of the commodity. The explanation here is obvious. An increase in the sales price raises the marginal contribution which in turn, lowers the BEP. The volume of output and sales being constant, any lowering of BEP leads to the emergence of profits, since the level of output is automatically higher than the BEP output.

EXAMPLE

Suppose a firm raises the price of its output from Rs 3 to Rs 4 per unit, the MC% would be [(4 – 2)/4] or 0.5 or 50%. The BEP with a fixed cost of Rs 20,000 as mentioned in the earlier examples, would be Rs 40,000 instead of Rs 60,000. And with a sale value of Rs 1,20,000, the profits will be reaped to the extent of Rs [(1,20,000 × 0.5) – 20,000] = Rs 40,000 as against Rs 20,000, when the price was Rs 3 per unit.

These changes are shown in Fig. 20.3.

However, one should not forget that raising of price in order to earn profits depends largely upon the elasticity of demand for the product in question and also the prices charged by competing firms in the industry.

20.3.3 Varying Costs and Level of Profits

Changes in the fixed costs and the variable costs, both influence the BEP. If these costs rise, achievement of the BEP is delayed or, in other words, BEP shifts upwards with no change in other variables. The result is that profit either contracts or disappears or losses may even be incurred. On the other hand, a decrease in these costs lowers the BEP and consequently profits either arise or expand. An example can make clear these changes and their impact on the BEP.

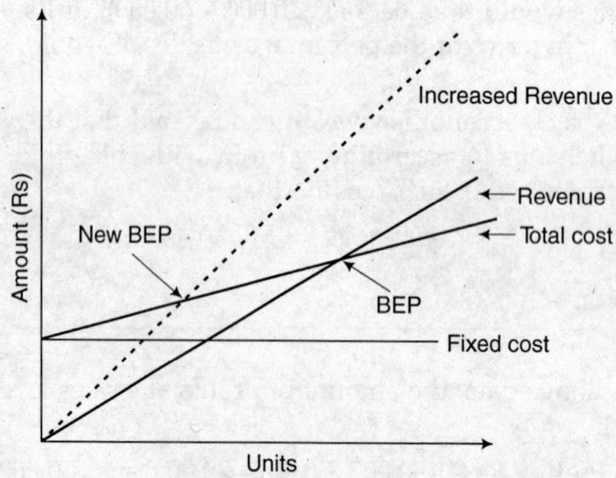

FIG. 20.3 Higher profit with increase in sale price

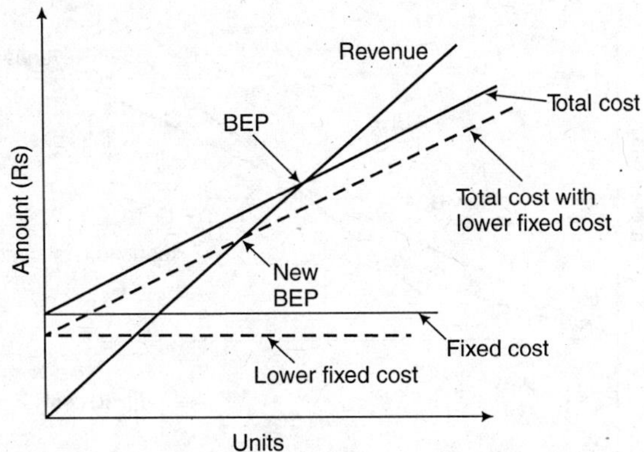

FIG. 20.4 Changes in fixed cost and the impact on BEP

EXAMPLE

Suppose cost control methods bring down the fixed costs to Rs 18,000 from Rs 20,000. If the sale price and the variable cost remain constant at Rs 3 and Rs 2 respectively, BEP will shift backward to Rs 54,000 from a previous level of Rs 60,000, and if the firm produces the same level of output, that is, 20,000 units, profits for Rs 2,000 will emerge.

The effect of decrease in fixed cost is shown in Fig. 20:4.

Similarly, the impact of the changes in variable cost can be shown with an example. If such costs drop, BEP will shift favourably and profits will emerge.

EXAMPLE

If a decrease in the prices of raw material or its efficient use reduces the variable cost from Rs 2 to Rs 1.40, the BEP with a fixed cost of Rs 20,000 will shift from Rs 60,000 to Rs 37,500. If the firm produces the same 20,000 units, profits will accrue to the extent of Rs 12,500.

The impact of decrease in the variable cost on the BEP is shown in Fig. 20:5.

Sometimes the firm has some control over the relationship between fixed costs and variable costs. In the above examples fixed cost is Rs 20,000 and variable cost is Rs 2 per unit. If the firm purchases modern equipment that increase the fixed cost on account of maintenance, insurance, etc., to Rs 25,000, but at the same time, increased efficiency of the new machine lowers the variable cost to Rs 1.50 per unit. In this case the marginal contribution rises to 0.5 or 50% in turn lowering the BEP, and, as a consequence, increasing the quantum of profits similarly as in case of increase in the sales price.

In short, changes in cost, sale price and the volume of sales change the BEP and influence the amount of profits. This means that the break-even analysis determines the relationship between profits on the one hand, and cost, price and the sale volume on the other.

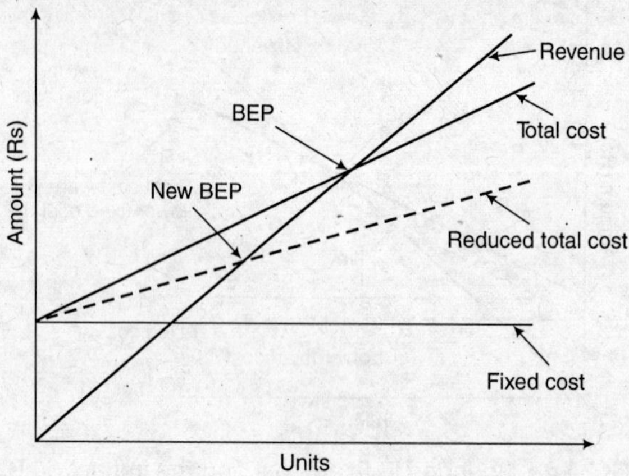

FIG. 20.5 Changes in variable cost and their impact on BEP

20.4 SALES-MIX AND BREAK-EVEN ANALYSIS

The determination of BEP becomes a little cumbersome if more than one product is involved. The added task in such cases is to calculate the weighted average of the marginal contributions. Since different products have different costs—fixed and variable, as also different sale prices, their marginal contribution has to differ. It is because of this difference that a weighted average is computed.

EXAMPLE

Suppose a firm sells two products—A and B. For Product A, the variable cost is Rs 2 and the sale price is Rs 4 per unit. For Product B, the variable cost and the sale price are Rs 3 and Rs 5 respectively per unit. The fixed cost of the firm is Rs 40,000. Now the marginal contribution for Product A would be [(4 – 2)/4] or 50%. Product B has a marginal contribution of [(5 – 3)/5] or 40%. If the relative share of these two products in the total sales is equal, the weighted average of the marginal contributions would be:

$$\{[(50 \times 1) + (40 \times 1)]/2\} = 45\%$$

The BEP sales would be: (Rs 40,000/0.45) = Rs 88,000

If the relative proportion of the two products changes to 3:1, the weighted average of the marginal contribution will change to:

$$\{[(50 \times 3) + (40 \times 1)]/(3 + 1)\} = 47.5\%$$

The BEP in this changed condition would be;

Rs (40,000/0.475) = Rs 84,210.53

20.5 USES OF BREAK-EVEN ANALYSIS

The usefulness of the break-even analysis is clear from the introductory section of the present chapter. Nevertheless, it would not be wrong to highlight some other uses of this analysis.

First, the break-even analysis helps in contemplating whether a new product should be added to the existing product line in the light of its estimated revenue and cost, or, whether, certain items should be dropped from the product line. This way, sound product planning can be done with the help of this analysis.

Second, this analysis helps in make-or-buy decisions which manufacturing firms often encounter. For example, an automobile manufacturer is posed with the question as to whether he should buy a spark plug or whether he should manufacture it. If the variable cost is less than the price that has to be paid to an outside supplier, it may be better to manufacture than to buy it.

Third, the break-even analysis is a useful technique for calculating the effects of installing equipment or its replacement on the basis of costs, revenues and profits.

20.6 LIMITATIONS OF BREAK-EVEN ANALYSIS

Despite the usefulness of the break-even analysis in the decision-making process, there are certain limitations to its usefulness. The results shown are often not completely accurate under all conditions, insofar as there are a number of factors which could influence them appreciably. For example, an increase in selling price may cause a reduction in the sales volume which is generally not taken into account in this analysis. Again, if the firm sells more than one product, the break-even chart of the firm as a whole, showing cost and revenue, does not truly represent these variables for any one product. Yet again, this analysis does not take into consideration the capital employed which may be a very important factor. Last, but not least, fixed costs are constant only over a relevant range of output, beyond which they change. Their presentation on a straight horizontal line is thus misleading. Nevertheless, if proper care is taken of these factors, this analysis is certainly an important tool of decision-making.

SUMMARY

Break-even analysis shows the relationship between the cost, price and the volume of output, and helps determine the level of output that covers the total cost and yields a desired amount of profit. In this way it serves as a tool of profit planning.

The first step in this analysis is to determine the break-even point (BEP) which indicates that very point of output that barely covers the cost, or where total revenue is equal to total cost. The process to arrive at BEP is to divide the fixed cost by the percentage of the contribution margin. In case the firm produces more than one product, the fixed cost is divided by the weighted average of percentage of the contribution margin. After BEP is determined, it is easy for the finance manager to plan for profits. This is done by either increasing the sales volume, or by increasing the price of the product, or decreasing the cost, both fixed and variable.

Despite a few limitations, this analysis is very useful not only in profit planning but also in deciding about replacement, buy-versus-manufacture or about adding a new product to the existing line of production, and for taking certain other decisions.

POINTS TO REMEMBER

1. What is break-even analysis? Why is it significant?
   - Break-even analysis deals with the determination of the output size that can be had with zero profit.
   - It is an important tool for profit planning.
   - It helps in make/buy decisions.
   - It is useful in decisions regarding replacement of machine.
2. How is break-even point determined?
   - It lies at a point where the sum of fixed and variable costs = revenue from sale or in other words,

$$Q = FC/(P - VC)$$

3. In which circumstances, does BEP change?
   - Increase/decrease in volume of sales
   - Increase/decrease in sale price
   - Increase/decrease in fixed cost
   - Increase/decrease in variable cost
4. Can sales be planned to earn a desired profit?
   - Yes. Planned sales = (FC + desired profit)/MC%
5. How do you arrive at BEP in case of sales-mix?
   - FC is divided by the weighted average of MC%

DESCRIPTIVE QUESTIONS

1. Explain the significance of the break-even analysis. What are the limitations it is subjected to?

2. What do you mean by Break-even Point? How do you arrive at it? Explain it with the help of a graph.
3. Explain how a desired amount of profit is planned through changes in the break-even point.
4. What do you mean by margin of safety? Explain its relevance in the context of break-even analysis.
5. Describe sales mix. How is it related to BEP?

OBJECTIVE-TYPE QUESTIONS

1. Mark true or false.
   (a) BEP denotes a point where revenue exceeds cost.
   (b) BEP is meaningless if there is no fixed cost involved in production.
   (c) Break-even analysis does not explain any relationship between cost, output and profit.
   (d) The amount of sales at BEP is reflected through the ratio of fixed cost and margin of contribution.
   (e) BEP can be changed through changes in the sale price.
   (f) BEP cannot be changed through changes in the fixed and variable costs.
   (g) Margin of safety is the difference between actual sales and BEP sales.
   (h) In case of sales mix, weighted average of contribution margin is relied upon for arriving at BEP.
2. Choose the most suitable answer.
   (a) The results of break-even analysis cannot be relied upon, because:
      (i) increase in sale price may lower the volume of sales
      (ii) it does not take into account the amount of capital employed
      (iii) both of the above
   (b) In case of sales mix, BEP depends on:
      (i) weighted average of contribution margin
      (ii) contribution margin of any one product
      (iii) none of the above
   (c) The margin of safety depends on:
      (i) fixed and variable cost
      (ii) actual sales and BEP sales
      (iii) none of the above
   (d) Sales at BEP is equal to:
      (i) Fixed cost divided by price
      (ii) Fixed cost divided by the difference of price and variable cost
      (iii) None of the above

(e) Margin of contribution % is equal to:
  (i) the difference of price and variable cost divided by price
  (ii) the difference of fixed cost and variable cost divided by price
  (iii) none of the above.

NUMERICAL PROBLEMS

1. If fixed cost is Rs 50,000, variable cost is Rs 15 per unit and sales price is Rs 20 per unit, find out BEP in terms of:
   (a) no. of units, and
   (b) value.
2. Based on the figures in Q. 1., above, compute the volume of production/sales if the firm desires to earn a profit amounting to Rs 30,000.
3. Find the margin of safety if the actual sales amount to Rs 90,000 and the BEP sales amount to Rs 50,000.
4. A firm produces two products, A and B. the total fixed cost is Rs 50,000. The variable cost and sale price per unit is Rs 3 and Rs 5 respectively for Product A and Rs 4 and Rs 6 for Product B. Both of the products are produced in equal proportions. Find out the BEP.
5. A company produces three products – A, B and C. The combined (non-separable) fixed cost is Rs 10 lakh to be allocated in the ratio of 2:3:5 respectively to A, B and C. The respective sale price is Rs 50, Rs 60 and Rs 90 with variable cost of Rs 30, Rs 40 and Rs 50. The separable fixed cost is respectively Rs 3 lakh, Rs 3 lakh and Rs 4 lakh for Products A, B and C. Find out the break-even point in terms of quantity for each of the products.
6. With a fixed cost of Rs 60,000, sale price per unit of Rs 15 and variable cost per unit of Rs 10, compute BEP. Will BEP change in terms of quantity if sale price moves up to Rs 16?

SOLVED NUMERICAL PROBLEMS

1. Find the BEP of production in terms of unit and in terms of value if the price of the product is Rs 250 per unit; variable cost is Rs 150 per unit and the fixed cost is Rs 1,50,000.

Solution

In terms of unit:

BEP = FC/(SP – VC)

= 1,50,000/(250 – 150) =1,500 units

In terms of value:

BEP = FC/MC%

MC% = (SP – VC)/SP

= Rs (250 – 150)/ 250 = 0.40 = 40%

= Rs 1,50,000/0.40 = Rs 3,75,000

2. If the product's demand is price-inelastic, the firm raises the price of the product from Rs 250 to Rs 300 with the same variable cost of Rs 150 and the unchanged fixed cost of Rs 1,50,000. Will the BEP change from that when it remains unchanged?

Solution

BEP with an increase in SP:

Rs 1,50,000/(300 – 150) = 1,000 units

3. The firm finds a very tough competition and is forced to reduce the price of the product from Rs 250 to Rs 210 with the same variable cost of Rs 150 and the unchanged fixed cost of Rs 1,50,000. Will the BEP change from that when it remains unchanged?

Solution

BEP with a cut in SP:

Rs 1,50,000/(210 – 150) = 2,500 units

4. The firm faces tough competition and takes up economy measures with the result that both fixed cost and variable cost come down. Fixed cost shrinks to Rs 1,40,000 and variable cost falls to Rs 140 per unit. The sale price remains unchanged at Rs 250 per unit. Find the new BEP.

Solution

BEP with reduced fixed and variable cost:

= Rs 1,40,000/(250 – 140) = 1,272.72 or 1,273 units

5. If a company plans to earn at least Rs 2,00,000 in order to maintain a desired level of earning per share, what would be the amount of production with a given fixed cost of Rs 1,50,000, variable cost of Rs 150 per unit and sale price of Rs 250 per unit?

Solution

Planned level of output = (FC + Profit)/(SP – VC)

(1,50,000 + 2,00,000)/(250 – 150) = 3,500 units

6. A firm produces three complementary products with a combined fixed cost of Rs 2,00,000. Product A has a price of Rs 20 with a variable cost of Rs 12 per unit. Product B has a sale price of Rs 8 with a variable cost of Rs 6 per unit and Product C has a sale price of Rs 25 with a variable cost of Rs 10 per unit. Find the BEP in terms of value of the output if the three products are produced in the ratio of 30:30:40.

Solution

Marginal contribution of:

Product A = (20 – 12)/20 = 0.40 = 40%

Product B = (8 – 6)/8 = 0.25 = 25%

Product C = (25 – 10)/25 = 0.60 = 60%

Weighted average of marginal contribution

$= 0.40 \times 0.30 + 0.25 \times 0.30 + 0.60 \times 0.40$

$= 0.435 = 43.5\%$

BEP = Rs 2,00,000/43.5% = Rs 4,59, 770.11

Mini Case

Paras Biscuits produces biscuits for last 10 years. In the beginning, its scale of operation was very small. But with growing demand for its product, it increased the size of its production. A couple of years back, it bought a bigger machine to sustain increasing production. But unfortunately, only 80% of the capacity is utilised presently. The total turnover is Rs 8,00,000 at the rate of Rs 25 per unit.

The details of the cost structure show that material cost is Rs 7.00 per unit. Labour cost per unit is Rs 6.75. Semi-variable cost is Rs 1,80,000 that includes variable cost of Rs 4.00 per unit. Fixed cost is Rs 85,000 up to 80% of the output, beyond which it goes up by Rs 20,000.

The owner of the factory likes to know the answer to the following questions:

Questions:

1. What would be the level of activity at the break-even point?
2. If it likes to earn 10% of the sales, what would be the number of units to be produced?
3. If the owner likes to make a profit of Rs 1,00,000, what should be the size of output?
4. What would be the sale price if BEP is brought down to 40% of the activity?

SELECT FURTHER READINGS

Levy, H. and R. Brooks (1986). "Financial Break-even Analysis and the Value of the Firm", *Financial Management*, 15 (Autumn): 22–26.

Raun, D.L. (1964). "The Limitation of Profit Graphs, Break-even Analysis and Budgets", *Accounting Review*, 39 (Oct.): 366–71.

21

LEVERAGE

OBJECTIVES

To explain what leverage actually means

To elucidate the ROI leverage

To discuss different forms of marginal-analysis leverage, such as operating leverage, fixed-charge leverage and combined leverage

To explain financial leverage

In general sense, a lever is the term used to refer to anything used to move something up, and leverage is therefore the advantage gained from the operation of a lever. This term is also used in corporate finance with a somewhat similar connotation. The discussion of leverage in this area of study is related to the acceleration of profits through changes in certain financial variables, which means in turn that leverage is a tool of profit planning.

Since the purpose of leverage is to raise profits, a high degree of leverage gives a big push upward to profits. Sometimes, however, it may act in the opposite direction, with a higher degree of leverage causing greater losses to the firm. It is for this reason that leverage is said to be a double-edged blade. If properly used, it serves its purpose well and its effects are favourable, on the other hand, when not properly employed, its effect may be unfavourable and it may prove a costly device.

Leverage can operate in different ways. Based on the ways in which it operates, it can primarily be grouped under three heads:

1. Return-on-Investment (ROI) Leverage
2. Marginal-Analysis Leverage
3. Financial Leverage

Their nature and operation will be discussed here.

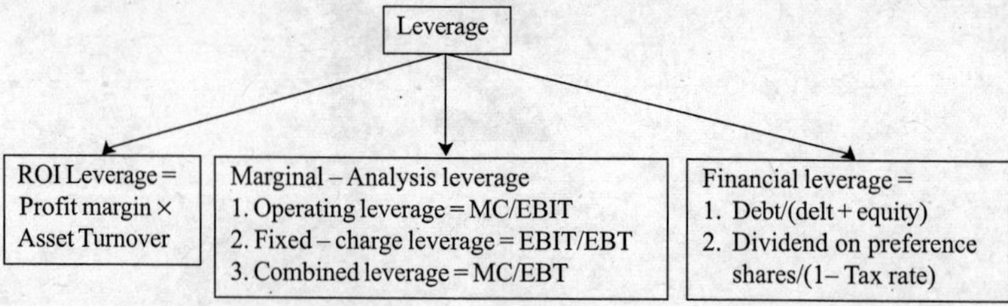

21.1 RETURN-ON-INVESTMENT LEVERAGE

Roi indicating a firm's efficiency in earning profits is a function of both the profit margin and asset turnover.

It has already been pointed out in Chapter 19 that the ROI indicating a firm's efficiency in earning profits is a function of both the profit margin and asset turnover. Based on Eq. 19.6 in Chapter 19, we can state that, ROI is a function of:

1. Operating profit
2. Sales
3. Asset turnover

Any improvement in ROI can be brought about by reducing various costs – production, selling and administrative – so as to raise earning before interest and taxes (EBIT) and thereby the profit margin. At the same time, ROI can be raised through reducing investment in assets with the same amount of sales or raising the volume of sales with the same amount of assets. These two alternatives may be used singly or together.

EXAMPLE

Suppose that a firm's sales is Rs 20,000, the operating profit amounts to Rs 5,000 and the assets are valued at Rs 10,000. Its ROI will then be:

$$\text{Profit margin} = 25\%$$
$$\text{Asset turnover} = 2$$
$$\text{ROI} = (25\% \times 2) = 50\%$$

If profit margin rises to 30% as a result of cost control measures and if assets are reduced to Rs 8,000, ROI will move up to:

$$\text{ROI} = (30\% \times 2.5) = 75\%$$

ROI leverage shows how a small change in the profit margin and asset turnover causes a much larger change in the ROI.

21.2 MARGINAL-ANALYSIS LEVERAGE

Marginal-analysis leverage relates the profit measure to certain other aspects of a firm's operations or financial situation. When it is concerned with the operating situation, operating leverage is said to exist, and, on the other hand, when it is concerned with the financial situation, it is the fixed-charges leverage that exists, when both types of the leverage exist, it is termed combined leverage. Thus marginal-analysis leverage is of three types. They are as follows:

1. Operating leverage
2. Fixed-charges leverage
3. Combined leverage

21.2.1 Operating Leverage

Operating leverage exists when changes in revenue (sales) produce greater changes in the operating profit.

Operating leverage exists when changes in revenue (sales) produce greater changes in the operating profit. This happens because fixed operating costs constitute a part of the total cost structure. Here it may be borne in the mind that fixed operating costs include fixed production, administrative and distribution costs, and not the interest on debt. Interest on debt is a fixed financial cost. The larger the fixed operating cost, the greater is the part of marginal contribution that is applied to cover the fixed cost. Once the break-even point is reached, the entire marginal contribution takes the form of operating profit, with the result that a 1% increase in sales will lead to a more than 1% increase in operating profit.

The degree of operating leverage (DOL) is computed by dividing the marginal contribution by the operating profit. In the form of an equation, DOL can be expressed as follows:

$$DOL = Marginal\ contribution/EBIT$$

or,

$$DOL = (Revenue - variable\ cost)/(Revenue - variable\ cost - fixed\ operating\ cost)$$

or,

$$DOL = Percentage\ change\ in\ EBIT/Percentage\ change\ in\ units\ sold \quad ...(21.1)$$

The greater a firm's DOL, the more its EBIT will vary with respect to fluctuations in sales. This would be evident with the help of an example.

EXAMPLE

Find the DOL if a firm sells 10,000 units @ Rs 5 per unit; variable cost is Rs 3 per unit and fixed operating cost is Rs 10,000.

$$DOL = Rs\ (50{,}000 - 30{,}000)/(50{,}000 - 30{,}000 - 10{,}000) = 2/1$$

If the sales volume increases by 20% to 12,000 units, the operating profit will rise to:

$$Rs\ (60{,}000 - 36{,}000 - 10{,}000) = Rs\ 14{,}000$$

This shows that with a DOL of 2/1, the operating profits rise by 40% (from Rs 10,000 to Rs 14,000) with only a 20% increase in the sales volume. In other words, a 1% increase in sales leads to 2% increase in operating profits.

Again if the fixed operating cost increases due to some changes in the methods of production, DOL will increase. With an increase in DOL, a given increase in sales will lead to a far greater change in operating profits.

EXAMPLE

Find the DOL with a fixed operating cost of Rs 12,000, the other variables being the same as in the preceding example.

DOL = Rs (50,000 – 30,000)/(50,000 – 30,000 – 12,000) = 2.5/1

In this case, if sales are raised by 20% to 12,000 units, the operating profit will be Rs (60,000 – 36,000 – 12,000) = Rs 12,000.

This shows that when DOL increases from 2/1 to 2.5/1, an increase in sales of 20% will raise profits by 50% – from Rs 8,000 to Rs 12,000.

Comparing the two examples, one finds that with a 20% increase in sales:

1. At a DOL of 2/1, the profit increases by 40%.
2. At a DOL of 2.5/1, the profit increases by 50%

It does not, however, mean that operating leverage has only favourable effects on profits. It has unfavourable effects too. If sales drop due to lack of demand, EBIT will decline more sharply.

EXAMPLE

Find the change in operating profits with a 20% fall in sales at DOL of 2/1 and of 2.5/1, the other variables remaining the same as in the preceding example.

At a DOL of 2/1, the sale volume declines to 8000 units or by 20%.and EBIT declines to Rs 6,000 or by 40%.

At a higher degree of DOL of 2.5/1, a drop in sales by 20% will make operating profit decline by 50%.

> With the existence of fixed-charge leverage, a change in the operating profit or EBIT leads to a larger change in the earning before taxes.

In case of a very high DOL, the entire EBIT may be wiped out and a loss may be reported. This is why, as a general rule, firms do not like to operate under a very high degree of operating leverage, particularly when they fear a drop in sales due to changes in demand. If, however, DOL is high, the firms would prefer a large margin of safety, meaning that they operate sufficiently above the break-even point.

21.2.2 Fixed-charge Leverage

Fixed-charge leverage exists when the capital structure comprises debt or other fixed-charge funds. These fixed charges are fixed financial costs, different from fixed operating costs. With the existence of fixed-charge leverage, a change in the operating profit or EBIT leads to a larger change in the earning before taxes (EBT). The degree of fixed-charge leverage, (DFCL) can be expressed as follows:

$$DFCL = EBIT/EBT$$

or

$$DFCL = (Revenue - var.\ cost - fixed\ oper.\ Cost)/ (Rev. - var.\ cost - fixed\ oper.\ cost - fixed\ financial\ cost) \quad ...(21.2)$$

EXAMPLE

Find DFCL if EBIT is Rs 10,000 and the firm has to pay a fixed amount of interest to the tune of Rs 2,000.

$$DFCL = [10{,}000/(10{,}000 - 2{,}000)] = 1.125/1$$

Using the preceding variables, it can be computed as follows:

$$DFCL = [(50{,}000 - 30{,}000 - 10{,}000)/(50{,}000 - 30{,}000 - 10{,}000 - 2{,}000)] = 1.125/1$$

The DFCL shows that any increase in EBIT would be accompanied by a greater increase in EBT. Suppose EBIT increases by 50% to Rs 15,000 at a 1.125/1 DFCL, the increase in EBT, based on the above example, would be 62.50%. DFCL with a fixed financial cost of Rs 5,000 would be 2/1. Thus at a higher DFCL, an increase in EBIT by 50% to Rs 15,000 will raise EBT by 100% from Rs 5,000 to Rs 10,000

However, fixed-charges leverage also has unfavourable effects. If EBIT declines from Rs 10,000 to Rs 9,000, that is, by 10%, EBT will be only Rs 7,000 (with fixed financial charges of Rs 2,000) registering a fall of 12.5%. The higher the DFCL, the greater will be the percentage fall in the EBT. In case of a very high DFCL, EBT may be wiped out. That is why firms do not prefer a high DFCL, particularly when earnings are volatile.

21.2.3 Combined Leverage

Combined leverage is a combination of the operating leverage and the fixed-charge leverage. In other words, the degree of combined leverage (DCL), is equal to the product of DOL and DFCL. In the form of an equation DCL can be expressed as follows:

> Combined leverage is a combination of the operating leverage and the fixed-charge leverage.

$$DCL = DOL \times DFCL \qquad ...(21.3)$$

Interpreting Eq. 21.3,

$$DCL = (Revenue - var.\ cost)/(Revenue - var.\ cost - fixed\ oper.\ cost - fixed\ fin.\ cost)$$

or,

$$DCL = Marginal\ contribution/EBT ...(21.4)$$

The purpose of the combined leverage is to compare the changes in revenues with changes in EBT. Based on the above examples where DOL is 2/1 and DFCL is 1.25/1, the DCL would be (2 × 1.25) or 2.5/1.

21.3 FINANCIAL LEVERAGE

Financial leverage has already been explained at greater length in Chapter 14. The readers are requested to go through it in that chapter. Based on the discussion in Chapter 14, financial leverage is different from the operating leverage:

- Operating leverage influences the operating income. Financial leverage influences the EBT.

- Operating leverage is concerned more with the production activities. Financial leverage is concerned with the financing decision.
- Operating leverage normally involves the business risk. Financial decision involves the financial risk.
- The degree of operating leverage depends upon the size of fixed cost. The degree of financial leverage depends on the size of debt in the capital structure.

Financial leverage is synonymous with fixed-charges leverage. However, it should be made clear that financial leverage is different from fixed-charges leverage insofar as financial leverage exists only when:

1. The capital structure comprises debt or other fixed-cost capital;
2. ROI must not be equal to the percentage of interest or other fixed charges.

The second factor is particularly relevant because if ROI is equal to the fixed charges, the firm is earning on the money exactly what it pays for the use of the money, which does not make any sense. Borrowing makes sense only when the ROI is greater than the fixed charges. For example, if ROI is 12% as against a 10% interest rate, this means that 2% is available as EBT, a part of which will be paid as taxes, the other part being available to the shareholders. In this case, financial leverage is favourable. There may, however, be cases when financial leverage is unfavourable, when ROI is less than the interest rate meaning thereby that the firm is losing money by way of payment of interest.

Naturally, a firm which intends to raise its earning per share (eps) and attract investors, applies a higher degree of financial leverage. However, those firms that fear volatility in their earnings try to introduce financial leverage only within narrow limits. This is because a drop in EBIT may lead to a sizeable diminution in the eps and thereby a sharp squeeze on the value of their shares.

21.3.1 Financial Leverage with Preference Shares

In a manner similar as to debt, preference shares also carry fixed charges. This is why a firm having preference shares in its capital structure is known to be a levered one. However, there is a difference between debt and preference shares. The difference being that the interest is tax-deductible, while dividends on preference shares are not. This means that for a favourable financial leverage, ROI must be greater than the sum of taxes and the dividends which can be expressed as follows:

$$ROI > \frac{Dividend\ yield}{(1 - tax\ rate)} \qquad ...(21.5)$$

EXAMPLE

If a Rs 100 preference share carries a 5% coupon rate and the tax rate is 30%, what will be the ROI to make a favourable financial leverage?

$$\text{ROI} > [0.05/(1 - 0.3)] = .0714 \text{ or } 7.14\%$$

SUMMARY

Leverage is used to raise profits and is therefore a tool of profit planning. Broadly speaking, there are three types of leverages. First, return-on-investment leverage which is brought into action either by decreasing the size of the assets so as to increase the asset turnover, or by decreasing the cost so as to raise the EBIT, or by incorporating these two methods at the same time.

Second, marginal-analysis leverage which takes the form of either operating leverage or fixed-charge leverage or a combination of the two. Operating leverage exists because of the existence of fixed operating costs. The greater the degree of this leverage, the larger is the change in the operating profit as a result of any change in the volume of sales. Similarly, fixed-charge leverage exists because of the existence of fixed-charge securities in the capital structure. It shows how a change in the operating profits leads to a greater change in the EBT. The degree of the combined leverage (DCL) is nothing but a product of the degree of operating leverage (DOL) and the degree of fixed-charge leverage (DFCL).

Financial leverage is similar to fixed-charge leverage but exists only when the ROI is not equal to fixed charges. The existence of financial leverage leads to a rise in the EPS provided that ROI is greater than the fixed charges. In case of preference share, ROI must be greater than the sum of taxes and the dividends.

POINTS TO REMEMBER

1. What is leverage? What are its different types?
   - Leverage is a profit-raising tool.
   - Its types are:
     - ROI leverage
     - Marginal-analysis leverage, such as operating leverage, fixed- charge leverage and combined leverage
     - Financial leverage
2. What is ROI leverage?
   - ROI leverage = Profit margin x asset turnover. It means that profits can be raised through raising either/both of the two ratios
3. What is operating leverage?
   - It exists when changes in contribution margin produce greater changes in operating profit. DOL = MC/EBIT

4. What is fixed charge leverage?
   - It exists when changes in EBIT lead to greater changes in EBT. DFCL = EBIT/EBT
5. What is combined leverage?
   - It is a product of operating leverage and fixed-charge leverage. (MC/EBIT) × (EBIT/EBT) = MC/EBT
6. How is financial leverage different from fixed-charge leverage?
   - Both exist when capital structure possesses fixed-cost capital. But financial leverage exists only when ROI must not be equal to interest rate.

DESCRIPTIVE QUESTIONS

1. Define leverage. Is it true to say that leverage is a double-edged sword?
2. Define ROI leverage. How can ROI be raised?
3. What do you mean by marginal-analysis leverage? Explain its different forms.
4. Distinguish between fixed-charge leverage and financial leverage. Comment on the relationship between financial leverage and EPS.

OBJECTIVE-TYPE QUESTIONS

1. Mark true or false.
   (a) ROI can be raised by raising the profit margin.
   (b) ROI will be lower if the asset turnover is higher.
   (c) Operating leverage exists when changes in revenue produce greater changes in operating profit.
   (d) The larger the fixed operating cost, the greater the part of margin of contribution that is applied to cover the fixed cost.
   (e) The greater the DOL, the greater will be change in EBIT as a result of fluctuation in sales.
   (f) The DFCL is obtained by dividing operating profit by EBT.
   (g) DCL is the product of DOL and DFCL.
2. Choose the most suitable answer.
   (a) Financial leverage exists when:
      (i) debt is present in the capital structure
      (ii) ROI is equal to the interest rate
      (iii) both of the above
   (b) ROI can be improved by
      (i) raising profit margin
      (ii) raising asset turnover
      (iii) both of the above

(c) DOL can be obtained by:
   (i) dividing margin of contribution by operating profit
   (ii) dividing margin of contribution by EBT
   (iii) neither of the above
(d) DFCL can be obtained by:
   (i) dividing the margin of contribution by EBT
   (ii) dividing EBIT by EBT
   (iii) neither of the above
(e) DCL is obtained by:
   (i) dividing DOL by DFCL
   (ii) multiplying DOL by DFCL
   (iii) neither of the above

NUMERICAL PROBLEMS

1. Find out ROI, if profit amounts to Rs 20,000, sales amounts to Rs 1,00,000 and assets amount to Rs 50,000.
2. On the basis of the following figures:

   Revenue = Rs 1,00,000

   Variable cost = Rs 60,000

   Fixed operating cost = Rs 10,000

   Fixed financing cost = Rs 5,000

   Compute:
   1. DOL
   2. DFCL
   3. DCL
3. Compute DOL if total output is 5,000 units, sale price per unit is Rs 100, variable cost per unit is Rs 70 and total fixed cost is Rs 1,00,000. What will be the change if output increases by 10%?
4. If marginal contribution is Rs 60,000, fixed operating cost is Rs 20,000 and interest payment is Rs 10,000, find out DFCL. Will DFCL change if marginal contribution moves up to Rs 80,000?
5. If a Rs 100 preference share carries 7% dividend rate, the tax rate is 30% and if ROI is 9%, compute the degree of financial leverage. Would it make a favourable financial leverage?
6. Find out the percentage in the contribution earned if the firm has an operating leverage of 1.20 compared to 1.25 in the preceding year and the current fixed cost is 25% more than in the preceding year.
7. Find out the percentage change in the EPS if sales increase by 5%, EBIT is Rs 112 million, EBT is Rs 32 million and fixed cost is Rs 70 million.

SOLVED NUMERICAL PROBLEMS

1. How much the operating profit has to be raised in order to have a return on investment of 30%, with given sales for Rs 3,00,000 and an asset for Rs 2,00,000?

Solution

Return on investment = profit margin × asset turnover

or $0.30 = x/3{,}00{,}000 \times 3{,}00{,}000/2{,}00{,}000$

or $0.30 \times 3{,}00{,}000 = x \times 3{,}00{,}000/2{,}00{,}000$

or $x = 90{,}000 \times 2{,}00{,}000/3{,}00{,}000$

or $x = 60{,}000$

The operating profit has to be raised to Rs 60,000 in order to get ROI of 30%.

2. A firm takes up economy measures and is able to reduce the operating cost, and raises the operating profit from Rs 50,000 to Rs 60,000. The sales amount to Rs 3,00,000 and the assets are valued at Rs 2,50,000. Find out ROI (a) prior to economy measures, and (b) after the economy measures.

Solution

(a) ROI prior to economy measures

$= 50{,}000/3{,}00{,}000 \times 3{,}00{,}000/2{,}50{,}000$

$= 0.167 \times 1.2 = 0.20 = 20.0\%$

(b) ROI following the economy measures

$= 60{,}000/3{,}00{,}000 \times 3{,}00{,}000/2{,}50{,}000$

$= 0.20 \times 1.2 = 0.24 = 24.0\%$

3. A firm has a sale for Rs 3,00,000. The cost of goods amounts to 60% of the sale value. The operating cost is further 10 % of the sale value. Find the degree of operating leverage.

Solution

DOL = MC/EBIT

MC = Sale value – cost of goods

= Rs 3,00,000 – 0.60 × 3,00,000 = Rs 1,20,000

EBIT = MC – operating cost

= Rs 1,20,000 – 0.10 × 3,00,000 = Rs 90,000

DOL = 1,20,000/90,000 =1.33

4. How much does the operating cost need to be reduced to get a DOL of 1.2, with a given contribution margin of Rs 1,20,000?

Solution

DOL = MC/EBIT

or $1.2 = 1{,}20{,}000/x$

or $x = 1{,}20{,}000/1.2$

or $x = 1,00,000$

or EBIT = Rs 1,00,000

Operating cost = Margin of contribution – EBIT

= 1,20,000 – 1,00,000 = Rs 20,000

The operating cost has to be reduced to Rs 20,000 in order to get a DOL of 1.2

5. Find the degree of fixed-charge leverage if EBIT is Rs 50,000 and the payment of interest on debt amounts to Rs 20,000.

Solution

DFL = EBIT/EBT

= Rs 50,000/(50,000 – 20,000) = 5/3 =1.7/1

6. Find the degree of combined leverage if DOL is 1.3/1 and DFL is 1.17/1. If lower payment of interest raises the DFL to 1.25, what would be the DCL?

Solution

DCL = DOL × DFL

= DCL = 1.3/1 × 1.17 = 1.52

DCL after the change in DFL

= 1.3/1 × 1.25 = 1.625

7. Find the minimum ROI that makes a favourable financial leverage with 10% Rs 100 preference shares and a tax rate of 30%.

Solution

ROI > {0.10/(1 – 0.30)}

or ROI > 0.1429

or ROI > 14.29%

Mini Case

Avantika Batteries manufactures small batteries for electronic goods. The owner asks the finance officer to chalk out a detailed production planning to maximise the profit in face of severe competition in the market. The finance manager finds out the level of expenditures, and accordingly, he suggests the measures. The present level of different costs and the sale price of three different groups of products are as follows:

Variables	Prod. A	Prod. B	Prod. C
Output (units)	2,50,000	70,000	3,00,000
Fixed cost (Rs)	3,00,000	6,00,000	7,00,000
Variable cost (Rs/unit)	20	80	15
Interest paid (Rs)	25,000	60,000	–
Sale price Rs/unit	30	70	15

There is a wide difference in the variables relating to the three groups of products. The finance manager has to find out the different types of leverages to frame a sound financial policy.

Questions:

1. Find out the degree of operating leverage.
2. Find out the degree of combined leverage.
3. Find out the degree of financial leverage

SELECT FURTHER READING

Ghandi, J.K.S. (1966). "On the Measurement of Leverage", *Journal of Finance*, 21 (Dec.): 476–80.

22

FINANCIAL FORECASTING

OBJECTIVES

To explain the techniques of forecast of a single variable

To describe the process of complete forecast of a firm's financial position using both the cash-flow approach and the balance-sheet approach

The financial analysis discussed in the foregoing chapters of the present part of the book, is based on the past and current financial performance. Interpretation of the past and current financial data is no doubt important, but it is not sufficient. A firm has to plan for future activities. Planning for the future requires an estimate and an interpretation of future financial data. In fact, the very goal of a firm is to have a continued growth of its activities. It intends to capture a growing share of the market for its products. Accordingly, it intends to expand sales, which require in turn an expansion in the necessary assets and in the funds to finance these growing assets. On the other hand, if a firm forecasts a drastic cut in sales due to changes in demand, it will have to plan for curtailing its assets accordingly, and to release the funds already tagged with the assets. All these activities require careful planning, at the root of which lies financial forecasting. In other words, financial forecasting helps a firm in the planning and designing of its future activities. If these activities are properly planned, risk is considerably reduced, and at the same time, profitability increases. Financial forecasting is, therefore, vital for the continuing success of a firm.

22.1 FORECAST OF SINGLE FINANCIAL VARIABLE

While forecasting the total financial condition of the firm, the first step is to forecast individual financial variables. These forecasts are then combined into a forecast of the complete balance sheet. In the present section, the various approaches to the forecast of individual variables will be dealt with, while the succeeding section will show how they are combined into an integrated forecast.

22.1.1 The financial Variables

The most important ingredient in the firm's planning process is the forecast of sales. It is the sales forecast that forms the basis for the forecast of other variables. The projection of sales in the coming years depends on:

1. The past trend in sales that is expected to carry on in the coming years. For example, if the sales volume has grown over the past five years at the rate of 5% per annum, the forecast for the next year's sales might be 5% above the current level; and
2. Some casual events that might materially affect the trend. These events may be the initiation of a major sales campaign or a change in the firm's pricing and other policies.

> The most important ingredient in the firm's planning process is the forecast of sales. It is the sales forecast that forms the basis for the forecast of other variables.

There are statistical devices for deriving the trend value and fitting them into a logistic curve in order to arrive at a sales forecast. These techniques lie outside the scope of the present book. For these the reader is advised to consult any book on statistics.

After the forecast of sales is made, it is easy to forecast other variables. These variables include the items of the income statement, viz., various incomes and expenses, and the items of the balance sheet, such as, different assets and liabilities. These variables are related to the volume of sales. Their relationship is fixed to a great extent, and so the size of these variables can easily be estimated if the volume of sales is given. Generally, two methods are used for this purpose. One involves the use of ratios and is known as the percent-of-sales method. The other is the use of regression analysis: simple linear; curvilinear; and multiple. However, the use of subjective decision in this respect cannot be ruled out.

22.1.2 Techniques of Forecast

Different techniques are used to forecast a single financial variable. These are statistical techniques. The purpose of the present chapter is not to explain these different techniques as they are the subject matter of a book on statistics. However, a brief comparative picture of them is given here.

Use of Ratios: The ratios for the current period are used to forecast future data. For example, if the size of inventory is currently 40% of the sale value, and if the sale value in the next year is expected to reach Rs 2,00,000, the size of inventory during the next year would naturally be:

$$\text{Rs } (0.40 \times 2{,}00{,}000) = \text{Rs } 80{,}000$$

There are, of course, certain variables that are not directly related to sales in the short-run. For instance, in the short-run, the size of plant and machinery does not change with a change in the volume of sales. However, the plant and machinery requirements for the next two or three years can be arrived at on the basis of the past average ratio of these assets to sales. Again, there are certain variables that are not directly related to sales, but, on the contrary, are related to purchases. For instance, accounts payable depends on the volume of purchases. There is, however, an almost definite relationship between sales

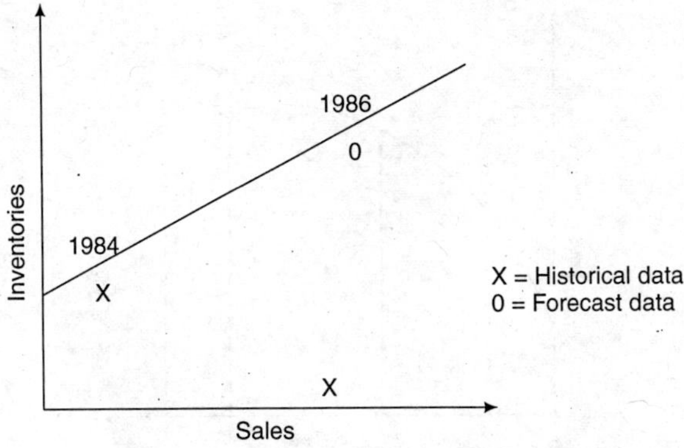

FIG. 22.1 Simple linear regression

and purchases, the volume of sales can be an indirect base for forecasting the volume of accounts payable. Let us suppose that purchases account for 40% of sales, and that the accounts payables are formed to the extent of 20% of the purchases amount. If the sales forecast for the next year is 10% above the current year's sale of Rs 2,00,000, the accounts payable forecast will amount to:

$$\text{Rs } (0.40 \times 2{,}20{,}000 \times 0.20) = \text{Rs } 17{,}600$$

Simple Linear Regression Analysis: Apart from the use of ratios or the percent-of-sales method, linear scatter diagram or simple linear regression analysis is used to determine the relationship between two variables. Fig. 22.1 shows a linear scatter diagram where the estimate of sales is shown on the horizontal axis and that of inventories on the vertical axis. Different points in the figure represent the particular values of inventory at given sales during different years. A line known as the regression line is drawn showing an average current and past relationship between sales and inventory and is extended in the same direction which would reveal the level of inventory for sales in the coming year.

The equation for the regression line is:

$$I = a + bS$$

where:

I = inventory
S = sales
a and b = constants determined using the least squares method.

The ratio of inventory to sales would be:

$$I/S = a + bS/S = a/s + b \qquad ...(22.1)$$

The simple regression analysis is normally preferred to the use of ratios. The reason being that the use of ratios or the percent-of-sales method assumes that the ratio of certain balance sheet items vary directly with sales. This shows a linear relationship that passes through the origin. In actual practice, however, this may not always be true. The slope of the line representing this type of relationship may vary, and it may lead to errors in forecast.

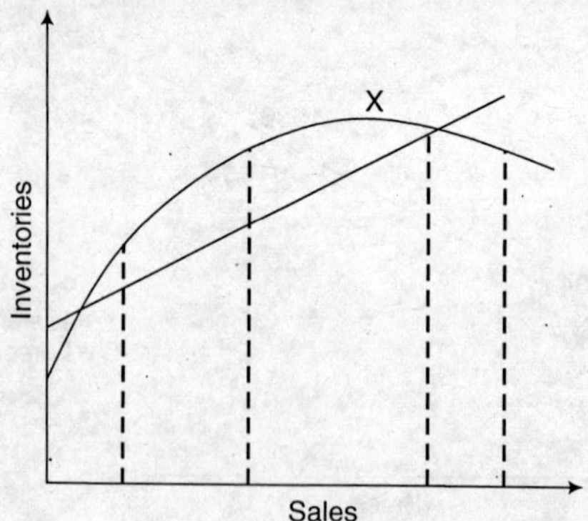

FIG. 22.2 Curvilinear simple regression

The scatter diagram, on the other hand, does not assume that the line of relationship passes through the origin. Rather it helps calculate the relationship at two points in time, extending a line through these two points. In the short-run period, differences in results following these two techniques may not be large, but, in the long run, they may be significant entailing in turn upon proper planning.

Curvilinear Regression: The simple linear regression analysis as shown in fig. 22.1 does not represent a decreasing relationship between sales and inventory beyond a certain point. However, it may so happen that a 1% increase in sales does require only a less than 1% increase in inventory. In that case, linear regression analysis may not provide accurate results. The analysts would then have to resort to curvilinear regression analysis. Fig. 22.2 shows a curvilinear regression line where a decreasing relationship between sales and inventory begins after point X is achieved. If at all, the analyst uses the linear regression analysis in this case, the estimates of the inventory requirements would be higher than the normal one, as shown in Fig. 22.2.

Multiple Regression Analysis: Multiple regression analysis is a more sophisticated approach to forecasting a firm's assets. The reason is that simple linear regression analysis assumes that the sales are a function of only one variable, which is generally not the case. Similarly, inventories are also influenced by various factors other than sales. The result is that deviations from the regression line appear. Although the curvilinear regression analysis minimises such deviations, it cannot rule them out completely. That is why an analyst uses the multiple regression analysis. Our purpose here is not to discuss this analysis at length as it can be found in any textbook on statistics. Nevertheless, a two-variable regression equation can be shown where the inventories are determined by sales as also the lead time.

The estimated equation will be as follows:

$$I = a + bS + cL \qquad \ldots(22.2)$$

where:

L = the lead time

S = sales

a, b, and c = the co-efficient of multiple regression equation which are again estimated using the method of least squares.

Thus we see that the multiple regression analysis solves more complex problems. However, its use must be balanced against the increased cost of using it.

22.2 COMPLETE FORECAST OF FINANCIAL POSITION

After the forecasts of individual variables is made, they are combined to develop a complete forecast of the firm's financial position over time. To this end, a couple of approaches are used. While one is known as the cash-flow approach, the other is the balance-sheet approach.

22.2.1 Cash-flow Approach

A cash-flow forecast is developed on the basis of the estimates of various cash receipts and payments. Cash receipts include cash sales along with the collection of bills receivable and other incomes, such as, issue of shares and debentures, maturity of investments and sale of any of the assets. Payments include the cost of goods paid in cash, interest and amortisation payments, dividend payments and expenses relating to fixed assets.

Prior to attempting a cash-flow forecast, the analyst prepares a proforma income statement or an income-statement forecast. This is important insofar as the analyst comes to know if the planning for the future activities brings any profit to the firm. Moreover, there are certain cash outflows, like the payment of corporate taxes, etc., that can easily be estimated from the proforma income statement. Table 22.1 and 22.2 show the balance sheet and the income statement respectively of a firm for the current year, on the basis of which the forecasts for the next year will be attempted.

The income statement forecast as presented in Table 22.3 assumes at the outset that there are seasonal variations in sales. The volume of sales in the third quarter is the largest, while that in the first quarter is the least. This is one of the reasons that the forecasts are shown quarterly, and, in the end, they are summed up to show the annual figure. Based on the past figures, the volume of sales during the next year is expected to grow by 10 %, that is, to Rs 12,10,000. The cost of goods is 60% of the value of sales in the current year, and so it is expected to go up to Rs 7,26,000 during the next year. The amount varies directly with sales with the result that it is not evenly distributed among different quarters. The

TABLE 22.1 *Balance Sheet of ABC & Co. as on 31 December, 2002 (Current Year)*

Liabilities	*Amount (Rs)*	*Assets*	*Amount (Rs)*
Accounts payable	32,000	Cash	20,000
Accrued expenses	18,000	Marketable securities	30,000
Mortgage (16%)	10,000	B/R	36,000
		Inventory	1,54,000
Mortgage (10%)	1,20,000		
Ordinary shares	4,00,000	Plant and machinery (net)	5,70,000
Retained earnings	2,40,000	Other assets	10,000
	8,20,000		8,20,000

TABLE 22.2 *Income Statement of ABC & Co. for the Year Ending 31 December, 2002 (Current Year)*

	Amount (Rs)
Net sales	11,00,000
Less: Cost of good sold	6,60,000
Contribution margin	4,40,000
Less: Wages	1,10,000
Depreciation	30,000
Other operating expenses	1,10,000
Operating profit	1,90,000
Less: Interest	13,600
Earning before tax (EBT)	1,76,400
Less: Taxes @ 30%	52,920
Net income after taxes (NIAT)	1,23,480
Dividend	40,000
Addition to retained earning	83,480

wages and other operating expenses each during the current year are 10% of the sale value, so both are expected to go up to Rs 1,21,000 during the next year. The existing plant and machinery will be sufficient to meet the required production in the next year, and therefore, the amount of depreciation will remain constant. Similarly, the same amount of borrowing will be sufficient meaning thereby that the interest charges will also remain constant. It may be pointed out that wages being mostly variable expenses vary with the sales during

TABLE 22.3 *Proforma Income Statement for the Year Ending 31 December, 2003*

	1st quarter	*2nd quarter*	*3rd quarter*	*4th quarter*	*Amount in Rs* *Total*
Net sales	2,50,000	3,00,000	3,60,000	3,00,000	12,10,000
Less: Cost of good sold	1,50,000	1,80,000	2,16,000	1,80,000	7,26,000
Gross margin	1,00,000	1,20,000	1,44,000	1,20,000	4,84,000
Less: Wages	25,000	30,000	36,000	30,000	1,21,000
Depreciation	7,500	7,500	7,500	7,500	30,000
Other operating expenses	30,250	30,250	30,250	30,250	1,21,000
Operating profit	37,250	52,250	70,250	52,250	2,12,000
Less: Interest	3,400	3,400	3,400	3,400	13,600
Earning before taxes (EBT)	33,850	48,850	66,850	48,850	1,98,400
Less: Taxes @ 30%	10,155	14,655	20,055	14,655	59,520
Net income after taxes (NIAT)	23,695	34,195	46,795	34,195	1,38,880
Dividends	—	20,000	—	20,000	40,000
Addition to retained earnings	23,695	14,195	46,795	14,195	98,880

TABLE 22.4 *Cash-Flow Forecast of ABC & Co. for the Year 2003*

Amount in Rs

	1st quarter	*2nd quarter*	*3rd quarter*	*4th quarter*
A. Collections	2,49,333	2,66,666	3,20,000	3,40,000
B. Operational cash Outflows:				
Payments to suppliers	1,02,000	1,70,000	2,04,000	1,32,000
Wages	25,000	30,000	36,000	30,000
Depreciation	7,500	7,500	7,500	7,500
Other operating expenses	39,416	30,250	30,250	30,500
C. Operating Cash inflow (outflow)	75,417	28,916	42,250	1,40,000
D. Other incomes	—	—	—	—
E. Other payments:				
Interest	3,400	3,400	3,400	3,400
Taxes	16,925	24,425	33,425	42,425
Dividends	—	20,000	—	20,000
F. Funds required (available)	95,742	18,909	(5,425)	(92,425)
G. Use of cash and securities	50,000	—	—	—
H. Cumulative funds required (available)	45,742	64,651	59,226	(33,199)

different quarters, but other expenses are almost fixed and distributed uniformly among the different quarters. The corporate tax rate is assumed to remain constant in view of no changes expected in the government's fiscal policy. As far as dividend is concerned, the firm would like to maintain stability in dividend in terms of the amount and pays it after every 6 months. The funds that remain after payment of dividend are retained with the firm.

After a clear picture of the expected income and expenditure is obtained, the analyst tries to attempt a cash-flow forecast. It is the cash-flow forecast that indicates the amount of funds the firm should arrange. Table 22.4 shows a cash-flow forecast. Generally, a firm sells goods on credit. So the collection of the bills is shown under this head. Assuming a net 60 term of credit, the collection during the 1st quarter of the next year relates to sales made in the closing months of the current year. In other quarters, collections will relate also to sales in the quarter just preceding. In the last quarter, a part of the sale value remains uncollected. Bad debt losses may reduce collections, but we do not assume any existence of such losses in the example given.

The second item on the cash-flow forecast is represented by operational cash payments that include payment to suppliers, and operating expenses such as wages, depreciation and other administrative and selling expenses. It is assumed that purchases are made on net 30 terms, although, in the last quarter the firm manages to purchases raw material on net 60 term of credit. The difference between the first item (receipts) and the second item (payments) indicates the net operational cash flow. In case other incomes exist, they should be added to the operational cash-flow. On the contrary, other payments, such as dividends, interest and taxes are deducted from it. In Table 22.4, it is assumed that the interest and taxes are paid quarterly, but the dividends are paid every 6 months. After these adjustments are made, the cash-flow forecast shows the amount of funds required (or available). The cumulative requirements of funds are also shown. It is found that at the end of the 1st quarter, the firm requires Rs 95,742. This amount is partly met by the cash holdings of the firm and also by converting the marketable securities into cash. They come to only Rs 50,000 leaving the amount of funds required as Rs 45,742. This amount rises to Rs 64,651 as the 2nd quarter too shows a fund requirement of Rs 18,909. In the 3rd quarter, there is an availability of funds of Rs 5,425 and again of Rs 92,425 in the 4th quarter, which results in a fund availability of Rs 33,199 with the firm at the end of the year.

22.2.2 Balance-sheet Approach

The proforma balance sheet provides estimate of the funds required and available in a manner similar to the cash-flow forecast. Therefore, the balance-sheet approach is a substitute for a cash-flow forecast. The proforma balance sheet can be developed with the help of the proforma income statement and the cash-flow forecast. Alternatively, it can also be developed on the basis of a proforma income statement alone.

Forecast Based on Proforma Income Statement and Cash-flow Forecast: The procedure is based on the following formula.

$$\underset{\text{(forecast)}}{\textit{Ending balance}} = \left(\underset{\text{(known)}}{\textit{beginning balance}} + \underset{\text{(forecast)}}{\textit{flows in}} - \underset{\text{(forecast)}}{\textit{flows out}} \right) \quad \ldots(22.3)$$

Table 22.5 presents a proforma balance sheet developed on the basis of Table 22.3 and 22.4. On the assets side, the first item is cash. It is represented by the amount of funds available with the firm at the year end (from Table 22.4). Second, bills receivables is computed as follows:

	Amount (Rs)
Sales forecast	12,10,000
Add: current year's balance	36,000
	12,46,000
Less: forecast collection	11,76.000
	70,000

Third, the entire material purchased is expected to be used, so the inventory balance of the current year would remain at the end of the next year. Similarly, there is no change in plant and machinery and in other assets. So they remain constant at the end of the next year.

On the liabilities side, the first item is accounts payable. It is computed as follows:

	Amount (Rs)
Cost of goods forecast	7,26,000
Add: current year's balance	32,000
	7,58,000
Less: forecasted payments for material	6,08,000
	1,50,000

TABLE 22.5 *Proforma Balance Sheet of ABC & Co. as at 31 December, 2003*

Liabilities	*Amount (Rs)*	*Assets*	*Amount (Rs)*
Account payable	1,50,000	Cash	33,199
Accrued expenses	18,000	B/R	70,000
Mortgage	10,000	Inventory	1,54,000
Mortgage (10%)	1,20,000	Plant and machinery (net)	5,70,000
Ordinary shares	4,00,000	Other assets	10,000
Retained earnings	1,39,199		
	8,37,199		8,37,199

Accrued expenses, short-term and long-term borrowings and the share capital are expected to remain constant and so there is no change in respect of them in the proforma balance sheet. Retained earnings show the assets minus liabilities.

Primary Balance Sheet Forecasts: As it is stated, the proforma balance sheet can also be developed without a cash-flow forecast. In this case, the individual balance sheet items are estimated using one of the single variable techniques. Dividend payments and retained earnings are shown in the income statement. The balancing of the balance sheet is done by plugging in additional cash required. If the total of asset side is larger than that of the liabilities side, additional funds must be obtained. If the case is just the opposite, this will mean that the firm has additional assets.

SUMMARY

Financial forecasting is the backbone of financial planning in any firm. If the forecast is accurate, planning particularly for assets and for the funds to finance them will be successful and this will in turn reduce the risk and raise profitability to a great extent. The first step in financial forecasting is to forecast the individual variables of the income statement and the balance sheet. First, sales is forecast on the basis of the past and current trend. Then, on the basis of the sales figure, other variables are estimated. The method used is either the percent-of-sales method or regression analysis. However, this requires a good deal of subjective judgement.

After individual variables have been estimated, they are combined into an income statement forecast and a cash-flow forecast leading to the preparation of a proforma balance sheet. They show a complete picture of the financial condition of the firm. In particular, the complete financial forecast shows the amount of funds the firm requires to carry on future activities or the amount of funds available with the firm as a result of these activities. It also helps a firm in controlling its finances for future activities.

POINTS TO REMEMBER

1. Why is financial forecasting important?
   - In order to cope with the demand in future, future activities are planned and for that future financial variables are estimated.
2. How do you forecast a single financial variable?
   - First of all, sales are projected and then on that basis, other variables are estimated insofar as the other variables have some kind of relationship with sales.
   - The past trend of a single variable is also considered.
3. What are the different techniques of forecast?
   - Use of ratios
   - Simple, curvilinear and multiple regression analysis
4. How is a complete forecast made?
   - Proforma income statement
   - Proforma cash-flow statement
   - Proforma balance sheet

DESCRIPTIVE QUESTIONS

1. How are sales and other variables forecast?
2. Comment on the use of regression analysis for making forecasts.
3. How do you make a complete forecast of the financial position of a firm?
4. Explain the cash-flow approach for making a complete forecast.
5. Explain the balance-sheet approach for making a complete forecast.

OBJECTIVE-TYPE QUESTIONS

1. mark true or false.
   (a) Forecasts of single variables are combined to arrive at a complete forecast.
   (b) The projection of sales depends on past trends along with some casual events affecting the trend.
   (c) Regression analysis is used to make forecasts.
   (d) Ratios are normally not used to make forecasts.
   (e) The forecast of variables has nothing to do with projected sales.
   (f) Cash-flow approach and the balance-sheet approach are the two methods of making a complete forecast.
   (g) Balance-sheet approach is a substitute for a cash-flow forecast.

2. Choose the most suitable answer.
   (a) Proforma balance sheet can be developed on the basis of:
      (i) cash-flow forecast only
      (ii) proforma income statement
      (iii) neither of the above
   (b) A cash-flow forecast is developed on the basis of:
      (i) estimates of cash receipts
      (ii) estimates of cash payments
      (iii) both of the above
   (c) Sales forecast depends on:
      (i) past trend
      (ii) casual factors affecting the trend
      (iii) both of the above
   (d) Proforma income statement:
      (i) considers seasonal fluctuation in sales
      (ii) does not consider seasonal fluctuation in sales
      (iii) considers only annual fluctuation in sales

NUMERICAL PROBLEMS

1. The income statement for the year ending 2003 shows the following figures:

   Sales = Rs 2,00,000

   Cost of goods sold = Rs 1,20,000

   Fixed operating cost = Rs 20,000

   Interest payment = Rs 5,000

   Taxes @ 30%

   In 2004, sales are expected to rise to Rs 3,00,000. Find out the net profit based on proforma income statement and using percent-of-sales method.
2. A company has the following financial data:

   Assets/sales ratio = 0.8

   Trade credit/sales ratio = 0.40

   Net profit margin = 7%

   Dividend pay-out ratio 50%

   Previous year's sale = 2000 units

   Compute the maximum sales growth rate that can be financed through internal funds only.

3. A company's financial position during 2003 was as follows:

   Sales = Rs 30,000

   Assets = Rs 20,000

   Bills payable = Rs 2,000

   Profit = Rs 1,500

   Retention ratio = 50%

   Find out the additional fund requirement during 2004 if sales are expected to increase by 10%.

SOLVED NUMERICAL PROBLEMS

1. P epare a proforma income statement if the sales in the current year amounting to Rs 6,00,000 are to move up in the next year by 10%. The cost of goods and the operating cost account for 60% and 10% respectively of the sale value. The interest payment during the current year is Rs 50,000. But, for increased sales, additional debt will be required and that will raise the interest payment to Rs 60,000. The tax rate is expected to remain unaltered at 30%.

Solution

Income Statement

Items	*Current year's actuals Rs*	*Projected figures for next year Rs*
Revenue from sales	6,00,000	6,60,000
Less cost of goods	3,60,000	3,96,000
Margin of contribution	2,40,000	2,64,000
Less operating cost	60,000	66,000
Operating profit	1,80,000	1,98,000
Less interest	50,000	60,000
Earning before taxes	1,30,000	1,38,000
Less taxes	39,000	41,400
Net income after taxes	91,000	96,600

2. The current year's balance sheet is as follows:

Liabilities	*Amount Rs*	*Assets*	*Amount Rs*
Bills payable	6,00,000	Cash	4,00,000
Bank credit	1,10,000	Marketable securities	1,00,000
Current liabilities	7,10,000	B/R	2,50,000
Share capital	3,00,000	Inventory	3,60,000
Retained earnings	2,00,000	Total current assets	11,10,000
Debt	2,00,000	Fixed assets minus dep.	3,00,000
Total	14,10,000	Total	14,10,000

   Assuming 10% increase in sales, prepare a proforma balance sheet for the next year.

Solution

Liabilities	*Amount Rs*	*Assets*	*Amount Rs*
Bills payable	6,29,280	Cash	4,19,520
Bank credit	1,10,000	Marketable securities	1,04,880
Current liabilities	7,39,280	B/R	2,75,000
Share capital	3,00,000	Inventory	3,52,397
Retained earnings	1,92,517	Total current asset	11,51,797
Debt	2,20,000	Fixed assets minus dep.	3,00,000
Total	14,51,797	Total	4,51,797

Notes:

Asset side:

1. Since sales are to increase by 10%, the growth in cash including marketable securities, as per Baumol Model, should be the square root of 1.10 or 1.0488 or by 4.88%. Marketable securities account for 25% of cash. The figure of these two items will change accordingly.
2. The average size of receivables is currently 41.67%. Thus the size of B/R will change accordingly.
3. The size of inventory will also grow by the square root of 1.10% or by 4.88%

Liabilities side:

1. Bills payable will also increase by 4.88%.
2. Larger activities will be partially financed by additional debt.
3. The changes will have an impact on retained earnings.

CASE STUDY

Income Statement of Apollo Tools Pvt. Ltd. Forecast for the Next Financial Period

The following is the income statement of Apollo Tools Pvt. Ltd. for two years, 2005–06 and 2006–07.

	2005–06 Rs	2006–07 Rs
Sales revenue	25,67,000	30,74,000
Less cost of goods sold	17,11,000	20,88,000
Gross profit	8,56,000	9,86,000
Less operating expenses		
Selling expenses	1,08,000	1,00,000
Administrative expenses	1,87,000	1,94,000
Depreciation	2,58,000	2,74,000

	2005–06 Rs	2006–07 Rs
Total operating expenses	5,53,000	5,68,000
Operating Profit	3,03,000	4,18,000
Less interest paid	91,000	93,000
EBT	2,12,000	3,25,000
Less taxes @ 30%	63,600	97,500
NPAT	1,48,400	2,27,500
Less dividend on preference shares	10,000	10,000
Earnings available to equity shareholders	1,38,000	2,17,000
EPS (10,000 shares)	13.80	21.70
DPS (40% dividend pay-out ratio)	5..52	8.68

The company is planning to implement a modernisation programme costing Rs 4,00,000 as a result of which variable cost is expected to drop during FY 2007–08 by 10% and the sales are expected to grow by 12%.

Questions:

1. Prepare a proforma income statement for FY 2007–08 based on per cent-to-sales method.
2. Do you feel that the company will need external financing for the modernisation programme?

SELECT FURTHER READINGS

Parker, G.G.C. and E.L. Segura (1971). "How to Get a Better Forecast", *Harvard Business Review*, 49 (Mar.–Apr.): 99–109.

Weston, J.F. (1958). "Forecasting Financial Requirements", *Accounting Review*, 33 (Jul.): 427–40.

Part VI

Special Topics in Financial Management

This part of the book discusses certain special topics that form an integral part of corporate financial management. They are, for instance:

1. Corporate combination that is normally known as mergers and acquisitions;
2. Corporate financial distress that is also known as corporate failure; and
3. International financial management, especially the exchange rate and foreign exchange market.

23

CORPORATE COMBINATIONS

OBJECTIVES

To discuss various forms of corporate combination and the motives behind such combination

To show how the consideration value is determined—the amount that the acquiring company pays to the target company

To explain the modes of payment of the consideration value

To delineate merger and take-over regulations in India

To show the accounting procedures of corporate combination

To explain divestitures, spin-offs and equity carve-outs

One of the key areas in financial management deals with expansion. Expansion takes two forms. One is internal expansion where a firm expands gradually over time in the normal course of business, in order to meet increasing demand for its products through the acquisition of new assets, replacement of the technologically obsolete equipment and the establishment of new lines of products. The financial implications of internal expansion have already been discussed in Part II of this book dealing with capital budgeting.

The other form of expansion is known as external expansion where a firm acquires a running business and grows overnight. It is better to denote external expansion as corporate combination as it is a broader term embracing mergers and all other forms of external expansion. It is corporate combination that forms the subject matter of the present chapter.

23.1 FORMS OF CORPORATE COMBINATIONS

23.1.1 Classification by Corporate Structure

If one classifies corporate combination by corporate structure, there are broadly three types of combination. The first type is known as merger where a firm acquires or purchases another firm. The acquiring firm continues to survive but the acquired firm loses its existence. To make it clear through an example, if Firm A acquires Firm B, the combined firm will be known as Firm A, Firm B has therefore ceased to exist.

In the second type of combination, known as consolidation or amalgamation, all the combining firms lose their identity and a new firm comes into being. For example, if Firm A and Firm B combine to form a new firm, Firm C, this is an amalgamation.

> If one classifies corporate combination by corporate structure, there are broadly three types of combinations—merger, consolidation and acquisition.

The third type of the combination is known as acquisition where the acquiring firm and the acquired firm both remain in existence. The acquiring firm is known as the holding company or parent company and the acquired firm is known as the subsidiary. The parent company owns shares in the subsidiary and thereby exercises control over it. The advantage of this form of combination is that the subsidiary retains its identity and goodwill. If the holding company wishes to decombine, it simply sells its equity holding in the subsidiary. In mergers and consolidation, the reverse process is not so easy.

23.1.2 Classification by Financial Relationship

Looking at the corporate combination from the viewpoint of economic and financial relationship, one further finds its three forms or types. Horizontal combinations where two or more firms engaged in similar lines of activity combine. For example, if two firms manufacturing automobiles merge, it will be called a horizontal combination. It helps create economies of scale because the size of the combined firm is larger allowing it to reap such gains.

On the other hand, a vertical combination occurs among firms involved in different stages of the production of a single final product. If an oil exploration firm and a refinery unit merge, it is an example of vertical integration. It reduces cost of transportation, and of communicating and coordinating production. Uncertainty over input supply is overcome as also the marketing of goods of a particular unit is assured through backward and forward linkages.

A third type of combination is called a conglomerate combination. it involves two or more firms in unrelated activities. Three types of conglomerate combinations are often found. The first is product-extension combination which broadens the product lines of the firm. The second is a geographic market-extension combination that involves two firms operating in different and non-overlapping geographic areas. The size of the market expands after the merger. Lastly, those conglomerates representing neither of the two are known as pure conglomerate combinations. There are financial conglomerates where a financial company manages the financial functions of other companies in the group. Similarly, there are managerial conglomerates combining the management of companies under one roof.

23.1.3 Classification based on Technique

Again from the viewpoint of technique, combinations can be grouped under three heads. They are as follows:

1. Friendly take-over;
2. Hostile take-over or tender offers; and
3. Leveraged buyout (LBO).

As far as friendly take-overs are concerned, there are a lot of negotiations regarding the consideration value, mode of payments, etc. The take-over deal is not disclosed until it is finalised. To this end, the acquiring company signs a confidentiality letter whereby it promises not to disclose the fact to any third party. When negotiations are on and all the relevant issues are sorted out, a letter of intent is signed. Finally, after the formal announcement is made to the press, a contract is signed.

Friendly take-overs require a lot of negotiations regarding the consideration value, mode of payments, etc.

When the negotiations fail, the acquiring firm makes its offer directly to the shareholders of the target firm asking them to tender their shares in lieu of a fixed amount per share. In order to lure the shareholders, the fixed amount is normally higher than the market price of the share. This is nothing but a hostile take-over. In hostile take-overs, the time devoted to negotiations is minimal because what is involved is the discreet purchase of the shares of the target company. There are a couple of ways in which the shares of the target company can be acquired. One method is known as a dawn raid where the acquiring company makes a sudden purchase of the shares of the target company. The other is one in which an irrevocable call option over some one else's shares is secured. After the initial stake is finalised, the acquiring company makes a bid. In order to grab the shares, it quotes a much higher price that deters other parties from making a similar bid. Such a bid is called as pre-emptive strike. On the other hand, if the company does not see a formidable competitor, it quotes a very low bid, often lower than the worth. This is called a low-ball offer.

In a leveraged buy-out (LBO), the buyer, which may be an outside group of investors, borrows funds to the extent of a major share of the purchase price and pledges the bought assets as collateral for the loan. In other words, LBO takes place when a group of investors acquires a firm in a transaction financed mainly by debt. The LBO is one of the modes of buy-outs that are different from the acquisition or take-over insofar as they (buy-outs) involve a group of individuals, and not a firm, buying the target firm. When the group represents target firm's management, it is known as management buy-out. If it represents employees, it is known as employee buy-out.

In hostile take-overs, the time devoted to negotiations is minimal because what is involved is the discreet purchase of the shares of the target company.

The LBO leads to synergistic effects meaning that purchase will raise the income to an extent sufficient to service the debt. The financing structure of an LBO depends on the quality of the assets that determines the cash-flow characteristics and on the perceived risk.

The acquiring company goes for an LBO only when the target company possesses potential in future, which means that if properly managed, the future cash flows of the target company will substantially increase. LBOs are quite common in the USA. However, in India, this practice yet to become popular.

In a leveraged buyout (LBO), the buyer borrows funds to the extent of a major share of the purchase price and pledges the bought assets as collateral for the loan.

23.2 MOTIVATIONS BEHIND COMBINATION

Combination is preferable to the start-from-scratch mode of investment. The more important reasons why it is opted for are as follows:

1. Reaping synergistic advantage;
2. Enjoying monopoly power;
3. Benefits of diversification;

4. Increased debt capacity;
5. Tax saving;
6. Undervalued assets; and
7. Agency issues.

First, combination provides synergistic advantages or the advantage of economies of scale. Firms that operate individually do not reap those benefits that are available when they are combined. This occurs because combination allows firms to reap economies of scale on different counts, especially on the counts of production, technological research, management, finance and marketing, etc. For example, when the fixed cost in Firm A does not cross the relevant range even after it acquires Firm B, the combination will lead to a saving in fixed cost that Firm B was previously incurring. This would result in a lower cost of production. Similar savings would occur in other relevant areas as well. These economies are most likely to occur in the case of horizontal combinations where opportunities exist for avoiding duplicate facilities.

To be more specific, synergistic effect is manifest on account of:

(a) Increase in revenue;
(b) Decrease in Cost;
(c) Reduced capital requirements.

Revenue increases on account of availability of **marketing gains**. Mergers helps strengthen distribution network, optimise the product mix and make advertising more effective in order to enhance the marketing gains. Revenue increases also on account of the availability of strategic benefits that are normally related to technology. Last but not least, it is the increased monopoly power in the wake of merger that enhances the marketing gains.

Cost is reduced on various counts. First, it is the achievement of the economies of scale explained in the preceding paragraphs. Second, it is the achievement of the economies of vertical integration. It is because the vertical mergers co-ordinate well the different processes of the same final product. Third, if the technology transfer is the main cause of merger, the merger may permit the use of cost-cutting technology. Fourth, it is sometimes the easy availability of raw material or intermediate goods behind mergers and acquisitions. If it is there, the cost will be lower. Fifth, merger helps improve the managerial efficiency that in turn reduces the cost.

Last but not least, as the size of the firm increases following merger, the current assets/ sales ratios tend to be lower with the result that the capital requirements are lower.

Second, combination reduces the risk of competition. It helps increase the market share and thereby the market power. The monopoly returns accrue to the firm even in the absence of any synergy or economies of scale. However, emergence of monopolistic character has certain disadvantages for consumers, for example, it may cause an unwarranted price rise.

Third, combination reduces financial risk through a greater amount of diversification. More particularly in the case of conglomerates, assets of completely different risk classes are acquired and, consequently, there is the possibility of negative correlation between the rates of return from these different classes of assets. If so, the return from the total portfolio of assets would be comparatively stable.

Fourth, combination leads to diversification that raises the debt capacity of a firm. Because of greater stability in the rates of return or in the cash flow after merger, the firm goes ahead and employs leverage in the capital structure. This helps in bringing down the cost of capital and raises the value of corporate wealth.

Mahindra & Mahindra has gone for a series of acquisitions. It is going for its eleventh acquisition deal in a span of three years which will be an equity buyout of a South African forging firm, known as SP Metal Forgings. The South African firm is a large exporter to the EU, the UK and Israel and provides parts for BMW, Peugeot, Renault, Nissan and Ford. The earlier ten acquisitions that took place in the past three years are as follows:

Year	Company	Business	Cost(Rs crore)	Stake %
Nov. 2004	SAR	Gear cutting	14.5	51
Nov. 2004	Jianling tractors	Tractor	35.5	80
May 2005	Amforge	Forging	128.5	47
Nov. 2005	Axes Technologies	Telecom solutions	240.0	100
Dec. 2005	PlexionTechnology	Design & engg.	37.0	88
Jan. 2006	Stokes Group	Forging	27.2	99
Sep. 2006	Jeco Holding AG	Forging	408.0	68
Nov. 2006	Hinoday Industries	Ferrous casting	–	66
Jan. 2007	Schoneweiss & Co.	Forging	–	90
May 2007	Punjab Tractor	Tractors	951.0	44

Based on: Business Standard, 21.11.2007

Fifth, it is sometimes tax savings that cause firms to combine. Suppose Firm A is earning high profits. It combines with Firm B which is incurring losses. After combination, the total profit will be lower than Firm A's profit alone with the result that the amount of tax would be lower. Sometimes the unused tax shield of one firm may appear as a merger incentive for the other that is more profitable.

Sixth, in many cases, the firms do not operate up to their potential because of inefficient management. In such cases, the acquiring company gets the valuable assets of the target company at a considerably lower price. In other cases, companies do not estimate their assets correctly. For example, oil exploration companies may undervalue their underground reserves. If an acquiring company knows this fact, it may be tempted to go for an acquisition so that it can get these assets at a lower price than the normal price.

Seventh, the agency problem or the possible conflict between the managers and the owners of a firm that may lead to combination. When the managers are able to share the gains that accrue to the shareholders after the merger, they too are the motivating force behind the combination. Normally, the managers are provided with share options in the merged firm. They are often provided with golden parachutes that save them from job termination. In such cases, they would not resist any effort towards combination.

In international business, mergers and acquisitions (M&As) are very common nowadays because of the above-mentioned reasons. However, there are certain other factors that also make international M&As imperative. First, they may occur when the domestic market is saturated and the firm is desirous of further expansion for reaping the gains from external economies. Second, they occur when international marketing faces a high tariff wall. In such cases, an M&A with host-country firms helps avoid tariffs. Third, they also occur when a firm that enjoys superior technology or managerial efficiency wishes to reap advantages from it in the international market, or when a firm wishes to acquire improved foreign technology in order to make a lead in the domestic market. Last but not least, international M&As are resorted also to assure a regular source of raw material that is not available domestically.

23.3 GAINS AND COSTS OF M&As

The discussion of the motivating factors makes it clear that there are gains from M&As. The gains manifest ultimately in the risen value of the firm that needs discussion at some length here.

To leave apart the long-term gains in terms of enlarged market or greater output, there are immediate gains that accrue on account of either reduced cost or risen revenue or both. At the same time, there are costs too. The costs manifest in the form of consideration value given by acquiring firm to the target firm in excess of the market value of the shares of the target firm. The net gain is represented by the excess of gains over the cost.

Let us take an example to show the gains and the cost:

	Acquiring firm	Target firm	Merged firm
Revenue (Rs)	6,00,000	3,00,000	9,75,000
Operating expenses (Rs)	4,00,000	2,50,000	6,00,000
Operating profit (Rs)	2,00,000	50,000	3,75,000
MPS (Rs)	50	30	
No. of shares	1,00,000	75,000	

Note: Operating profits increase in the merged firm due to shrunk expenses.

Here the operating profit rises by Rs 1,25,000 in the wake of the merger. So this amount should be treated as gain. If this gain is treated for perpetuity, the present value of gains with a discount rate of 10% would be:

Rs 1,25,000/0.10 = Rs 12,50,000

On the contrary, there are costs in the sense that the acquiring firm has paid, say, Rs 31 per share or Re 1 per share more than the market value of shares in the target company. So the cost will be:

Re 1 x 75,000 shares = Rs 75,000

The present value of net gains will be:

Rs 12,50,000 – 75,000 = Rs 11,75,000

23.4 DETERMINATION OF CONSIDERATION VALUE

Combination is a gainful strategy only when the value of the combined firm (V_{AB}) is greater than the sum of the value of the two firms ($V_A + V_B$) computed individually in the absence of the merger. This gain can be expressed in the form of an equation as follows:

$$\text{Gain} = V_{AB} - (V_A + V_B) \quad \text{...(23.1)}$$

However, the gain so derived has to be compared with the cost of M&A that is arrived at after deducting the value of the target firm from the price that the acquiring firm pays to the target firm. This means that the net gain from M&A accruing to the acquiring firm exists only when:

$$\{V_{AB} - (V_A + V_B)\} > (\text{Price} - V_B) \qquad ...(23.2)$$

Combination is a gainful strategy only when the value of the combined firm (V_{AB}) is greater than the sum of the value of the two firms ($V_A + V_B$) computed individually in the absence of the merger.

Thus, in this context, it is very significant to know what price the acquiring firm should pay the target company for acquisition, and what would be the impact of the changes in this price on the post-merger value of the firm. This price is known as the consideration value that is fixed within two extremes. One is the floor price of the package, any price below which is not acceptable to the target company. It is basically the market value of the shares of the target company. For example, if Firm A acquires Firm B and if the market value of Firm B's share is Rs 15, the consideration value must at least be Rs 15 per share. In practice, it is more than Rs 15 as a premium is necessary to attract Firm B for acquisition.

However, this does not mean that the amount of premium will swell infinitely. If it moves up or swells beyond a certain limit, the value of the acquiring firm will start to reduce and the very objective of the merger will have been lost. This limit is known as the ceiling price where the earning per share (EPS) of the acquiring firm in the post-merger period is equal to that in the pre-merger period. In other words, the ceiling price would be equal to the product of the EPS of the target firm and the price-earning (P/E) ratio of the acquiring firm.

Suppose the financial data of the two firms are as follows:

	Firm A	Firm B
Present earnings (Rs)	20,000.00	8,000.00
Shares (no.)	5,000.00	3,000.00
EPS (Rs)	4.00	2.67
Market value of shares (Rs)	32.00	16.00
P/E ratio	8.00	6.00

At the floor price, the value of Firm B in the post-merger period will be the same as its value during the pre-merger period. The owners of Firm B will get 16/32 × 3,000 or 0.5 share in Firm A for each share that they own in Firm B. Thus the wealth of Firm B in the post-merger period will be Rs (32 × 1500 shares) or Rs 48,000, which is equal to Rs (16 × 3,000 shares) which is again Rs 48,000 during the pre-merger period.

At this floor price paid, the EPS of Firm A after the merger will increase to Rs (20,000 + 8,000)/(5,000 + 1,500 shares) or to Rs 4.31. Assuming a price-earning ratio of 8, the value of one share of Firm A after the merger will be Rs (4.31 × 8.0) or Rs 34.48 and the value of the merged firm will be Rs (34.48 × 6,500 shares) = Rs 2,24,120 which is higher than the sum of the value of the two firms in the pre-merger period. Using Eq. 23.2, the net gain from merger will be:

Rs {[2,24,120 – (1,60,000 + 48,000)] – (48,000 – 48,000)} = Rs 16,120.

The higher the price above the floor price, the lower will be the gain to the acquiring firm as well as the higher will be the gain to the target company. However, Firm A may pay a large premium to Firm B in order to attract the latter toward acquisition. The ceiling will reach where

The higher the price above the floor price, the lower will be the gain to the acquiring firm as well as the higher will be the gain to the target company.

the price will be equal to the product of EPS of the target company and the P/E ratio of the acquiring firm. In the above example, it is Rs (2.67 × 8) or Rs 21.36. At this price, Firm B will receive 0.6675 share in Firm A in lieu of its one share or in all 2,003 shares in Firm A, meaning that there will be in all 7,003 shares in the merged firm. The EPS will be Rs (28,000/7,003 shares) or = Rs 4 which is equal to pre-merger EPS in Firm A. Assuming a P/E ratio of 8, the value of the merged firm will be Rs (32 × 7,003 shares) or Rs 2,24,096. Thus at both the ceiling price and the floor price, the value of the merged firm is almost the same. However, at the ceiling price, the net gain to the acquiring firm would just be zero because the gain from the merger will be reaped entirely by the target company.

In practice, the actual price is determined between these two limits depending upon the bargaining power of the acquiring firm and the target firm respectively, and accordingly, the net gain is shared partially by the acquiring firm and partially by the target firm. Suppose the consideration value is Rs 20 per share of Firm B. In this case, Firm A will issue 0.625 share for every share in Firm B which will be in all 1875 shares. The value of owners' wealth in Firm B would now be Rs (32 × 1875 shares) or Rs 60,000 as compared to Rs 48,000 in the pre-merger period. The EPS of the merged firm would be Rs (28,000/6,875 shares) or Rs 4.07. Assuming a P/E ratio of 8, the value of the merged firm will be Rs (32.56 × 6875 shares) or Rs 2,23,850 which is higher than the sum of the value of the two firms in the pre-merger period. The net gain to the acquiring firm as per Eq. 23.2 will be:

$$\text{Rs } \{[2,23,850 - (1,60,000 + 48,000)\} - (60,000 - 48,000)\} = \text{Rs } 3,850$$

Thus at a price agreed upon between the floor and the ceiling, both the acquiring firm and the target firm will reap the benefits; and, as a result, both will therefore agree to the merger. However, there are cases when the acquiring firm goes for acquisition also when its net gain is zero. This is however done only if certain other significant benefits will accrue to the acquiring firm.

The consideration value has so far been discussed in the absence of any changes in the international environment. In international combination, however, such changes cannot be overlooked. The first among such changes is a change in the exchange rate. The lower the existing spot rate of the currency of the target-company country, the lower is the price to be paid by the acquiring firm. If it is higher, the salvage value will be higher from the viewpoint of the acquiring firm. If the future spot rate is expected to be higher, the acquiring firm will receive a greater cash flow.

Second, the required rate of return will influence the value of the acquisition. This is because the cost of capital varies from one country to another, which is why the acquisition of a firm in a particular country may be more beneficial than the acquisition of another in some other country.

The value of acquisition differs in case of different countries because the ability to use financial leverage varies among countries.

Third, the value of acquisition differs in case of different countries because the ability to use financial leverage varies among countries. Since acquisition is financed mostly through borrowings, acquisition of firms in a country where flexibility in borrowing is greater is more common. For example, in the usa, a high debt ratio is not preferred, the acquiring firm does not therefore get much incentive on this count.

Last but not least, there are legal formalities regarding taxes and accounting. If they are favourable, they create competitive advantages for acquiring firms. This means that when these rules are more favourable and liberal, the acquiring firm may bid a higher price for acquisition.

23.5 MODES OF MERGER FINANCING

After the consideration value is determined, payment is made to the target firm. There are different modes of payment. They are as follows:

1. Cash payment;
2. Exchange of equity shares;
3. Exchange of preference shares and debentures; and
4. Payment under deferred payment plan.

23.5.1 Cash Payment

Payment in cash is the least cumbersome. Moreover, it has a favourable effect on the eps. The reason is that the number of shares outstanding does not increase, whereas the inclusion of the earnings of the target firm leads to a swell or increase in the earnings of the acquiring firm. However, this does not mean that this is the best way of paying the consideration value. It is a taxable transaction and so net gains will be lower. Again, the payment of cash is possible only when the firm has sufficient cash. If not, the acquisition of funds from other sources would be costly. Yet again, the shareholders of the acquired firm would prefer the exchange of shares and not a cash payment in order to reap the synergistic benefits of the merger.

23.5.2 Exchange of Equity Shares

This mode involves the exchange of equity shares. Shares in the acquiring firm are given to the shareholders of the target firm. The basis of this exchange is either the eps or the market price of the shares of the two firms or additionally certain other factors are taken into consideration. Suppose Firm A acquires Firm B and the former has an EPS of Rs 4 and the latter an EPS of Rs 3. The owners of Firm B will get 0.75 share in Firm A for each share that they hold in Firm B. If, again, the market price is the basis and the shares of Firm A and B sell at Rs 20 and at Rs 10 respectively, the owners in Firm B will get 0.5 share in Firm A for every share that they hold in Firm B.

The merit of this mode is that it is tax-free. However, the effect on the EPS of the surviving firm is not as favourable insofar as the number of outstanding shares will increase.

The merit of the exchange of equity shares mode of merger financing is that it is tax-free. However, the effect on the EPS of the surviving firm is not as favourable insofar as the number of outstanding shares will increase.

23.5.3 Preference Shares and Debentures

Sometimes the fixed earning securities accompany the equity shares. There are a number of reasons for it. First, there is a section of investors in the target firm who prefer fixed return to supplement their current income. They therefore prefer preference shares and debentures in the acquiring firm. Second, the acquiring firm may not be interested in the dilution of voting rights and may prefer to issue debentures. Third, when the dividend policy of the two firms—the acquiring firm and the target firm—differs significantly, it is very difficult for the surviving firm to design its dividend policy so that it suits the owners of the target firm. In such cases, convertibles are of great help insofar as they may allow the acquiring firm to comply with the income objectives of the target firm without changing its own dividend policy. Fourth, the target firm often prefers to supplement the equity shares with convertible securities in view of the fact that they combine senior security protection along with a portion of growth potential of equity shares. Fifth, the dilution of earnings may be minimised by the issue of convertible securities. Since they are not a part of the owner's equity financial instruments, the eps does not decline.

23.5.4 Deferred Payment Plan

The deferred payment plan is comparatively a recent mode of making payment. In it the acquiring firm makes an initial payment of cash or equity shares, and if earnings go on increasing, it makes additional payment. The amount of additional payment depends upon the growth in earnings, capitalisation rate and the market value of shares.

This mode of payment makes the negotiation of the merger smooth. The target firm is agreeable even to a low consideration value if the mode of payment is according to its choice. The acquiring firm pays the additional amount only when earnings justify it. Again, it does not allow the number of equity shares increase, and as a result, the impact on the eps is not unfavourable.

23.6 MERGERS AND TAKE-OVER REGULATIONS IN INDIA

The Indian Companies Act, 1956, restricts a company to acquiring the shares of another public company only up to 25% of its total paidup capital. Whenever such holdings exceed 10% of its subscribed capital, the company has to inform the Central Government.

The Indian Companies Act, 1956, provides for combination among industrial and business enterprises. As per the Act absorption or amalgamation are possible only when such activities are permitted by the memorandum of association of the concerned firm. If such provisions are not contained in the firm's memorandum, they should be approved by the shareholders and also by the Company Law Board. Besides, the stock exchange listing the shares of the combining companies should also be informed.

The Act restricts a company to acquiring the shares of another public company only up to 25% of its total paid-up capital. Whenever such holdings exceed 10% of its subscribed capital, the company has to inform the central government. If it is a hostile take-over, a company can refuse to register the transfer of shares.

Moreover, the Act protects the interests of the minority shareholders. Any purchaser can force a minority shareholder to sell his/her shares only when the offer has been approved by 90% of the shareholders, and the approval has been intimated to the minority shareholder.

Apart from the Companies Act, the Securities and Exchange Board of India (SEBI) has provided guidelines for take-overs. The guidelines cover the different aspects of take-overs. They are as follows:

1. In case of acquisition of 5% or more of the equity shares, the decision has to be intimated to the stock exchange.
2. If the acquisition does not exceed 10%, it is not mandatory on the part of the acquiring company to inform the other shareholders. But when the acquisition

exceeds this limit, an offer is to be made to other shareholders for the purchase of a minimum of 20% of the shares. The offer price should not be lower than the average of the weekly prices during the past six months.

3. The offer should include the information regarding the intention to continue the acquired business and the reason behind the offer.

23.7 ACCOUNTING PROCEDURES FOR COMBINATIONS

23.7.1 Acquisition

In case of acquisition, the target firm ceases to exist and so it closes its accounts. Two accounts are particularly relevant in this case. They are:

1. Realisation Account;
2. Shareholders' Account.

On the credit side of the Realisation Account are entered the liabilities taken over by the acquiring firm and also the purchase consideration. On the debit side of the Realisation Account are entered the assets taken over by the acquiring firm. In case the liquidation expenses borne by the vendor firm, they are also entered on the debit side. The amount by which the credit side exceeds the debit side shows the profit on realisation.

The other account is the Sundry Equity Shareholders' Account. To the credit side, is transferred the equity share capital, reserves and funds and the credit balance of the Profit and Loss Account or any other account showing accumulated profits. The balance of the Realisation Account is also transferred to this account. All these corresponded to the share in the acquiring firm.

As far as the books of the acquiring firm are concerned, the immediate effect of acquisition is manifest in the balance sheet where the liabilities and assets swell by the amount of liabilities and assets taken over. The impact of the purchase consideration is an additive factor on the new balance sheet.

Sometimes the acquiring firm holds some shares in the vendor firm that needs to be adjusted in the purchase consideration. On the other hand, if the vendor firm holds some shares in the acquiring firm, these shares are deducted from the total number of shares while allotting shares to the vendor firm. Again, if both the firms hold shares in each other, it becomes necessary to determine the value of the shares of both firms, as the value of one share will influence the value of the other. The procedure will be clear from an example.

EXAMPLE

ABC & Co. Ltd agrees to acquire the business of XYZ & Co. Ltd as on 31 December, 2003 and to take over the assets and liabilities at their balance sheet value, in exchange for which it is to issue 12 shares of Rs 10 each for every share of Rs 100 each in XYZ. The expenses of the acquisition, Rs 10,000 are to be borne by the acquiring firm. The balance sheets of the firms are as follows.

Balance Sheet of XYZ & Co. Ltd as on 31 December, 2003

Liabilities	Amount (Rs)	Assets		Amount (Rs)
Capital (5000 equity shares of		Land & Building		3,00,000
Rs 100 each fully paid)	5,00,000	Plant		2,00,000
Sundry creditors	58,000	Debtors	55,000	
Trade creditors	42,000	Less reserves	5,000	
Contingencies	10,000			50,000
		Stock		25,000
		Cash at bank		35,000
Total	6,10,000	Total		6,10,000

Balance Sheet of ABC & Co. Ltd as on 31 December, 2003

Liabilities	Amount (Rs)	Assets	Amount (Rs)
Authorised capital (2,00,000 equity		Land & Building	5,00,000
shares of Rs 10 each)	20,00,000	Plant	3,00,000
Issued capital		Goodwill	1,00,000
(1,00,000 shares of Rs 10 each)	10,00,000	Stock	60,000
Reserves	60,000	Debtors	1,20,000
Creditors	1,20,000	Cash	1,00,000
Total	11,80,000	Total	11,80,000

Solution

Books of XYZ & Co. Realisation Account

		Amount (Rs)			Amount (Rs)
To Assets:			By Liabilities:		
Land & Build.	3,00,000		Sundry creditors	58,000	
Plant	2,00,000		Trade credit.	42,000	
Debtors	55,000		Bad debt res.	5,000	
Stock	25,000				1,05,000
Bank	35,000		By ABC & Co. Ltd		6,00,000
		6,15,000			
To Shareholder's Account		90,000			
Total		705,000	Total		705,000

Shareholders' Account

	Amount (Rs)		Amount (Rs)
To Shares in ABC & Co.	6,00,000	By Realisation Account	90,000
			10,000
		By Contingency Fund Account	
		By Share Capital Account	5,00,000
Total	6,00,000	Total	6,00,000

Books of ABC & Co. Ltd
Balance Sheet as on 1 January, 2004.

Liabilities	Amount (Rs)	Assets	Amount (Rs)
Authorised Capital		Goodwill at cost	2,00,000
(2,00,000 shares of Rs 10 each)	20,00,000	Land & Building at cost	8,00,000
Issued & Subscribed Capital		Plant	5,00,000

(1,60,000 shares of Rs 10 each)		16,00,000	Stock	85,000
Paid-up capital			Debtors	1,75,000
(1,60,000 shares of Rs 10 each)		16,00,000	Cash at bank	1,25,000
Reserves		65,000		
Other Liabilities:				
Goods supplied	1,78,000			
Acceptance	42,000			
		2,20,000		
Total		18,85,000	Total	18,85,000

23.7.2 Holding Companies

The accounting procedure in case of holding companies involves the preparation of a consolidated balance sheet of the holding and the subsidiary companies, although in India, this is not mandatory. The shares in the subsidiary company that are held by the holding company should be treated as the assets and the liabilities of the subsidiary company. Thus the consolidated balance sheet shows the assets and liabilities of the subsidiary company in addition to those of the holding company. There is no problem if the entire share capital in the subsidiary company is held by the holding company. But when some of the shares are held by the outsiders, their proportionate share is shown in the consolidated balance sheet as the creditors under the head, "minority shareholders". The claim of the minority shareholders will consist of the face value of the shares held by them plus proportionate share in the profits of the company and reserves, along with a proportionate share in the increase in the value of the assets of the company minus their proportionate share in the loss, if any. After the treatment of minority interest, the assets and liabilities of the holding and the subsidiary companies are aggregated.

It is likely that the shares of the subsidiary company are bought at a higher/lower price than book value. If it is less, the difference is shown in the consolidated balance sheet as capital reserves. If it is higher, the difference is shown as goodwill. Goodwill minus the holding company's share of capital profits appears as an asset in the consolidated balance sheet. Profits accumulated in the subsidiary prior to acquisition are treated as capital profits. The subsidiaries proportionate share is shown as capital reserves in the consolidated balance sheet. However, its share of the current profits is added to the profits of the holding company.

EXAMPLE

The following are the balance sheets of ABC & Co. Ltd being the holding company and XYZ & Co. Ltd its subsidiary company. Prepare a consolidated balance sheet showing the interest of minority shareholders of the subsidiary company.

Balance Sheet of ABC & Co. Ltd as on 31 December, 2003

Liabilities	Amount (Rs)	**Assets**	Amount (Rs)
Share capital		Property net of depreciation	7,60,000
(1,00,000 shares of Rs 8 each		Plant net of depreciation	1,12,000
fully paid-up)	8,00,000	Shares in XYZ & Co. Ltd	
General reserves	4,00,000	(9000 shares of Rs 8 each)	1,44,000

	Amount (Rs)		Amount (Rs)
Creditors	2,40,000	Stock	2,40,000
P&L Appropriation Account	80,000	Debtors	1,60,000
		Cash at bank	1,04,000
Total	15,20,000	Total	15,20,000

Balance Sheet of XYZ & Co. Ltd as on 31 December 2003

Liabilities	Amount (Rs)	Assets	Amount (Rs)
Share capital		Investment at cost	16,000
(10,000 shares of Rs 8 each)	80,000	Stock	40,000
Creditors	16,000	Debtors	56,000
P&L Appropriation Account	1,20,000	Cash	1,04,000
Total	2,16,000	Total	2,16,000

Solution

Consolidated Balance Sheet of ABC & Co. Ltd alongwith its subsidiary XYZ & Co. Ltd as on 31 December 2003

Liabilities		Amount (Rs)	Assets		Amount (Rs)
Share capital			Property net of depreciation		7,60,000
ABC:	8,00,000		Plant net of depreciation		1,12,000
XYZ:	8,000	8,08,000	Stock		
Capital reserves	1,08,000		ABC:	2,40,000	
Less excess cost			XYZ:	40,000	2,80,000
of shares in XYZ	72,000	36,000	Debtors		
Gen. Reserves.			ABC:	1,60,000	
ABC:	2,40,000		XYZ:	56,000	2,16,000
XYZ:	16,000	2,56,000	Cash at bank		
Proportion of undistributed			ABC:	1,04,000	
profits of XYZ to outsiders		12,000	XYZ:	1,04,000	2,08,000
P&L Appropriation Account		80,000			
Total		15,92,000	Total		15,92,000

23.8 PURE DIVESTITURES, SPIN-OFFS AND EQUITY CARVE-OUTS

Firms do not always go in for the combination. Sometimes, especially parent companies, go for a reverse process of selling the assets of their subsidiary. A parent firm divests or sells off a part of its operation when it does not earn adequate rate of return or when it intends to narrow down the scope of its operation. In some cases, it sells off its assets when it needs cash for different purposes. This process is known as divestiture. Divestitures may take three forms. They are as follows:

1. Pure divestitures or sell-offs;
2. Spin-offs; and
3. Equity carve-outs.

23.8.1 Pure Divestitures

Pure divestiture is a process in which a part of the operation of the subsidiary is sold out to a third party either for cash or for securities or for a combination of the two. Divestiture is a voluntary one when the parent company makes the sale because of its own interests and not under any legal compulsion. What are the benefits for the parent company? Firstly, it may be a defence against hostile takeovers. Secondly, it helps bring in the required cash and thus helps improve liquidity. Thirdly, sell-off is a way to part with the unprofitable divisions.

> Pure divestiture is a process in which a part of the operation of the subsidiary is sold out to a third party either for cash or for securities or for a combination of the two.

If divestiture is voluntary, it is done in the interests of the firm and so it does have a positive impact on the shareholders' wealth. Black and Grundfest (1988) found in their empirical study that there was abnormal increase in the shareholders' wealth for the sellers in the sequel of divestitures.

> Reliance Industries Ltd. (RIL.) is India's largest private sector company with a turnover of Rs 1,18,354 crore and a profit of Rs 11,943 crore. In November 2007, it divested 4.01 per cent of its stake in Reliance Petroleum Ltd. (RPL) which amounted to Rs 4,023 crore. To be specific, it sold 18.04 crore equity shares out of its holding of 75% in RPL through the stock exchange. This move has broad-based the shareholding pattern and helped increase funds flow that will have a positive effect on the share prices.

23.8.2 Spin-offs

Sometimes a parent company separates the operation of its subsidiary from its own through distributing its shares in the subsidiary among its existing shareholders on a pro rata basis. In the sequel, the subsidiary becomes a new company and the existing shareholders in the subsidiary own the spun-off subsidiary.

Spin-offs are different from the sell-offs insofar as the parent receives no cash out of spin-off; and moreover, the initial shareholders of the spun-off divisions are the same as the parent shareholders. Spin-offs are common because they sometimes increase the company's focus. It is because it is easier to value the parent and the subsidiary after spin-off.

Synonymous with spin-offs, there are split-offs where a firm offers some of its shareholders its shares in subsidiary in exchange for their shares in the parent company. In this case too, the subsidiary becomes a new company but unlike spin-offs, the proportionate ownership of the two firms changes as those shareholders not party to the split-off process lose control over the subsidiary.

23.8.3 Equity Carve-outs

In equity carve-outs, some of the subsidiary's shares are sold out to the public in general and not to the existing shareholders. This process is different from the spin-offs insofar as the equity carve-out involves only a part of the subsidiary's equity. Moreover, shares are sold out for cash in case of equity carve-out, whereas, there is no cash exchange in case of spin-offs. Again, carve-outs are often subject to stringent disclosure requirements. Michaely and Shaw (1995) have found that profitable firms use mostly carve-outs, while loss-making firms use spin-offs.

SUMMARY

Firms may also expand through combinations which are often known as mergers and acquisitions (M&As). M&As may be vertical, horizontal or conglomerate. They are acquisitions and amalgamation. Again, they are hostile take-overs, friendly take-overs and leveraged buyouts. The formation of a holding company is also a form of combination.

There are a number of forces that encourage combination. These are reaping of the synergistic effects, doing away with the competition, reaping oligopolistic gains and diversification benefits. Tax consideration and personal consideration are also found in certain cases.

Sometimes, firms go for the reverse of combination. The process is manifest in different forms, such as divestitures, spin-offs and equity carve-outs.

In the process of M&As, the determination of the value of the acquired firm is important. It is normally determined on the basis of market value of the shares. The comparative P/E ratio is the best guide in this respect.

The payment to the target firm is made in form of cash, equity shares, preference shares or a combination of the same.

The target firm closes its accounts showing the effect of combination in its realisation account and the shareholders' account. The acquiring firm shows it through its balance sheet. In case of a holding company, a consolidated balance sheet is prepared combining the assets and liabilities of both the holding company and its subsidiary company. In India, there are specific rules and regulations governing mergers and take-overs.

POINTS TO REMEMBER

1. What are the forms of corporate combination?
   (a) Based on corporate structure
   - Merger
   - Acquisition
   - Consolidation

(b) Based on financial relationship
- Horizontal
- Vertical
- Conglomerate

(c) Based on technique
- Friendly take-over
- Hostile take-over
- Leveraged buy-out

2. What are the motivations behind combination?
   - Reaping synergistic advantages
   - Enjoying monopoly power
   - Reaping diversification benefits
   - Increased debt capacity
   - Tax saving
   - Reaping gains from undervalued assets
   - Agency issues
3. What are the gains from and costs of M&As?
   - Gains in terms of increased profit
   - Cost in terms of paying consideration value in excess of MPS in the target firm
4. How do you determine the consideration value?
   - The purpose is to raise the post-merger value of the firm.
   - The ceiling price is represented by the product of P/E ratio of the acquiring firm and the EPS of the target firm.
   - Floor price is equal to the MPS of the target firm.
5. What are the modes of merger financing?
   - Cash payment
   - Exchange of equity shares
   - Preference shares and debentures
   - Deferred payment plan
6. What are the provisions of the Indian Companies Act?
   - Acquisition only up to 25% shares of the target company
   - Related information to be supplied to the stock exchange and to the central government in specific cases
7. What is pure divestiture?
   - Parent company sells a part of the operations of the subsidiary to a third party.
8. What do you mean by spin-offs?
   - Parent company distributes the shares of the subsidiary among the existing shareholders.
9. What is equity carve-out?
   - Parent company sells the share of the subsidiary to the public in general and not to the existing shareholders.

DESCRIPTIVE QUESTIONS

1. Explain the different forms of combination.
2. Corporate combinations have certain motives behind them. Explain.
3. How is consideration value determined? Explain how the gains from acquisition are shared by the acquiring firm and the target firm.
4. What are the modes of payment of the consideration value? Explain their relative merits and demerits.
5. Describe the features of the M&A regulations prevalent in India.
6. Distinguish between pure divestiture, spin-offs and equity carve-outs.
7. Mention in brief the accounting procedure related to M&As.

OBJECTIVE-TYPE QUESTIONS

1. Mark true or false.
   (a) In equity carve-outs, the subsidiary's shares are not sold to the public in general.
   (b) Pure divestitures may be voluntary as well as compulsory.
   (c) In the case of holding/subsidiary companies, preparation of the consolidated balance sheet is mandatory in India.
   (d) SEBI needs to be informed if the acquisition involves more than 5% of the equity shares.
   (e) In a deferred payment plan of payment of consideration value, the acquiring company makes the additional payment even if there is no growth in earnings.
   (f) Equity shares are exchanged for the payment of consideration value.
   (g) The floor price of the consideration value is equal to the market value of the shares of the target company.
   (h) Vertical combinations occur among the firms involved in similar activities of business.
   (i) Conglomerates are found among unrelated firms.
   (j) Friendly take-overs are often more time consuming.
2. Choose the most suitable answer.
   (a) Horizontal combinations occur among firms involved in:
      (i) a similar line of business activities
      (ii) different stages of production of the same final product
      (iii) unrelated business activities
   (b) Hostile take-overs:
      (i) are less time consuming
      (ii) are more time consuming
      (iii) involve a lot of negotiation

(c) Combination helps in:
   (i) achieving economies of scale
   (ii) reducing the tax burden
   (iii) both of the above

(d) The ceiling price of the consideration value is equal to:
   (i) the market value of the shares of the target company
   (ii) the product of the EPS of the target company and the P/E ratio of the acquiring company
   (iii) neither of the above

(e) M&As in India have to conform to the provisions of:
   (i) The Indian Companies Act, 1956
   (ii) SEBI guidelines
   (iii) Both of the above

NUMERICAL PROBLEMS

1. Firm X is acquiring Firm Y. The financial position of the two firms is as follows:

	Firm X	Firm Y
Present earnings (Rs)	40,000	18,000
Shares (no.)	10,000	6,000
EPS (Rs)	4	3
MPS (Rs)	60	30
P/E ratio	15	10

If Firm X pays Rs 40 for each share in Firm Y, find the value of the merged firm and the gains from the merger.

2. Firm A has a taxable income of Rs 1,40,000 and Firm B has incurred a loss of Rs 20,000. The tax rate is 30%. Find out if there is any tax saving as a sequel to the merger of A and B.

3. A is acquiring B and pays 40% premium for B's shares. The financial position of the two companies prior to acquisition is given here respectively in the second and third columns below. Fill in the fourth column to show the post-merger scenario.

	A	B	A + B (post-acquisition)
Net profit (Rs)	1,00,000	20,000	
No. of shares	50,000	25,000	
MPS (Rs)	120	30	
Total market price (Rs)	60,00,000	7,50,000	
EPS (Rs)	2	0.80	
P/E ratio	60	37.5	

SOLVED NUMERICAL PROBLEMS

1. Company A with 10 lakh outstanding shares of Rs 40 each acquires Company B which has 5 lakh outstanding shares of Rs 20 each. The latter will be ready for acquisition only when it gains at least Rs 25 lakh from this move. Find how much Company A should pay per share to Company B.

Solution

Payment per share = (Share value of target company + gain)/No. of shares
= (5,00,000 shares × Rs 20 + Rs 25,00,000)/5,00,000 shares
= Rs 25 per share

2. Company A with 10 lakh outstanding shares of Rs 40 each acquires Company B which has 5 lakh outstanding shares of Rs 20 each. Their P/E ratio is 10 and 8 respectively. Find the price-earning ratio of the merged firm if Company A gives one share for every 2 shares in Company B.

Solution

Prior to acquisition:
A's earning = (10,00,000 shares × Rs 40)/10 = Rs 40,00,000
B's earning = (5,00,000 shares × Rs 20)/8 = Rs 12,50,000
After merger:
No of shares = 10,00,000 + 2,50,000 = 12,50,000
Earnings = Rs 40,00,000 + 12,50,000 = Rs 52,50,000
Price of the shares = 12,50,000 × Rs 40 = Rs 5,00,00,000
P/E ratio of the merged firm = Rs 5,00,00,000/52,50,000 = 9.52

3. Company A decides to acquire Company B in the expectation that the latter will improve its value by Rs 20 lakh over and above its 10 lakh shares selling at Rs 10 each. It gives Rs 12 per share as consideration value. Will this consideration value be acceptable to Company B? Will Company B gain if the consideration value is raised to Rs 15 per share?

Solution

Company B's value = Rs 10 × 10,00,000 shares + Rs 20,00,000 = Rs 1,20,00,000
Value per share = Rs 1,20,00,000/10,00,000 shares = Rs 12 per share
This is the floor consideration value that may be acceptable to Company B.
In case of Rs 15 per share, the gain would be
= (Rs 15 × 10,00,000 shares) – Rs 1,20,00,000 = Rs 30,00,000

4. The financial variables of the acquiring company, A and the target company, B are given hereunder.

	Company A	*Company B*
EPS (Rs)	15	17.50
Price of shares (Rs)	100	80
P/E ratio	6.67	4.57
No. of shares	20,000	40,000
Total earnings	3,00,000	7,00,000
Market value	20,00,000	32,00,000

The primary reason behind the acquisition is to raise EPS of the merged firm at least to Rs 16. Find (a) How many shares will be exchanged for one share in the target firm? (b) What will be P/E ratio of the merged firm?

Solution

(a) No. of shares offered per share in the target company so that the EPS in the merged firm is Rs 16:
= Earnings of the merged firm/EPS in the merged firm
= Rs (7,00,000 + 3,00,000)/16 = 62,500 shares
= 62,500 shares – 20,000 shares of the acquiring firm = 42,500 shares to be given to B
= 42,500 shares/40,000 shares = 1.0625 shares to be given per share in B

(b) P/E ratio = Total value/Total earnings
= Rs (20,00,000 + 32,00,000)/(3,00,000 + 7,00,000)
= 5.2

5. If the operating profit of the merged firm rises by Rs 75,000 and the acquiring firm pays Rs 2 per share more than the market value of the share in the target company, find the NPV of gains to shareholders in the acquiring firm, given 10.0% as discount rate and 50,000 shares in the target company.

Solution

PV gains in perpetuity = Rs 75,000/0.10 = Rs 7,50,000
Less cost of paying more = Rs 2 × 50,000 shares = 1,00,000

Rs 6,50,000

6. Company A is acquiring Company B. The former pays 0.5 of its shares to the shareholders in the target company for each share held by them. The financial variables of the two companies are as follows:

	Company A	*Company B*
Profit (Rs lakh)	75	15
No. of shares	12,50,000	4,00,000
EPS (Rs)	6.00	3.75
MPS (Rs)	72.00	30.00
P/E ratio	12	8

Calculate the EPS of the acquiring firm after merger. Find out the premium to be received by the shareholders of the target firm if the P/E ratio of the merged firm is 12.

Solution

Combined profit = Rs 75,00,000 + 15,00,000 = Rs 90,00,000
Combined shares = 12,50,000 + 0.5(4,00,000) = 14,50,000
EPS of the combined firm = Rs 90,00,000/14,50,000 = Rs 6.21
Market price after merger = P/E × EPS = 12 × 6.21 = Rs 74.52
Premium = {0.5 (74.52) – 30.00}/30.00 = 0.242 = 24.2%

Study Topic: Takeovers Regulations in India

SEBI Regulations

- Takeovers mean substantial acquisition of the shares of the target company in order to control/manage the target company.
- The word substantial means differently for different purposes.
- For the purpose of disclosure, it means holding of 5 per cent or more of the shares or voting rights if the target company is informed within four working days, 15 per cent or more if the target company is informed within 21 days from the financial year ending 31st March as well as the record date fixed for the dividend declaration, etc.
- For the purpose of control, it means appointment of majority of directors and making of policy decisions.
- The documents need to be filed with SEBI within 14 days from the date of provisional announcement and depositing Rs. 50,000 as fee.
- The merchant banker needs to submit a due diligence certificate.
- The acquirer sends OD and bank acceptance to the shareholder through the merchant banker within 45 days from the date of PA. The offer remains open for 30 days.
- The stock exchanges where the share are listed are informed about the deal at least four working days before the date of actual allotment

Procedures

- Merchant banker advising on the acquisition
- Collecting information regarding the target and examining the shareholders' profile as well as the debt profile
- Evaluating the Articles of Association
- Public pronouncement through the newspaper - one in English newspaper and the other in the regional language, within four days of finalizing the agreement.
- The announcement must include the identity of the acquirer, purpose of acquisition, total number of shares to be acquired, offer price and the modes of its payment, the highest and the average price to be paide by the acquirer to shares of the target company during the 12-month period prior to announcement, date of opening and closure of the offer and other details of the financial arrangements in the context of the acquisition.
- Preparation of a letter of offer within 14 days of announcement and its approval by the SEBI.
- Handing over the offer letter to the target company.
- Mailing of the offer letter to the shareholders within 45 days.
- Opening of an escrow accountand depositing the required amount as security for performance.
- Making of paymentwithin 30 days of the closure of the offer.
- If there is an upward revision of the price, that needs to be paid seven days before the closure of the offer.

—Based on SEBI Documents

REFERENCE

Black, B.S. and J.A. Gundfest (1988). "Shareholder Gains from Takeovers and Restructurings", *Journal of Applied Corporate Finance*, 1 (Spring): 5–15.

Michaely R. and W. Shaw (1995), "The Choice of Going Public: Spin-offs ve Carveouts", *Financial Management*, Autumn.

SELECT FURTHER READINGS

Bradley, M. et al. (1988). "Synergistic Gains from Corporate Acquisitions and their Division between the Stockholders of Target and Acquiring Firms", *Journal of Financial Economics*, 21 (1): 3–40.

Myers, S.C. (1976). "A Framework for Evaluating Mergers". In Myers, S.C., ed., 1976, *Modern Developments in Financial Management*. New York: Praeger.

Reinhardt, U.F. (1972). *Mergers and Consolidations: A Corporate Finance Approach*. Morristown, N.J.: General Learning Press.

Shleifer, A. and R.W. Vishney (1988). "Value Maximisation and Acquisition Process", *Journal of Economic Perspectives*, 2 (1): 36–56.

24

CORPORATE FINANCIAL DISTRESS

OBJECTIVES

To explain the concept of financial distress
To pinpoint the ratios on the basis of which financial distress can be predicted
To evaluate different ways of handling corporate failure

When not properly managed, a company may become financially distressed and then, if not checked, may finally cease to operate. That is why it is essential for a finance manager to be alert and to watch various indicators that show the advent of financial distress. If at all, financial distress does appear, the finance manager must have an idea of the tools that may be used as a remedial measure on such occasions. The present chapter discusses the very concept of financial distress, the symptoms that indicate any advent of such occasions and finally the ways in which to tackle it.

24.1 CONCEPT OF FINANCIAL DISTRESS

Financial distress, which is often referred to as financial failure, is a broad term and it can be interpreted in different ways. They are as follows:

1. Economic failure
2. Financial failure that includes,
   (i) Illiquidity
   (ii) Insolvency

Economic failure occurs where the firm's revenue is not sufficient to cover its costs or when the internal rate of return (irr) is less than the firm's cost of capital.

24.1.1 Economic Failure

Here the word, "failure" does not mean a firm's dissolution or collapse. Economic failure occurs where the firm's revenue is not sufficient to cover its costs or when the internal rate of return (IRR) is less than the firm's cost of capital. In other words, it can be said that economic distress occurs when a firm ceases to operate profitably. Such a situation may arise when the costs are not managed properly and/or if the sales do not generate sufficient revenue. It may happen also when the assets are not properly utilised.

24.1.2 Financial Failure

Financial failure occurs when the firm is operating profitably but it is unable to meet its contractual obligations to its creditors. This is why financial failure is often called contractual failure.

Financial failure may emerge on two counts. One is the illiquidity of the firm. The other is insolvency. Illiquidity is the case in which a firm's assets are sufficient to cover its liabilities, but liquidity (cash) is lacking at a particular point of time with the result that it cannot meet its contractual obligations. It is thus a temporary phenomenon and is often reversible.

Insolvency occurs when a firm's total liabilities exceed the value of the firm which means a negative net worth. This means that the firm is structurally incapable of meeting its contractual obligations.

In order to distinguish illiquidity from insolvency, it is often said that illiquidity is technical insolvency that emerges on account of a shortage of cash. On the other hand, insolvency is known as bankruptcy insolvency where the firm's total liabilities exceed the fair market value of its assets. The former is a comparatively less serious condition, than the latter.

24.2 SYMPTOMS OF FINANCIAL DISTRESS

Although financial distress cannot be predicted with certainty, yet there are certain indicators on the basis of which a finance manager can predict it. These indicators are nothing but financial ratios. Beaver (1986) finds in his study of 79 large firms some specific ratios that indicate the possibility of financial distress. They are as follows:

> Illiquidity is technical insolvency that emerges on account of a shortage of cash. On the other hand, insolvency is bankruptcy insolvency where a firm's total liabilities exceed fair market value of its assets.

1. Cash flow/Total debt
2. EBIT/Total assets
3. Cash flow/Total assets
4. Net income/Total assets
5. Sales/Total assets
6. Total debt/Total assets

It is suggested that the reader consults Chapter 19 of this book for a detailed discussion of the computation of these ratios. The first five ratios are related to certain forms of income that are divided by total debt or total assets. Failing firms have comparatively low ratios vis-a-vis non-failing firms. The sixth ratio is concerned with the debt burden. Failing firms are naturally associated with a high total debt/total asset ratio.

A similar study conducted by Altman (1968, 1993) reveals that certain financial ratios have a definite role in making a firm a distinctly failing one. He relies on five ratios, a sum of which determines the score. The score distinguishes a failing firm from the others. The five ratios are as follows:

1. Net working capital/Total assets
2. Retained earnings/Total assets
3. EBIT/Total assets
4. Total market value of shares/Book value of total debt
5. Sales/Total assets

These ratios indicate respectively: the investment of funds in the current assets; profitability relative to time; return on investment or the general earning power; financial leverage position; and the management's ability to generate sales out of the firm's assets. Failing firms are characterised by a low investment in current assets, being comparatively young, lower earning power, high debt burden and lower asset turnover. Altman feels that firms with a score of less than 1.81 are bound to face financial distress. Those above 1.81 but less than 2.99 are on the boundary line. But those above 2.99 do not land in financial distress.

Similarly, Gilson (1989) reveals that financially distressed firms are normally large, highly levered, with lower profitability and with lower dividend paying capacity and more likely to have negative accounting earnings. However, Menon and Schwartz (1990) are of opinion that financial ratios are simply one of the predictors of the corporate failure. The other predictors are management incentives and other strategic factors.

In the Indian context, Jayadev (2006) has analysed the financial factors responsible for predicting companies' financial distress. His study is based on Altman's Z-score model. Although he has made minor modifications in the sense that he has considered debt/book value of equity in place of debt/market value of equity. Based on his analysis, financial distress can be predicted one year prior to default if working capital/total asset ratio is -0.938 + 0.111, return on equity/total assets ratio is 0.027, EBIT/total asset ratio is 3.054, debt/equity ratio is 0.166 and sales/total assets ratio is 1.030.

24.3 MANAGEMENT OF CORPORATE FAILURE

24.3.1 Determinants of the Mode of Handling Failure

There are many ways of handling corporate failure—ranging from a mere contingency plan and out-of-the-court settlements to reorganisation as per the court's order and to liquidation of the firms. The selection of a particular approach depends on:

1. Nature of the failure;
2. Extent of the failure;
3. Choice of the different parties related to the firm.

If distress is to a large extent structural, there is no way out but to liquidate the firm. If, however, it is a contractual failure, reorganisation schemes are often implemented. When contractual failure is accompanied by economic failure, liquidation is the right course of action.

Again, if the failure is at the first stage, it can be managed simply through a contingency plan. If on the other hand it has already developed into the later stages, different schemes of reorganisation including voluntary settlements are required. If the financial ratios have crossed manageable limits, liquidation becomes more and more imminent.

Similarly, it is the choice of the shareholders/creditors/management that determines the mode of combating failure. For example, if the creditors and the shareholders are not agreeable to simple measures like composition and extension (to be discussed later), the company will have to move the court for a solution.

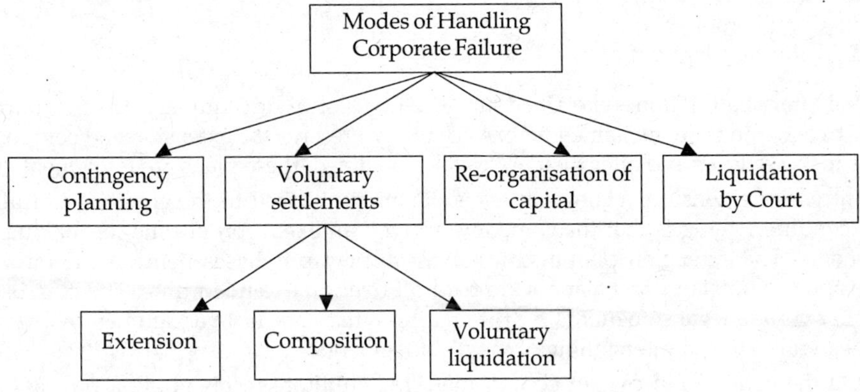

24.3.2 Contingency Planning

Contingency planning is useful only when distress is in the first phase or is yet to take a definite shape. The primary task before the finance manager is to mobilise resources. As a short-term measure, uncommitted reserves are built up that involves stretching of payables and exploitation of unused lines of credit. These sources of funds are often spontaneous inasmuch as the company accedes to them with the least possible efforts. Additionally, the company may go in for short-term borrowings but this requires negotiation with the lenders.

Contingency planning is useful only when distress is in the first phase or is yet to take a definite shape. The primary task before the finance manager is to mobilise resources. As a short-term measure, uncommitted reserves are built up that involves stretching of payables and exploitation of unused lines of credit. A company can reduce various expenses relating to production and distribution of the product.

Apart from the building up of uncommitted reserves, the company can reduce various expenses relating to production and distribution of the product. The current rate of dividend can also be trimmed.

As a medium-term measure, the company can cut capital expenditure or the expenditure on research and development. It may also sell a part of the fixed assets in order to mobilise resources.

After resources have been mobilised, a plan is chalked out as to how to deploy the mobilised resources. A particular sequence may be followed where the most liquid resources are used first and then the less liquid ones are used. Another sequence with just the reverse order of liquidity may also be followed. In fact, the selection of the sequence depends on the nature of the distress as well as on whether the finance manager is conservative or aggressive. If the finance manager is conservative, he stresses more on maintaining liquidity.

24.3.3 Voluntary Settlements

Voluntary settlements are out-of-court settlements allowing the company to continue as a going concern. They involve the following:

1. Extension
2. Composition
3. Voluntary liquidation

Voluntary liquidation is explained subsequently along with liquidation by the court. The other two methods are explained here. A company presents the extension and composition plans to its creditors and after their approval is obtained, these plans are implemented.

In case of extension, a company pays the amount owed to the creditors in full. The only condition being is that the company is given an extension of time for making such payments. The extension plan also involves all new purchases being made on a cash basis and the outstanding balances are paid off over an extended time. The plan usually includes certain legal safeguards for the creditors that vary from assignment of the assets as collateral to the countersigning of the disbursements.

On the contrary, in case of composition, the creditors receive only a pro rata share of their claims. They agree to this plan because they know that, if this is not done, the company will become bankrupt and that would delay the payment. If there are some dissenting creditors, they are paid off in full if there are only a few of them. This is done to expedite the composition procedure.

> In case of composition, the creditors receive only a pro rata share of their claims.

Now the question is whether the out-of-court settlement is a better way out. It avoids unnecessary expenses that may be legal, administrative and investigative. Moreover, the bargaining process is considerably simplified and a congenial atmosphere is created. However, there is always a question mark as to how far the creditors trust the management. It is more often that the creditors do not agree to such plans. Furthermore, the law of the land sometimes does not favour private restructuring, especially when fraudulent intent is anticipated. If at all the law permits private restructuring, it is not binding on the different parties related to the company. Michel and Shaked (1990) give an example of how shareholders were not agreeable to recovery of cash that was part of an out-of-court settlement.

24.3.4 Reorganisation

A reorganisation or reconstruction scheme is another method of tackling financial distress while allowing a company to continue as a going concern. The reorganisation scheme may be either internal or external. External reorganisation involves mergers and consolidation that has already been discussed in the preceding chapter. So it is the internal reorganisation that will be discussed here.

Internal reorganisation or reconstruction stands for a capital reduction plan in conformity with Sections 100 to 105 of the Indian Companies Act, 1956. The plan can take either of the following forms:

1. Reduction or extinction of the liability of members on account of uncalled capital;
2. Writing-off or cancellation of any paid-up capital which stands unrepresented by available assets;

3. Paying-off of capital being in excess of requirements;
4. Any other way approved of by the court.

In case of reduction or extinction of liability on account of uncalled capital, the shareholders benefit to the extent that they are not required to pay any further amount on the shares held by them. However, the security of the creditors extending to uncalled capital diminishes. When a part of capital is returned to the shareholders, creditor's security in this case also reduces. It is for this reason why creditors resent such plans.

When a company suffers from continuous losses either on account of a defective investment policy or due to certain other factors, the balance sheet shows accumulated losses in form of goodwill. In such cases, depreciation is lowered with the result that the assets appear in excess of their reasonable value. A capital reduction plan removes such an anomaly.

A capital reduction plan involves the following steps in sequence. They are as follows:

1. Estimation of loss;
2. Writing-off of the loss;
3. Paying compensation to different parties; and
4. Arrangement of working capital.

The first step is to estimate the losses. To this end, the debit side of the profit and loss account, the unwritten-off amount of fictitious assets and the intangible assets are summed up.

As regards writing-off of the losses, liabilities are reduced in the following order:

1. Equity share capital;
2. Preference share capital;
3. Unsecured loan; and
4. Loan secured by a floating charge.

If the loss is big, the entire equity capital may be reduced to zero. Therefore, the equity shareholders are the greatest sufferers. However, they agree to such plan in order to avoid liquidation.

The next step in the capital reduction scheme is to compensate different parties who suffer loss on account of the writing-off of the losses. The equity shareholders are not compensated inasmuch as an increase in their earnings in the sequel of capital reduction plan makes them better-off. However, the rate of dividend on preference shares is raised. The creditors are paid in form of cash. In certain cases, the interest rate is also raised.

The last step is to increase the working capital pool. Additional capital is arranged for this purpose. The modes of arrangement of additional capital are as follows:

1. Issue of shares in the market;
2. Requesting debenture-holders to extend the loan;
3. Short-term borrowings.

These steps of the reorganisation process are evident in the balance sheet of the company. The following example will make it clear.

EXAMPLE

The following is the balance sheet of ABC & Co. Ltd as on 31 December, 2003.

Liabilities	Amount (Rs)	Assets	Amount (Rs)
Authorised capital		Goodwill	10,000
30,000 8% preference shares	3,00,000	Plant & machinery	1,70,000
80,000 ordinary shares	8,00,000	Premises	1,40,000
Issued capital		Stock	2,80,950
30,000 8% preference shares	3,00,000	Debtors	3,58,000
30,000 ordinary shares fully paid	3,00,000	Cash	1,500
6% debentures	1,50,000	Profit & loss Account	39,500
Sundry creditors	2,49,000		
Total	9,99,950	Total	9,99,500

Reorganisation takes place on the following lines:

(a) 8% preference shareholders have to forego any arrears of dividend and such shares are to be converted into 6% preference shares of Rs 10 each.

(b) The ordinary shares of Rs 10 each are to be divided into five shares of Rs 2 each. Out of five shares, three shares are to be surrendered to the firm and two out of every three shares so surrendered will be allotted to the preference shareholders in proportion to their holdings as 10% preference shares. The remaining shares are to be cancelled or are utilised for writing off of losses, in writing down plant and machinery to Rs 1,62,000 and in eliminating goodwill.

Solution

The following is the balance sheet of ABC & Co. Ltd as on 31 December, 2003.

Liabilities	Amount (Rs)	Assets	Amount (Rs)
Authorised capital		Plant & machinery	1,62,000
30,000 6% preference shares	3,00,000	Premises	1,40,000
60,000 10% preference shares		Stock	2,80,950
of Rs 2 each	1,20,000	Debtors	3,58,000
3,40,000 ordinary shares of Rs 2		Cash	1,500
each	6,50,000		
Issued capital			
30,000 6% preference shares	3,00,000		
60,000 10% preference shares	1,20,000		
60,000 ordinary shares fully paid	1,20,000		
6% debentures	1,50,000		
Sundry creditors	2,49,000		
Capital reserves	2,500		
Total	9,42,450	Total	9,42,450

24.3.5 Liquidation

Liquidation means the selling of a company's assets and the distribution of the proceeds, after meeting the necessary expenses, among the creditors and shareholders of the company according to established norms. It is different from reorganisation and other methods of corporate failure management that believe in the continuity of the firm as a going concern. On the contrary, the company comes to an end as a sequel to liquidation.

Liquidation versus Reorganisation: Now the question is why should liquidation be preferred when reorganisation can be adopted that allows the firm to continue as a going concern. The basic principle behind the reorganisation versus liquidation decision is that reorganisation should be preferred only when the going-concern value after reorganisation is greater than the liquidation value. But this is not always the case. Sometimes the liquidation value is greater than the going-concern value and in such cases, liquidation is suggested.

> Liquidation means the selling of a company's assets and the distribution of the proceeds, after meeting the necessary expenses, among the creditors and shareholders of the company according to established norms.

Voluntary Liquidation: If the creditors feel that the company has become insolvent, voluntary liquidation occurs, in which case the Registrar of Companies is informed. Sometimes, voluntary liquidation is supervised by the court. In both the cases, a liquidator is appointed who sells the assets, meets the necessary expenses and distributes the realised value among the creditors and shareholders. He submits a detailed account to the creditors and shareholders. Whatever may be the mode of voluntary liquidation, it is quick and less expensive. The only problem is that the shareholders and creditors rarely come to an agreement with the result that the matter is often referred to a court for settlement.

Liquidation by the Court: When the varying interests of the creditors and the shareholders complicate voluntary liquidation, it is the court that begins the process of liquidation. The court appoints a liquidator to whom the company submits a Statement of Affairs showing the assets and liabilities and other details. The liquidator then sells the assets, meets the necessary expenses and meets the claims of different parties.

The proceeds of the assets are available to the different claimants essentially in the following order:

1. Legal charges;
2. Liquidator's remuneration;
3. Cost of liquidation;
4. Preferential creditors;
5. Secured creditors;
6. Unsecured creditors;
7. Preference shareholders;
8. Equity shareholders.

Preferential creditors are the government and the employees of the company as per the provisions of the law. They are paid in full. If assets are found inadequate, they are paid on a pro rata basis.

As regards secured creditors, it is assumed that they realise their own securities and so the liquidator does not make any payment to them. If the value of the collateral is greater than the amount of debt, the surplus is realised by the liquidator.

The equity shareholders are described as contributories. They first pay the uncalled amount demanded from them but are the last claimant to the liquidated value. Their cake may be bigger/smaller depending upon what remains after the distribution of the liquidated value among the creditors and the preference shareholders.

The liquidator prepares a detailed account of the various receipts and payments and submits it to the court.

24.4 MANAGEMENT OF FINANCIAL DISTRESS IN INDIA

Industrial sickness was long the subject of the Reserve Bank of India. In 1976, the H.N. Ray Committee was appointed to suggest measures in this context, but nothing substantial could be done. Another committee, known as Tiwari Committee, was appointed in 1981 to suggest measures on dealing with the financial distress. The Committee suggested for a legislation in this respect and the establishment of a quasi-judicial body. As a result, the Sick Industrial Companies Act (SICA) came into existence in 1985. The Board for Industrial and Financial Reconstruction (BIFR) was set up in 1987. An appellate body was also formed. It was Appellate Authority for Industrial and Financial Reconstruction (AAIFR).

The main objective of SICA is to detect well in time any sickness and expedite the revival of potentially viable units or closure of unviable industrial companies. In the beginning, only private sector companies could avail of the facility. But in 1991, it was also the government companies that were brought under the purview of the SICA/BIFR.

Accumulated losses must be higher than or at least equal to the company's net worth in order to be a financially distressed company, provided the company should have completed at least 5 years after its incorporation, must have obtained a factory licence and have 50 or more workers.

The measures are either legal or financial restructuring or toning of the management. The measures have already been discussed. A company possessing the above qualification has to register with the BIFR within 60 days of its net worth becoming negative. The BIFR appoints an operating agency to look into the matter and to suggest a viable rehabilitation scheme. A rehabilitation plan is designed within another 90 days' time and is implemented thereafter.

Again, in 2002, the government enacted Securitization and Reconstruction of Financial Assets and Enforcement of Security Interest Act to give some leeway at least to the secured creditors. It also permits the creation of asset reconstruction companies to lighten the burden of non-performing assets of banks and financial institutions.

SUMMARY

Failure does not necessarily mean a firm's dissolution or collapse. Economic failure occurs when a firm does not operate profitably. Financial failure occurs either when a firm is not able to meet its contractual obligations either on account of illiquidity or when its liabilities exceed the value of its assets.

Corporate failure can be predicted to a large extent with the help of financial ratios. These ratios normally relate to the earning power, debt burden, net working capital, etc., of the firm.

There are a number of measures to handle failure. Their application depends on the nature of failure, gravity of failure, and the choice of the creditors and shareholders. Contingency planning is adopted when distress is in its early phases. Voluntary settlements are one of other measures comprising extension and composition. Again, a reorganisation scheme involves writing-off of losses through capital reduction schemes. Lastly, liquidation is adopted when other methods are not useful and when the liquidated value is greater than the going-concern value. Liquidation is either voluntary or through the court. A liquidator is appointed by the court who sells the assets and distributes the proceeds among the creditors and shareholders as per the norms.

POINTS TO REMEMBER

1. What are the different types of corporate financial distress?
   - Economic failure
   - Financial failure on account of illiquidity
   - Financial failure on account of insolvency
2. How do you anticipate financial distress?
   - Weak financial ratios
   - Weak management incentives
   - Weak strategic factors
3. What are the determinants of the mode of handling failure?
   - Nature of failure
   - Extent of failure
   - Choice of different parties related to the firm
4. What are the modes of handling failure?
   - Contingency planning
   - Voluntary settlements – Extension, Composition and Voluntary liquidation
   - Re-organisation of capital
   - Liquidation by court

DESCRIPTIVE QUESTIONS

1. Distinguish between economic failure and financial failure.
2. Explain how corporate financial distress is predicted.
3. "Measures to handle corporate financial distress vary from one case to the other". Discuss. Explain in this context the role of contingency plans and voluntary settlements.
4. Describe financial reorganisation. What are the steps taken in this respect?
5. Explain liquidation of a company. Is it always preferable to financial reorganisation?

OBJECTIVE-TYPE QUESTIONS

1. Mark true or false.
   (a) Financial distress occurs when the IRR is greater than the cost of capital.
   (b) Insolvency occurs when cash in the firm is not sufficient to meet contractual obligations at a particular point of time.
   (c) Insolvency occurs when the firm's liabilities exceed its total assets.
   (d) Fast erosion in earning power leads to corporate failure.
   (e) Contingency plan is primarily concerned with the mobilisation of resources.
   (f) Extension means extension of time for making payments to the creditors.
   (g) Composition refers to the making of payments to the creditors on a pro rata basis.
   (h) Most often there is a clash of the interest of the creditors and the shareholders.
   (i) Liabilities are increased for the purpose of writing off of losses.
   (j) Equity shareholders have a prior claim to the liquidated assets as compared to the preference shareholders.
2. Choose the most suitable answer.
   (a) Insolvency occurs when:
      (i) liabilities exceed the value of assets
      (ii) liabilities are lower than the value of assets
      (iii) the firm is short of desired liquidity
   (b) Economic failure occurs when:
      (i) liabilities exceed the value of assets
      (ii) the firm is short of desired liquidity
      (iii) revenue does not cover cost
   (c) Corporate financial distress can be predicted on the basis of:
      (i) falling earning power of the firm
      (ii) falling debt burden of the firm
      (iii) neither of the above
   (d) Financial reorganisation involves:
      (i) mobilisation of resources
      (ii) capital reduction plan
      (iii) both of the above
   (e) A liquidator is appointed in case of:
      (i) voluntary liquidation only
      (ii) liquidation by court only
      (iii) both of the above
   (f) Contingency plan involves:
      (i) mobilisation of resources
      (ii) capital reduction plan
      (iii) both of the above

NUMERICAL PROBLEMS

1. A company is forced into liquidation. At the time of liquidation, its balance sheet is as follows:

	Amount (Rs)
Total assets....	35,00,000
Liabilities:	
Secured creditors	5,00,000
Unsecured creditors	5,00,000
Preference share capital (fully paid-up)	5,00,000
Ordinary share capital	20,00,000

Show how the liquidated amount can be distributed among the different claimants if:

(a) the assets are liquidated at Rs 10,00,000;

(b) the assets are liquidated at Rs 15,00,000;

(c) the assets are liquidated at Rs 20,00,000.

2. At the time of liquidation, the balance sheet of a company is as follows:

	Amount (Rs)
Total assets....	15,00,000
Liabilities:	
Secured creditors	2,00,000
Unsecured creditors	1,00,000
Preference share capital (fully paid-up)	5,00,000
Ordinary share capital	7,00,000

The liquidation expenses are Rs 15,000; liquidator's fee is Rs 20,000 and the value of the liquidated assets is Rs 7,80,000. Show how the liquidated amount can be distributed among different claimants.

3. A company has run into financial distress. It has Rs 1,50,000 as outstanding debt and Rs 75,000 as the value of current assets. The creditors are agreeable to share the value of current assets. What amount should they get?

SOLVED NUMERICAL PROBLEMS

1. The B/S of ABC & Co. as on 31st March 2007 is as follows:

Liabilities	*Amount Rs*	*Assets*	*Amount Rs*
Auth. & issued capital:		Inventory	1,00,000
8,000 shares/ Rs 100 each	8,00,000	B/R	20,000
6% debentures	14,00,000	Investments	7,000
Accrued interest	70,000	Cash & near-cash assets	1,00,000
Trade creditors	4,30,000	Loss	10,73,000
Income tax to be paid	30,000	Land & build.	5,00,000
		Plant & mach.	9,30,000
Total	27,30,000	Total	27,30,000

The re-organisation scheme approved by the court is as follows:

1. Each share shall be sub-divided into 20 fully-paid equity shares of Rs 5 each.
2. After sub-division, 95% of the holding will be surrendered by the shareholders.
3. Of the surrendered shares, 46,000 shares of Rs 5 each are to be converted into 10% participating preference shares of Rs 5 fully-paid.
4. Debenture-holders' claim to be reduced to Rs 2,30,000 that will be satisfied by the issue of participating preference shares.
5. Income tax liability is to be met.
6. The claims of the unsecured creditors shall be reduced by 80% and for the balance, equity shares of Rs 5 are to be given.
7. Shares surrendered and not re-issued are to be cancelled.

Prepare the re-organised balance sheet.

Solution

Liabilities	*Amount Rs*	*Assets*	*Amount Rs*
Share capital:		Inventory	1,00,000
46,000 pref. shares/Rs 5 each	2,30,000	B/R	20,000
26,000 ord. shares/Rs 5 each	1,30,000	Investments	7,000
Capital reserves	12,97,000	Cash & near-cash assets	1,00,000
		Land & build.	5,00,000
		Plant & mach.	9,30,000
Total	16,57,000	Total	16,57,000

2. Sagar & Co. is liquidated owing to heavy losses shown in the following balance sheet.

Liabilities	*Amount Rs*	*Assets*	*Amount Rs*
8,000 preference shares of Rs 40 each	3,20,000	Land & building	1,00,000
12,000 ord. shares of Rs 40 each	4,80,000	Other fixed assets	8,00,000
Bank loans	16,00,000	Stock	21,00,000
8% debentures	4,00,000	B/R	4,00,000
Int. outstanding on deb.	32,000	Losses	2,32,000
Sundry creditors	8,00,000		
Total	36,32,000	Total	36,32,000

Prepare Liquidator's Final Statement of Accounts after considering the following facts:

Liquidation expenses are Rs 12,000 and Liquidator's remuneration is Rs 40,000. Bank loan was secured by pledges on stock. Debt and interest thereon was secured by floating charge on assets. Fixed assets were realised at book value and the current assets were realised at 80% of book value.

Solution

Liquidator's Final Statement of Accounts

Receipts	*Amount Rs*	*Payments*	*Amount Rs*
Assets realised:		Liquidation expenses	12,000
Land & building	1,00,000	Liquidator's remuneration	40,000
Other fixed assets	8,00,000	Debentures 4,00,000	
Debtors	3,20,000	Add interest 32,000	4,32,000
Surplus from securities	80,000	Sundry creditors	8,00,000
(Stock) Rs			
		Preference shareholders	16,000
		@ Rs 2.00 per share	
Total	13,00,000	Total	13,00,000

CASE STUDY

Case - US Banks in Distress

There was an increase in the number of banks failure in the USA during the year 2010 over that in 2009. Precisely it was 157 compared to 140 failures in 2009. The list of the banks included in the distressed list of the FDIC too got larger. Resultantly, the entire banking structure in the USA stood changed.

Most of the distressed banks were found lending to the real estate sector or lending to other sectors that was secured by real estate. If one looks at the price of the real estate sector since 1996, it is evident that the prices were galloping upward for almost the entire decade. It was only beginning from the last quarter of 2005 that the prices tended to plummet. The decline in the prices was supplemented by increase in the unemployment rate as well as decrease in the commercial activities – ultimately leading to accumulation of the non-performing assets (NPAs) of the banks. The Draconian sword was hanging over the banks whether they would be able to meet their financial obligations.

Various ratios were put into use to distinguish between the financially sound banks and financially vulnerable banks. Some more important of the ratios are:

1. **Provision ratio:** It is calculated by taking ratio of *Provision for loan losses* and *Total assets*. Increasing Provision ratio indicates that loan distributed by bank is becoming more risky and bank is expecting more loan defaults. Increasing Provision ratio also indicates decrease in the value of total assets. With greater provision charged, net income of bank gets reduced. Thus increasing provision ratio indicates financial instability in the bank.
2. **Net NPA to Asset ratio:** It is calculated by dividing Net NPA (Total NPA-Net allowance) by Total assets. The increase in Net NPA to assets ratio indicates that

the increase in provision is not proportionate with the increase in the risk of the loan. As NPA is more than expected, it decreases the equity of the bank and thus indicating that bank is in financial distress.

3. **Net NPA to equity ratio:** It is calculated by using Net NPA divided by Total equity. Increased ratio indicates financial instability of the bank as equity is getting eroded due to increase in the NPA. High ratio indicates that equity of the banks has been diluted and banks are under debts that they would not be able to repay. High ratio is indicative of weak financial position of the banks. High ratio indicates that bank's equity is not enough to protect the bank from its current level of its nonperforming assets. If there is further increase in the level of non-performing assets, equity of the bank will completely be eroded.
4. **Asset quality ratio:** It is calculated by taking ratio of Provision to NPL. This ratio indicates how much of NPL is secured by way of providing provision. Decrease in asset quality ratio indicates that Provision charged is not enough to cover the NPL and thus bank is in financial distress. The value of its assets is decreasing due to increase in proportion of NPA in its assets portfolio and due to which it would not be able to cover its liability.
5. **Tier 1 ratio:** It is the ratio between Tier 1 capital and risk weighted assets. Lower ratio indicates financial instability as bank does not possess enough equity to protect itself against the risk of decreasing assets value.
6. **Total risk based ratio:** It is the ratio between total capital and risk weighted assets. Lower ratio reflects incapability of bank to cover the risk of decreasing value of its assets.
7. **Gross NPA to Gross loan ratio:** It indicates quality of credit portfolio of the banks. High gross NPA ratio indicates the low credit portfolio of bank and vice-versa.
8. **Gross NPA -Provision/Gross Loan-Provision ratio:** This ratio indicates the degree of risk in the portfolio of the bank.
9. **Total Provision/Gross NPA ratio:** This ratio indicates the degree of safety measures adopted by the bank as it has direct bearing on the profitability, dividend and safety of shareholders fund. If the provision ratio is low, it indicates that bank has made lower provision.

Most of the banks in USA that have been closed by FDIC or included in the list of distressed banks have their loan concentration in real estate including loan secured by real estate (primarily houses). When the prices of houses and real estate started to fall as indicated by the AIA billing index and Moody's real estate index, banks were not able recover their loans. It is because market value of underlying assets decreased and as a result, NPA of the banks started rising. It eroded the equity of the banks as indicated by the Net NPA to Equity .This ratio also indicates the level of problem persisting among the banks. High ratio indicates that equity of the banks has been diluted and banks are under debts that banks would not be able to repay which leads to their closure.

List of some of the banks that are expected to close by the year end of 2010 are:

Region	Bank	Net NPA to equity ratio
Georgia	Crescent Bank & Trust Company	7146.70
Illinois	Nor States Bank	106.18
Illinois	Midwest Bank & Trust Bank	325.05
Florida	Horizon Bank	193.29
Maryland	First Mariner Bank	353.52
Michigan	Macatawa Bank	160.46
Michigan	Fidelity Bank	231.42
Michigan	First Bank in Howell	330.42
Tennessee	American Patriot Bank	163.94
Ohio	Ohio Legacy Bank	103.69
Oregon	Premier West Bank	115.69
Oregon	Bank of Cascade	398.65
Washington	American West Bank	610.18

REFERENCES

Altman, E.I. (1968). "Financial Ratios, Discriminant Analysis and the Prediction of Corporate Bankruptcy", *Journal of Finance*, 23 (Sep.): 589–609.

——— (1993). *Corporate Financial Distress and Bankruptcy*. New York: John Wiley & Sons.

Beaver, W.H. (1986). "Financial Ratios as Predictors of Failure", *Journal of Accounting Research,* (Supplement): 71–111.

Gilson, S.C., (1989). "Management Turnover and Financial Distress", *Journal of Financial Economics*, 25 (1): 36–46.

Jayadev, M. (2006). "Predictive Power of Financial Risk Factors: An Empirical Analysis of Default Companies", *Vikalpa*, 31(3).

Menon, G.L. and K. Schwartz (1990). "Predicting Bankruptcy for Firms in Financial Distress", *Journal of Business Finance and Accounting*, 7 (Spring): 53–60.

Michel A. and I. Shaked (1990). "The LBO Nightmare: Fraudulent Conveyence Risk", *Financial Analysts Journal*, 46 (Mar.-Apr.): 41–50.

SELECT FURTHER READINGS

Argenti, J. (1976). *The Corporate Collapse: The Causes and Symptoms*. New York: Halsted Press.

Wruck, K.H. (1990). "Financial Distress, Reorganisation, and Organisational Efficiency", *Journal of Financial Economics*, 27 (4): 419–44.

25

INTERNATIONAL FINANCIAL MANAGEMENT

OBJECTIVES

To explain the concept of fixed and floating exchange rate regime

To describe how exchange rate is quoted

To explain how the exchange rate in the spot market is determined and the factors influencing such process

To discuss exchange rate determination in the forward market and the relevance of interest-rate parity theory in this context

To describe the distinctive features of the foreign exchange market and the various activities in it, such as, arbitrage, hedging and speculation

To explain the features of the market for derivatives, that is, the market for currency futures and for currency options

With growing liberalisation and globalisation of economic policies, corporate financial decisions cannot remain isolated of the changes in the international economic scenario. Changes in the exchange rate, behaviour of the foreign exchange market, international interest rate scenario, etc., influence corporate financial decisions. It is for this reason that international financial management has come to be an integral part of the study of financial management. However, the discussion in the present chapter will be limited to the discussion of the basics of the exchange rate and the foreign exchange market.

25.1 EXCHANGE RATE REGIME

It is the International Monetary Fund (IMF) that determines the shape of the exchange rate regime. It has given its member countries two options as to the type of exchange rate regime they are to follow. These options can broadly be grouped as:

1. Pegged exchange rate regime; and
2. Floating rate regime.

The distinctive features of these two options need some explanation.

> A currency is pegged either to a single currency or to a basket of currencies. This means that the value of a particular currency is fixed in terms of the value of the other currency or the weighted average value of the currencies in the basket, of course, within a given fluctuation band.

25.1.1 Pegged versus Floating Exchange Rate Regime

In the system of pegging, a currency is pegged either to a single currency or to a basket of currencies. This means that the value of a particular currency is fixed in terms of the value of the other currency or the weighted average value of the currencies in the basket, of course, within a given fluctuation band. In case of the floating exchange rate regime, on the other hand, the value of a currency in terms of another currency depends on the demand and the supply position of the latter in the foreign exchange market. Since the demand and supply position is subject to change, the exchange rate is not fixed: rather it is flexible. The determination of the exchange rate in a floating-rate regime is discussed in a subsequent section of this chapter.

The advocates of the floating-rate system put forth two major arguments. First, that the exchange rate varies automatically according to the changes in macroeconomic variables. As a result, no gap appears between the real exchange rate and the nominal exchange rate. The country does not need any adjustment that is often required in a fixed-rate regime and so it does not have to bear the cost of adjustment (Friedman, 1953). The other argument is that this system possesses insulation properties meaning that the currency remains isolated of the shocks emanating from other counties. It also means that a government can adopt an independent economic policy without impinging upon the external sector performance (Friedman, 1953).

However, MacDonald (1988) finds that the exchange rates among the countries on a floating rate system during 1973–85 were far more volatile than was warranted by changes in fundamental monetary variables.

Besides, developing countries in particular do not find floating rates suitable. This is because their economy is not diversified, and since their export is subject to frequent changes in demand and supply, they face frequent changes in exchange rates. This is more so when foreign demand for their products is price-inelastic. When the value of their currency depreciates, export earnings usually sag in view of inelastic demand abroad. Again, greater flexibility in exchange rates between a developed and a developing country generates greater exchange risk in the latter. This is because of the low economic profile of developing countries, and also because they have limited access to the forward market and other risk-reducing mechanisms.

25.1.2 Independent and Managed Floating

A floating rate system may be either independent or managed. Theoretically speaking, the system of managed floating involves intervention by the monetary authorities of the country for the purpose of exchange rate stabilisation. The process of intervention interferes with the market forces and so it is known as "dirty" floating, as against independent

Intervention is direct as well as indirect. When the monetary authorities stabilise the exchange rate by changing interest rates, this is indirect intervention. On the other hand, in the case of direct intervention, the monetary authorities purchase and sell foreign currency in the domestic market.

floating which is known as "clean" floating. However, in practice, intervention is a global phenomenon. Keeping this fact in mind, the IMF is of the view that while the purpose of intervention in the case of an independent floating system is to moderate the rate of change and to prevent undue fluctuation in the exchange rate, the purpose in a managed floating system is to establish a level for the exchange rate.

Intervention is direct as well as indirect. When the monetary authorities stabilise the exchange rate by changing interest rates, this is indirect intervention. On the other hand, in the case of direct intervention, the monetary authorities purchase and sell foreign currency in the domestic market. When they sell foreign currency, its supply increases, and as a result, the domestic currency appreciates against the foreign currency. When they purchase foreign currency, its demand increases, and the domestic currency tends to depreciate vis-à-vis the foreign currency. The IMF permits such intervention. If intervention is adopted for preventing long-term changes in the exchange rate away from equilibrium, it is known as "leaning-against-the-wind" intervention. On the contrary, if the purpose is to support the current trend of exchange rate movement towards equilibrium, it is known as "leaning- with-the-wind" intervention.

As per Plaza Agreement of 1985, G-5 nations had intervened in the foreign exchange market in order to make the US dollar consistent with the prevailing economic indicators.

Intervention helps the value of domestic currency move up or move down through the expectations channel. When the monetary authorities begin supporting the foreign currency, speculators begin buying it forward in the expectation that it will appreciate. Its demand rises and in turn its value appreciates vis-à-vis the domestic currency.

Intervention may be sterilised or non-sterilised. When the monetary authorities purchase a foreign currency through created money, the money supply in the country increases. This leads to inflation, and it is an example of non-sterilised intervention. However, if securities are simultaneously sold in the market to mop up the excess supply of money, intervention does not lead to inflation. This is a sterilised intervention. A study by Obstfeld (1983) reveals that non-sterilised intervention is common, because sterilised intervention is not very effective. However, on the whole, Loopesko (1984) confirms the effect of intervention on exchange rate stabilisation.

Furthermore, there has also been a case of coordinated intervention. As per the Plaza Agreement of 1985, G-5 nations had intervened in the foreign exchange market in order to make the US dollar in consistence with the prevailing economic indicators.

25.2 EXCHANGE RATE QUOTATION

25.2.1 Direct and Indirect Quote

Exchange rates are quoted either directly or indirectly. A direct quote gives the home-currency price of a certain quantity of a foreign currency, usually one unit or 100 units. If India quotes the exchange rate between the rupee and the US dollar in a direct way, the quotation will be written as Rs 40/US $. On the other hand, in indirect quoting, the value of one unit of the home currency is presented in terms of the foreign currency. If India adopts an indirect quote, the banks in India will quote the exchange rate as US $0.025/Re

25.2.2 Buying and Selling Rate

Normally, two rates are published—one being the buying rate and the other being the selling rate. The buying rate is also known as the bid rate. The selling rate is known as ask rate or offer rate. The bid rate is always given first followed by the ask-rate quote. Suppose if rupee-US dollar rate is Rs 40.00–40.30/US $, the former is the buying rate and the latter is the selling rate. The former is the rate at which the banks purchase a foreign currency from the customer. The selling rate is the rate at which the banks sell any foreign currency to their customers. Since the banks need some amount of profit in these transactions, the selling quote is higher than the buying quote. The difference between these two quotes forms the banks' profit and it is known as the spread. The bid-ask spread is often stated in percentage terms that can be computed as follows:

Two rates are published—one being the buying rate and the other being the selling rate. The buying rate is also known as the bid rate. The selling rate is known as ask rate or offer rate. The bid rate is always given first followed by the ask-rate quote.

$$\text{Spread} = \{[(\text{Ask price} - \text{Bid price})/\text{Ask price}] \times 100\} \quad \text{...(25.1)}$$

25.2.3 Forward Rates

The quotes for the forward market are also published in the newspaper and periodicals. There are two ways of quoting forward rates. While one is known as an outright quote, the other is known as a swap quote. The outright quote for the US dollar in terms of rupees can be written for different periods of a forward contract as follows:

Spot	One month	Three months
Rs 40.00–40.30/$	Rs 39.80–40.20/$	Rs 39.60–40.10/$

The swap quote, on the other hand, only expresses the difference between the spot quote and the forward quote. It may be noted that decimals are not written in swap quotes. It can be written as follows:

Spot	One month	Three months
Rs 40.00–30/$	Rs (20)–(10)/$	Rs (40)–(20)/$

Swap quote, on the other hand, only expresses the difference between the spot quote and the forward quote. It may be noted that decimals are not written in swap quotes.

In the above quotes, it is found that the longer the maturity, the greater is the change in the forward rates. Again, with a longer maturity, the spread also widens. This is because of uncertainty in the future that increases with lengthening of maturity.

The change in forward rates may be upwards or downwards. With such movements, disparity arises between the spot and forward rates which is known as the forward rate differential. If the forward rate is lower than the spot rate, it will be a case of forward discount. On the contrary, if the forward rate is higher than the spot rate, it would be known as forward premium. Forward premium or discount is expressed as an annualised percentage deviation from the spot rate. It is computed as follows:

$$\text{Forward premium (discount)} = \{[(n\text{-day forward rate} - \text{spot rate})/\text{spot rate}] \times 360/n\} \quad \text{...(25.2)}$$

Where:

n = the length of forward contract expressed in number of days

Applying the above example of one-month forward quotation, we get:

$$\{[(39.80 - 40.00)/40.00] \times 360/30\} = -0.06$$ or 6% forward discount.

FOREX MARKET

EXCHANGE RATE MAJOR CURRENCIES

	Yesterday	1 day ago	1week ago	1 month ago	1 year ago
Re/US $	39.340	39.330	39.370	39.740	44.910
Re/Euro	57.570	57.510	57.370	56.780	57.400
Re/Pound	80.660	80.350	81.510	81.440	84.720
Re/Yen	0.357	0.356	0.360	0.344	0.380
Re/China (Yuan)	5.290	5.290	5.290	5.260	5.705

Source: Development Credit Bank

DOLLAR FORWARDS (IN %)

	1 month	3 months	6 months	12 months
(a) USD Libor	4.77	4.98	4.85	4.50
(b) Forward Premium	2.70	1.68	1.59	1.26
(c) Implied Deposit (a+b)	7.47	6.66	6.44	5.76

CROSS CURRENCY RATES

	INR	USD	EUR	GBP	CHF	JPY	CAD	AED	SAR	CNY
Rupee (INR)	–	39.340	57.570	80.660	35.170	35.660	40.240	10.720	10.590	5.290
US $ (USD)	0.025	–	0.683	0.488	1.119	1.103	0.978	3.670	3.715	7.437
Euro (EUR)	0.017	1.463	–	0.714	1.637	1.614	1.431	5.370	5.436	10.883
Pound(GBP)	0.012	2.050	1.401	–	2.293	2.262	2.004	7.524	7.617	15.248
Swiss Franc(CHF)	0.028	0.894	0.611	0.436	–	0.986	0.874	3.281	3.321	6.648
Yen (JPY, 100 Yen)	0.028	0.906	0.619	0.442	1.014	–	0.886	3.326	3.367	6.741
Canadian $(CAD)	0.025	1.023	0.699	0.499	1.144	1.128	–	3.754	3.800	7.607
UAE Dhiram(AED)	0.093	0.272	0.186	0.133	0.305	0.301	0.266	–	1.012	2.026
Saudi Rial(SAR)	0.094	0.269	0.184	0.131	0.301	0.297	0.263	0.988	–	2.002
China(Yuan)(CNY)	0.189	0.134	0.092	0.066	0.150	0.148	0.131	0.493	0.500	–

Source: *Business Standard, 20 November 2007.*

25.2.4 Cross Rates

Sometimes the value of a currency in terms of another is not known directly. In such cases, one currency is sold for a common currency, and the common currency is exchanged for the desired currency. This is known as cross rate trading and the rate established between the two currencies is known as the cross rate. Suppose a newspaper quotes the exchange rate between the US dollar and the Canadian dollar and also between the US dollar and the Indian rupee but does not quote the exchange rate between the Indian rupee and the Canadian dollar. Thus the rate of exchange between the rupee and Canadian dollar will be found out through the common currency: the US dollar. This technique is similar for both the spot cross rates and the forward cross rates.

EXAMPLE

A newspaper quotes Rs 35.00 – 35.20/US $; and, at the same time, it quotes CRs 0.76 – 0.78/US $. Find out the exchange rate between the Indian rupee and Canadian dollar.

The selling rate of the Canadian dollar in India can be found out by selling rupees to bank for US dollars at Rs 35.20/US $, and then buying Canadian dollars with the help of US dollars at C$ 0.76/US $. This means:

Rs 35.20/US $ 1 × US $ 1/C$ 0.76 = Rs 46.32/C$

The buying rate of a Canadian dollar in India can be found out through buying Indian rupees from the bank for US dollars at Rs 35.00/US $ and selling Canadian dollars for US dollars at C$ 0.78/US $. This means:

Rs 35.00/US $ 1 × US $ 1/C$ 0.78 = Rs 44.87/C$

Combining the two, one gets:

Rs 44.87 – 46.32/C$

25.3 DETERMINATION OF EXCHANGE RATE IN SPOT MARKET

25.3.1 The Process of Determination

It is the interplay of the forces of demand and supply that determines the exchange rate between two currencies in a floating rate regime. The exchange rate between, say, the rupee and US dollar depends upon the demand for US dollars and the supply of US dollars in the Indian foreign exchange market. The demand for foreign currency comes from individuals and firms who have to make payments to foreigners in foreign currency mostly on account of the import of goods and services and purchase of securities. The supply of foreign exchange results from the receipt of foreign currency normally on account of export or sale of financial securities to foreigners.

In Figure 25.1, the exchange rate designated by the price of the US dollar (foreign currency) in terms of rupees, is shown on the vertical axis and the supply of, and demand for, the US dollar is shown on the horizontal axis. The demand curve slopes downward to right because the higher the value of the US dollar, the costlier are the imports and the importers curtail the demand for imports. In the sequel, the demand for foreign currency

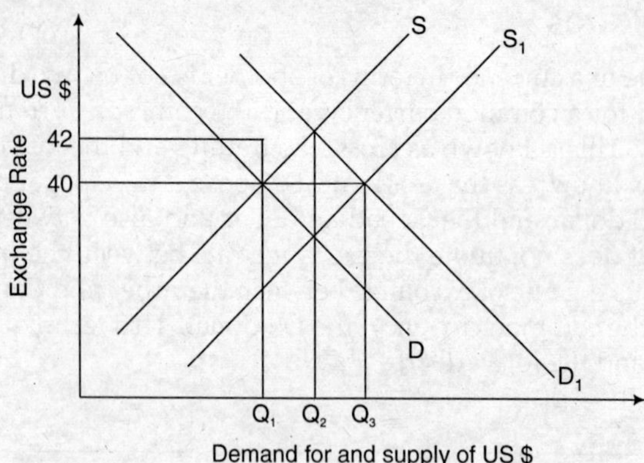

FIG. 25.1 Exchange rate determination

falls. Similarly, a higher value of US dollar makes exports cheaper and thereby stimulates the demand for exports. The supply of the US dollar increases in the form of export earnings. This is why the supply curve of the US dollar moves upward to the right with a rise in its value. The equilibrium exchange rate arrives where supply curve intersects the demand curve at Q_1. This rate as shown in the above figure is Rs 40/US $.

If demand for imports rises owing to certain domestic factors, the demand for the US dollar will rise to D_1 and intersect the supply curve at Q_2. The exchange rate will be Rs 42/US$. But if exports rises as a sequel to a decline in the value of rupee and the supply of dollar increases to S_1, the exchange rate will again be Rs 40/US $. Quite evidently, the frequent shifts in demand and supply conditions cause the exchange rate to adjust frequently to a new equilibrium.

25.3.2 Factors Influencing Exchange Rate

Impact of Inflation: It is normally the inflation rate differential between two countries that influences the exchange rate between their currencies. The influence of the inflation rate is explained by the Purchasing Power Parity (PPP) theory (Cassel, 1921; Officer, 1976). The theory suggests that at any point of time, the rate of exchange between two currencies is determined by their purchasing power. If e is the exchange rate and P_A and P_B are the purchasing powers of the currencies in the two countries, A and B, the equation can be written as follows:

$$e = P_A / P_B \qquad ...(25.3)$$

In fact, this theory is based on the *theory of one price* in which the domestic price of any good equals its foreign price quoted in the same currency. To explain this, if the exchange rate is Rs 2/US $, and the price of a particular commodity is Rs 100 in India, then as per the theory it must be US $ 50 in the USA. In other words:

(US $ price of a commodity × price of US $) = Rupee price of the commodity ...(25.4)

If inflation in one country causes a temporary deviation from the equilibrium, arbitrageurs will begin operating, as a result of which equilibrium will be restored through changes in the exchange rate. Suppose, the price of the commodity soars up in India to Rs 125, the arbitrageurs will buy that commodity in the USA and sell it in India earning a profit of Rs 25. This will go on till the exchange rate moves to Rs 2.5/US \$ and the profit potential of arbitrage is eliminated.

The exchange rate adjustment as a sequel to inflation may be further explained as follows. If the Indian commodity becomes costlier, its export will decline. At the same time, its import from the USA will expand as imports will become cheaper. Higher imports will raise the demand for the US dollar raising in turn its value vis-à-vis the Indian rupee.

However, this version of the theory, which is known as the absolute version, holds good if the same commodities are included in the same proportion in the domestic market basket and the world market basket. Since this does not normally occur in real life, this is a serious limitation of the theory. Moreover, it does not cover non-traded goods and services where transaction cost is significant.

In view of the above limitation, another version of this theory has evolved which is known as the relative version of the PPP theory. The relative version states that a change in the exchange rate that would retain the original level of relative price of tradeable to non-tradeable goods in the economy, would establish an equilibrium exchange rate. It further states that the exchange rate between the currency of any two countries should be a constant multiple of the general price indices prevailing in the two countries. In other words, percentage change in exchange rate should equal the percentage change in the ratio of price indices in the two countries. To put this in the form of an equation, where I_A and I_B are the rates of inflation in Country A and Country B, e_o is the A's currency value for one unit of B's currency in the beginning of the period and e_t is the spot exchange rate in period t:

$$\frac{e_t}{e_o} = \frac{(1+I_A)^t}{(1+I_B)^t} \qquad \text{...(25.5)}$$

EXAMPLE

If India has inflation rate of 5% and the USA has a 3% rate of inflation and if the initial exchange rate is Rs 40/US \$, the value of the rupee in a 2-year period will be:

$$e_2 = 40\ (1.05/1.03)^2 = \text{Rs } 41.57/\text{US } \$$$

Such an inflation-adjusted rate is known as the real exchange rate. When the government sticks to a particular exchange rate without caring for prevailing inflation, a gap emerges between the real and the nominal exchange rates which entails upon export competitiveness. It is for this reason that this theory suggests that a country with high rate of inflation should devalue its currency relative to the currency of countries with lower rates of inflation.

A number of studies have empirically tested the two versions of the PPP theory. The absolute version has been tested by Isard (1977) and McKinnon (1979). Both of them had found violation of the theory in the short-run, but in the long-run, they found the theory holding good to a certain extent. As regards the relative version, the studies made till the early 1980s normally found the relationship existing between the rate of inflation and the exchange rate, especially in the long run (Aliber and Sickney, 1975; Dornbusch, 1976; Mussa, 1982). But subsequent studies have found clear-cut violations of the theory even in the long-run (Adler and Lehmann, 1983; Edison, 1985). Taylor (1988) finds very little evidence of the PPP theory to holding good. In a review of 14 cases, MacDonald (1988) found that in 10 cases, the theory was not applicable even in the long-run, however, in four cases it held good in the long-run.

There are primarily three factors that cause the PPP theory to not hold good in real life. First, the assumptions of this theory do not necessarily hold good in real life. Second, there are other factors, such as interest rates, governmental interference, etc., that influence the exchange rate. In the early 1990s, some of the European countries experienced higher inflation rates than the USA, their currency did not however depreciate against the dollar in view of the high interest rates that attracted capital from the USA. Third, when no domestic substitutes for imports are available, goods are imported even after their prices rise higher in the exporting countries.

Interest Rate: The experts differ on how changes in the interest rate influence the exchange rate. The flexible price version of the monetary theory explains that any rise in domestic interest rate lowers the demand for money. Lower demand for the domestic currency in relation to supply of the foreign currency causes depreciation in the value of domestic currency. On the contrary, the sticky price version of the monetary theory has a different explanation. It is that a rise in interest rate increases the supply of loanable funds which means a greater supply of money and a depreciation in domestic currency. But at the same time, it shares the view of the balance of payments approach where a higher interest rate at home as compared to a foreign country attracts capital from abroad lured by higher returns. The inflow of foreign currency increases the supply of foreign currency and raises the value of domestic currency.

However, suggests Fisher, this proposition cannot be thought of in isolation of inflation, inasmuch as inflation negates the return on capital to be received. If the interest rate is 10% and the rate of inflation is 10%, the real return on capital would be zero. This is because the gain in the form of interest compensates for the loss on account of inflation. In fact, it was Irving Fisher who decomposed nominal interest into two parts – the real interest rate and the expected rate of inflation. And so, the relationship between nominal interest rate and the expected rate of inflation is known as the Fisher Effect.

The Fisher Effect states that whenever an investor thinks of an investment, he is interested in a particular nominal interest rate which covers both the expected inflation and the required real interest rate. In form of an equation, it can be shown as follows:

$$(1 + r) = (1 + a)(1 + I) \qquad \text{...(25.6)}$$

Where:

r = the nominal interest rate

a = the real interest rate

I = the expected rate of inflation

EXAMPLE

The required real interest rate is 4% and the expected rate of inflation is 10%, the required nominal interest rate will be:

$$(1.04 \times 1.10) - 1 = 14.4\%.$$

Suppose, the interest rate in the USA is 4% and the inflation rate in India is 10% higher than in the USA. A US investor will be tempted to invest in India only when the nominal interest in India is more than 14.4%.

The concept of real interest rate applies to all investment—domestic and foreign. An investor invests in a foreign country if the real interest rate differential will be in his favour. But when such a differential exists, arbitrage begins in form of international capital flow that ultimately equals the real interest rate across countries. Suppose, the real interest rate is 5% in India and 4% in the USA, capital will begin flowing from the USA to India. In the USA, a declining volume of capital will raise the real interest rate, while an increasing volume of capital in India will push down the interest rate. The capital flow will continue till the real interest rate in both countries becomes equal. This means that the process of arbitrage helps equate the real interest rate across countries. Moreover, since the real interest rate is equal in different countries, a country with a higher nominal interest rate must face a higher rate of inflation.

An investor likes to hold assets denominated in currencies expected to depreciate only when the interest rate on those assets is high enough to compensate for the loss on account of the depreciating exchange rate.

However, for this type of arbitrage, it is necessary that the capital market be homogeneous throughout the globe so that the investors do not differentiate between the domestic capital market and foreign capital markets. In real life, a homogeneous capital market is not found in view of government restrictions and varying economic policies in different countries. As a result, the interest rate varies among countries. Mishkin (1984) finds that investors have a strong liking for the domestic capital market in order to insulate themselves from foreign exchange risk. Arbitrage will not occur even if the real interest rate on foreign securities is higher. The Fisher Effect is helpless on this count. Again, the Fisher Effect normally holds good in case of short-maturity government securities and very little in other cases (Abdullah, 1986).

Empirical tests present different results. Gibson (1970, 1972) and Fama and Schwert (1977) are in favour of the Fisher Effect; while the studies of Mishkin (1984) and Cumby and Obstfeld (1984) do not support the Fisher effect.

There is also Fisher's open proposition that is known as the International Fisher Effect or the generalised version of the Fisher Effect. It is a combination of the conditions of the PPP theory and Fisher's closed proposition. It may be recalled that the PPP theory suggests that the exchange rate is determined by inflation rate differentials, while the latter states that the nominal interest rate is higher in a country with a higher inflation rate. Combining these two propositions, the International Fisher Effect states that the interest rate differential shall equal the inflation rate differential. In form of an equation, it can be written as follows:

$$\frac{1+r_A}{1+r_B}=\frac{1+I_A}{1+I_B} \qquad ...(25.7)$$

The rationale behind this proposition is that an investor likes to hold assets denominated in currencies expected to depreciate only when the interest rate on those assets is high enough to compensate for the loss on account of the depreciating exchange rate. As a corollary, an investor holds assets denominated in currencies expected to appreciate even at a lower rate of interest because the expected capital gain on account of exchange rate appreciation will make up for the loss in yield on account of low interest rate.

25.4 EXCHANGE RATE DETERMINATION IN FORWARD MARKET

The IRP theory states that equilibrium is achieved when the forward rate differential is approximately equal to the interest rate differential. In other words, the forward rate differs from the spot rate by an amount that represents the interest rate differential.

The forward exchange rate is normally not equal to the spot rate. The size of forward premium or discount mainly depends on the current expectation of future events. Such expectations determine the trend of the future spot rate towards appreciation or depreciation and thereby determine the forward rate that is equal to, or close to, the future spot rate. Suppose, the US dollar is expected to depreciate, the holders of US dollars will start selling it forward. These actions will help depress the forward rate of the US dollar. On the contrary, when the US dollar is expected to appreciate, holders will buy it forward and the forward rate will improve.

25.4.1 Interest Rate Parity Theory

The determination of the exchange rate in the forward market finds an important place in the Interest Rate Parity (IRP) Theory. The IRP theory states that equilibrium is achieved when the forward rate differential is approximately equal to the interest rate differential. In other words, the forward rate differs from the spot rate by an amount that represents the interest rate differential. In this process, the currency of a country with a lower interest rate should be at a forward premium in relation to the currency of a country with a higher interest rate. Equating the forward rate differential with the interest rate differential, we find:

$$A \times \frac{(n\text{-}day\ F - S)}{S} = \frac{(1+r_A)}{(1+r_B)} - 1 \qquad \text{...(25.8)}$$

On the basis of the IRP theory, the forward exchange rate can easily be determined. One has simply to find out the value of forward rate (F) in Eq.25.8. The equation shall be re-written as:

$$F = S/A\ \{(1 + r_A/1 + r_B) - 1\} + S \qquad \text{...(25.9)}$$

EXAMPLE

Suppose the interest rate in India and the USA is respectively 10% and 7%. The spot rate is Rs 40/US $. The 90-day forward rate can be calculated as follows:

$$F = 40/4\ \{(1.10/1.07) - 1\} + 40$$

or

$$F = \text{Rs } 40.28/\text{US } \$.$$

This means that the higher interest rate in India pushes down the forward value of the Indian rupee from 40 a dollar to 40.28 a dollar.

25.4.2 Covered Interest Arbitrage

If the forward rate differential is not equal to interest rate differential, covered interest arbitrage will begin and it will continue till the two differentials become equal. In other words, a positive interest rate differential in a country is offset by annualised forward discount. Negative interest rate differential is offset by annualised forward premium. Finally, the two differentials will be equal. In fact, this is the point where forward rate is determined. The process of covered interest arbitrage may be explained with the help of an example.

EXAMPLE

Suppose, the spot rate is Rs 40/US $ and the 3-month forward rate is Rs 40.28/US $ involving a forward differential of 2.8 %. The interest rate is 18% in India and 12% in the USA involving an interest rate differential of 5.37%. Since the two differentials are not equal, covered interest arbitrage will begin. The successive steps shall be as follows:

1. Borrowing in the USA, say, US $ 1,000 at 12% interest rate.
2. Converting the US dollar into Indian rupees at the spot rate to get Rs 40,000.
3. Investing Rs 40,000 in India at 18% interest rate.
4. Selling the Indian rupees 90-day forward at Rs 40.28/US $.
5. After 3 months, liquidating the Rs 40,000 investment which would fetch Rs 41,800.
6. Selling Rs 41,800 for US dollars at the rate of Rs 40.28/US $ to get US $ 1,038.
7. Repaying loan in the USA which amounts to US $ 1030.
8. Reaping profit: US $ (1038 – 1030) = US $ 8.

Therefore, as long as inequality continues between the forward rate differential and the interest rate differential, the arbitrageurs will reap profits and the process of arbitrage will continue. But with this process, the differential will be wiped out because:

1. Borrowing in the USA will raise the interest rate there;
2. Investing in India shall increase the invested funds there and thereby lower the interest rate there;
3. Buying the Indian rupee at the spot rate will increase the spot rate of the Indian rupee;
4. Selling the Indian rupee forward will depress the forward rate of the rupee.

25.5 FOREIGN EXCHANGE MARKET

25.5.1 Distinctive Features

The foreign exchange market, where different currencies are bought and sold, does not denote a particular place. Rather it is an over-the-counter market. It consists of trading foreign exchange market is classified either as the spot market or the forward market. It is the timing of actual delivery of foreign exchange that differentiates between spot market and forward market transactions. In the spot market, currencies are traded for immediate delivery at a rate existing on the day of transaction.

desks at major agencies dealing in foreign exchange throughout the world that are connected by telephones, telex, etc. Again, it is a round-the-clock market meaning that transactions can take place at any time in a 24-hour day. This is necessary because different countries are located at different longitudes. If an Indian bank buys dollars at 12 A. M., it will be midnight in the USA. From this point of view, the foreign exchange market has to operate round-the-clock.

The foreign exchange market is classified either as the spot market or the forward market. It is the timing of actual delivery of foreign exchange that differentiates between spot market and forward market transactions. In the spot market, currencies are traded for immediate delivery at a rate existing on the day of transaction. For the purpose of making bookkeeping entries, delivery takes two working days after the transaction is complete. If a particular market is closed on Saturday and Sunday and if the transaction takes place on Thursday, delivery of currency will take place on Monday. Monday in this case is known as the value date or settlement date. Sometimes there are short-date contracts where the time zones permit the delivery of the currency even earlier. If the currency is delivered the same day, it is known as a value-same-day contract. If it is done the next day, the contract is known as a value-next-day contract.

In view of the huge amounts involved in these transactions, there is seldom any actual movement of currencies. Rather debit and credit entries are made in the bank accounts of the seller and the purchaser. Most of the markets have an electronic system for transfer of funds that saves time and energy. The system existing in New York is known as Clearing House Inter-bank Payment System (CHIPS).

In the forward market, contracts are made to buy and sell currencies for future delivery, say, after a fortnight, one month, two months and so on.

In forward market, on the contrary, contracts are made to buy and sell currencies for future delivery, say, after a fortnight, one month, two months and so on. The rate of exchange for the transaction is agreed upon on the very day the deal is finalised. The forward rates with varying maturity are quoted in the newspaper and those rates form the basis of the contract. Both the parties have to abide by the contract at the exchange rate mentioned therein irrespective of whether the spot rate on the maturity date resembles to the forward rate. In other words, no party can back out of the deal even if changes in the future spot rate are not in its favour.

The value date in case of a forward contract definitely lies beyond the value date applicable to a spot contract. If it is a one-month forward contract, the value date will be the date in the next month corresponding to the spot value date. Suppose a currency is purchased on the 1 August. If it is a spot transaction, the currency will be delivered on 3 August. But if it is a one-month forward contract, the value date will fall on 3 September. If the value date falls on a holiday, the subsequent date will be the value date. If value date does not exist in the calendar, such as 29 February (if it is not a leap year), the value date will fall on 28 February.

25.5.2 Major Participants

The participants in the foreign exchange market are individuals, firms, banks, governments, and occasionally international agencies. Individuals are normally tourists who exchange currencies. They are also migrants sending a part of their income to their family members living in their home country. Firms are generally importers and exporters. Exporters prefers to receive payments in their own currencies or in a strong convertible currency. Importers need foreign exchange to make payments for imports. When firms and individuals approach the local branch of a bank, the local branch in turn approaches the regional office or head office foreign exchange department. The latter actually deals in foreign exchange with other banks on behalf of its customers. Thus there are two tiers in the foreign exchange market. One tier involves transactions between the ultimate customers and the banks. The other tier consists of the transactions between two banks. It is the second tier of the market that accounts for the largest segment of the total foreign exchange transactions in the market. The reason is that the purpose of inter-bank transactions is not only to meet the foreign exchange demands of the ultimate customers but also to reap gains out of movements in foreign exchange rates.

Commercial banks dominate the foreign exchange market but the monetary authorities also participate in the market to help stabilise the value of the domestic currency.

It is either because of the length of the transactions that must pass through the two tiers of the market, or because of the profit motive involved in these transactions that there is often a gap between the amount of purchase and the amount of sale of a currency by banks. If a bank buys less of a currency than it contracts to sell, the position is known as a short position in that currency. The reverse occurs, when a bank buys more of a currency than it contracts to sell, this is known as a long position in that currency. When the quantum of sale and purchase is equal, such equality denotes a square position.

It is a fact that commercial banks dominate the foreign exchange market but the monetary authorities also participate in the market. Their purpose in doing so however is different. It is to help stabilise the value of the domestic currency. Sometimes international agencies purchase and sell foreign currencies in the foreign exchange market, however that is not a routine affair.

Again, the participants in the market may also be grouped according to their behaviour and their motive behind foreign exchange transaction. They are as follows:

1. Non-banking entities that simply exchange currencies in order to honour their obligations or to get the desired currency;
2. Non-banking entities, such as traders that use the foreign exchange market for the purpose of hedging their foreign exchange exposure on account of changes in the exchange rate. They are known as hedgers;
3. Banks that exchange currencies on behalf of their customers. In such cases, their profit is limited to the amount of spread between the bid and the ask rates;
4. Arbitrageurs that exchange currencies because of varying rates of exchange in different markets. The varying rates are the source of their profit;
5. Speculators that buy or sell currencies when they expect movements in the exchange rate in a particular direction. The movement of exchange rate in the desired direction gives them profit.

25.5.3 Currency Arbitrage in Spot Market

Despite developments in the telecommunication system, rates of exchange vary in different markets. The arbitrageurs take advantage of this inconsistency and reap profits through buying and selling currencies. They buy a particular currency at a cheaper rate in one market and sell it at a higher rate in another. This process is known as currency arbitrage. This process influences the demand for, and supply of, the particular currency in the two markets that ultimately leads to the removal of inconsistency in the two markets, with the value of the currency in the two markets becoming uniform.

Suppose:

In New York: \$ 1.9800 – 10/£; and

In London: \$ 1.9700 – 10/£.

The arbitrageurs will buy the dollar in New York and sell it in London making a profit of \$ (1.9800 – 1.9710) or \$ 0.009 per pound sterling.

In the above example, two markets and two currencies are involved. This is why it is known as two-point arbitrage. There may be three-point arbitrage or even more.

25.5.4 Arbitrage, Hedging and Speculation in Forward Market

Forward buying and selling of a currency for hedging depends upon whether the hedger finds himself/herself in a long position or in a short position. An export billed in foreign currency creates a long position for the exporter. On the contrary, an import billed in foreign currency leads to a short position for the importer.

Forward market arbitrage has already been explained earlier under the head, covered interest arbitrage. Let us now discuss hedging. Under the process of hedging, currencies are bought and sold forward. Forward buying and selling depends upon whether the hedger finds himself/herself in a long position or in a short position. An export billed in foreign currency creates a long position for the exporter. On the contrary, an import billed in foreign currency leads to a short position for the importer.

Take first the case of a long position. The Indian exporter, for example, signs a contract for mica export to the USA for US \$ 1,000. The export proceeds are to be received within three months. The exporter fears a drop in the value of the US dollar that may diminish the export earnings in terms of the rupee. To avoid this diminution, the exporter goes for a three-month forward contract and sells forward US \$ 1000. Suppose the spot as well as the forward rate is Rs 40/US \$. If the dollar depreciates to Rs 39 after three months, the export earnings will diminish to Rs 39 thousand in the absence of a forward contract. But since the exporter has already sold forward a similar amount of dollars, the loss occurring due to the depreciation of the dollar will be met through the forward contract. By selling the dollar under the forward contract, it would fetch Rs 40 thousand that will be equal to the original export value.

However, the forward deal does not only have advantages, it also has certain disadvantages. The advantage is that if the value of the dollar falls, the exporter will not have to face a loss of income. The disadvantage however is that if the value of the dollar appreciates, the exporter will not benefit from the appreciation. Moreover, when a part of the merchandise is not accepted by the importer, the exporter will have to arrange for dollars in order to honour the forward contract.

In the event of a short position where the Indian importer buys goods from the USA, say, for US $ 1,000 and where the importer fears an appreciation in the value of US dollar, the forward deal will involve buying of dollars. If dollar appreciates to Rs 41 after the three-month period, the importer will have to pay Rs 1,000 more. But if a forward deal has been entered into for purchase of a similar amount of dollars, the importer will purchase US $ 1,000 with Rs 40,000 and pay US $ 1,000 to the exporter. In this way the importer will be saved a Rs 1,000 loss. Here again, the forward deal is fraught with both advantage and disadvantage. If the dollar appreciates, the importer has eliminated losses. But if the dollar depreciates, the importer will not benefit from the depreciation.

Speculators are also very active in forward market operations. Their purpose is not to reduce the risk but to reap profits out of changes in exchange rate over time. The source of profit to them is the difference between the forward rate and the future spot rate.

Again, it is not only the arbitrageur or the hedger who makes use of the forward market. Speculators are also very active in forward market operations. Their purpose is not to reduce the risk but to reap profits out of changes in exchange rate over time. This is why they are not very concerned with the direction of the exchange rate change. Rather the source of profit to them is the difference between the forward rate and the future spot rate.

Suppose a speculator expects a depreciation in the value of the dollar over and above the forward rate, he will sell US $ 1,000 three-month forward at the rate of Rs 40.50/US $. If, on maturity, the US dollar depreciates to Rs 40, the speculator will get Rs 40,500 under the forward contract. At the same time, he will exchange Rs 40,500 at the then future spot rate of Rs 40/US $ and will get US $ 1,012.50. Both activities—selling and purchasing of US dollars will be simultaneous. Thus without making any investment, the speculator will make a profit of US $ 12.50 through the forward market deal. Again, if the speculator expects an appreciation in the dollar, he will buy the dollar in the forward market and, on the maturity, he will sell it in the open market reaping profits.

The above example is a very simple one. Many other examples can be cited about speculation in the forward market. In fact, this type of speculation depends upon the expected movement of the future spot rate.

Futures contract is standardised involving a fixed amount of different currencies. The date of delivery is also fixed, whereas, in a forward contract, neither the size of the contract nor the delivery date is fixed. The forward market is an over-the-counter market, while futures contracts are finalised in a pit through brokers. In every futures deal, the clearing house is necessarily involved as a party.

25.6 MARKET FOR DERIVATIVES

25.6.1 Market for Currency Futures

Besides the spot and forward markets, currencies are also traded in the market for currency futures and the market for currency options. These two markets are known as the market for derivatives insofar as the prices in these markets are driven by the spot market price. The market for currency futures came into being in 1972 in the USA. It is at present found at many important financial centres.

A currency futures contract involves trading of an underlying currency at a specified exchange rate and for a fixed maturity period. In many other respects too, it is different from a forward contract. The size of a futures contract is standardised involving a fixed amount of different currencies. The date of delivery is also fixed, whereas, in a forward contract, neither the size of the contract nor the delivery date is fixed. The forward market is an over-the-counter market, while futures contracts are finalised in a pit through brokers. In every futures deal, the clearing house is necessarily involved as a party. If a party is the buyer of a currency, the clearing house is the seller of the currency. If another party is the seller of a currency, the clearing house serves as the buyer of the currency.

forward contracts are settled on maturity. But in the case of currency futures, the rates are matched everyday with movements in the spot rates; and on this basis, gains and losses are settled everyday. This process is called marking to the market.

Trading in currency futures is subject to specific margin and maintenance requirements. Margin is justified on the grounds that the traders represent a source of credit risk to the exchange or the clearing house. Long futures traders may not have sufficient funds to buy the underlying foreign currency. In order to cover the risk, they are required to deposit margin money with the clearing house. This is normally in form of cash deposits, although liquid securities are also used. The initial margin amount varies from one exchange to another. It is returned on the completion of the contract. If it is in form of securities, the interest earned thereon is also paid to the traders. In case of forward contracts, there is no question of margin and maintenance requirements.

In case of forward contracts, the deal is settled on maturity. But in the case of currency futures, the rates are matched everyday with movements in the spot rates; and on this basis, gains and losses are settled everyday. This process is called marking to the market. The process of marking to the market can be explained with the help of an example.

Suppose an investor buys Canadian dollar (Can. \$) futures (Can. \$100,000) at US \$ 0.75 on a Monday morning which is to mature within two days. At the close of Tuesday, if the price moves up to US \$ 0.755, the investor will make a profit of [100,000 × (US \$ 0.755 - 0.750)] or US \$ 500. But if the price falls to US \$ 0.749, the investor will have to bear a loss. The amount of loss will be deducted from the margin money. If the loss is big and, as a result, the margin money falls below a certain level, which is known as the maintenance margin, the investor receives a margin call for depositing the margin money within a specified period. Again, on Wednesday, the prevailing price on that particular day will be compared with the price prevailing on Tuesday and the gain or loss will be determined. On the maturity day, the investor receives the amount of the contract after the adjustment of the profit/loss. However, it may be mentioned that in very few cases, the amount of the contract flows to the investor. In majority of the cases, there is a matching contract in opposite direction. The investor gets only the difference.

The purpose of the daily settlement procedure is to create a safer futures market so that less creditworthy investors may participate. Contrary to this, forward contracts witness cash flows only on the date of maturity, this makes them more risky. Nevertheless, forward contracts are widely used. The reason being is that:

1. They are available at many financial centres;
2. Forward contracts have no standard size and the amount can be tailored to individual needs; and
3. Maturity of thousands of transactions taking place daily is not necessarily compatible with the fixed maturity of the futures.

When a trader has to enter a currency futures contract, he informs his agent who in turn informs the commission broker at the stock exchange. The commission broker executes the deal in the pit for a commission/fee. After the deal is executed, the commission broker confirms the trade with the agent of the trader (client or principal). The agent details the principal about the transaction and the futures price. The principal deposits the margin money with the clearing house at the very start of the next day. Settlement takes place every working day that is known as marking to the market. The final settlement is made on maturity.

25.6.2 Market for Currency Options

A currency options contract is similar as a forward contract or a futures contract in the sense that the buyer of the currency options possesses the right to buy or sell foreign currency after the lapse of a specified period, at a rate determined on the day the contract is made. The currency options contract however has a distinctive feature that is not found in either a forward or a futures contract. It is that the buyer of currency options has the freedom to exercise the options if the agreed-upon rate turns in his favour. If not, he may let the options expire.

The options market is of three types, viz., listed currency options market, over-the-counter options market and currency futures options market.

The options market is of three types, viz., listed currency options market, over-the-counter options market and currency futures options market. The listed currency options market is found as a part of the stock exchanges. The size and the maturity of such contracts is normally fixed. The option buyer or the seller enters into the deal with the clearing house, of course, with the help of a broker. In case of the over-the-counter market, options deals are finalised with the banks. The size of the contract is normally bigger and the banks repackage the size of the contract according to the clients' needs. In currency futures options market, the options are marked to market, meaning that they undergo daily settlement as in the case of a futures contract.

Broadly speaking, there are two types of options. In a call option, the buyer of the option agrees to buy the underlying currency, while in a put options contract, the buyer of the option agrees to sell the underlying currency.

Again, the call and put options are of two types. One is known as the European option which is exercised only on maturity, and the other is the American option that may be exercised even before maturity. It is normally in the buyer's interest to exercise the option before the maturity. This is why American options command a higher price than European options.

In recent years, several more variants of options have become available. For example, one is known as a forward reversing option. In this case, the call option premium is paid only when the spot rate is below a specified level. The premium is quoted by the seller who charges the premium only when the options are not exercised. This way the buyer gets a liberal term.

Second, there are preference options. In this case, the buyer gets an additional privilege to designate the option either as a call option or as a put option. This privilege is however only exercised after the lapse of a specified period.

Third, in case of average rate options, it is the arithmetic average of the spot rate during the life of the option that is taken into account instead of the spot rate on maturity. This type of option enables the buyer to hedge a series of daily cash inflows over a given period in one single contract.

Fourth, a look-back option provides the holder the right to purchase or sell foreign currency at the most favourable exchange rate realised over the life of the option. For example, the buyer of a call has the right to buy the underlying currency at the lowest exchange rate realised between the creation of call and the expiry date. The buyer of a put has the right to sell the underlying currency at the highest exchange rate during the life of the option. All this means that the strike rate in a look-back option is not known until the expiry date. Naturally, because of this speciality, the premium of a look-back option is normally higher than the premium of a traditional option.

Exercise price, or strike price, is the price at which options are exercised.

Fifth, the buyers, who are confronted with foreign exchange risk in respect of many currencies, buy a basket option where the underlying currency is not simply one but many.

For a clear understanding of currency options, the readers must be acquainted with a few terms that are used in this context. The various terms are explained below.

1. The option-buyer is a person or a firm who gets the right to buy options. If the option-buyer agrees to buy the underlying currency, he is the buyer of a call option. If he agrees to sell the underlying currency, he is known as the buyer of a put option. The option-buyer is also known as the option-holder.
2. The option-seller is the party that has an obligation to perform if the option is exercised. This is the party who charges the premium for granting such privilege to the buyer. The option-seller is also known as the option-writer.
3. Exercise price is the price at which options are exercised. It is also known as the strike price.
4. At-the-money is the situation when the strike price is equal to the spot price on the maturity date.
5. If, in a call option, the strike price is lower than the spot rate, the situation is known as in-the-money. In case of a put option, an in-the-money situation warrants the spot rate being lower than the strike price. It is an in-the-money situation when the option-buyer exercises the option because then only can the option-buyer gain. Out-of-the-money is just the opposite situation of in-the-money. This means that the spot rate should be lower than the strike rate in case of a call option; and the spot rate should be higher than the strike rate in case of a put option.
6. Premium is the value or price of the option that the option-buyer pays to the option-seller at the time of signing of the contract. It is also known as the option value or the option price. It is not returned even when the option is not exercised. The amount of premium is the sum of the option's intrinsic value and the time value. The intrinsic value denotes the extent to which an option would currently be profitable to exercise. In other words, it represents the gains accruing to the holder on the exercise of the option. In the case of a call option, it is the excess of the current spot rate over the strike price. The intrinsic value of a put option will naturally be represented by the excess of strike price over the current spot rate. Thus it can be said that when the option

Premium is the value or price of the option that the option-buyer pays to the option-seller. The amount of premium is the sum of the option's intrinsic value and the time value.

is in-the-money, it has some amount of intrinsic value. The intrinsic value of an option—put or call—may be positive. It may be also zero but it cannot be negative insofar as the option-buyer will not exercise the option if the option is out-of-the-money.

Time value of the option, on the other hand, represents the sum of money that a buyer is willing to pay over and above the intrinsic value. Time value of an option exists because the spot rate of the underlying currency is expected to move towards an in-the-money position between the signing of the contract and the maturity date. On the maturity date, the time value of the option is zero and the premium is entirely represented by the intrinsic value. Again, if there is an at-the-money position that means that there is no intrinsic value, the option premium is entirely represented by the time value. Between these two positions, the premium is represented partly by the intrinsic value and partly by the time value.

EXAMPLE

Suppose the strike price of a call option is Rs 60.00/£. The premium is Rs 0.05 per unit of the British pound. The spot rate is Rs 60.02/£.

The amount of premium = Rs (0.05 × 62,500) = Rs 3,125.

Intrinsic value = Rs [(60.02 – 60.00) × 62,500] = Rs 1,250.

Time value = Rs (3,125 – 1,250) = Rs 1,875.

Here the size of British pound options contract is £ 62,500.

The gains accruing to the option-buyers are unlimited, while the loss borne by them is limited to the amount of premium paid by them. On the other hand, the option-seller's risk of loss is unlimited. Gain is limited to the amount of premium it receives. This is why the market for currency options provides an asymmetry between income and risk of loss. In case of a call option, the buyer will gain if the spot price is greater than the sum of the strike price and the premium. For the seller of the call option, profit profile is simply the mirror image of the loss profile of the option-buyer. If the buyer does not exercise the option, the gain accruing to the seller will be equal to the amount of the premium. If however the buyer exercises the call option, the seller will have to face a loss equal to the excess of the spot price over the strike price that can be any amount.

In case of a put option, the buyer will let the option expire if the spot rate is greater than the strike rate. The buyer will be face a loss equivalent to the amount of premium. Profit will accrue to the buyer only if the spot price is lower than the sum of the strike price and the amount of the premium. As far as the seller is concerned, profit will be equal to the amount of premium. The amount of loss will be infinite depending upon how much lower the spot price is.

Hedgers and speculators operate in the market of currency options. The importer buys a call or sells a put or goes for the both at the same time. An exporter buys a put, sells a call or goes for the both at the same time. Similarly, speculators buy two or more calls or two or more puts or a combination of call and put depending upon the expected trend in the exchange rate vis-à-vis the strike rate.

SUMMARY

Exchange rate regimes can be broadly grouped as either fixed (pegged) or floating. A floating rate regime has been found to be superior to the fixed rate regime but has also been found to have very high oscillations. A floating rate regime may be independent. It may also be managed, where the monetary authorities are found intervening in the foreign exchange market to stabilise rates.

Exchange rates are quoted either directly or indirectly. There are buying and selling quotes, spot and forward quotes and also cross quotes. In a floating rate regime, exchange rates are determined by the market forces of demand and supply. The interest rate differential and the inflation rate differential influence the exchange rate.. The determination of the forward rate is primarily subject to interest rate differentials.

The foreign exchange market may be either spot or forward depending upon the timing of delivery of the currency transacted. The participants are individuals, traders, banks and international institutions, but it is the arbitrageur, hedger and speculator that dominate the market.

There is also the market for derivatives, such as the market for currency futures and the market for currency options. In these markets too, the hedger and speculator operate in a significant way.

POINTS TO REMEMBER

1. Distinguish between pegged exchange rate and floating exchange rate regimes.
   - In a pegged exchange rate regime, the value of a currency is fixed in terms of other currency or basket of currencies.
   - In a floating exchange rate regime, the exchange rate is determined by market forces. So it is not fixed.
   - In a floating exchange rate system, there appears no gap between nominal and real exchange rate. Additionally, it has insulation properties. But wide fluctuations in exchange rate are found in many cases.
2. Distinguish between independent and managed floating.
   - Independent floating, as opposed to managed floating, does not have market intervention by monetary authorities, normally central bank of the country. Even if there is intervention, the purpose is to moderate the rate of exchange.
   - Intervention may be direct/indirect, sterilised and non-sterilised, or still stabilising/destabilising.

3. What are the different types of exchange rate quotes?
   - Direct and indirect
   - Buying/bid and selling/offer quote
   - Spot rate and forward rate quote
   - Cross rate quote
4. How is exchange rate determined in spot market?
   - Exchange rate is determined by the forces of supply and demand. Greater the demand, higher is the value of currency. Greater the supply, the lower is the value of the currency vis-à-vis other currency.
5. What are the factors influencing exchange rate?
   - Inflation rate
   - Interest rate
   - Market intervention by the central bank
   - Psyche of the participants
6. How is exchange rate determined in forward market?
   - It is the interest rate parity theory which explains that interest rate differential is equal to forward rate differential.
   - If the two differentials are not equal in the short run, covered/uncovered interest arbitrage takes place that ultimately equalises the two.
7. Mention the features of foreign exchange market.
   - Over-the-counter
   - Round-the-clock
   - Convertible currencies are bought and sold
   - Spot and forward market
8. Who are the major participants in the foreign exchange market?
   - Arbitrageurs
   - Hedgers
   - Speculators
   - Non-banking entities exchanging currencies to honour their obligations
9. Distinguish between arbitrage, hedging and speculation.
   - Arbitrage means making profits out of varying exchange rates in different markets on a particular point of time.
   - Hedging means minimising risk on account of changes in the exchange rate.
   - Speculation means making profit on account of changes in exchange rate over a period of time.
10. What are the markets for derivatives?
    - Currency futures located normally at stock exchanges where a fixed amount of currency is traded for a fixed delivery.
    - Currency options that may be a part of organised market or may be over-the-counter. The option buyer has a privilege of not exercising the options contract – the privilege not found in forward/futures market.

DESCRIPTIVE QUESTIONS

1. Distinguish between a pegged exchange rate regime and a floating exchange rate regime. Is the latter superior to the pegged exchange rate regime?
2. Distinguish between independent floating and managed floating. Explain how the monetary authorities intervene in the foreign exchange market to stabilise the exchange rates.
3. What do you mean by cross rates? How are they determined?
4. Floating exchange rates are determined by the market forces of supply and demand. Explain.
5. Describe how the inflation rate differential influences the exchange rate.
6. Discuss the Fisher Effect and explain its relevance to exchange rate determination.
7. Discuss the Interest rate parity theory and its role in determining the forward exchange rate.
8. Describe the distinguishing features of the foreign exchange market. Who are the major participants in it?
9. Hedging in the forward market is like a double-edged sword. Explain.
10. Discuss the features of the market for currency futures.
11. What are the different types of currency options contracts? Explain how the buyers and the sellers of options benefit from the option deals.
12. Write notes on:
    (a) Direct and indirect quote
    (b) Spread between buying and selling rates
    (c) Forward rate differentials
    (d) Currency arbitrage in spot and forward markets

OBJECTIVE-TYPE QUESTIONS

1. Mark true or false.
   (a) Disparity between the real exchange rate and the nominal exchange rate does exist in the pegged exchange rate regime.
   (b) Pegged exchange rate regime has insulation properties.
   (c) Domestic currency is on the denominator in the direct quote.
   (d) Ask/offer rate and selling rate carry the same meaning.
   (e) Forward rate differential is greater in shorter maturities.
   (f) The purpose of arbitrage is to minimise/eliminate exchange rate risk.
   (g) Settlement date in spot market transactions falls after a week.
   (h) Exporters are in a short position in respect of the currency they are to receive.
   (i) Marking to market is found in forward market transactions.
   (j) The intrinsic value of an options contract may be negative when it is out-of-money.

2. Choose the most suitable answer.
   (a) Sterilised intervention by the monetary authorities is expected to:
      (i) increase the money supply in the country
      (ii) bear no ultimate effect on the money supply
      (iii) neither of the above
   (b) Demand for foreign currency is primarily influenced by:
      (i) size of export
      (ii) size of import
      (iii) neither of the above
   (c) Domestic currency tends to depreciate owing to:
      (i) high inflation rate
      (ii) lowering of inflation rate
      (iii) constant inflation rate
   (d) Covered interest arbitrage takes place when:
      (i) forward rate differential is equal to interest rate differential
      (ii) forward rate differential is not equal to interest rate differential
      (iii) neither of the above
   (e) Speculators buy a foreign currency in the forward market if:
      (i) the future spot rate of the currency is expected to be lower than the forward rate
      (ii) the future spot rate of the currency is expected to be higher than the forward rate
      (iii) the future spot rate of the currency is expected to be equal to the forward rate
   (f) Marking to market in the market for currency futures is done:
      (i) only on the maturity date
      (ii) every day
      (iii) on the date of signing of the contract
   (g) Options are exercised when they are:
      (i) in-the-money
      (ii) out-of-money
      (iii) at-the-money
   (h) The time value of an options contract on the date of maturity is:
      (i) zero
      (ii) negative
      (iii) more than the intrinsic value

NUMERICAL PROBLEMS

1. On the basis of the following figures, find out:
   (a) The intrinsic value of a British Pound options contract assuming: (i) call option; and (ii) put option
   (b) Gain/loss to the option buyer assuming: (i) call option; and (ii) put option

(c) Gain/loss to the option seller assuming: (i) call option; and (ii) put option
   (i) Spot rate on maturity US $ 1.68/£
   (ii) Strike rate US $ 1.60/£
   (iii) Premium US $ 0.05/£

2. Three one-month forward deals were contracted respectively on the 27, 28 and 29 January 2004. What would be the settlement date?
3. If the rate of exchange is:

   US $ 2.0000 – 2.0100/£ in New York

   US $ 1.9800 – 1.9810/£ in London

   Explain how an arbitrageur would gain.
4. If a direct quote is Rs 45/US $, how can this rate be presented in an indirect quote?
5. Find out the bid-ask spread if the exchange rate is Rs 45.00 – 45.50/US $.
6. Find out the cross rate for SF/Euro if, Euro 4.25 – 4.28/US $ and SF 65.20 – 65.30/US $.
7. If the nominal interest rate is 15% and rate of inflation is 6%, find out the real interest rate.
8. Calculate the 3 month forward rate (using the Interest Rate Parity Theory) if the spot rate is Rs 45/US $ and the interest rate in India and the USA is respectively 8% and 5%.
9. Based on the PPP theory, what will be the exchange rate after 2 years if the present exchange rate is Rs 45/US $ and the inflation rate in India and the USA is respectively 8% and 5%?
10. If the inflation rate in India and the USA is respectively 7% and 4% and if interest rate in the USA is 6%, find the interest rate is India based on Fisher's equation.

SOLVED NUMERICAL PROBLEMS

1. If direct quote is Rs 39/US $, how can this exchange rate be presented under indirect quote?

   Solution

   US $ 1/Rs 39 = US $ 0.0256/Re.
2. If indirect quote is US $ 0.025/Re, how can this exchange rate be shown under direct quote?

   Solution

   Re 1/US $ 0.025 = Rs 40/US $.
3. Consider the following bid-ask prices: Rs 40 – 40.40/ US $. Find the bid-ask spread.

   Solution

   Bid-ask spread = {(ask rate – bid rate)/ask rate} × 100

   (40.40 – 40.00)/40.40 = 0.0099 or 0.99%
4. Find out the forward rate differential if spot rate of US $ is Rs 40.00 and one-month forward rate is Rs 40.80.

Solution

Forward rate differential = {(For. rate – spot rate)/spot rate} × A × 100

360/30 {(40.80 – 40.00)/40.00} × 100 = 2.0% It will be known as a forward premium as the value of US dollar has increased.

5. Find the one-month forward rate of US dollar if spot rate is Rs 45.00 and the forward premium is 12%.

Solution

360/30 {(x – 45.00)/45.00} = 0.12

or (x – 45) = 0.12 × 45 × 30/360

or x = 45 + 0.45 or x = 45.45

6. Find Rs/€ exchange rate if Rs 43.93 – 43.95/US $ and € 0.83 – 0.84/US $.

Solution

Bid rate = Rs 43.93/0.84 = Rs 52.30/€

Ask rate = Rs 43.95/0.83 = Rs 52.95/€

= Rs 52.30 – 52.95/€

7. If exchange rate at the end of 2006–07 is Rs 43.91/US $ and if the rate of inflation in India and USA during 2007–08 is respectively 7% and 4%. Find:
   (i) inflation rate differential between the two countries, and
   (ii) the exchange rate at the end of 2007–08.

Solution

Inflation rate differential = $(1 + I_A)/(1 + I_B) - 1$

Inflation rate differential between India and USA:

(1.07/1.04) – 1 = 0.0288 = 2.88%

Exchange rate at the end of 2007–08:

= (1.07/1.04) × 43.91 = Rs 45.18/US $

8. If the rate of inflation in India and the USA is 7% and 4% respectively and if interest rate in the USA is 6%, find the interest rate in India.

Solution

1.07/1.04 = 1 + x/1.06

or 1 + x = 1.07/1.04 × 1.06

or x = 0.0906 = 9.06%

9. If interest rate in India and the USA is 9.06% and 6% and if spot exchange rate is Rs 43.91/US$, find the exchange rate during the next year.

Solution

1.906/1.06 × 43.91 = Rs 45.18/US $.

10. Find out the amount of profit out of covered interest arbitrage if interest rate in India and the USA is respectively 9% and 4.50% and spot and the 6-month forward exchange rates are respectively Rs 45.00 and Rs 45.20.

Solution

There will be covered interest arbitrage insofar as the interest rate and forward rate differentials are not equal.

To start with, borrowing $ 1,000 in the USA, converting it into rupee for 45,000 and investing the rupee for six months will fetch Rs 47,025. Selling Rs 47,025 forward will fetch $1,040. After repaying dollar loan along with interest for 1,022.50, the arbitrageur profits $ 1,040 – 1,022.50 = $ 17.50.

11. Presently, the spot rate is Rs 44.50/US $. A speculator feels that, after a week, US dollar should appreciate to Rs 44.60. What should he do if he has Rs 10,000 at his disposal?

Solution

The speculator should buy US dollar today to get 10,000/44.50 = US $ 224.72. After a week, he should sell those dollars to get 224.72 × 44.60 = Rs 10,022.47. The profit from speculation will be: Rs 10,022.47 – 10,000.00 = Rs 22.47.

12. Suppose spot rate on April 1 is 1.785/£. Pound futures contract is sold at $ 1.790 for June delivery and at $ 1.785 for September delivery. Expecting that pound will depreciate fast after June, a speculator buys the former and sells the latter. Later he finds that pound may appreciate by June but may not depreciate subsequently. So he reverses the two contracts respectively at $1.78 and $ 1.76. Suppose the exchange rate on both the maturity dates is $ 1.795/£. Find how much the speculator gains/loses.

Solution

Buying pound futures contract:

Gain per pound from the original contract = $ 1.795 – 1.790 = $ 0.005 and gain from the reverse contract = 1.795 – 1.760 = $ 0.035. Total gain $ 0.040 per pound

Selling pound futures contract:

Loss per pound from the original contract = $ 1.795 – 1.785 = $ 0.010 and from the reverse contract = $ 1.795 – 1.780 = $ 0.015. Total loss = $ 0.025 per pound

Net gain = $ 0.040 – 0.025 = $ 0.015 per pound = $ 0.015 × £ 62,500 = $ 937.50.

Had there been no reversal of the contracts, the speculator would have lost to an extent of $0.005 – 0.010 = $ 0.005 per pound or in all $ 0.005 × £ 62,500 = $ 312.50.

Note: (1) It ignores marking to market. (2) The size of pound contract is £ 62,500.

13. A pound options call contract has strike rate of $ 1.820/£ and a premium of $ 0.08. Spot rate on maturity is $ 1.830/£. Find gain/loss to options buyer/options seller.

Solution

Since S > (X + P), options buyer will gain. If options buyer gains, options seller has to lose.

Gain to the options buyer = $ 1.830 – 1.820 – 0.08 = $ 0.02/ £.

Total gain = $ 0.02 × £ 62,500 = $ 1250.

The seller of pound gets $ 0.10 less than the rate in the open market but he gets a premium for $ 0.08. Thus his loss per pound is $ 0.02. Total loss is $ 0.02 x £ 62,500 = $ 1,250.

14. The exchange rate in two markets is as follows:

New York: \$ 1.9800 – 10/£

London: \$ 1.9700 – 10/£

Find out how arbitrageurs will make gains.

Solution

Selling pound in New York for \$ 1.9810 and buying pound in London for \$ 1.9700 and thus making a profit of \$ 1.9810 – 1.9700 = \$ 0.0110

CASE STUDY

RBI Intervention and the INR/USD Exchange Rate

RBI's intervention in the foreign exchange market started well in 1990s in the wake of the adoption of the managed floating exchange rate regime. Although the purpose in general has been to check undesirable volatility in the exchange rate, RBI states the objectives as follows:

1. To influence the trend movements in the exchange rates because they perceive long-term equilibrium values to be different from actual values
2. To maintain export competitiveness
3. To manage volatility in order to axe risk in financial market transactions
4. To protect the currency from speculative attack

The intervention has now turned more significant in view of large inflows on account of foreign investment – both FDI and FII. The quantum of FDI has suddenly soared up from US \$7.722 billion in FY 2005–06 to US \$19.531 billion in FY 2006–07. The investment by FIIs too was large. The net investment was as big as US \$3.225 billion during FY 2006–07, although the gross investment was much bigger. During the first four months of FY 2007–08, FDI and FIIs' net investment were respectively of the order of US \$6.609 billion and US \$11.774 billion.

It was natural for INR to appreciate in the sequel of huge supply of US dollar in the foreign exchange market. INR, which was once at a low of 46.88 per US dollar during April 2006, appreciated to 41.19 during April 2007 and further to 39.77 during September 2007. Indian imports turned cheaper following appreciation. But the exports turned costlier in the international market with the result that the export value was badly affected. The textiles sector, informational technology sector and a few others were a case in point, although some of the other exports were not hit so badly. Thus making exports competitive is on the top of the present-day agenda and for which RBI has stepped in for large market intervention.

If one looks at the RBI intervention, it is clear that in the whole of the financial year, 2006–07, RBI bought US dollars and never sold them in the foreign exchange market. The same trend continued in the following six months. The rationale behind it was to maintain the demand for dollars and help them not to fall. But now the question is whether the intervention has been effective.

The short-run efficacy of intervention depends on a host of factors including market positioning, timing of intervention and quantum of intervention vis-à-vis market turnover. But, in this context, a very big problem on the count of the FIIs' investment cannot be overlooked. It is that during the later months of FY 2006–07 and the first half of FY 2007–08, the gross inflow of FIIs' investment was on an average around ten times the net figure. If RBI bases its intervention of buying US dollars from the market on the net investment basis, it would be definitely a wrong judgement to contain any appreciation in the value of rupee. On the contrary, if the basis is the gross investment, large intervention is unwarranted. The figures in table below show that the buying of US dollars as percentage of FIIs' net and gross investments has been oscillating in a wide range. Thus we can say that the intervention should have been still more fine-tuned.

Again, RBI's buying of US dollars in relation to the turnover in the foreign exchange market, as the figures in the table below show, has been fluctuating. It shows the lack of fine-tuning between the two variables. And so, we cannot expect too much from the intervention, although the impact of intervention is visible at times. For example, when the intervention as percentage of turnover in the foreign exchange market was the highest at 2.66 per cent, the rupee appreciation was one of the lowest at 0.25 per cent.

RBI Intervention, FIIs' Investment and Turnover in the Foreign Exchange Market

Period	RBI's buying of US $ in mill.	Buying of US $ as % of turnover in FX market	Buying of US $ as % of FIIs' gross investment	Buying of US $ as % if FIIs' net investment	INR/USD exchange rate	% change in exchange rate
Nov. '06	3,198	0.71	44	192	44.74	–
Dec. '06	1,818	0.41	21	-241	44.28	1.03
Jan. '07	2,830	0.61	26	-758	44.16	0.27
Feb. '07	11,862	2.66	97	807	44.27	-0.25
Mar. '07	2,307	0.40	19	283	43.47	1.81
Apr. '07	2,055	0.33	19	146	41.19	5.24
May '07	4,426	0.81	33	303	40.57	1.51
June '07	3,192	0.48	23	181	40.70	-0.32
Jul. '07	11,428	1.61	56	271	40.44	0.64
Aug. '07	1,815	0.25	12	-104	40.90	-1.14
Sep. '07	11,867	1.48	64	218	39.77	2.76

Based on RBI figures and the study of Financial Express dated 2.12.2007

Questions:

1. How does inflow of foreign investment influence the exchange rate of INR/USD?
2. Do you find any relation between RBI intervention and the INR/USD exchange rate?

3. Why has RBI gone for only buying USD and not for selling it?
4. Do you find that the quantum of RBI's intervention has some sort of relation with the FIIs' investment or with turnover in the foreign exchange market?

REFERENCES

Adler, M. and B. Lehmann (1983). "Deviations from Purchasing Power Parity in the Long Run", *Journal of Finance,* 38 (5): 1471–87.

Aliber, R.Z. and C.P. Stickney (1975). "Accounting Measures of Foreign Exchange Exposure: The Long and Short of It", *The Accounting Review,* 50 (1): 4–57.

Cassel, G. (1921). *The World's Monetary Problem.* London: Constable.

Cumby, R.E. and M. Obstfeld (1984). "International Interest Rate and Price Level Linkages under Flexible Exchange Rates: A Review of the Evidence". In J.F.O. Bilson and R.C. Marston, *eds., Exchange Rate Theory and Practices.* Chicago: University of Chicago Press, pp. 121–52.

Dornbusch, R. (1976). "Expectations and Exchange Rate Dynamics", *Journal of Political Economy,* 84 (6): 1161–76.

Edison, H. (1985). "The Rise and and Fall of Sterling: Testing Alternative Models of Exchange Rate Determination", *Applied Economics,* 17 (6): 1003–21.

Fama, E.F. and and G.W. Schwert (1977). "Asset Returns and Inflation", *Journal of Financial Economics,* 5 (1): 115–46.

Friedman. M. (1953). "The Case for Flexible Exchange Rates", *Essays in Positive Economics.* Chicago: University of Chicago Press, pp. 157–203.

Gibson, W.E. (1970). "Price Expectations Effects on Interest Rates", *Journal of Finance,* 25 (1): 19–34.

——— (1972). "Interest Rates and Inflationary Expectations", *American Economic Review,* 62 (5): 854–65.

Isard, P. (1977). "How Far We Can Push the Law of One Price", *American Economic Review,* 67 (5): 942–48.

Loopesko, B. (1984). "Relationship among Exchange Rates, Intervention and Interest Rates: An Empirical Investigation", *Journal of International Money and Finance,* 3 (2): 257–77.

MacDonald, R. (1988). *Floating Exchange Rates: Theories and Evidence.* London: Allen & Unwin.

McKinnon, R.I. (1979). *Money in International Exchange.* Oxford: Oxford University Press.

Mishkin, F. (1984). "Are Real Interest Rates Equal Across Countries? An Empirical Investigation of International Parity Conditions, *Journal of Finance,* 39 (5): 1345–58.

Mussa, M. (1982). "A Model of Exchange Rate Dynamics", *Journal of Political Economy,* 90 (1): 74–104.

Obstfeld, M. (1983). "Exchange Rates, Inflation and the Sterilisation Problem: Germany 1975–81", *European Economic Review*, 23 (2): 161–89.

Officer, L.H. (1976). "The Purchasing Power Parity Theory of Exchange Rates: A Review Article", *IMF Staff Papers*, 27 (1): 1–60.

Taylor, M.P. (1988). "An Empirical Examination of Long-run Purchasing Power Parity using Cointegration Techniques", *Applied Economics*, 20 (10): 1369–81.

SELECT FURTHER READINGS

Frankel, J. A. (1993): *On Exchange Rates*. Cambridge, Mass: MIT Press.

Krueger, A.O.(1983). *Exchange Rate Determination. Cambridge: Cambridge University Press.*

ANSWERS

OBJECTIVE-TYPE QUESTIONS

Chapter 1

1. (a) T (b) F (c) T (d) T (e) F (f) T
2. (a) iii (b) ii (c) i (d) i

Chapter 2

1. (a) T (b) F (c) T (d) F (e) T
2. (a) ii (b) i (c) ii (d) ii (e) ii

Chapter 3

1. (a) T (b) F (c) T (d) T (e) T (f) F
2. (a) i (b) ii (c) i (d) i

Chapter 4

1. (a) F (b) F (c) T (d) F (e) T (f) T
2. (a) i (b) ii (c) iii (d) i (e) i (f) iii

Chapter 5

1. (a) F (b) T (c) T (d) T (e) F (f) F
2. (a) iii (b) i (c) iii (d) ii (e) i

Chapter 6

1. (a) T (b) T (c) F (d) T (e) T
2. (a) iii (b) ii (c) i (d) ii

Chapter 7

1. (a) F (b) F (c) T (d) F (e) F (f) T
2. (a) i (b) ii (c) iii (d) ii

Chapter 8

1. (a) F (b) T (c) F (d) F (e) F (f) T
2. (a) ii (b) i (c) i (d) ii (e) i

Chapter 9

1. (a) T (b) F (c) T (d) T (e) T (f) T
2. (a) i (b) i (c) i (d) i (e) i (f) ii (g) i

Chapter 10

1. (a) F (b) T (c) T (d) T (e) F
2. (a) ii (b) i (c) iii (d) ii (e) i

Chapter 11

1. (a) F (b) F (c) F (d) T (e) F
2. (a) ii (b) i (c) i (d) iii (e) ii

Chapter 12

1. (a) T (b) F (c) F (d) T (e) F (f) F
2. (a) i (b) iii (c) ii (d) i (e) ii

Chapter 13

1. (a) T (b) F (c) F (d) T (e) F
2. (a) iii (b) i (c) i (d) ii (e) i

Chapter 14

1. (a) F (b) T (c) F (d) T (e) T
2. (a) iii (b) ii (c) ii (d) ii (e) ii

Chapter 15

1. (a) F (b) T (c) T (d) F (e) T (f) T (g) F (h) F
2. (a) ii (b) i (c) ii (d) ii (e) i (f) i

Chapter 16

1. (a) F (b) F (c) T (d) F (e) T (f) T (g) T (h) T (i) T
2. (a) ii (b) ii (c) ii (d) i (e) i

Chapter 17

1. (a) F (b) T (c) T (d) F (e) F (f) F (g) T
2. (a) iii (b) i (c) iii (d) ii (e) i

Chapter 18

1. (a) F (b) F (c) T (d) T (e) T (f) T (g) F (h) F (i) T (j) F
2. (a) ii (b) iii (c) iii (d) iii (e) ii (f) ii

Chapter 19

1. (a) F (b) F (c) F (d) T (e) T (f) T (g) T (h) T (i) T (j) T
2. (a) iii (b) i (c) i (d) iii (e) ii

Chapter 20

1. (a) F (b) T (c) F (d) T (e) T (f) F (g) T (h) T
2. (a) ii (b) i (c) ii (d) ii (e) i

Chapter 21

1. (a) T (b) F (c) T (d) T (e) T (f) T (g) T
2. (a) i (b) iii (c) i (d) ii (e) ii

Chapter 22

1. (a) T (b) T (c) T (d) F (e) F (f) T (g) T
2. (a) ii (b) iii (c) iii (d) iii

Chapter 23

1. (a) F (b) T (c) F (d) T (e) F (f) T (g) T (h) F (i) T (j) T
2. (a) i (b) i (c) iii (d) ii (e) iii

Chapter 24

1. (a) F (b) F (c) T (d) T (e) T (f) T (g) T (h) T (i) T (j) F
2. (a) i (b) iii (c) i (d) ii (e) iii (f) i

Chapter 25

1. (a) T (b) F (c) F (d) T (e) F (f) F (g) F (h) F (i) F (j) F
2. (a) ii (b) ii (c) i (d) ii (e) ii (f) ii (g) i (h) i

NUMERICAL PROBLEMS

Chapter 2

1. Rs 26,435
2. Rs 1,39,298
3. Rs 83,333
4. Rs 292.60
5. Qly: 6.24%; Mly: 6.17%
6. 24 years
7. 7.5%
8. (a) Rs 116.64; (b) Rs 116.99; (c) 117.16
9. Rs 1,698.55
10. (a) Rs 4,00,000; (b) Rs 8,33,333; (c) Rs 62,500
11. Rs 23,938.67
12. Rs 20,328.00

Chapter 3

1. 10.2%
2. 11.08%
3. Std. Dev. = 164.01
4. Portfolio return = Rs 726; portfolio risk = Std. Dev. = 164.207
5. (a) 14.50%;
6. (a) X = 13%; Y = 14.4%; (b) Variance: X = 0.00066; Y = 0.00218; SD: X = 0.0257; Y = 0.0467; (c) Cov. XY = 0.00048; Corr. Co-ff. 0.4 (d) portfolio return = 13.56%; portfolio risk = 0.02858
7. 15.6%
8. 19.5%
9. Variance 12.25
   Standard deviation 3.5
10. 0.7568

Chapter 4

1. Rs 800.40
2. Rs 1,153.85
3. 16%
4. Rs 10,000
5. Rs 935.83
6. 9.2%
7. Rs 1.58, Rs 1.65, Rs 1.74, Rs 1.91, Rs 2.11
8. Rs 10
9. 10%
10. 8.77%
11. 12.50%
12. Rs 1,58,514

Chapter 5

1. NPV: X = Rs 1,365, Y = Rs 313; PI: X = 1.14, Y = 1.03; IRR: X = 20.5%, Y = 13.5%; MIRR: X = 15.4, Y = 12.9
2. NPV = Rs 61. IRR should not be relied upon as there is more than one IRR.
3. Rs 21,350
4. Rs 21,000
5. Rs 351
6. Proposal A will be accepted.
7. Rs 14,700
8. IRR = 7.10%
9. Rs 2,49,000
10. 11.3%

Chapter 6

1. (a) Based on NPV, Project Y, Z and X should be accepted; (b) Projects X and Y
2. NPV with inflation-adjusted cash flow = Rs 26,646; NPV without such adjustment = Rs 15,193

3. NPV for Project X = Rs 9358; NPV for Project Y = Rs 5,359
4. Proposal B with higher ANPV will be accepted.
5. Year 1 = 0.9565, Year 2 = 0.9149, Year 3 = 0.8752
6. Postponement will be preferred.
7. Rs 1.6 crore
8. A combination of A, C and E
9. Rs 53,007

Chapter 7

1. (a) 8.4%; (b) 6.5%
2. 5.90%
3. (a) 16%; (b) Rs 3 per share; (c) 16.9%
4. 10.20% without floatation cost and 10.42% with floatation cost
5. (a) 17%; (b) 15%; (c) 18%
6. 11.44%
7. 14%
8. 10.6%
9. 11.81%
10. 18.8%

Chapter 8

1. 91 days
2. 73 days
3. 73 days
4. 73 days
5. GOC = 193 days; NOC = 120 days
6. GWC = Rs 72,000; NWC = Rs 35,000
7. Asset turnover ratio changing from 2.5 to 1.54
   Return on investment changing from 30% to 18.46%
8. Rs 33,000
9. Pre-reduction return on capital = 18%
   Post-reduction return on capital = 19.57%

Chapter 9

1. Rs 57,735
2. D = Rs 9832; Upper limit = Rs 49,496; Return point = Rs 29,832; Average cash balance = Rs 33,109
3. Rs 1,227.40
4. Rs 20,000, Rs 60,000 and Rs 1,00,000 respectively during January, February and March.
5. Cash released for Rs 15,00,000; Benefit = Rs 1,45,000
6. Rs 42,426
7. Rs 9,68,245

Chapter 10

1. ACP = 39 days; AR = Rs 1,08,333; Changed AR = Rs 51,944
2. Rs 1,895

3. ERR being 35% is greater than required rate of return and hence liberalisation of credit policy is justified.
4. AR = Rs 2,00,000; Saving in the financing cost = Rs 20,000
5. 39 days
6. Net cost of financing = Rs 4,748; Effective rate = 16.75%
7. 39.9 days
8. 45 days
9. 32 days

Chapter 11

1. EOQ = 14.142 tonnes; No. of orders 71; 5 days
2. 5.7 days
3. The sum of order cost and carrying cost for 20 tonnes is lower and hence a bigger order than EOQ is justified.
4. 3.994 tonnes
5. The moment the stock falls to 9.5 tonnes.
6. Rs 200
7. 400 units

Chapter 12

1. 74%
2. Additionally to pay Rs 135.26
3. 33%
4. 6.66%
5. Rs 2,750
6. (a) 10%; (b) 11.11%
7. Rs 30,000

Chapter 13

1. Rs 4,00,000
2. Rs 1,00,000
3. Based on earning theory, the amount of capital should be Rs 5,00,000. Thus it is a case of overcapitalisation. Earnings to be raised by Rs 20,000.

Chapter 14

1. (a) Rs 33,333; (b) Rs 23,333; (c) Rs 29,333
2. Rs 3,50,000
3. Unlevered firm: 20%; levered firm: 14.8%
4. MM approach: any ratio; Traditional approach: Leverage has to consider the risk of shareholders and even creditors.
5. (a) 14%; (b) 24.5%
6. Rs 15.75
7. 11.15%
8. 16.31%
9. Rs 18,66,667

Chapter 15

1. 25 rights per new share
2. Value of one right is Rs 2.22; value of ex-right share is Rs 57.78
3. (a) Rs 2,33,000; (b) Rs 2,50,000; (c) Rs 2,30,000
4. Rs 1,00,000
5. NPV is negative by Rs 39,288 and hence refunding is not suggested.

Chapter 16

1. Rs 13,870.40
2. 2.8%
3. Rs 72,096
4. 10%
5. NAL is Rs 7,344 and hence lease option should be opted for. Again, IRR is 6.1% which is lower than the after-tax cost of debt, so leasing should be preferred.
6. Rs 17,698.49
7. Rs 6,309.15

Chapter 17

1. Walter model: Rs 88; Gordon model: Rs 100
2. (a) pay-out ratio = zero, (b) Rs 96.
3. Rs 165 in both the cases
4. Dividend will be paid in the third and fourth year at the rate of Rs 0.40 and Rs 0.60 per share respectively.
5. (a) Rs 0.80, Rs 0.88, Rs 0.72, Rs 0.92, Rs 0.84 respectively from the first to the fifth year, (b) Rs 1.00. No extra dividend.
6. Rs 4
7. Rs 40,000 will be invested in the project with 20% IRR. Dividend pay-out ratio will be 20%.
8. Rs 62.5
9. Rs 130
10. Rs 400

Chapter 18

1. Rs 1,95,000
2. Rs 1,05,000
3. Rs 2,50,000
4. Rs 57,000
5. Cash increased by Rs 2,000
6. Decrease in working capital = Rs 450; funds from operation = Rs 2,750; increase in cash position = Rs 50.
7. EPS: Rs 3.30; DPS: Rs 2.10
8. Contribution margin = Rs 1,20,000
   EBIT = 60,000
   EBT= 45,000
   NIAT = 31,500

Chapter 19

1. (a) current ratio = 1.93/1
   (b) quick ratio = 1.18/1
   (c) receivable turnover ratio = 13.64
   (d) inventory turnover ratio = 12.35
   (e) profit margin = 23%
   (f) ROI = 53.70%
   (g) return on equity = 59.24%
   (h) EPS = Rs 18.60
   (i) capitalisation rate = 155%;
   (j) debt-equity = 63.69%
   (k) debt-asset = 38.91%
   (l) book value = Rs 31.40
   (m) dividend yield = 15.5% (assuming Rs 12 as MPS).
2. Rs 75,000
3. Rs 2,00,000
4. 2/1
5. (a) 20%
   (b) 25%
   (c) 5%
6. 50%
7. Rs 1,00,000
8. Rs 50,000

Chapter 20

1. (a) 10,000 units (b) Rs 2,00,000
2. 16,000 units
3. 44.4%
4. Rs 1,36,425.65
5. A = 25,000 units, B = 30,000 units and C = 22,500 units
6. BEP = 12,000 units, New BEP = 10,000 units

Chapter 21

1. 40%
2. DOL = 4/3; DFCL = 6/5; DCL = 8/5
3. 3/1 to be changed as 33/13
4. 4/3 to be changed as 6/5
5. ROI < tax-adjusted dividend. Leverage is not favourable.
6. 50%
7. 28.4%

Chapter 22

1. Net profit Rs 64,750. (Note: Fixed op. cost will remain constant).
2. 8.75%
3. Rs 1,250

Chapter 23

1. The value of the merged firm is Rs 8,70,030 which is higher than the combined value of the two firms prior to merger by Rs 90,030, out of which Rs 60,000 is shared by Firm Y and the rest by Firm X.
2. Tax saving of Rs 6,000
3. Net profit = Rs 1,20,000; No. of shares = 58,750; MPS = Rs 122.55; Total market price = Rs71,99,812.50; EPS = Rs 2.04; and P/E ratio = 60.

Chapter 24

1. (a) only creditors, (b) creditors and preference shareholders in full; (c) ordinary shareholders will also get Rs 5,00,000.
2. After meeting liquidation expenses and liquidator's fee, creditors will be paid in full. Preference shareholders will get only Rs 4,45,000. Ordinary shareholders will not get anything.
3. Rs 0.50 per rupee of debt.

Chapter 25

1. (a) (i) Re 0.08 per pound; (ii) Zero; (b) (i) Gain = Re 0.03 per pound; (ii) Loss = Re 0.05 per pound; (c) (i) Loss = Re 0.03 per pound; (ii) Gain = Re 0.05 per pound
2. 27 February 2004; 28 February 2004; and 29 February 2004
3. Selling pounds in New York and buying pounds in London yielding a profit of Re 0.03 per pound
4. $ 0.0222/Re
5. 1.099%
6. SF 15.2336 15.3647/Euro
7. 8.49%
8. Rs 45.3277/US $
9. Rs 47.61/US $
10. 9.6%

GLOSSARY

Abandonment value: The value of a project after its assets are sold externally.

ABC method of inventory management: Expensive items of inventory are more closely controlled than the less expensive items.

Accounting rate of return: Accounting profit divided by some measure of investment.

Accounts receivable: It is a current asset arising out of credit sales.

Accrued expenses: Expenses owed but not yet paid.

Adjusted present value: A sum of project's discounted cash flows (assuming all-equity financing) and the value of any tax-shield benefit of interest related to project financing minus floatation cost, if any.

Agency problem: Problems arising out of separation of ownership from control. It is manifest in managerial decisions not being in the interest of the owners of the company.

Agency relationship: The relationship between shareholders (principal) and the managers (agent).

Aggressive Policy: Matching short-term liabilities not only with variable current assets but also with permanent current assets and stressing more on profitability than on liquidity.

Ageing receivables: The process of classifying receivables according to their age as on a given date.

Amortisation schedule: Loan repayment schedule along with the interest up to the maturity.

Annual percentage rate: An interest rate that includes also the additional interest earned on account of compounding.

Annuity: A series of equal cash flow at regular intervals.

Arbitrage: Buying assets cheap and selling them dear in different markets in order to make profits.

Asymmetric information hypothesis: It assumes that investment banks have better knowledge than the issuer of a security about investors' demand. It also assumes disparate-quality information among the investors.

Average collection period ratio: Accounts receivables divided by net sales per day showing efficiency in collection of amounts receivable on credit sales.

Balance sheet: A financial statement showing a firm's assets and liabilities as on a specific date.

Balloon payment: A method of repaying a loan where the entire principal amount is paid at maturity and not in instalments.

Bankruptcy: A situation in which a firm's financial position is such that it is unable to pay its debts. In such cases, its assets are surrendered to a court for administration.

Beta: A statistical concept measuring the sensitivity of the return on a security to changes in the market rate of return.

Bond: A long-term debt instrument issued by a company. It is also known as a debenture.

Bond-refunding concept: Provision of a call feature in bonds so as to cut future interest cost.

Bondholder expropriation hypothesis: A concept showing how the firm's value is raised at the expense of its bondholders.

Book value: The value of assets as per a firm's balance sheet.

Break-even analysis: An analysis showing the relationship between profit on the one hand and cost, sales volume and sales price on the other.

Break-even point: A point at which revenue equals operating cost with the result that the net operating income is zero.

Business risk: Inherent uncertainty in the physical operation of a firm manifesting ultimately in fluctuating operating income.

Buy out: Conversion of a state-owned unit into a private-owned company.

Call provision: It specifies that the company (issuer) has the right to buy its preference shares or debentures at a given price from their holders.

Capital-asset pricing model: A model explaining the relationship between risk and return. In this case, the required rate of return is equal to the risk-free rate plus a premium based on the systematic risk.

Capital budgeting: The process of and selecting of long-term investment projects.

Capitalisation rate: The discount rate used for arriving at the present value of expected future cash flows.

Capital market: Market for medium-term and long-term finances and financial instruments.

Capital rationing: A situation when the amount of funds for long-term investment is limited.

Capital structure: The ratio in which equity shares, preference shares and debt form the capital base of a firm.

Cash budget: Statement of anticipated receipts and payments of cash.

Certainty equivalent: The amount of cash representing the part of uncertainty in cash flow. Its adjustment equates the uncertain cash flow with the cash flow with certainty.

Clearing float: Time consumed between the deposit of a cheque and its clearing.

Clientele effect: Investors buy a company's share as a result of company's attractive long-term policies.

Combined leverage: A factor measuring the effect of a change in sales on net income.

Commercial paper: Short-term, unsecured promissory notes often issued by high-rated companies.

Commitment fee: A fee charged by a lender on the unused part of credit.

Common-size statement: A statement showing financial variables in percentage terms. Balance sheet items are shown as a share of total assets, and Incomes are shown as a share of net sales.

Compensating balance: Non-interest bearing demand deposits with the bank. This is the minimum balance maintained with a bank.

Congeneric mergers: Merger between related business interests.

Conglomerate merger: Merger between unrelated business interests.

Conservative policy: Matching current assets as much as is possible with long-term capital and stressing more on liquidity than on profitability.

Consolidation: The merger of two firms into a new firm, in which the two old firms cease to exist.

Contractual failure: It occurs when the company fails to fulfil its debt commitments.

Contribution margin: Revenue needed to meet fixed cost. It is equal to revenue minus variable cost.

Conventional project: project having net initial cash outflow followed by operating cash inflows.

Conversion price: The price per share at which an equity share is exchanged for a convertible security.

Conversion ratio: The number of equity shares for which a convertible debt security is exchanged. It is equal to the face value of the convertible security divided by the conversion price.

Convertible security: A debt security convertible into equity shares.

Coupon rate: The interest rate mentioned in a bond.

Covenant: Restrictions imposed by a lender on the borrower.

Credit standard: The minimum required creditworthiness of a firm applying for credit.

Current assets: Cash and other assets that are convertible into cash within one accounting year or within the normal operating cycle.

Current liabilities: Obligations to be repaid within one accounting year or within the normal operating cycle.

Current ratio: Current assets divided by current liabilities.

Current yield on a bond: The annual interest on a bond divided by the current price of the bond.

Debenture: A long-term debt instrument not secured by any property.

Debt-equity ratio: Debt divided by the book value of equity.

Debt ratio: Debt divided by total assets.

Default risk: Risk borne by bondholders that they will not be getting back their principal along with interest.

Depreciation: A deduction of a part of the asset's cost from income for each year during the asset's life.

Dilution: Reduction in earning per share due to an increase in the number of shares.

Disbursement float: Delay in the clearance of payable cheques by the bank.

Discount rate: The rate used to bring down the future cash flows to the present value.

Diversifiable risk: It is the risk specific to the company that can be reduced through diversification of investment.

Divestitures: Selling off part of a firm for cash/securities. It is also known as a sell-off.

Dividend pay-out ratio: That part of a firm's earnings paid out as dividend.

Dividend yield: Dividend per equity share as a percentage of its market price.

Draft: It is an instrument through which the drawer of a draft instructs the drawee to make payment of the amount mentioned therein to a payee. The payee is normally the drawer.

Economic failure: Inability of a firm to earn adequate return on investment.

Economic order quantity: A size of order for inventory that minimises the inventory cost.

Effective annual interest rate: Rate of interest earned after adjusting the nominal rate by compounding during a particular year.

Efficient financial market: Where the current price of securities reflects all available and relevant information.

Equity carve-out: The public sale of shares in a subsidiary.

Ex-dividend: A share is ex-dividend when a new purchaser does not get the right to receive dividend on the share to be paid in the immediate future.

Expected value: Weighted average of possible outcomes where weight is based on probabilities of occurrence.

Extension: An agreement between the firm and its creditors to postpone repayment of debt.

Face value: The actual stated value of a security.

Factoring: The sale of accounts receivable. The purchaser is known as a factor.

Financial distress: When a firm is unable to meet its financial obligation.

Financial intermediaries: Financial institutions that borrow and lend money.

Financial lease: A non-cancellable lease that is meant to continue for the life time of the asset.

Financial leverage: The introduction of fixed-charge securities into a firm's capital structure.

Financial risk: Uncertainty in a firm's return from investment. The larger the variation, the greater the risk.

Fixed charge: Fixed payment under a contractual agreement, such as, interest on debt, etc.

Floatation cost: The costs involved in issuing securities.

Fixed-asset turnover ratio: The ratio of sales to fixed assets.

Fixed cost: That part of the total cost that does not change with changes in output.

Float: Difference between the cash balance as per the cash book and the balance as per the bank ledger.

Forfaiting: The sale without recourse of medium and long-term export receivables to banks.

Forward contract: An arrangement requiring the delivery of currency/securities on a future date.

Forward exchange rate: An exchange rate applicable to a forward contract.

Funds-flow statement: A financial statement showing the working capital position.

Going-concern value: The value of a firm as a running business entity.

Goodwill: A firm's intangible asset. It normally arises when an acquiring firm gets a larger value from the acquired firm.

Gross profit: Sales minus cost of production.

Gross working capital: It is the sum of current assets.

Holding company: The company that holds a majority of the equity shares of another company/companies.

Homemade leverage: Adoption of a process of leverage at the personal level.

Horizontal mergers: When firms that are in the same business combine or merge.

Hurdle rate: The minimum required rate of return from an investment.

Income statement: A financial statement showing income and expenses and various types of profit.

Indenture: A legal agreement between the bond issuing company and the bondholders.

Independent proposals: When rejection/acceptance of a proposal has nothing to do with the rejection/acceptance of another proposal.

Inflation: A rise in the general price level.

Insolvency: A firm's inability to meet its financial obligations.

Interest coverage ratio: The extent to which interest payment is covered by profits. It is pre-tax profit divided by one plus interest.

Interest rate risk: The loss/gains to borrower/lender on account of changes in interest rate.

Internal rate of return: A specific discount rate that makes the net present value zero.

Inventory turnover ratio: It is the cost of goods sold divided by inventory.

Investment bank: A bank employed by a company to sell its shares and to perform certain other functions related to the issue.

Junk bonds: A high-yield, high-risk and below-investment grade bond.

Just-in-time: It is a method of inventory management in which inventory reaches the site of production only when it is needed. The holding cost is zero.

Lead time: Time that elapses between the placing of an order and the delivery of goods.

Lease: A contract under which the lessor (owner of an asset) permits the use of that asset to another, known as the lessee in return for a periodic rental payment.

Letter of credit: A instrument issued by the importer' bank to the exporter guaranteeing payment if goods traded are in order.

Leverage: The use of fixed cost funds for the purpose of raising profitability.

Leveraged buy-outs: Debt-financed purchase of a company's shares.

Leveraged lease: A type of lease where the lessor borrows to acquire the assets to be given on lease.

Line of credit: The maximum limit to the extension of credit facilities to a buyer.

Liquidation: The sale of a company's assets after its winding up.

Liquidation value: The value realised from the sale of a company's assets following liquidation.

Liquidity: A measure of the ability of an asset to be converted into cash.

Liquidity ratio: Various ratios that indicate the extent to which liquidity is present in a firm, such as, current ratio, acid ratio, etc.

Listing: The permission for a security to be traded on an organised stock exchange.

Lock-box: A post-office box maintained by a company's bank to expedite customers' remittances and to speed up the cash inflow.

London inter-bank offer rate: The interest rate charged by major London-based banks on inter-bank lending of Eurodollars.

Maintenance lease: see operating lease.

Management buy-out: It is a leveraged buy-out where the pre-buy-out management gets a share in the equity capital.

Market risk: It is the systematic risk or undiversifiable risk that cannot be reduced through diversification.

Matching policy: Matching the maturity of finances with the usual life of the asset.

Maturity value: The face value or par value of bonds/debentures.

Merger: The combination of two or more firms.

Money market: Market for short-term funds, normally with maturity periods of less than one year.

Money market mutual funds: Firms that pool the resources of large number of investors for further investment.

Mortgage bonds: Bond secured by a mortgage.

Mutually exclusive proposals: The acceptance of one proposal means the automatic rejection of the other proposal.

Negative float: Increase in the amount of cash tied up in the collection cycle.

Negative pledge clause: It is a covenant where the asset of the borrower cannot be used for the purpose of lien.

Net lease: Lease where the lessee is responsible for the maintenance of the leased assets.

Net present value: Difference between discounted value of inflows and discounted value of outflows.

Net working capital: Current assets minus current liabilities.

Non-conventional project: Initial cash inflow followed by net operating cash outflow.

Open-end mortgage: A type of mortgage where the collateral can be used for some other debt also.

Operating cycle: Time elapsed between commitment of cash for production and the collection of receivables.

Operating expenses: Expenses related to operation, such as administrative costs, production cost, etc., but not the cost of material.

Operating lease: A type of lease where the lessor provides for the maintenance of the leased equipment.

Operating leverage: Changes in sales that lead to changes in net operating income. This is because of the fixed costs.

Operating margin: Operating income divided by sales.

Opportunity cost: Rate of return foregone on the next best comparable alternative.

Optimal capital structure: That mix of equity shares, preference shares and debt that leads to the minimum weighted average cost of capital.

Over-subscription privilege: The right to buy unsubscribed shares on a pro rata basis under a rights offering.

Par value: The stated value or the face value of a security.

Participating preference share: A preference share that entitles its holder to also participate or share in the dividend meant for the equity share holders.

Pay-back period: The period during which the initial investment is expected to be recovered. The expected period is the target pay-back period that may differ from the actual pay-back period.

Permanent current assets: That part of the current assets which is stable throughout the year.

Portfolio: A combination of assets meant for investment.

Positive float: The opposite of negative float (See negative float).

Pre-emptive rights: The right of the existing shareholders to buy new shares whenever offered by the company. It checks any dilution in their share in the company's equity.

Preference share: Such shares carry a fixed rate of dividend. Moreover, they have prior claim to dividend as compared to the equity shares.

Price-earning ratio: The market price of share divided by the earning per share.

Primary market: The market in which the securities are initially sold.

Prime rate: Interest rate charged by banks on short-term, low-risk loans.

Probability distribution: A set of possible values and their associated probability of occurrence.

Profitability index: Present value of operating and terminal cash flow divided by the initial investment.

Profitability ratio: Any ratio that measures or indicates profitability, such as profit divided by sales, etc.

Proforma financial statement: A projected balance sheet or income statement as on a future date.

Promissory note: A financial instrument through which one promises to pay a stated amount after a specific period.

Quick ratio: Current assets other than inventory divided by current liabilities. It is also known as the acid-test ratio.

Recapitalisation: It occurs when a firm sells bonds to buy back its equity shares.

Refunding: Redeeming old debentures through the issue of new ones.

Reorganisation: Reorganisation of the capital structure of a financially distressed company.

Repurchase: The buy back of shares.

Required rate of return: The minimum expected rate of return that a project should yield in order to be accepted.

Residual dividend policy: A policy in which dividend is payable to shareholders only when no investment opportunities exist for investment of the earnings.

Restrictive covenants: Restrictions imposed by the bondholders on issue of bonds by a company.

Retained earnings: That part of profits which are not distributed as dividend but retained for reinvestment.

Reverse split: Reduction in the number of the company's shares. It is the opposite to share split.

Revolving credit agreement: A formal contractual commitment to provide maximum amount of credit to a firm.

Rights: A privilege enjoyed by the shareholders to buy new shares offered by the company before they are sold to the public.

Rights-off: It is just the opposite of rights-on.

Rights-on: A share is called rights-on when it entitles its owner to a right that is about to be issued by the company.

Risk-adjusted discount rate: When the risk factor is adjusted to the discount rate for bringing down the future cash flows to the present value.

Risk-averse: A term that describes an investor who demands a higher expected return for bearing a growing amount of risk.

Safety stock: Inventory kept in reserve for meeting unexpected demand.

Sale-leaseback agreement: A type of lease where the company sells the asset owned by it and then uses the asset as a lessee.

Salvage value: The price of a company's assets after the life time of the assets.

Secondary market: It is the market where the securities are sold the second time and thereafter.

Secured credit: Short-term credit backed by accounts receivable/inventory.

Security market line: The straight line showing return-risk relationship in respect of projects under the capital-asset pricing model.

Sell-off: The sale of a company's asset. It may be partial sale or a complete sale known as voluntary liquidation.

Semifixed cost: When a portion of cost is fixed and the other portion is variable.

Semistrong efficient market: A market in which the price of shares reflects only publically available resources.

Serial bonds: Bonds issued at the same time but with varying maturities.

Share-split: When shares are divided into parts. It helps increase the number of outstanding shares, but the total value of share remains the same.

Sinking fund: A fund created to enable retirement of a security prior to maturity.

Spin-off: Distribution of a parent's share in subsidiary among the parent's shareholders on a pro rata basis.

Smoothened residual dividend policy: A form of liberal residual dividend policy.

Spontaneous financing: Trade credit that emerges spontaneously in the wake of a firm's day-to-day operation.

Stock dividend: When dividend is distributed in form of shares. It is known as a bonus share issue in India.

Stock-out: The absence of the desired amount of inventory to meet an order.

Strong form efficient: A market in which the price of shares reflects all publicly and privately available information.

Subscription price: The price at which existing shareholders buy shares under a rights offering.

Subsidiary: A company controlled by another company, known as the parent company.

Sunk cost: The amount of money that already stands invested or spent on a project.

Systematic risk: see market risk, the risk that cannot be diversified.

Take-over: The acquisition of a company.

Target payback ratio: The ratio of residual funds to total earnings.

Tax shield: It helps reduce the taxable income.

Technical analysis: Financial forecast on the basis of historical data.

Term loans: Unsecured loans with specific maturities.

Term structure of interest rates: Relationship between yield to maturity and time to maturity of bonds.

Time value of money: Productivity of money in form of interest earned is based on the time value of money.

Times interest earned ratio: It is similar to the interest coverage ratio.

Trade acceptance: A draft signed by an importer.

Trade credit: Credit extended between firms, known as bills payable or bills receivable.

Trade liabilities: Liabilities owed to suppliers.

Underwriting: Purchase of shares from the issuer by an investment bank for their resale. Underwriting is done when all the shares are not bought by the investors during the initial offer.

Unsecured loan: When debt is not backed by a pledge of assets.

Unsystematic risk: Variation in the rate of return on a particular security that is not explained by variation in the market as a whole. This type of risk can be reduced through diversification.

Variable cost: The cost that moves up and down with a movement in the size of output.

Vertical integration: When firms engaged in different stages of production combine in order to make a single final product.

Warrant: Long-term option to purchase equity shares at a specific exercise price over a given period of time.

Yield curve: Relationship between yields and term to maturity.

Yield to maturity: The expected rate of return from a bond if bought at the current market price and held till maturity.

Zero-coupon bond: A bond having no interest feature sold at deep discount. Discount serves the purpose of interest.

MATHEMATICAL TABLES

Table 1: Present Value of Re 1 Due at the End of n Periods

Period	*1%*	*2%*	*3%*	*4%*	*5%*	*6%*	*7%*	*8%*	*9%*	*10%*
1	.9901	.9804	.9709	.9615	.9524	.9434	.9346	.9259	.9174	.9091
2	.9803	.9612	.9426	.9246	.9070	.8900	.8734	.8573	.8417	.8264
3	.9706	.9423	.9151	.8890	.8638	.8396	.8163	.7938	.7722	.7513
4	.9610	.9238	.8885	.8548	.8227	.7921	.7629	.7350	.7084	.6830
5	.9515	.9057	.8626	.8219	.7835	.7473	.7130	.6806	.6499	.6209
6	.9420	.8880	.8375	.7903	.7462	.7050	.6663	.6302	.5963	.5645
7	.9327	.8706	.8131	.7599	.7107	.6651	.6227	.5835	.5470	.5132
8	.9235	.8535	.7894	.7307	.6768	.6274	.5820	.5403	.5019	.4665
9	.9143	.8368	.7664	.7026	.6446	.5919	.5439	.5002	.4604	.4241
10	.9053	.8203	.7441	.6756	.6139	.5584	.5083	.4632	.4224	.3855
11	.8963	.8043	.7224	.6496	.5847	.5268	.4751	.4289	.3875	.3505
12	.8874	.7885	.7014	.6246	.5568	.4970	.4440	.3971	.3555	.3186
13	.8787	.7730	.6810	.6006	.5303	.4688	.4150	.3677	.3262	.2897
14	.8700	.7579	.6611	.5775	.5051	.4423	.3878	.3405	.2992	.2633
15	.8613	.7430	.6419	.5553	.4810	.4173	.3624	.3152	.2745	.2394
16	.8528	.7284	.6232	.5339	.4581	.3936	.3387	.2919	.2519	.2176
17	.8444	.7142	.6050	.5134	.4363	.3714	.3166	.2703	.2311	.1978
18	.8360	.7002	.5874	.4936	.4155	.3503	.2959	.2502	.2120	.1799
19	.8277	.6864	.5703	.4746	.3957	.3305	.2765	.2317	.1945	.1635
20	.8195	.6730	.5537	.4564	.3769	.3118	.2584	.2145	.1784	.1486
21	.8114	.6598	.5375	.4388	.3589	.2942	.2415	.1987	.1637	.1351
22	.8034	.6468	.5219	.4220	.3418	.2775	.2257	.1839	.1502	.1228
23	.7954	.6342	.5067	.4057	.3256	.2618	.2109	.1703	.1378	.1117
24	.7876	.6217	.4919	.3901	.3101	.2470	.1971	.1577	.1264	.1015
25	.7798	.6095	.4776	.3751	.2953	.2330	.1842	.1460	.1160	.0923
26	.7720	.5976	.4637	.3607	.2812	.2198	.1722	.1352	.1064	.0839
27	.7644	.5859	.4502	.3468	.2678	.2074	.1609	.1252	.0976	.0763
28	.7568	.5744	.4371	.3335	.2551	.1956	.1504	.1159	.0895	.0693
29	.7493	.5631	.4243	.3207	.2429	.1846	.1406	.1073	.0822	.0630
30	.7419	.5521	.4120	.3083	.2314	.1741	.1314	.0994	.0754	.0573
35	.7059	.5000	.3554	.2534	.1813	.1301	.0937	.0676	.0490	.0356
40	.6717	.4529	.3066	.2083	.1420	.0972	.0668	.0460	.0318	.0221
45	.6391	.4102	.2644	.1712	.1113	.0727	.0476	.0313	.0207	.0137
50	.6080	.3715	.2281	.1407	.0872	.0543	.0339	.0213	.0134	.0085
55	.5785	.3365	.1968	.1157	.0683	.0406	.0242	.0145	.0087	.0053

Period	*12%*	*14%*	*15%*	*16%*	*18%*	*20%*	*24%*	*28%*	*32%*	*36%*
1	.8929	.8772	.8696	.8621	.8475	.8333	.8065	.7813	.7576	.7353
2	.7972	.7695	.7561	.7432	.7182	.6944	.6504	.6104	.5739	.5407
3	.7118	.6750	.6575	.6407	.6086	.5787	.5245	.4768	.4348	.3975
4	.6355	.5921	.5718	.5523	.5158	.4823	.4230	.3725	.3294	.2923
5	.5674	.5194	.4972	.4761	.4371	.4019	.3411	.2910	.2495	.2149
6	.5066	.4556	.4323	.4104	.3704	.3349	.2751	.2274	.1890	.1580
7	.4523	.3996	.3759	.3538	.3139	.2791	.2218	.1776	.1432	.1162
8	.4039	.3506	.3269	.3050	.2660	.2326	.1789	.1388	.1085	.0854
9	.3606	.3075	.2843	.2630	.2255	.1938	.1443	.1084	.0822	.0628
10	.3220	.2697	.2472	.2267	.1911	.1615	.1164	.0847	.0623	.0462
11	.2875	.2366	.2149	.1954	.1619	.1346	.0938	.0662	.0472	.0340
12	.2567	.2076	.1869	.1685	.1372	.1122	.0757	.0517	.0357	.0250
13	.2292	.1821	.1625	.1452	.1163	.0935	.0610	.0404	.0271	.0184
14	.2046	.1597	.1413	.1252	.0985	.0779	.0492	.0316	.0205	.0135
15	.1827	.1401	.1229	.1079	.0835	.0649	.0397	.0247	.0155	.0099
16	.1613	.1229	.1069	.0930	.0708	.0541	.0320	.0193	.0118	.0073
17	.1456	.1078	.0929	.0802	.0600	.0451	.0258	.0150	.0089	.0054
18	.1300	.0946	.0808	.0691	.0508	.0376	.0208	.0118	.0068	.0039
19	.1161	.0829	.0703	.0596	.0431	.0313	.0168	.0092	.0051	.0029
20	.1037	.0728	.0611	.0514	.0365	.0261	.0135	.0072	.0039	.0021
21	.0926	.0638	.0531	.0443	.0309	.0217	.0109	.0056	.0029	.0016
22	.0826	.0560	.0462	.0382	.0262	.0181	.0088	.0044	.0022	.0012
23	.0738	.0491	.0402	.0329	.0222	.0151	.0071	.0034	.0017	.0008
24	.0659	.0431	.0349	.0284	.0188	.0126	.0057	.0027	.0013	.0006
25	.0588	.0378	.0304	.0245	.0160	.0105	.0046	.0021	.0010	.0005
26	.0525	.0331	.0264	.0211	.0135	.0087	.0037	.0016	.0007	.0003
27	.0469	.0291	.0230	.0182	.0115	.0073	.0030	.0013	.0006	.0002
28	.0419	.0255	.0200	.0157	.0097	.0061	.0024	.0010	.0004	.0002
29	.0374	.0224	.0174	.0135	.0082	.0051	.0020	.0008	.0003	.0001
30	.0334	.0196	.0151	.0116	.0070	.0042	.0016	.0006	.0002	.0001
35	.0189	.0102	.0075	.0055	.0030	.0017	.0005	.0002	.0001	*
40.0107	.0053	.0037	.0026	.0013	.0007	.0002	.0001	*	*	
45	.0061	.0027	.0019	.0013	.0006	.0003	.0001	*	*	*
50	.0035	.0014	.0009	.0006	.0003	.0001	*	*	*	*
55	.0020	.0007	.0005	.0003	.0001	*	*	*	*	*

*The factor is zero to four decimal places.

Table 2: Present Value of an Annuity of Re 1 per Period for n Periods

Number of Period	*1%*	*2%*	*3%*	*4%*	*5%*	*6%*	*7%*	*8%*	*9%*
1	0.9901	0.9804	0.9709	0.9615	0.9524	0.9434	0.9346	0.9259	0.9174
2	1.9704	1.9416	1.9135	1.8861	1.8594	1.8334	1.8080	1.7833	1.7591
3	2.9410	2.8839	2.8286	2.7751	2.7232	2.6730	2.6243	2.5771	2.5313
4	3.9020	3.8077	3.7171	3.6299	3.5460	3.4651	3.3872	3.3121	3.2397
5	4.8534	4.7135	4.5797	4.4518	4.3295	4.2124	4.1002	3.9927	3.8897
6	5.7955	5.6014	5.4172	5.2421	5.0757	4.9173	4.7665	4.6229	4.4859
7	6.7282	6.4720	6.2303	6.0021	5.7864	5.5824	5.3893	5.2064	5.0330
8	7.6517	7.3255	7.0197	6.7327	6.4632	6.2098	5.9713	5.7466	5.5348
9	8.5660	8.1622	7.7861	7.4353	7.1078	6.8017	6.5152	6.2469	5.9952
10	9.4713	8.9826	8.5302	8.1109	7.7217	7.3601	7.0236	6.7101	6.4177
11	10.3676	9.7868	9.2526	8.7605	8.3064	7.8869	7.4987	7.1390	6.8052
12	11.2551	10.5753	9.9540	9.3851	8.8633	8.3838	7.9427	7.5361	7.1607
13	12.1337	11.3484	10.6350	9.9856	9.3936	8.8527	8.3577	7.9038	7.4869
14	13.0037	12.1062	11.2961	10.5631	9.8986	9.2950	8.7455	8.2442	7.7862
15	13.8651	12.8493	11.9379	11.1184	10.3797	9.7122	9.1079	8.5595	8.0607
16	14.7179	13.5777	12.5611	11.6523	10.8378	10.1059	9.4466	8.8514	8.3126
17	15.5623	14.2919	13.1661	12.1657	11.2741	10.4773	9.7632	9.1216	8.5433
18	16.3983	14.9920	13.7535	12.6593	11.6896	10.8276	10.0591	9.3719	8.7556
19	17.2260	15.6785	14.3238	13.1339	12.0853	11.1581	10.3356	9.6036	8.9501
20	18.0456	16.3514	14.8775	13.5903	12.4622	11.4699	10.5940	9.8181	9.1285
21	18.8570	17.0112	15.4150	14.0292	12.8212	11.7641	10.8355	10.0168	9.2922
22	19.6604	17.6580	15.9369	14.4511	13.1630	12.0416	11.0612	10.2007	9.4424
23	20.4558	18.2922	16.4436	14.8568	13.4886	12.3034	11.2722	10.3711	9.5802
24	21.2434	18.9139	16.9355	15.2470	13.7986	12.5504	11.4693	10.5288	9.7066
25	22.0232	19.5235	17.4131	15.6221	14.0939	12.7834	11.6536	10.6748	9.8226
26	22.7952	20.1210	17.8768	15.9828	14.3752	13.0032	11.8258	10.8100	9.9290
27	23.5596	20.7069	18.3270	16.3296	14.6430	13.2105	11.9867	10.9352	10.0266
28	24.3164	21.2813	18.7641	16.6631	14.8981	13.4062	12.1371	11.0511	10.1161
29	25.0658	21.8444	19.1855	16.9837	15.1411	13.5907	12.2777	11.1584	10.1983
30	25.8077	22.3965	19.6004	17.2920	15.3725	13.7648	12.4090	11.2578	10.2737
35	29.4086	24.9986	21.4872	18.6646	16.3742	14.4982	12.9477	11.6546	10.5688
40	32.8347	27.3555	23.1148	19.7928	17.1591	15.0463	13.3317	11.9246	10.7574
45	36.0945	29.4902	24.5187	20.7200	17.7741	15.4558	13.6055	12.1084	10.8812
50	39.1961	31.4236	25.7298	21.4822	18.2559	15.7619	13.8007	12.2335	10.9617
55	42.1472	33.1748	26.7744	22.1086	18.6335	15.9905	13.9399	12.3186	11.0140

Number of Period	*10%*	*12%*	*14%*	*15%*	*16%*	*18%*	*20%*	*24%*	*28%*	*32%*
1	0.9091	0.8929	0.8772	0.8696	0.8621	0.8475	0.8333	0.8065	0.7813	0.7576
2	1.7355	1.6901	1.6467	1.6257	1.6052	1.5656	1.5278	1.4568	1.3916	1.3315
3	2.4869	2.4018	2.3216	2.2832	2.2459	2.1743	2.1065	1.9813	1.8684	1.7663
4	3.1699	3.0373	2.9137	2.8550	2.7982	2.6901	2.5887	2.4043	2.2410	2.0957
5	3.7908	3.6048	3.4331	3.3522	3.2743	3.1272	2.9906	2.7454	2.5320	2.3452
6	4.3553	4.1114	3.8887	3.7845	3.6847	3.4976	3.3255	3.0205	2.7594	2.5342
7	4.8684	4.5638	4.2883	4.1604	4.0386	3.8115	3.6046	3.2423	2.9370	2.6775
8	5.3349	4.9676	4.6389	4.4873	4.3436	4.0776	3.8372	3.4212	3.0758	2.7860
9	5.7590	5.3282	4.9464	4.7716	4.6065	4.3030	4.0310	3.5655	3.1842	2.8681
10	6.1446	5.6502	5.2161	5.0188	4.8332	4.4941	4.1925	3.6819	3.2689	2.9304
11	6.4951	5.9377	5.4527	5.2337	5.0286	4.6560	4.3271	3.7757	3.3351	2.9776
12	6.8137	6.1944	5.6603	5.4206	5.1971	4.7932	4.4392	3.8514	3.3868	3.0133
13	7.1034	6.4235	5.8424	5.5831	5.3423	4.9095	4.5327	3.9124	3.4272	3.0404
14	7.3667	6.6282	6.0021	5.7245	5.4675	5.0081	4.6106	3.9616	3.4587	3.0609
15	7.6061	6.8109	6.1422	5.8474	5.5755	5.0916	4.6755	4.0013	3.4834	3.0764
16	7.8237	6.9740	6.2651	5.9542	5.6685	5.1624	4.7296	4.0333	3.5026	3.0882
17	8.0216	7.1196	6.3729	6.0472	5.7487	5.2223	4.7746	4.0591	3.5177	3.0971
18	8.2014	7.2497	6.4674	6.1280	5.8178	5.2732	4.8122	4.0799	3.5294	3.1039
19	8.3649	7.3658	6.5504	6.1982	5.8775	5.3162	4.8435	4.0967	3.5386	3.1090
20	8.5136	7.4694	6.6231	6.2593	5.9288	5.3527	4.8696	4.1103	3.5458	3.1129
21	8.6487	7.5620	6.6870	6.3125	5.9731	5.3837	4.8913	4.1212	3.5514	3.1158
22	8.7715	7.6446	6.7429	6.3587	6.0113	5.4099	4.9094	4.1300	3.5558	3.1180
23	8.8832	7.7184	6.7921	6.3988	6.0442	5.4321	4.9245	4.1371	3.5592	3.1197
24	8.9847	7.7843	6.8351	6.4338	6.0726	5.4509	4.9371	4.1428	3.5619	3.1210
25	9.0770	7.8431	6.8729	6.4641	6.0971	5.4669	4.9476	4.1474	3.5640	3.1220
26	9.1609	7.8957	6.9061	6.4906	6.1182	5.4804	4.9563	4.1511	3.5656	3.1227
27	9.2372	7.9426	6.9352	6.5135	6.1364	5.4919	4.9636	4.1542	3.5669	3.1233
28	9.3066	7.9844	6.9607	6.5335	6.1520	5.5016	4.9697	4.1566	3.5679	3.1237
29	9.3696	8.0218	6.9830	6.5509	6.1656	5.5098	4.9747	4.1585	3.5687	3.1240
30	9.4269	8.0552	7.0027	6.5660	6.1772	5.5168	4.9789	4.1601	3.5693	3.1242
35	9.6442	8.1755	7.0700	6.6166	6.2153	5.5386	4.9915	4.1644	3.5708	3.1248
40	9.7791	8.2438	7.1050	6.6418	6.2335	5.5482	4.9966	4.1659	3.5712	3.1250
45	9.8628	8.2825	7.1232	6.6543	6.2421	5.5523	4.9986	4.1664	3.5714	3.1250
50	9.9148	8.3045	7.1327	6.6605	6.2463	5.5541	4.9995	4.1666	3.5714	3.1250
55	9.9471	8.3170	7.1376	6.6636	6.2482	5.5549	4.9998	4.1666	3.5714	3.1250

Table 3: Future Value of Re 1 at the End of *n* Periods

Period	*1%*	*2%*	*3%*	*4%*	*5%*	*6%*	*7%*	*8%*	*9%*	*10%*
1	1.0100	1.0200	1.0300	1.0400	1.0500	1.0600	1.0700	1.0800	1.0900	1.1000
2	1.0201	1.0404	1.0609	1.0816	1.1025	1.1236	1.1449	1.1664	1.1881	1.2100
3	1.0303	1.0612	1.0927	1.1249	1.1576	1.1910	1.2250	1.2597	1.2950	1.3310
4	1.0406	1.0824	1.1255	1.1699	1.2155	1.2625	1.3108	1.3605	1.4116	1.4641
5	1.0510	1.1041	1.1593	1.2167	1.2763	1.3382	1.4026	1.4693	1.5386	1.6105
6	1.0615	1.1262	1.1941	1.2653	1.3401	1.4185	1.5007	1.5869	1.6771	1.7116
7	1.0721	1.1487	1.2299	1.3159	1.4071	1.5036	1.6058	1.7138	1.8280	1.9487
8	1.0829	1.1717	1.2668	1.3686	1.4775	1.5938	1.7182	1.8509	1.9926	2.1436
9	1.0937	1.1951	1.3048	1.4233	1.5513	1.6895	1.8385	1.9990	2.1719	2.3579
10	1.1046	1.2190	1.3439	1.4802	1.6289	1.7908	1.9672	2.1589	2.3674	2.5937
11	1.1157	1.2434	1.3842	1.5395	1.7103	1.8983	2.1049	2.3316	2.5804	2.8531
12	1.1268	1.2682	1.4258	1.6010	1.7959	2.0122	2.2522	2.5182	2.8127	3.1384
13	1.1381	1.2936	1.4685	1.6651	1.8856	2.1329	2.4098	2.7196	3.0658	3.4523
14	1.1495	1.3195	1.5126	1.7317	1.9799	2.2609	2.5785	2.9372	3.3417	3.7975
15	1.1610	1.3459	1.5580	1.8009	2.0789	2.3966	2.7590	3.1722	3.6425	4.1772
16	1.1726	1.3728	1.6047	1.8730	2.1829	2.5404	2.9522	3.4259	3.9703	4.5950
17	1.1843	1.4002	1.6528	1.9479	2.2920	2.6928	3.1588	3.7000	4.3276	5.0545
18	1.1961	1.4282	1.7024	2.0258	2.4066	2.8543	3.3799	3.9960	4.7171	5.5599
19	1.2081	1.4568	1.7535	2.1068	2.5270	3.0256	3.6165	4.3157	5.1417	6.1159
20	1.2202	1.4859	1.8061	2.1911	2.6533	3.2071	3.8697	4.6610	5.6044	6.7275
21	1.2324	1.5157	1.8603	2.2788	2.7860	3.3996	4.1406	5.0338	6.1088	7.4002
22	1.2447	1.5460	1.9161	2.3699	2.9253	3.6035	4.4304	5.4365	6.6586	8.1403
23	1.2572	1.5769	1.9736	2.4647	3.0715	3.8197	4.7405	5.8715	7.2579	8.9543
24	1.2697	1.6084	2.0328	2.5633	3.2251	4.0489	5.0724	6.3412	7.9111	9.8497
25	1.2824	1.6406	2.0938	2.6658	3.3864	4.2919	5.4274	6.8485	8.6231	10.835
26	1.2953	1.6734	2.1566	2.7725	3.5557	4.5494	5.8074	7.3964	9.3992	11.918
27	1.3082	1.7069	2.2213	2.8834	3.7335	4.8223	6.2139	7.9881	10.245	13.110
28	1.3213	1.7410	2.2879	2.9987	3.9201	5.1117	6.6488	8.6271	11.167	14.421
29	1.3345	1.7758	2.3566	3.1187	4.1161	5.4184	7.1143	9.3173	12.172	15.863
30	1.3478	1.8114	2.4273	3.2434	4.3219	5.7435	7.6123	10.063	13.268	17.449
40	1.4889	2.2080	3.2620	4.8010	7.0400	10.286	14.974	21.725	31.409	45.259
50	1.6446	2.6916	4.3839	7.1067	11.467	18.420	29.457	46.902	74.358	117.39
60	1.8167	3.2810	5.8916	10.520	18.679	32.988	57.946	101.26	176.03	304.48

Period	12%	14%	15%	16%	18%	20%	24%	28%	32%	36%
1	1.1200	1.1400	1.1500	1.1600	1.1800	1.2000	1.2400	1.2800	1.3200	1.3600
2	1.2544	1.2996	1.3225	1.3456	1.3924	1.4400	1.5376	1.6384	1.7424	1.8496
3	1.4049	1.4815	1.5209	1.5609	1.6430	1.7280	1.9066	2.0972	2.3000	2.5155
4	1.5735	1.6890	1.7490	1.8106	1.9388	2.0736	2.3642	2.6844	3.0360	3.4210
5	1.7623	1.9254	2.0114	2.1003	2.2878	2.4883	2.9316	3.4360	4.0075	4.6526
6	1.9738	2.1950	2.3131	2.4364	2.6996	2.9860	3.6352	4.3980	5.2899	6.3275
7	2.2107	2.5023	2.6600	2.8262	3.1855	3.5832	4.5077	5.6295	6.9826	8.6054
8	2.4760	2.8526	3.0590	3.2784	3.7589	4.2998	5.5895	7.2058	9.2170	11.703
9	2.7731	3.2519	3.5179	3.8030	4.4355	5.1598	6.9310	9.2234	12.166	15.917
10	3.1058	3.7072	4.0456	4.4114	5.2338	6.1917	8.5944	11.806	16.060	21.647
11	3.4785	4.2262	4.6524	5.1173	6.1759	7.4301	10.657	15.112	21.199	29.439
12	3.8960	4.8179	5.3503	5.9360	7.2876	8.9161	13.215	19.343	27.983	40.037
13	4.3635	5.4924	6.1528	6.8858	8.5994	10.699	16.386	24.759	36.937	54.451
14	4.8871	6.2613	7.0757	7.9875	10.147	12.839	20.319	31.691	48.757	74.053
15	5.4736	7.1379	8.1371	9.2655	11.974	15.407	25.196	40.565	64.359	100.71
16	6.1304	8.1372	9.3576	10.748	14.129	18.488	31.243	51.923	84.954	136.97
17	6.8660	9.2765	10.761	12.468	16.672	22.186	38.741	66.461	112.14	186.28
18	7.6900	10.575	12.375	14.463	19.673	26.623	48.039	85.071	148.02	253.34
19	8.6128	12.056	14.232	16.777	23.214	31.948	59.568	108.89	195.39	344.54
20	9.6463	13.743	16.367	19.461	27.393	38.338	73.864	139.38	257.92	468.57
21	10.804	15.668	18.822	22.574	32.324	46.005	91.592	178.41	340.45	637.26
22	12.100	17.861	21.645	26.186	38.142	55.206	113.57	228.36	449.39	866.67
23	13.552	20.362	24.891	30.376	45.008	66.247	140.83	292.30	593.20	1178.7
24	15.179	23.212	28.625	35.236	53.109	79.497	174.63	374.14	783.02	1603.0
25	17.000	26.462	32.919	40.874	62.669	95.396	216.54	478.90	1033.6	2180.1
26	19.040	30.167	37.857	47.414	73.949	114.48	268.51	613.00	1364.3	2964.9
27	21.325	34.390	43.535	55.000	87.260	137.37	332.95	784.64	1800.9	4032.3
28	23.884	39.204	50.066	63.800	102.97	164.84	412.86	1004.3	2377.2	5483.9
29	26.750	44.693	57.575	74.009	121.50	197.81	511.95	1285.6	3137.9	7458.1
30	29.960	50.950	66.212	85.850	143.37	237.38	634.82	1645.5	4142.1	10143.
40	93.051	188.88	267.86	378.72	750.38	1469.8	5455.9	19427.	66521.	*
50	289.00	700.23	1083.7	1670.7	3927.4	9100.4	46890.	*	*	*
60	897.60	2595.9	4384.0	7370.2	20555.	56348.	*	*	*	*

*FVIF > 99,999

Table 4: Future Value of an Annuity of Re 1 per Period for *n* Periods

Number of Period	*1%*	*2%*	*3%*	*4%*	*5%*	*6%*	*7%*	*8%*	*9%*	*10%*
1	1.0000	1.0000	1.0000	1.0000	1.0000	1.0000	1.0000	1.0000	1.0000	1.0000
2	2.0100	2.0200	2.0300	2.0400	2.0500	2.0600	2.0700	2.0800	2.0900	2.1000
3	3.0301	3.0604	3.0909	3.1216	3.1525	3.1836	3.2149	3.2464	3.2781	3.3100
4	4.0604	4.1216	4.1836	4.2465	4.3101	4.3746	4.4399	4.5061	4.5731	4.6410
5	5.1010	5.2040	5.3091	5.4163	5.5256	5.6371	5.7507	5.8666	5.9847	6.1051
6	6.1520	6.3081	6.4684	6.6330	6.8019	6.9753	7.1533	7.3359	7.5233	7.7156
7	7.2135	7.4343	7.6625	7.8983	8.1420	8.3938	8.6540	8.9228	9.2004	9.4872
8	8.2857	8.5830	8.8923	9.2142	9.5491	9.8975	10.260	10.637	11.028	11.436
9	9.3685	9.7546	10.159	10.583	11.027	11.491	11.978	12.488	13.021	13.579
10	10.462	10.950	11.464	12.006	12.578	13.181	13.816	14.487	15.193	15.937
11	11.567	12.169	12.808	13.486	14.207	14.972	15.784	16.645	17.560	18.531
12	12.683	13.412	14.192	15.026	15.917	16.870	17.888	18.977	20.141	21.384
13	13.809	14.680	15.618	16.627	17.713	18.882	20.141	21.495	22.953	24.523
14	14.947	15.974	17.086	18.192	19.599	21.015	22.550	24.215	26.019	27.975
15	16.097	17.193	18.599	20.024	21.579	23.276	25.129	27.152	29.361	31.772
16	17.258	18.639	20.157	21.825	23.657	25.673	27.888	30.324	33.003	35.950
17	18.430	20.012	21.762	23.698	25.840	28.213	30.840	33.750	36.974	40.545
18	19.615	21.412	23.414	25.645	28.132	30.906	33.999	37.450	41.301	45.599
19	20.811	22.841	25.117	27.671	30.539	33.760	37.379	41.446	46.018	51.159
20	22.019	24.297	26.870	29.778	33.066	36.786	40.995	45.762	51.160	57.275
21	23.239	25.783	28.676	31.969	35.719	39.993	44.865	50.423	56.765	64.002
22	24.472	27.299	30.537	34.248	38.505	43.392	49.006	55.457	62.873	71.403
23	25.716	28.845	32.453	36.618	41.430	46.996	53.436	60.893	69.532	79.543
24	26.973	30.422	34.426	39.083	44.502	50.816	58.177	66.765	76.790	88.497
25	28.243	32.030	36.459	41.646	47.727	54.865	63.249	73.106	84.701	98.347
26	29.526	33.671	38.553	44.312	51.113	59.156	68.676	79.954	93.324	109.18
27	30.821	35.344	40.710	47.084	54.669	63.706	74.484	87.351	102.72	121.10
28	32.129	37.051	42.931	49.968	58.403	68.528	80.698	95.339	112.97	134.21
29	33.450	38.792	45.219	52.966	62.323	73.640	87.347	103.97	124.14	148.63
30	34.785	40.568	47.575	56.085	66.439	79.058	94.461	113.28	136.31	164.49
40	48.886	60.402	75.401	95.026	120.80	154.76	199.64	259.06	337.88	442.59
50	64.463	84.579	112.80	152.67	209.35	290.34	406.53	573.77	815.08	1163.9
60	81.670	114.05	163.05	237.99	353.58	533.13	813.52	1253.2	1944.8	3034.8

Number of Period	12%	14%	15%	16%	18%	20%	24%	28%	32%	36%
1	1.0000	1.0000	1.0000	1.0000	1.0000	1.0000	1.0000	1.0000	1.0000	1.0000
2	2.1200	2.1400	2.1500	2.1600	2.1800	2.2000	2.2400	2.2800	2.3200	2.3600
3	3.3744	3.4396	3.4725	3.5056	3.5724	3.6400	3.7776	3.9184	4.0624	4.2096
4	4.7793	4.9211	4.9934	5.0665	5.2154	5.3680	5.6842	6.0156	6.3624	6.7251
5	6.3528	6.6101	6.7424	6.8771	7.1542	7.4416	8.0484	8.6999	9.3983	10.146
6	8.1152	8.5355	8.7537	8.9775	9.4420	9.9299	10.980	12.136	13.406	14.799
7	10.089	10.730	11.067	11.414	12.142	12.916	14.615	16.534	18.696	21.126
8	12.300	13.233	13.727	14.240	15.327	16.499	19.123	22.163	25.678	29.732
9	14.776	16.085	16.786	17.519	19.086	20.799	24.712	29.369	34.895	41.435
10	17.549	19.337	20.304	21.321	23.521	25.959	31.643	38.593	47.062	57.352
11	20.655	23.045	24.349	25.733	28.755	32.150	40.238	50.398	63.122	78.998
12	24.133	27.271	29.002	30.850	34.931	39.581	50.895	65.510	84.320	108.44
13	28.029	32.089	34.352	36.786	42.219	48.497	64.110	84.853	112.30	148.47
14	32.393	37.581	40.505	43.672	50.818	59.196	80.496	109.61	149.24	202.93
15	37.280	43.842	47.580	51.660	60.965	72.035	100.82	141.30	198.00	276.98
16	42.753	50.980	55.717	60.925	72.939	87.442	126.01	181.87	262.36	377.69
17	48.884	59.118	65.075	71.673	87.068	105.93	157.25	233.79	347.31	514.66
18	55.750	68.394	75.836	84.141	103.74	128.12	195.99	300.25	459.45	700.94
19	63.440	78.969	88.212	98.603	123.41	154.74	244.03	385.32	607.47	954.28
20	72.052	91.025	102.44	115.38	146.63	186.69	303.60	494.21	802.86	1298.8
21	81.699	104.77	118.81	134.84	174.02	225.03	377.46	633.59	1060.8	1767.4
22	92.503	120.44	137.63	157.41	206.34	271.03	469.06	812.00	1401.2	2404.7
23	104.60	138.30	159.28	183.60	244.49	326.24	582.63	1040.4	1850.6	3271.3
24	118.16	158.66	184.17	213.98	289.49	392.48	723.46	1332.7	2443.8	4450.0
25	133.33	181.87	212.79	249.21	342.60	471.98	898.09	1706.8	3226.8	6053.0
26	150.33	208.33	245.71	290.09	405.27	567.38	1114.6	2185.7	4260.4	8233.1
27	169.37	238.50	283.57	337.50	479.22	681.85	1383.1	2798.7	5624.8	11198.0
28	190.70	272.89	327.10	392.50	566.48	819.22	1716.1	3583.3	7425.7	15230.3
29	214.58	312.09	377.17	456.30	669.45	984.07	2129.0	4587.7	9802.9	20714.2
30	241.33	356.79	434.75	530.31	790.95	1181.9	2640.9	5873.2	12941.	28172.3
40	767.09	1342.0	1779.1	2360.8	4163.2	7343.9	22729.	69377.	*	*
50	2400.0	4994.5	7217.7	10436.	21813.	45497.	*	*	*	*
60	7471.6	18535.	29220.	46058.	*	*	*	*	*	*

*FVIFA > 99,999

AUTHOR INDEX

SUBJECT INDEX